An Honest Writer

An Honest Writer

The Life and Times
of James T. Farrell

ROBERT K. LANDERS

ENCOUNTER BOOKS
SAN FRANCISCO

First edition published in 2004 by Encounter Books, an activity of Encounter for Culture and Education, Inc., a nonprofit tax exempt corporation.

Encounter Books website address: www.encounterbooks.com

Manufactured in the United States and printed on acid-free paper.

The paper used in this publication meets the minimum requirements of ANSI/NISO Z39.48-1992 (R 1997)(*Permanence of Paper*).

FIRST EDITION

Library of Congress Cataloging-in-Publication Data

Landers, Robert K.
    An honest writer : the life and times of James T. Farrell / Robert K. Landers.
    p. cm.
    Includes bibliographical references and index.
   ISBN 1-893554-95-3 (alk. paper)
    1. Farrell, James T. (James Thomas)—1904–1979. 2. Novelists, American—20th century—Biography. I. Title.

PS3511.A738 Z76 2004
813'.52—B22
2003064219
10 9 8 7 6 5 4 3 2

For Susan

Contents

Introduction

JAMES T. FARRELL WAS ONCE a literary titan, mentioned in the same breath with Hemingway, Faulkner and Dos Passos; and *Studs Lonigan,* his trilogy of novels about a swaggering young "tough guy" from a lower-middle-class Irish family on Chicago's South Side, was considered a modern classic. But this powerful work has fallen into neglect, and a century after his birth in 1904, Farrell is a largely forgotten figure. He and his finest achievements—*Studs Lonigan* and his series of five novels about the O'Neills and the O'Flahertys—deserve better.

Studs Lonigan and other vivid characters in those works were rightly declared by the pioneering critic Joseph Warren Beach in 1941 to be "among the memorable people in English fiction." But Farrell's naturalistic novels provide more than memorable people. They afford a richly detailed picture of life in an American city as it was actually lived by ordinary people, particularly Irish-Americans, in the early decades of the twentieth century. "You forget that you are seeing this life through the eyes of a selecting novelist," marveled critic Carl Van Doren. "It seems merely to be there before you."

Whether in praise or in disparagement, it was often said of Farrell's works that they were "sociology" as much as art. And indeed they were. Novelist Gerald Green, the author of *The Last Angry Man*, on learning in 1976 that he and Farrell shared the same publisher and editor, asked the editor to convey his admiration to the author of *Studs Lonigan* and the O'Neill-O'Flaherty novels. "Nothing in modern sociology, no journalism, including [Jimmy] Breslin's, or [Daniel Patrick] Moynihan's 'Beyond the Melting Pot,'" said Green, "can ever tell us anything new or enriching about the urban Irish, once we have read James T. Farrell. A giant."

Art and sociology work together in Farrells's best writing. The O'Neill-O'Flaherty novels long seemed to be chiefly about Farrell's

ix

alter ego, Danny O'Neill, an upward-bound counterpoint to the doomed Studs Lonigan; and the four books of the series published in the 1930s and 1940s—*A World I Never Made, No Star Is Lost, Father and Son*, and *My Days of Anger*—were informally known as "the Danny O'Neill novels." But eventually, and particularly after the appearance of the fifth novel, *The Face of Time* (1953), it became more apparent that the series was really less about Danny than about Danny's family members—who were Farrell's own family members immortalized in fiction—and the milieu in which he grew up.

This was Farrell's great subject: the world of his boyhood and youth. His extended family—the parents from whom he was separated at an early age, his grandmother and the other relatives with whom he lived when he was growing up—remained at the forefront of his creative awareness throughout his life. Turning them into fictional characters, he wrote about them again and again, in some of his best books and in later works as well.

As the decades in which Farrell grew up have receded into the past, the sociology in his books has become social history. Without their close correspondence to the actual Irish-American experience of the period, his naturalistic novels, for all their vivid characters and cumulative power, would deserve far less of our attention; with that correspondence, they deserve far more than they recently have received. "Sooner or later," Canadian novelist Morley Callaghan predicted in 1976, "people will want to know what life was really like in Farrell's time…and then they will read him."

The literary realism in Farrell's best works was not achieved in the manner so conspicuously urged not long ago by the flamboyant writer Tom Wolfe, who wanted novelists to leave neofabulism, magical realism and other voguish dead ends behind, and "head out into this wild, bizarre, unpredictable, Hog-stomping Baroque country of ours and reclaim it as literary property." Farrell didn't need to head out anywhere. He simply drew on his memory and imagination to recreate in astonishing detail, and with keen psychological insight, the world as it was on Chicago's South Side when he was growing up—a vanished world that is at once remote and familiar, and as absorbing as anything to be found in our "Hog-stomping" country today.

Despite Farrell's great accomplishment at his peak, there is no denying (despite some of his champions' best efforts) that as a writer he had serious faults. He was a writer not by nature but by force of will. And what a mighty will it must have been, for the words poured forth almost without stop. Yet he found it difficult to refine and polish his prose. He was not a stylist. And he wrote far too much. Some of his more than fifty published books deserve the oblivion into which time has cast them.

But not all of them, certainly not *Studs Lonigan* and the O'Neill-O'Flaherty novels. "In spite of the *longueurs* and occasional flatnesses of the naturalistic method, the cumulative effect of Farrell's work is impressive and powerful," historian Arthur Schlesinger Jr. once observed. "He has re-created a segment of America in our time and peopled it with characters…who are part of our literary heritage; he has thus transfixed a moment of history."

Doing that, Farrell inspired many younger writers. Reading *Studs Lonigan* when he was a freshman at Harvard "changed my life," Norman Mailer has recalled. The trilogy expanded his sense of what literature could encompass, much as reading one of Sherwood Anderson's books did for Farrell himself. "Now, I realized you could write books about people who were something like the people you had grown up with. I couldn't get over the discovery." *Studs Lonigan* helped inspire Mailer to become a writer.

Another journalist and novelist, Pete Hamill, has said, "[Farrell] taught me and other city writers to look with pity and terror and compassion at the people we knew and at ourselves, to give value to the casualties of the urban wars, to speak in some way for those who have no voices."

And many of the voiceless responded to Farrell's works with great enthusiasm, especially to *Studs Lonigan*. When an Army corporal lent his favorite book to young draftee Frank McCourt, called up after the Korean War began, it turned out to be the second volume in the Lonigan trilogy—"a paperback, falling apart," as McCourt writes in his recent memoir, *'Tis*.

> The corporal tells me I'm to guard this book with my life, that he reads it all the time, that James T. Farrell is the greatest writer that ever lived in the U.S.A., a writer that understands you an' me, kid, not like those blue-ass bullshit artists they have in New England. He says I can have this book till I finish basic training and then I have to get my own copy.

But while "do[ing] battle so that others did not remain unfulfilled as he and his family had been" became Farrell's aspiration (as it became the budding writer Danny O'Neill's), that lofty desire proceeded from a profound alienation from the voiceless he knew—from his family, his people, his community. "I think our generation [of writers] will be remembered as the one in which everyone hated, often without visible reason, the town in which he was born," critic Van Wyck Brooks wrote darkly in March 1941, just months before America's entry into World War II. Farrell, John Dos Passos, William Faulkner, Ernest Hemingway and so many other "writers of great power," Brooks complained, "seem to delight in kicking their world to pieces, as if civilization were all a pretence and everything noble a humbug."

If a close scrutiny of Farrell's life inevitably sheds light on his great subject—the world of his boyhood and youth—it also offers the opportunity to ponder anew not only the connection between such alienation and the creativity that Farrell and other writers of the time exhibited, but also the link between that alienation and those writers' propensity for political extremism.

Like so many others who entered the "adversary culture" during the Depression, Farrell was drawn to the solution offered by the American Communist Party. Unlike so many others in the "red decade" of the 1930s, however, he retained his independence of mind and awakened early to the horrors of Stalinism. And with a fine disregard for the likely damage to his literary reputation and the hostile reception his future books could expect to receive in certain influential leftist quarters, he courageously spoke out—not just once but again and again. "People look back on that time," he said decades later, "and think it was all simple factionalism. Sectarian factionalism. It wasn't in my case. I saw the leftwing movement as a world force, and I tried to be precise in my criticism. It wasn't a sectarian stand, and it wasn't anybody's line."

His was "a lonely road," journalist Murray Kempton observed. "Ten years later, [Hollywood screenwriter] Albert Maltz, facing expulsion from the Communist Party, would declare that he did not wish to face Farrell's fate. Farrell's fate, the unspeakable, was to walk alone."

Though Farrell was right about Stalinism, he remained a radical for more than a decade after his break with the Communists, finally freeing himself from Trotskyist and Marxist illusions only with the onset of the Cold War. He mutated into an anti-Communist liberal, opposed to McCarthyism at home as well as to Communism abroad, and joined with others of like mind during the 1950s on the American Committee for Cultural Freedom and in the Congress for Cultural Freedom. He remained an anti-Communist liberal (or social democrat) the rest of his life. Farrell's political evolution perhaps holds important lessons for later generations—about the perils of excessive reliance on abstract theory in politics, about the real merits of the tough-minded liberalism that New Leftists so condemned in the 1960s and that tenured radicals of today continue to despise, and about the value of integrity and courage as one makes one's way through the labyrinth of events.

Farrell's lonely journey was destined to be literary as well as political. His courageous political stance against Stalinism was partly responsible for his isolation, but only partly. The postwar turn away from naturalism also contributed to the neglect he would endure. And so did Farrell himself, by allowing inferior work of his to be published. His 1946 novel, *Bernard Clare*, observed one critic, "would be more appropriate as [the young writer protagonist's] first fumbling effort than as James T. Farrell's 18th or so published book."

Still another factor in the neglect of Farrell was, in a word, snobbery. One eminent critic made it clear that he was willing to read only so much about the "unreflecting and limited people" portrayed in his novels. An anonymous reader agreed: "He writes about the people I've spent all my life trying to get away from." Even Farrell's own wife would finally have enough of "those awful people." But of course those awful people were *his* people, unlettered Irish immigrants and their progeny, the unchampioned voiceless whose plight and humanity he sought to represent and convey.

On his journey Farrell did, though, have at least one companion: truth, or at least truth as best he understood it at the time. It is his "rigorous loyalty to his vision of the truth," said his friend Schlesinger, that characterizes his "place in American letters.... His vision is the vision of the naturalist, who writes about men and women with a literal honesty that would be remorseless if it were not informed by compassion."

Over the decades Farrell came to be often lauded as an honest writer. Some critics tried to make the praise faint by pointing out that honesty is, after all, among the virtues that a reader expects from a serious writer as a matter of course. Perhaps so. But serious writers who are honest bearers of inconvenient truths are not always welcome. The Communists, of course, never treated the renegade Farrell with anything but vituperative scorn, while

Catholics were slow to appreciate the frankness and truth of his portraits of the faithful in Chicago. And readers who didn't care to have anything to do with "those awful people" in his novels, or who recoiled from his unsentimental depiction of life as too often (in his words) "gray" and "dreary," shunned his books. Faced with the prospect of such hostile receptions, the writers of Farrell's time proved that, in sad fact, honesty like his is rare and precious. Like George Orwell, he deserves to be remembered and honored for it.

But stubbornly to go one's own way, as Farrell did, has its own hazards. For all his novelist's insight, he could be obtuse and even willfully blind about people and events. He was immensely self-centered—like a child in many ways. And at times, his behavior was appalling.

"Do writers have to be such monsters in order to create?" the Irish novelist Edna O'Brien asks at one point in her recent biography of James Joyce. "I believe that they do," she said. "It is a paradox that while wrestling with language to capture the human condition they become more callous, and cut off from the very human traits which they so glisteningly depict."

Artists are naturally self-centered, Farrell's longtime editor, Jim Henle, once observed. "Obviously, if a man or woman weren't self-centered, he or she would never become an artist. To be an artist you must believe [that] you and everything that happens to you—your thoughts, desires, emotions, etc.—are important." But Farrell, he added, was not "meanly self-centered." His egocentricity did not preclude "a generous interest in other human beings.... He could throb with interest—and expect you to share it—re his blood pressure, his parochial school past, his views of West German rearmament, etc., etc.—but he could push these aside in a moment if a policeman clubbed a picket or if new details were available re slave labor camps in Siberia."

Because of that larger interest he took in suffering humanity, Farrell's odyssey through most of the twentieth century is an unusually fascinating one. And, fortunately, during much of this journey, he kept detailed notes. Here, then, is the story of an honest writer.

Part 1

Young Farrell

Prologue
The Wound

THE BOY WOULD NOT STOP screaming. He was back home—and he didn't want to be.

For two weeks, young James Thomas Farrell had been staying with his grandparents, John and Julia Daly, in the apartment they shared with their grown son and daughters. And in all those early summer days of 1906, the two-year-old with curly blond hair had been the household's center of attention.

His grandmother especially had doted on Jimmy, in what were for the boy surroundings of unaccustomed comfort. The Dalys' apartment in the Grand Boulevard section of Chicago's South Side had steam heating, electricity, an indoor toilet, a telephone and even the services of a colored maid. No such amenities existed in his parents' tenement flat on the city's Southwest Side. Jimmy's father, James Francis Farrell, was a teamster—a mere "tinker," in the derisive yet perhaps not wholly unaffectionate description of Julia Daly, herself married to a former teamster—and he could not, at least not yet, house his family in the style to which his in-laws had grown accustomed.

But the absence of steam heating and electricity may not have seemed all that important to young Jimmy. He was probably more impressed upon his return home by the discovery that, in addition to his older brother, Earl, there was now a newborn sister, Helen, in whom his mother seemed to take an excessive interest, and by the realization that he could no longer easily turn to his grandmother or his young aunts for the loving attention they had been lavishing upon him. Instead, there appeared before him early that evening the tired and less indulgent countenance of his father, home after a long day's work.

Overwhelmed by these enormous changes, little Jimmy began

to scream. He cried and cried, until at last his weary mother could stand no more.

"Jim, you better take him back to my mother's!" Mary Daly Farrell told her husband.

And so it was done. Jim Farrell took his bawling son the few blocks to Wentworth Avenue and the streetcar. They rode south, then switched at 47th to an eastbound car. Along the way, there were suspicious glances, perhaps even some accusatory words, directed at Jim Farrell; and he protested his innocence: He had *not* been beating the child.

Finally, at Indiana Avenue, father and son got off and walked the short distance to the Daly apartment. Julia Daly opened the door. "Ma Jule," the boy said, in words that his Aunt Ella was later to repeat many times, "heaten the bottle and put me to bed."

It was the most significant event of young Farrell's life, a psychic wound that turned out to be inseparable from the creative strength of the novelist to come.* It gave rise to questions that would haunt him and haunt his fiction: *Why had his parents given him away? Was there something wrong with him? Or with them?* It was a self-inflicted injury, by a child who didn't understand what was happening.

Nor, apparently, did his parents. They had not intended that he should grow up in the Daly household, estranged from his natural family: they had thought only to quiet their screaming son. Although the family was poor and the addition of a third youngster was not an unmixed blessing, Jim Farrell was a proud man, devoted to his wife and children. He would never have readily agreed to give his son away to his in-laws or to anybody else. Yet as one day followed another, as the days turned into weeks, and the weeks into months, what had not at first been intended—except perhaps by Julia Daly—became the way it was and the way it would be. Jimmy Farrell would live with the Dalys.

_____

*Exploring the connection between trauma and art, Edmund Wilson found "the conception of superior strength as inseparable from disability" in Sophocles' play *Philoctetes*, in which the hero's incurable wound and invincible bow are somehow linked. The connection is not one of causation, however. Wilson's study, *The Wound and the Bow* (1941), as critic David Castronovo has noted, shows "how trauma becomes obsessive subject matter and how certain [artists] and their works are not fully conceived of apart from it."

Chapter One

The Farrells and the Dalys

WHEN THEIR FIRST CHILD, William Earl, was born on March 27, 1900, Jim and Mary Farrell had been married for almost a year and were living in a flat on Archer Avenue, in a working-class area southwest of the Loop, Chicago's central business district. Six feet two, with dark brown hair, broad shoulders and long, powerful arms, Jim Farrell had just turned twenty-nine a few days earlier. He was handsome in a rough-hewn way, with a dimpled chin and sensitive eyes. Next to him, Mary Farrell, who was barely five feet tall, seemed even shorter than she was. She had striking black hair and a pleasant face, but her main appeal came from within. She would turn twenty-six in September (though she told the census-taker who came in June that she was only twenty-three).

The neighborhood—where they were still living when Jimmy was born four years later—was far from ideal. Trains rumbled by just a few blocks away; tracks leading to depots in the southern part of the Loop lay to their east and west, and to the north were railroad freight yards. Beyond the tracks to the west was the normally polluted South Branch of the Chicago River. Wafting up from the southwest was the stench of the Union Stock Yards, slaughterhouses and packing plants, soon to be made infamous by Upton Sinclair's muckraking novel *The Jungle* (1906). And to complete the environmental degradation there was the nearby Levee, the vice district that was under the baronial protection of First Ward Aldermen "Bathhouse John" Coughlin and Mike "Hinky Dink" Kenna.

The Farrells' flat was in a four-story, stone-front brick tenement at 2127 Archer. Three other families, headed by working men from Croatia, Germany and Kentucky, lived there with them. Next door, in a two-story wood-frame building—where Jim Farrell had probably boarded before his marriage—were two more families: a German tailor and his wife and son, and an Italian schoolteacher and his German wife (who had an Italian barber boarding with them). Of the nearly 1.7 million people then living in the city, more than one-third were foreign-born and more than three-fourths had foreign-born parents.

Once, no more than a biblical lifespan earlier, the occupants of 2127 and 2125 Archer, taken all together, would have constituted a majority of Chicago's population. In 1830, when the original town plan was drawn up, Chicago had fewer than fifty inhabitants. They occupied a dozen log cabins in the vicinity of Fort Dearborn, an isolated Army outpost at a bend in the Chicago River close to where the river emptied into Lake Michigan. The transformation of this tiny village of fur trappers into what poet Carl Sandburg would call "the City of the Big Shoulders" began—once the large Indian population in the area was induced to leave—with the construction of the Illinois and Michigan Canal. With the 1825 opening of the Erie Canal, linking Lake Erie at Buffalo, New York, with the Hudson River at Albany, attention had turned to Chicago and the prospect of a canal that would connect the Great Lakes and the Mississippi River. From its mouth at Lake Michigan, looking west, the Chicago River formed a tree-shaped "Y," with one arm extending northward and the other southward. The Illinois and Michigan Canal would join the river's South Branch to the Illinois River (and thence the Mississippi), thus creating a network for water-borne commerce throughout the young nation. Archer, running southwest from the city's center, served as the path of supply for the immigrants, mainly Irish and German, who built the canal.

The Irish laborers who came to Chicago during the 1830s lived in wooden shanties that they constructed along the banks of the South Branch. New to America or not, the workers brought with them the boisterous ways they had known at home. British visitors to America during the 1820s and 1830s were surprised to discover along such canal banks what seemed virtual replicas of peasant villages in Ireland, each shanty complete (in the words of one disdainful observer) with a pig, a cow and other "sterling Irish comforts." Whiskey drinking, which subcontractors encouraged, was common among the workers, as were brawls over employment and territory.

Even before the canal opened for traffic in 1848, the waterway spurred Chicago's growth. When the city was incorporated in 1837, one year after canal digging began, Chicago had more than four thousand inhabitants; by 1850, with the canal in operation, the population had increased to almost thirty thousand. But by then the first train had come to Chicago, bringing with it the future. Serving as gateway between East and West, the city became the main wholesale market for the entire midcontinent. Wheat, corn, lumber, hogs and cattle began flowing to Chicago by rail. The city's population soared from more than 112,000 in 1860 to nearly 300,000 in 1870.

The newcomers included Jim Farrell's father, James Farrell of County Tipperary in Munster. He was among those who left Ireland after the Great Famine, which had lasted from 1845 through the early 1850s. More than one million peasants had perished in the famine and more than two million others had fled the island, most of them escaping to America. Poverty and hunger did not end with the famine, and neither did emigration. Farrell, then in his early twenties, journeyed to the United States before (or just after) the Civil War began, disembarking at New Orleans. He became a soldier in the Confederate Army, serving, along with a good many Irishmen, with the Louisiana Tigers, whose bravery on the battlefield was equaled only by their drinking and brawling in camp.

The war over, James Farrell may have lived for a time in Kentucky. By the end of the decade he was married to an Irish-born woman named Honora Kelly and was living in Chicago. He was an unskilled laborer, as were six out of ten Irish-born workers living in the city around 1870. By then the era of massive emigration from Ireland was over. Chicago's first-generation Irish population, which had swelled to about 40,000, would grow by fewer than 4,500 in the next decade.

Hostility toward the Irish was not as rampant in the Midwest as it was in the East, but it was more evident in Chicago than in other midwestern cities. The Irishman is "a born savage—as brutal a ruffian as an untamed Indian…" fumed the *Chicago Evening Post* in 1868. "Breaking heads for opinion's sake is his practice. The born criminal and pauper of the civilized world…a wronged, abused, and pitiful spectacle of a man…pushed straight to hell by that abomination against common sense called the Catholic religion." Not surprisingly in that harsh light, many want ads in Chicago newspapers still ended with the phrase, "No Irish Need Apply."

Such attacks only made the Catholic identity of the Irish more important to them. They developed strong ties with their parish priests and came to regard the construction of churches as an expression of Catholic power. After the Great Chicago Fire of 1871 destroyed seven Catholic churches, Irish pastors launched campaigns to replace their frame churches with brick structures; the financing came from the working men and women of the parishes.

The great conflagration—which broke out on October 8, 1871, in a barn on DeKoven Street, west of the South Branch, and then spread north and east—cut a huge swath of destruction through the center of the city. It left as many as three hundred dead, one hundred thousand homeless and a charred wasteland of nearly three square miles. The rebuilding of Chicago began apace, and that meant steady employment for laborers like James Farrell.

On March 23, 1871, little more than six months before the fire, Farrell's wife, Honora, gave birth to a son: James Francis. Hardly more than one year later, on April 12, 1872, while giving birth again, Honora died. She was thirty-two years old.

James Farrell married again. A census enumerator in June 1880 found the middle-aged laborer living on Armitage Road with his second family—his new wife Bridget, younger by a dozen years, and daughters Nelly (six years) and Mary (one month). James Francis, now nine, was said to be "at school."

In fact, he had been sent to an orphanage. Perhaps it was after running away from home, but in any case he felt abandoned and he resented his father's new family. Decades later, when James Francis and Mary Farrell were married and had children of their own, he still would have nothing to do with his stepmother and her daughters. His good-hearted wife, however, had the women over for tea several times; they came during the daytime, when Jim was not at home.

THE STREETS OF EARLY twentieth-century Chicago were crowded with teamsters and their horse-drawn wagons, hauling everything from ice, coal and milk to laundry and furniture. There were some 35,000 such men in the city, and Jim Farrell was one of them. At some point he went to work for Wells, Fargo & Company express; in later years he worked for American Express Company.

The express business had begun decades earlier as a way of shipping cash and other valuables safely; it had grown to provide fast and secure transport of various other things, including fragile items and perishables such as fresh fruit, vegetables and fish. Promising their customers speed and taking responsibility for damage or loss, the express companies arranged with the railroads to carry the commodities in exchange for 40 to 60 percent of receipts.

Farrell's daily routine centered around the wholesale produce market at South Water Street, a short east-west street, just south of the Chicago River and north of the Loop—"the busiest street in the world," some said. Stores, three or four stories high, lined both sides. Teamsters brought produce to and from the stores, which were not near any railroad terminal. From all regions of the country came fresh fruit and vegetables, poultry and eggs, butter and cheese, as well as fish, nuts, dry beans and frogs' legs. Some of it ended up on tables in Chicago; the rest went elsewhere. Teamsters took shipments to the depots as well as to local hotels, restaurants and clubs.

Teamsters worked hard. They usually began at six in the morning and, with an hour off for lunch, finished up around six in the evening. And they worked six days a week, fifty-two weeks a year, with no vacations and only two holidays, the Fourth of July and Christmas Day—both unpaid. For their labor, most teamsters received less than fifteen dollars a week. That was after they were unionized.

Teamsters were used in virtually every industry. Many manufacturers and most wholesale merchants didn't own their own teams, so they contracted with team owners to do hauling for them. The teamsters' role was vital. No industry could keep going if the drivers decided to put down their reins.

That the teamsters were willing to exercise their collective power once they discovered it owed a good deal to the sort of men they were. A writer named Ernest Poole (a former settlement house worker and later a Pulitzer Prize–winning novelist) tried in 1904 to describe the typical Chicago teamster who, unlike the "wretched tailor" who was "sweated" (grossly overworked and underpaid by his employer), had learned to fight back:

> You can see him any day in the rush and jam of the downtown street, an Irish-American, rough, swaggering, big-hearted, honest. He is up in life now, but four years ago he was decidedly down. His wage and hours were like those of the sweatshop victim, on whom so much sympathy has been rightly poured.... His whole waking life was an endless fight for precedence. In the South Water Street jam

9

the police gave up making arrests, for there were fights every hour, while at bridges, markets and railway stations, wherever the tangle was thickest, the teamster amply made good the name which the County Hospital doctors have given him—"the roughest, toughest scrapper of the working classes."

Certainly, Jim Farrell fit that mold. "Men did not come tougher than my father," his novelist son remembered. He would not back down from anyone.

Novelist Farrell—who never had a close relationship with his father—also habitually noted another characteristic: his loyalty to organized labor. "My father was a union man," he once wrote. "In 1904, in the big teamsters' strike in Chicago, my father was...a union slugger. Not a paid one, a mercenary, but a union man who was in a fight for his dignity, and his family, and for his fellow working men." There is some truth in this heartfelt picture, both about Jim Farrell himself and about the value that he and men like him saw in organized labor. But the novelist repeatedly got more than the year of the strike wrong. (It took place in 1905.) Had he ever delved into the early history of the teamsters' union and into what happened during that big strike, he would have discovered the dubious character of the union's leaders, the questionable purpose of the strike, and the tragic racial violence that resulted from it. The history is more complicated than the novelist seems to have realized.

The teamsters' union had come to be, as one account put it, "cordially hated, not only by the employers, but by all the other unions. For though the leaders were continually posing as the champions of any and every striking organization, the strikers were invariably left in the lurch" once the teamster leaders gained their venal ends. Whatever they originally had in mind with the 1905 strike—whether a straightforward show of union strength or a blackmailing scheme—the strike was an utter failure. Its costs included 21 people killed and 415 reported injured. Jim Farrell, an honest union man, presumably did his share of the "slugging" against scabs. And employers' importation of hundreds of black strikebreakers from St. Louis and the river towns further south undoubtedly had strengthened his racial prejudice. "My father was very, very much against the colored," Helen Farrell remembered.

A few years later, Jim Farrell climbed down from his wagon and left teaming. During 1908 and 1909, he was employed as a bartender. By 1910, however, he was back working as a teamster again. Perhaps that is when he first went to work for American Express.

━━━➤◦◄━━━

BEFORE HER MARRIAGE, MARY DALY FARRELL had worked as a domestic for a wealthy family in the Prairie Avenue area. When she wed Jim Farrell, she left domestic service behind.

She began having children right away. Although she was pregnant nearly every year, fourteen or fifteen times in all, only seven children survived. Earl was the first and would always be her favorite. The second was Jimmy—James Thomas Farrell—born on February 27, 1904, after the family had left Archer Avenue and moved around the corner to a flat in a three-story building at 369 West 22nd Street. His birth took place at home, with a midwife named Lottie Klein assisting the attending physician, one Dr. Carter. Soon after, the infant was baptized at St. John Church, at 18th and Clark Streets. Two years later, when Helen was born—and Jimmy was taken to the Dalys to stay—the family was living a little further south, on Princeton Avenue, near 27th Street.[*]

Looking back nearly six decades later to the night, so fateful for him, when he was taken back to his grandmother, the novelist wondered what it might have been like for his father after dropping him off. "I think of my father, taking the ride back....And then, on the next morning, my father getting out of bed early, before dawn. He had to fix his own breakfast.... But how could he have felt, what might [he] have felt on the morning after my tantrum and return to my grandmother's?" What his father probably felt was bewildered annoyance, which over time hardened into hurt resentment. A dozen or more years later, Jim Farrell was walking with his youngest daughter on Calumet Avenue, headed for the elevated station, and as they approached 59th Street, they saw young Jimmy in

---

[*] Some scholars, notably Edgar M. Branch and Alan M. Wald, have suggested that it was because of the Farrell family's poverty, especially, as Branch put it, "with children coming regularly," that Jimmy was sent to live with the Dalys. This is an oversimplification. Poverty may have been a necessary precondition, but it was not a sufficient one. The four Farrell children born after Jimmy went to live with the Dalys all remained in their parents' household. That Jimmy (and later his sister Helen—see Chapter Two) did not, then, cannot have been due solely to the family's poverty.

the distance, coming toward them; when Jimmy saw them he dashed into traffic to avoid them. The girl felt her father's hand tighten on hers. "Goddamn Daly pup," he muttered.

A year or so after Jimmy went to live with the Dalys, the Farrells moved to a two-story tenement at 2430 LaSalle Street. The house was divided into four flats, two above, two below; it had a porch all around, and entrances front and back. Heat came from a wood stove, light from kerosene lamps. Out back was a single outhouse for the four families. Down the street, at 25th, were a meat packing firm, which always gave off a distinctive odor, and a saloon. Chicago at the turn of the century had more saloons than groceries, meat markets and dry goods stores combined.

Jim Farrell occasionally stopped in at that corner saloon for a drink. If the saloon was typical, teamsters would drop in during the afternoon to quench their thirst, use the free toilet, and let their horses drink from the watering troughs. Then, during the late afternoon, wives and children would come to take out beer for the evening meal in buckets, cans or pitchers, which were called "growlers." There were few, if any, growlers brought back to the Farrells' flat, however: Mary Farrell did not want alcohol in her home.

Her husband was seldom inebriated, but every so often he did succumb. His youngest daughter remembered him, when drunk, warning her mother: "Woman, if you don't shut your mouth, I'll put my fist right down your throat." But his daughters never saw him hit her. Almost always, in fact, he deferred to his wife's wishes: "All right, we'll do it that way," he would say.

In allowing her second son to live at the Dalys', Mary Farrell no doubt believed that the boy might well be better off there. Certainly, she was a good mother to her other children. "She was very warm and very affectionate," her youngest daughter, also named Mary, recalled, "and [she] knew how to keep children amused when it was raining outside or it was snowing. We had a lot of fun growing up, even though we were very poor." Three children were born to her in the LaSalle Street flat (which had only two bedrooms): Richard Joseph ("Joe"), on June 24, 1908; John Henry ("Jack"), on June 10, 1910; and Mary Elizabeth, on August 27, 1911. Each was baptized soon after birth at All Saints Church, at 25th Place and Wallace Street.

Being so often pregnant, and with so many young children demanding her attention, Mary Farrell did a poor job of keeping the house clean. "She was more interested in how her kids were than how the house was and she'd spend time with us," her daughter Helen remembered. Decades later her son, in harsh but more-or-less accurate detail, drew a fictional portrait of the Farrells' LaSalle Street home: The father ("Jim O'Neill")

> went into the bedroom off the dining room where Lizz [his wife] lay on the bed in a corner, her belly swollen under the soiled white sheet.... He glanced around, junk all over, the dresser in the corner piled with it, rags, clothes, junk, and the table on the left with a slab of grocery box in place of one leg, it, too, was piled and littered with every damn thing in the house.... Again he looked around, and noticing the kerosene lamp amid the litter on the small table, he silently cursed to himself. He wondered would he and his family ever have a decent home where they could live like human beings and bring the kids up right.

The condition of their flat sometimes so bothered Jim Farrell that he would spend much of Sunday, his one day off, cleaning it up. Farrell's Sundays were almost invariably devoted to home and family. Mary Farrell was a pious woman, and the Farrells regularly went to Sunday Mass. Because Jim Farrell had been an orphan, he was especially determined that his children should have the benefits of being part of a loving family. He almost always cooked the family's Sunday dinner. And then he would sit down and read the Sunday newspaper. Sometimes he would take Helen and Joe to visit relatives on his mother's side of the family. Other Sunday afternoons, he and Mary would take the children on the streetcar to Lincoln Park for an outing.

In time, the Farrells had a seventh child, Francis ("Frankie"), born on May 23, 1914. By then the family had moved down the block into a two-story tenement that housed only two families instead of four, but otherwise was not much of an improvement. Soon after Frankie was born, the Farrells moved again, this time to a cottage at 236 West 45th Place that they had all to themselves. When they lived there, the five younger children—Helen, Joe, Jack, Mary and Frankie—went each day to meet their father coming home from work. They sat, all in a line, on the curb and waited for him to get off the streetcar. No other father had such a reception awaiting him. When Jim Farrell arrived, he would scoop Mary and Frankie up into his arms, and with the other children hanging on they would walk happily home. Jimmy was never among them.

———⟫•◦•⟪———

ONE AFTERNOON, JIMMY FARRELL, then about five years old, was playing in back of the Dalys' low-rise apartment house on Indiana Avenue when an older boy decided to assert his primacy. Jimmy soon rushed upstairs to his grandmother and tearfully told her what had happened:

"Mudder, the big boy hit me!"

Julia Daly's response was swift and vehement:

"Son, you go out and don't you come back in here until you can bring me a pound of his flesh."

Jimmy wiped his eyes, ran back outside, and tore into his tormentor. More than five decades later, the fight was still vivid in his memory: "I beat him up, wrestled and shoved him to the ground, and scratched. I had taken my grandmother's words literally. I screamed, but he screamed more loudly. My screams were in anger, but his were from pain." The older boy at last ran off, but Jimmy went back upstairs with a sense of failure. When his grandmother saw that he was crying again, she began to ask for her switch so that she herself could deal with the troublemaker outside. But then Jimmy told her what he had done and explained his tears: "Mudder, I can't get the flesh off."

Julia Daly patted him on the head, told him he was a good boy and gave him a glass of milk and a cookie. Never again did Jimmy Farrell go home crying. "Ever since that afternoon," he wrote in late middle age, "I have fought my own battles."

The old woman who taught him to do that was a feisty Irish peasant who smoked a corncob pipe and seemed to relish conflict. She was "a proud little woman" (in Jimmy's phrase), though not, ordinarily, an affectionate one. But she dearly loved young Jimmy. When she took him for a walk and they passed some girls, she would cry out: "Girls, turn your face to the wall, here's me grandson." No girl, in her view, could be good enough for Jimmy.

As a girl herself, Julia Brown Daly had lived in Athlone, a town on the river Shannon, in the Irish Midlands. About 1860, fifteen-year-old Julia Brown and her sister, Mary, who was a year or two older, left their troubled island for America. After a forty-five-day crossing, they found themselves in New York. Before the decade was out, Mary Brown entered a convent and Julia Brown, after working as a domestic servant in Brooklyn, married John Daly,

14

whom she'd known in Athlone and who had come over to America the year after she did. They first went to live in Green Bay, Wisconsin, and then moved to Chicago, where John Daly worked as a day laborer and later as a teamster.

Julia Daly had a son named James in 1868, but he died before he was two. In her grandson Jimmy, Julia Daly may well have seen again the first-born child that she had lost nearly four decades before. The Dalys had a second son in 1869, but he too didn't live long. Then, on August 26, 1871, their first child who would survive into adulthood was born: Richard Thomas Daly. He would be known as "Tom" (and Jimmy would be given a middle name in his honor). Three years later, on September 22, 1874, Mary Rose Daly—Jimmy's future mother—was born. In the years that followed, Julia and John Daly had five more children, three of whom would survive into adulthood: Bill, born on February 9, 1879; Ella, born on June 10, 1883; and Bessie, born on March 13, 1886. Tom and Bill were to become traveling salesmen, Ella became a hotel cashier, and Bessie worked as a stenographer. Their mother could neither read nor write (despite what she seems to have told census-takers), yet her cantankerous spirit reigned over the Daly household until she died.

THE GRAND BOULEVARD COMMUNITY in which the Dalys lived was about four miles south of the Loop and a world away from the Farrells' working-class neighborhood. Grand Boulevard itself was a broad, tree-lined thoroughfare on which many wealthy Chicagoans had built elegant homes—it had been a popular route for recreational carriage rides. From 51st Street, where it formed an entrance to Washington Park, the boulevard ran north to 39th Street and beyond, toward downtown. Native-born Protestants, Irish Catholics and German Jews lived in the Grand Boulevard community. West of the boulevard, on such parallel avenues as Michigan, Indiana and Prairie, were two- and three-story apartment buildings occupied by middle-class families, with one apartment on each floor. The Dalys' flat was at 4816 Indiana.

Sometimes, Jimmy's grandfather—a short, wiry man with gray hair and a clipped mustache—took him to Washington Park to feed the ducks in the pond. Or they walked to the end of the streetcar line, where John Daly chatted and drank beer with the guys.

When Jimmy was six, his grandfather fell sick with cancer and spent his days resting on a small cot in the dining room of the apartment. Father Edward L. Dondanville, from Corpus Christi Church at 49th and Grand Boulevard, came to visit. On one such visit, Jimmy impressed the priest with his precocious fund of baseball knowledge. Jimmy's older brother, Earl, had a large collection of pictures of baseball players (which came then in cigarette packages) and he had given Jimmy his duplicates; Uncle Tom and Aunt Ella had given him others. Father Dondanville held Jimmy's cards in his hands and asked him to identify the players and their teams. Jimmy not only did so, but also told him whether the players batted right- or left-handed. Although he was too young to be able to read the cards, he'd learned about the players from Earl. Father Dondanville dubbed the bright lad "Young Ty Cobb."

Visits from parish priests to families such as the Dalys were quite common in those days and by no means limited to sick calls. Usually a priest would come at least once a week to have tea with Julia Daly. Like her daughter Mary, Julia was very pious. She looked up to priests and nuns as holy men and women of God. And also like her daughter, she was quite superstitious, in the tradition of her rural Irish ancestors.

"If there was anything in this world that she hated more than a) another female, b) married men, and c) black Protestants," Jimmy Farrell recalled decades later, "it was Satan."

He elaborated: "No one could curse the Devil like my grandmother.

"—That Spawn of Hell, that Limb of Hell.

"She would let go at him.

"—He'll not get me grandson.

"She would cross herself without holy water and claim to have given the Devil the scoot.

"—Catch me wasting that blessed water on the Limb of Hell!"

In between bouts with the Devil, Julia Daly was drawn to the drama of death. Through reports from her daughter Mary, she vicariously attended wakes of Farrell relatives. Julia was always eager to hear of deaths, especially of violent ones. She liked to have the death notices in the newspaper read aloud to her, and she delighted in hearing accounts of murders or other violent crimes.

Julia also seems to have welcomed, even encouraged, discord in her own home. Being unable to read, she was easily bored. When she found it too quiet, she "would stir things up" and get her off-

16

spring wrangling with one another, her granddaughter Mary recalled. "There was a lot of fighting at the Dalys'. You couldn't get two or three of them together at any one time that you didn't have a donnybrook going on, [with them] running up and down the hall, screaming at each other."

In December 1910, Jimmy's grandfather died. At the wake in the Daly home, Jimmy chased Helen around the coffin, according to her account. The funeral ended in Calvary Cemetery in Evanston, just north of the city, but burial was put off until spring because the ground was frozen.

Earlier that year, the Dalys had moved to another apartment on Indiana Avenue. After John Daly's death—perhaps out of a superstitious belief on the part of Julia that one should not continue to live in a home where a person has died—they moved a short distance to an apartment at 4953 Calumet Avenue, closer to Grand Boulevard.

But death pursued them. In May 1911, Julia's daughter Bessie, a pretty, sweet-natured young woman with long auburn hair, died of tuberculosis. She was twenty-five. Bessie was buried just three days after her father's coffin had been lowered into the ground. The Dalys—widow Julia, her son Tom, her daughter Ella and her grandson Jimmy Farrell—moved yet again, going a few blocks away to a second-floor apartment at 5131 Prairie Avenue, west of Washington Park.

⟫•0•⟪

TOM DALY, A BACHELOR ALL his life, was the family's chief breadwinner. Around the turn of the century, he had become a traveling salesman—a "commercial traveler"—for James A. Lawrence & Company, a Chicago boot-and-shoe firm; his younger brother, Bill, also worked there as a shipping clerk. Just before Jimmy Farrell joined the Daly household, Bill married a wealthy woman from Madison, Wisconsin, where he went to live.

Tom Daly excelled at selling shoes to retail merchants. In 1901 he left Lawrence & Company for Schwab Brothers, and two years later went to another Chicago shoe manufacturer, the Cole-Davis Company. Some time after that, he became a traveling salesman for a Massachusetts shoe firm, the Upham Brothers. His territory was Illinois, Missouri, Minnesota, Wisconsin and Iowa. He remained with the company for many years.

The commercial traveler's job was more difficult than it had been in the 1870s and 1880s, when relatively few products were available. In the new era, scholar Timothy B. Spears has observed, traveling salesmen made an effort to shed the image of "the 'old-time drummer,' whose bawdy jokes, flashy clothing and free drinks they now considered crude and inefficient." The modern commercial traveler was strictly business. He relied upon "scientific salesmanship" to win over potential customers. The mind was his battlefield. To be successful (according to *Hints on Salesmanship,* a 1911 manual), a salesman had to develop "a strong personality which is capable of persuading and controlling the minds of others."

A thoroughly modern commercial traveler—and undeniably a success—Tom Daly made about $10,000 a year working for Upham Brothers, his nephew recalled. "He believed in success, and in gaining it by hard work." Although Daly's formal education didn't go beyond the eighth grade, he was forever bent upon self-improvement. Toward that end, he read a lot of "serious books," on the order of *The Letters of Lord Chesterfield,* and he habitually used the genteel language that he thought would mark him as a cultivated gentleman. He liked to call Jimmy "Sport," and some of the women and girls in the family "Princess" or "Countess." He wanted those around him to reflect the refinement, elegance and good manners that he strove for. In fact, he insisted upon it. "Nix on that," he would say when he perceived a lapse by someone. Formality was the rule at meals when he was around, even at breakfast. And at table Tom offered instruction, as necessary, on how to eat and behave. "He was always bossy," in Helen Farrell's view. When he wasn't around—and he was frequently on the road—meals tended to be eaten informally in the kitchen.

Tom Daly was only about five feet three inches tall. "He had, as many short men do, this Napoleonic complex, and he had it but good," said his niece Mary. When Tom was home, as the novelist ruefully described, he

> was always dominant, and life at home had to turn and revolve around him. His needs were prior to our (my) needs. Not only the course of events in the house changed: my emotions changed. Fear, anxiety, a secondary position. Much emotion was wasted, worrying about when he came home, and then, more was wasted, wishing for him to go away, for the time when he would go away. With this, he

had a habit of running down most of what you did, of having to know more than you did, and of having to turn anything into a victory of his personality.

Yet while he was "commanding, even Napoleonic, he never crossed my grandmother, and she never crossed him."

Like his mother, Tom attended Mass every Sunday, receiving Holy Communion at least three or four times a year. Yet his soul was not so permeated by grace as to prevent him from harboring the common prejudices against blacks and Jews. On occasion he would talk darkly of "niggers" and "kikes."

But Tom loved young Jimmy and tried to be like a father to him, albeit a father who was often away from home. He evidently felt himself much superior to the boy's real father, who, for all his hard work, had so much less "success." Sometimes on Sunday the Farrells would visit the Dalys, sitting around and feasting on ice cream. "There was friendliness," Helen Farrell remembered, "but there wasn't any [rapport] with my father." (Whereas when John Daly was alive, he and his son-in-law, both being teamsters, had got along well.) Except for Jimmy, Tom Daly showed the Farrell children, particularly the boys, little affection. Jimmy saw a good deal of his older brother Earl before the four-year difference in their ages put too much distance between them, but Tom Daly did not consider Earl a good influence. He would belt Earl when the boy said or did something he deemed wrong. And he would hit Joe Farrell too. As a consequence, when Joe became old enough, he simply refused to go over to the Dalys'.

Once, when the boys' little sister, Mary, was eight or nine, Tom Daly struck her and she went home crying. Jim Farrell was furious. "My father took me by the hand, and I don't think I touched the ground all the way" back to the Dalys' apartment, she remembered. When they got there, Jim Farrell—tough, strong, six feet two—lifted his Napoleonic brother-in-law up by his vest until his feet were off the ground. "If you ever lay a hand on my little girl again," Farrell said, "I'll kill you."

⟶➤•◀⟵

JIMMY'S AUNT ELLA DALY, who was twenty-seven years old in 1910, worked as a cashier in the posh dining rooms of the Grand Pacific

Hotel, at Clark Street and Jackson Boulevard. Palatial inns such as the Grand Pacific had begun to appear in Chicago in the late 1860s and early 1870s, their existence made viable by the railroads and the passengers they brought to the city. During the last quarter of the nineteenth century, the Grand Pacific was the famed Palmer House's main rival in hotel grandeur.

Ella was an attractive woman, about five feet four, well built, with brown hair and eyes to match. She wore glasses, which—*pace* Dorothy Parker—did not deter men from making passes. She was smart: a crackerjack cashier, very good at doing quick calculations and good at making conversation. And she was a warm, generous person who loved Jimmy, calling him "Little Brother" and doing things for him and playing with him.

At the Grand Pacific, Ella met a lot of wealthy and influential men. Wirt H. Cook, a lumberman from Duluth, Minnesota, who was sixteen years her senior and married, was one of them. Their affair was serious, at least on her part. He promised to marry her, and she believed him. Whatever his intent, he was the love of Ella Daly's life. But Cook's conflict with a Chicago lumberman—at the center of a national political scandal—apparently helped to bring their affair to an end.

The scandal concerned the bribery of Illinois legislators to elect Republican William Lorimer to the U.S. Senate in May 1909. (The Seventeenth Amendment to the Constitution, providing for direct popular election of senators, was still in the future.) Just before the election, Edward Hines, who was involved with Cook in a company that was logging timber in northeastern Minnesota, came to Cook's room at the Grand Pacific to discuss company business. After a few minutes, according to Cook's later testimony, Governor Charles S. Deneen, a Republican, telephoned. Then Hines, invoking the names of President William H. Taft and Nelson Aldrich, the powerful U.S. senator from Rhode Island, told Deneen that Lorimer had to be elected. "I will be down on the next train," Hines said, "prepared to furnish all the money that is required."

Friction grew between the two businessmen, and at a stockholders' meeting in March 1911 there was a showdown. Cook accused Hines of conducting the company's business so as to benefit his other interests; Hines denied it and denounced him as a blackmailer. The directors sided with Hines, and Cook's interest in the company was bought out.

The next month, Cook told a state senate committee investigating the alleged bribery in the Lorimer case about the overheard telephone conversation between Hines and the governor, and about other pertinent conversations and meetings. A few months later, he told his tale to a U.S. Senate committee.

Satisfying as all this may have been to Cook, it did carry a risk: that Hines might somehow use his affair with Ella Daly to try to discredit him. But Hines could only have done so with Ella's cooperation. Detectives working for Hines one night grabbed Earl Farrell and tried to pump him for information, and Ella herself may have been questioned. But she remained loyal to her lover.

With the ouster of Lorimer from the U.S. Senate in July 1912, the danger to Wirt Cook passed. He no longer needed Ella's loyalty. And as he was no longer involved with Hines, he had no reason to make frequent business trips to Chicago. At some point he simply stopped seeing Ella Daly. When he did come to the city, he managed to avoid her.

For a long time, Ella did not accept what had happened. For years she talked of "W. H.," as she called him, and of how he had promised to marry her. She would study the newspapers closely and when, now and then, she saw him mentioned as having arrived in town, she would get Earl, or occasionally Jimmy, to call hotels around town to find out if he was there. He never was. She came to see herself as a tragic heroine; but she was appearing in a play staged mainly in her own mind.

A lapsed Catholic, Ella seldom went to church and found no relief from her sorrows in the faith of her childhood. Instead, she sought solace in the bottle. She drank a lot— mostly whiskey, sometimes gin. She went on binges, and sometimes her brother Tom put her in People's Hospital on 22nd Street to dry out.

The loss of W. H. Cook was not Ella's only woe. Life at home cannot have been easy for her—or for anyone else in that tumultuous household. It was not a happy home. Her mother was contentious and unaffectionate, her brother was domineering and had a nasty temper, and she herself was an alcoholic given to histrionics. Among the Farrells, in contrast, "there were problems, as there are with all [families], but nothing like that," Jimmy's sister Mary remembered. "We didn't have this yelling and screaming and calling each other names, getting down to calling each other *sluts* and *whores* and *bastards* and *pimps*. It just never went on at our house."

As the novelist himself wrote long after that fateful night in

1906 when, as a squalling two-year-old, he was brought back to the Dalys': "It was a turbulent domestic world [in] which I was to live." And yet, for all the discord in his home, Jimmy was loved and even spoiled.

Chapter Two
Jimmy—and Studs

IN SEPTEMBER 1911, AT age seven, Jimmy Farrell entered the first grade at the Corpus Christi parochial school, just a few blocks from home. Run by the Sisters of Mercy, the school was only a few years older than he was, having opened in 1901 along with Corpus Christi Church. During the preceding decades there had been a new outbreak of anti-Catholicism in the country. The American Catholic hierarchy decided at the Third Plenary Council in Baltimore, 1884, that preservation of the faith required parochial schools. Chicago's Catholics had already arrived at that conclusion: in 1880, twenty-nine of the city's thirty-one parishes had schools.

At Corpus Christi and other parochial schools, the Church-approved truths of Christian doctrine were set down in question-and-answer form in a series of "Baltimore Catechisms." For Jimmy, the catechism's stern, legalistic lessons were not just lines to be memorized and recited and put out of mind. In the spring of 1912 he made his First Holy Communion, receiving the wafer of bread that, he was taught, had been transformed into the body of Jesus Christ. To make a good Communion, one had to be in a state of sanctifying grace, which meant that he had to go to Confession to tell his sins to a priest and obtain God's forgiveness. Jimmy was uneasy about taking part in this awesome drama. He found himself wishing he were not a Catholic, he recalled long afterward. "If I sinned, I had to confess. And in some instances, make penance. If I didn't, I could go to Hell."

Yet of course much of Jimmy's inner life and development took place outside of school and church. Baseball was his passion. In 1911 he saw his first White Sox game, and on August 27 he was on hand as Big Ed Walsh pitched a no-hitter against the Boston Red Sox. Over that season and the next two, Jimmy went to somewhere between forty and fifty big-league games. Uncle Tom would take him to White Sox owner Charles Comiskey's new ballpark at 35th and Shields, or he'd go with Earl. After Julia Daly began attending Ladies' Day games in 1912, she also would take him. And the next year, he sometimes went on his own.

When he was eight, Jimmy began going to Washington Park to play ball himself. "Every morning in summer, a group of men would be out, fooling around, and sometimes they would play a scrub game.... I used to play catch with some of them, watch them hit out and catch flies, and listen in wonderment when they talked of baseball." He began to dream of becoming a big-league star himself and imagine men in Washington Park talking of his exploits.

The next spring, the future baseball legend learned from his second-grade teacher, Sister Hilda, that he needed glasses. Despite the inevitable nickname, "Four Eyes," he continued to chase his dream of stardom. As he developed in the coming years and the dream took firmer hold, he would go at baseball in almost the same way that he later would go at writing: compulsively, relentlessly, and with the stubborn conviction that, whatever others might say, glory—perhaps even a sort of immortality—would one day be his.

HELEN FARRELL, JIMMY'S SIX-YEAR-OLD sister, went to Madison, Wisconsin, in 1912 to stay for the summer with her uncle Bill Daly and his well-to-do wife, Emma. They had been married for several years but had no children of their own.

Jim Farrell was against letting his older daughter go away, but his wife supported the idea, and he acquiesced. When the summer was up, Helen did not come back; Aunt Emma and Uncle Bill just kept her. Mary Farrell, who was aware of the disparity between her family's living standard and that of her siblings, seems not to have objected strenuously. Her husband did, but to no avail.

Ella Daly also wanted little Helen back in Chicago. She declared that she would stop drinking if Emma and Bill would just bring Helen home. They did not put her to the test. During the ensuing months, Emma and Bill came with Helen to Chicago a few times, but they carefully avoided the Farrells and didn't let the Dalys know that Helen was with them. When they went to have dinner with the Dalys, they left her behind in the care of someone at their hotel; once it was an elevator operator, who let her ride up and down with him.

About a year after Helen came to Madison, Emma became sick

and had to go into a sanitarium in Milwaukee for a few weeks. She and Bill didn't know what to do with Helen, so finally the girl was brought back to Chicago, to her parents, brothers and baby sister. Reunited with her family, Helen found that she didn't want to leave them again. "So I told my aunt I didn't want to go back." Emma was not pleased.

For the next several years, Helen lived at home but spent a great deal of time over at the Dalys'. She was there so much, in fact, that for a while, after the Farrells had moved into the cottage on 45th Place in 1914, she was enrolled as a student not only at St. Cecilia's, the nearby parochial school, but also at the public school near the Dalys'. Somehow, with a great many written excuses for Helen's absences at both schools, Aunt Ella and her complaisant mother managed to pull it off.

⟹≫-0-⟸⟸

"THEY WHO OF ALL OTHERS are famed for their beautiful home life are—many of them—content to live in flats, to move every May or October day, to be ever on the wing like stormy petrels." So the *New World*, the archdiocesan newspaper, once remarked about the curious tendency of Chicago's Irish to spurn the advantages of homeownership, remain renters, and move often. Despite their relative prosperity, the Dalys followed this pattern. On May 1, 1915, they left 5131 Prairie Avenue and the Corpus Christi parish behind and moved further south into the Washington Park community, to a first-floor apartment at 5704 Indiana Avenue in the parish of St. Anselm Church. Ella Daly may have been, at least indirectly, the stormy petrel responsible for the move.

Some time before, still pining for Wirt Cook and feeling sorry for herself and perhaps having had a bit to drink, Ella had gone to bed with a man named James H. Mullen, a widower who lived in the apartment downstairs. Julia Daly was livid. Her daughter, her own flesh and blood, not only had committed a mortal sin against Almighty God but had done so in their own building, almost in their own home! Suppose their neighbors and fellow parishioners at Corpus Christi found out! The only solution, she may well have thought, was to move.

Moving day was a Saturday, and early that afternoon Jimmy and his older brother were scouting out his new environs and came upon two boys, one around Jimmy's age, the other about a

25

year and a half older. "Say," said young Jimmy, in a tone that evidently seemed a little impudent to the neighborhood boys, "where do you guys play ball around here?" Their first thought (as Jimmy later learned) was to "clean up" on the fresh kid and his older companion, but for some reason—probably fifteen-year-old Earl didn't look like a pushover—they did not. One of the boys, the one about Jimmy's age, later became his friend. His name was Johnny Johnson. The other boy—who had not yet turned thirteen and was still wearing knee pants—was to became important to Jimmy too, but in a different way. His name was William P. Cunningham. His friends called him "Studs," a nickname he may have acquired as a result of his supposed resemblance—being short with broad shoulders—to a short nail with a large head, or because, on some occasion lost to history, he wore a dress shirt with studs when his peers did not.

Decades later, people who had known him as a youth would remember Studs Cunningham, with his cap tilted at a cocky angle and his swagger and bullying toughness, and say he was just like James Cagney, the movie star.

Cunningham's father, Patrick F. Cunningham, who was about forty-five in 1915, had come from County Cork, had worked as a plasterer and then a plastering contractor, and had done very well. He and his family lived in a comfortable apartment on South Wabash Avenue, two blocks west of the Dalys' new address. Mrs. Cunningham, the former Bridget Feeney, had also been born in Ireland. She didn't like the name Bridget, perhaps because her mother had the same name, or perhaps because so many "Bridgets" had found work in America as live-in domestics during the nineteenth century that the name had come to be associated with household service. She wanted her friends to call her Beatrice. The Cunninghams were "lace-curtain Irish," anxious not to be confused with disreputable "shanty Irish." And they were good Catholics who went to Mass regularly and raised their five children to do the same.

When Jimmy Farrell met Studs Cunningham, the older boy was just completing the seventh grade at St. Anselm's and Jimmy was about to transfer into the fourth grade there.* The two boys were never really friends; Jimmy was rarely, if ever, inside the Cunningham home on Wabash Avenue (or their subsequent home a

---

*Cunningham, born on September 13, 1902, was less than two years older than Jimmy but was three grades ahead of him. Jimmy had not entered first grade until he was seven and a half, while Studs evidently had started school when he was just turning six.

block away on Michigan Avenue). But for a time Jimmy looked up to Studs, who was "one of the best fighters of the boys who hung around Indiana [Avenue]," as the novelist would long afterward recall. To young Jimmy, whose father feared that Tom Daly was turning him into a "dude," the tough-guy demeanor of Studs Cunningham clearly had a certain fascination. To Studs and his friends, on the other hand, Jimmy was just a little squirt. For sport they would sometimes get him into a fight with some other kid; fortunately he always managed to win. "Studs used, sometimes, to tell me I could fight. For a period, he treated me better than Earl [did]. I was always interested in him, and wanted his good will." He wanted Studs to come to his twelfth birthday party in February 1916, but his brother Earl told Julia Daly that the boy was a bad influence, and she didn't allow it.

Little more than a year after their first meeting, Studs Cunningham graduated from St. Anselm's. Long afterward, when Jimmy Farrell was at work on his first novel, he looked back to that day and imagined Studs getting ready for the graduation ceremony. The scene became the unforgettable opening of *Young Lonigan* (1932):

> Studs Lonigan, on the verge of fifteen, and wearing his first suit of long trousers, stood in the bathroom with a Sweet Caporal pasted in his mug. His hands were jammed in his trouser pockets, and he sneered. He puffed, drew the fag out of his mouth, inhaled and said to himself:
> Well, I'm kissin' the old dump goodbye tonight.
> Studs was a small, broad-shouldered lad. His face was wide and planed; his hair was a light brown. His long nose was too large for his other features; almost a sheeny's nose. His lips were thick and wide, and they did not seem at home on his otherwise frank and boyish face. He was always twisting them into his familiar tough-guy sneers. He had blue eyes; his mother rightly called them baby-blue eyes.
> He took another drag and repeated to himself:
> Well, I'm kissin' the old dump goodbye.
> The old dump was St. Patrick's grammar school...

Cunningham—short, stocky, muscular—looked very much like Lonigan, except perhaps for the wide lips. And he was on the verge of fourteen, not fifteen, when he kissed St. Anselm's goodbye. After he left, one of his friends was to recall much later, Cunningham fell in with a bad crowd. He took to hanging out at a poolroom near the elevated station on 58th Street, between Prairie and Calumet. When summer was over, he entered Loyola Academy, a Jesuit-run high school for boys in Chicago's Far North Side. He did very poorly, however, and in December he dropped out. Before long, Studs went to work for his father and started to learn the plastering trade.

Jimmy and Studs Cunningham seldom saw each other in the succeeding years. But Studs left an indelible impression on the younger boy's voracious mind.

⟹▸•◦◂⟸

DURING THE WINTER OF 1916–1917, Bill Daly left Madison, Wisconsin. His wife had died, and he decided to return to Chicago. There was not really enough room for him in the Dalys' Indiana Avenue apartment. So on May 1, 1917, the Dalys and Jimmy Farrell moved once again. Their new address was 5816 South Park Avenue, a three-story graystone building directly opposite Washington Park.

The Dalys' second-floor flat had eight rooms, including a large front parlor (where they put their Victrola phonograph and the piano that Aunt Bessie had played) and a back parlor that Tom Daly used as a library. He had a lot of books and he would often sit in there in his easy chair, reading. Tom and thirteen-year-old Jimmy slept on twin beds in the front bedroom; Bill had a room to himself; Julia had her own room adjoining the kitchen; and the fourth bedroom, adjacent to the small dining room, was occupied by Ella Daly and Helen Farrell, who now came to live in the household too.

During the preceding years, Helen had been shuffled back and forth between the Farrells' home and the Dalys' so often that she scarcely knew where she belonged. Julia had not especially wanted her to live with them, but Ella, who doted on Helen, contended that the girl was needed to keep the old woman company on nights when Ella was working. Jim Farrell had long resisted the campaign to take away another of his children, often going to the Dalys' to get Helen and bring her home. But Mary Farrell had not resisted, telling her husband that her mother needed Helen. Now that the Dalys had so much room, the argument was finally settled: Helen went to live with them. But she frequently went back to her parents' home and usually had dinner there, something Jimmy rarely did.

Mary went over to the Dalys' nearly every day to sit with her mother, have tea and share the latest gossip. When Jimmy and Helen came in from school, Helen would talk with their mother, but Jimmy was very soon out the door. Decades later, Jimmy provided an unsympathetic and somewhat exaggerated portrait of his mother (in the guise of "Lizz O'Neill"), "wearing a man's tattered coat. She was dirty, and there was a soiled rag tied under her chin. She wore an old, crushed hat, and her uncombed hair straggled from under it. Her face needed washing. Her dress was stained." Mary kept losing teeth in childbirth, as happened to pregnant women who didn't take in sufficient extra calcium, and she suffered from neuralgia, bunions and other minor ailments. She didn't think that, in the end, she would be judged by her appearance.

In contrast, her brother Bill was very much concerned with his appearance. It took him hours to get dressed before going out. Unlike his brother Tom, though, he was not very ambitious. He would find work as a shoe salesman, his niece Helen remembered, but then some months later he would try to tell his boss how to run the company and end up losing his job. "He'd work six months and then he'd be out of a job, and then it would be six months or a year before he worked again."

Working or not, Bill did not spend any time contemplating eternity. Unlike his sister Mary and their mother, he abhorred any thought of final judgment, or indeed any mention of death. He had abandoned Catholicism for an almost hysterical insistence on positive thinking. He strenuously objected to what he called "crepe-hanging." Sunday dinner at the Dalys', his niece Mary remembered, "always ended up in a free-for-all, because somebody would start talking about something, and Bill would call it 'crepe-hanging.'"

<hr />

AFTER THE UNITED STATES declared war on Germany in the spring of 1917, displaying patriotic sentiments was the order of the day. For a pregame ceremony at Comiskey Park on Opening Day, the White Sox players donned army uniforms, shouldered Springfield rifles and marched around the field in somewhat ragged drill formation. Then they changed into their baseball outfits and played ball.

The Sox, managed by Clarence "Pants" Rowland, did very well that season. By June 8 they were in first place—and they didn't give it up. In the World Series, they went up against the New York Giants.

Tom Daly was then on the road, but he had sent Jimmy a money order for five dollars so that he and Earl could see a few of the Series games. At the World Series opener, held in Comiskey Park on Saturday, October 6, Jimmy and Earl sat high up in the right-center-field bleachers and had a great time watching the pitchers' duel between Ed Cicotte and the Giants' Slim Sallee. Chicago took that first game, 2-1. "I went home thrilled and happy," Jimmy recalled.

But the exciting afternoon did not end happily for him. When he got home, he discovered that his dog, an Airedale that Tom Daly had found in Boston and shipped home for him, had run away. She was never found. Before long, Tom produced another Airedale, dubbed "Liberty." When Jimmy's friend Joe Cody—who lived next door with his aunt and cousin—got a dog, he picked up on the theme and named it "Bell."

Three days after seeing his first World Series game, Jimmy, along with his sister Helen and Studs Cunningham's sister Loretta, was confirmed at St. Anselm's by Archbishop George W. Mundelein. James Thomas Farrell—who occasionally set aside his dream of becoming a baseball player so that he could imagine himself fighting in the Great War—was now (in theory, at least) a soldier of Christ.

———➤•○•◄———

THE LITTLEST FARRELL, FRANKIE, a lively and winning youngster, turned four in the spring of 1918. When he was an infant, the Farrells had moved into the cottage at West 45th Place and Wells Street in the Fuller Park community, where they were a bit more comfortable than they had been in their previous abodes. The toilet was still outdoors, but at least they had it all to themselves. Jim Farrell's cousin, Johnny Kelly, who was chief plumber at the Palmer House, installed a gas line in the cottage for them so they would have gas for lighting and a gas stove for cooking. For heat, they had a coal-burning potbelly stove that stood in the opening between the dining room and the parlor. But even the two stoves were not enough to keep the drafty wooden cottage warm in wintertime.

Comfort of a different sort was available nearby in the form of St. Cecilia Church. Mary Farrell often dashed over there, perhaps finding not only solace in prayer but respite from the demands of her children and, in the edifice itself, a beauty not otherwise present in her drab surroundings. Given the usual slovenly condition of their home, however, Jim Farrell may well have thought his wife spent too much time at St. Cecilia's. He did regard as excessive the donations she made to the church. Although his pious and easygoing wife, pregnant again in 1918, didn't manage money very well, Farrell always brought his slender pay envelope home to her unopened.

That year, on the other hand, saw a dramatic improvement in the family's material circumstances. Jim Farrell was promoted to wagon dispatcher and received a substantial raise in pay, to $175 a month. The new job meant he had to work nights. But before long he would be making $225 a month. And Earl, who graduated that spring from Tilden Technical High School, would soon be going to work at the express company himself. At last, Jim Farrell and his family were able to move up in the world, to join the "steam heat" Irish.

Farrell's good fortune came during a time of great change for the express business. In December 1917, President Woodrow Wilson had the federal government take over the railroads to meet wartime needs. Suddenly, the express companies—their contracts with the railroads no longer honored—began losing thousands of dollars a day. Out of the negotiations that soon commenced between the express firms and the government came a single, government-regulated express company, eventually to be known as American Railway Express.

But before Jim Farrell started working nights for the new firm, and before his family moved up to steam heat, tragedy struck. On Wednesday, June 19, 1918, Helen Farrell became sick. She felt weak all over and had a sore throat, a fever and a cough. The next evening, Julia Daly went to fetch the nearest doctor. He looked Helen over but could not identify her illness. He promised to return with another physician. Julia decided not to wait. She had Jimmy telephone Dr. James J. Roach, a close friend of Tom Daly's. Dr. Roach came right over and immediately recognized that Helen had diphtheria. She was rushed to the Municipal Contagious Disease Hospital. Jimmy was given a shot.

Diphtheria, which mainly threatens children, had been a common—and fearsome—feature of urban life during the nineteenth century. In 1880 there were 1,463 deaths in Chicago from the disease, or more than 290 for every 100,000 inhabitants. But a

31

treatment for the disease was soon found: medical researchers were able to isolate diphtheria's bacterial cause, finding also that healthy children who showed no symptoms of the disease could be "carriers," and they developed an effective antitoxin treatment.

The antitoxin worked best if administered during the first days of the illness. The longer it was delayed, the less effective it was likely to be. In a special investigation into seventy-five diphtheria deaths in 1917, the Chicago Department of Health found that only six had not been preventable.

By Tuesday, June 18, 1918—two days before Helen was hospitalized—it was apparent to the Farrell family that four-year-old Frankie was sick. His mother knew that Dr. Roach was a close friend of her brother Tom's, and so—perhaps that day, certainly the next day, and again the day after that, several times in all—she had Earl go to a store on Wentworth Avenue where there was a telephone and call Dr. Roach to have him come and examine Frankie. They waited and waited in the cottage, with Mary nursing the boy night and day. But Tom Daly's close friend never showed up. Perhaps he feared that the Farrells would not be able to pay for a house call. Whatever the reason, the family never forgave him.

Early Friday morning at the cottage, six-year-old Mary and her brothers Joe and Jack came into the parlor, where their pregnant mother was sitting on the couch. She was holding Frankie, rocking back and forth. And she told them he was dead. They knelt down.

Frankie was buried that afternoon. In such cases, the threat to public health dictated that interment be carried out swiftly and privately. Jim Farrell, Earl and little Mary accompanied the white hearse bearing the small coffin to Calvary Cemetery. "Poor little fellow," the father said, crying all the way.

When they got back to the cottage, the ambulance was there to take the children to the Municipal Contagious Disease Hospital. The Health Department was making a special effort that month (and the next) to get as many diphtheria patients as possible to the hospital rather than letting them stay at home in quarantine.

Mary Farrell's travail was not yet finished. With her youngest child freshly buried and her others (except for Jimmy) taken off to the hospital, she gave birth that same afternoon to a child who either was stillborn or lived only a short time.

After this ordeal, the family quit their cottage at 45th and Wells that summer and moved into a comfortable first-floor apartment in a six-flat building at 5939 Calumet Avenue, just a short block away from the Dalys' apartment. Their new home had steam heat, an indoor bathroom, hot and cold running water, gas and electricity. Finally the Farrells had arrived. But the memory of Frankie stayed with them. "I thought after my mother lost Frankie that she would never laugh again," Helen said. Mrs. Farrell wore black for two years.

——————➤•◦•◄———————

FOR FOURTEEN-YEAR-OLD JIMMY, his family's tragedy was eclipsed by his love of baseball. He continued to dream of becoming a big-leaguer: "Nothing seemed to me as important." From early spring to late autumn, he played ball. He played with other boys and he played with men. He played on any team that would have him. On summer days he headed for the ballfield after breakfast, again after lunch and then after supper. He was always playing or practicing baseball. "All through my boyhood I believed I was growing up to have a destiny, to become known to many, to thousands."

Jimmy's fervor seemed to set him apart. "His intensity, and the grandiose ambitions it fed, even during his boyhood," he was to write of his alter ego Eddie Ryan in *The Silence of History* (1963), "had been a reason why he felt himself to be different from other boys, and thus, as having something wrong with him, something which often made him fear that he was a goof."

The boys in the neighborhood measured themselves and others by their ability to fight. "As you know, Jim," Andy Dugar, a friend from Indiana Avenue, reminded him decades later, "if you and I hadn't known how to protect ourselves with our 'dukes' as we used to say on 58th St., we would have been pushed around a lot more than we were."

"Mostly the tough boys let me alone," Jimmy recalled on another occasion. "I was a good fighter, one of the best in the neighborhood.... I had a left hook, and a hard, mean right, and could box. I had natural athletic ability." Observant and smart, Jimmy used his intelligence to help him win battles. "I used to watch how every kid fought or boxed, and I would figure out how I would fight him, if I had to."

Jimmy entered eighth grade at St. Anselm's that fall. He had not been much interested in his schoolwork before, but now, inspired by his teacher, a tall, dark nun named Sister Magdalen, he became engrossed in his studies. One rainy Saturday afternoon, he recalled, "I sat by our parlor window in the apartment on South Park Avenue looking out at the wet trees and the dying greenness of Washington Park." He wanted to be outside playing, up around 60th or 61st Street, where he might see Dorothy, a little blonde girl who also went to St. Anselm's and whom he worshiped from afar. But he stayed inside. He had to write a composition about President Andrew Jackson's war on the Bank of the United States.

Jimmy usually found it hard to write and kept his compositions short. But this time the subject interested him, and he wanted to impress Sister Magdalen. So, as Julia Daly puttered about in the back of the apartment, he wrote and wrote. "Swept along, I filled page after page of my composition book.... For the first time in my life I experienced that absorption, that exhilaration, and that compulsion which drives you to sit alone and write with the immediate world about you walled out of your consciousness and with your impulses to have fun in the present put to sleep."

———————❖———————

DURING THE SPRING AND SUMMER of 1919, many racial clashes broke out in Washington Park. White gangs from the neighborhood of 59th and Wentworth Avenue—including some of the tough Irish who belonged to Ragen's Colts, a notorious "athletic club" sponsored by a politician named Frank Ragen who found its members' proficiency in intimidation useful—objected to black youths using the park's baseball diamonds. Ball games in the park often led to gang fights, which were usually broken up by park policemen. Jimmy, who so frequently went to Washington Park to play ball, must have been aware of the gang fights and may well have seen some of them.

On a Saturday night in late June, a showdown between white and black gangs was set to take place in the park, but police got wind of it. Two hundred policemen rushed to the scene and kept an all-night vigil. The white hoodlums—some of them, it was believed, members of Ragen's Colts—consequently avoided the park and instead sought out isolated blacks to assault. They murdered two black men.

Racial violence in the city soon got worse. One stiflingly hot Sunday afternoon in late July, a seventeen-year-old black youth cooling off in Lake Michigan apparently was hit by a rock thrown by a white man and drowned; a white policeman refused to make an arrest and the Chicago race riot of 1919 commenced. It might well have ended with the first clash had it not been for gangs of young toughs, especially white gangs, Ragen's Colts prominent among them. They kept the rioting going for more than four days.

"Day and night," recounts historian William M. Tuttle Jr., "white toughs assaulted isolated blacks, and teenage black mobsters beat white peddlers and merchants in the black belt," the South Side area where 90 percent of the city's black population lived:

> As rumors of atrocities circulated throughout the city, members of both races craved vengeance. White gunmen in automobiles sped through the black belt shooting indiscriminately as they passed, and black snipers fired back. Roaming mobs shot, beat, and stabbed to death their victims. The undermanned police force was an ineffectual deterrent to the waves of violence which soon overflowed the environs of the black belt and flooded the North and West Sides and the Loop.

The immediate neighborhood in which the Dalys and Farrells lived was spared, and Jimmy himself was not even in Chicago. Tom Daly had taken him to Grand Junction, Michigan, for two weeks of fishing and the rural life. But the rioting in Chicago affected him nevertheless. Monday night, a white seventeen-year-old he knew named Clarence "Clackey" Metz, who lived on the other side of Washington Park, was caught up in the action. He and four friends, instead of going to a movie as they had intended, joined a mob bent on assaulting blacks. Metz ended up on 43rd Street, bleeding to death from a stab wound (inflicted by a victim trying to defend himself). His demise was later to inspire one of Farrell's most effective short stories, "The Fastest Runner on Sixty-first Street," and in *The Young Manhood of Studs Lonigan* (1934) the killing of "Clackey Merton" appears as a *casus belli* in the eyes of Studs and his pals, belatedly eager to join in the mayhem. When Lonigan, brandishing a baseball bat, and the others (variously armed with a straight razor, brass knuckles, a .22 revolver, a hunting knife and clubs and sticks) get word of "a gang of niggers" on Wabash Avenue, they head that way.

> *The streets were like avenues of the dead. They only caught a ten-year-old Negro boy. They took his clothes off, and burned them. They burned his tail with lighted matches, made him step on lighted matches, urinated on him, and sent him running off naked with a couple of slaps in the face.*

To their disappointment, this was all that Lonigan and the unorganized "58th Street" gang could accomplish. It was, of course, quite enough.

⟶⟫-◊-⟪⟶

UNDER THE INFLUENCE OF Sister Magdalen, his eighth-grade teacher at St. Anselm's, Jimmy Farrell not only became interested in his studies but also came to imagine—albeit very reluctantly—that he had a vocation for the priesthood. (Conveniently, Quigley Preparatory Seminary on the Near North Side had just recently opened its doors.) Jimmy had not been enthusiastic about the prospect of becoming a priest because it would mean giving up both of his most important dreams—becoming a ballplayer and winning Dorothy, his blonde schoolmate. Still, he couldn't help but think that perhaps God wanted him to make those sacrifices.

With Jimmy's graduation from St. Anselm's that spring of 1919, Sister Magdalen's spell began to break. At a class picnic in Jackson Park a few days after graduation, he kissed Loretta Cunningham, Studs's younger sister. "It was the first time in my life that a girl had kissed me on the lips," he would remember. "I was very happy and very guilty, because I was going to be a priest, and I couldn't kiss girls." He soon decided that he didn't have a vocation for the priesthood after all. That September, instead of going off to Quigley Preparatory Seminary, he entered St. Cyril High School, a few miles southeast of his home.

Chapter Three
Growing Up

RESOLVED: *THAT THE CHICAGO CUBS are a better baseball team than the Chicago White Sox.* It was absurd, of course. The White Sox in September 1919 had never seemed more awesome. Yet that was the resolution that Jimmy Farrell had to uphold. On Friday, September 12, at the end of his first week at St. Cyril's, his elocution teacher, Frater Dionysius, had proposed a debate on baseball and asked for volunteers. Jimmy's hand shot up. The debate was to be held when the class met again the following Friday.

Eager to show off his baseball knowledge, Jimmy set aside his own passionate allegiance to the White Sox and worked enthusiastically to overcome the plain truth. Writing out his argument in a composition notebook, he discussed the histories of both teams and compared all of their current players, position by position. He dwelled at length on those individual Cubs whom he deemed superior to their White Sox counterparts and played up the strengths, real or imagined, of the other Cubs. Day after day, he scoured the record books and his own considerable fund of baseball lore. When the time for the debate arrived, his notebook was nearly filled.

"I was the first speaker," he recalled long afterward. "I was rather small. A curly-haired boy with gold-rimmed glasses, wearing blue short pants and a red sweater. I walked to the front of the room, my notebook in my hand. Usually shy and timid, cautious when first in a new environment, I was neither shy nor cautious." Reading aloud what he had written or, at times, speaking without consulting his notebook, Jimmy presented his case. His classmates were astonished at first, but many soon grew bored. His extremely detailed argument in support of what everyone knew to be false seemed endless. It took up most of the hour, and the debate had to be continued another day. Whatever his classmates may have thought, Jimmy was pleased with himself. He believed that he had been "something of a sensation."

When the debate finally concluded on the next Friday, it was judged a draw—which was, in effect, something of a victory for Jimmy. After all, the White Sox had clinched the American League pennant just two days earlier and seemed almost certain to beat the Cincinnati Reds in the World Series.

In October, as it happened, there was a stunning upset: The Reds took the championship, five games to three. Jimmy was disappointed. Like most other Americans, he never suspected that the Series had been fixed.

⟹•○•⟸

ST. CYRIL'S, RUN BY THE Carmelite order, was a small regional school, its enrollment only about two hundred boys when Jimmy entered. Just two of his St. Anselm's classmates came to St. Cyril's with him. When he was in his twenties and looking back with a jaundiced eye, Jimmy said that the atmosphere during his first year there had been "stagnant, [with] no football or baseball teams, no school magazine, no dramatic events, unless a country-school sort of elocution and public-speaking contest be described as dramatic, no school spirit, almost nothing." Nevertheless, hard as it was for the disenchanted young graduate to admit it, he and his classmates had indeed been learning in high school.

During Jimmy's first two years at St. Cyril's, he was a good student, albeit not an outstanding one. The subjects he studied included Latin, geography, algebra, history and English, and his marks were generally in the eighties. Jimmy's first English teacher was Father Leo J. Walter, the school's Prefect of Discipline and, despite his title, a kindly man. Jimmy welcomed the priest's weekly composition assignments, although his enthusiasm diminished when the time came to do them, for he lacked self-confidence. But his compositions generally were well received. At least one was even read aloud in class by Father Leo.

In November 1919, Father Albert H. Dolan, a newly ordained priest in his mid-twenties who was a stern disciplinarian, came to St. Cyril's. He was "a man of energy," Jimmy remembered some years later, and after his arrival "the atmosphere changed." Father Dolan took over Jimmy's English class. "All over again I had to gain confidence in myself. Unlike Father Leo, Father Dolan might not like my compositions. But he did. And he, too, gave me good marks. He read some of my compositions in class." Jimmy was still not among the best students, even in English.

⟹⟩◦⟨⟸

ONE NIGHT IN JUNE 1920, an automobile drew up only a block or so from the Dalys' apartment building at 5816 South Park Avenue. A man emerged from the car, went up to the house at 5922 South Park and then, after a few minutes, sped away. The explosion from the bomb he left behind shattered windows throughout the block and almost demolished the front of the house at 5922, which was the home of Jesse Binga, a prominent black banker and real estate agent. It was not the first time that Binga's home had been bombed; nor would it be the last. But he resolutely refused to move.

In *The Young Manhood of Studs Lonigan,* Farrell wrote about one of the bombings at *"a low, two-story, red stone house between Fifty-ninth and Sixtieth on South Park Avenue,"* the home of *"Abraham Clarkson, the leading colored banker of Chicago."* A crowd swiftly gathered, most hoping that Clarkson would get the message. But by now, they knew that he wouldn't.

> *For Abraham Clarkson had been bombed before, and had stated defiantly that he would move from his home to another one only in a casket. It was nerve for the nigger to say that and go on ruining a white man's neighborhood, living amongst people who didn't want him. Secretly, many of those present wished that he had been killed. Some of the Catholics wished only that it had wounded him, un-mortally, for didn't he always give Father Gilhooley a hundred dollars in the annual Easter and Christmas collections.*

Between 1917 and 1921, there were fifty-eight bomb explosions in Chicago at the homes of blacks who had moved into new neighborhoods, or at the homes or offices of real estate agents, white or black, who were blamed for bringing in blacks. More than half of the explosions took place within an area not much larger than two square miles—and inside it were the homes of the Dalys and the Farrells.

Hundreds of thousands of blacks had migrated from the rural South to Chicago and other northern cities, their movement prompted by the wartime labor shortage in the industrial North and by the shift of southern farmers away from cotton because of

39

the ravages of the boll weevil. Between 1916 and 1919, historian Allan H. Spear has noted, some fifty thousand blacks came to Chicago—"to crowd into the burgeoning black belt, to make new demands upon the institutional structure of the South Side, and to arouse the hostility of the Negro community's white neighbors."

The behavior of many of the rural blacks who came to the city was no more unimpeachable than had been the behavior of the shanty Irish in decades past. "The Negroes suffered from disease; they were 'immoral' by the standards of white society, having a high illegitimate birthrate, a high crime rate; their slums were appalling," one scholar has observed. Even many of the established black residents rejected the newcomers because of their woefully deficient habits and attitudes. Yet whites, for the most part, were not inclined to make much distinction between blacks who met their standards of morality and deportment and those who fell short.

When the Farrells lived in the cottage at West 45th Place and Wells Street, a black couple had lived next door. Although Mrs. Farrell treated the woman in a friendly way, their other white neighbors spoke resentfully of "the niggers" living so near. Little Mary Farrell, whom the black woman would sometimes invite in for milk and cookies, found the neighbors' hostility hard to understand. "Her house was always neat and clean, and the windows were shining, and the curtains. It was the cleanest house in the neighborhood! What was wrong with her?"

The shameful animosity that Irish-Americans in general had toward blacks was strong and longstanding. "As early as May 11, 1850," historian Carl Wittke has noted, "the *New York Tribune* had commented on the strange phenomenon that the Irish, having escaped so recently themselves 'from a galling, degrading bondage,' should vote against all proposals to give greater rights to Negroes and should come to the polls on election day shouting, 'Down with the Nagurs! Let them go back to Africa, where they belong.'" With their own bitter history of oppression, the Irish had much in common with the blacks—and perhaps just for that reason, their contempt for them seemed to know no bounds.

The bombings of Jesse Binga's house, like the deaths of Clackey Metz and others who had participated in the race riot, may well have driven home to Jimmy the pernicious consequences of racial prejudice. But such prejudice was all around him. Some of his friends were in the "Merry Clouters," a gang that—to judge from a

Farrell short story of that name—took equal delight in singing in harmony and harassing blacks in Washington Park. Racial prejudice was in the park, in the school, in the church and in the home. And it was no doubt in the conversation of the men of the Wagon Call Department of the American Railway Express Company, with whom Jimmy worked as a telephone clerk that summer after his first year at St. Cyril's. Eventually, in *Studs Lonigan* and other works, he would bring the commonplace racial prejudice among the Irish-Americans of Chicago squarely into American literature.

———————

AFTER SCHOOL RESUMED IN September 1920, the "Black Sox" scandal finally came to light: eight Chicago White Sox players, in exchange for money from gamblers, had thrown the 1919 World Series. Jimmy didn't want to believe it.

Later that month he went to a Sunday game between the White Sox and the Detroit Tigers, which the Sox won easily. Afterward he went under the stands with other fans and stood near the steps leading from the home team's clubhouse. "Shoeless" Joe Jackson and another of the "Black Sox" appeared and, without acknowledging the fans' encouraging calls, walked impassively by. Jimmy and others followed them. Then, as he would long remember, a fan called out: "It ain't true, Joe." And as the two players walked slowly on, not turning back, the crowd (though not shy Jimmy) took up the cry: "It ain't true, Joe."

But the truth could not be denied. Jimmy's days of worshiping baseball players came to an end. As he later reflected, "I was growing up."

Even so, he remained enthusiastic about athletics. He played basketball and baseball for St. Cyril's during his second year at the school, and also became athletic editor of the *Oriflamme*, a student magazine that Father Dolan established that fall. (Its name meant "golden flame," a reference to the fire that the Lord Almighty sent down to Mount Carmel to show the Israelites who the true God was.)

Jimmy contributed accounts of games to the magazine, a job which often required powers of imagination. "The [St. Cyril] teams had a habit of losing, and I...was forced to find new excuses for each defeat. Our team never lost fairly and squarely. It was always through bad breaks." Nor did St. Cyril teams ever give up before the game was over. "Actually, they gave up numerous times, but that wasn't for publication." The deviations from the harsh truth he felt obliged to make bothered Jimmy somewhat.

The February 1921 issue of the *Oriflamme* contained a very brief story (only 305 words) by Jimmy, entitled "Danny's Uncle." In light of Jimmy's own family situation, it is suggestive that the protagonist, Danny O'Neil (whose name is just one "l" short of the name of the writer's later alter ego), lives with his parents, and that Danny, with a well-aimed snowball, knocks off and ruins the silk hat of a "solemn-faced" man who turns out to be his wealthy uncle.

Father Dolan "tried to stimulate literary activity among the better pupils," the novelist later recalled. "We were not ashamed to reveal some of our feelings in our compositions." But not all of their feelings, of course: "We never would have written of our romantic daydreams about girls."

Less than a block away from St. Cyril's was Loretto Academy, a regional Catholic high school for girls. But for all the contact they had with the boys of St. Cyril, the girls of Loretto might have been on the other side of the planet. There was virtually no interaction between the two schools.

During their first two years at St. Cyril's, Jimmy and his classmates committed no graver transgression than smoking. He and most of the others seldom talked about sex. "I was slow in developing, and was shy with girls." He continued to dream of the unattainable Dorothy, worried at times that perhaps he really did have a vocation for the priesthood, and "scarcely ever spoke to a girl."

⟹⊶⊷⟸

"AFTER A LAPSE OF SEVERAL YEARS, St. Cyril High School will again put a team on the gridiron," reported the *New World*, the archdiocesan weekly, in September 1921. Jimmy became (as he later put it) "more or less of a star" on the new team. In an account of a 47-6 loss by St. Cyril to St. Rita Prep that November, the *New World* noted: "The St. Cyril boys in Farrell, Grace and McMillan brought applause for their play and hard fighting uphill all the way."

Sports—football, basketball, baseball—remained Jimmy's chief interest. A stellar member of the football team, he also became quite skilled at basketball, acquiring the nickname "Jumps" and serving as team captain in his senior year. And he was good at baseball, too—but not as good as he wanted to be. Once, to his acute embarrassment, he struck out with the bases loaded three times in a single game. In *Father and Son* (1940), he wrote about the day when Danny O'Neill did likewise: "In a pinch, it was always the same. He lost his confidence. When he didn't have time, a few seconds in which to think, it was different. That was why he was better in football and basketball than he was in baseball."

Toward the end of his third year, Jimmy began to slack off in his studies and turned his attention instead to the opposite sex. He would screw up his courage, ask a girl out—and usually get rejected. "I daydreamed through my classes, and I yearned for all the girls who wouldn't go out on dates with me."

With Prohibition now in effect, drinking became especially alluring to some of the St. Cyril boys. One Friday night in the fall of 1922, with a football game scheduled the next day, Jimmy went to a party and "for the first time in my life I was partly drunk." He and some of his teammates didn't get to bed until 4 A.M. Later that day they lost the game against St. Mel's, although Jimmy's subsequent account in the *Oriflamme* managed to make defeat seem almost victory. A line inserted into his story by the editor-in-chief claimed that "Farrell...played his usual spectacular game." Maybe he did.

Jimmy began not showing up for afternoon football practice. When coach Harry Curran asked him one day to explain his absences, Jimmy said that he already knew everything the coach had to teach. His dereliction didn't get him thrown off the squad— but that, the coach said, was only because he was needed.

That fall, in a game against De La Salle of Joliet that was played on a muddy field in the pouring rain, Jimmy injured his knee. He finished out the season, making a fifty-yard run against St. Philip's in the final game. But he was left with a permanent "bum" knee.

At his final football banquet, Jimmy made clear his preference for unwelcome truth over convenient fiction. He objected to "the indiscriminate praise that was sprinkled so freely on an unsuccessful team." This heresy won him a reprimand by Father Dolan.

"What is school spirit?"

That was one of the questions posed to students by the *Oriflamme* in a contest whose purpose, the magazine said in its January-February 1923 issue, was "to increase the excellent school spirit at St. Cyril."

The winning one-sentence answer to that particular question, as decided by Father Dolan and his fellow judges, was submitted by James Farrell, Class of '23. "School spirit," Jimmy declared, "is an ardent and enthusiastic participation in all school activities." This profundity gained him the prize, one dollar, but not before Father Dolan—who, as the novelist later recalled, "liked to play somewhat sadistic practical jokes on students"—quietly informed him that he was going to withhold the dollar because Jimmy's uncle had failed to pay his tuition that year. This was true. Tom Daly and the Upham Brothers shoe firm, it seems, were experiencing some difficulties. But the understanding priests of St. Cyril had allowed Jimmy to continue at the school for his final year. When Father Dolan was done with his little joke, Jimmy got his prize.

Although Jimmy advocated "school spirit" and certainly seems to have displayed it often enough, he in fact was not an "ardent and enthusiastic" participant in *all* of the school's activities. One year at the annual retreat, a week set aside for the spiritual renewal of the boys of St. Cyril, there was "a scandal, perpetrated mainly by the writer," he recalled in an unpublished essay written in his twenties.

"Having several dollars, I invited every one in our group (about eight) to attend a Balaban and Katz show rather than the afternoon sermon." (Balaban and Katz ran a number of "picture shows" in Chicago and booked many vaudeville acts.) Before long, about fifteen boys took off and "saw amongst other things, girls dancing with scanty apparel on their sensuous, young bodies." But the boys' absence from the retreat was discovered. "Two of my pals were forced to kneel before the entire student body at chapel in acknowledgement of their guilt, and the others were publically [*sic*] reprimanded. Only the writer escaped, having gotten a forged excuse for sickness."

The school booster thus, on occasion, became a furtive rebel. But he and most of the other boys of St. Cyril did not let their wayward impulses carry them very far. No experienced confessor could have been greatly shocked by their transgressions. "Bumming from school," Jimmy wrote, "was considered almost as brave as pool-playing or shooting craps. Fights were few, although there was much cruel, unthinking humor. We talked and wondered much about sex, and two or three more daring fellows had affairs [or] relationships with loose girls."

In 1922, AT THE AGE OF fifty-one, Jimmy's father had a stroke, his second. It affected his right side. He now needed a cane to walk and his speech was somewhat slurred. It became harder and harder for him to work; before long, he could not work at all. His oldest son, Earl, came to the family's rescue. Earl Farrell had been working in the express company's office during the day and taking a business course at night. Now he quit his office job and took better-paying work as a helper on one of the wagons; to save money, he also gave up night school. With what Earl earned, and a little help from the Dalys, the Farrells managed to get by.

Jim Farrell made the best of his diminished situation. He liked music and often reclined in his Morris chair, listening to records on the Victrola—light opera, light classical music, Stephen Foster songs. And he would read—not only the newspaper but the volumes in an encyclopedia-like set that he owned, and Shakespeare. He loved Shakespeare, his youngest daughter remembered.

He must have worried a great deal about his wife and children. The youngest, Mary, was only eleven. Now and then his thoughts must have turned to his second son, the one who had grown up with the Dalys in relative comfort and who had always been so distant from him. In *Father and Son*, after Jim O'Neill has a stroke, and with his oldest son, in consequence, now working on the wagons, there is an encounter between Jim and his son Danny:

> "Well, when you get out of school in June, we'll get you back in the company, and it's going to be O'Neill's Express Company."
>
> He wouldn't be able to go to college and make a name for himself as a college football star. He wouldn't be able to be in a fraternity and live the life of a college man.
>
> They sat for a few silent moments.
>
> "Papa, I can quit now and go to work," Danny said, but he hated to have to do this.
>
> "You finish it out this year. I'll be back at work sooner than it looks, too. I'm feeling better already. I'll get a week or two more of rest, and then I'll start taking walks. I'll be in shape in no time."

Did such a conversation ever take place between Jim Farrell and his son Jimmy? It might have. But it seems much more likely that it was a conversation that the son, long afterward, wished had taken place, an offer of help that he wished he had made. In any case, Jimmy remained in school. And before long he made his father very angry.

In February 1923, shortly before his nineteenth birthday, he

went on a toot in the Chicago neighborhoods of Pullman and Rose-
land, and drank wood alcohol in the guise of bootleg whiskey. By
his own later account, he "almost died."

When Tom Daly brought the errant youth home from the hospital, Ella Daly was at the door to meet them.

"Why did you do it, Little Brother?" she asked.

"I'm sorry," Jimmy replied.

His father's response was a good deal stronger than Ella's. The
episode prompted the ailing Jim Farrell to intervene forcefully in
his son's life. "My father made me work—made me take a job—on
hourly rates as a freight handler for the express company over at
Monroe and Desplaines," Jimmy recalled almost three decades later.
His father also forbade him to play sports any more. Given his own
situation, Jim Farrell must have felt that it was time for Jimmy to
put away childish things and come to the aid of his family. By
Jimmy's own account, however, he didn't do that.

"The work [at the express company] was too heavy, and in
addition to which, I had no inclination for it," he recalled. "At all
events, partly out of malingering, partly out of the fact that I did
definitely strain my groin lifting heavy boxes, I quit."

Nor did he give up sports. He continued to play basketball
but, so far as the newspapers were concerned, under the name of
"Hart" or other aliases. Evidently his father never found out.

———⟫◦⟪———

DURING HIS YEARS AT St. Cyril's, Jimmy earned a total of seven letters
in football, basketball and baseball. "'Jumps,'" said his senior yearbook, "is one of the best all-around athletes ever turned out at St.
Cyril's." Had the high school been coeducational, his athletic
prowess might have enabled him to get some traction with girls.
But it wasn't, and he didn't.

His lack of success with the opposite sex was not for lack of
effort. He joined the high school fraternity, Alpha Eta Beta, and he
learned to dance at the newly opened Trianon Ballroom, at 62nd
and Cottage Grove Avenue. But there was something about him that
made the girls stand off. Perhaps it was his intensity, or his lack of
self-confidence—or the volatile mixture of the two. He was brash
at times with certain adults, such as coach Curran or Father Leo,
who he had reason to suspect would indulge him, and he was used

to dealing forcefully with boys his own age. But with girls he became shy and awkward. The more he tried to impress them, the more he failed—and the lower he sank in his own eyes, and quite possibly in theirs, too.

In his affecting short story "Senior Prom," Farrell described how it was for young Danny O'Neill during the spring of his senior year: "When ten different girls had turned him down for a date for the Alumni Dance in April, Danny was hurt and deeply embarrassed. He couldn't understand why girls wouldn't date him and wondered what was wrong with him.... He had had the same difficulty in getting dates before, and he had become convinced that many girls talked about him and laughed at him behind his back." Danny went as a stag to the Alumni Association's annual dance, but soon after it, he resolved to get a date, "a beautiful girl," for the Senior Prom at the end of May. As the prom drew closer he became more and more worried: "To show up without a date at the Senior Prom would be like placing the brand of failure upon himself. But it seemed that girls just didn't want to go with him."

Danny (like young Farrell himself) did manage to get a date for the prom. But pretty as Sis Hansen was, neither she nor the prom quite lived up to his daydreams. She showed no interest in him and at the dance openly flirted with another boy. Finally, a cab brought Danny and his date back to her home. She gave him perfunctory thanks, said good night, and warded off his clumsy attempt to kiss her.

> "Aren't you going to kiss me good night?" he asked, tense. She smiled coldly and was gone.
>
> Hurt and dazed, he watched her walking up the steps of the inner hallway. He stood for a moment, defeated. Then he walked out. His shoulders slumped and after one glance up at the darkened window of her parlor, he slowly trudged home.
>
> What was the matter with him? What was wrong with him? He looked at the sky and the shrubbery of the park across the street, and he was just hurt with a sense of defeat. His dreams of Sis and of love were dust.

GRADUATION CAME ON MONDAY, June 18, 1923. Jimmy's parents were not present (possibly because of what may have been a conflicting engagement: his brother Joe's graduation from St. Anselm's). But Julia Brown Daly was on hand to see her cherished grandson receive his high-school diploma.

Jimmy's classmate Richard Parker delivered the class oration. A half-dozen other graduating students also took part in what the *New World* called "an exceptionally fine literary program." Jimmy was not among them.

Gold medals for various academic achievements were handed out. Parker got one for Latin, and Bob Lusk, the *Oriflamme* editor-in-chief, received two gold medals—one for senior English and another for science essay. Other boys were similarly honored. But Jimmy was not among them.

Archbishop (soon to be Cardinal) Mundelein, who had presided at Jimmy's confirmation six years before, presented the diplomas to him and the forty-five other graduating students. "His Grace," the *New World* reported, "then addressed the graduates, complimenting them for their splendid performance and hoping for a greater St. Cyril's." Mundelein wanted, and soon got, a physical expansion of the high school to accommodate the community's growing population. And to dispel the notion that it was just for the boys who lived in the St. Cyril parish, the enlarged school was given a new name: "Mount Carmel High School."

But in June 1923 the school was still St. Cyril's. And in the *St. Cyril High School Yearbook* issued that month, "the appointed prophets" foretold the futures of graduating seniors. "Farrell," the prophets said, "will have paid all his debts and will have been elected to the Athletic Hall of Fame."

To nineteen-year-old Farrell himself, who already had begun work as a telephone clerk at the express company, the future may have seemed less certain.

⸻ ⟩⟩•○•⟨⟨ ⸻

THAT NOVEMBER, DURING THE week of Thanksgiving, Jim Farrell had another stroke. On Saturday the 24th, as he lay helpless in bed, Mary Farrell went out to arrange for his hospitalization. Left alone with him in the apartment were twelve-year-old Mary and her brother Jack, who was a year older. Playing in the dining room, they could hear their father gasping for breath. They took turns going into the bedroom to look at him.

When he became quiet, Mary long afterward remembered,

Jack went into the bedroom and then came back with "a funny expression" on his face. "Papa is dead," he said. Mary went into the bedroom. She patted her father on the forehead and kissed him on the cheek. "Goodbye, Papa," she said.

The two children then sat in the dining room, waiting in silence for their mother to come home. When she did, she tried to close her husband's eyes and she put a cloth over his head. Then she went over to the Dalys'. Before long, Helen Farrell came running over to the Farrell flat, "crying very hard."

At this, Jack and little Mary finally burst into tears. Their father was gone.

And gone with him was any possibility that he and his secondborn son might eventually come to a better understanding of each other. Now, any such reconciliation could take place only in the mind and imagination of the surviving Jim Farrell.

Chapter Four

A Modern Man

YOUNG FARRELL HAD LONG since become familiar with the demands and routines of the express company's wagon department, having first been introduced to them in the summer of 1920. He had endured the men's ragging, listened to their banal conversations, and experienced the monotony of their work. His brothers Earl and Joe might be content to remain at the company for the rest of their lives, but he wanted something different. "Sometimes, I would think of writing," he later recalled.

During the summer of 1924, Farrell began to read serious books. His father had read Shakespeare and his uncle Tom Daly perused volumes he considered conducive to self-improvement, but young Farrell's own reading had never gone much beyond the sports pages and what his teachers at St. Cyril's had required. Now, however, with the excitements of his school days over and the need to advance himself apparent, he began his self-education.

The newspapers that summer were full of stories about "the crime of the century": the kidnapping-murder of fourteen-year-old Bobby Franks by two older youths, Nathan Leopold Jr. and Richard Loeb. All three were from wealthy families in the Hyde Park neighborhood, near the University of Chicago. A host of "alienists" (psychiatrists) descended on the city in connection with the case, and the resulting buzz about "abnormality" and other interesting conditions may well have influenced Farrell's initial choice of books: Sigmund Freud's *Psychopathology of Everyday Life* and an introductory work on psychoanalysis by A. A. Brill. He also read G. K. Chesterton's *New Jerusalem*, the Christian apologist's recent account of his travels in Palestine.

When he encountered an unfamiliar word, Farrell wrote it down and later looked up the meaning. "Every night I would look up five of these words, and then write a sentence using each of them."

But he knew that he would need more than an enlarged vocabulary to escape from the sort of existence in which he now felt trapped. That September, accordingly, thinking he eventually would become a lawyer, he embarked on a course of classes at DePaul University night school. Soon his eyes began to give him trouble. The vision in his right eye would never be good, but thanks to what eventually turned out to be a false diagnosis by a specialist, Farrell now feared that "the price of study and of writing would be blindness."

Defying his apprehensions, he kept at his studies: "I was struggling to gain self-confidence and to equip myself for the future." In a book assigned in his English class, he found an essay that evoked "an instantaneous feeling of recognition on my part." It was a gloomy essay, he thought, but "it seemed to register a sadness that was in the order of life." Sitting in his urban classroom, tired after "a nerve-racking day of work in the express office," he listened to the blare of motor horns in the darkness outside and imagined young men like himself passing with their girls on the street below, on their way "to see shows, to dance, to enjoy themselves and kiss and pet on dates." He felt a sadness that seemed much like that expressed by the essay's author, whose name—Theodore Dreiser— was new to him.

But sadness was not a constant companion. "Next Saturday evening, St. Cyril's Alumni Association will stage a dance at Father Hilary's new auditorium.... I will favor all with my most august presence," he wrote to "Red" Conners, who had been on the high school football team with him and was now a freshman at the University of Notre Dame. In another letter, to his friend Andy Dugar, who had moved to Los Angeles, Farrell reported that while work and school were "the main things demanding my attention," he occasionally took the time "to attend a dance or see a show." These days, he told Dugar, he seldom saw their old "58th Street" buddies, except for Paul Caron, with whom "I pal around." Tall, handsome and clever, Caron—besides having shared with Farrell the distinction of being able to lick Dugar in a fight—had a way with girls that Farrell much envied.

Like many another man at twenty, Farrell found life confusing and earnestly sought to understand the meaning of it all. Working toward his future, he became extremely conscious of time. He read the last chapter of Walter Pater's *Renaissance* (1873) and was "profoundly stirred" by the neopagan aesthete's infamous words:

Not the fruit of experience, but experience itself, is the end. A
counted number of pulses only is given to us of a variegated, dramatic life. How may we see in them all that is to be seen in them by
the finest senses?....To burn always with this hard, gem-like flame, to
maintain this ecstasy, is success in life.

Eager to burn bright, Farrell quickened his pace. In February
1925 he applied to the University of Chicago to begin classes in
the fall, anticipating that by then he would have completed a year
at DePaul. The next month, however, he abandoned night school so
he could quit the express company and work instead as a gas station attendant for the Sinclair Oil and Refining Company. He
earnestly told the supervisor who hired him that he wanted to
work his way up from the bottom "and become a lawyer and work
as a lawyer for this corporation." Initially, he filled in at various gas
stations for men who were off; subsequently, he was assigned to
the station at 42nd and Michigan, where he worked the evening
shift, 3:00 to midnight, six days a week. A company rule was
waived, giving him permission to study while on duty.

Farrell's new job was not without its hazards. One night, he
left the station a little late, then realized he had forgotten something. "I went back in the station, turned the inner lights on to get
what I had forgotten, and came out and locked the door. I was
almost shot without knowing it." Across the street was a cop named
Doyle, who had whipped out his gun and was preparing to shoot.
"In those days," Farrell explained in a 1942 diary entry, "there was a
big reward for a policeman apprehending a burglar or robber who
was holding up or robbing a gas station." But with Doyle that night
was Studs Cunningham, drawn there by the policeman's prior
accounts of the many brothels and prostitutes in the area. "Studs
recognized me, and said that's young Farrell. Otherwise, I would
have been shot." Studs Cunningham, he believed, saved his life.

———❖———

IT WAS NOT FAR—no more than a mile or so—from his home to the
University of Chicago, but it must have been an exciting day for
him that June, and a proud one for Julia Daly, when Jimmy first set
off to go where no Farrell or Daly before him had gone. At twenty-
one, he stood about five feet, eight inches tall and had thick, curly,
dark brown hair and his father's broad shoulders and long arms. He
wore horn-rimmed glasses with extremely thick lenses, and, if he

dressed that day as he typically did in the next few years, he had on a rather shabby blue suit, with his tie loosely knotted and the collar of his white shirt slightly askew. In all likelihood he carried a brief-case, not yet as crammed with books and papers as it would come to be. Leaving his home, he crossed to the other side of South Park Avenue, entered Washington Park at 58th Street, and then pro-ceeded through the park, walking in his somewhat odd way, a rolling gait, almost lurching, his right arm tending to move forward with his right leg and his left arm doing the same with his left leg. He knew the park well, of course. For him (as for Eddie Ryan in *The Silence of History*) it held "many associations, many memories, many dreams that never came true, many brooding boyhood sad-nesses, many recollections of running, shouting boyhood play." Soon Farrell emerged at 57th Street, crossed Cottage Grove Avenue—he was in the city's Hyde Park section now—and walked to Cobb Hall on the campus.

The university, with its imposing limestone buildings in the Gothic style, was only a dozen years older than Farrell himself. It was "a new model American university," historian Frederick Rudolph has written, "one which divided the 12 months of the year into four academic quarters and invited its students to take a mini-mum three or an accelerated four." But more important than undergraduate instruction, as its first president, William Rainey Harper, did not hesitate to proclaim, was academic research. A Chicago school of sociology soon developed around professors William I. Thomas (before scandal forced him to leave in 1918) and Robert E. Park, a former newspaperman who inspired studies of urban life. Similarly, in philosophy, a Chicago school of pragmatism grew up around John Dewey (before he departed for Columbia University in 1904 after a quarrel with Harper) and his associate George Herbert Mead. Both schools of thought influenced Farrell's own thinking and *Studs Lonigan*.

Except for his Catholicism, it was not unusual in the 1920s for someone of Farrell's modest background to be attending the Uni-versity of Chicago. After the Great War, the Ivy League schools in the East began to attract the scions of Chicago's wealthy and well-born, and the local institution had to content itself, for the most part, with undergraduates from middle- and lower-middle-class fam-ilies who could not afford to send their offspring away to school. Tuition at the University of Chicago in 1925–1926 was $74 per quarter. Most students lived at home and commuted to the campus, just as Farrell did. Unlike him, however, most were Protestant. The university did not discriminate against Catholics; they generally excluded themselves.

Such "diabolical" institutions (as the archdiocesan weekly, the *New World*, warned its readers on various occasions) taught "strange doctrines"; they were "materialistic" and lacking in "moral atmosphere"; they were "under the influence of socialism," "full of debauchery and drunkenness," and "subversive of all religious belief." Not all Catholics in the city agreed, needless to say.

Farrell was not oblivious to the reputed dangers. One week after his matriculation, he reported in a letter to Paul Caron that one had to guard one's faith carefully. Farrell's courses that summer quarter were in history: "Early Medieval Europe" and "Later Medieval and Early Modern Europe." He somehow managed to get an A in the first and a B in the second without having to abandon his faith.

But the challenge to religious belief, as Farrell was soon to discover, was not confined to the campus of the University of Chicago. That summer, a Tennessee schoolteacher named John Scopes went on trial. With the eager help of the American Civil Liberties Union, he had gotten himself charged with having violated Tennessee's new law that (on paper at least) banned the teaching of evolution in the public schools. The "monkey trial," as H. L. Mencken gleefully called it, at which defense attorney Clarence Darrow mercilessly grilled the "Great Commoner," William Jennings Bryan, about his belief in the literal truth of the Bible, was a cruel farce, a degrading sideshow. Yet in its distorted way, the trial did reflect a larger truth: the relentless advance of science—indeed, modernity itself—now seemed to call religious faith seriously into question. "Illusions have been lost one by one," journalist Joseph Wood Krutch was to write in *The Modern Temper* (1929). "God, instead of disappearing in an instant, has retreated step by step and surrendered gradually his control of the universe.... [And] man is left more and more alone in a universe to which he is completely alien."

At the University of Chicago, so near to where he had spent his boyhood years, young Farrell now glimpsed the perplexing modern world. Earnest, intelligent, ravenous for knowledge, he could hardly have failed to notice the great gulf that yawned between "enlightened" modern opinion and what he had always been taught.

━━➤●◀━━

ONE SATURDAY MORNING IN early November 1925, Farrell took a train south to Champaign, Illinois. Tom Daly, who was "on the road," was staying in a hotel there, and he and Farrell planned to go to a football game that afternoon: the University of Chicago "Maroons," coached by Amos Alonzo Stagg, were taking on the University of Illinois and its famed captain, Red Grange. Unfortunately for all concerned, it was raining.

Farrell and his surrogate father had lunch in a restaurant at the hotel, talking about the weather and how the gridiron would be a sea of mud. Until a few months before, Farrell had entertained the hope of playing for the Maroons himself the following year; but he wrenched his "bum knee" so many times between May and September that he reluctantly gave up that aspiration. (Later, when he tried out for the freshman basketball team, he pivoted once, popped his knee—and finally retired from school sports.)

Most of the people in the crowded and noisy restaurant seemed to Farrell to be in good spirits. But he and his uncle did not share in the general mood. Farrell felt that he ought to say something to his uncle "that would break through to him." But he couldn't.

At the game, they sat together, "looking as though we were father and son." Like the 69,000 other spectators, they were cold and wet. On the field, as the *Chicago Tribune* reported the next day, the rival teams "slipped and slushed through a veritable quagmire." Illinois quarterback Grange was unable to find his feet, but the punting of a teammate gave Illinois the edge. After more than two hours, the wretched game finally ended with Illinois the victor but Chicago not disgraced.

After they left, Farrell and his uncle had dinner, and then, since it would be a while before the train for Chicago departed, they went to Daly's hotel room. "Uncle Tom seemed to want to say something that he couldn't get himself to say, or else that he did not know how to say," Farrell recalled decades later. "There was an embarrassment which we both shared."

Daly asked how things were at home, and Farrell said they

55

were all right. That meant: Ella Daly had been staying sober. She was working now at the LaSalle Hotel, an imposing 22-story edifice at LaSalle and Madison, in the financial district. She may have been drinking a little less, but she still had a problem with the sauce.

If Tom had any inkling of what was to happen to his own employer, Upham Brothers, within the next year and a half, he must have worried about that, too. For Charles S. Upham, the treasurer of the Massachusetts firm and son of one of its cofounders, would soon die, Upham Brothers would halt its operations, and Daly would lose a great deal of money—something like $30,000 according to Farrell's recollection—which he had invested in the company over the years.

Sitting in the hotel room with him, Farrell felt, as he later said, "a great sadness about my uncle and his life." For years, Tom had traveled and stayed a night or two in one hotel after another, in one midwestern city or town after another. "I sensed a great loneliness in him. We were inarticulate with each other. The loneliness of the hotel room was like a penetrating sadness."

⇒►·0·◄⇐

THAT SAME MONTH, NOVEMBER 1925, Farrell was transferred from the filling station at 42nd and Michigan to one at 25th and Wabash, in the black belt. He worked at the gas station from 2 to 9 P.M., seven days a week, made at least $140 a month and gave half of it to his mother (who, with Earl, Joe and the two younger children, Jack and Mary, had moved into a nicer apartment across the street from their old one); he also gave $5 a week to his grandmother.

Traffic was light at his new station and that gave him time to read. But sometimes his mind was so much on his studies that he forgot to collect from a customer; then, to make up the difference, he resorted to "pulling the pumps," i.e., giving subsequent customers less gas than they paid for. Almost all of the attendants "grafted or cheated a little, if not more," he remembered long afterward.

At the university that autumn quarter, Farrell was taking a political economy course on "Industrial Society" and a history course on "Later Modern Europe." He also continued reading on his own. He read Sinclair Lewis's *Babbitt*, published three years before, giving him a picture of the American businessman strikingly different from the one Tom Daly had always presented. The derisive portrait seemed to Farrell a truer one. "For months, after I had read *Babbitt*, I was thinking of the book, talking of it, looking at people and testing them against Babbitt."

He threw himself into his studies and independent reading. His horizons were being widened, he was absorbing facts and asking questions, and he was developing intellectually. In other respects, though, college so far proved to be something less than Farrell had hoped. For months, he had gone without a date.

Nor did he have one that New Year's Eve. But he was not unoccupied on that last day of 1925: He finished reading Samuel Butler's *Way of All Flesh* (1903), a work that one critic has described as "a hymn of hate against Victorian Christianity and the Victorian bourgeois family." Farrell, perhaps significantly, was not put off by it. On the contrary—as he wrote two days later, earnestly setting down his thoughts on paper—he considered it "an excellent novel."

"Butler's philosophy is twisted up somewhat," he reflected. "He contends that pleasure is the best guide for human action. He says that it is better for a man to have sinned than to have been sinned against. He discards idealism in religion and human actions and seems to be [a] material[ist]." But he added: "Butler is not all wrong in his views.... If we are material[ists] we must admit his conclusions."

━━➣●◆━━

FATHER MICHAEL GILMARTIN, PASTOR of St. Anselm's, was very proud. His parish had a magnificent new church, a $350,000 Romanesque structure with twin towers and inside, three Carrara marble altars. Gilmartin's friend Patrick Cunningham, the plastering contractor, had done a good job on the interior. The church's main entrance was on spacious Michigan Boulevard, and now the combination church-and-school building on 61st Street, built when Gilmartin had formed the parish in 1909, could be used exclusively for the school. The pastor had secured Cardinal Mundelein's permission to build the new church in 1924, and the edifice, blessed by Mundelein in December 1925, was now finished. The pastor was sure it meant that his parish's future was bright. Many of his parishioners were much less sanguine.

In the preceding years, as the black belt had expanded and blacks began to move into the area, many of the Irish of St.

Anselm's feared that their neighborhood was doomed. Gilmartin refused to believe it and insisted that a new church would keep the neighborhood white. In *The Young Manhood of Studs Lonigan*, Farrell has one of Studs Lonigan's pals, Red Kelly, explain to him:

> "St. Patrick's is a coming parish, Studs. And the new church is going to make it. It's going to stop all this wild talk about the jiggs moving around here and running the neighborhood. Gilly is a smart man, and what he said last Sunday in church is the goods. Michigan Avenue is going to be made a boulevard. Property values around here will sky-rocket. The new church will clinch the matter. You watch, it'll make people stay here, and the new ones of the right kind with money will move in and buy property. Gilly knows his stuff."

As it turned out, Gilmartin did not know his stuff. By the time the church was dedicated, the migration of whites out of the area was well under way. Before the decade was out, the Dalys, the Farrells and the Cunninghams would all join the exodus, and in 1932 the parish would be turned over to a new pastor and the Society of the Divine Word Fathers. St. Anselm's would become a thriving black Catholic parish.

Mary Farrell would leave something lasting behind, however. It was an extravagant gesture on her part, requiring a donation that her late husband undoubtedly would not have approved. Inside the new St. Anselm Church, on the left wall near the front was a plaster representation of one of the Stations of the Cross: "Jesus is made to bear His cross." And on a brass plaque was this inscription: "In Memory of James Francis Farrell and Honora Kelly Farrell."

<hr />

FOR YOUNG JIM FARRELL, lonely and yearning and unsure of himself, family and faith were becoming increasingly unwelcome burdens. The first in his family to attend college, and daring to dream of rising high in the world, he was on his own—and he could not help but think that his family, with its members' various faults and failures, all so well known to him and so long a source of embarrassment and even shame, was somehow holding him down.

He also couldn't help but think that the Catholic faith in which his family had reared him might be part of his problem. The most important question from an intellectual standpoint was whether Catholic doctrine was true. He had read some of Saint Augustine's *City of God*, probably in connection with his course in the history of early medieval Europe, but he was becoming less and less sure that acceptance of the Faith of Christ was the right course. And if it was not, if the faith of Augustine and Bede, of Aquinas and Chesterton, was not true, then of course it should be rejected—even though, in Farrell's case, that would be almost to reject his own family and his own past. But *was* Catholic belief, *was* all that he had been taught from an early age about God and man, false?

Determining the truth or falsity of Catholic belief was a daunting enough challenge, but there was also the less abstract matter of sex. The Church insisted that premarital sex was sinful, and a Catholic young man who took his faith seriously could not escape the knowledge that he was supposed to, in a word, *wait*. Although his lack of success with girls made the question more academic than he would have wished, it still preyed upon his mind, putting him, as it did Eddie Ryan in *The Silence of History*, into "a slough of gloom."

"Faith is a private matter," Farrell later wrote—and so, he might have added, is its loss. Precisely how it occurred in his case is not entirely clear, and may not have been clear even to him. Yet he seems to have become convinced that unbelief came to him one morning as a sudden revelation, somewhat as he later described it happening to Danny O'Neill in *My Days of Anger* (1945).

What was most significant about the revelation was Farrell's unquestioning acceptance of it. He had no serious doubt that the good news of salvation, as it were, was at hand. In "one fell swoop," he later wrote, "the confusing and contradictory thoughts I had which made judgment and decision difficult" were cast aside. Had they not been, had any serious doubt remained in his mind, he could as well have remained a believer, asking God to help him in his unbelief. Instead, with characteristic intensity, Farrell became a true unbeliever.

He could not long keep this news to himself, unless he wished to be judged in his own eyes a hypocrite and a coward. Others in his place might have reasoned that since God did not exist, hypocrisy and cowardice were no longer vices to be shunned, that all was now permitted. Thus, a young Catholic who utterly ceased to believe could still go to Sunday Mass, still make the Sign of the Cross and kneel in apparent prayer, still receive Communion as if he were genuinely convinced that the wafer of bread had been transubstantiated into the Body and Blood of

Christ—and no one else would know the difference. But that course was not open to young Farrell. As he had been earnest in belief, so now he would be earnest in unbelief. And that meant he would have to stop going to Mass—and *that* meant he would have to confront his family. In *My Days of Anger*, Danny O'Neill does just that:

> "I'm not going to mass."
> "What's that?" his uncle asked, puzzled.
> "I'm not going to mass. There is no God," Danny bitterly proclaimed.
> "What?"
> "I'm an atheist," he said defiantly.
> "What the hell are you telling me?" Uncle Al shouted, almost jumping out of the chair.
> The die was cast. There could be no retreat. No concessions could be granted.

And the household explodes. The reaction in the Daly household to Farrell's apostasy was probably even stronger. "A bombshell like that," Farrell's sister Mary said, "would have produced much yelling, wringing of hands, running up and down the hall, door slamming, name calling, swearing and commotion in general. Much blame would have been put on the University of Chicago." And Farrell's pious mother, who had hoped that he would become a priest, must have been especially disturbed by his loss of faith. "She prayed a lot," Mary said, "and I'm sure many of her prayers were for Jimmy."

That spring of 1926, he was taking an English course in public speaking. If, as seems likely, he proceeded to do in class what Danny O'Neill did, he delivered "a verbal bombshell" in the form of a four-minute speech, concluding: "Therefore, I say there is no God." It was probably soon thereafter, in that same class, that Farrell made another explosive assertion, another rejection of a common belief, another implicit rebuke to his family and community: "I opposed all theories of racial superiority, and proclaimed my view that I believed in full justice and equality for Negro citizens." His father would have been aghast.

That same year, Farrell read with enthusiasm the English philosopher Bertrand Russell's essay "A Free Man's Worship," which for many intellectuals then, a historian of the period has noted, was "a challenging statement of the only attitude it seemed possible for modern man to assume."

In sweeping and sonorous prose, Russell addressed the swelling naturalist congregation:

> That man is the product of causes which had no prevision of the end they were achieving; that his origin, his growth, his hopes and fears, his loves and his beliefs, are but the outcome of accidental colloca-tions of atoms; that no fire, no heroism, no intensity of thought and feeling, can preserve an individual life beyond the grave; that all the labors of the ages, all the devotion, all the inspiration, all the noon-day brightness of human genius, are destined to extinction in the vast death of the solar system, and that the whole temple of man's achievement must inevitably be buried beneath the debris of a uni-verse in ruins—all these things, if not quite beyond dispute, are yet so nearly certain that no philosophy which rejects them can hope to stand. Only within the scaffolding of these truths, only on the firm foundation of unyielding despair, can the soul's habitation be safely built.

It was an impressive sermon, and Farrell was very moved by it. He was now a modern man.

———————

"I OVERTURNED ALL OF THE values of my boyhood and became a very rebellious young man," he remembered almost a quarter-century later. "As I did, I came to the conclusion that I did not want to be a success in the usual terms: I did not want to be a Babbitt."

To avert that dread possibility, he abruptly quit the employ of the Sinclair Oil and Refining Company, thus freeing himself from the vow he had made to the supervisor to rise to become a Sin-clair lawyer. Soon thereafter, making no similar pledge of corporate fealty, he went to work for the Standard Oil Company, first at a gas station at 47th and Bishop near the odorous stock-yards, and later, in the fall, at a station a little farther north, at 35th and Morgan in Bridgeport, a slum now inhabited by Poles, Lithua-nians and Italians.

In the four quarters that he had thus far completed at the University of Chicago, Farrell had done very well, getting all A's or B's in his courses and "winning a freshman honor scholarship because I was one of the twenty highest students." After taking the summer off, he returned in the fall to take courses in philosophy, economics and sociology, in which, again, he was to receive all A's or B's.

When he had first come to the university, Farrell had intended to major in social sciences and become a lawyer. Now he began to move in a different direction.

Chapter Five
To Be a Writer

ONE SNOWY MORNING IN January 1927, Farrell accosted Professor James Weber Linn in Cobb Hall and told him that he wanted to take English 210, the advanced course Linn taught in English composition. Farrell lacked the necessary credits, having previously taken only two English courses (though he'd gotten A's in both of them). Linn, who had never met Farrell before, at first tried to dissuade him, but finally relented. The professor told Farrell to submit a piece of writing, and he would then decide whether to let him into the class.

A popular teacher, Linn also wrote a column for the *Chicago Herald and Examiner*, and it was in that journalistic guise that Farrell had first encountered him. The column, Farrell recalled in a 1955 memoir, "seemed sophisticated, intelligent and always interesting. I saw in Linn a man of knowledge and education, living in a world far beyond mine." Farrell was drawn to that world, but he also was now self-consciously a rebel. In selecting a subject on which to write, he chose one that he supposed might antagonize the professor.

Farrell knew that Linn had supported the U.S. effort in the Great War, while he himself had become convinced that the people, here and abroad, who had opposed the war had been right. "My heroes," he explained decades later, "were [those] who had held out, Randolph Bourne, Ramsay MacDonald, George Bernard Shaw, Bertrand Russell, Rosa Luxemburg, Lenin, Trotsky." Strangely missing from his list is a national figure who was much closer to home than any of those he named: social reformer and pacifist Jane Addams. Young Farrell probably didn't know of her stand during the war, and may not even have known that she was James Weber Linn's aunt. He almost certainly didn't know that Linn's older brother, as a YMCA volunteer, had been killed in the fighting in the Argonne

Forest. And so, no doubt thinking himself quite bold, challenging Linn even as he sought his approval (and also, perhaps not incidentally, giving himself an excuse in case that approval was denied), Farrell wrote about "the war of steel and gold."

Linn, whose gruff exterior and vague resemblance to Theodore Roosevelt had won him the campus nickname "Teddy," did not agree with the substance of Farrell's puerile essay, but that made no difference. "He said," Farrell recalled, "[that] he did not know if I should ever develop the skill and imagination to be a writer, but that my writing qualified me for admission to his course."

"Teddy" Linn—"a rather big man," in Farrell's description, "with a round, youngish face and bushy eyebrows"—was more than just a popular teacher: he was a superb one. For thousands of his students, recalled J. D. Thomas, Class of 1929, who went on to become an English professor himself, Linn "was [our] greatest inspiration toward the love—as distinguished from the study—of literature."

On the first day of class in the advanced composition course, the fifty-year-old teacher, a nervous man and a chain smoker with graying hair and a gray suit, sat at his desk, frequently twisting his body about in his chair, and, with what Farrell recalled as simplicity and honesty, talked about himself. In his youth, he had wanted to be a writer. He graduated from the University of Chicago in 1897 and, after working for the *Chicago Record* for a while, returned to the university to do graduate work. In 1903, he became an English instructor. He could then afford to get married, which he did the next year. Teaching enabled him to support his family, but he continued to write. He didn't imagine that he would ever be a great writer, but he kept at it and eventually became a newspaper columnist. The lesson for Farrell and the other students was manifest: *Persist!*

"He told us [that] he did not know if any of us could become writers," Farrell remembered. "If we desired to, we must write and write. He promised to read everything we submitted, and encouraged us to turn in as much as we could write."

Farrell—who was "very determined" (in his own later self-description), though still "lacking in self-confidence"—took Linn at his word, and over the next few months buried him in an avalanche of words. "I wrote on scraps of paper in the gas station. I wrote in pencil. I scrawled." Despite the almost illegible handwriting, Linn read it all. And he "tried to be fair in his judgments of my work when I would say things that were opposed to what he thought and believed."

The humane Linn believed in civilization and in the virtues on which he thought it rested: "courage, confidence, earnestness, intelligence, and honor." And he believed that literature should shun the "abnormal": "We sit by the fire of humanity, warming our hands and hearts. Outside in the darkness are terrible shapes of wild beasts, mauling each other, destroying each other, involving one another in nastinesses incredible. We may invite them to sit with us, if we so desire. Personally, I do not desire." But to young Farrell—unsure of himself, lacking religious faith, ashamed of his family and the recurrent discord in his home, able to recall many instances of cruelty and brutality just beyond his doorstep, weighed down by an accumulation of felt slights and indignities, and depressed by his repeated failures with the opposite sex—the wild beasts did not seem so remote.

———⊳◦⊲———

BEFORE HE ACQUIRED A serious girlfriend (according to the woman who was that girlfriend), Farrell became sexually experienced. His fiction provides some clues to his early encounters. In *My Days of Anger*, in the quiet early morning hours of his twenty-first birthday, Danny O'Neill crosses "the Rubicon of sex," doing so with an intoxicated female acquaintance in his own bed; meanwhile, an approving and also inebriated male friend of theirs waits in the parlor and a just awakened Mrs. O'Flaherty has returned to her own room after greeting the two visitors. Somewhat implausible as all this may seem, something like it may well have happened to Farrell, although if it did, it is doubtful that the river crossing was very successful. In *Lonely for the Future* (1966) there is a reference to "an awkward, not completed [sexual] experience" Eddie Ryan had "over two years" before, when he would have been about twenty-one.

Farrell's next probable sexual encounter, born of loneliness and increasing desperation, was more base. In *Lonely for the Future*, an episode he had related decades earlier in *My Days of Anger* as having happened to Danny O'Neill appears again with only minor differences. In the later version, Eddie Ryan is remembering what happened: He closes up the gas station at 35th and

Morgan and, as usual, takes a trolley car to the 35th Street elevated station. Ordinarily he would transfer to a southbound local train. But on that particular night, after he gets off the streetcar, he stands and looks around—until a coarse-looking whore propositions him. She leads him to a dimly lit room above a delicatessen. He is shocked by "the ugliness of the entire scene." The transaction is brief. And afterward, waiting for a train, Eddie is "ashamed."

Despite the shame, it would not be the last time Ryan goes with a prostitute. The same is true of Danny O'Neill—and also, it would seem, of young Farrell. Indeed, at some point in his youth he would contract gonorrhea.

⇒►०◄⇐

ANNABELLE MCCLURE, NINETEEN years old and "a striking blonde," was one of some two hundred young people who on the evening of March 1, 1927, gathered in the basement club room of the Essex Hotel, at 5721 Cottage Grove Avenue. They were there for the opening of a "Slow Club."

"I'm simply tired of going out with men who expect a good-night kiss," Miss McClure explained. "So many of my girl friends say the same thing. We've decided to stop cheapening ourselves. So when I read that they were organizing a Slow Club where I could go and have a good time without being obliged to pay for it in caresses, I decided that it was the place for me."

"Boys and girls will be able to find in the club sane fun without making fools of themselves," asserted Miss Olive Potter, a seventeen-year-old "artist model" who was, according to the *Chicago Tribune*, the organizer of the club. Persons between the ages of sixteen and thirty-two were welcome to join, provided they agreed not to drink or pet. Miss Potter was being assisted by John Sullivan of 5128 Calumet Avenue, the newspaper said.

The idea of "Slow Clubs" for wholesome young people who were out of step with the "jazz age," with its "necking," "flask-toting" and "automobile parties," had originated the preceding November in Philadelphia and then spread to Chicago. This was the anti-flaming-youth counterrevolution, the *Tribune* reported, "opposed in principle to the panting sheik, the amorous lounge lizard and careless young maidenhood."

But this particular Slow Club was not at all typical. Jack Sulli-van, the main force behind it, had no desire to slow down Jazz Age youth. He and Paul Caron and a few others wanted to have some laughs and raise money for the Oasis Club, a bohemian forum that Sullivan apparently had helped to organize. Farrell and Caron frequented the Oasis, which met in the hotel basement, and they and Sullivan became fast friends. (At one Oasis gathering, Farrell had debated the question "Is Life Worth Living?" with Oasis manager Frank Midney, an older man and a socialist who had once run for mayor of Cleveland. Farrell seems to have taken the side of despair, and lost.) But to judge from his fictionalized account in *Lonely for the Future*, Farrell was reluctant to have much to do with the cynical Slow Club scheme.

"Oasis 'Slow Club' Has Real Revolt" proclaimed the *Tribune* on March 15, reporting what happened the previous evening. "The blowup occurred after the 'steam roller,' handled by the experienced parliamentarians of the Oasis club, elected its hand-picked officers. Miss Olive Potter, in whose name the first meeting was called in the Oasis club room, declined the chair in favor of the secretary-treasurer, Mr. Sullivan." William and Andrew Karzas, the brothers who owned the popular Trianon and Aragon ballrooms, had offered their premises for the Slow Club's use. Sullivan shocked the assembly by declaring that in his view a public ballroom has a better effect socially on young people than churches do.

"Do you really mean what you say?" demanded an emissary of the Chicago recreation commission, which was seeking to assist the various Slow Clubs being organized in the city.

"That is my opinion," Sullivan reaffirmed. "The Trianon ballroom has a better effect socially than our churches."

An uproar ensued and a group of young people withdrew to form their own, more decorous club.

The Oasis Slow Club continued for at least a few months. Caron, Sullivan and some others, Farrell recalled in a 1957 letter, "slowed down" youth "by drinking like hell and making as much love as anyone could. Caron started making bootleg liquor." In Farrell's later fictionalized account, "George Raymond" (Caron), who is illegally selling washtub gin at the club, makes it his chief aim to seduce the virginal girlfriend of the club's bouncer—and succeeds. But his effort divides those running the club into two camps. Raymond and Alec McGonigle (Sullivan) are expelled, and "for good measure" so is Eddie Ryan. After Raymond's conquest of the girl, he has a fight with the bouncer. Raymond wins, but badly hurts his left hand. Something like this happened in real life. As Farrell recalled:

"It ended in a brutal fight between Paul and some other guy over a girl; they fought in Jackson Park, and Paul broke several bones in his hand; the other guy's face was a mess."

Caron, Farrell said, was "a remarkable fighter. He and I once prevented a race riot at 63rd and Ellis by cleaning up some drunken Irish." But he was even more remarkable—especially in Farrell's envious eyes—as a Don Juan. In a letter written from New York some months after the fight in which he injured his hand, Caron told Sullivan that he had just gotten a letter from a girl, an evidently heartbroken young woman—perhaps the one at the center of the Slow Club dispute—who had returned the ring he had given her and now wanted it back along with some money she had loaned him. In reply he sent her "a picture of Satan with a quotation from Aristotle in original.... My next letter to her (if I send one) will be a treatise on 'What I lost by knowing her.'" Later in the same missive, he boasted: "Am now receiving letters from Elouise (The Texas girl) and Mary Louise (My one and only)."

Caron, who had shed his Catholic faith soon after Farrell did, was a Jazz Age Nietzschean—a glib, handsome, intelligent, amusing and fearless young man, always well dressed. He was also willful and shamelessly manipulative. "H. R. H. 'Hellfire' Caron," he signed a 1925 letter to Farrell, written when Caron, soon to find work as a traveling salesman, was living in Dallas with "Elouise" (a.k.a. Ella Louise)—"[the] sweetest girl in the commonwealth"—while keeping up his correspondence with "both Mary Louise and Ethel" back in Chicago.

It is easy to see why Farrell found Caron fascinating. But Caron saw something in Farrell, too: an intelligence to match his own, an earnestness that he had lost, an emotional depth that he would never have. "Don't think that I at times don't feel lost without Jimmy to 'chew the fat with,'" he wrote to Farrell from Texas. "I consider our friendship on a higher plane than any other I have made."

<hr />

ALTHOUGH FARRELL WAS NEGLECTING his courses in economics and psychology that winter quarter, he kept churning out words—thousands of them, tens of thousands—for Professor Linn. Standing over his little desk at the gas station in Bridgeport, his hands dirty and greasy from servicing cars, Farrell wrote with pencil on the backs of company forms about "anything I thought of."

"I wrote of moods, sketches of people, descriptions of the streets, of the long lines of factory girls going to and coming from work in the central manufacturing district, prostitutes on the streets, fantasies." Linn saw promise in one crude effort that concerned men working in an express company; eventually it would become Farrell's second novel, *Gas-House McGinty* (1933). Linn also saw potential in an insufficiently developed short story called "Calico Shoes," about a Bohemian woman who has been severely injured in an accident and her Lithuanian husband who exploits her condition; it too, after revision, was eventually published (in 1934). Farrell had more immediate success with a quasi-journalistic effort that he submitted to Linn, a six-hundred-word sketch of people he encountered in an eatery in the Loop. The prose was rather clumsy, and yet the piece had creativity and an earthy vitality. Linn decided to run the sketch in his "Round About Chicago" column in the *Chicago Herald and Examiner*. It is of course possible that he was just desperate for a column that day, but it seems more likely that he was being characteristically generous to a student who, for all his roughness as a writer, seemed unusually promising. In any case, on March 16, 1927—two days after the "real revolt" that Jack Sullivan sparked at the Oasis Slow Club—Farrell broke into print with "Pie Juggling in the Loop."

"This column today," Linn wrote by way of introduction, "is supplied by J. F. Hold me responsible only for recognizing a journalist in the making. Here goes:

" 'I sit in a wicker-backed chair in a loop sandwich shop. The homely waitress has taken my order for ham on toast and coffee....' "

On that day, March 16, 1927, when young Farrell for the first time saw words of his own in print for all to read, he knew there could only be one path for him. "I made a kind of pledge to myself," he would recall in the mid-1960s. "It was to be life or death with me, even literally so. It was to be all or nothing, and I would strive to be a writer. I was willing to take a chance, and to risk failure. If I were to fail, I might end up in the gutter—so I then thought. In risking [that], I would 'burn my bridges behind' (a phrase I then used very often)." He would accept no constraints but "honor, truth, sincerity, honesty."

Soon thereafter, Farrell read a book that pointed the way: Sherwood Anderson's *Tar: A Midwest Childhood* (1926). Although reviewers and potential readers had given it little notice, *Tar* was a charming series of dramatized autobiographical tales about Tar Moorhead (the author's stand-in), growing up in rural Ohio.

Reading *Tar* at the gas station at 35th and Morgan, Farrell "burned and thrilled with excitement." And the thought came to him: "If the inner life of a boy in an Ohio country town of the nineteenth century was meaningful enough to be the material for a book like *Tar*, then perhaps my own feelings and emotions and the feelings and emotions of those with whom I had grown up were important." His ambition to write, and his confidence that he could, were strengthened. "I thought of writing a novel about my own boyhood, about the neighborhood in which I had grown up."

Now resolved to be a writer, Farrell—who got a B from Linn in advanced composition that quarter and got C's in the two other courses—decided to leave school. And he tried to write a novel. "I went back to my short-pants days, and attempted to create a character who [was] much like myself, and who would reveal himself and tell a story of others around him and of himself; this would be done in a stream-of-consciousness flow."

Standing at the desk in the gas station and starting to write in pencil, he was sure he had found a way to write that would work, that the writing would just flow right out and keep flowing. But after a few pages, he came to "a dead halt." He was uncertain if what he had written had any merit at all. Finally, he abandoned the attempt. And he threw the pages away.

━━➤•0•◄━━

AGAINST TEDDY LINN'S ADVICE, Farrell quit his job at the gas station that July and hitchhiked to New York City with Paul Caron. "I was 23. I'd had enough of Chicago," Farrell recalled. "I had to take a total risk. I was a writer, and I had to find my world."

North of Bear Mountain in upstate New York, they got a lift in a Studebaker and the driver was able to take them all the way into the city. They entered Manhattan at night, and as they sped through the deserted streets New York seemed weird and uninviting, a city without people. But then, as they passed by Cavanagh's Restaurant on 23rd Street and Farrell glimpsed the customers inside—"so happy…so prosperous, so distant, so strange"—he knew that he was in the New York he had imagined: vibrant, exciting, at the center of things. The elegant diners in Cavanagh's were "proof that life was going on. I felt that I would become part of it, if that was what I wanted, but that if I did not, did not want it, that would be all right, too." He remembered the scene at the end of Balzac's novel *Père Goriot* in which young Eugène de Rastignac looks upon Paris and vows, "Henceforth there is a war between us." In his imagination Farrell made a similar gesture. "I had come to New York to write, to make war, to plunge through the future."

The driver dropped them on 23rd Street close to Eighth Avenue. The nearby YMCA had no rooms available, so they tried a cheap hotel and then a second one, but the smell in the rooms drove them off. They trudged on in the heat of the late July night, finally ending up in Union Square. Observing "a fair number" of appealingly disreputable men and women in the park, the explorers found their way to a bench near the center, where they sat, watching and listening to "a Bolshevik defending an idea with idealistic words that got lost in the night and the noise, a streetwalker turning away from two young fellows who laughed as she went, a guy with a loud voice and no use for Al Smith."

Farrell was tired but excited. "It was adventurous and romantic again to be on the bum, on my own, and in New York." Eventually he fell asleep, awaking with the dawn.

They soon found a cheap single room with one small bed, which they shared. For an aspiring writer, minor discomforts were a small price to pay for the heady experience of being in "the world's greatest city."

Within two weeks of his arrival in New York, Farrell had sent off a dispatch to Linn, who used some of it in his *Herald and Examiner* column for August 6. Linn's readers were informed that "J. F." had this to say from New York:

> Wanderlust has sent me here, as a prelude to a long period of bumming. I have had some interesting experiences—sleeping with the 'boes in Union Square Park; living two days in Greenwich Village without knowing it; competing with the Dempsey-Tunney fight returns by debating religion and anarchy on a street-corner; watching the urchins fight for a nickel a side to amuse the noonday crowds; and swimming in the murky picturesqueness of the East River. I need an audience—so look out!

"I'm looking out, Jimmy," the warm-hearted teacher-columnist added, before moving on to other matters.

Farrell rapidly found work as a clerk in a United Cigar Company store at 96th and Broadway on the Upper West Side, and soon was transferred to another United Cigar store at 72nd and Broadway. His starting salary was $24 a week. Caron found employment as an elevator operator in the expensive Dorset Hotel, then as an ad salesman for a classified telephone directory: R. H. Donnelly's "Red Book." Their jobs enabled them to move out of their cramped quarters and into separate rooms in the Mills Hotel at 36th Street and Seventh Avenue, where the rent was only fifty cents a night.

Farrell, Caron informed Jack Sullivan on August 19, "Hopes to remain here till fall 1928 and then go to New Orleans. Has difficulty in washing socks clean and is elected champion musser [*sic*] of packed suitcases—Confesses to spasmodic semi-erections of the penis from lack of exercise and is taking bending exercises in the morning to reduce the girth of his abdomen. Laments the loss of his typewriter which we plan to take out [of hock] at the end of this week."

Three days later, Caron began selling "Red Book" ads and Farrell, along with his friend, was caught up in a mass demonstration against the impending executions of Nicola Sacco and Bartolomeo Vanzetti. In the seven years since two gunmen had held up and murdered a paymaster and his guard in South Braintree, Massachusetts, American liberals had become convinced that the men convicted of the crime—both admitted anarchists and both carrying guns when they were arrested—were innocent. In liberal eyes, the shoemaker Sacco and the fish peddler Vanzetti were harmless philosophical anarchists, victims of the postwar "Red Scare" and anti-immigrant prejudice. The prosecution had been corrupt, the judge narrow-minded, the jury made up of bigots. Even the president of Harvard, who headed a committee appointed by the governor to review the case, had betrayed the truth in the interest of the established order. And now, despite worldwide protest (which was actually Communist-organized, for the most part), Sacco and Vanzetti were to be executed.

Farrell was moved by the plight of the two men and angry at the injustice he was sure it represented. His friend Caron was emotionally detached from the drama, and his co-workers at the cigar store were indifferent to Sacco and Vanzetti's fate, but Farrell was not. On the night of the executions, he got off work between eight and nine and felt himself drawn to Union Square, "pulled there by an unseen force." He met Caron, and they took the subway downtown to 14th Street and Seventh Avenue, and then walked eastward to the square.

Earlier there had been fiery speeches by anarchist Carlo Tresca and others. By now the throng of five thousand outside the Union Square East offices of the Communist *Daily Worker* newspaper was largely silent, waiting for the terrible news to come. In describing the scene in his novel *Bernard Clare* (1946), Farrell said the silence could only be compared to

the silence of a church when the priest approached the sacred parts of the mass. And how different this was! There, in church, the people knelt in awe and adoration, or at least in habit that simulated awe and adoration. They were bent down before their God, Who was symbolically to repeat His sacrifice on the cross. Here, men and women stood, and their very silence was a weapon that they were hurling like a lance at these armed police, at all of the armed authority of the nation.

Police ringed the square, and as Farrell stood in the park he felt "a cold passion. If necessary, I would have fought to the death that night. If my eyes met a cop's eyes, I wouldn't turn my gaze away and my expression must have been a grim one."

At 12:25 A.M., as a sign appeared in a second-floor window of the *Daily Worker,* telling the crowd that the end was nearing, fourteen motorcycle policemen raced down Fourth Avenue and through the square with sirens screeching—"an ear-rupturing noise that announced Power."

A few minutes later, another sign appeared in the window: "Sacco murdered." There were a few hisses and moans from the crowd, but otherwise it "was curiously undemonstrative," a *New York Times* reporter on the scene noted.

A new sign appeared: "The Workers' Party must not forget its martyrs." And then finally this: "Vanzetti murdered."

Police began to circulate through the crowd, and it broke up. The silent vigil was over.

Later that day, when he read a newspaper story about the executions, young Farrell burst into tears.

For many American liberals, the conviction and execution of Sacco and Vanzetti marked an important turning point. Now they knew that "the system" was corrupt, that class warfare was a reality. As novelist John Dos Passos, eight years older than Farrell, famously put it: "all right we are two nations."

Long afterward, Farrell was to learn that Carlo Tresca, whom he got to know during the 1930s, told others before he was assassinated in 1943 (quite possibly by a Soviet agent) that Sacco was guilty and Vanzetti innocent. "I was shocked, angry and felt betrayed," Farrell said. Although he and Tresca had never discussed the case, Farrell thought that "someone should have admitted something somewhere along the line" to him.

———➤◦◄———

BEFORE THE SUMMER OF 1927 was over, Farrell caught sight of a "real" writer. He and Caron were sitting on the steps of the New York Public Library, looking down at the passing scene on Fifth Avenue, when they saw a slender man with long, blond hair walk by, carrying under his arm a copy of *Replenishing Jessica*, a novel by poet Maxwell Bodenheim, formerly of Chicago and now of Greenwich Village.

Farrell, who had read "with great amusement" Ben Hecht's *Count Bruga*, a roman à clef with a satiric portrait of Hecht's friend Bodenheim, said to Caron:

"Paul, I'll bet that's Maxwell Bodenheim."

And it was.

"I was excited merely to see a man who had published books," Farrell remembered. "I wished that we had tried to speak with him."

The brush with that semblance of literary greatness bolstered Farrell's own ambition. He spent many hours in the library's general reading room. By mid-September he had quit the United Cigar store, moved out to the Borough of Queens and taken a better-paying job selling ads for Donnelly's Red Book. "I was able to sell enough in a few hours a week to keep my job. I spent more time in libraries than I did selling." He read *Sister Carrie*, *An American Tragedy*, and others of Theodore Dreiser's novels. They made a profound impression on him: "More than anything else, I felt wonder and awe: I was strengthened in my feeling that human emotions, feelings, desires, aspirations are valuable and precious. I gained more respect for life, more sympathy for people, more of a sense of human feelings and thoughts as of major value in this, our common life." During his months in New York he also read much of Nietzsche, and "whenever I was too strongly inclined to think and act in terms of Nietzschean arrogance, I would think of the Dreiserian world. The impression Dreiser left was too strong for me to fall unchecked into an acceptance of the Nietzschean idea of the superman."

Eventually, Farrell moved back to Manhattan, first to a rooming house above a drug store at Eighth Street and Fifth Avenue, then to the Chelsea YMCA at 23rd Street and Seventh Avenue.

Sometimes he wandered about Greenwich Village. He would go to Hubert's Cafeteria on Sheridan Square. "It was always crowded with young people—bohemians, long-haired fellows and short-haired girls." But he remained too shy to talk with any of them.

He read books and went to the Metropolitan Museum of Art, to lectures, concerts and the theater. And he kept writing. When he first came to New York, he was working on the short story "Calico Shoes." He also wrote some sketches that he sent to Linn, who used one of them in his August 25 column. At some point, Farrell "tried to get going on a novel about the corner of 58th Street and Prairie Avenue," but once again he gave up after a few pages. "I couldn't develop my characters and invent a sequence of situations and events that would swing along as a novel."

By the end of 1927, Paul Caron was back in Chicago, writing to Farrell and thanking him for the tie he had sent as a Christmas present. Farrell meanwhile rang in the new year by running through the halls of the YMCA at four in the morning, "preaching blasphemy.... I claimed, as I remember, to be the embodiment of the Second Coming." Before long, he too was back home in Chicago.

Chapter Six

Dorothy — and Lonigan

THE CUBE WAS A little theater that some University of Chicago students had started in February 1928 in the Jackson Park Art Colony, a faded bit of bohemia a few blocks east of the campus and near the park. Manager Nick Matsoukas and his fellow students had established the theater in a one-story storefront at 1538 East 57th Street, one of twenty-six leftover storefronts from the 1893 World's Columbian Exposition that later served as cheap studios for artists and writers. Although its heyday was over, the Art Colony survived, and Farrell—who registered for the spring quarter at the university but then withdrew in early June before completing his course work—became involved with the Cube.

On June 23, a Saturday night, Maxwell Bodenheim was due to give a reading at the theater. A notice of the reading posted on a tree outside Woodworth's Book Store on 57th Street had attracted the attention of a red-haired coed on her way home from classes. She knew nothing about the poet, but the thought flashed into her mind that she could attend the poetry reading and write a paper about Bodenheim and his work for the class she was taking with James Weber Linn.

And so that Saturday night, wearing a pink georgette dress with ruffles, she went to the Cube. The theater was long and narrow, with the stage at one end, and with black walls and bright red benches seating about one hundred people. "We waited and waited and waited," she recalled, until at last Bodenheim "showed up, as drunk as could be." The poet could hardly stand upright when he came out onto the stage. He tried to recite his poetry, but couldn't. Finally, he simply collapsed. The young woman was shocked. "Oh my, I couldn't understand that. A *poet* getting drunk like that! And falling down on the stage!"

Bodenheim hung around for a while and talked drunkenly

76

with some of the students. One of them was Farrell, at last convers-
ing with a real writer. Bodenheim told him that he expected one
day "to die in the gutter," like the nineteenth-century French poet
Paul Verlaine.

Farrell also had his eye on the pretty redhead in the pink
dress. He had seen that she was scandalized by Bodenheim's performance. And she was aware that he kept staring at her. Eventually,
a man named John Howe, who worked at the university and knew
them both, introduced them. Her name was Dorothy Butler.

Farrell suggested that they go to Gus's candy store on the corner, near the park, and get some popcorn. "And we went in there,"
she remembered, "and he bought me instead an ice cream cone."
The proprietor had lately become acquainted with Farrell, but he
had known Dorothy since she was a little girl. He cautioned the
young man: "You be careful now, you take her right home." Farrell
did so, but he asked her out before parting. She told him to call her.
He did not delay.

Six years younger than Farrell, Dorothy Butler resided in a
comfortable apartment at 5600 Blackstone Avenue with her
younger sister, Virginia, and their widowed mother, Margaret.
Dorothy had lived all her life in Hyde Park, with the University of
Chicago nearby. Her mother, who was part Dutch, hailed from
upstate New York; her father, Patrick, although born in Chicago
when his parents were visiting America, had grown up in Ireland.
By a remarkable coincidence, Dorothy's parents shared the same
birthdate: St. Patrick's Day, 1876. Her father had been a lawyer and
had been in the grocery business, along with her uncles. They
owned a chain of several hundred stores—the Consumers' Sanitary
Butter and Coffee Stores (later sold to the even larger Kroger
chain). Her father had died in early 1925 at age forty-eight, and her
mother never remarried. Although not quite rich, the Butler family
was well off.

Dorothy, who had entered the University of Chicago in the
fall of 1927, was a graduate of St. Xavier Academy, a parochial high
school for girls. But like her mother, who rarely went to Mass, she
was only a nominal Catholic.

Aside from the blow of her father's death, Dorothy had had a
sheltered childhood. But her mother, with many friends to occupy
her attention and a live-in housekeeper to take care of household
matters, was a somewhat distant figure. Though she treated her
daughters well and provided them with much, she didn't seem

especially *interested* in them (or so Dorothy thought, looking back in her eighties). As Dorothy advanced into young womanhood, she appears to have been essentially on her own.

The others in the circle she was now entering were older and more experienced. The Cube's new dramatic director, Mary Hunter, for instance, had a much more worldly background. Born in California the same year as Farrell, she had attended Wellesley College in Massachusetts for several years, and during school vacations worked as a script girl in Hollywood for playwright-director William de Mille, the father of her dear friend Agnes, the future choreographer. Mary had known even then that she wanted to be a director (and in time she would become a well-known Broadway director). An attractive brunette, she eventually became a close friend of Farrell's (and romantically involved with Jack Sullivan). In her eyes, Dorothy Butler seemed "very innocent, a little bewildered, and a little terrified. But she adored Jimmy, she absolutely worshiped the ground he walked on."

No one else was so worshipful. In the eyes of almost everyone else who knew him, Farrell was an oddball, albeit a talented and good-natured one. "Jimmy the Genius," Nick Matsoukas called him. Pudgy and disheveled and wearing thick, gold-rimmed glasses, Farrell was very awkward in social situations. With his lurching gait, his shoulders hunched over, and his head with its shock of curly dark brown hair moving from side to side, he reminded Mary Hunter of a bear.

But he was a dancing bear. Sometimes when he visited Dorothy at her home, she remembered, they would turn on the Victrola or the radio and dance. He loved to waltz. So did Mary Hunter, and occasionally, at a nightclub, she and Farrell would dance together. He was "a divine dancer," she said. "We'd bump into a lot of people, but the spins were wonderful, just wonderful."

Off the dance floor, Farrell the eccentric would reappear. He had a tenor voice, which, given his broad-shouldered physique, seemed rather incongruously high-pitched. When he was enthusiastic about some subject, he would speak very emphatically and wave his arms, the words pouring forth in a torrent almost faster than he could articulate them; as his excitement mounted, his eyebrows would shoot up and he would look out over his glasses as he energetically held forth. Sometimes, though, "if he was fumbling for a thought," Mary Hunter recalled, "he would sort of mash up his words," making it difficult for others to be entirely sure what he was saying. At other times, he would withdraw into himself. He was often dreamy, abstracted, lost in thought.

"Jimmy was erratic and wandered about and didn't always keep appointments and things of that sort," Mary Hunter said. "But I found him delightful. It seemed to me that he was a man deeply absorbed and just beginning to know that he was gifted, and highly gifted, and not quite knowing what to do with it, because nobody had ever thought [that he was] before."

———————

JULIA DALY, NOW IN HER eighties, fell and broke her hip in late 1928, and thenceforth was confined to a wheelchair. Ella Daly took care of her. Ella was able to do so because she had been fired from her job at the LaSalle Hotel after auditors discovered a shortage in her cashier's "bank." The hotel cashiers weren't supposed to borrow money from their banks, but Ella and others did, hoping that the auditors wouldn't show up before they returned the money. The chief cashier, Jim Crawford—with whom Ella had slept once, or perhaps more—would tip her off when the auditors were about to arrive. But Crawford left the LaSalle in 1927 to work at the owners' massive new hotel on Michigan Avenue, the Stevens. His departure left Ella unprotected, so a shortage was discovered and she lost her job. (Through Crawford, however, she would obtain part-time employment as a cashier at the Stevens.)

Fortunately, Tom Daly was working again. Although Upham Brothers had ceased operations in 1927, Daly was working at a wholesale shoe firm on South State Street by the fall of 1928. He continued to work there for the next few years until, in the midst of the Depression, he lost that job and eventually ended up on relief, or at least on the brink of it.

Meanwhile, the Dalys had joined the exodus of whites from the South Side. In May 1928 they moved to East End Avenue on the South Shore. Helen Farrell remained behind, staying with the Farrells; later that year, she got married. The next year, with Earl Farrell about to get married, his mother and sister Mary moved in with the Dalys for a while, before getting an apartment of their own with Joe and Jack Farrell.

Julia Daly's fall seems to have made her offspring more aware of how limited the time remaining to their mother was. They ceased, or at least reduced, their continual bickering. And in Ella

Daly's case, the sobering impact was literal: if she didn't stop drinking, at least she cut back.

———➤•●•◄———

FARRELL DID WELL ENOUGH IN his English composition courses that summer of 1928, but didn't complete the work for his philosophy course. He skipped the university's autumn quarter to concentrate on writing, doing reviews and articles for the *Daily Maroon*, the student newspaper, and other publications. His first *Maroon* contribution, a review of an exhibition at the Art Institute of Chicago, was published under a pseudonym: "Dorothy Butler." He had submitted it that way because he'd had a spat with the editors. But the quarrel was quickly forgotten. Soon, writing in the *Maroon* and elsewhere under his own name, Farrell was complaining about the university library's failure to subscribe to *This Quarter* and other literary periodicals; exposing the practice of "pulling the pumps" and other such stratagems employed in the "Filling Station Racket in Chicago"; and objecting to the "undiscriminatory [*sic*] praise" being heaped upon Negro art solely because of the artists' skin color.

In January he became the campus correspondent for the *Chicago Herald and Examiner*, replacing a young man who was moving on to a fulltime job with a St. Louis paper. Editor Duffy Cornell hired Farrell for the part-time position after talking with him for only five minutes or so. Its chief attraction for him was the pay, which, depending on how much space he was able to fill, usually amounted to $20–$25 a week and sometimes $30. He needed the money, but the job also provided other, less tangible benefits. Newspaper work was regarded as romantic, held the promise of excitement, and made his ambition to be a writer appear more plausible. "This part-time job gave me a function in society," he reflected long afterward, "and that was probably good for me at the time." Writing for a newspaper, he thought, made him seem less of "an oddball's oddball."

He managed to dig up some stories that officials at the university were not pleased to see in print, including one about a coed who had committed suicide after being informed that she would not be graduating. But for the most part he found covering the campus news not very exciting. One of his principal tasks was to find willing coeds and set up what were called "leg" photos. "I had to arrange for regular leg pictures, and I did not mix 'profession' with hormonic pleasure. I got the girls, the legs, the photographer, the names of the legs and girls, and no dates nor openings." ("Verbal as he was," recalled Mary Hunter, "Jimmy never had a line.")

He was given off-campus assignments, too. But at the end of August, he would be sacked. The reason: not enough leg pictures.

⟫•0•⟪

AT THE WESTERN END OF the Jackson Park Art Colony, just around the corner from 57th Street, on Harper Avenue, stood what was implausibly known as the "Coudich Castle," a hive occupied by artists, writers, newspapermen, students and a strange European couple named Coudich, who ran the place. The uncastlelike apartment house consisted of two buildings, each at least four stories high, and the rents were cheap. Mary Hunter lived in a two-room apartment in the back.

Around the corner, on 57th Street, was Cable Court, where cable cars used to turn around. Mary, Jack Sullivan, Nick Matsoukas, Dorothy Butler, Farrell and others loved to play a children's game there called "pussy-in-the-corner." When they tired of that, they went to Jackson Park and played "run-sheep-run" and other kids' games. When her friend Agnes de Mille visited once, Mary Hunter recalled, she was "absolutely astounded that semi-grownup people would play games out in the middle of the night on a street corner." But Agnes nevertheless joined them in a massive treasure hunt and "had a thoroughly good time."

Farrell and the other semi-grownups didn't confine themselves to children's games, however. One day, Mary Hunter lent Farrell the key to her flat and he brought Dorothy Butler there. In that apartment in the Coudich Castle, Dorothy remembered, she lost her virginity.

Having thus given herself completely to the man she adored, Dorothy apparently gave less and less of herself to her schoolwork. She found her classes boring, and now she had James (as she called him). And so, by her decision (or perhaps the college's), she dropped out after the winter quarter of 1929.

She did not tell her mother. As far as Margaret Butler knew, Dorothy remained a student at the University of Chicago. Each quarter, she pocketed the tuition money and kept up the pretense at home that she was taking courses and going to classes. Day after day, she would rise early in the morning and leave home, supposedly headed for class. She would while away the hours at the library or at less studious haunts, finally returning home around dinnertime. And she kept this up for two years! Dorothy appeared in one play at the Cube and sometimes fancied herself an actress; at least she was good enough to fool her mother.

━━━━━━━━➤•◀━━━━━━━━

STUDS CUNNINGHAM—"BILL," AS he was called by his family—died at home on Sunday, March 10, 1929, with his sister Loretta whispering the Act of Contrition in his ear and his anguished parents looking on.

Just a few days before, the young plasterer had gone off to work with what seemed like a cold. His mother urged him to stay home, but he wouldn't. When he returned at day's end, he was much worse. A doctor was summoned, and he said that Bill had lobar pneumonia. The doctor and the family did what they could for him.

Bill's death "was a terrible shock," Loretta remembered, "because he was such a strong kid."

The wake was held Monday and Tuesday in the Cunningham home on the South Shore. Among those who attended was Jim Farrell, who had last seen Cunningham in November, near the Chicago Public Library on Randolph Street. (In a 1946 letter, Farrell wrote about the encounter: "I casually ignored him, and he put out his hand and asked me if I didn't want to say hello to him. This was a personal victory for me.") On Wednesday there was a Requiem High Mass in Our Lady of Peace Church, and then Cunningham, just twenty-six years old, was laid to rest in Holy Sepulchre Cemetery.

Farrell had never been close to Cunningham ("I never talked twenty minutes seriously with him in my whole life"), and the older youth's aura of fearsome power had long since vanished. By the time Farrell was nineteen, he later thought, he "probably could have handled" the reputed tough guy. ("He was a right hander, and didn't know how to use his left. I'd have blocked his roundhouse right, and counterpunched with my right, and with my shoulders, I had a really mean right.") But now, as he contemplated Studs's death, Farrell seems to have had a sense not only of a life cut short, but of a life misspent.

"He went to Loyola for one year, loafed about for a similar

period; and then he became a plasterer for his father," Farrell wrote that spring in a short story called "Studs." "He commenced going round to the poolroom. The usual commonplace story resulted. What there was of the boy disappeared in slobbish dissipation. His pleasures became compressed within a hexagonal of whores, movies, pool, alky, poker, and craps."

A few weeks after the funeral, Farrell started classes at the university again. Two of his friends, George Brodsky, an aspiring poet and writer whom he had met at the Cube, and Felix Kolodziej, a shy farm boy from Wisconsin, were taking Professor Linn's course in advanced composition and they persuaded Farrell to take it with them. He also repeated the philosophy course he had failed to finish the previous summer. This quarter—his eighth at the university—was to prove his last.

For Linn, Farrell once again turned out thousands of words:

> I wrote stories, sketches, book reviews, essays, impressions, anec-
> dotes. Most of these manuscripts related to death, disintegration,
> human indignity, poverty, drunkenness, ignorance, human cruelty.
> They attempted to describe dusty and deserted streets, street cor-
> ners, miserable homes, pool rooms, brothels, dance halls, taxi dances,
> bohemian sections, express offices, gasoline filling stations, scenes
> laid in slum districts. The characters were boys, boys' gangs, drunk-
> ards, Negroes, expressmen, homosexuals, immigrants and immigrant
> landlords, filling-station attendants, straw bosses, hitch hikers, bums,
> bewildered parents. Most of the manuscripts were written with the
> ideal of objectivity in mind.

"Studs" was one of the manuscripts he submitted. "At Studs's wake last Monday evening," Farrell wrote,

> everybody was mournful, sad that such a fine young fellow of
> twenty-six should go off so suddenly with double pneumonia; blown
> out of this world like a ripped leaf in a hurricane. They sighed and
> the women and girls cried, and everybody said that it was too bad....
> The undertaker...laid out Studs handsomely. He was outfitted in a
> somber black suit and a white silk tie. His hands were folded over his
> stomach, clasping a pair of black rosary beads. At his head, pressed
> against the satin bedding, was a spiritual bouquet, set in line with
> Studs' large nose. He looked handsome, and there were no lines of
> suffering on his planed face. But the spiritual bouquet (further assur-
> ance that his soul would arrive safely in Heaven) was a dirty trick. So
> was the administration of the last sacraments. For Studs will be mis-
> erable in Heaven, more miserable than he was on those Sunday

nights when he would hang around the old poolroom at Fifty-eighth and the elevated station, waiting for something to happen. He will find the land of perpetual happiness and goodness dull and boresome, and he'll be resentful. There will be nothing to do in Heaven but to wait in timeless eternity. There will be no can houses, speakeasies, whores (unless they are reformed), and gambling joints; and neither will there be a shortage of plasterers.

Professor Linn praised the story enthusiastically and read it aloud in class.

Thus buoyed up, Farrell took "Studs" to another English professor, fifty-eight-year-old Robert Morss Lovett, who also was an editor of the liberal *New Republic*. (The magazine was then located in New York, and Lovett's flexible academic schedule enabled him to spend part of the year in the East.) Lovett had first become aware of Farrell in May 1929, when he heard about the young man's criticism of the student Dramatic Association for not inviting blacks to participate. The recent production of *Goin' Home*, Farrell had observed in a *Maroon* article, "was a play of negro sentiment, written in sympathy with the notion that a negro has no home in this white man's world. On campus there are a number of sincere, and competent negro actors.... Had the Dramatic Association been seriously interested in its supposed work, it [would] have invited these negroes to participate." (Farrell's friends at the Cube, who included a black student named Katherine Dunham, the future dance legend, shared his views. In January, after the Drama Association had refused to let her become a member, they put on four Negro plays at the Cube with Negro casts.)

After reading "Studs," Lovett summoned Farrell to his office. Looking like "a kind of large and brooding walrus of a man, soft-spoken, gentle," the professor advised him to turn the story into a novel. "I had already begun to think of doing this," Farrell later related, "and Professor Lovett's advice clinched the matter for me."

<hr />

Whoever reads this account will be as disturbed as they would be if they should discover a drunkard in the gutter. It is such a story. Perhaps it is cruel, unsympathetic, one long puke. So be it. The account is true. It pleases me as little as it will my readers. It pleases me as little as life does with its confusions fogs loose ends sordid tragedies garbaged lives.

So begins Farrell's very short story "Slob," which appeared in the June 1929 issue of *Blues*, a little magazine edited in Columbus, Mississippi. His first published story, it had nothing to do with Cunningham or Lonigan, and it is a profoundly revealing document.

The "slob" in question is Nora, a woman of forty-five—the same age as Ella Daly (until her birthday that June).

> Wrinkles are beginning to line her face. Her bobbed, permanently-waved hair is disordered into travesty. Her eyes are swollen behind tortoise-shell rimmed glasses. She is stupidly drunk.... Her head flops upon the table....
>
> Her brother, who has been scrambling eggs, straightens her in the chair and exhorts her to eat. He and his nephew attempt to feed her, the latter holding her head while the former pours tomato juice down her throat. She wriggles and insists on eating by herself. They finally give up and she picks up a slice of tomato, allowing the juice to get all over her chin. She wipes it away with the back of her hand.
>
> Come on and eat something. Here I got some warm eggs and ham for you, the brother says.
>
> I wass a gooooooo girull once. I wass a goooo girl once. Yes I wass.
>
> Sure you were but come on and eat now. You've been drunk for a week....
>
> He assists her to rise and guides her slowly into the bedroom. He forces her to lay down in the bed. She lays there like a log. Her legs slowly widen and her dress curls upwards. He turns away with a look of disgust. Then he covers her. He goes out of the room. She urinates in the bed.

As the story continues, Nora yells a lot and accuses her brother, Harry, of beating her, of being a son of a bitch, of making a whore out of her. She tries unsuccessfully to get out of bed, then falls back into it; he goes into the kitchen and cries; the nephew suggests that she be placed in an insane asylum. She manages to get up and leave the bedroom, only to pitch face-forward onto the floor. Harry asks the nephew to help him pick her up. "The nephew says to let her lie there and forget about her. They pick her up and carry her back to bed."

Nora continues to carry on. In the end, Harry hits her on the jaw, "she reels and then falls on the bed senselessly. She snores heavily and he covers her up. Then he goes into his room and cries. The smell of her body and the odor of gin from her breath fill the room."

Shortly after the story appeared, Farrell received a note from Clifton P. Fadiman, then a young editor with the New York publishing firm Simon & Schuster: "I read with the greatest pleasure and interest 'Slob' in *Blues* and I am impelled to write and ask you whether you may not be possibly contemplating a longer work of fiction which you might care to submit to us. I can assure the manuscript an eager and interested reading."

What a lift this inquiry must have given Farrell! He had only one published story to his credit—and yet that single story had been enough to attract the flattering attention of a New York editor.

On a sunny afternoon soon thereafter, Farrell sat with Mary Hunter on the campus green and talked about what response to make to Fadiman. "Students passed us, hatless lads and girls in their summer dresses," Farrell remembered in an essay a quarter-century later. "I spoke of possible scenes, of how my book would lead to Studs's death, of a character who later became Weary Reilley. Mary took what I said very seriously and made comments. In a sense, *Studs Lonigan* was born that afternoon."

The birth actually was not quite that simple. As his correspondence with Fadiman makes clear, Farrell at first had more than one novel in mind. He told the editor on June 24:

> At present, I have no long work completed, but I have been working on two novels. One is a realisitc [*sic*] story of a corner gang at Fifty Eighth and Prairie Avenue of this city. The neighborhood beackground [*sic*] is that of a middle class community which slowly disintegrates into a rooming house section, finally succumbing to the advance of the negro. I shall send you shortly, a draft of a story which suggests the method of handling, and the types of characters to be described.
>
> The other novel is a tale of a boy in a Catholic high school of this city during the early part of the jazz age. It will deal with the innumerable conflicts resulting from the development of an adolescent sexualism, [*sic*] and the failing struggle to conform these impulses to the type of athlete idealized in this particular environment
>
> I am unable to specify the date of conclusion for either of these works, as I am at present employed on a Chicago newspaer, [*sic*] which occupys [*sic*] a considerable portion of my time. However, I am setting to work on these immediately.

Fadiman—a 1925 graduate of Columbia University who was born the same year as Farrell and had just started working for Simon & Schuster—responded right away: "I shall look forward to the material on either or both of the two novels, both of which sound extremely interesting."

Not quite two weeks later, on July 10, Farrell wrote to the editor again:

> In going through the material, which I mentioned in my previous letter, I find that it is too uneven in quality, and too disorganized for me to send you. Hence, I am withholding it.
>
> I am going ahead with one of the long works I indicated, the corner gang novel. It is to center about a particular location, Fifty Eighth and Prairie Chicago. This is the heart of a neighborhood which has slowly undergone a transition inevitable in modern urban development. Originally, it was a quiet bourgeosie [*sic*] section; slowly it disintegrated into a rooming house area. Now it is inside the zone of Chicago's negro population, and is seemingly to repeat the major aspect of its transition.
>
> In this background I inted [*sic*] to treat a number of boys who grow up, and who, mainly, drift to the poolroom and its complements as the only outlet of their impulses for the romantic and the adventurous. The characters form a vivid set of contrasts, and include such different types as George Lott, ranking Davis cup star, Frank Egan who was recently sentenced to Joliet for rape, after a spectacular trial, a young fellow who went up for violation of the Mann Act, a misguided young man who died from internal complications of gnorohea [*sic*], a Quixotic medievalist who has done everything from check-forging to elevator starting, sound substantial oil salesmen, small-time politicians, hoboes, poolroom loafers, nymphomaniacs, cab drivers, middle class virgins, high school athletes, and others.
>
> This diverse group is in a sense my old gang, the fellows I grew up with, whose stories I listened to, who I played ball with and later got drunk with. I know them intimately, and have absorbed the background out of which they came. Similarly [*sic*], I have moved far enough away from it, to have developed something of a perspective; but am still close enough to it, to write the story with some degree of sympathy and comprehension.
>
> It seems a vital aspect of contemporary city life, and I am impelled to do it immediately. At present, my time is so interrupted that I am unable to give it the continuous effort essential to give a work quality. However, I am going on, and devoting all my available time to it.
>
> I shall probably be in New York sometime this summer, or early in the fall, and I should like to dis- [*sic*] this matter with you then.

On July 16, with a prudent blend of enthusiasm and caution, Fadiman concluded this round of their correspondence: "I like the outline of your book enormously. More than that I cannot say until I see a few sample chapters." He added: "By all means, call me up as soon as you are in the city and let's arrange a long luncheon so we can discuss the novel."

In August, Farrell took off for New York, armed with letters of introduction from Robert Morss Lovett to editors at the *New Republic*, the *Nation*, and the *Books* section of the *New York Herald Tribune*. He had lunch with Fadiman, who gave him at least one more letter of introduction, to an editor at the *New York Post*. Farrell apparently hoped to earn enough from book reviews and other occasional journalism to allow him to stay in New York. He lived frugally at the Mills Hotel, the Chelsea YMCA, and then for a while with friends—including Paul Caron, who earlier that year had married a beautiful young woman named Sarajo Loeb and was living on Riverside Drive. Farrell's book reviews began to appear, but staying in the city proved impractical. In October, he returned to Chicago.

During his time in New York, he had worked hard on his novel. And by September he had written several hundred pages. Although he was modeling his protagonist on Studs Cunningham, Farrell was also drawing on his own life and imagination to make the character come alive.

Once, on a very hot day, Dorothy remembered, she and Farrell had climbed a tree in Jackson Park and, sitting together on a large branch, had eaten their lunch. They stayed up there for perhaps an hour, holding hands and kissing, feeling the cooling breeze and watching the people, unaware of them, passing below. For his novel, then, Farrell moved the tree to Washington Park, got rid of the lunch, and had Studs and Lucy Scanlan stay up on the branch all afternoon. First composed that summer—and then written and rewritten "at least 25 times," according to his recollection—it is one of *Young Lonigan*'s most memorable scenes. But, contrary to Dorothy, it may well have been entirely imaginary. Farrell told an interviewer: "The scene with the tree, when Studs is with the girl Lucy Scanlan, is something I wanted to do, but I was too shy." And, it seems, it was something he had wanted to do when he was eleven, with a ten-year-old girl named Helen Shannon, long before he met Dorothy.

———————

As HE WORKED ON HIS book, Farrell also began to read the works of

John Dewey. When a friend had asked him in 1928 what he thought of Dewey, he replied with a dismissive crack: "Boy Scout." But since then he had grown somewhat wiser—he had rejected bohemianism. In an essay published in June 1930, he wrote, with only slight exaggeration, that after the "harsh realization" that there was no God, he and his generation had fallen for "a new religion. St. Bohemia opened her arms to us; we knelt and prayed; we accepted a new credo; we practiced the rites and performed the ceremonies of this new religion. Our church reversed all the patterns of the bourgeois. It made supposed vice[s] virtues, and idealized them with the intensity of medieval devil worshippers." Yet slowly the falsity of "St. Bohemia's religion" became apparent.

And so Farrell now turned to Dewey's "experimentalism" (or "instrumentalism"). Its impact was strong and lasting. As he affirmed decades later, Dewey was "the major influence on my writing.... The Deweyan conception of character, of habit, influenced me very much."

In *Human Nature and Conduct* (1922), Dewey wrote: "The poignancy of situations that evoke reflection lies in the fact that we really do not know the meaning of the tendencies that are pressing for action." (Farrell was to quote that sentence at the front of *Young Lonigan*.) Dewey continued:

> We have to search, to experiment. Deliberation is a work of discovery. Conflict is acute; one impulse carries us one way into one situation, and another impulse takes us another way to a radically different objective result.... In short, the thing actually at stake in any serious deliberation is.... what kind of person one is to become, what sort of self is in the making, what kind of a world is making [*sic*].

In writing what he expected to be a single novel about Studs Lonigan's wasted life and tragic death, Farrell could easily have made his protagonist a casualty of a character defect or, alternatively, a victim of his degraded environment. Had Farrell chosen either course to the exclusion of the other, his novel would surely have seemed contrived and unsatisfactory. Dewey, with his stress on the interaction between human nature and the social environment, may well have saved the budding novelist from that mistake. Lonigan, as he appeared in print, would be a victim of what Farrell often called the "spiritual poverty" that surrounded him, but he also fell victim to his own poor choices during his short life.

The philosopher under whose sway Farrell had now come turned seventy that October and was one of the leaders of American liberalism. Although he had supported U.S. participation in the Great War (which Farrell continued to look upon as "a war of steel and gold"), Dewey had denounced the executions of Sacco and Vanzetti, and in an influential series of articles in the *New Republic* in the waning months of 1928 had given his favorable "impressions" of Soviet Russia. The Russian people whom he had encountered on a visit that year seemed full of "courage, energy, and confidence in life." A great experiment was taking place there, he declared, "an enormous psychological experiment in transforming the motives that inspire human conduct." And he was optimistic about the outcome, as were liberals in general.

In a survey of "Liberals in Chicago" that Farrell undertook in the November 1929 issue of *Plain Talk* (for which he was paid the considerable sum of $100), his admiration for Jane Addams, Clarence Darrow *et al.* was manifest, but he also seemed to harbor the suspicion that liberalism itself had proven hopelessly ineffectual. Robert Morss Lovett, Farrell said, was "a splendid example of the American intellectual liberal at his finest"—and yet Lovett (whose only son had been killed in the war) had almost disavowed the liberal faith, "declaring that the American liberal had failed in the two critical situations of the last decade: the war and the Sacco-Vanzetti case." With the class struggle imminent, Lovett believed that "it was the duty of the liberal to contribute his energy and his intellect to the proletarian cause."

Farrell himself had come to think that socialism was inevitable, and that Soviet Russia was showing the way. Two decades later, he wrote:

> A sense of socialism came out of the social and cultural atmosphere. Further than that, I reasoned...that men had acquisitive and aesthetic impulses. Society could be so organized that greater play was given to one or the other set of impulses. Capitalism gave free play to acquisitive impulses. Socialism would give more play to aesthetic impulses. Socialism was not a utopia. It would be a different order of society in which the generous and acquisitive impulses of men would provide them with outlets that would satisfy their needs for prestige and dignity, and that with this, there would be more economic justice.

It was an appealing dream, and it became more so as the Great Depression, then just beginning, deepened.

"THIS IS ROT! WHY! This fellow can't even write."

That was the initial reaction of Edward Titus, the editor-publisher of *This Quarter*, to some short stories that Farrell had sent in the spring of 1930 to the little Paris magazine. Titus, who was married to the wealthy cosmetics empress Helena Rubenstein, was a man of conservative literary tastes. His associate editor, Sam Putnam, however, was not. When the large packet of Farrell stories first arrived, Putnam (as he later recalled) took them home with him that evening and started reading them.

"These get better and better," he told his wife.

"Have you discovered another genius?" she asked, somewhat sarcastically.

"I don't know—yet. I think maybe I have."

A midwesterner and former art and literary critic for the *Chicago Evening Post*, Putnam saw

> my own Chicago…coming to life in these tales and sketches of back-o'-the-yards "punks." Of course, I never knew the back-o'-the-yards as Farrell does, but I knew enough about it to realize that this was the genuine article. I was enthusiastic, to put it mildly. That very evening I dashed off a note to the author: "I think your stuff is swell. Send us some more." I did not know what "old man Titus" would think about these stories, but I was determined that they were going to be published—if necessary, I would start a magazine of my own!

Since Titus found Farrell's stories repugnant, a battle took place between the two editors, going on for weeks. "In the meanwhile," Putnam recounted, "by every boat, there arrived a fresh batch of stories [from Farrell]; I had never seen such an output and with the quality standing up so well to the quantity." ("For God's sake," Titus exclaimed, "tell that chap out in Chicago to stop sending us his tripe!") In the end, Farrell's short story "Studs" was published in the July–September issue of *This Quarter* (and Farrell was paid $25). Putnam broke with Titus for good soon thereafter, feeling that getting Farrell published had been the only thing he had accomplished during his brief time with the magazine.

Meanwhile Farrell, besides turning out short stories, essays and book reviews at a prodigious pace, was working on his novel. Early in 1931, he showed his by then massive manuscript to Lloyd "Bus" Stern, who had been a friend since boyhood. Stern suggested that the first section was a novel in itself. "I saw the merit of the idea," Farrell later recalled, and he began "sending it out then and there as *Young Lonigan*."

Clifton Fadiman, the editor at Simon & Schuster who had first expressed interest in a Farrell novel, delivered his verdict in a letter dated February 4: "I am afraid I cannot cotton to this. It seems to me rather crudely and over-emphatically written; you stress your irony too much for it to be very effective. You have got some really genuine material here but you seem to go at it with both hands."

Disappointed but far from defeated, Farrell then mailed *Young Lonigan* off to another New York publishing house, Covici, Friede. Back came the manuscript and a politely unilluminating March 12 rejection letter from Harry Block, the firm's literary editor.

Farrell next sent the manuscript to a third New York publishing firm, Brewer & Warren. Joseph Brewer, the firm's president, wrote back at length on March 31. Although Farrell had promise as an author, *Young Lonigan* "obviously could not be published because the very expressions which you use, as well as a number of the scenes and overt acts, would more certainly than fate stir up the Society for the Suppression of Vice and we should have expensive law suits on our hands."

First from a host of magazines and newspapers, and now from publishing houses, Farrell was getting used to rejection. "From 1928 to 1931," he reflected in an unpublished 1964 essay, "I believe I had more rejections than most writers receive in their entire lives."

But in the spring of 1931, Farrell had something else to worry about: Dorothy Butler was pregnant. It was not the first time. The year before, she had had an abortion. Farrell, who provided the $50 for the doctor, had waited outside while Dorothy, accompanied by a friend who had had an abortion herself, went in to see him. Before long, the deed was done. "That was the end of that," in Dorothy's view. But Farrell, his dormant Catholic conscience perhaps aroused, was troubled by it. No more abortions, he had vowed then.

Farrell's feelings for Dorothy must have been more complicated (or else much less complicated) than hers for him. Grateful as he must have been when she first came into his life, and even more so when she gave herself completely to him, he had not remained entirely faithful to her. He found himself attracted to Mary Hunter, and she—although she was going with Jack Sullivan—found herself somewhat drawn to him as well. Farrell made amorous advances, and one night she gave in. But she knew, even if he perhaps did not, that it would never work out. Their brief romance went no further. Neither Jack Sullivan nor Dorothy Butler found out.

Yet now Dorothy, for the second time, was carrying his child. And this time, he wanted them to keep the baby. Perhaps, after all, he really did love Dorothy. What were they to do?

"Well, I wanted to go to Paris," Dorothy remembered. Two of her aunts had gone there a few years before; their talk had inspired in her the desire to see it for herself. She had spoken of this with James even before she became pregnant, but he had not been receptive. He had read Ernest Hemingway's *The Sun Also Rises* (1926) about the "lost generation," of course; it had become a cult book in American colleges a few years earlier, inspiring some young Americans to rush off to Paris to experience chic disillusion first-hand. Attractive as that siren call may have been to Farrell—and it must have had some appeal—it had not seemed practical. He was trying to write about Studs Lonigan's Chicago, not Hemingway's Paris. And without a job, he had scarcely any money, other than what his writings intermittently brought in and what Dorothy gave him.

But now they had to do something. It was obvious, to her at least, that if she had the child, they had to be wed. If they kept the marriage and her pregnancy secret, he would not come under familial pressure to get a job and could concentrate on his writing. And if they went off to Paris, she could have the baby there and after a time they could return, respectably married with child. As for money, she still had some of the "tuition" money she'd taken from her mother over the preceding two years, which they could use to get to Paris. And so, she and James agreed, that was what they would do.

But they could hardly let their families in on their plans (even though Mrs. Butler liked James, and everyone in the Daly and Farrell families liked Dorothy). Cover stories were needed. His would be that he was going off to New York to get his novel published. Her story would be that she had won a scholarship to study in Paris. Farrell managed to obtain some University of Chicago stationery, typed up an announcement of the scholarship, signed a university official's name to the letter, and mailed it to Dorothy.

When she showed it to her mother, Mrs. Butler was suitably impressed and, of course, very pleased for her daughter. She helped her get ready for the trip and gave her some money.

On Monday, April 13, 1931, James Thomas Farrell and Dorothy Patricia Butler were secretly married at Chicago's City Hall. Ted Marvel, a singer and preacher's son from Kansas City, whom Farrell had first met at the Chelsea YMCA in New York, served as best man.

Later that same day, Farrell left for New York. Mary Hunter and Jack Sullivan saw him off at the train station. Unaware of the furtive wedding, they supposed that his departure marked the end of his affair with the amiable but somewhat "balmy" Dorothy, and they thought he was doing the right thing. Indeed, Mary Hunter recalled, they were "totally delighted" for him.

In New York, Farrell stayed at the Chelsea YMCA. He visited, among other places, the office of the *New Masses* ("A Monthly Publication of Workers Art and Literature") on East 19th Street, met Mike Gold, the editor, and left the *Young Lonigan* manuscript with Walt Carmon, the managing editor, who promised to submit it to Vanguard Press. Farrell said that if his book was accepted, he'd give a 10 percent commission to the *New Masses.*

On an impulse, Farrell also paid a visit to Horace Gregory, a poet whose work he admired and who lived in Sunnyside, Queens. Within minutes of Farrell's arrival, Gregory later recalled, "he had broken through my air of reticence, and we were talking as though we had known each other half our lives. He was earnest, voluble, hilarious, full of plans and lively anecdotes. We had a drink to his future success."

Meanwhile, Dorothy had come to New York with her mother. On Friday, April 17, Mrs. Butler saw her daughter off on the SS *Pennland*, bound for Cherbourg. As she waved goodbye, Margaret Butler had no idea that her son-in-law was also aboard, nor even that she had a son-in-law.

Chapter Seven
Paris

MR. AND MRS. JAMES T. FARRELL arrived in Cherbourg with about $65 between them. They took the train to Paris, stayed a few nights in a hotel near the gare de l'Est on the Right Bank, then crossed to the Left Bank, where before long they found an inexpensive hotel off the boulevard St. Germain des Près.

It was springtime in the City of Light, and there was much to see and absorb. The people on the streets seemed to Farrell "strange and mysterious beings, living in a world that was not my world," and speaking a language he only half understood. "I was constantly in danger of being overwhelmed," he said later of his early Paris days. "There was so much beauty, so much charm, so much grace in this city, in its orderly streets and its harmoniously arranged parks, its historic sites and buildings, its churches and galleries."

They soon found Sam Putnam—and Montparnasse, the famed haunt of the avant-garde. Putnam, who had become a Farrell champion when he worked for Edward Titus's *This Quarter*, was now editor of his own little magazine, the *New Review*, and was to prove very helpful to Farrell during his time in Paris.

Despite its bohemian attractions, Montparnasse had become somewhat passé by the time Farrell arrived. The 1920s were over. The generation of writers that had experienced the Great War had come and, for the most part, gone. Five years had elapsed since *The Sun Also Rises* appeared, and nine years since the heroic publication of James Joyce's *Ulysses* by Sylvia Beach's Shakespeare & Company. Paris, as Malcolm Cowley, literary editor of the *New Republic*, noted, had ceased to be "the center of everything 'modern' and esthetically ambitious in American literature."

Putnam took Farrell to Shakespeare & Company for a short

visit. Sylvia Beach was not at all sure she liked the young new-comer; perhaps he struck her as a bit uncouth. Farrell, Putnam wrote in his memoirs, represented "a new America that was coming up, one we did not know existed, an America that was shortly to find expression in the social-literary movement of the 1930s." In the disillusion brought on by the war, the isolated world of the private imagination had beckoned; now, with the Great Depression, realism began to come into vogue again.

Although welcomed by Putnam, Farrell's literary realism was disdained by the sort of avant-gardist associated with such magazines as Eugene Jolas's *transition* (which, as it happened, had suspended publication in mid-1930). "Realism in America has reached its point of saturation," the editors had declared in 1927. "We are no longer interested in the photography of events, in the mere silhouetting of facts, in the presentation of misery." Putnam's *New Review*, in contrast, stressed the "sacramental significance of reality" and wanted, above all, "a return to content."

It didn't take Farrell long to decide that "Montparnasse was not for him," Putnam recalled. "He was not in any sense a Montparnasse type. He felt ill at ease with us and we with him. We did not speak the same language."

Even if Farrell had been more in tune with *transition*'s "Revolutionists of the Word," or at least, like Putnam, could speak the "language," he could hardly have afforded to become a Montparnasse literary flâneur—not with his limited funds, a pregnant wife and no steady source of income. (Just weeks after their arrival in Paris, he and Dorothy began to run out of money; she resorted to cabling an uncle for help.) It was all very well to sit in the café Le Select listening to expatriate literati expound on Joyce or Gertrude Stein or some abstract literary theory, but Farrell soon turned his attention back to the Chicago of his memory and imagination—and to the real challenge of making his way as a writer. He didn't think that he would be missing much. In the Parisian cafés, he reported to Walt Carmon of the *New Masses*, "everyone talks and little is said."

In May, Farrell had lunch with Ezra Pound in a restaurant on the rue Carmartain. The poet, who had left Paris in 1924 for Rapallo, Italy, was on the masthead of the *New Review* as associate editor. Earlier in the year, Putnam had sent him two Farrell stories he was considering for publication: "The Scarecrow," about a pathetic, sluttish fourteen-year-old girl, and "Jewboy," an excerpt from *Young Lonigan* about a boy rejected by the girl at the center of a "gang shag" (or "gang bang") because he was Jewish. "Certainly the stuff we are here to print," Pound commented. The two stories should be published together, he advised Putnam. "Effect cumulative, and shows that a new writer is here." Pound judged that "The Scarecrow" was "much the more important" of the two stories. (He even claimed enigmatically that the story provided "An answer to several questions asked by the late Henry James." Just what the Master's now-answered questions might have been, the poet failed to disclose.) Despite his advice, Putnam decided to publish "Jewboy" by itself in the August-September-October issue.

Noted among the literati for his generosity to other writers, Pound arranged for Farrell to take "The Scarecrow" and three other stories to Desmond Harmsworth, a young Englishman living on the Île St. Louis who had recently started up a publishing firm. Harmsworth and his partner read the stories, and he spoke well of them—but he didn't see fit to publish them. (Later in the year, Farrell had a similar, perhaps even more frustrating experience with a London publisher named Jacob Schwartz, who praised his stories but finally decided that he didn't dare publish them.)

Pound tried to assist Farrell again that spring by including him among the authors he recommended to Caresse Crosby. After the sensational suicide of her husband, Harry, she was seeking to turn their small Black Sun Press, which specialized in finely printed limited editions, into a commercial firm. This, too, came to nothing.

Farrell pursued other possibilities. He sent "The Scarecrow" to Peter Neagoe, a Romanian native and recently naturalized American, who at Putnam's suggestion was editing an anthology of work by American writers in Europe. Neagoe, who was married to a painter and living in Mirmande, an artists' colony in the South of France, liked the story but thought it could be made shorter and strengthened in certain ways. (He eventually published a different Farrell story, "Soap," in his anthology *Americans Abroad*, which appeared in December 1932.)

The eager young writer also heard from Bob Brown, a Chicago native and former freelance writer in his mid-forties who had invented what he called a "Reading Machine," a compact precursor of the microfilm reader that, as he envisioned it, "would carry words endlessly to all reading eyes in one unbroken line" and supplant that antiquated device, the book. "The written word," Brown insisted (in a book), "hasn't kept up with the age. The movies have outmaneuvered it. We have the talkies, but as yet no readies." Residing in a colony at Cagnes-sur-Mer on the Riviera, Brown was now intent upon perfecting his Reading Machine, and toward that end was gathering "readies" for an anthology he planned to publish. He invited Farrell to contribute, and the young writer obliged. "You have the idea perfectly," Brown told him. In one contribution, Farrell "readified" a story penned by his brother Jack (now twenty-one and one of the handful of people whom he had let in on the secret of his marriage to Dorothy). The resulting readie began: "Miss Ryan...keen dress model from work...walking...stark naked...into his dreams...her face beams...smiles...a comeon daddy...."

Readies for Bob Brown's Machine, which, in addition to Farrell's efforts, included readies from Gertrude Stein, Ezra Pound, Kay Boyle, Eugene Jolas, Robert McAlmon and others—some forty contributors in all—appeared later in the year. Farrell, who got no money for his work, was unimpressed by most of the writing in the volume. (Brown admitted to him that—with the notable exceptions of the readies by Kay Boyle, her lover Laurence Vail, a painter, and Farrell himself—he was, too.)

With the help of Putnam and Pound, the freshness of his material, and his own talents and hard work, Farrell began to make his presence felt among the expatriate literati. But in terms of his subsequent career, he probably would have done as well if he had not crossed the Atlantic. For back in New York, his *Young Lonigan* manuscript had been enthusiastically received by James Henle, president of Vanguard Press.

"Well, our friend Farrell is the best man you have sent to me to date," Henle wrote to Walt Carmon at the *New Masses* on May 12.

> *Young Lonigan* is a moving study. Of course, it is intensely brutal and I am not sure that it gains by forcing this feature; if you read it you will note that the passages where he relies on implication rather than explicitness are infinitely more effective.
>
> I am sorry that he didn't come to see me before he left for Paris. He evidently has a revision of this manuscript in mind (from what you tell me) and I should like to talk to him about it. In addition to the point I have made, I think there is a certain obscurity in the opening twenty or thirty pages that should be cleared up.

Later in May, Farrell received word from Henle that Vanguard Press was interested in publishing *Young Lonigan*. The exciting news came shortly before he and Dorothy left their hotel and moved to Sceaux-Robinson, a suburb of Paris. Together with Reuben and Esther Mencken, friends from the University of Chicago and the Cube who had preceded them to Paris, they rented a *pavillon* that Putnam and his family had previously occupied. Henle's offer was soon followed by a contract providing Farrell with an advance against royalties of $100 down and $150 more on delivery of the revised and completed manuscript.

Not long after getting Henle's good news, Farrell received some bad: Paul Caron, his Nietzschean buddy, had died from a cancerous tumor of the brain. Farrell wept. Some years later, he was told by Caron's family that toward the end "Paul kept talking of me, and that shortly before he died, talking with wheezes, and with forced breaths, so that his words came slowly, he said—Always...keep...in touch...with Jimmy."

Farrell's own family in Chicago still believed him to be in New York, but cracks had begun to appear in that little fiction. "Mother & I received your lovely long letter & it pleased her indeed," Ella Daly wrote him (c/o the *New Masses*) on May 30. "You were very considerate, yet she still wants to know your address, where you live & etc. So you explain to Mother what your room is like[,] how much you pay...."

Farrell decided then it was time for his fictional self to merge with his real one. He told the Dalys that not only did Vanguard want to publish his book, but he had just left New York for Paris.

"Your letter received," Ella responded on July 1. "[W]ords cant [*sic*] express how happy we all were that your book was accepted. Good luck." His sudden decision to go to France, now that a New York press was going to publish his book, apparently did not strike the Dalys as extremely odd, perhaps because they knew that Dorothy was in Paris. "Mother as usual said you traveled enough to NY. What did you want in Paris. But at that she was pleased. Uncle Tom is away most of the time. I know it pleases him." Imagining that her nephew must now be coming into money, Ella, always good at wheedling cash from people, wasted little time in putting in the family's claim: "[W]e will appreciate any thing you can do for us as its [*sic*] hard with mother sick nothing but expenses How much do you think your book will bring not that I [want] to be personal only I am so happy you worked so hard and you deserve it."

Money was on Farrell's mind, too. The Menckens would soon

depart Sceaux-Robinson for Russia, leaving the Farrells to come up with the full rent—about 600 francs (or $23) a month—which they did not have. Farrell kept telling their landlady "that I was hoping to get some money." She was "tightfisted and rich"—but she also was kind to the young American couple with a baby on the way, and never evicted them.

Farrell worked hard, revising *Young Lonigan* and writing other fiction. On a typical morning, Dorothy said, he would "get up early and write" while she remained in bed. "After a while, he'd get lonesome. He'd bring me in a cup of coffee and I'd get up, and then we'd talk for a long, long time." Eventually they would have something to eat and go out for a while. Later in the day, or at night, he would write some more.

Henle, his editor at Vanguard, had him add a new first chapter to *Young Lonigan*, to introduce Studs to the reader more effectively. Fearing the censors, he also had Farrell delete a chapter about a "gang shag." Slightly more than a quarter-century later, the deleted chapter appeared in print as a short story, "Boys and Girls."

With his revision of *Young Lonigan* accomplished and spurred by the hope of getting an advance on a second novel, Farrell, in a burst of concentrated effort, dashed off in a mere ten days (or so he later claimed) a first draft of a novel about an express company. "The Madhouse, a Romance of Commerce and Service," as he titled it, would be published two years later as *Gas-House McGinty.*

Meanwhile, Farrell and Dorothy decided the time was right to tell their families that they had been married, ostensibly in Paris. Just before receiving Dorothy's letter, however, Mrs. Butler somehow discovered from another source that her daughter and James Farrell were man and wife. She liked James, but was understandably upset. After learning of her reaction, Farrell, in a letter to his friend Ted Marvel (who had recently visited Mrs. Butler), mounted his high horse:

> Amen I say to you unless you have been washed in the blood of the Lamb, Glory hallelujah, and the bourgeosie will weep and wail and gnash their teeth because their notions are not respected and the neighbors can't all come in and all agree that yes our nice little morals codes are so nice and never broken. And yes, I haven't had my hair cut since June, and sometimes I only shave twice a week, and now writers can't make a living.... And I should just get caught marching up to jesus in a church and giving some bastard of a priest

five bucks or ten bucks to get snactified [*sic*] in holy matrimony. If anybody asks you about my marriage tell them I was married by the Pope, with Cardinal Gasparri assisting.

If Mrs. Butler was "so damn worried about her daughter living in a furnished room," he went on, why didn't she send her some money? "I mention this as a mere matter of logic, not that I'd ask her, etc." His own family, he confided, "wrote me nice letters and swallowed their disappointment. Jack said my grandmother is promising to whale my arse."

With his marriage now public knowledge back home and the need for money continually pressing upon him, Farrell, for all his bravado, began to doubt the wisdom of his decision to leave the University of Chicago. "I was foolish, and ignorantly thought that I couldn't be a writer if I remained there," he wrote to Whit Burnett, the Vienna-based editor of *Story*, which published one of his stories in its September-October issue. Apparently Farrell was also entertaining second thoughts about his choice of vocation. "At present," he told Burnett, "I am devoting myself wholly to fiction, but later plan, either to abandon or subordinate it to the study of philosophy." This he didn't do, but his interest in philosophy endured—not always to the advantage of his fiction, especially in his latter decades.

He was living in France indefinitely, Farrell continued, but he was "in no sense of the word, an expatriate," and he subscribed to "no Parisian literary credos or movements." Although his champions Putnam and Pound might be sympathetic to Italian dictator Benito Mussolini's fascism, Farrell, stubbornly (if circumspectly) going his own way, was not. "My sympathies are almost wholly left wing." (In a letter to his sister Mary two months later, he told her: "The communists are not always as crazy as they seem—although many communists are cracked. If I make any dough on my books, part of it is going to Communism.")

In late September, Henle cabled him to offer an advance of $200 for his express-company novel. ("The boy is certainly good," Henle wrote to Walt Carmon. "We'll make them all sit up and take notice.")

The next month, Farrell received another cablegram informing him that his grandmother had died. Julia Brown Daly, an Irish peasant who could not read a word he wrote, was probably the only one of his elders in the Farrell or Daly families whom he had loved without reservation. "When I had left Chicago in April, she had cried," he later remembered. "Now, I cried."

━━━━━━◆◦◆━━━━━━

IN NOVEMBER, WITH THEIR BABY expected soon, the Farrells (who were several months behind in their rent) left Sceaux-Robinson and moved to a hotel near the rue Delambre in Montparnasse, where they would be nearer to the American Hospital in Neuilly-sur-Seine. Once the baby was born, they intended to move into an apartment that, with the help of the Putnams, they had found in the suburb of Fontenay-aux-Roses. Mrs. Butler now sent them some money. The writer Kay Boyle—whom they had not yet met and who was living on the Riviera—after hearing of a fellow writer and his pregnant wife in Paris so poor they couldn't afford baby clothes, sent them some clothes that one of her daughters had worn. The Farrells bought a crib and waited.

The advances from Henle were their chief source of income (aside from the hundreds of dollars sent them by Dorothy's mother and uncle). The payments Farrell sporadically got for his other writings were far from lavish—and sometimes not even forthcoming. Edward Titus, the editor of *This Quarter* who had initially regarded Farrell's stories as "tripe," more recently had accepted one of them for an anthology he was planning. Getting him to pay for the story was another matter. Titus had claimed "that he gives five bucks a page advance, which means about eighty five bucks to me," Farrell complained, "but all I have to do is go down and fight for it, because that's the only way the bastard will pay." In all his time in Paris, he earned only $60 from such literary efforts.

In November, Farrell received some dispiriting news from Henle in New York: On advice of counsel, Vanguard Press, in order to avoid legal action on grounds of obscenity, would publish only a limited edition of *Young Lonigan* in the spring, and it would be dressed up to resemble a sociological case study. Farrell was angry and disappointed, but resigned. "I don't know what to say," he replied.

> Naturally it is very discouraging and also irritating, but I don't see that it does me any good, either to feel martyred, or to get angry and curse.... Obviously, I feel that such conditions should be fought, but how I don't know, and I wouldn't want you to take any serious financial risks with any of my books. I have confidence that you will do

whatever you can, and that the course of action you pursue will be
the wisest possible one. I think I understand the kind of stupidity a
publisher is up against, because I have met the same kind of stupidity, and have lost countless time bumping into it amongst my
relatives, in-laws, teachers, former employers and so on.... I can't do
any more wholesale revision of the book and appreciate your not
asking me to. If I try to make further expurgations, I shall ruin whatever value it might have, and hence, I don't know that there is
anything more to say.

Farrell thanked Henle for letting him sell the French rights to
Young Lonigan for his own profit. He also sent the editor, for possible use, letters he had written to three University of Chicago
professors whom he knew—sociologist Ernest Burgess, philosopher T. V. Smith and political scientist Harold Lasswell—asking
them for comments on *Young Lonigan* that (if favorable) might be
used on the dust jacket. If the book were to be "addressed to sociologists," the novelist suggested, "their comments would be
helpful."

For all his willingness to adapt to the situation, Farrell was
indeed very discouraged. Writing to Peter Neagoe in Mirmande, he
unhappily told him what had happened. Neagoe, in response, tried
to get him to look on the bright side: "If Henle is an enterprising
guy he can make the book a huge success, just because of its supposed restriction.... So, cheer up old boy. Besides you have your
second book and bushels of stories and you ain't quite as old as the
hills yet. And I don't know that bricklaying or 'something' would be
better. We guys are marked in our own way and got to stick to it
through thick and thin. I see nothing ahead of you but a path of
roses."

And soon, Neagoe reminded him, "you will be a happy papa."

In the second week of December, Dorothy went into labor. "It
took so long," she remembered. "It took about 35 hours of labor. It
was terrible." In his short story "Soap," published the next year in
Neagoe's anthology, Farrell wrote about the ordeal in fictional
form:

He recalled her moaning in the labor room, her screams filling the
corridor outside, as he had paced it, wrung with the fear that she
would not live. He had gone into the labor room, and seen her twisting and agonizing on the bed. She had curtly ordered him out of the
room, and he walked out, hang-dog. That had been at about eleven
o'clock in the evening. She had gone on like that until the next after-

noon, when the baby had been delivered. The nurse had come out with the swaddled, wrinkled faced baby under her arm. His son.

In real life, they named him Sean Thomas Patrick Farrell. "Thomas after [Farrell's] uncle," according to Dorothy, "Sean because we liked the name, and Patrick after my father."

Four days after Sean's birth, Farrell was awakened early in the morning by the hotel concierge and told to phone the hospital. He did, and was given the terrible news: his son was dead.

> And he had seen it in the nursery the day before it had died [Farrell wrote in "Soap"]. The little thing had looked cute, its face had been clear, the head well-shaped, the eyes a deep, rich blue. It had lain, sniffling, and gasping, unable to breathe, and suffering as it had taken in the oxygen. [The mother's] body had been torn and bruised by the baby, and she, too, had nearly died. And she had only been permitted to hold the baby in her arms for a few seconds on the third day. She had been brave when he told her that it was dead, but he had seen all her crushed maternal instincts on her struggling, wearied girl's face.

The infant was buried in a cemetery at Neuilly-sur-Seine. Dorothy, who had to remain in the hospital for a few weeks, could not be there with Farrell.

The day after Christmas, with Dorothy still not well, Farrell went to a party thrown by Kay Boyle and Laurence Vail in his studio in Paris. Farrell had written to Boyle of the baby's death, and had had drinks with her and Vail a few days before. When Farrell arrived at the studio, he stood for a moment in the doorway before coming in from the cold; to Kay Boyle he seemed a forlorn figure, with his cap pulled down over his eyes and carrying a parcel—the baby clothes. When (by her recollection long afterward, but not his) he announced what he had, the other guests, ignorant of the tragedy, burst into laughter. Then he explained. Something of a pall was doubtless cast upon the party, but the gloom cannot have lasted long. Farrell proceeded to get drunk along with everyone else.

"There were hard days in the winter of 1932, following the death of my son," he later recalled. He was about ready for "the breadline," he wrote to his sister Mary in a January 12 letter, when, on the preceding Friday, a check had unexpectedly arrived from his publisher. After learning of the baby's death, Henle, on his own initiative, had sent Farrell $100. The novelist had meanwhile sold the

French rights to *Young Lonigan* to "the biggest publishing house over here—the Nouvelle Revue Française—but there's not much money in it," he told his sister. "I'm giving a hog's share of my royalties to the translator to get a decent job done."

Farrell had Vanguard send galleys of *Young Lonigan* to "Mr. Pound," and invited him to comment. The poet thought that Farrell (or "Farrel" as he habitually addressed him) could tighten up the beginning, which he did. "Also rhythm," Pound told him. "Effect a bit too much Joyce of the Portrait [i.e., *Portrait of the Artist as a Young Man*]. You May say they were all irish, and the ijum the same. Only escape is to keep the langwudg but change the rhythm or movement."

"As to the Irishness of it, I generally feel that I'm an Irishman rather than an American," Farrell responded, and *Young Lonigan*

> was recommended at the nrf [Nouvelle Revue Française] as being [practically?] an Irish novel. I had read Joyce, and pretty well forgotten him in all details at least a year, and the Portrait a year and a half before even starting the book, and any similarity was all unconscious. I reread most of the Portrait a month or so ago, and while doing so, I did feel that, with differences of time, climate and country, there were certain similarities to the exterior conditions and experiences and even the personal ones portrayed there and the ones I bumped into in the course of growing up as a Catholic young man, attending a Catholic high school taught by Carmelites rather than Jesuits etc. In the scenes which I like best, I think there is a change in what one might as well call rhythmns [sic]. I mean in the playground scene, jewboy, the one at the beach, the one in the tree in the park, and the fight with Wary [sic]. Also the rhythmns [sic] are more or less unconscious, because I can never consciously write in rhymns [sic], and most of the time if my writing is rhythmical, it is a matter of good luck.

Farrell, now in a cheaper apartment on the rue de la Glascière, kept working that winter. Henle liked the short stories he had sent and told him that if *Young Lonigan* was well received, Vanguard might publish a book of his short stories in addition to the express-company novel. As a young writer, Farrell was now doing well—except monetarily.

As the weeks went by, what money he and Dorothy possessed began to run out. When his shoes wore out and one of the soles caught on something and ripped off, he could not afford to buy a new pair. A French friend gave him some tennis shoes, and—in the rather pitiable hope that the canvas shoes would be mistaken from a distance for oxfords—they covered them with dark shoe polish.

Then one day, when they were almost flat broke, they had to decide whether to buy bread or soap; Farrell bought bread and stole some soap. In desperation, Dorothy turned to her family, and her mother sent $100. A local minister also aided them.

In March, Henle sent Farrell a proof of what would be the introduction to *Young Lonigan*, written by Frederic M. Thrasher, a New York University sociologist who had just completed a study of "1,313 gangs" in Chicago. Robert Morss Lovett, the University of Chicago English professor who had encouraged Farrell to turn "Studs" into a novel and had given him letters of introduction to various editors in New York, was apparently instrumental in getting Thrasher to do the introduction. Farrell wrote the sociologist to thank him, noting in passing, "I believe that I was somewhat conscious of some of the things you point out, such as the inability of school, home, church, and social agency in the form of the playground to canalize the impulses of these particular characters."

Farrell, plugging away ceaselessly, rewrote a story, "Helen, I Love You" (in which "goofy" young Danny O'Neill, new in the neighborhood, stands up verbally to another boy in front of red-haired Helen Scanlan's house), and sent it off to H. L. Mencken's *American Mercury* in New York.

By April, however, both Farrell and Dorothy knew it was time to go home. With the help of Mrs. Butler and Travelers Aid, they returned to America on a Dutch liner, the *Statendam*. On April 17, a Sunday morning, they arrived in Hoboken, New Jersey, with $15 between them.

They had left more than Paris behind. "It was there," Farrell wrote, "that my youth really ended."

Part 2

Novelist and Radical

Chapter Eight
A Revolutionary Writer

"THIS NOVEL IS ISSUED IN a special edition, the sale of which is limited to physicians, surgeons, psychologists, psychiatrists, sociologists, social workers, teachers, and other persons having a professional interest in the psychology of adolescents."

So warned the dust jacket of *Young Lonigan: A Boyhood in Chicago Streets* (dedicated "To the Memory of Grandmother Julia Brown Daly"), which was published just days after the Farrells arrived in New York from Paris. And if that notice on the dust jacket was not enough to discourage the general reader, there was the book's unusually steep price: $3.75 (which was $1.25 more than the price would be for each of the later volumes in the trilogy).

The reader who surmounted these obstacles found a raw, relentless novel that makes extensive use of the tough-guy idiom of the streets, with its habitual ethnic slurs and brutal sexual candor. "I have a feeling this is a great book, but I'm a minister's son and I must admit that much of it is just too tough for me," said James Weber Linn—obviously proud of his protégé—to one of his students, who then stayed up all night and into the morning, devouring the novel with gusto.

Young Studs, freshly graduated from St. Patrick's, licks a hoodlum (and fellow graduate) named Weary Reilley in a fight and is soon hanging out with the toughs at 58th and Prairie. Their talk is of kikes and hebes, niggers and eight-balls, micks and pig Irish, and of chickens and hot dames, girlies and molls, of girls built like a brick outhouse, of good stuff gone to waste. Studs—unable to express his innocent love for Lucy Scanlan—is stirred by the sight of his sister in her nightgown. Eager to learn more about the can house (whorehouse) on 57th Street, he takes part, it is indirectly made clear, in a gang shag with Iris, "who took all kinds of guys up to her house when her mother wasn't home." This last sordid

episode serves, or at least should have served, as a powerful counterpoint to the tender scene earlier with Studs and Lucy in the tree
in Washington Park. The absence of the chapter directly telling of
the gang shag weakens the novel—but the critics apparently didn't
sense that anything was missing.

Some reviewers let the dust jacket be their guide. The sage
who examined *Young Lonigan* for the *Chicago Herald and Examiner*, the Hearst paper that had fired Farrell from his job as campus
correspondent, disposed of the book in three paragraphs and concluded that it might be of interest to social scientists who "like
their case histories fictionized." The anonymous reviewer for the
New York Times Book Review concluded that *Young Lonigan* was
not a novel at all. "The artistic powers of the author, save where he
exercises a selective faculty to make his scenes more typical, are in
suspension. His to record and report"—and, in the reviewer's opinion, to produce a mere "novelist's notebook, a painstaking record
from which another Mark Twain might construct an important epic
of youth."

Other critics were more perceptive. The *New York Herald Tribune* hailed the book as "a classic…a profound study of a certain
kind of American adolescence and of a background that is representative of hundreds of breeding places of youth in American
cities." The novel was not pornographic, the anonymous reviewer
noted, but neither was it sentimental. "Its fidelity to truth is too
close to admit of facile response."

"Mr. Farrell's unblinking, open-eyed veracity reminds one of
Theodore Dreiser at his best," Farrell's friend Horace Gregory
declared in the *Nation*. The action of the book—street fights, kissing games and such—includes nothing out of the ordinary, but the
"deadly" nature of young Lonigan's environment soon becomes
apparent. Farrell scrupulously refrains from exaggerating his protagonist's impulses and desires, Gregory observed, yet even without
"dramatic" effects, his novel achieves a cumulative power, and the
final chapters linger in the reader's imagination.

In the *New Republic*, Edward Dahlberg, the Boston-born
author of the impressionistic "proletarian" novel *Bottom Dogs*
(1929), asserted that Vanguard Press had done Farrell "a grave injustice" by presenting his "very promising" first novel in the way it
had. *Young Lonigan* was "not a study of the *psychopathia sexualis*
of American boyhood," Dahlberg pointed out. "The emphasis, in
reality, is on the texture of the language. Farrell's American idiom

has a fresh pliancy and a kind of headlong vigor." The novelist rendered "the speech of Chicago's street arabs" with "a convincing naturalness and hard integrity."

"My book is out, but I don't know how it is selling," Farrell wrote to his sister Helen in May. "Some of the reviews are good and some are bad, and so on." *Young Lonigan* was not selling well. By the end of the year, only an anemic 420 copies had been purchased. (Under his contract with Vanguard, Farrell was not to earn any more money from the book until 1,742 copies were sold.) Yet the protective camouflage in which Vanguard had enveloped *Young Lonigan* was not entirely responsible for the lack of interest. The next two volumes in the trilogy—*The Young Manhood of Studs Lonigan* and *Judgment Day*—also set no sales records.

AFTER THEIR RETURN TO NEW YORK, the Farrells moved into an apartment on Union Square kept by Walt Carmon's mistress, Frances Strauss. Carmon—who a year earlier had forwarded the *Young Lonigan* manuscript to Vanguard—had until recently been managing editor of the *New Masses*; Strauss remained the magazine's business manager.

Vanguard Press and the *New Masses* began with an almost biological connection: they had grown from the same seed money. In 1922 a young Harvard dropout named Charles Garland, frustrated in his desire to renounce his paternal inheritance of $1 million, had used the unwanted money to establish the American Fund for Public Service. The Garland Fund (as it became known) made benefactions to various liberal and radical organizations, including the Communist Party and some of its auxiliaries. It was thanks to Garland's largesse that the *New Masses* and Vanguard Press came into existence in 1926.

At the outset, most of the *New Masses'* editors and contributors were liberals or independent radicals, but the Communists were in effective control, and before long the magazine's true color became apparent. In 1928, Michael Gold, the guiding spirit of the magazine and the leading evangel in America for "proletarian literature," became the main editor. Born Itzok Granich, he had grown up among impoverished Jewish immigrants on Manhattan's Lower East Side. Although his father had not been a worker but rather a failed entrepreneur, and Gold himself had briefly attended Harvard, he

111

did his best to seem a proud member of the working class. ("He affected dirty shirts," smoked "stinking, twisted Italian three-cent cigars, and spat frequently and vigorously on the floor," recalled Joseph Freeman, the first editor of the *New Masses*.) As Gold was to demonstrate repeatedly over the years, he shared with Saint Ignatius Loyola, the sixteenth-century founder of the Jesuit order, the conviction that it is necessary to be ready always to believe "that the white that I see is black, if the hierarchical Church so defines it"—except that in Gold's case, the hierarchical church was the Communist one, headed now in Moscow by Joseph Stalin. In 1928, having outmaneuvered his "Left" rivals in the Politburo, Stalin moved far leftward to outflank his erstwhile Bolshevik allies on the "Right" and complete his consolidation of power. The Communist International (Comintern) announced that world capitalism had entered a more precarious stage, a "Third Period" demanding Communist militancy. Reflecting these developments, the *New Masses* under editor Gold—in a transformation undoubtedly made at the party's behest—became an increasingly overt Communist instrument.

Vanguard Press took a different course. Having decided to found a publishing house, the Garland Fund's trustees persuaded Rex Stout (the future mystery writer) to become president and poured what eventually amounted to $155,000 into the firm. In its first years (with managing director Jacob Baker actually running things), Vanguard published inexpensive, hardbound reprints of works by such authors as Darwin, Hegel, Marx, Lenin, Edward Bellamy and Upton Sinclair. In May 1928 Vanguard bought out another small firm and started issuing general books at regular trade prices. Then in December 1928, with the Garland Fund money exhausted, Jim Henle, a former journalist, bought a half-interest in the firm and became Vanguard's president; a few years later he acquired the other half. As Farrell's editor, Henle was to become one of the most important figures in his life as a writer.

A dozen years older than Farrell, the dapper Henle was intelligent, literate and witty. He was also a decent man, devoted to his wife and two sons. Born in Louisville to a German Jewish family, a graduate of Columbia University, he had written for the old *Masses*, had been a reporter on the *Socialist Call*, the *Brooklyn Eagle* and the *New York World*, and then had become managing editor of *McCall's* magazine.

After buying Vanguard with his wife's money, Henle proved

over the ensuing decades to be an extremely good editor, with an eye for talent that others had failed to notice. A small firm with a handful of employees, Vanguard Press published not only Farrell's novels but first works by Calder Willingham, Saul Bellow and "Dr. Suess" (Theodore Geisel). Still, of all the writers with whom Henle worked, Farrell was, in a personal sense, the most important. Their professional relationship developed into a close friendship. They saw each other often and, in time, talked on the phone and wrote letters to each other almost daily, exchanging ideas and comments on literature and national and world events, as well as on editorial matters. Henle's missives typically were thoughtful, sensible and to the point; Farrell's were earnest, prolix and at times quite penetrating. Henle had the editorial virtues that the gifted but disorderly novelist lacked; he helped Farrell bring his best works into being.

<hr />

DOROTHY DIDN'T LIKE THE bedbugs in the Union Square apartment, and they soon left it, moving directly to the Sutton Club Hotel on East 56th Street, according to her recollection. Their exit may not have been entirely voluntary, however; or else there may have been an intermediate apartment that they were forced to leave—since Farrell later remembered that they went to the Sutton after having been "evicted from our apartment (a not too uncommon experience during the Depression)." In any case, they arrived at the Sutton. Farrell had become acquainted with Julian Shapiro, a boyhood friend of the hotel's manager, novelist Nathanael "Pep" West (who was then working on *Miss Lonelyhearts*). West often let fellow writers room at the Sutton free of charge, and he invited the penniless Farrells to stay for a while. "He did it simply and unobtrusively as though it were a matter of course," Farrell remembered. After a week or two in the hotel, the Farrells moved into an apartment in Greenwich Village. Before the year was over they moved several more times

One afternoon that spring, Farrell paid a visit to the *New Masses* office, now located on West 15th Street. There he met the editor who was Carmon's replacement and whose name sixteen years later was to resound throughout the nation: Whittaker Chambers. His descent into the Communist underground still some months in the future, Chambers had been hired by Mike Gold and Joseph Freeman on the strength of four stories he had written for the *New Masses* that had been very warmly received in Moscow, and with the blessing of Alexander Trachtenberg (who headed the party's New York publishing firm, International Publishers, and served as "cultural commissar"). On that spring afternoon, he and Farrell talked about "art as a weapon," a function on which the editor-*cum*-revolutionary insisted. Farrell said that he held a different view of writing and intended to write in his own way. Writers of his sort, Chambers asserted, would be forgotten within a decade. The prospect of oblivion did not frighten him, Farrell responded.

"A writer always has to take a chance," he explained to someone else not long afterward. "He is not certain just what value anything he writes may have and he runs the chance of looking quite foolish." Since a writer of fiction relies so heavily on his unconscious, Farrell pointed out, he is not entirely aware of what he is trying to do or what he has done: "I don't think the unconscious is merely a Freudian nightmare. I agree with Dewey when he said that the mind of civilized man is resident in the unconscious." Yet a writer, at least one such as himself, seeks "to order and to work out a meaning to life" in his writing, using the concrete and particular rather than the abstract and general. "This effort is primarily an aesthetic one." But besides being "a literary performance," a piece of fiction can also embody social criticism. *Young Lonigan* "is intended in part as social criticism.... The American communities give the individual little help in any effort to grow up and become civilized. I tried to imply these things, without shouting about them, and without giving them a kind of an emphasis that would spoil my attempt to make *Young Lonigan* a literary performance."

Farrell—whose short story "Helen, I Love You" appeared in the July issue of Mencken's *American Mercury*—was now back at work on his next "literary performance": *Gas-House McGinty*, a novel about a Chicago express company's wagon call department (headed by the title character). The book was to be published the following February. Though his friend Horace Gregory praised it in the *New York Herald Tribune* as a novel of "extraordinary power" with "a wide streak of realistic poetry running through the prose," the reviewer for the *New York Times Book Review*, Fred T. Marsh, saw more clearly that *Gas-House McGinty* was lesser Farrell. "In [*Young Lonigan*] the boys and girls of Chicago streets stood out, very real and very affecting figures against the carefully filled-in background. In the new novel the people, even McGinty, have less individuality." Only 819 copies were sold in the first three months after publication.

Living in New York, Farrell was as much in exile as he had been in Paris, with his imagination intensely focused on that place from which he was bitterly estranged, the city of his youth. "I am exceedingly soured on Chicago," he wrote to his sister Mary. "It is mainly a case of being soured on people I knew there, most of whom are ineffectual, and should not need to cause one to waste [one's] time, but I just wouldn't even want to go within a radius of the place they live." Should she run into such people who claim to be his friends, he advised her to tell them "it is more likely that I shall deny it and remark that they are goddamn liars."

Farrell's alienation from his own people, the Irish Catholics of Chicago, was extreme. They lived in "spiritual poverty." They did not love knowledge and beauty as he did; they did not strive to understand the world or yearn to create a lasting work of art as he did; they did not share his lofty aspirations or appreciate his own determined, even heroic, efforts to fulfill them. His people, he believed, had held him back: their limitations had become his limitations, which, as he became aware of them, he had to fight all the harder to overcome. "He would do battle so that others did not remain unfulfilled as he and his family had been," he was to write of Danny O'Neill near the end of *My Days of Anger*. "For what he had seen, for what he had been, for what he had learned of these agonies, these failures, these frustrations, these lacerations, there would never be forgiveness in his heart. Everything that created these were his enemies."

Angry, combative, frequently wearing a grim expression and still something of an eccentric, the twenty-eight-year-old Farrell was drawn, as a moth to the flame, to that extremist sect of the alienated, the Communist Party U.S.A. In 1932, after a spurt of growth, it had about 14,500 members nationwide, most of them foreign-born and 40 percent of them unemployed. New York was the party's headquarters and chief stronghold. New York Communists, overwhelmingly Jewish, were prominent in the party's cadre throughout the nation. The party imagined its natural constituency to be workers in basic industries, but neither Jews nor Finns (the party's other large group, concentrated in the upper Midwest) were prominent in heavy industry. Irish Catholics, like Italian and Polish Catholics, were conspicuous by their absence from party ranks. Thus, even among the profoundly alienated, Farrell stood out.

Perhaps this only enhanced his romantic image of himself, defiantly shaking his fist at the indifferent universe, at the God Who did not exist, at the Roman Catholic Church and at Chicago's Irish Catholics.

The Great Depression, which seemed to signal the collapse of American capitalism or at least demonstrate its inadequacy, gave the Communist Party its opportunity. The Depression did not directly affect Farrell's own situation: he was jobless by choice and accustomed to poverty already. With Vanguard and Henle's help, and what he earned from his stories and book reviews (and from selling his copies of the books he reviewed), he and Dorothy managed to scrape by. But his thinking was of course affected by the country's terrible economic crisis. While he found most of the individual Communists whom he met repellent, he told his sister Mary, "I am generally quite sympathetic to communism....We are headed sure as Hell for a shambles and a collapse, and the communists are the only ones making any intelligent gesture against this possibility."

But while he had marched with the Communists on May Day, 1932, parading in the rain from Union Square to Rutgers Square, Farrell was not yet ready intellectually to accept Marxism. That the economic crisis demanded a solution, "that people are starving, that war lies in the future as a threat to our whole civilization and our very lives, that the promise of American life has not, and most likely cannot, ever be fulfilled under the present system," he wrote in the *New York Sun* in October 1932, "[does not] prove that dialectic materialism is a statement of scientific method, or that economic determinism can be applied as a fundamental concept in the judgment of, say, the work of Proust, or that the Marxist system is the only system which can explain life, and that it can explain all of life."

Other American writers, artists and intellectuals were also wrestling with Marxism and the implications of the Depression. More than fifty of them—including John Dos Passos, Sidney Hook, Granville Hicks, Edmund Wilson, Malcolm Cowley, Sherwood Anderson, Theodore Dreiser, Lincoln Steffens and Langston Hughes— signed a manifesto endorsing the Communist Party ticket in the 1932 presidential election. Communism was the only way out of the crisis of capitalism, they believed. "As responsible intellectual workers, we have aligned ourselves with the frankly revolutionary Communist Party." Farrell, not yet a sufficiently prominent "intellectual worker" to be invited to add his name to such a list, did not support the Communist ticket. Not that it would have made any difference: out of 39,816,522 votes cast in the November presidential election, the Communist candidate, William Z. Foster, received a minuscule 102,991. The Socialist candidate, Norman Thomas, did considerably better, getting 884,781 votes, but that was only 2.2 percent of the total vote. Most of the American electorate—a majority made up of 22.8 million voters—chose to invest their hopes in the Democratic candidate, Franklin Delano Roosevelt.

═══▶●◀═══

THE COMMUNISTS "FREQUENTLY CAN see revolution around the corner just as clearly as our politicians and business leaders have spotted prosperity around that same corner," Farrell noted in December. This pithy comment came in a *New York Sun* review of Reinhold Niebuhr's *Moral Man and Immoral Society*, a review that is quite revealing, both in what Farrell says and in what he does not.

Niebuhr, the American Protestant theologian who would become famous for his "Christian realism," considered himself at the time a "Christian radical." In *Moral Man* he argued that there is a fundamental difference between the morality of individuals and the morality of social groups such as nations and classes. Liberals such as John Dewey, who looked to intelligence, the advance of social science and education to produce social progress, "completely disregarded the political necessities in the struggle for justice in human society," Niebuhr maintained. They failed to recognize that collective power, whether in the form of imperialism or of class domination, could be overcome only by some other kind of power. Communism, like every vital religion, has a millennial hope: the dream of achieving a perfect egalitarian society. This is an illusion, but a useful one in bringing about radical social change, Niebuhr believed. To achieve such change, he was willing to countenance the use of violence under certain circumstances.

Farrell seems to have been rather overwhelmed by the brilliant preacher's acute insights and sonorous pronouncements. Instead of expressing reservations and objections or making counterarguments, he mostly confined himself to approving paraphrase and a few complementary observations. He did not rise in defense of Dewey, whose works had previously so impressed him. Nor did he make derisive comments about Niebuhr's Christianity. He expressed contempt instead for "most American intellectuals," who, he said sneeringly (the mask of Chicago tough guy in place), "might be described as the 'Second Coming Boys'"—the liberals, clergymen, democratic socialists and Communists who were looking hopefully to the dawning of a new age. "By the simple application of common sense," he said, "Mr. Niebuhr scores tellingly against various of these types...who await the millennium."

Noting Niebuhr's position on revolutionary violence, Farrell, like the Christian radical, recognized that revolution has its dangers, namely "those of a long-drawn-out and devitalizing conflict and the erection of newer injustices through bureaucracy." Yet Farrell did not strongly convey, as Niebuhr himself had, how dreadful the dangers really are. Societies "risk the welfare of millions when they gamble for the attainment of the absolute," the theologian had pointed out. "And, since coercion is an invariable instrument of their policy, absolutism transmutes this instrument into unbearable tyrannies and cruelties."

And so indeed it did. Even as both men were writing, Stalin was inflicting famine and terror on millions of Soviet peasants, especially those in the Ukraine and adjoining grain-growing areas, who had militantly resisted collectivization of their farms. In the resulting catastrophe, according to Robert Conquest's authoritative history, perhaps seven million died of starvation. Niebuhr (who took somber note in *Moral Man* of the great amount of force that the Russian dictatorship was using to impose collectivization on the peasantry) soon repudiated his notion that the Communist myth was a useful one. The younger, more innocent Farrell—angry at what he saw as the stunted lives of his own people, believing (along with many others) that American capitalism was on the verge of collapse, and alert to the growing menace of fascism—continued to be drawn to the utopian illusion.

———⊱•◦⊰———

FARRELL ATTENDED THE COMMUNIST May Day revels again in 1933. "Workers of the World, Unite," exhorted a large banner carried by some of the Reds as they marched toward Union Square, where the Socialists were holding their own demonstration.

The Comintern had not been especially dismayed when Adolf Hitler came to power in Germany in January. It had viewed his rise during the preceding years as a sign of German capitalism's growing weakness, bringing the great day of revolution nearer. Still, some tactical adjustments were now considered in order. It was time to desist from denouncing Socialists as "social fascists" and to dust off the idea of a "united front from below."

Accordingly, the New York Communists on this May Day were eager to have rank-and-file Socialists join their late-afternoon demonstration at Union Square. Socialist leader Norman Thomas, mindful of the Communists' bad faith in the past, was wary when he spoke to the 15,000–20,000 Socialists at their rally and made no mention of a united front. But after the Socialists' time was up and the city's mounted police had begun to herd them out, Communist Carl Winter found the microphone and shouted, his voice amplified to a tremendous volume: "Socialists, stay. Do not go. We invite you to stay for the Communist meetings." This so stunned the policemen, the *New York Times* reported, "that they stopped in their tracks. The Socialists may have been surprised, too, but they cheered and stayed."

To writer Edmund Wilson, present along with Farrell that day, it seemed that "the only thing that had made any impression on [Farrell] about the May Day demonstration was the comrades sucking Eskimo Pies and pop with banners that said, We Want Bread!"

One doubts that was the *only* thing the novelist noticed. But Farrell's alertness to such ironies was evidence not only of his eye for telling detail but of his stubborn independence of mind. This last quality made some of the more pious revolutionaries a little uneasy.

Farrell had "a rich proletarian background," Edwin Rolfe wrote in his *New Masses* review of *Gas-House McGinty*, but the novelist was regrettably still lacking in "social insight." There was "a vagueness, a lack of direction in these workers [in *Gas-House McGinty*], reactions which—even though the action of the novel takes place more than 10 years ago—seems [*sic*] unreal in the year 1933."

Farrell—who was working on the second and, as he then assumed, final volume of the Lonigan saga—read Marx's *Capital* in the Modern Library edition that year. But as the more than seventy-five book reviews of various sorts that he wrote in 1933 for the *New York Sun*, the *New Republic* and other publications show, he didn't confine his reading to Marx or Marxist devotional literature. Among the books he reviewed were James Gould Cozzens's novel *The Last Adam* ("decidedly readable and competent"), Montaigne's essays ("charming, and packed with wisdom, pertinancy, clarity of thought, and discrimination"), and George Orwell's *Down and Out in Paris and London* ("genuine, unexaggerated, and intelligent"). Nor did Farrell automatically bestow comradely approval upon the efforts of "revolutionary" writers. While he rated Josephine Herbst's *Pity Is Not Enough* "one of the most important novels of the year" and said that it measured "the price of what we call success in a manner that is thoroughly honest, sincere and sympathetic," he was far harsher in his judgment of Jack Conroy's "proletarian novel" *The Disinherited:*

> Mr. Conroy is extremely careless, if not slapdash, in his method and in his characterizations. He persists in dragging minor characters back into the narrative without motivation. His story is weakened by unconvincing coincidences. A number of his characters are aimless drifters; but while their buffetings under the capitalist system may support a theory, their misery is not communicated to the reader.... The writing, considered notable by some reviewers for its brutal realism and simplicity, is merely commonplace and undistinguished except for an occasional moving flash.

Increasingly sympathetic to Communism though he was, Farrell was not about to surrender his mind to it. He remained very much his own man.

———➤•◯•◄———

"I HAVE FEARS," FARRELL WROTE in early August 1933 to Dorothy, who was staying in Chicago at her mother's. "It is the first time in my life I can work under conditions that are describable as ideal and I fear I shan't get used to it." Hard at work on the second Lonigan volume, he was a guest at Yaddo, a retreat for artists on a 440-acre wooded estate in Saratoga Springs, New York.

Farrell and the other artists—most of them leftwing in their politics—slept and ate in a baronial mansion, a three-story, graystone dwelling with fifty-five rooms, expensive Persian rugs on the floors, books and paintings lining the walls, and bric-a-brac everywhere (including a pair of large sleighs in the hall, reportedly a gift from the Queen of the Netherlands). Outside were more splendors: vast lawns, white marble fountains, a rose garden, groves of towering white pines, artificial ponds, and scattered about, the private studios that were the working quarters for Farrell and the other guests. His own studio, he told Dorothy, was "a barn, quite large, and clean [with] a small table, chair with canvas seat, small stove, bookshelves, deck chair, round table…cot, and a large desk."A box lunch was delivered there each day, so he could continue working through the afternoon with only minimal interruption."The place is, honestly, like a dream," he said with a touch of awe.

The dream had first been that of Katrina Trask. She and her husband, Spencer, a New York investment banker and philanthropist, had known tragedy as well as success and great wealth: all four of their children had died in childhood. In 1899, as the now-childless couple strolled through the woods of their estate, Katrina, a writer herself, had a vision of what Yaddo should become."Here will be," she is supposed to have said, "a perpetual series of house parties—of literary men, literary women, and other artists…. Look, Spencer, they are walking in the woods, wandering in the garden, sitting under the pine trees—men and women—creating, creating, creating!"

The vision was not realized immediately, however. In fact, more than a quarter-century was to pass before artists were invited to Yaddo to create, create, create. Spencer Trask experienced financial reverses in the Panic of 1907 and was killed in a train wreck two years later. His widow, by then a near-invalid, subsequently closed the mansion and, to save funds for Yaddo's future, lived in the renovated caretaker's cottage. In 1921, a year before her death, Mrs. Trask married George Foster Peabody, who had been Spencer Trask's business partner and long chastely in love with her. After her death, Peabody worked to fulfill her Yaddo dream. And in the summer of 1926, with Elizabeth Ames, a war widow then in her early forties, presiding as Yaddo's executive director, the "house parties" finally began in Saratoga Springs (or Saratoga, as the town was also known).

Energetic, shrewd and a little deaf, Mrs. Ames had a butler, a chef, a housekeeper and a host of maids to assist her in coddling the creative. She also acquired a reputation (perhaps somewhat exaggerated) for trying to break up any of her guests' romantic relationships she deemed unsuitable. Thinking that Mrs. Ames might consider Farrell's marriage unsuitable, his old friend Mary Hunter (now a regular on a popular radio show, "Easy Aces," and living in New York with her husband, Jack Sullivan), had warned him of her reputation. But when Farrell came to Yaddo in August, he found the director "very charming" and "quite nice" to him, and was impressed by how well she managed her diverse guests.

Farrell stood out at Yaddo, recalled Horace Gregory (who was there too, along with his wife, poet Marya Zaturenska): "Against the backdrop of Yaddo's fanciful interiors, Farrell seemed an archetypical Irish-American primitive. He was unique, and he knew it. His tremendous industry in turning out several thousands of words a day set him well apart from the other guests." (And his example, one surmises, may not have endeared him to the less industrious among them.)

For the most part, Farrell was very pleased to be at Yaddo. He liked his room in the mansion, he liked his studio, he liked being able to work without interruption, and he liked being coddled by Mrs. Ames and her staff. But he missed Dorothy.

Mrs. Ames, evidently perceiving this, came to his rescue. Breaking her rule about nonartist spouses, she invited him to have Dorothy join him in September and stay with him in the farmhouse (about a fifteen-minute walk from the mansion) for as long as they liked, until the end of October. "I didn't hint or anything for this," he told Dorothy. But he was delighted. "Always I keep thinking if Dorothy was only here—and now you can be. I love you."

Determined to complete work on the second Lonigan volume while he was at Yaddo, Farrell was alternately "disconsolate and then confident" about the novel, "but I suppose it will turn out well." At some point he had come to realize that the wild New Year's Eve party that he had imagined, with Studs lying drunk and unconscious near the fireplug at 58th and Prairie, would have to conclude this volume, and that the death scene he had in mind for Studs would have to be postponed for a third.

His intensive labor on the novel—he worked mornings and afternoons until about four o'clock, when his eyes gave out and he broke for tea, and then, after supper and a few games of Ping Pong, put in several more hours—seems to have made him something of a wreck. "I don't know how long I can stand daily grind," he wrote Dorothy, "because I am not well and fear a nervous breakdown—I don't want to be told to relax because I cannot—I'm determined to finish this book and relaxation is an impossibility until I do."

And he was worried about Dorothy, about her health and about what she might be doing in Chicago. He was upset when he learned that his brother Jack had taken her to a dance and not mentioned it to him. He insisted that she write to him every day without fail, and was angry with her when she didn't. "Dear it's this way," he explained to her. "You get to know everybody here. It's dull in consequence. It offers me little relaxation. I don't want to go to town and spend money. I don't want to go to movies and strain my eyes. I don't want to drink—read either. It intrudes on my work. Getting mail from you is my only relaxation."

To his immense relief, Dorothy finally arrived at Yaddo in mid-September. A month later, with the final draft of the novel presumably finished, they left for New York and spent the fall in the city. Then, in January 1934, they returned to Yaddo. Thanks to the generosity of Mrs. Ames, the novelist and his wife were to live, off and on, at this magnificent retreat in the foothills of the Adirondacks for some time to come.

⊰⊷•⊶⊱

"WE'RE ALL SETTLED NOW," Farrell wrote to his sister Helen on January 25 from Yaddo, which was covered with more snow than he supposed he had ever seen, "and I'm waiting for my book to come out next Tuesday and almost praying that it sells."

The Young Manhood of Studs Lonigan—dedicated to Farrell's Uncle Tom, and taking Lonigan from 1917, when the United States entered the Great War, to a lurid New Year's Eve party that ushered in the fateful year of 1929—was published on January 30. In the novel, Lonigan, with the opposite sex frequently on his mind ("She had everything she owned pressed right up to him, yumyum, and she made him want it like he almost never wanted it before"), goes to work for his father as a painter's apprentice, yearns for love (with Lucy), and now and then daydreams of having an exciting life (as "Lonewolf Lonigan," a burglar with a gat; or "Yukon Lonigan," hunting gold in Alaska; or even "Mayor Lonigan," presiding over Chicago). His actual life is far more prosaic: "hanging around the poolroom, now and then a smalltime crap game or round of poker; benders on Saturday night, and maybe a couple of times during the week; sometimes a can house." Lonigan manages, with his crudity, to turn a precious date with Lucy into a night never to be repeated. Still a practicing Catholic, he occasionally goes to Confession and does his best to avoid impure thoughts before receiving Communion on Sunday—and then quickly gets back on the road to perdition. Meanwhile, the South Side neighborhood changes. Though Father Gilhooley gets his new church built, the blacks keep moving in and the Lonigans and others move out. And then comes, for "the boys" from the old neighborhood, the gruesome

123

New Year's Eve party—the climax of the novel—at which Weary Reilley beats and rapes a girl. Finally, as the New Year dawns, a drunken figure is visible in the falling snow, huddled by the curb near the fireplug at 58th and Prairie, his eyes puffed black, his nose swollen and bent, his suit and coat bloody, dirty and smelling of vomit. "It was Studs Lonigan, who had once, as a boy, stood before Charley Bathcellar's poolroom thinking that some day, he would grow up to be strong, and tough, and the real stuff."

On the day the novel was published, Lewis Gannett, in his *Herald Tribune* column ("Books and Things"), took just a brief paragraph—under the inaccurate subhead "A Gangster's Boyhood"—to deliver his dismissive summary judgment: "The book is rough, tough, and foul-mouthed, like the slum boy it pictures, and sex-obsessed but disgustingly convincing. It is rather a clinical portrait than a work of art." The next day, in his "Books of the Times" column in the *New York Times,* John Chamberlain seemed to respond: "[The] adjective 'clinical' is usually applied in a derogatory sense, as if to say, 'This is not art.' However, if a work of art consists of presenting material in its most effective—i.e., its most artistic—form, then 'The Young Manhood of Studs Lonigan' is a work of art."

Jim Henle was cautiously optimistic. "It is too early to be sure about anything," he wrote Farrell, "but it does look as though we have a chance to put your book over and we are going to do our damndest to accomplish this. Everyone seems to feel, as I did when I read it, that you are growing and that it represents a distinct advance. As you know, there are a great many promising first novels, but so seldom is that promise fulfilled. If I am wrong about you, I don't belong in the publishing business."

Most of the subsequent reviews applauded Farrell's accomplishment. The anonymous critic for the *New York Times Book Review*, however, while acknowledging the book's "power and truth" and marking Farrell as a writer to watch, complained that as a social portrait *Young Manhood* was somewhat deficient in that the author slighted "the influences which might have helped Studs" and failed to include "any characters who are stronger than their environment." (The reviewer seems to have overlooked Danny O'Neill, sitting in the Upton Service Station in the Black Belt, reading Thorstein Veblen's *Theory of Business Enterprise* and dreaming of becoming a writer and ridding himself completely of the hateful "world of 58th Street.")

The most perceptive review was again by the freelance writer Fred T. Marsh, writing this time in the *New Republic:*

> Farrell is writing a series of novels dealing with an element in American life that has been scarcely touched upon in fiction. He has forged a technique both original and exactly suited to his purpose. That purpose is to make the world see and know and come to understand his people for what they are, inside and out. Thus, the representation is flatly naturalistic but brilliantly accurate and convincing; and at the same time the psychological note is always present....
>
> One fears that a great deal of nonsense will be written about this extraordinary work. It is not about "gangsters" as that word has come to be used in connection with organized crime. It is not about the Chicago "slums," or about hobos, sports, gunmen and suchlike colorful and exotic characters. It is not about the despised and rejected of men. Studs comes from a respectable Irish-American-Catholic home, one generation removed from the home of an immigrant laborer. The Lonigans are well-off. The Fifty-eighth Street gang is a shifting bunch of "tough" youngsters, street-corner sports, poolroom sharks and so on....A gang like this may be found in hundreds of big-city neighborhoods and in every small city from New England to California. Studs is as indigenous as Babbitt to American city life.

In the *New Masses*, Edward Dahlberg tried to reassure the comrades of Farrell's political soundness:

> It is true, there are no strikes or demonstrations in Farrell's novels. Besides that, there is scarcely a figure or a character that can be salvaged, and yet these books are highly serviceable to both workers and intellectuals.... Some day, in our future, classless society, readers will examine *The Young Manhood of Studs Lonigan,* and say, "Look, what we were, and see what we have come through."

<hr />

FARRELL, EVER THE EARNEST OBSERVER, was among twenty thousand men and women crowded into New York's Madison Square Garden on the afternoon of February 16, 1934, for a mass meeting. It had been called by Socialists and various trade unions as a gesture of solidarity with the Austrian Socialists just vanquished in a bloody, four-day civil war in Vienna with the quasi-fascist regime of Chancellor Engelbert Dollfuss. Within ten minutes, the protest rally itself turned into a bloody melée: some five thousand Communists who

had made their way inside the Garden disrupted the meeting with
the intent of taking it over.

"Chairs were flung from balconies and boxes," the *Herald Tribune* reported, "curses and shouts and the uproar of fist fights
drowned out the futile set speeches from the rostrum. More than
100 persons were injured, 20 seriously enough to be treated by
physicians." Among those treated was Clarence Hathaway, editor of
the Communist *Daily Worker*, who had attempted to seize the
podium, only to be beaten by angry Socialists with fists and chairs
and thrown over a railing to the floor.

In a joint statement afterward, the Socialists and trade unions
declared "that the Communist psychology and conduct as mani-
fested at this meeting do not differ from Fascist psychology and
conduct, and that communism has become a pariah among the
workers and all fighters for democracy and liberty."

Farrell, too, was evidently appalled by what he saw. In *Yet
Other Waters* (1952), he was to give a fictional rendition of what
happened and have his writer-protagonist, Bernard Carr, exclaim:
"What the hell did they want to accomplish with this hooliganism?
The Communists have disgraced themselves permanently in the
American radical movement after this disgusting spectacle."

Other radical writers and intellectuals agreed. In an "Open
Letter to the Communist Party," John Dos Passos, Edmund Wilson
and twenty-three others (including Farrell's erstwhile mentor
Robert Morss Lovett, who was later to acquire a reputation as, in
one polemicist's biting words, a "ubiquitous 'decoration' for endless
Communist fronts") protested the party's "disruptive action" and
bemoaned "the culpability and shame of the Communists." In V. F.
Calverton's *Modern Monthly*, which favored an independent, Amer-
icanized radicalism, editor Calverton, philosopher Sidney Hook and
sixteen others denounced the Communists' "act of insane hooliganism." In an "Open Letter to American Intellectuals," they urged those
"sympathetic with the revolutionary movement" to resign from the
Communist Party if they were members, "to repudiate...the Communist auxiliary organizations, well described as 'innocents' clubs'
in most instances," and to join in building radical A. J. Muste's
nascent American Workers Party, which aimed to lead the revolutionary way to "a free workers' democracy."

If Farrell heard that clarion call, he did not heed it. Outraged
as he no doubt was by the Communist "hooliganism" at Madison
Square Garden, as well as, perhaps, by the flagrantly untrue account

of it published in the *Daily Worker*, his reaction cannot have been as uncomplicated as that of his fictional protagonist Bernard Carr. Indeed one wonders if, on some level, the Communists' fascist-like behavior did not impress him with how *serious* they were about revolution. The Communists were not just talking and writing— they were acting to change the world. And if their action was misguided and even disgraceful, as in this case, well, there were bound to be many unfortunate incidents in the course of a revolution.

Whatever his precise reasoning may have been, Farrell in the ensuing months moved closer to the Communists and became more politically *engagé*. In March, as a member of a delegation from the National Committee for the Defense of Political Prisoners (associated with the Communists' International Labor Defense), he visited Leon Blum, a "militant laundry worker," in Great Meadows Prison, Comstock, New York. In June, Farrell's name appeared with those of Dos Passos, Cowley, Dahlberg, Hicks and others on an "Open Letter" urging novelist Thomas Mann, in exile from Nazi Germany and visiting the United States, to speak out in behalf of the Jews and political dissidents who were suffering Nazi persecution. In September, Farrell joined a Communist-sponsored picket line of literati outside the offices of the Macaulay Publishing Company in New York, in support of a strike called after five employees were fired for union activity. The next month, Farrell appeared in the pages of the *Daily Worker* in a fund-raising appeal. Beneath the headline "'Daily' Cannot Exist On Faith Alone, Says Farrell on D. W. Drive," and next to a photo of himself, the novelist made his pitch:

> It is quite apparent that the present is a crucial historical period in American life. The nation seethes with bitter and unchanneled unrest, and the necessity for a change of our social system has been and continues to impress itself upon many minds [*sic*]. Sudden and emphatically important shifts in mass attitudes await us in the imminent future. On the one hand, the seeds of a revolutionary movement have been planted. And on the other hand, the signs of incipient Fascism are clearly to be distinguished.
>
> In such circumstances, the role cast for revolutionary journalism is an essential one....

For all his active support for the revolutionary movement, Farrell did not close his eyes to the divisions within it or his mind to the thoughts of heretics. At Yaddo that summer, he had become friends with George Novack, a former advertising manager for

E. P. Dutton who had joined the Communist League of America (Trotskyist) the preceding fall. Leon Trotsky, exiled by Stalin in 1929, was now powerless and on the run in France, though he had scattered bands of sympathizers there and elsewhere. As a guest at Yaddo, the Trotskyist Novack found himself "the lone oppositionist amidst 13 Communist members or sympathizers." Communist sympathizer Farrell, who had previously read Trotsky's *Literature and Revolution*, now read his *History of the Russian Revolution.* He was impressed, but still harbored doubts about the banished author.

Taking part in a *New Masses* symposium on Marxist criticism that July, he irascibly declared: "*New Masses* criticisms of my work have never raised challenging issues that warrant reply." He also complained that the magazine's critics had lauded "dreary writing, largely, it seems, because of the author's revolutionary subject matter or his good intentions. If authors must be praised for their revolutionary good intentions, I would suggest a division of function. Besides reviews and criticisms, let there be a new department created under the title of Department of Professional Encouragement."

Farrell's independence continued to make the comrades somewhat uneasy. Reviewing his *Calico Shoes and Other Stories*, published in late September, the *New Masses* said that it "offers further testimony to Farrell's gifts of observation, his ear for the rhythms of workers' speech, his grasp of technical problems in varied forms of short fiction—and his remoteness from the revolutionary working class movement."

Meanwhile, in the one place on earth where that movement had triumphed, the great experiment continued. On December 1, Sergei Kirov, boss of the Leningrad party organization and, in Stalin's eyes, dangerously independent, was murdered. The distinguished British historian Robert Conquest, not one to exaggerate, writes:

> This killing has every right to be called the crime of the century. Over the next four years, hundreds of Soviet citizens, including the most prominent political leaders of the Revolution, were shot for direct responsibility for the assassination, and literally millions of others went to their deaths for complicity in one or another part of the vast conspiracy which allegedly lay behind it. Kirov's death, in fact, was the keystone of the entire edifice of terror and suffering by which Stalin secured his grip on the Soviet peoples.

But of course that was not immediately apparent, although the assassination was front-page news the next day in the *New York Times*. (And it was to be many years before it became evident that Stalin himself very likely had arranged the murder.)

"It has been a good year, an exceptionally good year," declared Granville Hicks, looking back in the *New Masses* on the "revolutionary literature"—the plays, poetry, short stories and novels—of 1934. The New England–born son of an office worker, and a *summa cum laude* graduate of Harvard who had studied for the ministry for two years and then taught English literature at Smith College and Rensselaer Polytechnic Institute, Hicks was the author of *The Great Tradition* (1933), a Marxist interpretation of American literature, and now literary editor of the *New Masses.*

In Hicks's retrospective on the year, *The Young Manhood of Studs Lonigan* was among fifteen novels that he listed as being "by avowed revolutionaries or close sympathizers." But some of these works, he noted with slight disappointment, "are revolutionary only in a rather broad sense of the word." *Young Manhood* was one of them. "Everyone knows where he stands," Hicks wrote of Farrell.

> But his novel pretty much disregards the insight Marxism can give into the psychology of the petty bourgeois.... I have a curious sense that Farrell is still in a preparatory stage. He has extraordinary powers of observation and a remarkable memory, but his sense of human values is distorted. That he will develop into a clear and powerful writer I do not doubt, but I sometimes wish he would hurry up.

———◈———

"THE CAPITALIST SYSTEM CRUMBLES so rapidly before our eyes that...today hundreds of poets, novelists, dramatists, critics, short story writers and journalists recognize the necessity of personally helping to accelerate the destruction of capitalism and the establishment of a workers' government."

So began a January 1935 "call" in the *Daily Worker* and other radical organs—signed by Farrell and sixty-three other literati (out of the "hundreds" supposedly champing at the bit)—for a congress of American revolutionary writers to be held in New York in the spring. "We are faced by two kinds of problems," declared the statement, whose other signatories included Theodore Dreiser, Jack Conroy, Malcolm Cowley, Edward Dahlberg, Joseph Freeman, Michael Gold, Horace Gregory, Clarence Hathaway, Josephine

Herbst, Granville Hicks, Alexander Trachtenberg and Nathanael West. One problem was how to take effective action against "the dangers of war and fascism" that were "everywhere apparent." The other problem was how to present in their own literary works "the fresh understanding of the American scene that has come from our enrollment in the revolutionary cause."

At the congress—which, the call unaccountably failed to mention, was to be modeled on the Soviet Writers' Congress held in Moscow the year before—revolutionary writers "who have achieved some standing in their respective fields" would assemble for "fundamental discussion." The congress, said the signers of the call, should create a "League of American Writers" that, *inter alia*, would "fight against imperialist war and fascism," oppose "the influence of bourgeois ideas in American literature," and (certainly not least) "defend the Soviet Union against capitalist aggression."

Although the capitalist system was presumed to be rapidly disintegrating, its end was not considered so near as to disrupt anyone's private plans that depended upon its continued functioning. Earlier in the month, Dorothy Farrell had begun work at Yaddo as Mrs. Ames's personal secretary, with the expectation of receiving a regular income indefinitely, and Farrell himself, staying in New York at the Brevoort Hotel on lower Fifth Avenue while he labored to finish the final Lonigan volume, *Judgment Day*, evidently expected that the capitalist system would remain sufficiently intact for him eventually to receive royalties from the novel's sales.

<hr />

ON A COLD SATURDAY IN LATE January, Farrell had breakfast with his friend Nathanael West in a drugstore across from the Brevoort (where West, too, was staying). "Come on along with me, Pep, and get arrested," Farrell said.

Ever since ninety-two women (only a fraction of the total work force) at Ohrbach's department store on East 14th Street had gone out on strike in mid-December, demanding a forty-hour work week, a 10 percent wage increase and recognition of the Office Workers Union, mass picketing there had become a regular Saturday event, despite an injunction against it.

"The girls on strike have shown amazing courage," the *New Masses* reported. "They have picketed in rain and sleet and they have withstood the brutality of the police without flinching." On this particular Saturday, Farrell, West, Edward Dahlberg and several other writers "carried signs which protested the injunction and marched in double formation in front of the store."

Since the injunction specified that it should be read in full to violators, Dahlberg insisted that this be done—and so it was, to him, for forty-five minutes, while picketing outside the store continued. Dahlberg was later accused of violating the injunction, while Farrell and the others were charged with disorderly conduct.

Their picketing at Ohrbach's finished, the group went across Union Square to S. Klein's dress store, where another strike was under way, and picketed there. While thus engaged, according to the perhaps not wholly unbiased *New Masses* account, "they were assaulted by the police and ridden down by the mounted cops." Finally, the writers were loaded into a police wagon and taken to the station house. The policemen there "couldn't imagine how a 'good Irishman' like Farrell could have been implicated in such a scrape." After eight hours in jail, Farrell (who ultimately received a suspended sentence) returned around midnight to the Brevoort and resumed work on the final draft of Studs Lonigan's death scene in *Judgment Day*.

WITH FARRELL AND 215 other writer-delegates seated on the platform (along with 150 writers up there as guests), the First American Writers' Congress opened on Friday, April 26, 1935, before a standing-room-only crowd of four thousand spectators. The initial, and only public, session of the three-day conclave was held in the hall of the Mecca Temple, the largest Masonic Shrine in the city, on West 55th Street. Granville Hicks, presiding as chairman, announced the receipt of greetings from the Comintern's International Union of Revolutionary Writers and from Maxim Gorky, the Russian writer who was deemed "the father of proletarian literature."

Beneath the hall's tiled dome, which was surmounted by the Scimitar and Crescent, various radical luminaries addressed the assembly. Malcolm Cowley, the fellow-traveling literary editor of the *New Republic*, decried "the brutality of our society" with its heartless upper classes, declared that art and culture "cannot live in such a world" and lauded "the overflowing vitality of literature and culture in the Soviet Union." No dissent on that point was heard. "The Soviet Union has destroyed the lie that the masses cannot build culture," Mike Gold affirmed. "They are building the mightiest culture in the world."

Before the congress had begun, as Farrell long afterward told an interviewer, Communist Party cultural commissar Alexander Trachtenberg, who was principally in charge of planning the event, had convened all the speakers to make sure their speeches would be free of ideological deviation—an effort that could hardly have been necessary in Gold's case. Yet there were signs, on this day and the two succeeding ones (when the congress shifted to the New School for Social Research for its closed sessions), that on certain questions the party line was in flux.

As the implications of Hitler's triumph in Germany sank in, Moscow had become less certain that a fascist Europe was really to be welcomed. Not until the Comintern's Seventh World Congress in Moscow in August would the new "tactical" line be clearly spelled out: the Third Period, in which the revolution was near and Communist militancy was required, was over, and a worldwide Popular Front—which would go beyond a "united front" and include even bourgeois elements—was to be instituted to combat the extreme danger of fascism. But even before the American writers gathered in New York, some changes had been made. In the *New Masses* the preceding September, Joseph Freeman had noted that "our literary movement...has abandoned its sectarian attitude."

In his address at the Mecca Temple, Earl Browder, general secretary of the Communist Party U.S.A., said: "While recognizing the dynamic role of the avowed Communists, there are many writers in this Congress who have certain misgivings about the possibility of fruitful work in this united front. Most of these doubts are based upon lack of information about the policy of our Party in this field; some of them arise from the fact that Party policy is sometimes distorted by overzealous Communists, particularly the most recent recruits without proletarian background."

Among those attentively listening was John Chamberlain, the daily book columnist for the *New York Times.* He later reported that the general secretary "made a few sarcastic references to the now liquidated period when the 'infantile disease of leftism' raged in Communist literary publications; he warned against the zeal of new converts; he lamented the fact that 'bourgeois' accessions to the Communists often feel they must 'do penance' for their birth and early circumstances." To Chamberlain, all this suggested a welcome "right-about-face in the Communist ranks." Later in the conference, he was shocked to hear Mike Gold say, "We have no blue-print for the proletarian novel." Chamberlain remembered when Gold had had precisely such a blue-print.

Over the next two days, papers on various aspects of the writers' great struggle were delivered, including a much-discussed one by novelist Edwin Seaver on the proletarian novel. Attempting to define the genre, he argued that the author need not be a worker or even write about workers, but had to align himself with the working class and use the Marxist interpretation of history. Edward Dahlberg addressed the menace of fascism, urging his fellow writers to "take history in our hands and help write it from the creative point of view of those who labor and produce." Matthew Josephson asserted that "Soviet Russia...offers us a glimpse of what future societies may be like." Malcolm Cowley, while denying that the revolutionary movement is "a church that calls upon [the writer] to have faith, to surrender his doubts," described "the principal gift" that the movement can offer to writers as "the sense of human life, not as a medley of accidents, but as a connected and continuing process.... It gives the values, the unified interpretation without which one can write neither good history nor good tragedy." Proletarian novelist Jack Conroy said that to him, "a strike bulletin or an impassioned leaflet are of more moment than three hundred prettily and faultlessly written pages about the private woes of a gigolo or the biological ferment of a society dame." Perhaps still smarting from Farrell's criticism of his "commonplace" writing, Conroy said that writers such as Michael Gold in his quasi-autobiographical novel, *Jews Without Money*, had demonstrated "how one may combine simple, and what some ultra-aesthetic critics might call banal and commonplace, words into an exciting and colorful pattern. And any literate worker doesn't need a glossary or a key to comprehend what they're driving at."

One paper that went unread at the congress was an eloquent and, in the circumstances, quite remarkable essay by John Dos Passos, whom the Communists had held up as the leading revolutionary writer in America. Already disillusioned with Stalinism and what was happening in the Soviet Union in the wake of the Kirov murder, Dos Passos had taken new interest in the foundations of Anglo-Saxon democracy. "To fight oppression, and to work as best we can for a sane organization of society, we do not have to abandon the state of mind of freedom," he declared. "If we do that we are letting the same thuggery in by the back door that we are fighting off in front of the house." His paper was not read because it wasn't received in the mail until Monday, when the congress was over—or so at least Dos Passos was told by Malcolm Cowley.

Just as stubbornly going his own way as the older Dos Passos but not yet disillusioned with the Stalinists, Farrell spoke at the congress on Sunday (the day after *Judgment Day* was published). His subject: "The Short Story." As if he wanted to make his independence unmistakably clear from the outset, he immediately launched into an attack on the delinquencies of "revolutionary criticism" in dealing with the short story, denouncing "that species of over-politicized and ideologically schematized criticism which has been too dishearteningly frequent in the literary sections of revolutionary journals." (In *Partisan Review*, he similarly objected to Seaver's thesis on the proletarian novel, decrying "the creation of a kind of revolutionary scholasticism that can only breed sterility.") That done, he turned to the short story.

At a time when "there was an increasingly apparent contradiction between the hopes of the American dream and the manner in which human destinies unraveled in actual life," Farrell said, a revolt against the "plot short story" had occurred. Its "mechanical formula" (consisting of "conflict, based on rising action, and upon a clash of opposing views, which created a mounting suspense, and was resolved in the denouement") had proven too constricting. Often, the characters were unconvincing as human beings, and seemed mere "appendages to moral codes and viewpoint…rooted in the ideology which is the intellectual bodyguard of capitalist democracy." Now, in the twentieth century, the literature of realism and social protest had overturned the familiar pattern: "The happy ending became the unhappy ending. The plot short story became the plotless short story. Sin, instead of virtue, was rewarded…. Success led to discontent rather than to content." This writing, he said, had shown the human cost of capitalist democracy in America.

> In these last years then, the short story has been introducing us to a new kind of American life, to the life of poor farmers and sharecroppers in backward rural areas, to the scenes, sights, and dialects of the urban streets, to the feelings of Slavic immigrants, the problems and discontents of sweat-shop workers, the feelings and oppressions of the factory proletariat, the conduct and aspirations of revolutionary organizers, the attitudes of Negro intellectuals toward white folks, the traditions and backgrounds of labor history, the brutality of the prize ring and the life behind it.

But many of the "new revolutionary short stories," Farrell went on, lacked "what might be called internal conviction." Trying to express a revolutionary viewpoint or feeling, the authors failed to make "their aim functional within the story so that it impresses the reader as a natural and integral aspect of the story"; instead, the revolutionary viewpoint or feeling seemed "to be glued onto it." Many revolutionary short stories also "have been too generalized," portraying hunger, suffering or oppression without the concrete details or observations that would make the stories linger in the reader's mind.

Valid as this literary criticism may well have been—and the young black writer Richard Wright, for one, was enormously impressed by what Farrell had to say—this paper was but one of many delivered at the congress. When the last one had been read that final day, and the last delegate had spoken, Michael Gold, presiding, announced the approach of "a very serious and historic moment": the formation of the League of American Writers.

The new organization consisted of a seventeen-member executive committee and an encompassing national council. The executive committee, whose members included Gold, Cowley, Freeman, Josephine Herbst, Hicks, Seaver and Trachtenberg, was headed by novelist Waldo Frank. At least ten of the committee members were Communists. Although Frank was not, he was close enough. ("Communism must come, and must be fought for," he had declared at the opening session.) The literati decorating the larger national council included Conroy, Dahlberg, Horace Gregory, Robert Morss Lovett, playwright Clifford Odets, Lincoln Steffens, Richard Wright, Nelson Algren and James T. Farrell.

When that "historic" work was done, Gold called upon Waldo Frank to speak. As he walked down the aisle to the platform, the delegates rose. Visibly moved, Frank stood before the audience and said:

> We have to create our philosophy of revolutionary writing as we live our lives. We have to create it out of our experience, as men and women living in this revolutionary age, and also out of our experience as writers....All that has gone before might be called a sort of false dawn, or, if you will, the very earliest part of the dawn before the sun rises.

When Frank was done and the applause had died down, Farrell—perhaps still, as he had been earlier, in a "gaily disruptive" mood—arose and suggested that the delegates conclude the congress's final session by singing the "Internationale." And so, lifting their voices in revolutionary song, Farrell and his literary comrades brought the American Writers' Congress to a close.

━━━━━►➤-◦-◄◄━━

THE SUN WAS BRIGHT IN New York on May Day as Farrell again marched in the Communists' parade. The Socialists, declining once more to forge a "united front" with the Reds, staged their own parade. Nevertheless, a carnival spirit prevailed throughout the rival parades and mass demonstrations in Union Square. Two days later, the *Daily Worker* presented the impressions of Farrell, along with some of the other writers who had participated:

> I saw massed thousands marching with waving red flags, fists raised to the chorus of the International[e], slogans symbolizing the struggle against capitalism, against war and Fascism. Such an event leaves an indelible impression, an impression of solidarity, unity, revolutionary purposes and hopes. I realized how these masses in New York's magnificent demonstration were only a fragment of those millions all over the world.
>
> And all these marching masses, these songs, plays, slogans, told one story—the story of who owns the future, who will win it. I feel the demonstration in New York was one mighty symbol of our common revolutionary hopes.

Chapter Nine
"A Kind of Inevitability"

FARRELL FOUND MORE THAN revolutionary hope in that May Day parade of 1935: he found Hortense Alden, a beautiful actress who had been one of the stars of *Grand Hotel*, the smash Broadway hit of 1930-1931. The attraction between the two—she descending from the height of her fame, he just approaching the height of his—was mutual. Soon, with Dorothy out of the way, working at Yaddo, they became lovers.

Hortense was a glamorous woman, intelligent, worldly and always "on stage." She was about five feet six inches tall, slender and shapely, with delicate features. Unlike many actresses, she was well read and appreciated literature. A perfectionist in whatever she did, she had pronounced opinions and did not suffer fools gladly.

There was a certain mystery about her. She was even more estranged from her own past than Farrell was from his; whereas he wanted to expose his early life to the world, she kept hers shrouded in secrecy. When she died forty-three years later, her son didn't know the names of her parents or anything about them, and was under the impression—as Farrell himself evidently was—that Alden was the family name she had acquired at birth.

In fact, eighteen years before she met Farrell, on February 1, 1917, a young woman named Hortense Berger, claiming to be from Bloomsbury, New Jersey, won a beauty contest at a ball in Newark sponsored by the state branch of the Motion Picture Exhibitors of America. The next day, the *Newark Star-Eagle* reported that the contest judges "picked Hortense Berger—or Hortense Alden, if you want the stage name she has taken—as the winner of the prize, a position with a movie company.... She said she was born in Dallas, Tex., sixteen years ago, and when she was four played a minor role in a stock company. Her mother was with the Boston Opera

137

Company," a short-lived (1909–1914) but highly regarded cultural venture in the Athens of America. Although Hortense Berger said she was from Bloomsbury, an alert *Newark Evening News* reporter noticed that she had "a New York address at 511 West 139th street." At that same address, the city directory for 1917 reveals, a salesman named Bernard J. Berger, presumably her father, was living.

Even then, when she was only sixteen years old and just transforming herself into Hortense Alden, there were hints that she could be difficult: "Her long black curls, brown eyes, pink and white complexion and suggestions of temperament, as they call it on the stage, won out for her over a half hundred contestants," the *Evening News* reporter observed.

Two years after her Newark triumph, Hortense Alden appeared onstage in Washington, D.C., and a month later in New York, in a musical comedy called *Tumble In* (though her part as "Hortense" was so minor that it went unmentioned not only in the reviews but also in a cast list that accompanied one of them). Two years later, in a Theatre Guild production of Franz Molnar's *Liliom*, a play about a carousel barker, she made her Broadway debut, demonstrating in the role of Marie, noted *Theatre Magazine*, that she "can do a character part with skill." In the ensuing years, she went on to other plays and other parts. In March 1925—when she was playing "the flirtatious Emelia" in *The Firebrand*, a romantic comedy about the sixteenth-century Italian sculptor Benvenuto Cellini—the *New York Times* carried an account of her career that obviously emanated from Hortense or her agents. The newspaper said that she had "arrived on Broadway from her native Texas by way of New Orleans, Louisville, Chicago and Greenwich Village," and offered some colorful details:

> She studied music and dancing in New Orleans and, then, without the permission from her parents, left the city with a troupe of Lyceum Bureau entertainers. The following Summer found her singing in a musical comedy stock company in Louisville, and in the Fall she threw in her lot with a road company. Before long she was stranded in Chicago, as might have been expected, so she sang in a cabaret for a few weeks. And then she met a New York show girl who offered to pilot her to New York, to Greenwich Village and to the offices of the Broadway producers.

This account, however, may contain at least as much fiction as fact. Her sister, who was known to Farrell as "Bettina Alden," told him after Hortense died that she had never been able to sing or dance, and had never appeared as a singer in Louisville or Chicago.

Be that as it may, Hortense did tour for two seasons (1927–1928) with the gifted acting couple Lynn Fontanne and Alfred Lunt, in Theatre Guild productions of George Bernard Shaw's *Arms and the Man* and several other plays. Then, in March 1930, she appeared with the famed Russian-born actress Alla Nazimova in an adaptation of Ivan Turgenev's *A Month in the Country*, a Theatre Guild production "made memorable," according to one account, by Nazimova's "magnificent performance" as Natalya Petrovna. Hortense (who played Katia) was also much taken with Nazimova, who was twenty-two years her senior—she became her protégé and, it is said, her lover. But soon it was on to a new play (Aristophanes' *Lysistrata*, which opened in June), a new part (Myrrhina) and a new lover: Clifford Odets, then in his mid-twenties and not yet the celebrated leftwing playwright.

Hortense Alden, wrote Farrell's fellow revolutionary novelist Edward Dahlberg (whose friendship with Farrell may have ended over her),

> was an unadulterated dizzard, but unusual. One month she was enraptured with Karl Marx and felt it her bounden duty to lie with a Stalinist in order to understand more minutely *Das Kapital*. Again, she fell in love with Dostoevsky and insisted upon having sexual commerce with a commentator on *Notes from Underground*. The last time I saw her she was under the spell of William Blake's poems. Always puzzled by her I never knew whether she was a nymphomaniac or an erotical laboratory worker. She had resolved that she could never interpret Marxist culture unless she had connection with one who possessed the tool to produce it.

However unorthodox her self-education, Hortense Alden was a superb actress, a fact that became widely recognized when she appeared in *Grand Hotel*, which opened at the National Theatre on Broadway in November 1930. She had one of the principal roles, that of Flaemmchen, "a handsome and complaisant stenographer" (in one reviewer's description). In a single week during the Christmas holidays, the play took in a record $43,000. In February, beneath a drawing of the actress, the *Times* one Sunday simply noted: "Hortense Alden, the Complaisant Stenographer of 'Grand Hotel,' Which, It Seems Hardly Necessary to Add, Is at the National." Her acting made a tremendous impression on those who saw it.

Among them was F. Scott Fitzgerald, who a few years later, although unable to recall her name, declared in print that he had seen her twice in the play "and I think she's one of the greatest actresses in the world."

The play ran on Broadway for almost thirteen months, grossing more than $1.25 million (another record). On December 5, 1931, a Saturday night, the curtains closed on the last of 561 performances, and the engagement at the National Theatre ended. *Grand Hotel* (which had had no preliminary out-of-town performances) then went on tour. The very next morning, Hortense and fifty-five other players, five musicians, and a stage crew of ten left on a special train for Chicago, where on Tuesday night the play opened at the Grand Opera House. Once again, the melodrama was well received.

Yet within days, for reasons as unknown now as they must have been inexplicable then to producer Herman Shumlin, the temperamental Hortense decided she didn't wish to continue on the tour and gave him her notice. The producer had made her a star with *Grand Hotel;* now, suddenly, she was leaving him in the lurch.

"She was a wonderful actress," said playwright Randolph Carter, who met her later in the decade and became a close friend. "If she hadn't been so temperamentally difficult, I think she would have been one of our greatest stars."

But she was more than a fine actress. Hortense Alden was a beautiful, intelligent and literate woman. That spring of 1935, Jim Farrell (who had been fleetingly unfaithful to his wife before*) was enchanted by her.

<hr />

WHILE THE NOVELIST HAD BEEN working to complete the Lonigan tril-

---

*Much to Dorothy's dismay when she found out, Farrell had a "brief affair" with a woman named Nadine ("Deene") Young in early 1935. A more doubtful liaison has been alleged by novelist Gore Vidal. He claims in his memoir *Palimpsest* (New York: Random House, 1995) that Farrell once told him, and that dancer Nora Kaye later confirmed, that the two of them had been married when Kaye was "fourteen or so," and that the marriage had been annulled. If Kaye was born in 1920, as her *New York Times* obituary (March 1, 1987) and other accounts say, then she would have been fourteen in 1934. Just why Farrell would have committed bigamy with her is unclear, and Dorothy Farrell and others close to him agree that no such marriage took place. Farrell may have known the dancer, but aside from Vidal's account, no evidence that he did has turned up.

ogy, editor Jim Henle's faith in the project had never wavered. "It's like building blocks," he declared more than once, his Vanguard associate Evelyn Shrifte remembered. "When all three volumes come out, then that book will be known as a masterwork."

Judgment Day takes Studs Lonigan into the early years of the Great Depression (years that his real-life prototype, Studs Cunningham, did not live to see). Having caught pneumonia in 1929 after the notorious New Year's Eve party, Lonigan never fully recovers his health. And Lucy is lost to him—she is only a recurrent memory. But he has a girlfriend, Catherine, to whom he becomes engaged, despite his feeling that "there was something common about her."

Paralleling Studs's decline is the economy's. His father's house-painting business is doing poorly, and the tenants in the apartment building that the elder Lonigan owns are having their own money woes and falling behind on their rent. But the Depression is only temporary, according to such authorities as utilities magnate Solomon Imbray (read: Samuel Insull). Impressed, Studs takes a flyer on Imbray stock—and watches most of his savings disappear. So his worries multiply. The elder Lonigan—who listens closely to the demagogic radio priest Father Moylan (read: Father Charles Coughlin)—rails against foreigners, "the Jew international bankers" and "these Reds here agitating to overthrow the government [and] exciting the niggers down in the Black Belt."

Studs is initiated into the Order of Christopher (read: Knights of Columbus), "proud to be entering an order of men so closely connected with the Church. Remembering his catechism from grammar school, he told himself that the Church was One, Holy, Catholic, and Apostolic, built upon the rock of Peter, and that it would last until Judgment Day." But for Studs—and for the Church and America too—Judgment Day soon draws near.

With Studs sick and on his deathbed (and his fiancée pregnant), his distraught father returns to their old South Side neighborhood and comes upon a Communist parade. ("Goddamn Reds. They shouldn't be permitted to march in the street.") "Like a man in a trance" he watches the marchers pass by—chanting, singing, carrying signs and banners (NO WORK NO RENT; REMEMBER SACCO AND VANZETTI; DEFEND THE SOVIET UNION)—and he thinks of his own troubles, of his dying son. "And still they were passing. Suddenly, like a man making an intellectual discovery, Lonigan realized that these people were happy. He could see them laugh. He could see how, between their yells and cries, they grinned, and their faces seemed alive." Danny O'Neill's kid brother and sister parade past. Finally the last column passes, the marchers "singing with raised right fists":

> *'Tis the final conflict,*
> *Let each stand in his place,*
> *The International Soviet*
> *Shall be the human race.*

In *Judgment Day*, the perceptive critic William Troy noted in the *Nation*, there is nothing to compare "for sheer terror" to the New Year's Eve party in *Young Manhood*, "in which Mr. Farrell crystallized his vision of the contemporary world in a scene that is like an epitome of all human depravity and evil.... The truth is that ...this last volume does not, through its first three-quarters, approach the qualities of its two predecessors in the series. But this judgment must immediately be followed by the qualification that the last quarter, which is devoted to Studs Lonigan's illness and death, brings the whole series to a brilliant and momentous close." The reader comes "to feel—what one feels only in the greatest works of fiction—that the individual catastrophe is but the symbolical parallel to some vaster and more consequential catastrophe in the world at large."

"Mr. Farrell's art attains a new depth," *Herald Tribune* columnist Lewis Gannett wrote. Noting that he had dismissed *The Young Manhood of Studs Lonigan* as "rather a clinical portrait than a work of art," he admitted that "perhaps I was carried too far by disgust for the material with which Mr. Farrell so honestly and sometimes so painfully deals. The Lonigan books are art, powerful if purgative art." The *Chicago Tribune*'s Fanny Butcher agreed. While she was "shocked" to learn "the intimate thoughts and actions of such as Studs Lonigan," she said that "critically speaking, the shock is salutary, for with the impact of fact comes also the impact of the author's art, which, now that the trilogy is finished, looms as important and meticulous literary photography with a social interpretation, not mere photography, as the first two books gave one to think."

The comrades and their sympathizers were, of course, delighted by the Communist parade near the novel's end, pointing the way to the future. In the *New Masses*, Josephine Herbst said that "*Judgment Day* should illuminate the first two volumes for those who persist in thinking of the story of Studs Lonigan as an isolated history of a Chicago neighborhood tough." In the *New York Times Book Review,* Harold Strauss wrote that Farrell's "acceptance of the Marxist analysis...has given [his] work greater depth and significance."

But Farrell was an artist, not a propagandist, William Troy pointed out. His trilogy "is a representation rather than an indictment of our culture." As an artist, he had successfully steered a course "between the Charybdis of contemporary subjectivism and the Scylla of Marxist orthodoxy." As a result of his "balanced view of life," though, he tended "to include more in his picture than is always necessary." There was a relaxation of intensity, which "without a bias either of temperament or doctrine...must be supplied by the aesthetic process alone." If Farrell could submit himself to an aesthetic discipline that would enable him to gain more control over his material and "to do greater justice to the breadth and clarity of his perception," the critic concluded, "there will be nothing to prevent him from becoming one of the truly great writers of our time."

———⫸•⫷———

IN EARLY JUNE 1935, FARRELL—rather impulsively, it seems, and without any obvious purpose unless it was simply to gather impressions and material—journeyed from New York to Washington. It was, as it happened, a momentous time in the nation's political life. On May 27, the Supreme Court had invalidated the National Recovery Administration, the agency for industrial planning that was a principal New Deal instrument (albeit an increasingly ineffectual one) for restoring the economy's health. In a carefully prepared performance at a press conference four days later, President Roosevelt denounced the decision, saying the court had relied on a "horse-and-buggy definition of interstate commerce." What historians have called the "Second Hundred Days" then commenced. "Reverting to his old role of Chief Legislator," historian James MacGregor Burns has written, "the President bluntly told congressional chieftains that certain bills *must* be passed. Congress, which had been dawdling, was suddenly spurred into action, with the progressives in each chamber now riding high."

Arriving in the sweltering capital by train on Thursday, June 6, Farrell seems to have been oblivious to the immense significance of what was happening. As a radical, he perhaps could

143

not imagine that the president and Congress together could do much of anything significant for the common good. "I watched one circus called the Senate of the United States, and another circus called the Congress of the United States," he wrote to Hortense that night, stumbling a bit over the nomenclature. "In Congress, they were all just asking could they extend their remarks into the record, which means they were building up their box scores. In the Senate, they were arguing, with from 10 to 30 more or less awake, and more or less present, [about] a bill…concerning holding companies."

That bill to restrict the power of giant utility holding companies over their operating subsidiaries was one of FDR's "must" measures then before Congress, but others were more important. New York senator Robert Wagner's National Labor Relations Act (to be signed into law in July) secured workers' right to collective bargaining, and the Social Security Act (to be signed into law in August) provided for old-age pensions, unemployment insurance and other forms of assistance to those in need. To these far-reaching pieces of legislation, certainly among the most significant of the entire New Deal era, Farrell appears to have paid virtually no attention.

He was quite impressed, though, on meeting the very *un*influential New York representative Vito Marcantonio, a nominal Republican and active fellow traveler: "probably the most able, radical, and consistently clear man in Congress," Farrell informed Hortense, adding that "the fellow is alive, and intelligent and a regular guy." Since the congressman was sponsoring a performance of Clifford Odets' play *Waiting for Lefty* in Washington later in the month, Farrell told her, he had promised to get him "a copy of your friend Odets' book."

The next morning, thanks to an obliging newspaperman, Farrell was able to attend a presidential press conference. President Roosevelt sat at a desk, with Secret Service men behind him and correspondents gathered in a semicircle in front. "Roosevelt is suave," Farrell reported to Hortense. "He can very suavely manage to say nothing. In spots the conference seemed almost suggestive of being a high school seminar. Some of the newspapermen lap it and him up. A few, I guess, don't. It was uninspiring." More interesting to Farrell was a conversation he had the night before in "a cheap restaurant" with an eighteen-year-old southern boy whose "ambition is to get a suit of clothes" and with it, perhaps, "a girl."

After his first night in a too-expensive hotel ($3.50 a night), Farrell stayed with the *Daily Worker*'s Washington correspondents, a husband and wife. On Saturday night, "Comrade Jerry"—V.J. Jerome, Alexander Trachtenberg's fellow "cultural commissar"—came to Washington. During his visit, he went with Farrell to "one of those sportland places" with pinball machines. "It was the best kind of relaxation he could have had, and so he left very happy," Farrell told Hortense. On Tuesday at the Senate, and then again on Wednesday, Farrell observed Senator Huey Long in action. The Louisiana demagogue—who just months later was to be assassinated—was regarded by many as a potential American Hitler. "He has got something," Farrell wrote to Hortense after his initial view of the "Kingfish." "What I mean [is] he has got what Babe Ruth and Jack Dempsey both got. Call it a kind of tone or manner, or personality. Or still better simple ham acting and the capacity for a certain amount of self-dramatization."

On Wednesday, Long launched a filibuster against FDR's effort to extend, at least in "skeletonized" form, the National Industrial Recovery Act, which the high court had so weakened. The senator began speaking at 12:15 P.M. and was still going strong in the wee hours of the morning. "Just when he seemed to be getting dull," Farrell said, "he would pull a surprising recovery." By around four in the morning, according to Farrell, many of the senators were drunk. Vice President John Nance Garner, presiding over the Senate, "was so drunk he could hardly talk." At last, Long gave up—and the Second Hundred Days continued.

During his stay in Washington, Farrell had much more than national politics on his mind: he was dreaming frequently of Hortense. "And so—Darling I am sure I am in love with you," he wrote to her two days after he arrived. "I adore your letters and get a sense of you in them—a sense of certain things, feelings, of yours which I so much cherish—And when I think of you, which is so very often, I too have this sense of possibilities, of many possibilities."

She had a great interest in music, and therefore he was eager to be instructed. "I know little of music," he confessed. "I am your humble and adoring pupil."

He was now conscious of other failings he had, and sought to diminish them in her eyes by suggesting that she could help him to overcome them. "I find that I talk too much," he wrote to her on Wednesday, June 12. "What I mean is I say the wrong things. Not always the wrong things. But I say them the wrong way. I indulge too much in the wrong kind of irony, satire, and sarcasm and so— well I win for myself fishy eyed remarks. And that's the wrong way to succeed, isn't it, so won't you teach me differently, my darling?"

The next night, watching fireworks marking the end of a Shriners' convention in Washington, and planning to leave a few days hence, he wished that she were with him. "I like fireworks. We would have liked fireworks if we were seeing and hearing them together. Well, that's that, and so we'll like something else we see and hear together, on Sunday, and maybe something else on Monday. Won't we? Yes. I'll bet on it."

⸺⸻●⸻⸺

AFTER SPENDING MOST OF the week in New York, Farrell left on Friday for Saratoga Springs in a car driven by Elinor Rice Novack, whose Trotskyist husband, George, was again a guest at Yaddo. Her father had died that spring, and she had used some of her inheritance to buy a secondhand Chevrolet, the first automobile she had ever owned.

For much of the way, the drive north along the Hudson River was very pleasant. The nearby hills, Farrell later remembered, were "shaggy with trees," the river was "deep blue," and the mountains far ahead were "washed in a blue mist until they looked like a distant sea." But then came the rain.

In Rhinebeck, New York, they found themselves going slowly downhill on a slippery road. The car's tires were bald, a condition no one had pointed out to the inexperienced driver. Rounding a curve, the vehicle skidded and crashed into the back of an ice truck parked by the side of the road. The whole front of the car was demolished.

The ten or so seconds of skidding before the crash, Farrell recalled, had seemed to last forever, long enough to reflect calmly, "Well—here goes—a smashup—maybe the show is up." Then the collision threw him forward with a jolt and his head hit the windshield. He got out of the car and discovered that while he'd had the breath knocked out of him, he wasn't seriously injured. Neither was Elinor. "The smashup is over—and the show ain't over."

They made it to the nearest train station. She decided to return to New York; he, with a bruised left rib, elected to go on to

146

Saratoga Springs. Still a little nervous and shaken up when he arrived at the station there, he was met by Dorothy and some of his friends and fellow guests at Yaddo: writer Peter Neagoe, whom he had known from his Paris days; novelist Nathan Asch (son of the famed Yiddish writer Sholem Asch); poet Jim Daly, and George Novack. "Dorothy was quite lovely to me, and had everything fixed up," Farrell wrote to Hortense, "and the gardener sent over beautiful roses, and so that was that."

Receiving a note from Hortense the next day, Farrell showed it to the apparently unsuspecting Dorothy. Telling Hortense in a letter that he had shown Dorothy her note, Farrell added, in an impressive manifestation of either a belief in the awesome power of truth or a guilty conscience (or perhaps both): "She is very sweet to me—to everyone—and she looked quite handsome last night. She's got to dress up every night, more than the others because of her job. She's working very hard too, but that is good for her. It means functioning on her own in a line where she can develop real capacities which she possesses. She's really a darling."

Time would take care of the situation, he assured his lover a few days later. "Yaddo. Well darling, it is hard, and it should not be hard. You see now darling it is not the same. We don't want to see ourselves, often, do certain things. There is always a painfulness in change. In the disorganization and the reorganization of our sentiments. Well anyway, it is painful darling...I have got not to let myself be soft or sentimental. Somehow the most painful thing in life is to be unrelenting. And anyway darling, I see so very extremely clearly—that time must do some solving of some problems. It probably will. But anything but time right now would be very bad."

With his mind frequently on Hortense and his romantic situation, and with his sore side and recent brush with death, Farrell felt somewhat detached from the life around him. The other writers and artists were quiet and serious (and to George Novack's dismay, little inclined to engage in political argument); Mrs. Ames appeared relaxed and content, not in one of her note-writing frenzies; and Dorothy was busy as her assistant. Yaddo seemed tranquil now, and Farrell didn't feel his usual compulsion to work. Soon after his arrival, Peter Neagoe jokingly begged him not to finish another book over the weekend, and threatened to arrange a picket line of writers outside his studio if he did. But Farrell was relatively inactive, dashing off a sketch of the filibustering Huey Long for the *New Masses* (which ran it under the headline: "Another Washington Circus"), and playing softball, despite his bruised rib.

Ensconced in "very elegant" quarters in the Yaddo mansion, as he told Hortense, Farrell received word from an agent who was trying to get him screenwriting work in Hollywood that "one of the most important executives" at Warner Brothers had indicated the studio might be "very much interested in having you out here" if Farrell could come up with an idea for "a screen characterization that would suit" actor Paul Muni. Earlier in the year, Farrell had strongly advised Nathanael West against going to Hollywood; now he was considering going there himself. "I don't know that I want to go," he told Hortense. "California is so far away from Hortense at present.... And I don't know anyway that I want to go to Hollywood." Still, he added, there was the money to consider. (Later that year, MGM offered him a screenwriting job at $250 a week; he was tempted, but turned it down.)

But Hollywood was the future (or not); Yaddo was the present. With his mind often on the absent Hortense, Farrell found the evenings—with Mrs. Ames and the guests gathered, after supper, in "that enormous room near the frilled, intricate, carved, over-carved, enormously carved throne, with its yellow pillows, and opposite it on the other side, the pictures of the Lady Trask and the Broker Trask"—excruciatingly boring, he told Hortense. "There are silences. There are remarks made for impressions. There are those who cannot talk to [Mrs. Ames]. One must talk loud, because she is deaf. One hears one's own voice raised. Everyone else hears one's own voice raised. When one makes one of those necessarily trivial remarks that go to make up the content of so much of our talk, well, one hears it, everyone hears it, and it makes one feel like a fool. The evenings are long. They are boring. They are deadening." He detected a great deal of "repression" at Yaddo, although this "oppressed" him less than others, he said, "because I can manage to do things, to say things, or to goof and nobody minds my goofing because I am a goof anyway." (There are worse things to be called than a "crazy Irishman," V. J. Jerome had told him in Washington.)

To escape the pall, Farrell, with his newfound enthusiasm for music, took to going off to the music room and playing records. "Incidentally," he wrote Hortense, "on Bach. One piece I have always played here whenever I play music, for over two years—St. Mathews [*sic*] Passion."

Hortense was in the process of reading through Farrell's published works, most recently *Gas-House McGinty*. "It has become the orphan amongst my books," he told her, "the only one I worry about getting reissued when the first edition is exhausted, the only one that is never referred to when my work is written about." With his various books now receiving her close scrutiny, Farrell may have become a little self-conscious about his stylistic limitations. In one of his letters, after quoting a passage from the philosopher George Santayana that he admired, he said:

> Sometimes I wish I could write with this easy and composed grace. But I never shall. It is for someone else. Somehow I feel a kind of tension, a lack of composure, and intellectual ease, and also an inability to master such a kind of literary style. I'd love to write one thing with the same kind of natural grace that Santayana manages in his writings. But then. Well we can always appreciate what we cannot do.

On Friday, only a week after he had arrived at Yaddo, Farrell left by train for New York and Hortense. He intended to join her there in seeing Josephine Herbst off for Paris and Hitler's Germany (where the novelist was determined to do some reporting), to do some work for the *New Masses*, and then to return to Yaddo in August. "Don't mention I'm coming in," he wrote to his lover early in the week. "I don't want to see many people. Hardly anybody but Hortense."

<hr />

"DARLING," HE WROTE TO Dorothy from New York on July 10,

> from things we have both said to each other, it is apparent that we have both realized that there has been a change between us, and we don't function toward one another as we used to.... And sooner or later, such a condition must be assimilated, and if we can do that, and try not to be rash, bitter, angry, mad at each other, it may be the better for both of us. Also, Dorothy, I think that if the causes be attributed to external circumstances, or to other people, we will [be] superficial in looking at what is and has been happening to us. Because, darling, we have been too much to each other to think that somebody else, some circumstance, some separation could be so important as to bust in between us. I think, darling, that the cause is really more deep seated. It is not a matter of whether we made mistakes. Everybody makes mistakes. All men and women who are

married make mistakes. It isn't mistakes. It is, rather, a kind of inevitability.

Farrell—who, in theory at least, now had no more use than Friedrich Engels did for the "bourgeois" institution of marriage— went on in a vaguely Deweyesque vein and at considerable length. He argued that life is "a process" and change only natural, albeit often "sad and distressing." Living entails recognizing that fact, assimilating the experience and learning from it. He was not to blame; she was not to blame.

> I am convinced that rather than dictate to our emotions and pas-
> sions, they dictate to us…. It is one of the paradoxes of love, I think,
> of love, of emotions of love, that by their very preciousness, by their
> force and strength within oneself, they wear themselves down, and
> tend to exhaust themselves. And then they lead to something else—
> often something deeper. Affection. Understanding. Friendship. And
> that darling may be what has been going on between us.

He proposed "a temporary separation until the fall, and then for us to see how to [*sic*] feel toward one another. And in that way, we won't be rash, and jump to conclusions." He urged her to try not to be angry with him, and in conclusion said he would be wait-ing for her answer.

Farrell wrote at least two drafts of the letter. He seems to have wanted to secure a separation that would let Dorothy down gently, in stages, without his having to confront her directly in person or feel any guilt about his behavior. But he may have sensed, through the Deweyesque fog, that sending her this letter would not be right. Apparently he could not bring himself to do it. Dorothy never saw it.

⟢⟐⟐⟐⟐

IN MID-AUGUST, FARRELL returned to Yaddo and was greeted with warmth and cordiality. But again, he felt detached. By the middle of the next day, he and Dorothy had still talked only of relatively inconsequential matters. She had lately put herself on a strict diet and lost some weight; Farrell thought she looked "lovely" but also "pale and haggard," and he worried that she might carry her regi-men too far. He spoke to her about that danger—but not yet of the subject that was really on his mind. She evidently knew that in

150

New York he had not been staying at the Hotel Brevoort, and once, he told Hortense, she "tried adroitly to find out where I had been living," but that was all. Dorothy habitually made it a point not to be inquisitive. Although she may have sensed that something was amiss, she apparently did not suspect what it was. "I shall talk with her...definitely and [in] as clear cut [a way] as the situation permits in the next few days," Farrell assured Hortense in a letter he wrote the morning after his return.

As it turned out, he broke the news to his wife of "the change between us" that very afternoon. They were in bed in their suite in the mansion, having made love shortly before, she long afterward recalled. She thought he had been acting a bit strangely since his return, and asked him what was the matter. Finally he told her: he was in love with another woman, Hortense Alden, and wanted to be with her.

With no experience of broken marriages in her family, Dorothy was greatly shocked. "I couldn't believe it," she remembered. "I couldn't believe it." She tried to remain outwardly calm, but could not hold back her tears. "I was terribly upset. He was my husband [and] I loved him dearly." She later made some excuse and didn't go down to dinner that evening.

"Dorothy and I have talked," Farrell reported to Hortense, "and I discarded even the attempt at subterfuges. I told her, and while we were both unhappy, and upset, I am very glad that I did. I am too fond of Dorothy, and I have been too much in love with her, and she has been too much to me in my life for me to permit myself the avoidance of responsibilities by using subterfuges." It would have been wrong, he said, to allow their relationship to end in lies. "If I did that, I should not have retained my own self-respect, and would have had no right to expect respect from her." Dorothy deserved honesty, he believed, and he was going to give it to her, "whatever scenes and discomforts" he had to face as a result. But Dorothy—in part, at least, because she was inhibited by her job assisting Mrs. Ames—made no scenes.

In his sudden relief and his rush of feeling for his wife, Farrell initially entertained the illusion that somehow they would remain close to each other. "She is going to take her vacation in October, and come to New York, and stay at the Brevoort," he informed Hortense. "I am going to see her naturally, a lot. I am going to come up here for a week or two in November around Thanksgiving. We are going to spend Christmas and the holiday season together...." But gradually he abandoned those unrealistic plans.

In the succeeding days, Farrell became again more the detached observer, wishing Dorothy well, but from a distance. "She does not see the values of using pain a little," he wrote to Hortense. "[Pain] is not compensated for...but it can be assimilated, and be the basis of what we call growth. And independence is a great virtue, and something that should well be experienced by all people at some time. And she will learn that, I both think and hope."

On Sunday, Dorothy and then Farrell spoke with Mrs. Ames; according to him, she "was very shocked...and in a way regretful," but also indulgent. She told him "how she could well understand such a situation. That a man could find he needed more than one woman, and all the rest of it, and that not following one's impulses and emotions was just to scatter ghosts between people, and that bourgeois marriage after all was very unhealthy, and an institutionalizing thing."

Sixteen years later, Farrell would confide to his diary that perhaps "what did most to wreck my marriage with D[orothy] was that I couldn't know when to believe and when not to believe her." It appears that he was not the sole maker of fictions in their family. Dorothy's two-year deception of her mother into thinking that she was still a college student was only the most remarkable of her flights of imagination. In her naiveté, recalled Mary Hunter, Dorothy "tried to make herself interesting by saying things that weren't necessarily true—what she'd done or whom she'd seen, and so forth. [It was] a desperate effort to make herself interesting to other people." This penchant for make-believe evidently persisted into her adulthood. Dorothy would continue to work at Yaddo after Farrell left her, but some months later Mrs. Ames would write to him of her: "While she is so beautifully free of malice, of undue curiosity, she has a great tendency to phantasy, and what is actually worse of being rather seriously deceitful. T[i]me and again she has embarrassed me and worse." That judgment may have been too severe. But innocent and even relatively infrequent as Dorothy's little fictions may have been, it is easy to see how, once detected or suspected, they could have begun to erode her husband's trust, making him doubt her even when she was telling the truth. Nevertheless, it was *he* who had been unfaithful and who now was leaving for someone else.

Despite the reservations that Yaddo's director came to have

about her assistant, Mrs. Ames appears to have played no role in the breakup of the marriage. But if she eventually joined Mary Hunter in thinking that Farrell and Dorothy were not meant for each other, she was not the only one. Peter Neagoe, for instance, who was Dorothy's friend as well as Farrell's, thought they were mismatched. "Dorothy talked to [Peter] about us, and me and her," Farrell told Hortense, "and he has been very kind and understanding to her. And at the same time, he said to [me], Jimmyboy (what he calls me) you know you are very right, and I'm quite glad. Dorothy is a fine girl, but she is not the girl for you, and it is very good that you are doing this."

In any case, he was doing it. By Sunday, two days after his fateful disclosure to Dorothy, they had said virtually everything they had to say to each other, and Farrell realized it was best that he depart. Mrs. Ames invited him to go up to Triuna Islands, three islands on Lake George that belonged to Yaddo, and stay there for a while. Farrell agreed.

"Dorothy is now nice," he reported to Hortense on Monday. "Calm. Sad but a little bit serene." On Tuesday, he left for Triuna Islands.

Some time after his departure—it may even have been after his return to New York—Dorothy confessed her true state of mind to the Yaddo chauffeur, a man named Jim Shannon. "If I had some strychnine," she told him, "I'd kill myself."

———⟫·◦·⟪———

IT WAS QUIET AT LAKE GEORGE; there were not many people around. Farrell rowed around the three islands and then swam. His rooms were in the upper story of a structure that looked to him a bit like a ship and formed part of a bridge connecting two of the islands. Unable to work or read much that first night, he was alone with his melancholy thoughts and reflections and the sound of lapping waters. He felt a sense of release. "I am sad," he wrote to Hortense. "But the sadness has altered. It is not so personal. It is, as you might say, a little of the sadness of the world." But, he said, he had no regrets.

In the ensuing days, he saw a little of the others on the islands (who included a bright, talented, twenty-three-year-old "kid" named John Cheever), but for the most part he kept to himself. He rowed and swam, went for walks, listened to music (Stravinsky's *The Fire-*

bird), and read (Faulkner's *As I Lay Dying*). And he worked—on a play that he and Hortense were trying to write together, and on his next novel, which was about his own family. He had started on "the family saga" in early 1934 (before turning to the final volume in the Lonigan trilogy), but now he was finding the going tough. ("I am still plugging," he told Hortense. "Fighting through a swamp, as it were.... But I won't let it go. I just got to dog and dog and dog the damn stuff. It's been this way before. It will be again. And I have only one way of coming out of it. Fighting and dogging through it.")

By Friday, Farrell was feeling "imprisoned" on Triuna Islands. "Today here, I get a feeling suddenly of being cramped, confined, bound almost, hemmed in and surrounded by waters that never let up, that pound, pound, pound." He looked forward to leaving the islands and seeing Hortense again.

He tried repeatedly to phone her all that afternoon and evening, and again Saturday morning, but there was no answer. Then, to his surprise and delight, she showed up in person, having driven up from New York with a friend. Hortense spent the night and went back to the city the next morning, followed closely by Farrell missives. Her visit, he said, had been "wonderful." A few days later, Farrell left the islands and, with only a brief stop at Yaddo, returned to New York too.

STUDS LONIGAN, THE THREE NOVELS brought together within hard covers, with an introduction by John Chamberlain of the *New York Times*, was published by Vanguard in November (less than two months after Farrell's second collection of short stories, *Guillotine Party and Other Stories*, had come out). The individual Lonigan novels had established Farrell's reputation; now, with their combination into one volume, his hitherto small readership began to grow much larger. By the following June, *Studs Lonigan* was selling as many copies in a month as *Young Lonigan* had in its first eight.

Assessing the trilogy in *Saturday Review*, editor Henry Seidel Canby, while wincing at the "sometimes unbearably brutal" subject matter, hailed Farrell as "an excellent story teller" and "a first-rate artist in current speech. His descriptions of the cheap squalid streets of Chicago, the poolroom bums, the smells and sounds of the animal life of vicious children trying to be sports, are vivid and convincing. So objective is he in his narrative that on the rare occasions when he allows himself to make a comment the effect is of a scratch in a perfect realistic painting."

Chapter Ten

"A Betrayal of Honest Writers"

ONE EVENING IN JANUARY 1936, Edmund Wilson came to supper at Farrell and Hortense Alden's apartment at 139 Lexington Avenue, staying until a half-hour before midnight. The talk was of Soviet Russia, which Wilson had visited as a journalist for several months in 1935. "He spoke very clearly and unbiasedly of Russia," Farrell wrote in his diary the next day.

By the time Wilson—an independent leftist who earlier in the decade had urged progressives to "take Communism away from the Communists"—arrived in Leningrad in late May, the sudden flood of arrests, deportations and executions following the December 1934 assassination of Kirov had almost subsided. The two old Bolsheviks Grigori Zinoviev and Lev Kamenev, arrested in December on charges of having inspired the murder at least indirectly, had been given a closed trial and prison sentences the next month. In early June, while Wilson was in Moscow, there was a further shock: Abel Yenukidze, the erstwhile secretary of the Central Executive Committee and member of Stalin's immediate entourage, was expelled from the Central Committee and the party for "political and personal dissoluteness." Soon, however, the regime seemed to relax and an outward calm began to prevail. But Wilson was too intelligent and too honest an observer to be completely taken in. Although he believed that Soviet Russia represented a great and decisive advance for humankind, he perceived that the great socialist experiment had developed some serious defects.

"He says that there is a real political terror," wrote Farrell, setting down Wilson's table talk, "and that people are extremely afraid to express themselves on politics, and that to get a sense of the degree, and to make an estimation of the nature and possibilities of political unrest beneath the surface, you have to get to know people extremely well." Wilson thought that the terror and "the elimination of Bolsheviks from the ruling caste there" were partly due to Stalin's "morbid fears…of people being against him."

Still, the "backwardness" of the Russian people made it necessary, in Wilson's view, for there to be "this ruling caste of the Communist party."To get "a real sense" of the Soviet Union and "the cult of Stalin," one had to grasp the Russian past, with its "slavery, ignorance, and illiteracy." But Wilson was now convinced, as Farrell said he himself was, "that there is little from either politics, or ideas, or literature that we can learn from the Russians."

In the spring, in a series of articles for the *New Republic* about his journey, Wilson, though expressing a newfound respect for America's republican institutions, was to insist that Americans were in no position to reprove the Russians until "we shall be able to show them an American socialism which is free from the Russian defects." In the meantime, "in spite of these defects, you feel in the Soviet Union that you are at the moral top of the world where the light never really goes out."

Stout and balding and, at forty, now entered upon middle age, Wilson (whose second wife had died in a fall down a flight of stairs little more than three years earlier) was, Farrell noted, "from what Hortense says, personally unhappy." But Farrell greatly admired him. "Wilson is a man who earns his ideas; he struggles and thinks and studies them; he assimilates and absorbs them, and takes no facile and meaningless short cuts to attitudes that have no basis in his mind and his feelings."

⇒►•◄⇐

DESPITE THE REPORTS OF "political terror" in the Soviet Union, Farrell remained steadfast in his revolutionary faith. Workers and farmers in the United States, he had written some months earlier in a *Daily Worker* review of leftist journalist John L. Spivak's *America Faces the Barricades* (1935), "are losing one hope after another, and gravitating toward a revolutionary position as a matter of trial and error."

Spivak had persuaded him "that bitter unrest has begun to sweep America and that the American masses have reached a stage of disillusionment where they can now stir." Yet Farrell was not optimistic that revolution was in the offing. With "the rigidity of [the] federal system of bourgeois democracy impressed upon the minds of the people," he wrote in his diary after the Supreme Court in early 1936 invalidated the New Deal's Agricultural Adjustment Act, the populace will be "easy prey for Fascist demagogues....That means that the outlook in America seems to be hopeless and gloomy, and one looks forward to America turning into another hell on earth. Unless Fascism can be checked."The "leftward movement" in America, he lamented, "is still so weak."

To Moscow, however, the prospect of revolution in the United States or other nations was less important now than winning over the bourgeois governments as allies against Nazi Germany. Hence the Popular Front. But for Farrell and other fervent believers in revolution who had not accepted the discipline of party membership, this new policy's literary implications presented serious problems.

Farrell (who in March was to win a $2,500 Guggenheim fellowship in creative writing) was rapidly becoming a "name" himself, and as such, potentially of no small value to the Communists. But the rising novelist was more than ever unwilling to subordinate his aesthetic judgments to the supposed needs of the revolutionary moment. Indeed, early in the year he decided to set down his thoughts about literature and literary criticism in an article, then made up his mind to turn the article into a small book, which Henle agreed to publish.

The comrades found Farrell's independence galling, especially when he criticized the works of revolutionary writers. Clara Weatherwax's *Marching! Marching!*, for example, a first novel about a strike by lumber workers on the Pacific Coast, was a *New Masses* prize novel and the leftist Book Union's January 1936 selection for its membership. In his *Herald Tribune* review, Farrell duly noted the author's "genuine sincerity and good intentions"—and then proceeded to savage the book (which he privately titled, "Stumbling Stumbling").The author knew her subject, he said, but she didn't know how to write well: her style was imitative, her dialogue was dead, her characters were stiff. "To me this book recreates no sense of life, establishes no convincing characterizations." It belongs, he concluded, "in the lower rank of the revolutionary writings."

Granville Hicks and the other comrades were not pleased. In a revolutionary gossip column that he was turning out in the *New Masses* under the pen name "Margaret Wright Mather," Hicks wrote: "Jim Farrell's review of *Marching! Marching!* in *Herald Tribune Books* wasn't so hot. J. Donald Adams, of Section Five [*New York Times Book Review*], is stupid. He slams the left-wing books himself or gets some other obviously incompetent hack to do it. Irita Van Doren, of *Books*, is smart. She assigns a left-wing novel to a left-wing novelist. Farrell is a fine novelist, but he likes only one kind of writing, the kind he does himself; so *Marching! Marching!* is lousy."

Farrell was outraged: "I argued out the objections to *Marching! Marching!* on grounds as objectively as I could," he told his diary. "And this is the way the boys play ball.... I decided to get Hicks, and turn him into a howling joke....The goddamn little sniping fake revolutionary jesus!" He fired off some "manifestoes and burlesques" (as he later described them) to various people in response.

Earlier that week, the *Daily Worker's* first Sunday edition had appeared, with a column by Farrell. Complete with a Hearst-style magazine section, the *Sunday Worker* had been inaugurated in the Popular Front-ish hope of attracting a mass readership that extended beyond the party faithful. Despite some reservations, Farrell had agreed to write a regular column. His first (about the plays of Albert Bein, whose *Let Freedom Ring* Farrell and Hortense Alden had championed) turned out to be his last. When he spoke with Joe North the following Saturday, the editor didn't even mention that the second column Farrell had written was not going to appear in Sunday's paper. Farrell inferred from this silence that the reason his column did not appear was not a lack of space, but rather "orders from above...or else [North's] fear of the Ninth floor," where "Pope" V. J. Jerome presided.

At the *New Masses*, meanwhile, Stanley Burnshaw assured Farrell that a review the latter was doing of Jim Daly's poetry was still wanted. Farrell revised it a half-dozen or so times—but to no avail. It never appeared. Nor, Farrell learned, did an evidently favorable review of *Studs Lonigan*. The reviewer, Nathan Asch, told Farrell that when he had spoken to the *New Masses* editors about their failure to publish it, Mike Gold had passed the buck to Isidor Schneider, and Schneider had passed it to Burnshaw. "This convinces me," Farrell noted in his diary, "that there's something wrong, and that they have done some Star-Chambering of me."

Working diligently on his little book about literary criticism, Farrell reread Hicks's *Great Tradition* (1933; revised, 1935) and found much in it that he strongly objected to. "I am convinced that Hicks' book must be attacked, and so, I am going to do Charlie Angoff [editor of the *American Spectator*] a piece on it, and let the boys rave their ears off. Now is the time, it seems to me, to break the iron chain of ineptitude that is a ring around contemporary revolutionary writing; and I am in a position to be a spearhead of it, and so that is what I intend to do."

———————

EARLY IN THE YEAR, FARRELL and Jim Henle met one morning with "a fellow named Moscowitz," who gave them to understand that he was right-hand man to Darryl F. Zanuck, vice president in charge of production at the Twentieth-Century Fox movie studio. Moscowitz told them he had received a wire from the West Coast asking him to find out how much the film rights to *Studs Lonigan* would cost. "He acted and talked as if he knew nothing else, and did not even know anything about the book," Farrell noted in his diary, "and so we told him our terms—we asked for twenty thousand dollars—but naturally we will take less. If we can get it."

Some months later, at a dinner party at the home of Elinor Rice Novack's sister and brother-in-law, Farrell met the movie actor James Cagney. "Cagney is absolutely made for [the part of Studs Lonigan]," Farrell decided. "And vice versa, Studs is made for Cagney. As a matter of fact, Cagney looks a little bit like Studs Cunningham did." Cunningham had been huskier, with broader shoulders, but there was a decided resemblance.

But Cagney, then thirty-six, was never to appear in the role of young Lonigan, for the simple reason that no movie of *Studs Lonigan* was to be made for almost a quarter-century more. It would have been next to impossible to make a film that was at all faithful to the book during that period, when the movie industry, under the sway of the Catholic "Legion of Decency," adhered to the Motion Picture Production Code of 1930. Ironically, though a movie truly faithful to the book would no doubt have received the legion's condemnation, it would not have deserved it. *Studs Lonigan* does not invite the reader to sympathize with the sexual and other misbehavior described—just the opposite. Indeed, as the literary critic Philip Rahv penetratingly observed, there is in Farrell's works "an underlying moral code which, despite his explicit rejection of the Church, seems...indisputably orthodox and Catholic."

———————

IN ACCORDANCE WITH THE Popular Front, Farrell and other revolutionary literati were now expected to embrace the works not only of fellow "proletarian" writers but also of "bourgeois" authors whom they had previously been encouraged to disdain. Farrell refused to do this, declaring it "a betrayal of honest writers."

In his diary, Farrell recorded how a disillusioned Robert Cantwell (a "proletarian" novelist whom Farrell, perhaps a bit envious of his more fluent prose style, sometimes called "Robert Cantwritewell") told him of a banquet at which Sinclair Lewis, "this broken down hulk of a writer, drunk," was honored by the comrades and their sympathizers, with "everybody making speeches full of praise and apple sauce about him, and Lewis sneering at them, cracking vile anti-Semitic jokes....And, Bob added, while they toady that way to Lewis, because he had a name and he is a Nobel prize winner, they have driven away better men from the movement, men like Wilson [and] Hemingway.... " Farrell vented his disgust:

> For years now, they have been bleating out their stupidity, and in the name of the workers, the revolution, culture, and the future of humanity. And now with the united front [proposed with the Socialists, the Communist Party's modest first step toward the Popular Front], they do it even more so. They are the intellectual leaders— Joe North—Stanley Burnshaw—Mike Gold—Joshua Kunitz—Robert Forsythe—Granville Hicks—Isidor Schneider, and such of the boys. How can one have respect for them. For many, it is impossible to assume, even, that they have any intellectual integrity. And to think of how many they may be misleading, confusing. It sometimes seems really criminal; one feels like crying out.

<hr />

FARRELL HAD BEEN INVOLVED in the creation of *Partisan Review,* an organ of the John Reed Club of New York (a Communist Party auxiliary intended, like similar clubs elsewhere, to win writers and artists to the revolution), and had contributed an excerpt from *The Young Manhood of Studs Lonigan* to its first issue (February-March 1934). Although the party late that year ordered the John Reed Clubs abolished, making way for the nascent League of (established) American Writers, *Partisan Review* continued to appear through most of 1935; its principal editors, William Phillips and Philip Rahv, were trying to figure out how they might keep it alive indefinitely, while the party pondered whether to kill it or make it the official organ of the new league. As it worked out, the magazine—with the approval of cultural commissar Trachten-berg—merged with novelist Jack Conroy's revolutionary periodical, *Anvil*, to become the monthly *Partisan Review and Anvil*. Farrell agreed to serve as a regular columnist, covering theater.

In the inaugural February 1936 issue, Farrell boldly criticized the latest offering—*Paradise Lost*—of Clifford Odets, a playwright much revered in Communist and leftwing circles. Farrell knew that Odets had been a friend of Hortense's and may have known that they had been lovers, but he probably tried to be objective.

Though he began by mocking Odets's inflated reputation, Farrell was careful to note the playwright's past accomplishments in *Waiting for Lefty* and *Awake and Sing*. But Odets's latest play—about the middle-class paradise lost and the paradise to come—was, Farrell said, "a burlesque" of his earlier work, "a play so consistently, so ferociously bad" that it left the reviewer gaping "in open-mouthed wonder." The play's title, he said, should have been: *Lay Down and Die*.

Mike Gold, in the *New Masses*, was quick to rise to Odets's defense. "It seems a pity," Gold said in favorably appraising the new *Partisan Review and Anvil*, that the editors had seen fit to include Farrell's column. "When one remembers that Farrell also attacked Jack Conroy's first novel, *The Disinherited*, saying in *The Nation*, that the book had 'no soul' (this from the author of the most soul-less novels in recent America); and that Farrell wrote a sour review of Clara Weatherwax's fine novel in *The Herald-Tribune*, one begins to wonder what is wrong, and whether Farrell has the objectivity, fairness and generosity—let us also add, common sense—to be a critic."

Farrell's friend Josephine Herbst responded from Yaddo with a blistering letter to the *New Masses* editors, attacking the anti-intellectual Gold and his muddled "political" mugging of the earnest Communist sympathizer Farrell, so odd in view of the comrades' fawning on the politically unreliable Sinclair Lewis. When her letter appeared in print, however, it was considerably toned down, with no criticism of the inept Clara Weatherwax, no mention of Lewis and no hint that Gold had been acting, in Herbst's eyes, more like a fascist than a Communist.

After the *New Masses* editors had received her letter, as well as a joint one from Phillips, Rahv, Asch, Gregory and others, they invited Herbst down to New York to straighten things out. She came, and stayed with Farrell and Hortense. When she returned to their apartment from the "fraction meeting" at which the matter was settled, she "couldn't talk to us [about it]," Farrell wrote in his diary. "At supper time, she made conversation, and Hortense relieved her by saying she looked tired, and ought to lay down and we would bring her coffee in to her in the bedroom. She jumped at the opportunity." An hour or so later, she emerged from her bedroom to claim that she had won a victory. "We both knew better," Farrell affirmed. He tolerated no trimming in such affairs.

"Josephine was taken into camp by the boys," he wrote, "and when her letter…was printed, it was a love letter. I was made a goat. The issue was falsified into one which would show that the Communist Party has not one line on culture, and [that] Mike's attack on me was his own opinion, and not that of the party." Though Herbst's printed statement was hardly a "love letter," Farrell's understanding of what happened seems to have been essentially correct.

He had come to realize, he wrote in his diary, that he had been "put onto Stalinist skids, and they are all greased for me, and they will enjoy nothing better than shooting me down them."

⇒»‑◦‑«⇐

"THE CUNNINGHAMS ARE QUITE sore at me," Farrell wrote to Hortense in early April from Chicago, where he had returned for a few weeks to soak up material from those who were his characters and potential characters. By this time, *Studs Lonigan* and the individual novels had given him a certain notoriety in his native city. "The general impression of [the Cunninghams], and of many others, is that I wrote the books in order to capitalize on what I knew of 58th street, and to make money. And they keep saying, I didn't know what I was writing and talking about." (Nearly six decades later, Studs Cunningham's sister Loretta was still saying this.) The assumption that Farrell's chief motive as a writer was pecuniary offended the idealistic author. Paul Caron's younger brother Joel, who was running an advertising agency, did not realize, Farrell said, "what an insult it was [to suggest] that I had written my books to make money, capitalizing on sensational trends in writing."

The old gang from 58th Street and environs had been no

163

more radicalized than Caron, Farrell found. "The boys…are getting more and more respectable." Harold O'Keefe ("Red Kelly") "is much married, with two kids." His brother had a political job. So did Jim Martin ("Fat Malloy"). Louis Lederer ("Phil Rolfe"), who had married Loretta Cunningham, "has left the bookie business, and started a bakery." Joe Cody ("Joe Coady"), once Farrell's next-door neighbor and friend, had become "after years at the University, nothing but a disgustingly cheap politician." Johnny Johnson ("Johnny O'Brien") was selling suits part-time and thinking of becoming a priest.

Early in his visit to Chicago, Farrell bumped into Tubby Collins ("Tubby Connell"), who was working as a glazier, and had a drink with him and his girlfriend, Marge, a telephone operator. When she asked Tubby what *Young Lonigan* was about, he gave what Farrell considered a "most revealing" answer: "Jimmy took this Cunningham family, they had a little money, and they thought that they were so much, and he showed them up, and showed up an Irish family, and what it was, instead of what it liked to make you think it was." Tubby's comment, Farrell later told Hortense, "suggests that many liked the idea of another 'lace-curtain' Irish family being shown up."

Some liked the idea of Studs Cunningham in particular being exposed. The fellow who had been Farrell's model for "Mose Levinsky, poolroom intellectual," a minor character in *The Young Manhood of Studs Lonigan*, and who was now working in the advertising department at the *Chicago Times*, told him how he hated Studs Cunningham, how Cunningham was no good. Once, he said (Farrell told Hortense), Studs and some of his pals "caught him in Washington Park and beat the hell out of him—just because he was a Jew."*

Other Chicagoans had their own bêtes noires and took pleasure in seeing Farrell pin them, wriggling, to the page. "Some lawyers in town could—I learned—kiss me," he told Hortense. The attorneys were delighted with his mocking depiction of the pompous "Dennis P. Gorman," who evidently bore more than a passing resemblance to a certain Chicago judge. Some of the portraits in the novels "are so devilishly accurate and to the point

---

*In Cunningham's later years, he may have become less bigoted. He at least became good friends with his sister's Jewish boyfriend (and future husband), Louis Lederer; they often played handball together on weekends. Lederer eventually became a top gambling expert for the notorious Chicago gangster Sam Giancana.

that they absolutely cannot be interpreted as anyone else but a certain prototype. I would have fared better, had I mixed up prototypes more." With some Chicagoans, he noted, identifying who was who in the novels had become a game. "The one character who puzzled them most was Weary Reilley. They can't make out Weary." (Frank Egan, the convicted rapist on whom Weary Reilley was based, had lived near 63rd Street and hadn't been part of the 58th Street gang.)

In general, Farrell reported to Jim Henle, people seemed to be "sore" about his novels—but "at the same time, proud." One fellow from the old neighborhood, Ed Kenny, was always trying to show that he was the character "Kenny Kilarney," though in fact he wasn't. (The actual model for the character had died several years before.) Ed Kenny, Farrell learned from Tubby Collins, "will always be saying, 'Look, that guy [Farrell] made me do that [in *Studs Lonigan*]. I never did that.'" And although ostensibly angry, "he will say it with pride, to show that he wishes he was in the book."

Farrell confided that he found it a strain to see all "the boys" of yesterday. He felt that he was acting a role with them. Their class and outlook were "petty bourgeois" and, in the writer's eyes, they were fodder for fascism. He was glad to get "a sense of the way the pattern of their lives has unwound, and I can fill in the last few years imaginatively. But this is likely to be the last time."

He paid a visit to the express company's wagon department. "I did not stay long," he recounted. "It was, in fact, just a little bit too ghastly to stay. I mean, well, I was so removed from the fellows, there was nothing to talk about, particularly since they were working—and in addition, I was a kind of [an] affront to some." Eleven years ago, he had been "the crazy punk," but now he appeared "with my status changed." The man who had been the model for "Gas-House McGinty" was "set off from the call department in a little caged-off room…and I think he knew I was in the office, but he did not look around or come out." All that Farrell could see of the proto-McGinty was his broad back. Meanwhile, Farrell's erstwhile boss, Percy Smith ("Wade Norris"), "resented my coming quite decidedly. Didn't speak to me. So, as I was leaving, I looked at him, rather buoyantly, and said—pointing—

"'Is that Mr. Smith?'

"'Yes, it's Mr. Smith.'

"'How are you?'"

"'O.K.'"

He spit out this last as if to say: "you sonofabitch, why don't you get the hell out of here."

⸺➤-○-◄⸺

THE DALYS, LIVING ALL TOGETHER in a one-room kitchenette apartment, were in rather sad shape. "There is something terribly pathetic about them," Farrell told Hortense. Uncle Tom, now sixty-four, was "a broken man. He does not have the same assertiveness, the same brashness, the same nervous self-confidence; he advice mongers in a more quiet vein." He was somehow managing to bring home about ten dollars a week and had lately taken to reading Karl Marx. Bill "just hugs his radio more desperately, and still talks about the psychology of wishing yourself into success in life." Ella was earning five to seven dollars a week cleaning people's houses and giving women shampoos. She now called herself a "communist," but she was doing some campaign work for the Democrats in the idle hope that a victory by the Cook County machine candidate who was challenging the incumbent Democratic governor would lead to patronage jobs for her and her brothers.

To Farrell, the Dalys seemed to be "just waiting to die." His mother provided a welcome contrast. "My mother was wonderful," he told Hortense. "Unlike the Dalys, she has a sense of life to her. She is a moron. But she is an alive moron." She told Jimmy and the others that when a policeman had "rolled" her son Joe, she had gone to the police station and confronted the cop. "She brandished her fists, yelled, acting out how she claims to have spoken to him. 'I walked up to him, and I said you sonofabitch. You rolled my son. How many children have you got. If you didn't have five children I'd take that star off you. I would. You can be thankful that you got your children. If you didn't you wouldn't be wearing that star, you sonofabitch.'"

Farrell thought that, of all of them, his mother was in some ways the one suffering the most. "She has no teeth," he explained to Hortense. "She can only eat certain kinds of food." She had gotten very fat and had constant indigestion. "Jack and I talked about trying to get her teeth—fifty bucks or so." (Later in the decade, the family did get Mrs. Farrell some new teeth. Daughter Mary went with her to the dentist, and she got a complete set, uppers and lowers. "Two days after she got them," Mary sadly remembered, "she was sick to her stomach, and she was throwing up. Her teeth fell in the toilet and she flushed the toilet—and that was it. We couldn't afford to get another set.")

The Dalys, to Farrell's disgust, were impressed that he had recently been mentioned in Walter Winchell's gossip column. "So you see—Walter Winchell is somebody to such people," Farrell said to Hortense. "They have no standards of their own." Like Americans in general, he reflected, members of his family imagined that a realm exists in which "celebrities are forever having social engagements, parties, seeing each other, drinking, eating, being gay." And his family members seemed to believe "that I lead that kind of a life too. And they like it that I should—and perhaps at the same time—they envy me."

Of all his siblings, Farrell seemed to feel closest now to Jack and Mary, both of whom were bright and shared his enthusiasm for revolution. Jack, whom he stayed with on his visit to Chicago, was married to "an intellectual Jewish girl…from a rich bourgeois family" and was going to school with the aim of becoming a doctor. Mary, less happily wed, was pregnant. Helen, who was even less happily married, seemed to Farrell less intelligent than Mary but warmer and more generous. As for his brothers Earl and Joe, both still working at the express company, Farrell sensed some "definite class differences." "They talk in terms of forty and fifty dollars a week as a good salary," he informed Jim Henle. "Well I don't get that. But I could. The mere fact that I could seems to set me off from them." His older brother Earl, he told Hortense, was "representative of many workers" in that he was "thoroughly corrupted by petty bourgeois ideology, ideals, ambitions, aspirations. For instance at one point [Earl's wife] Loretta said, 'Sure I some day expect to be rich.' … Their class is not going to move forward, and take things over to run a socialist state. They are going to get rich."

Not rich perhaps, but with the publication later in the year of *A World I Never Made*, Earl and the other leading figures among the Farrells and the Dalys were to be transformed into literary characters. Farrell showed at least some of the manuscript to Jack Farrell and his wife, Lillian. They both "grant very enthusiastically," he told Hortense, "that I have gotten all the family down very exactly and very realistically….

"God," Farrell added, "if I can carry this work through sweetheart—it will have an impact and deal with a sector of American life that no other novelist has touched in the same detail…. I have the most wonderful opportunity of any novelist my age in America.

It's my job then to take it and squeeze every last drop out of it."

It seems never to have occurred to him that, no matter how justified his great work of imagination and memory might be, he was in a sense betraying his family—the people who, whatever their faults and limitations, whatever their sins, had been closest to him, had given him life and sustained him when he was young.

⸺➤◦◄⸺

FARRELL'S *A NOTE ON Literary Criticism,* published in May, was hailed by Edmund Wilson as "quite a remarkable event." Writing in the *Nation,* he explained why:

> For one thing, it is one of the few intelligent discussions of literature from the Marxist point of view which have yet been written by Americans. But it is especially conspicuous as being the work of one of the ablest of the younger novelists. The book suffers a little, it is true, from Farrell's characteristic faults: it is diffuse and badly organized; it runs to footnotes as long as the chapters; and the line of the argument is not always kept clear. But it is inspiriting to see a novelist getting up to argue general principles with the critics and actually showing authority in that field in which they have been pretending to instruct him. And one is surprised, after reading Mr. Farrell's novels, which derive so much of their effectiveness from the total immersion of the author in the lives of unreflecting and limited people, to discover behind them a mind capable of philosophical abstraction and analysis.

Farrell argued in *Note* that two kinds of "leftism" had deformed revolutionary literary criticism. The first kind, exemplified by Mike Gold, was "the school of revolutionary sentimentalism," which "demands a literature of simplicity to the point of obviousness, and even of downright banality. Crying for songs of 'stench and sweat,' it tends to idealize the 'worker' and 'the worker-writer,' producing overdrawn pictures of both."

The second sort of leftism, represented by Granville Hicks, was the tendency toward "a mechanically deterministic 'Marxism,'" which "usually assumes implicitly, if not explicitly, that literature follows economics obediently and directly." But Marx and Engels's conception of dialectical materialism was more complicated. (Unlike many self-proclaimed Marxists, Farrell had actually read some of the weighty tomes in the revolutionary canon.) "When Marx and Engels traced and described the influence of economics on social processes," he wrote, "they did not do so in order to exclude other factors that influence social processes—factors like ideals, art, culture." Works of literature, Farrell declared—employing a quasi-Marxist jargon that he fortunately kept out of his fiction— can have "a human worth and a carry-over power which endow them with a relatively inherent persistence-value after they have been divorced from the material conditions and the society out of which they have been created."

As a philosopher, Farrell was an amateur, in both the good and the bad senses of that word. And he was not being entirely fair to his fellow amateur Hicks. Farrell didn't point out in his book, as he had in his assault on "Mr. Hicks: Critical Vulgarian" in the April issue of the *American Spectator*, that Hicks *agreed* with him that litera- ture did not directly follow economics. "Mr. Hicks," Farrell wrote in the *Spectator*, "is frequently willing to acknowledge this indirect- ness of relationships [between economics and culture]. But he does so only outwardly. In his specific analysis [in *The Great Tradi- tion*] he forces a direct relationship." If Hicks agreed with Farrell in the abstract but invariably found it hard to avoid a crude economic determinism in particular cases, then perhaps there was a funda- mental defect in the theory. Farrell might profitably have addressed that possibility, but he didn't. His revolutionary faith evidently did not permit it.

"The truth is"—as a more dispassionate analyst and scholar, R. N. Carew Hunt, later wrote—"that while Marx was ultimately led to admit an interconnection between [the economic substructure and the superstructure comprising all the manifestations of man's mind], he never clearly worked out what it was, and that if he had attempted to do so he would have had to abandon his theory."

Still, Farrell's polemic was, as Wilson said, an intelligent dis- cussion of literature and literary criticism from the Marxist point of view. In the revolutionary circles in which they moved, *A Note on Literary Criticism* was a breath of fresh air (though not universally welcomed as such). Farrell pointed out, for example, that the terms *bourgeois* and *proletarian* were descriptive categories, not stan- dards by which to judge works of literature. Nor was the class struggle the cartoonish conflict that it was often made out to be:

> The class struggle does not in any sense produce so complete a dif- ferentiation of human beings that there are no similarities between men who, objectively, belong to different social classes. Nor does it mean that the class struggle is a direct, potent, conscious factor at

every moment in a man's life; it does not cause him to act in every detail of every situation in a preconditioned way that makes him indistinguishable from other members of his class. The class struggle... is an objective set of relationships, fundamental in a society, and it has a devious, shifting, differentiating influence (sometimes direct, sometimes indirect) on individuals and on classes.

Farrell also disputed the oft-proclaimed notion of art as a weapon. Though literature did have "social influence," he said, it was rarely able to function as effective propaganda. "When revolutionary novels sell in such relatively small numbers, it is merely talking through one's hat to assert that they can serve as fiery instruments, changing word into deed overnight." Moreover, literature intended as narrow propaganda was usually full of "ineptitudes."

Brandishing quotes from Marx and other revolutionary saints, Farrell dealt telling blows to Gold, Hicks, the fellow-traveling Malcolm Cowley and the like, but he didn't stop there, as Edmund Wilson noted: "Mr. Farrell is to be congratulated for having stood up not merely to the local boys but also to the Russian panjandrums—such as [Karl] Radek, whose rubbish about Joyce in 'Problems of Soviet Literature' he has been able to shoot so full of holes that I hope nobody will ever again be impressed by it."

All in all, Farrell's book was an extraordinary performance and a significant event. At the *Partisan Review and Anvil*, the editors—William Phillips, Philip Rahv and Alan Calmer—welcomed it warmly. *A Note on Literary Criticism*, Calmer wrote, "is the first lengthy statement of a critical stand that must, I firmly believe, become the dominant emphasis of Marxian criticism if proletarian literature in the United States is to grow instead of stagnate. For... in place of the vulgar practices of 'leftism' which he demolishes, Farrell stresses the importance of literary and human values in dealing with central social experience."

The more orthodox comrades were, of course, less enthusiastic. At a farewell party for Mike Gold, who was going off to write a novel, "the boys"—Farrell noted in his diary that Phillips had told him—"were buzzing about the latest issue of *Partisan Review* . . . and Kyle Crichton called Alan Calmer a Farrell-lover. Jack Kunitz frothed at the mouth about me, about Phillips, and about Rahv, and said I was looking for trouble, I was anti-Party, and that I was an opportunist. Finally Jack was red faced, and could only curse. And Mike Gold last week went up to the *New Masses* and ranted until he almost ranted himself into reading the copy of *Partisan Review and Anvil* that he had under his arm."

Isidor Schneider—as Farrell, Phillips and Rahv had anticipated—was chosen by the comrades to review the book for the *New Masses*. ("In other words," Farrell wrote in his diary after running into Schneider having lunch with his wife and six-year-old daughter in a cafeteria, "Isidor has made himself the stooge and sucker. Oh Isidor Stooge!") Schneider later wrote in his review that "To accept his analysis would be to abandon Marxism altogether, to deny the achievements of Marxist literature and criticism."

A few weeks after Schneider's review appeared in the *New Masses*, Granville Hicks, the former ministry student turned Communist littérateur, weighed in with his appraisal (oddly headlined, "In Defense of James Farrell"): "In the course of his book [Farrell] misrepresents the opinions of half a dozen revolutionary critics.... It may be doubted, indeed, if there is any point at which *A Note on Literary Criticism* is genuinely valuable. But we must be careful not to assume that, because the book is an inadequate statement of Marxism, its central ideas are anti-Marxist. Mr. Farrell has built badly, but it is on a Marxist foundation. This we must recognize, for the sake not of the book, but of Marxism."

The *New Masses*, then, was not quite sure whether Farrell's analysis implied abandonment of Marxism, as Schneider had it, or was erected on a foundation of Marxism, as Hicks believed. The one thing the agitated comrades were sure of was that they didn't like Farrell's heresy.

⋙━◦━⋘

FARRELL ATTENDED THE DULL Republican convention in Cleveland that June, at which Kansas governor Alf Landon was nominated for president; then, later in the month, he went with Hortense to Philadelphia and the drawn-out Democratic convention that nominated Franklin Roosevelt for a second term. At both events, the novelist saw H. L. Mencken, whom he had first met the preceding August. (He and Hortense had been passing the Hotel Brevoort in New York one evening when she noticed Mencken sitting with poet Edgar Lee Masters. Hortense and Mencken knew—and disliked—each other, but she introduced Farrell to him, and he invited them to sit down. "We drank beer and talked for about an hour," Farrell later recalled. "Mencken and Masters were good friends, and they enjoyed each other's company. They liked to joke about [William Jennings] Bryan, the Fundamentalists, and the yokels, and they did so that evening.")

In Philadelphia, Mencken mentioned that Theodore Dreiser was in town and supplied the name of his hotel. Farrell was eager to meet Dreiser, whose *An American Tragedy* he considered "the *greatest* American novel of our century."

"I went there," Farrell later recalled, "phoned his room, and identified myself. He asked me to come up." Dreiser was cordial but seemed absorbed in his own thoughts. "We talked casually, and mainly about literature.... My impression then was of a big bulk of a man, self-centered, not too graceful; but also of a man who was kind and even soft. It was clear to me that he did not know my own writing." It was the mention of Mencken's name, apparently, that had won him entry to the older novelist's room. They talked for about forty-five minutes. As Farrell was leaving, a secretary came in and Dreiser, wanting to introduce his departing visitor to her, turned to him and asked him his name.

The day after the Democratic convention ended, Farrell and Hortense were back in New York, attending the final session of the Communist convention in Madison Square Garden. They arrived that afternoon as gubernatorial candidate Robert Minor was nominating general secretary Earl Browder to be the party's candidate for president of the United States. Farrell—who had been contemptuous of the potbellied politicians at the Democratic convention and considered the delegates remote from "the stream of American life"—was impressed by the Communist show. "The enthusiasm was spontaneous, and genuine, bursting forth into continuous roars, with demonstrations, the demonstrators carrying red flags," he wrote in his diary.

But Farrell was disturbed by the weak tone of the speeches and the platform. Instead of urging revolution, as in the past, the Communists were portraying the 1936 election as a choice between progress and reaction. Under pressure from Moscow, they were ostensibly opposing Roosevelt while actually giving him indirect support by making Landon the chief enemy. The Communists, Farrell noted, had retreated from the "basic Marxian position...that the bourgeois state and its parliament are the instruments of the ruling class. The Communists here take a position of working through the bourgeois parliament." Moreover, by urging that America stay out of war, the Communists, in order to further Soviet foreign policy, were implicitly distinguishing between "good" capitalist powers such as the United States and "bad" ones such as Germany, Italy and Japan. In Farrell's view, there was really "little difference" between the policy of "a bourgeois democracy" and that of "a fascist country on the imperial stage."

"The main task of a revolutionary party in America at the present time," it seemed to him, "is the task of education"—but the Communist campaign was providing "a course of education in social democratic measures." Farrell had not completely made up his mind about this, but he was "very skeptical."

Increasingly, in the coming weeks and months, he would turn to the works and thought of Leon Trotsky, the outcast but unbowed revolutionary hero. Back in early June, before he went off to the GOP convention, Farrell had talked with Edmund Wilson one night at the Brevoort until it closed, and then had gone back with him to his place. "Drank too much beer," Farrell recorded in his diary the next day. "Wilson said that these last years, Trotsky has been 'the Marxist conscience of the world.'"

Chapter Eleven

Renegade, in a World He Never Made

"OVER A HUNDRED PEOPLE were executed, and a larger number imprisoned after the killing of Kirov. And now this," Farrell reflected on August 20, 1936. Old Bolsheviks Zinoviev and Kamenev and fourteen others on public trial in Moscow had confessed to conspiring with the exiled Trotsky and the German secret police to assassinate Kirov and other Soviet leaders, including Stalin. Trotsky, in Norway, denounced the proceedings as "humbug," declared that the confessions had been coerced, and promised to make "the accusers the accused." He offered to present his case before an impartial international commission of inquiry.

Already troubled by the failure of France's Popular Front government to aid its sister Popular Front government in the Spanish Civil War—and by Stalin's evident willingness to abandon the proletariat of one country after another—Farrell cast a skeptical eye on the Moscow trial. Though *New York Times* correspondent Walter Duranty, preeminent apologist for Stalin in the mainstream American press, had pronounced it "inconceivable that a public trial of such men would be held unless the authorities had full proofs of their guilt," Farrell decided that the whole business looked "fluky." The way in which the accused conspirators stood up and tried to outbid each other as terrorists seemed suspicious; Trotsky, despite what the *Daily Worker* now had him saying, had always condemned individual terrorism; Kirov had not even been an important figure in the Soviet leadership; and Zinoviev, who was certainly a Marxist, confessed that if he and his fellow conspirators had succeeded, they would have put Russia on the road to fascism. It all made no sense. But within days, Zinoviev, Kamenev and the other defendants were found guilty and executed.

In conversations with Farrell while the trial was in progress, *Partisan Review* editors Rahv and Phillips were uncertain of its import. Rahv, born in the Russian Ukraine and a member of the Communist Party, and Phillips, born in New York to Russian immigrants and not a party member (though his wife was), "had this view," Farrell wrote in his diary on August 20: "If the accused are innocent, what kind of Bolsheviks are they, not making a political speech in court.... If they are guilty, well they are blackguards, and should be denounced." After another conversation the next day, Farrell noted that Rahv "is practicing suspended judgment [and] is beginning to think that there must have been a conspiracy." For the two editors, politics was closely bound up with the survival of their financially beleaguered magazine. Despite their campaign against literary "leftism" and their own growing political unease, *Partisan Review* (which no longer included the *Anvil* in its title) remained within the Communist orbit. In mid-August, Farrell had talked with them about the possibility of "dragging *Partisan Review* out from under the boys [and] giving it a vague Trotskyist orientation instead of its present vague Stalinist orientation." But nothing came of the idea right away. With the magazine's existence at stake, the editors were apparently unwilling to cut off any potential source of support. "Looks to me like the end of *Partisan Review*," Farrell wrote in his diary a month later. "Last night, Rahv and Phillips had a meeting with Tractenberg's stooge board of the League of American Writers to discuss an amalgamation. Rahv and Phillips said they were going to set conditions. But it remains, he who pays the piper calls the tune." As it turned out, the October issue of *Partisan Review* would be the last published under Communist auspices.

By early September, if not before, Farrell had become convinced that Moscow's charges against Trotsky were false. He decided to break politically with the Communists. He would speak up about his conviction that Trotsky was being framed. And he would support for president neither the Communist Earl Browder nor President Franklin Roosevelt (whom the Communists were covertly backing) but rather the Socialist candidate, Norman Thomas.

In early October, Farrell went to a "dull" meeting of a committee working for Thomas and his running mate, George Nelson of Wisconsin. (There Farrell met philosopher Sidney Hook, an independent radical and a leading American authority on Marxism. Farrell had heard that he was arrogant, but saw no sign of it that night. "Hook seemed like a nice guy, but didn't say much," he observed in his diary.) Later in the month, Farrell attended a dinner for the ticket and heard Thomas speak. In an article for the *Socialist Call,* Farrell explained why he was supporting him. "The Socialist Party has the only valid position on war and fundamental issues in this campaign," and it did not "mechanically separate the issues of Socialism versus Capitalism and progress versus reaction," as the Communists did. Moreover, it was necessary "to call imperialist war imperialist war," while the Communists were fostering "the same delusions that led to social patriotism in 1914 and 1917."

Even before that declaration was published, Farrell had made his political apostasy apparent. On the same day that news reports from Moscow announced the arrest of Soviet propagandist Karl Radek and others on charges of complicity in the alleged Trotskyist conspiracy, and told of the trial, or trials, yet to come, Farrell attended a party to explore the possibilities of raising funds for *Partisan Review.* There he brought up "the subject of the Russian trials, and announced my firm belief that it was a frameup of Trotsky."

Two days later, the *Socialist Call* published a Farrell satire mocking the Communists' Popular Front-ish willingness to settle for mere opposition to GOP presidential candidate Alf Landon.

In the comrades' eyes, Farrell's open political rebellion was far more serious than his earlier literary deviations had been: it marked him as a renegade. The very next day, the Workers Bookshop, which had sold more than a thousand copies of *Studs Lonigan,* canceled its order for one hundred copies of *A World I Never Made.* "I suspect that the 'local boys' are going to get vindictive toward me," Farrell reflected. "Well, that is life, that is literature, that is politics. They can't call their souls their own."

<hr/>

WITH *A WORLD I NEVER MADE* (whose title was from a line by A. E. Housman: "I, a stranger and afraid, / In a world I never made"), the Farrells and the Dalys were transmuted into literary characters. The novelist's grandmother, Julia Brown Daly, became Mary Fox O'Flaherty, his Uncle Tom became Al O'Flaherty, Aunt Ella became Margaret ("Peg") O'Flaherty, and Uncle Bill became Ned O'Flaherty. The Farrells, meanwhile, were transformed into the O'Neills. Jim and Mary Farrell became Jim and Lizz O'Neill, while Earl became

Bill O'Neill, Jimmy himself was Danny O'Neill (who had already appeared as a minor character in *Studs Lonigan*), Helen became Margaret ("Little Margaret") O'Neill, and so on.

A World I Never Made opens on a Sunday morning in August 1911, with seven-year-old Danny O'Neill—who lives with the O'Flahertys in their comfortable apartment on Calumet Avenue, not with his impoverished parents in their filthy tenement on LaSalle Street—attempting by surreptitious means to get out of going to Mass (and almost succeeding, until his choleric Uncle Al returns and forces him to go). The novel ends about five months (and some five hundred pages) later, on Christmas Day, as the O'Flahertys celebrate at home and await the arrival of the O'Neills. The O'Flahertys—just as prone to familial discord as the Dalys—are determined to avoid any quarrels on this day, but the reader knows by then how slim the chances are that the resolution will be kept.

With no obviously contrived plot, the novel is filled with countless incidents and episodes—many, probably most, drawn from real life, or at least real life as Farrell imagined it. Margaret O'Flaherty's affair with lumberman Lorry Robinson, a married man and a Protestant who is caught up in a political scandal, is an example; Ned O'Flaherty's proposal that he and his wife take Little Margaret and rear her as their own in Madison, Wisconsin, is another. Farrell enters the minds and portrays the behavior of his fictional family members with confidence and fervor, and the dialogue he invents for them is, with rare exceptions, utterly convincing.

"As Mr. Farrell tells their story, [his characters] move as by instinct through the experiences of these months," critic Carl Van Doren wrote in the *Nation*.

> They have consciences which, without always keeping them from what they know is misbehavior, continually haunt them. Their consciences make up nearly as much of the story as their acts. This helps to give to *A World I Never Made* that habitual tenderness which is quite as characteristic of Mr. Farrell's novels as their toughness. Easily multiplying endless incidents to show his characters in action, he sees them, feels through them, and thinks around them. He has an extraordinarily capacious mind which holds the persons and events of a novel as if they were, somehow, in solution, to be poured out in a full stream in which his own share as narrator may be lost sight of. You forget that you are seeing this life through the eyes of a selecting novelist. It seems merely to be there before you.

Bernard DeVoto, writing in the *Saturday Review,* agreed: "His book has abundantly the life that is so conspicuously absent from all contemporary fiction except the very best. His characters live in their own right, of their own parts and passions, and what they feel and do is true." Moreover, by adding compassion to the anger of his portrayal of the O'Neills and the slum in which they exist, Farrell "lifts himself to a higher estate in fiction than he had occupied before.... He is dealing with universals, and...he has, whether or not he intended to, abandoned the class struggle for the deadlier struggle between mankind and the gods."

In the *Studs Lonigan* trilogy, Farrell had created one truly memorable character: Studs Lonigan himself. In *A World I Never Made,* he created four: Mrs. O'Flaherty, Al O'Flaherty, Margaret O'Flaherty and Jim O'Neill. (Lizz O'Neill and Ned O'Flaherty do not quite rise above the level of caricature, and Danny could be any bright and sensitive seven-year-old boy with a liking for baseball.) Jim O'Neill, the intelligent, hardworking teamster who longs to better his family's condition and who has dignity and courage and none of the pretensions or illusions of the O'Flaherty brothers, is, as Van Doren noted, "the most moving character" in the novel (despite his racial prejudice and other failings). One wonders what led Farrell to draw this admiring portrait of his father. Was it guilt (since he had been so estranged from him in life)? Or ignorance (since, as Danny would reflect in a later volume, he "had never really known" his father)? Or ideology (since his father belonged to the sainted working class)? Or dramatic necessity (since the novel would have been poorer without the admiring portrait)? Or a belated apprehension of the apparent truth (since the portrait is consistent with the recollections of Farrell's sisters)? One can only speculate.

For DeVoto, it was not Jim O'Neill but Mrs. O'Flaherty who is the book's "principal triumph": "Sprinkling holy water to exorcise devils, cursing her daughter and sometimes beating her with her fists, pouring a flood of invective on everyone who offends her or any of her family, beerily weeping over Danny or her dead husband or the dead [daughter] Louise—she is truly magnificent.... [C]ontemporary fiction has few characters so alive or so memorable."

The reaction to *A World I Never Made* upon its publication was not everywhere so enthusiastic or perceptive. Among novelists, Farrell might be, as Van Doren said, "the truest historian of the

American city culture," and his chosen slice of Chicago could be "any of the poorer parts of any large American city," but there were many people who wanted nothing to do with any such intensely urban experience, in life or in literature. *Herald Tribune* columnist Lewis Gannett, who in the preceding years had reluctantly brought himself to recognize the Lonigan books as powerful "if purgative" art, now recoiled in genteel horror from Farrell's latest work. "This is a dirty book and disgusting," he declared on its day of publication. Though acknowledging the author's "obviously sincere determination to picture in all its honest ugliness" a world that was part of the American scene, and conceding Farrell's artistic right to do that, Gannett still shuddered at the result.

In Chicago, Fanny Butcher of the *Tribune* responded to Farrell's latest work with only slightly less aversion. She found *A World I Never Made* "profoundly shocking." But while the world Farrell depicts is remote from the experience of most "gentle readers," his realism "has about it such undeniable veracity, such minutiae of detail, of word and deed that no reader could persuade himself that such a world does not exist." Even so, the book was, "in its brutal realism, an indictment of humankind. It is so brutal, so frank, so factual that many readers will be filled with the kind of disgust that cannot bear another word."

This sort of realism, gentle readers were permitted to conclude, was not literature. But the naturalists—among whose number Farrell as a novelist had come to be counted—thought otherwise. Naturalism, whose founding father was the French novelist Émile Zola (1840–1902), attempted to apply natural science to literature, sought objective portrayals of life without moral judgment, and saw man's fate as the product of heredity and environment. Imported from Europe during the 1890s, naturalism (in its pure or, more often, impure form) was by now a well-established American literary tradition, running from Stephen Crane and Frank Norris to Theodore Dreiser and Dos Passos.

But naturalism as Farrell practiced it had its dangers. A *Chicago Times* writer indicated that the family depicted in *A World I Never Made* was Farrell's own. Jim Henle advised the columnist that "you have certainly let yourself [in for] a libel suit if any woman can identify herself with Aunt Margaret or any man with Uncle Al." But of course, there did exist a woman who could identify herself with Aunt Margaret, and a man who could identify himself with Uncle Al. And those individuals would have been less (or more) than human not to be wounded by Farrell's fictional treatment of them.

Tom Daly wrote a letter to his beloved nephew indicating his unhappiness. Farrell showed the letter to Henle, who responded: "Do you feel that it might be a good thing for me to write him and tell him of the impression *I* got of Al from the book—that of a thoroughly decent, honest, loyal, generous person. Evidently he doesn't like the picture of himself in the book—none of us are over-fond of honest mirrors—and perhaps a letter from an outsider would make him feel better." In Tom Daly's case it might have, at least a little. But one doubts that such a letter could have assuaged the hurt that Ella Daly felt at her fictional portrayal by her "Little Brother" (as she had called Farrell when he was young). "Ella was livid, Ella was heart-broken," her niece Mary remembered. And though Farrell's mother had her faith to comfort her, she too must have been pained when she saw his harsh, even contemptuous depiction of Lizz O'Neill.

Still, the hurt felt by Farrell's relatives was undoubtedly lessened by the fact that *A World I Never Made* was a product of imagination as much as memory—a fact easily lost to sight because of Farrell's great skill as a naturalistic novelist. In 1911, when the novel takes place, the author had, after all, been only seven years old. He was not present to record the dialogue at Ella's trysts with Wirt Cook, for example, nor was he on the road with Uncle Tom to take down his conversation with other salesmen. But Farrell's realism was such that it almost seems as if he must have been there. The reader forgets, as Van Doren noted, that "a selecting novelist" is at work. The life unfolding in the novel "seems merely to be there before you." But that was not true for all readers: Tom and Ella knew very well how much their nephew had invented. As a result, despite their wounded feelings they could still have the satisfaction of being able to say honestly to themselves—and if occasion arose, to others—that the characters in the novel were not really they. Even though, in all but the literal sense, the characters *were* they, at least as Farrell saw them.

———◆———

FARRELL WAS TROUBLED BY THE specter of censorship. Pope Pius XI earlier in the year had issued an encyclical lauding the Legion of Decency's crusade in the United States to promote "clean" movies, especially for the sake of the young, and calling upon the bishops of the world to join in the drive. This prompted Farrell to reflect upon what he saw as the embattled artist's need continually to defend his values and his efforts not only from corrupting influences within the literary world, but also from "outside assaults" by the Church, the "forces of reaction" and the "corrupting forces" that seek only profits. "If and when Mother Church, with its Legion of Indecency in America, manages to get the movies cleaned up," he said, "it will then proceed to the stage, and to books."

His visceral response to the threat of censorship apparently made it impossible for him to take a more nuanced view of the subject. In light of his preoccupation in his novels with childhood and youth, that is somewhat surprising. After all, in *The Young Manhood of Studs Lonigan* he had shown at one point how a movie Studs saw influenced his thoughts and dreams, and the novelist had also agreed with sociologist Frederic Thrasher that *Young Lonigan* pointed to the failure of church, school, home and social agency to "canalize the impulses" of Lonigan and his pals. Yet now Farrell seems not even to have considered the question of whether society, for the sake of its youth and its future, should regulate the mass medium of film.

In an essay for the *Nation* (published in October in two successive issues, under the title "The Pope Needs America"), he directly attacked the Church as "potentially a threat to progressive forces." Never before had the Catholic Church in America been "more alert, more militant, more on the offensive than it is at present." Unable to turn back "the clock of history," the Church was able to defend itself only "by becoming a staunch ally of capitalism, whether the latter takes the form of bourgeois democracy or fascism."

It was not only the Church's influence on Hollywood that concerned Farrell. He also worried about Hollywood's influence on American literature, as he made clear to a throng gathered at a *New York Times* book fair in early November: "The course of the writer today is difficult. He must choose between success and commerce." As Hollywood's influence grew, that choice was likely to become even harder. By relying on "a very simple common denominator of fiction and emotion," Hollywood was tending "to keep popular taste on a very simple level and to establish a fixed literary pattern so that in the future books which do not conform to the pattern will be thought generally not interesting."

Farrell, appearing with Carl Sandburg and others, delivered

the only speech of the evening. To his surprise, it received "loud and prolonged applause," and a horde of autograph seekers gathered about him, pushing paper, books and programs forward for him to sign. That had never happened before.

——⇒•0•⇐——

FARRELL CONTINUED TO PAY CLOSE attention to the plight of Trotsky, now interned in Norway by a Norwegian government bent upon appeasing the Soviet Union and prevented from formally defending himself against Stalin's charges. His followers in the United States and elsewhere were working with sympathetic liberals and radicals to give him that chance, however, even as Moscow prepared for another show trial.

American Trotskyists, five hundred or so partisans led by Max Shachtman and James P. Cannon, had earlier in the year dissolved their Workers Party (which had been formed in late 1934 from the Communist League of America [Trotskyist] and A. J. Muste's American Workers Party), and entered the Socialist Party en masse. Now, with the Trotskyists' active participation, a Committee for the Defense of Leon Trotsky was formed—and Farrell became a member. He was seeing his "impassioned" Trotskyist friend George Novack "pretty regularly these days" and thought that "things have been happening to prove him right on some things, even though that is a melancholy consolation."

Farrell and Hortense, who also became a member of the committee, went to a meeting on November 11 at Novack's home. "Not much achieved," the novelist wrote in his diary. "Voted to exclude the names of Shachtman and Cannon from the list of those on the letterhead of the committee." The group, it was agreed, should not appear to be an instrument of Trotsky's partisans.

Sidney Hook, who had been active in Muste's American Workers Party but had little sympathy for the Trotskyists, was very helpful in that regard. Throwing himself wholeheartedly into the struggle in the belief that "the issues transcended the case of Trotsky and his followers," the New York University professor performed the signal service of recruiting his septuagenarian mentor, John Dewey, as well as Norman Thomas to the cause.

Farrell also sought to gather support for the effort. At a cocktail party on November 17 for the old *Masses* cartoonist Art Young, whose book Vanguard Press was publishing that day, Farrell went around asking guests if Trotsky should have the right to asylum and the right to defend himself. More than three hundred people, including many Communists, were in attendance. Farrell obtained five signatures for the committee, including one from Lewis Gannett, the *Herald Tribune* reviewer who had been disgusted by *A World I Never Made*. Farrell and Mary McCarthy, a young writer three years out of Vassar whom he and Hortense had befriended and taken to the party, later "ragged" the inebriated Gannett, telling him they thought he "was square and honest, but that he had no right to review fiction. He was a bit defensive."

The ever-combative Farrell also made it a point to confront some of the comrades at the party, including cultural commissar Trachtenberg. "I got Tracty and shook my fist under his nose, and taunted him and the other Stalinists there, [daring them] to call me a careerist, a person not to be trusted, a derelict etc. to my face. Nobody did. Hortense got scared seeing this. It was done very good naturedly, however."

In his quest for signatures at the party, Farrell received some curious rebuffs, including one from Max Lerner, an editor at the *Nation.* He was there with Martha Dodd, a gorgeous woman who had been a student with Farrell at the University of Chicago and whom the novelist had run into the day before. Her father was now the U.S. ambassador to Germany. Meeting Farrell by chance on a bus, she remembered his name, something she had seldom done in Chicago. But somebody had told her that he "was a 'Trotskyist Socialist renegade,' and she launched into a defense of the Moscow trials, the policy of the Soviet Union, and the Communist Party." (Decades later, she and her husband, Alfred Stern, were to be accused of spying for the Soviet Union and indicted by a grand jury, and would then flee to Communist Czechoslovakia.) Farrell "razzed" Max Lerner about something he had written on the Moscow trials in the *Nation,* then introduced him to George Novack "to have George sic into him. George did. Max had to squirm." But Lerner gave no reason for his refusal to join the committee.

At one point during the party, Farrell thought to approach Mary McCarthy about Trotsky's plight. She was standing near the refreshment table, rather bleakly surveying the scene, she later recalled, when her "novelist friend... dimple-faced, shaggy-headed, earnest, with a whole train of people, like a deputation, behind him," came up to her and asked if she thought Trotsky was entitled to a hearing.

"Trotsky? I glanced for help at a sour little man I had been talking with, but he merely shrugged. My friend [Farrell] made a beckoning gesture and a circle closed in. What had Trotsky done? Alas, I had to ask." In August, when the Moscow trial took place, McCarthy had been in Reno obtaining a divorce, and then in Seattle; she was hazy on the details of the case. Farrell "supplied the background, speaking very slowly, in his dragging, disconsolate voice, like a schoolteacher wearied of his subject." She could tell from his "low, even, melancholy tone that he regarded the charges as derisory."

"What do you want me to say?" McCarthy protested. "I don't know anything about it."

"Trotsky denies the charges," Farrell patiently replied. "He declares it's a GPU [Soviet secret police] fabrication. Do you think he's entitled to a hearing?"

"Why, of course," she laughed, unaware that there were people who thought he was not.

"She says Trotsky is entitled to his day in court," Farrell announced to those around them

Soon, McCarthy also agreed that Trotsky was entitled to the right of asylum.

By asking her opinion on this momentous matter, Farrell meant to pay deference to his young friend (though she, not realizing this, went home "with the serene feeling that all these people were slightly crazy"). He had not sought her signature for the defense committee; Mary McCarthy was not yet "a name." Even so, within days she found herself on the committee's letterhead, thanks to him. (In adding her name to the "very distinguished" list, Farrell long afterward explained to her, "I was complimenting you, and making a small opportunity for you.") At first she was angry and intended to withdraw her name, but after receiving strange phone calls from people she barely knew—all urging her to resign from the committee, which, they advised her, was a reactionary tool, unjustifiably meddling in the Soviet Union's internal affairs— she changed her mind. Behind the phone calls, she correctly sensed, was the Communist Party "wheeling its forces into would-be disciplined formations, like a fleet or an army maneuvering." Members of the defense committee more prominent than herself, she later learned, "got anonymous messages and threats."

When Martha Dodd told Farrell that she had been warned that he was a "Trotskyist Socialist renegade" and not to be trusted, it was only one of many such aspersions that got back to him. "The local boys will do everything that they can to discredit me, to wreck my career, to impugn my intellectual integrity. And I have to fight them."

———➤-◊-◄———

A FEW DAYS AFTER THE PARTY for Art Young, Farrell left New York by train, traveling south. He was taking a vacation and heading for Key West. Hortense remained behind.

He stopped in Washington, D.C., where he saw Jacob Baker, who had run Vanguard Press in its early years and more recently had been in charge of "Federal One," the Works Progress Administration arts projects, which included the Federal Theatre Project.

"I shall try and get the talk around to the project," Farrell wrote to Hortense on the day he was to meet Baker, "and then, I'll tell him of your difficulties." Precisely what those difficulties were is not apparent, but her frustration as an actress is clear enough. She had not been on stage in New York since 1934 (in a play that closed after only eight performances), and in July she had been reduced to appearing in an exceedingly amateurish production of Shaw's *Arms and the Man* in Massachusetts. But Baker had been dismissed in the spring from his position in charge of the arts projects and evidently was unable to help. (A few months later the actress's spirits would briefly brighten when she secured a role in Randolph Carter's *Arms for Venus*. But the comedy would close after only twelve performances.)

Moving on from Washington, Farrell proceeded to Key West, where he met Ernest Hemingway. The older novelist had been born and reared in the Chicago suburb of Oak Park. Before their marriage, Farrell and Dorothy had become acquainted with members of Hemingway's family through friends in Oak Park.

Farrell waited a few days before sending him a note; Hemingway then came right over to Farrell's rooming house.

They seemed to hit it off. Hemingway laughed at Farrell's playful parodying of *Death in the Afternoon*—"Hemingway, I'm going to write a book, titled *Death at 3 P.M. on the Diamond*. Chapter One will be 'The Heroism of Ty Cobb's Hook Slide.' Chapter Two will be...."

Hemingway told Farrell that he'd been impressed by the fight scene in *Young Lonigan;* he could tell that the author knew his stuff. Hemingway kept to himself his opinion that although the novel had some very good parts, the writing was flat and repetitious.

Farrell, similarly, had some unspoken reservations about Hemingway's work. He seeks "the most simplified sensations and feelings," and in doing that, "simplifies character," Farrell wrote to Hortense. "There is not great range.... He does not create characters who can be remembered as Babbitt is remembered. He creates moods, feelings...a certain situation, and the relationships between two people in that situation."

After Hemingway left Key West for Cuba some days later, Farrell invited his wife, Pauline, to dinner. She was busy, she said—busy that night, busy the next. She liked Farrell, though she hadn't at first, she told him, adding that no one in Key West had taken to him initially. But as she had gotten to know him better, she had grown fond of him. And everyone else had, too, she assured him.

"The explanation of it all," Farrell wrote Hortense, "is just ebullience." After he arrived at Key West and regained his freedom from the restrictions of travel, he explained, he had become "a little bit ebullient"—and something of a puzzle to those around him. He asked a lot of questions, and "I said disconcerting things. I asked them what was their department of culture, and they would look at me. And so on."

But what had initially put off Mrs. Hemingway and the others, one suspects, was not so much his exuberance per se, or even some of his puzzling remarks, as his apparent unmindfulness of them and their reactions to him. "I never pay attention to an effect on people.... Rather to what they say...or to saying something that it concerns me to say. Or else to bantering at them. It was by bantering at people here that I, also, evidently disconcerted them."

Yet such displays of rudeness did not mean that he was unsympathetic or uninterested in others. Jim Henle was to reflect on this trait decades later: "During the course of a busy lifetime, Jim hurt the feelings of a great many persons. In most—perhaps in all—of these cases the hurt was unintentional—in fact, the author himself never suspected what he had done. A mere matter of omitting commonly essential phrases which—[I knew] because I knew him so well—were at the back of his mind, whether or not he expressed them."

Even Henle, though, was startled one morning when he told Farrell that he and his wife, Marjorie, would have to call off an engagement they had with Farrell and Hortense that evening. "'Marjorie has tonsillitis,' I explained. 'That's good,' he replied, 'because there's a lecture I want to attend.'" What Farrell "genuinely intended to say," Henle believed, was:

> "I'm sorry to hear that but now I can take advantage etc." He was always so intent upon his final goal that he was likely to omit all intermediate steps. In this case it was easy to supply the omission, yet for the moment even I was shocked. I repeated: "Marjorie is ill," and he repeated: "Yes, I'm glad because.... " Yet the last accusation one could make against him was that he was callous or indifferent to the suffering of others. He was extremely sympathetic and—more than sympathetic—helpful.... It was merely the easy phrase, the graceful disclaimer, the modifying and mollifying clause that he never mastered.

His brusqueness, whether others found it excusable or not, was deceptive—as Pauline Hemingway and others at Key West evidently came to realize after they got to know him better.

Farrell had to be back in New York by December 18, when he was scheduled to speak at a mass meeting sponsored by the Trotsky defense committee. Despite Key West's appealing climate, he was ready to leave more than a week before then. It was "a dead town," he decided, with "no intellectual life...that amounts to a damn." He could not live as Hemingway did. "I couldn't find life's meaning in hunting and fishing. Ideas, impressions, awareness, that's better fishing."

He returned to New York, where he had the satisfaction of being able to read in the *New Masses* Mike Gold's sarcastic attack on him and on Sidney Hook and other "migratory intellectuals" who had rejected the true faith, and then of being able to speak, along with Norman Thomas and others, at the mass meeting. The three-hour rally at the Center Hotel on West 43rd Street was held as Trotsky himself was about to leave Norway for Mexico, where, despite Communist protests, he had been offered asylum.

A throng of two thousand was jammed inside the hotel auditorium. Introduced as one who, "being an Irishman, likes a good fight," Farrell characterized the evidence presented at the Moscow trial as "utterly worthless and fantastic" and denounced the coverage by the Communist press. Trotsky was the real "strong man"* of

---

*"Stalin" is an adopted name meaning "man of steel."

Russia, because to go about "never knowing whether you will be killed by a Stalinist or Fascist—that takes real courage!"

———≫•◦•≪———

ON THE NEXT TO LAST DAY of 1936, by court order, nearly four hundred copies of *A World I Never Made* were seized by police and removed from the offices of Vanguard Press. This was done under the direction of John S. Sumner, attorney for the New York Society for the Suppression of Vice, which had been founded sixty-three years earlier by Anthony Comstock, the legendary anti-obscenity crusader. Magistrate Anthony F. Burke had issued a warrant after Charles J. Bamberger, an agent of the society, swore that Farrell's novel contained at least seventy-five indecent passages. A preliminary hearing was scheduled for February.

By mid-January, Jim Henle, who had been absent from the Vanguard offices for a minor eye operation, was back at work and starting to mount a vigorous defense. "We will take this case to the highest court in the state, if necessary," he stated. "It seems hardly likely to me that it will be possible to suppress so simple and honest and straightforward and moving a novel as *A World I Never Made.*"

Henle and his colleagues labored hard to fight the attempted suppression. "Vanguard Press," Farrell noted, "is humming...with everyone overworked because of the case." They entreated critics, authors, editors and others for support, and scores responded with enthusiasm. Carl Van Doren, Bernard DeVoto, Joseph Wood Krutch, Mark Van Doren, Reinhold Niebuhr, Clifton Fadiman, Maxwell E. Perkins, Ernest Hemingway, Louis Untermeyer and Glenway Wescott were just some of those who rallied around Farrell, Vanguard and the literary flag.

From Baltimore, H. L. Mencken, famous for his opposition to Comstockery, offered his assistance. "[Farrell] has done a series of really brilliant novels and short stories, and it is an outrage that so honest and competent a man should be harassed by philistine ignoramuses."

A younger and more fastidious critic, with a greater appreciation for moral and intellectual complexity, agreed. Lionel Trilling, an instructor of English at Columbia University who, like Mencken, had expressed a high opinion of Farrell's work before this litigious occasion, wrote to Henle that he found the attack on *A World I*

Never Made "utterly incomprehensible on any moral grounds. It is perfectly true that Mr. Farrell describes acts and records words which polite conversation does not admit, but nothing could be more obvious than that the whole book is motivated by a moral purpose."

Despite the outpouring of support he was receiving, Farrell was worried—not simply about the outcome of the case (though it seemed unlikely that the attempted suppression would succeed, in light of previous judicial rulings), but also about a Book of the Month Club award he was being considered for. He hoped the honor would make it "just about impossible for the courts to convict *A World I Never Made*." But he feared that the writers and critics on the awards committee "will [not] have the courage to give me one of these prizes, while I am under fire from Sumner," and he grumbled in his diary about the imagined shortcomings of various jurors, including the "inconsequential writers" Pearl Buck (author of *The Good Earth*) and Hervey Allen (author of *Anthony Adverse*).

But the committee members proved him wrong. On January 29 the club announced that one of its four $2,500 Fellowship awards for outstanding works that had been neglected by readers was going to Farrell for *Studs Lonigan*. ("And so," Farrell noted, "I gladly revise my opinion of the business.")

Being under fire from Sumner seems, if anything, to have helped him in the Book of the Month Club competition. "No other American writer burns with more honesty and sincerity of purpose than Mr. Farrell," said one committee member, Ralph Thompson of the *Times*, "and it is to be hoped that that fact will be borne in mind when...his publishers appear in court to answer to Mrs. Grundy for his latest work, *A World I Never Made*."

And that fact was borne in mind in Magistrate Henry H. Curran's court—not least, of course, by Vanguard's lawyers. In a legal memorandum, they presented *A World I Never Made* as "a sociological novel," quoting at length from a review by Ernest W. Burgess, the eminent University of Chicago sociologist. Beginning with the *Studs Lonigan* trilogy, Farrell's work attracted attention from both literary critics and sociologists, Burgess said, "because of its almost unprecedented subject matter and the originality and vitality of the author's style." The value of *A World I Never Made* to "sociologists...and others who aspire to acquaintance with the way people of our different social classes actually live and think and talk can hardly be overestimated."

At the two-day hearing, nearly a hundred letters in support of Farrell and his novel, along with twenty published reviews, were submitted to the court. Farrell and Henle testified for the defense, as did, on the second day, Bernard DeVoto, Carl Van Doren and columnist Heywood Broun. Each of the critics was "superb," Henle thought, "but Jim outshone them all. He kept his temper under Sumner's heckling and patiently—in reply to the other's questions—lectured the old gentleman on the relationship between sociology and literature. It was the old man who sputtered and the youth who was tolerant and indulgent…. [It] was plain the magistrate was sorry to see Jim step down from the witness stand, so completely had Jim won him."

The author's motives and the opinions of literary critics were irrelevant, insisted Sumner, a tall, slender man with thinning gray hair and a stern, ministerial face. What mattered was the law—and the "obscene, lewd, lascivious, filthy, indecent and disgusting book" that Farrell had written.

At the end of the hearing, Magistrate Curran took *A World I Never Made* home to finish reading it himself. Then, on February 11, he delivered his decision. Farrell's novel, while it contains some "coarse words" and "coarse episodes," must be considered as a whole, the judge said. And so he concluded:

> No, I don't think the book is pornographic. I think it is photographic, and something more. Certainly this author has a passion to show us that kind of life as he lived it, and he has "given it to us good," as the expression goes. To the last inch he sketches the degradation of it, but throughout he paints at the same time the happier sides of the human nature there, the warm hearts—the warm Irish hearts—which you would find if you had lived in Chicago twenty-five years ago.

Curran dismissed the complaint against *A World I Never Made.*

But that would not be the final major attempt to censor Farrell's works. Eleven years later, police in Philadelphia—acting on the complaint of a Baptist minister and in accordance with an unusual Pennsylvania law—raided the city's bookstores and gathered an "obscene" harvest of some two thousand volumes, including copies of *Studs Lonigan* and *A World I Never Made.* Farrell and Vanguard filed suit in federal court, as did other authors and publishers. Protestant and Catholic clergymen testified against the "filthy" books. Farrell defended his work in court, before an overflow crowd. The judge granted a restraining injunction against further seizures. But the last word in the whole affair belonged to a different jurist, Judge Curtis Bok, who presided over a criminal case brought against five Philadelphia booksellers accused of possessing Farrell's works and other offensive volumes with intent to sell them. The novels were not obscene, the judge ruled; rather they were "obvious efforts to show life as it is." In a fifty-three-page opinion that came nearly a year after the police raids, Judge Bok declared that censorship should be left to the community, not the law.

FARRELL WANTED VERY MUCH to be a member of the Commission of Inquiry that was to question Trotsky in Mexico. It was, he thought, as if Oliver Cromwell or Robespierre were to be interrogated—neither of whom "had the intellectual breadth that Trotsky has." Having co-founded the Soviet regime with Lenin and created the Red Army, Trotsky was both a man of (revolutionary) action and an intellectual. As such, he fascinated Farrell.

Early in January 1937, the novelist had reviewed *Behind the Moscow Trial* by Trotsky's intellectual American follower Max Shachtman (whose last name Farrell, with characteristic casualness about such details, repeatedly misspelled). The son of an émigré Jewish tailor from Warsaw, Shachtman grew up in New York, dropped out of City College in 1921, became a Communist organizer in Chicago two years later, and was expelled from the party as a Trotskyist (along with James P. Cannon) in 1928; the following year, he and other Trotskyists formed the Communist League of America. Shachtman met Trotsky for the first time in 1930 in Turkey, and later became his trusted "commissar for foreign affairs," arranging most recently his trip from Norway to Mexico. Now the Trotskyist thinker threw himself into exposing the Moscow trial. "His pamphlet," Farrell wrote in the *Socialist Call*, "is a brilliant work of analysis, which leaves the official version of the case without even one shred of credibility. He has conclusively demonstrated the utter valuelessness of the testimony." The second Moscow show trial (of Radek and sixteen others, accused of having formed a backup "Anti-Soviet Trotskyite Center") later that month did not cause Farrell to alter his appraisal.

The American Communists disagreed with him, of course. In February, before a throng of fifteen thousand in Madison Square Garden, Earl Browder praised the Soviet Union for "exterminating the agents of fascism and war lurking within its own borders," and denounced Trotsky as an "egomaniac firebrand" and "the advance agent of fascism and war throughout the world."

"The bitterness involved as a consequence of the Moscow trials is going to run very deeply," Farrell wrote in his diary. "There is now a line of blood drawn between the supporters of Stalin, and those of Trotsky, and that line of blood appears like an impassable river."

Much was potentially at stake for the Communists in how the world came to view the Moscow trials, and they made strenuous efforts to disrupt the Trotsky defense committee and its work. Some committee members, such as Mauritz A. Hallgren, an editor at the *Baltimore Sun,* decided their best course was to resign. After "deep and earnest thought," Hallgren explained, he had concluded "that there is a preponderance of evidence tending to prove that the defendants in Moscow were fairly tried and that their guilt in conspiring to overthrow the Soviet government has been established. I believe, too, that the same evidence shows that Trotsky participated in the conspiracy, or at least had knowledge of it.... Furthermore, I am now convinced that, whatever its subjective justification might be, the objective purpose of the American Committee for the Defense of Leon Trotsky is to aid the Trotskyists, perhaps unwittingly, in their efforts to destroy the present Soviet government." Even before the committee received his long letter of resignation, Hallgren had dispatched copies to the *Daily Worker* and the *New Masses.*

At a mass meeting on February 9 in New York—which the defense committee had arranged for Trotsky to address via a special telephone hookup—the Russian exile (as Sidney Hook was later to write) "slashed to pieces the main points of testimony bearing on his alleged meetings with the Moscow defendants, explained the mechanisms of terror that evoked the self-besmirching confessions, riddled the rationalizations of the Kremlin apologists into absurdity, offered a thumbnail sketch of the causes of 'the revolution betrayed,' and most significant of all, offered to appear before a public and impartial Commission of Inquiry to confront the charges made against him." The 6,500 people in attendance did not hear Trotsky's own voice as he accomplished all that, however, for—in an apparent act of sabotage—the telephone wire was cut somewhere south of Monterey. So Max Shachtman, who possessed a copy of the prepared text, read the outcast's eloquent words to the assembly. "Why does Moscow so fear the voice of a single man?" Trotsky asked.

> Only because I know the truth, the whole truth. Only because I have nothing to hide. Only because I am ready to appear before a public and impartial commission of inquiry with documents, facts and testimonies in my hands, and to disclose the truth to the very end. I declare: if this commission decides that I am guilty in the slightest degree of the crimes which Stalin imputes to me, I pledge in advance to place myself voluntarily in the hands of the executioners of the GPU. Do the accusers of the Kremlin hear me? I throw my defiance in their faces. And I await their reply!

One week later, John Dewey and Horace Kallen, of the New School for Social Research, issued a statement signed by Farrell and other members of the defense committee about all the phone calls, letters and visits that some of them had received, urging them to resign. In the seventy-seven-year-old Dewey's case, these efforts, along with a honeyed official invitation to go on a grand tour of the Soviet Union to see how much progress had been achieved since he had last been there, only stiffened his resolve to remain on the committee and—despite his family's strong misgivings—to go with the Commission of Inquiry to Mexico. "We have no concern whatsoever with Leon Trotsky's political views," he and the others asserted in their statement. Nor were they interested "in prejudging the question of the truth or falsity of the charges made against him. Our sole concern is to secure for him those plain human rights before the court of public opinion and under the law of the land to which, according to immemorial liberal tradition, all people in similar circumstances are entitled."

Four score and eight literary and intellectual worthies were not persuaded. In "An Open Letter to American Liberals," Corliss Lamont, a wealthy "author and lecturer" (and tireless Soviet apologist), and eighty-seven others—including Heywood Broun, Malcolm Cowley, Theodore Dreiser, playwright Lillian Hellman, Granville Hicks, journalist (and screenwriter-to-be) Ring Lardner Jr., Max Lerner, Robert Morss Lovett, *Middletown* author Robert S. Lynd, poet Dorothy Parker, novelist Henry Roth, novelist Tess Slesinger, social worker Lillian D. Wald, Clara (*Marching! Marching!*) Weatherwax and Nathanael West—urged liberals, especially those on the

Trotsky defense committee, to reconsider their position. After all, they argued, Trotsky has found asylum in Mexico, and the Mexican government and the American press have let him speak in his own defense. Why go any further? "The demand for an investigation of trials carried on under the legally constituted judicial system of the Soviet government can only be interpreted as political intervention in the internal affairs of the Soviet Union with hostile intent."

Although Trotsky opposed "individual terrorism," he did approve of "revolutionary terror." That he and his alleged accomplices had conspired to depose or even assassinate Stalin and his associates was not (the inconvenient facts of the matter aside) intrinsically implausible. Either way, the implications were momentous. Yet these writers and intellectuals were loath to pursue the truth, lest it prove embarrassing to the exalted Soviet Union.

Farrell, in contrast, sought the truth no matter whom it might embarrass. "The condition of the world, intellectually, gets more and more disheartening," he reflected. "Fewer and fewer people seem to strive to retain any objectivity of judgment." For a while in February, he and others feared that the defense committee might not survive the Stalinist assault. "The confusion, the refusal to think, the ignorance, and, in many cases, the yellowness of the American intellectual [are] now coming out," Farrell wrote in his diary. "If they succeed in breaking up this committee, the Stalinists will have new life, and they can terrorize us on any issue." He was appalled by their underhanded methods, which included bribes and threats. His fellow Vanguard author Ferdinand Lundberg was openly warned that the sales of his latest book would suffer if he took the wrong stand. "It is utterly revolting and disgusting."

But the Stalinists did not succeed in breaking up the committee, or in preventing a Commission of Inquiry, headed by John Dewey, from being formed. Farrell, however, was not chosen to be on it. The commission was supposed to be impartial, but Farrell had already concluded that Trotsky was framed and had said so in public. As a result, two other members of the defense committee's executive committee, journalists Suzanne La Follette and Ben Stolberg, vetoed his selection. (Ironically, La Follette herself seemed to Farrell to be "falling heavily for the Trotskyists.")

The subcommission (of the larger body) that was to interrogate Trotsky, then, ended up consisting of Dewey, La Follette, Stolberg, Otto Ruehle (a prominent German Socialist in exile from Nazi Germany) and Carleton Beals (an author of books on Latin

America and a friend of Stolberg's). Though not a commissioner, Farrell decided to go along as an observer. "I am just as pleased," he said. "I should be more free in Mexico if I were not on the commission, and I should be able to attend the meetings and hear everything just as well."

In early April, even as Malcolm Cowley was whitewashing the second Moscow show trial in the pages of the *New Republic,* Farrell joined Dewey, Stolberg and La Follette, along with George Novack and a commission secretary, Pearl Kluger (who was, like Novack, a Trotskyist), and boarded a train for Mexico, by way of St. Louis. When Dewey—perhaps conscious of Farrell's already impressive output of published works—had first met the novelist at a defense committee session in March, he said to him, "I thought that you were an older man." To the thirty-three-year-old Farrell (who himself was noticeably older than he had been a half-dozen years before, his face a bit fuller, his body a bit thicker about the waist), the philosopher had seemed old and tired at the meeting. Yet now, on the train, a much more vigorous figure appeared.

"He amazed everyone by the amount of work he was able to do," Farrell recalled some years later. "On the train he finished reading the official versions of the first two trials, and read from the writings of Trotsky. He spent many hours alone, reading in his small compartment." When he emerged, though, he was quite sociable.

> At mealtimes he would listen and talk, and he would sit with us now and then, smoking a cigarette and drinking a glass of beer. Whenever anyone spoke, he would listen very attentively, sometimes leaning forward a little in order to hear better…. His powers of attention, his dry wit, and his extraordinary keenness of mind were revealed with such modesty and simplicity that they came as a shock. I talked to him about American liberals, American philosophers, and education. His estimations of men were just, but not without sharpness. And as one talked to him, the years seemed to be stripped away. One lost some sense of the fact that this kindly old man was John Dewey. He was another human being, a member of this temporary group.

Dewey liked Farrell, and they became friends. But while Farrell admired the philosopher and what he was doing now, considering him "a great man," it was the defiant Trotsky who had already captured his imagination.

The exiled revolutionary was staying with his wife in painter Diego Rivera's villa on Avenida Londres in Coyoacán, which was then a suburb of Mexico City. It was there that the subcommission's hearings were to be conducted. Some of Trotsky's followers and sympathizers from New York, including journalists Herbert Solow and John McDonald, were helping him prepare for them. Farrell visited the house on the night before the hearings began and was pressed into service carrying adobe bricks for the brick-and-sandbag barricades that were being erected in the study (and hearing room) in front of three French windows that faced the street. "In and out of the room Mexicans and Americans paraded, carrying bricks for the rising barricades," Farrell remembered long afterward. He himself quit after a while because "it was affecting my sinuses," but the labors went on late into the night. Now and then, Trotsky appeared, with his trademark goatee. He watched the progress for a few moments, then went back to his work, and finally to bed.

Farrell returned to Mexico City. He was staying in an apartment there with George Novack, Pearl Kluger and Albert Glotzer, a Trotskyist court reporter who was recording the commission proceedings. Glotzer and Farrell, both baseball enthusiasts from Chicago, had quickly struck up a friendship. One night, quite possibly that one, Glotzer recalled, "Jim got the chills. I don't know what caused it. It was a very warm night in Mexico City. But I tended him, [using] blankets, overcoats, everything I could find, until he broke the chill."

The next morning, April 10, a Saturday, the hearings commenced, with a police guard outside the villa. That day and for the next seven, Trotsky held forth, speaking in English. It was a bravura performance. With eloquence, devastating logic and biting wit (as well as considerable documentation), the brilliant revolutionary demolished the Stalinist case against him. *"Either Lenin's Political Bureau was composed of traitors, or Stalin's Political Bureau is composed of falsifiers,"* he declared on the final day of the hearings. "There is no third possibility!"*

Farrell was bowled over by Trotsky's performance. He had "an

---

*One commission member, Carleton Beals, was not present to hear Trotsky say that. Ill at ease with the proceedings from the start, Beals had appeared oddly hostile to Trotsky, asking questions that seemed calculated more to embarrass him than to evoke pertinent testimony. Before the hearings resumed on the final day, Beals resigned, claiming that the commission's investigation was not "truly serious." Beals reportedly had been having financial problems, and Farrell was told that a Stalinist named Harry Block had "got to" him. In any event, his resignation—despite the best efforts of the Stalinists to use it against the commission—had little lasting impact.

extremely fertile and quick mind, throwing off ideas right and left, constantly and continually, shifting from subject to subject, analyzing the most minute details, then shifting to Marxian theory, questions of political strategy, [and] political estimations of men he worked with." The revolutionary's "utterly impersonal" approach also impressed Farrell. "He makes political estimates of men, not personal ones"—even in the case of his archenemy. "He emphasizes again and again—it is not Stalin. It is a system, an apparatus, a historical development, a period of reaction. He says, Stalin, too...once was a good revolutionary." The Soviet Union, in Trotsky's eyes, appeared in a similarly abstract light. Despite the "Stalinist bureaucracy," he argued during the hearings, the Soviet Union remained a workers' state—"a degenerated workers' state." That being so, he insisted, it was "the absolute duty of every revolutionist to defend the U.S.S.R. against imperialism, despite the Stalinist bureaucracy."

Trotsky, Farrell would write long afterward, "was a man of genius, of will, and of ideas.... His Marxian faith was a faith in ideas. We can properly say that Trotsky was a great man." (Even at that late date, when Farrell had come fully to grasp that Trotsky's genius and will and ideas had helped bring into being one of the worst tyrannies in human history, he still appears to have regarded Trotsky's nobility of purpose as unsullied.)

Farrell realized, albeit reluctantly, that his friend George Novack was a fanatic, and he was quite contemptuous of many of Trotsky's avowed followers. (Part of his reason for joining the defense committee, he told his diary, had been "to...protect Trotsky from the Trotskyists," who "are so religious in their adoration of Trotsky that it can be cut with a knife.") Yet the fanaticism and ruthlessness of Trotsky himself somehow escaped his notice.*

With the hearings finished, Farrell, joined now by Hortense,

---

*Trotsky had brutally suppressed the rebellion of sailors at the Kronstadt naval base in 1921—sailors who were passionate for revolution and democracy. "During the period when Trotsky held power," Robert Conquest has written, "he was, whatever his personal magnetism, a ruthless imposer of the party's will who firmly crushed the democratic opposition within the party and fully supported the rules which in 1921 gave the ruling group total authority." In exile, Trotsky in 1931 had endorsed the prosecution's trumped-up case in the Moscow trial of Menshevik leaders—which was just as transparently a frame-up as the more recent trials with Trotsky among the accused. (His endorsement in that trial had been "a great error," he told the Dewey commission.) For the Soviet regime's millions of non-Communist victims, Trotsky had shown little solicitude.

remained in Mexico a month longer to see the sights and get a better sense of the country. While thus engaged, he received in the mail one day a clipping from Jim Henle, a *New York Times* dispatch from Moscow. In a recently published article there, the *Times* reported, Farrell, Hook and certain other American writers were denounced as "Trotskyist robbers of the pen."

The Stalinists will stop at nothing, Farrell reflected. "There is no retreating from them. There is only a fight, because they are one of the forces [that] threaten to poison intellectual life in America."

Later that year, in the *Daily Worker*, cultural commissar V. J. Jerome would attack Farrell and other "scribblers and unskilled intellectuals in the literary field, who have sneaked back to the bourgeoisie through the gateway of Trotskyism"; condemn "the too common notion...that the literary battle is a thing apart from the political struggle"; and call for "the complete routing and annihilation of Trotskyism," be it "'literary' or otherwise."

In the Soviet Union, the Stalinists were doing much more than that. The Great Terror that had begun with Kirov's assassination in 1934 was reaching full force. In June, it was to be publicly announced that Marshal Mikhail Tukhachevsky, the deputy people's commissar for defense, and seven other high-ranking Red Army officers had been convicted of treason at a secret trial and then executed. But the Terror was not confined to officialdom. "Though the liquidation of card-holding Communists gave the Great Terror of 1937–38 its special character," historian Ronald Hingley has written, they did not constitute the majority of its victims.

> Far from it, for the onslaught fell on virtually all sections of the community: religious believers and atheists, Slavs and non-Slavs, illiterates and university professors, Stalin-lovers and Stalin-haters. It struck Moscow, Leningrad, the [Russian Soviet Federative Socialist Republic] as a whole, the Ukraine and Belorussia, as well as Caucasia and Central Asia, ranging from Minsk to Vladivostok, from the Arctic to the deserts. The very concentration camp commandants were kidnapped by Stalin's execution squads. No one could feel safe.

Much of this was hidden from Western view at the time, of course. But the show trials were not. (The third one—of "rightist" Nikolai Bukharin, former NKVD chief Genrikh Yagoda and others— was to take place in March 1938.) Yet many on the Left, including the liberal editors of the *New Republic* and of the *Nation*, refused to open their minds to the evidence of what was happening.

This was not true of John Dewey, the archetypal American liberal. Near the end of 1937, in an extensive interview with the *Washington Post* after his Commission of Inquiry had pronounced Trotsky not guilty, Dewey declared that "the great lesson" to be drawn from the inquiry and from the Moscow trials was "the complete breakdown of revolutionary Marxianism. Nor do I think that a confirmed Communist is going to get anywhere by concluding that because he can no longer believe in Stalin, he must now pin his faith on Trotsky." American radicals, said Dewey, needed to reconsider the whole question of using violence, rather than democratic methods, to achieve social progress. "The dictatorship of the proletariat has led and, I am convinced, always must lead to a dictatorship over the proletariat and over the party. I see no reason to believe that something similar would not happen in every country in which an attempt is made to establish a Communist government."

Farrell, too, was now firmly opposed to the Stalinists, though not yet ready to renounce Marxist revolution. He was sympathetic to Trotsky, but was not "pinning his faith" on him or enlisting in his army or embracing his theories. Indeed, that summer, as the American Trotskyists, under pressure from Trotsky, were about to leave the Socialist Party and there was talk that they might be expelled (which is what eventually happened), Farrell would find that he could make "neither head nor tail" of the two sides' conflicting stories. "This factionalism and sectarianism gets me. I want to keep away from it. I'm not a politician. And I want to rethink all of Marxism, revolution and everything else."

During his stay in Mexico, Farrell spoke several times with Trotsky. At their final meeting, the exiled revolutionary hero, ever intent upon his grand cause, asked Farrell what he intended to do when he returned to America.

"I'm going to write novels," Farrell told him.

Chapter Twelve

"Amidst a Kind of Ruin"

RETURNING FROM MEXICO on May 27, 1937, Farrell met that evening with Philip Rahv, William Phillips, Mary McCarthy, and several others seeking to develop "an opposition" at the second American Writers' Congress, which was to begin eight days later. "Rahv and Phillips want it non-political," he wrote in his diary, "and they plan merely to call for a proposal on a Marxist position in literature. Which is a little bit funny. The whole bunch were vague, and they did not know precisely what they wanted to do and to be, except that they wanted to be an opposition." Farrell had expressed his own opposition in the form of an article to appear in the June *Saturday Review*, pointing out the meager output of the younger proletarian writers since the 1935 congress heralding the dawn of a new age of revolutionary literature.

At that earlier conclave, the call to hasten the destruction of capitalism, as well as to defend the Soviet Union against capitalist aggression, had been quite straightforward. When one speaker suggested that for purposes of propaganda, the phrase "the people" might be more effective than "the worker," he was immediately subjected to a barrage of objections. But at the congress two years later, during the Popular Front era, that same substitution was virtually obligatory. Capitalism, assumed to be rapidly crumbling in 1935, was now scarcely mentioned. Revolutionary writing was also neglected, as Rahv observed in print some months later.

> If the first Call summoned writers to the struggle against *imperialist* war and fascism, the second contented itself with a timorous meliorism designed not to offend well-paid scenario writers and ancient contributors to *The Saturday Evening Post*. In the past, nothing short of the sovietization of 'the literature of the whole world' would do; today, the gates of the dialectic have been thrown wide open to any successful money writer.

Sponsored by the Communist-controlled League of American Writers, the 1937 congress began on the night of Friday, June 4, with a public meeting in Carnegie Hall. Among the speakers was Ernest Hemingway, recently returned from Spain. On Saturday and Sunday, closed sessions confined to the 353 writer-delegates—mostly Communists and Communist sympathizers—were held at the New School for Social Research. The "opposition" was a tiny band indeed, all of five in number. Rahv and Phillips had been persuaded by the impetuous McCarthy and a former *Fortune* magazine writer named Dwight Macdonald to join them and another writer, Eleanor Clark, in protest. They showed up Sunday morning at a "craft commission on criticism," presided over by Granville Hicks.

"Mary and Eleanor and Dwight got up to speak against the narrow interpretations of literature and politics and the factional control of the organization," Phillips recalled. "Though immeasurably more talented and intelligent, they were no match for the infighting skills of their opponents who were old hands at this kind of polemic.... Rahv and I, who were more familiar with the jargon and pseudo-arguments of the Communists, tried at the end to bail out our fellow dissidents, but our heart was not in it and we could not make much headway against a stacked meeting."

Farrell had intended to go to the public session on the conclave's first day, but found when he arrived that the tickets were sold out. On the basis of what he heard later from Rahv, Phillips and the others, he concluded that he hadn't missed much: "All in all, the congress seems to have been dead and deadly." Intellectually and morally, this harsh judgment was doubtless on target. Politically, though, the congress proved an immense success. Membership in the reorganized League of American Writers— headed now not by Waldo Frank (who had dared to dissent on the Moscow trials) but by a Hollywood writer and secret Communist named Donald Ogden Stewart—swelled during the next two years to about eight hundred.

Among the literati, Farrell and his anti-Stalinist friends were definitely in the minority. Though the pugnacious novelist was heedless of the consequences that opposition might have for his literary career, Rahv and Phillips were more circumspect—and with good reason. The Communist Party, Rahv would note in print the next year, had been quite successful in its "cunning and unscrupulous strategy...to manipulate the loyalties of hundreds of influential people in the arts, in journalism, and in the universities."

"It is not the open Stalinists, of course, who are most dangerous," Rahv pointed out, "but rather their 'liberal' allies and
apologists." The seemingly reasonable arguments of the latter did
what "the hysterical and monotonous lying of a Mike Gold" could
not: effectively keep the truth hidden from the many thousands of
people who were not party members and were in no position to
get at the facts themselves. "During the last few years," Rahv
observed, "the Stalinists and their friends, under multi-form dis-
guises, have managed to penetrate into the offices of publishing
houses, the editorial staffs of magazines, and the book-review sections of conservative newspapers." The result was "a kind of
unofficial censorship....This G.P.U. of the mind is attempting—
through intrigue, calumny, and overt as well as covert pressure—to
direct cultural opinion in America into totalitarian channels."

Rahv and Phillips were very conscious of this powerful force
as they sought to revive their defunct magazine. Early in 1937 they
had wavered back and forth about the Communist Party (to which
Rahv still belonged). Since they regarded Farrell as sympathetic and
politically astute, they often consulted him. Always, Phillips
recalled, he was "exuberant, boyish, witty, energetic, lively, interested in everything, very political." In January they discussed with
him the possibility of bringing out *Partisan Review* under the auspices of the Socialist Party; but after a meeting had been arranged
with Norman Thomas, the two editors, to Farrell's annoyance,
backed out. "The cat came out of the bag," he wrote in his diary,
when Phillips "asked me would I write for *Partisan Review* if it
continued without breaking with the Stalinist movement." But by
late March, this possibility had apparently been foreclosed. Rahv
and Phillips told Farrell "that they're fairly rapidly being read out of
the movement."

Shortly before, Phillips had met Fred Dupee, who had become
the literary editor of the *New Masses*. (After the congress in June,
Dupee was expelled from the party for associating with the oppo-
sitionists, and then fired from the *New Masses*.) Through him,
Phillips and Rahv met Dwight Macdonald, a Yale classmate of
Dupee's who was leaving *Fortune* and moving left. Dupee and Macdonald had a wealthy friend, an abstract painter named George L.
K. Morris, who proved to be the "angel" Rahv and Phillips had been
searching for.

Phillips and Rahv told Farrell about this after he got back

from Mexico. But in the ensuing weeks and months, as the two editors worked with Macdonald, Dupee, Morris, and Mary McCarthy (with whom Rahv was now romantically involved), and on the new *Partisan Review,* Farrell was conscious of being left out. He gave them sections of his forthcoming novel, and they chose a selection for the first issue. But they didn't ask him to write anything specifically for the magazine. "Not that I care," he told his diary, noting that their pay of two dollars a page was not munificent. "The reason they haven't asked me is, I believe—they are striving to make up their minds, and haven't succeeded. I might be too dangerous. They won't print Eastman, they said, [for] strategic reasons."

Max Eastman—the handsome poet-philosopher, champion of love and revolution, erstwhile editor of the *Masses* and the *Liberator,* apologist for Lenin, translator of Trotsky—had spoken at the Trotsky defense committee's mass meeting in December, along with Farrell, Norman Thomas and Max Shachtman. The *Socialist Call,* the Socialist Party's official organ, did not report his remarks in its news columns but instead chastised him in an editorial for letting "the repressive features of the Soviet state" become so magnified in his mind that he identified the Soviet Union with its bureaucracy and failed to see the regime's "basically working class nature." Eastman's position was almost as displeasing to the Socialists and Trotskyists as it was to the Stalinists.

Though Farrell had not alienated the Socialists or Trotskyists in that way, he may well have thought that his high profile in the Trotsky defense effort limited his utility in the eyes of the perpetually maneuvering Rahv and Phillips. Yet soon the two editors were as much "Trotskyite" renegades in the Stalinists' eyes as Farrell himself was. Rahv was expelled from the party, as was Phillips's wife (who declined to leave her husband, which was the condition for her remaining a party member).

But Rahv and Phillips and their new *Partisan Review* colleagues still did not encourage Farrell to write for them. More than politics was behind this, as Farrell himself came to suspect. (He also became convinced that Mary McCarthy, whom he considered "a bright and clever girl" but no "intellectual giant," had "something to do with it.") Much as the editors respected Farrell's political acumen and his accomplishment in *Studs Lonigan,* and much as Rahv and Phillips (and McCarthy) may have liked him, they were not enthusiastic about his writing. The season for "proletarian literature" had passed, and Farrell's literary naturalism was not really to their taste. They were drawn to the modernist works of T. S. Eliot, Franz Kafka, Thomas Mann and the like. "We were interested in the modernist thinking, and [Farrell] wasn't," Phillips recalled in 1994. "He really wasn't. There was something old-fashioned about his thinking."

He also was not a stylist, a failing that was not fatal in his powerful long fiction but grievously weighed down his nonfiction essays and reviews, as well as his short stories. For all of his indefatigable labors, he just could not seem to polish his prose. Farrell wrote in the same way that he talked, with the words pouring out of him like water, Phillips remembered. But the writing "wasn't polished enough, it wasn't careful enough."

McCarthy, writing in *Partisan Review* after World War II, would group Farrell with Theodore Dreiser and Eugene O'Neill as authors "whose choice of vocation was a kind of triumphant catastrophe; none of these men possessed the slightest ear for the word, the sentence, the speech, the paragraph; all of them, however, have, so to speak, enforced the career they decreed for themselves by a relentless policing of their beat."

But McCarthy (who, despite her severe view of his writing, would prove a friend) failed to appreciate the extent of Farrell's literary achievement, or the role that his imagination, not just his phenomenal memory, had played in it. "How is one to judge the great, logical symphony of a tone-deaf musician?" she asked of his work in her *Partisan Review* essay. The correct answer, surely, is: as one would judge any other symphony. Yet McCarthy, like the erstwhile Exeter and Yale aesthete Dwight Macdonald, was a stylist, so naturally enough, like Macdonald, she vastly overestimated the importance of style. It isn't everything, as McCarthy's own stillborn fiction demonstrates.

Farrell's gracelessness, his carelessness with words, not only helped to isolate him on the fringe of the *Partisan Review* crowd but also left him vulnerable to his enemies. And now that he had broken politically with the Communists, he had quite a few. Among the most influential was the *New Republic*'s Malcolm Cowley.

"Lillian Lugubriously Sighed" was the headline over a *New Republic* review in November of *The Short Stories of James T. Farrell*, a collection published two months earlier. The review, the lead one in the magazine, was by Otis Ferguson, an ex-sailor from Massachusetts who was wild about movies and jazz but not about

Farrell's published work. From what he deemed a crowded field of possibilities, Ferguson selected "'Oh!' Lillian lugubriously sighed" as his prize example of the author's "tone deafness." Ferguson had reviewed a book of his once before, but the review had not been published. Cowley (as he had told Farrell) considered the review "vicious" and hadn't let it appear. Now, however, things were different, and Cowley loosed the caustic Ferguson on the renegade.

Farrell is "a kindly and generous person in normal life," acknowledged Ferguson (whom Farrell had once helped). But

> when he becomes Farrell-the-writer he is equipped with the most complete stock of hatreds I have ever seen—everyone from the characters in his book to his fellow novelists and reviewers; add to this a certain unhumorous pompousness in throwing his intellectual weight around, and you can see how there must be quite an underground anti-Farrell school by now. And this round-up of all his short stories might very well serve as its textbook, for he is not a story teller and the short form highlights the faults without having much scope for the virtues.

Ferguson was not the first to notice Farrell's "hatred" for many of his characters. Some months before, in a review of his *Can All This Grandeur Perish? and Other Stories,* Alfred Kazin, a young, passionate critic who once had been excited just to meet Farrell, adverted to "the strident stories in which he baits the middle-class Irish whom he hates with so much relish." Kazin—who lauded Farrell for being so "superbly honest" an historian of "his own people"—had not been quite so blunt about his "hatred" a year and a half earlier, when reviewing *A World I Never Made.* Then, he had noted only that Farrell "cannot resist being furious here," that "a personal grievance...as well as a social one" holds the novel together.

Farrell himself, of course, didn't think he hated any of his characters; he thought he hated the environment that had made them as they were. When he was a Communist sympathizer, reviewers had taken that rationalization for granted; now that he was a renegade, his assumed personal grievances came under sharper scrutiny.

To a certain extent, Farrell's critics had truth on their side. Although he did not hate his characters, he did have contempt for many of them. And whereas in *A World I Never Made* the contempt is mixed with pity, in too many of his short stories it is undiluted—and quite off-putting.

This is not true of all of his stories, however. "Seventeen," for instance, a novelette-length story about youthful love and pregnancy, has compassion along with astringency. Reviewer Fred T. Marsh, perceptive as always about Farrell's work, thought that "Seventeen," though "a little awkward," showed (as *A World I Never Made* had) where his true talent lay. "Here genuine sentiment, rooted deeply in youthful emotional life, ennobling and beautifying the tawdriness which surrounds it, for a time captures the tale. Farrell is a little afraid of it. But he knows it is there. Here, rather than in the field of social conscience, it seems to me, lies Farrell's main future as a novelist."

But the Stalinists wanted to deny Farrell any future as a novelist, just as they wanted to stamp out the new, independent *Partisan Review.* ("No Quarter to Trotzkyists—Literary or Otherwise" was the headline above one of several *Daily Worker* attacks on the magazine, as the *Partisan Review* editors noted in their first issue, dated December 1937. "That we do not consider ourselves 'Trotskyists' and that *Partisan Review* has been founded precisely to fight the tendency to confuse literature and party politics—these facts Comrade Jerome chooses to ignore.")

Fellow Chicago novelist Nelson Algren, who was on the side of the Stalinists, gladly penned a harsh review of Farrell's collected short stories for a publication called the *Beacon.* He had a grudge against the renegade. In 1934, Jim Henle had asked Farrell's opinion of Algren's first novel, which Henle had commissioned and just received in manuscript. Farrell reported back that the work was in "very bad shape," with "all kinds of bad writing," but that it nevertheless had some "damn good things in it." He gave Henle a detailed, sixteen-page critique, full of corrections and suggested changes. Farrell no doubt thought his honest appraisal would help not only Henle but the author.

Algren didn't like it, however. He acceded to Henle's demands for various changes in order to get his novel published, but he was furious at Farrell—just how furious, Farrell evidently did not realize at the time. The following spring, in his speech at the American Writers' Congress, Farrell lauded an Algren short story ("So Help Me") as a penetrating assessment of "the cost of capitalistic society." But such praise was hardly enough to lift the spirits of Algren, who was dismayed by what he took to be the failure of his novel, *Somebody in Boots.* He was so depressed, in fact, that Dick Wright and his other friends from Chicago who were with him feared he might commit suicide. Wright and others appealed to Farrell for aid—and Farrell came through, arranging with Mrs. Ames for Algren to stay at Yaddo for ten days, and getting Vanguard to pay for his meals. But Algren seemed "almost insane" to Farrell. On the day he was to leave New York for Saratoga Springs, Farrell kept him busy for hours, walking around with him and continually talking to him, until the train finally departed. At Yaddo, Dorothy showed Algren to his room and tried to make him feel at home, but even as she did this, he told her he didn't belong there—and by the next morning, he had fled. More than two years later, reading Algren's attack in the *Beacon,* Farrell reflected: "Algren sure wants to get me.... Largely because I once helped Nelson when he was going out of his mind, and his friends and comrades came to me, and I made the mistake of trying to help him. For which, he will never forgive me."

Algren's mentor, proletarian novelist Jack Conroy, also had no fondness for Farrell, ever since he had laced into *The Disinherited.* After Otis Ferguson's caustic review of Farrell's work appeared, Conroy piled on with a letter to the *New Republic,* in which he tried to slay him with a derisive nickname—"James 'Tuffy' Farrell." Ferguson's review, Conroy said, "was much too mild, but compared to the usual one, which proceeds from the assumption that Tuffy is a combination of Balzac, Zola, Dostoevsky, Hardy, et al., it is remarkable."

Soon, Malcolm Cowley and his *New Republic* colleagues went further, running a letter denouncing "that pretentious windbag, James Farrell...a palpable fraud whose literary talents are so slender, whose faults are so many and obvious. Farrell's characters, far from being hard-boiled in any realistic sense, remind us (to borrow a phrase from N. West's admirable *Miss Lonelyhearts*) of 'a little girl making a muscle.' ... Added to his almost completely unrealistic approach are his heinous faults of grammar, construction and logic. Up Ferguson! Raus mit Farrell!" The letter, which appeared over the names of twenty-five people from East St. Louis, Illinois, was actually the work of Conroy and a friend. As Conroy long afterward related, they had gotten patrons of an East St. Louis bar, some of them illiterate or drunk, to sign the document. That Cowley and his fellow editors chose to publish it suggests how eager they were, as "liberal" allies of the Stalinists, to see Farrell's reputation tarnished.

Dwight Macdonald (whom Farrell had come to regard as a literary snob and a "genuine crackpot") wrote to the *New Republic* in protest of "the literary lynching.... James T. Farrell has his faults as a novelist, but surely that does not justify such a childish and malicious outburst as this." Fred Dupee also protested. And in the March 1938 issue of *Partisan Review,* the editors objected to the "personal and scurrilous attack" on Farrell. "Regardless of the merit of Mr. Farrell's work—and we do not agree with the East St. Louis camarilla—we deplore the publication of such a letter."

Farrell, of course, noticed the incidental qualifications in these defenses of his reputation. When the independent *Partisan Review*'s first issue had appeared (with, among other offerings, "Mrs. O'Flaherty and Lizz," a selection from his next novel, *No Star Is Lost*), he had hailed the reborn magazine and its potential "[to] have a genuine influence in American letters and in American thought about literature." But now he was disappointed by the editors' "weak" response to the attack on him. On the same page with their defense, he noticed, they had printed this comment on their inaugural issue from his "jealous" former friend Nathan Asch: "Except for the Farrell piece, I think the first issue is swell."

<hr />

SOON AFTER HE FINISHED GOING over the proofs of *No Star Is Lost*, Farrell left in May 1938 for Europe and a vacation. As he made the "slow and dull" voyage across the ocean on the SS *President Harding*, he had "[the] sense of being isolated from the world. And at the end of that isolation, a sick Europe [awaited]. A very sick Europe." From it, he believed, America should keep her distance. The United States was in no danger of attack from foreign soil, Farrell was sure, and involvement in "another War to Make the World Safe for Democracy" would mean "the establishment of virtual fascism" at home.

He arrived in London just before the weekend of what many would remember as the "May crisis," when it seemed that Europe was closer to war than it had been since the summer of 1914. London and Prague believed that Hitler was about to attack Czechoslovakia, and the Czechs began to mobilize. (The rumors of imminent aggression proved false, however. In the months thereafter, British prime minister Neville Chamberlain was to do his utmost to try to appease Hitler, working hard to make sure that Prague yielded to the dictator's demands and that the French abandoned their Czechoslovak ally.) Though Londoners were outwardly calm that weekend, Farrell sensed the tension and fear beneath the surface.

Meanwhile he was quickly swept up in a publicity tour that

his English publisher had arranged. He did not find it "a particularly pleasing ordeal," he wrote to a friend a few days later. There seemed to be a preconception that he was "a kind of Horatio Alger success," and the newspapermen and columnists he talked to appeared determined to stick to that line. Farrell was also interviewed briefly on radio. "It was all a bore, but it's now pretty nearly over."

Not quite. The BBC asked him to appear on the strange new medium of television on the evening of Thursday, May 26. Hortense, who had left New York after he did, arrived in London in the early morning hours that day, and she watched the television interview from a film projection room. She was "tremendously thrilled" by television, and Farrell was excited, too. "It is going to have a revolutionary effect in communication and perhaps also in popular entertainment," he told Jim Henle. Some days later, however, he added a prescient cautionary note: "I dread the commercialization of television in USA. Think of it. Skits to advertise razors showing men shaving, soap ads with skits showing Papa and Mama and Johnny boy and the grandmaw all using a certain brand of soap...."

Farrell and Hortense made a trip to Oxford one day and looked up A. J. Ayer, the logical positivist whose combative *Language, Truth and Logic* (1936) had caused a stir. He was a friend of a friend, and Farrell found him "an intelligent and likeable fellow, but terribly fastidious." He was disappointed that he could not seem to engage the philosopher in "really serious talk," and at lunch with Ayer and another scholar, the conversation was all about good food and where to find it—and "me, with my bad teeth, my indifferent taste, well I was a bit of a lost soul."

The weather in London was unpleasant, indeed "atrocious," and Farrell and Hortense soon were off to Paris. Farrell, who had gone about London carrying an Irish blackthorn walking stick, did not much like the "reserved" and "Puritanical" English. "The French are more natural, more alive, they talk more, they make more noise, they kiss and make love on the street, they go down [it] holding hands," he wrote to his brother Jack.

It had been six years since he left Paris with Dorothy. Now, world events made the city seem "a different and a sadder" place. He revisited some of his old haunts, accompanied by ghosts, some of whom materialized. Robert McAlmon, whose work as a writer Farrell considered, for the most part, "too literal and dull," summoned him and Hortense to his table at the Select café. "He was drunk [and] pathetic [and] terribly jealous of me," Farrell recorded, "and...he kept finding things about my books that he considered phony." Farrell saw Sylvia Beach one day and had supper with her a few days later. She was now quite sure that she disliked Farrell. He had offended her, when he first ran into her this June, by loudly boasting about living with a beautiful actress. He was, Miss Beach decided, a "pushy upstart."

It was Farrell's champion Sam Putnam who had introduced him to Sylvia Beach seven years earlier. Putnam was one of the ghosts who did not materialize, having returned to the States the year after Farrell did. But Farrell remembered him: "An intellectual desperado, with no capacity to make his personal relationships decent and lasting. Then, Sam saw Mussolini as the hope of art and literature, not to mention the world. Now, he sees Stalin in that light."

Though he was quick to notice the ingratitude of an Otis Ferguson or a Nelson Algren, Farrell himself was not one to let any feelings of thankfulness cloud his resolutely unsentimental appraisals of others. Indeed, he does not seem to have felt much gratitude at this stage in his life toward any of those—with the possible exception of Jim Henle—who had helped him achieve what he took to be his success. Not Putnam; not Ezra Pound (another admirer of fascism, with whom Farrell seems to have ceased corresponding in 1935); not Mrs. Ames ("A woman who is always making gestures without meaning to them," he and Hortense had decided the previous summer, after the Yaddo director regretfully told him that she could not "find a berth" for him just then on such short notice as he had given her); not Lovett (who had shown himself a political fool, ever eager to be manipulated by the Stalinists); and not James Weber Linn. In "The Professor," a short story in *Can All This Grandeur Perish? and Other Stories,* Farrell had drawn a cruel portrait of Linn as a professor and newspaper columnist who had once wanted to be a great writer but settled for mediocrity, and who came finally to see himself as he really was: "a failure, and, yes, something of a clown."

Farrell was so determined to be a great writer, and so unsure that he was or would be, that he found it necessary to denigrate, in one way or another, all those who had helped him, lest their assistance seem to call into question the intrinsic worth of his work, its ability to shine brilliantly on its own. And believing his portrayal of the professor to be accurate, he no doubt thought that Linn should, after all, finally face the truth about himself.

Farrell did feel a very strong obligation to truth. Though he now did not "like or respect" Linn, and felt that Linn's role in his career had been "an accident of time," and though he had given up trying to defend the Stalinist "stooge" Lovett, he still felt that, in writing of the origins of *Studs Lonigan,* as he recently had, he needed to acknowledge the encouragement that both men had given him. So, in his introduction to a Modern Library edition of the trilogy (due out in September), he had written: "In a sense, Professor Linn and Professor Lovett are the spiritual godfathers of *Studs Lonigan.*"

But the two disrespected godfathers were far from Farrell's mind during his stay in Paris. "My experiences here have been purely visual," he wrote to his brother Jack after some days in the city. "I have walked the streets, looked at cathedrals, peoples, sat in cafes and this is about all.... I have had, here, just the kind of rest I need. A 'moral holiday,' to quote an apt phrase of William James."

Two weeks after their arrival in Paris, he and Hortense went to Chartres and saw the magnificent cathedral that Henry Adams had said expressed "the deepest [emotion] man ever felt,—the struggle of his own littleness to grasp the infinite." They both were overwhelmed. "It is probably the most beautiful cathedral in the world," he wrote Jack.

Farrell wished that Meyer Schapiro, a brilliant art historian who taught at Columbia University, were with them at Chartres. (Farrell was "a genuine student [who was] happiest with scholars," Jim Henle would recall. "[He was the] only author I've ever known who preferred the company of scholars to that of motion picture stars—or other authors.") Schapiro, who was active in radical politics, had been a member of the Trotsky defense committee, and he and Farrell had become good friends. (It was he who had told him to look up A. J. Ayer at Oxford.) "A mouth in search of an ear" was Mary McCarthy's crack about Schapiro, whose imposingly erudite discourse was eloquent, impersonal and—as it sometimes seemed to even the most admiring of his auditors—interminable. But Farrell, with his own restless intelligence, extensive reading and wide-ranging interests, certainly provided the scholar and fellow anti-Stalinist radical with more than an ear. He had a mouth of his own, and he didn't hesitate to use it, even on subjects on which Schapiro was an authority. Farrell wrote to him from Paris:

> I felt [that] behind the loveliness, serenity, beauty, and charm at Chartres, there was the expression of a life that must have been fully

as sick as life today. So many miracles—restoring the blind, resurrecting the dead, giving health back to babies, and bringing them back to life, so many champions of the people, in the guise of saints, who gave alms to the poor, who healed the sick, and raised the dead, and fronted for the suffering soul before God Almighty, so much of this convinces me that there must have been many troubled minds, much fear of sickness which was not understood, a great deal of what is to us dreadful fanaticism, and that Chartres, with all its serenity, to repeat, is a memorial of an age which one cannot like, even if one respects certain of its supreme artistic achievements."

Little more than a week after their visit to Chartres, Farrell and Hortense went to Lisieux, in Normandy, where Saint Thérèse (1873-1897), the "Little Flower," had lived. In her name, Father Albert Dolan, Farrell's English teacher at St. Cyril's, had founded the Society of the Little Flower in 1923, the year that Farrell graduated. Subsequently, the priest had established various shrines in her honor. Farrell thought a visit to Lisieux might come in useful for his fiction. "I went in the line of duty, feeling that I should go," he wrote to Jim Henle, "but I do not know what I gained, except resentment, disillusionment with humanity, and a feeling of hopelessness. Mankind will do anything rather than face the fact that he is not the center of the universe, and that the medieval conception of the world is false....And at Lisieux, there is the not very masked commercialization of all this—the use of human ignorance as a means of economic gain, the sale of bad statues, miserable souvenirs of a visit to Lisieux."

Though they despised Lisieux, Farrell and Hortense very much liked France, particularly Paris, and decided to stay longer than the month they had originally planned. But finally it was time to leave, and they were off to Ireland.

"Dublin is not a lovely city, or a pretty city," he wrote to Henle in late July. "It is drab, and has little to interest the eye in the way that Paris has. It is very poor, too....This is an unfortunate race and what you see here is an unfortunate race in a backward country." Yet the Irish, he and Hortense found, were extremely warm and friendly. "The people are the main interest and they are very charming," he wrote to his old college friend Felix Kolodziej, who worked on his father's farm in Wisconsin. "I have never met with such hospitality in my life as that here. Your old friends, Mrs. O'Flaherty, Lizz O'Neill, and that Connerty one [as Lizz is given at times to refer to one of her neighbors], they are to be seen on almost every corner. You could take Lizz, plant her down here, and it would seem, in a week, as if she had been here all of her life."

Farrell had intended to take a vacation from writing during these months abroad, and thought he had "pretty much succeeded." But he didn't count his letter-writing; he kept up a voluminous correspondence, as usual. On July 30, for instance, he sent typewritten, single-spaced letters to Kolodziej (two pages), Henle (two-plus pages) and Schapiro (three pages), and then the next day, more letters—to Henle again (four pages), Kolodziej again (three-plus pages), Ferdinand Lundberg (four-plus pages) and his sister Mary (three pages).

In early August, Farrell and Hortense went on a tour of the countryside. The unspoiled beauty of Killarney in southwest Ireland—its deep-blue lakes, heather-clad mountains and lush green vegetation—especially impressed them. Killarney "is one of the loveliest sights I have ever seen," Farrell told Henle.

They returned to Dublin on August 5, a Friday. The next day, Farrell poured out enough words to fill some thirty single-spaced typewritten pages and mailed them off in the form of letters to Henle, Schapiro, Novack, Lundberg, and his brothers Earl and Jack. That night, he and Hortense went to a reception given by the Abbey Theatre to inaugurate a two-week festival of plays and lectures. During the ensuing days, they attended some of the plays. But Hortense decided she had had enough of Ireland and (perhaps eager to get back to their New York apartment, which had been robbed while they were in Paris) left for New York before the festival's first week had ended.

Farrell elected to stay a few weeks longer. It would be "rather lonely," he knew, without Hortense (or "Chica Dove," the pet name that he, a.k.a. "Lump," now used for her in his missives trailing her across the ocean). But he wanted "to make a round or two of the public houses in the slums here—the [playwright Sean] O'Casey world—and...go up to Mother's country in Westmeath." The insularity of the Irish seems to have both appalled and fascinated him. "Ireland is very parochial," he wrote to his brother Jack, "and many of the values of your and my boyhood run through the land. The moral and spiritual and intellectual and aesthetic content of the life of many is really no different from that of many in our boyhood neighborhoods."

An attack of indigestion laid him low, however, and he was

forced to revise his plans. There would be no trip to Westmeath nor any visits to Dublin pubs. But the physician he consulted, Dr. Robert Collis, offered to take him through the worst of the city's slums. "You might think that conditions in the cottage were pretty bad when you grew up," he wrote to Jack. "But they are luxury and a country club compared [with] some of the things I saw this morning in the slums of Dublin." He had seen them from the outside before, but now he saw the slums from the inside. "What I saw is truly dreadful," he wrote to his sister Mary.

> I was in an old crumbling house. Families of six, seven, eleven living in one room. In some instances, six sleeping in one bed. Buildings infested with rats, with falling ceiling propped [up] by boards, rain leaking through plasters, consumptive families in which the father has died in the same bed in which three and four are now sleeping, inadequate sleeping with even six in a bed so that some of the boys in the family have to sleep on the floor, places where with eleven in one room a baby has been born in addition, disease, filth, misery, conditions to dehumanize beyond measure.
>
> Ireland is a crazy country that has never become completely civilized. And it is church ridden beyond belief almost. And the Church is the factor which results in the poor people here breeding like animals so that malnutrition and undernourishment are constant factors, part of the social environment of the nation. The Church is more concerned with the babies of the poor being kept out of Limbo thanks to the Sacrament of Baptism than it is to the feeding of the children after they have been generously saved from Limbo.

Farrell also met Jim Larkin, the radical Irish labor leader who had roused Dublin's workers to rebellion earlier in the century, but had then grown discouraged and emigrated to America. Now he was back in Dublin, "a tired and embittered old man…but an exceedingly charming and human personality" in Farrell's description. Introducing the visitor around, Larkin said, "I want you to meet my friend Farrell. He's written a great novel, but you dare not read it for fear you'll lose your immortal soul." Farrell regretted that he hadn't looked Larkin up sooner: "Besides being such interesting company, he would have taken me all around Dublin."

Farrell left Ireland on August 27, aboard the SS *Manhattan*. Three days later, the shipboard newspaper brought disturbing news: the crisis over the Sudetenland had grown acute; there was talk of imminent world war. Munich, the surrender of the Sudeten-

land to Hitler, and Chamberlain's "peace for our time" were only a
month away.

——➤-◦-◄——

THE TITLE OF *NO STAR IS LOST*, published in mid-September 1938, was
taken, like the title of *A World I Never Made*, from an A. E. Housman
poem full of adolescent angst. As the earlier poem expressed a frustrated alienation from the laws of God and man, so this one
displayed a bleak vision of an indifferent universe: "*Stars, I have
seen them fall, / But when they drop and die / No star is lost at
all / From all the star-sown sky.*" The novel's expiring star turns
out to be Arty O'Neill, the youngest child of Jim and Lizz O'Neill,
who—like Farrell's youngest brother, Frankie—dies in a diphtheria
epidemic (which occurs in the book three years before it did in
real life).

In *No Star Is Lost*, set between the summer of 1914 and the
spring of 1915, Farrell further develops the characters introduced
in *A World I Never Made*. Mrs. O'Flaherty comes to seem more of a
witch; Lizz O'Neill, less of a caricature; and Farrell's alter ego,
Danny O'Neill, more of an individual, weighed down by the turmoil
in his home. The terrible difference that class can make is mani-
fested in the failure of Dr. Mike Geraghty, Al O'Flaherty's best
friend, to answer the repeated calls to attend to little Arty in the
impoverished O'Neill household, whereas he comes right away to
treat Little Margaret at the O'Flahertys'. The climactic chapter, in
which diphtheria ravages the O'Neill family, is almost as powerful
as the terrifying New Year's Eve party in *The Young Manhood of
Studs Lonigan*.

But some prominent reviewers of *No Star Is Lost* didn't see
the novel that way. Alfred Kazin in the *Herald Tribune*'s *Books*,
Clifton Fadiman in the *New Yorker*, and George Stevens in the *Saturday Review* (of which he was now the editor) found it too long
and too similar to its predecessor. "The painful truth," Kazin
declared, "is that there is nothing in this second volume that one
cannot get from the first. Mr. Farrell, with magnificent energy, is
turning round and round in the same vindictive circle.... [He] has
lost his sense of proportion; he is writing madly, bitterly...and he is
no longer saying anything. He is hacking his people to bits, stamping on them, scaling dead flesh, and the hatred has become

tiresome as it was once electrifying." Stevens, while lauding Farrell's "photographic realism," contended that the author was writing "out of memory—a detailed and inexhaustible memory—but it is memory, not imagination. It is a picture of life, not a vision." Fadiman complained that the continuing characters in the novel "do not develop. Peg O'Flaherty gets drunker, the O'Neills get more miserable, Grandma O'Flaherty becomes more and more of a murderous old harridan; but simple straight-line intensification is not growth or change." Farrell, he said, "is so deeply anchored in his childhood that he has lost, to a degree, his sense of proportion, a sense of the proper relationship between himself and his readers."

Farrell did indeed risk trying his readers' patience. *No Star Is Lost* is quite long (637 pages) and the characters do not make the sort of sudden and sharp departure from their established patterns of behavior that Fadiman and no doubt others craved. Yet surely it is legitimate for an artist to portray "growth" as it normally occurs in life and to deepen his readers' knowledge of his characters by letting them observe those characters intimately over a prolonged period, even over several novels. The reader of *A World I Never Made*, it is true, finds little that is startlingly new in *No Star Is Lost*; but he does find implicitly posed again and again, throughout the second novel as throughout the first, the same insistent, indeed eternal adolescent question: *Why?*

Why was Danny O'Neill taken from his natural family? *Why* must Jim O'Neill's family live in poverty? *Why* is Lizz O'Neill so slovenly, so superstitious? *Why* is Mary O'Flaherty so lacking in affection for her grown daughters? *Why* is Margaret O'Flaherty so bent on self-destruction? *Why* must the O'Flahertys fight with one another so much? *Why* did Dr. Geraghty not come to treat little Arty?

Farrell was indeed "deeply anchored in his childhood"—and his ability to recreate so faithfully, in such utterly persuasive detail, the world of his childhood, populated by living, breathing human beings, is precisely what makes his novels so impressive an achievement.

The other criticisms these reviewers made were even wider of the mark. The "hatred" (or more accurately, as previously noted, the contempt) that Kazin supposedly had found so "electrifying" in *A World I Never Made* is actually much less in evidence in *No Star Is Lost*. And the imagination whose alleged absence Stevens so lamented is more obviously apparent in the new novel—for

instance, in the memorable scene in which Mrs. O'Flaherty con-
verses with her dead husband in the graveyard where he is buried.

Reading these reviews, Farrell sensed that "a gang up on me"
might be in progress. He was especially offended by Kazin's portrayal of him as bitter and vengeful, consumed by hatred for his
own people; he considered this "personally insulting." In his diary,
he sneered at Kazin, who had been writing reviews for Cowley at
the *New Republic* for several years, as "Cowley's little altar boy."
Kazin himself, by his own later account, actually didn't much like
Cowley, but—despite Stalin's murderous purges, despite the
Moscow show trials, and despite reports of Communist perfidy in
Spain—he "shared [Cowley's] feeling that Fascism was the main
enemy and I feared any division on the left that might limit maxi-
mum resistance to Franco and Hitler." Kazin could hardly have been
unaware of Farrell's status as a political renegade. Perhaps this did
not affect his view of Farrell's latest work. But it might well have.
Certainly, in his 1936 review of *A World I Never Made*, Kazin had
discerned that Farrell had a "social" grievance as well as a "personal" one, whereas in his review of *No Star Is Lost* two years later,
the social grievance had disappeared and Farrell was "no longer
saying anything." Perhaps it was just that he was no longer saying
the right thing.*

In Cowley's *New Republic*, Robert Morss Lovett—who had provided the introduction to Farrell's collected short stories but had
been offended by "The Professor," the contemptuous and ill-disguised
portrait of Lovett's colleague, James Weber Linn—weighed in with a
review under the headline, "Farrell at the Crossroads." Saying that Farrell's work to date had dealt, for the most part, with life in "the mean
streets within a half-mile west of Washington Park, Chicago, and the
drab houses of the Irish families who have now given way to the

---

*The political sympathies of Kazin and other critics were on more conspicuous display
the next year, when they reviewed *The Adventures of a Young Man*, a semi-autobio-
graphical novel expressing author John Dos Passos's profound disillusionment with the
Communists. Kazin pretended that Dos Passos was disaffected with "the whole radical
movement in America," could not bring himself to state plainly the Communist perfidy
that prompted the radical protagonist's disillusion, and found Dos Passos to be suffering
from the same putative malady as Farrell—"pure hatred" of his characters. Farrell, detect-
ing a political "gang up" by reviewers, took up the cudgels for Dos Passos in "Dos Passos
and the Critics," an essay in the *American Mercury* (August 1939). "The reception given
The Adventures of a Young Man," Farrell said, "reads like a warning to writers not to stray
off the reservations of the Stalinist-controlled League of American Writers, to which more
than one of the critics belong."

Negroes," Lovett questioned how much longer "his public can be held to the severe contemplation of this sordid life."

"It looks as if Lovett has been gotten into the gang up," Farrell wrote. "The very first sentence is one stating that I am at the crossroads. Why? He doesn't say, except to point out that it might take great courage and resourcefulness on my part to learn to write something different. Lovett, having read nine works of fiction by me ought to see a plan and a development in which I am seeking to expand from a basis set in the works which I have already done. At all events, Lovett at an advanced age of about 70 writes an obituary notice of Farrell who is 34. Life teems with humor."

Not all the reviews of *No Star Is Lost* were hostile. In the daily *Times*, Ralph Thompson, who had not liked Farrell's short stories at all, hailed his new novel as "a tremendous piece of work" that "strikes with an even greater force" than its predecessors. In Farrell's "libelously faithful portrait of the world of Chicago Irish" could also be seen the world of the Irish of Boston and other cities. "It is a world that has been exerting a ponderable influence upon what we call American culture for a hundred years, and Mr. Farrell is its foremost chronicler."

Farrell, naturally, was delighted by Thompson's review. He thought it showed that Thompson had read the book carefully and with an open mind. "I must interpret his review of my short stories on the basis that he frankly hated them, and that that is his privilege. It is also Lovett's privilege, but there is misinterpretation and irrelevancy in Lovett's review that is inexcusable, and that suggests that the local boys went to work on him. How long will Mr. Farrell's public stand for his books. That sort of gag is occurring too familiarly in the first reviews. The hypothesis that the Stalinists have started a gang up on me has a great deal of circumstantial and internal evidence to substantiate it."

But if there was a "gang up," it is by no means obvious that it was a consciously conspiratorial one. Not that the Communists would have shrunk from engaging in such a collective mauling. But once Farrell's open political rebellion became known, there probably was no need for them to go much beyond ritualistic denunciation: their "liberal" sympathizers, acting more or less on their own, with all kinds of qualifications and reservations, would do the rest. Some of Farrell's critics, of course, were simply expressing their honest judgments of his work and the defects they found in it without regard to politics. But it was often hard to tell the honest critics from the others. This sort of confusion was what enabled the Stalinists to exert so much influence in American cultural life.

———▶-●-◀———

DICK PARKER, FARRELL'S CLASSMATE from St. Cyril's who had worked on the *Oriflamme* and played basketball with him, came to visit in September (just a few days before Hortense and Farrell moved into a new apartment at 185 Lexington Avenue, near 32nd Street). Parker had graduated from Dartmouth College in 1930 and had just received his doctorate from the University of Chicago. An Egyptologist, he was involved in an expedition based in Luxor, Egypt. Farrell was impressed and thought him "a decent chap, very decent," but was struck by how Parker, unlike himself, had confined his intellectual inquiry to a single field.

He came to supper, and Farrell and Hortense served steak. But as it was a Friday, Parker, a devout Catholic, felt obliged to pass up the meat. Farrell had assumed that such an intelligent man must have long since left the Church, but that was not the case. Farrell also discovered that his guest did not agree with him about the "pedagogical inadequacies" of their old school. Having distinguished himself at Dartmouth, Parker thought he had been as well prepared for the academic work there as any of his classmates.

They talked of Bob Lusk, who had been the *Oriflamme* editor-in-chief. After graduation, he worked for Father Dolan's Society of the Little Flower for a time, then got into the jewelry business, and was now employed in a political patronage job. He had written a few stories and tried to sell them, but without any luck. Now he had four daughters and a pregnant wife to support. ("Lusk will make a good story," Farrell observed in his diary the next day. "Now the poor fellow is in the iron grip of necessity. The society in which he placed his trust, his life, and his values has left him in this situation.")

Farrell's literary renown meant little to most of his erstwhile classmates. When his early books had been published, Parker reported, they'd said to one another: "Did you hear? Jimmy Farrell is writing dirty books now." Few, if any, of them had troubled to read those books.

Parker filled him in on how some of the fellows were faring. One had not stopped chasing girls after his marriage, was now separated from his wife and had lost his job. Another, who had owned a filling station with his brother, had lost ownership during the Depression and was now an employee at the same station. One fellow was running his father's laundry; another was in the grocery business and not doing very well; another, an epileptic, had drowned the previous summer.

"It was strange, almost eerie, talking with Dick, putting my mind back 15 years ago...," Farrell reflected. "I was the only rebel from the class. I rebelled against everything of any importance in the total environment of those days. They did not. They are nostalgic where I am bitter and critical and objective." They had let all the slights and hurts of adolescence fade from memory, but Farrell had not. For him, the wounds were still fresh.

—————»•०«————

" 'PEACE' NOW IS NOTHING to shout over," said Farrell—who, along with the rest of worried mankind, had been hanging on the radio news—to his brother Jack after the settlement at Munich was announced. He explained his fears:

> Something inexpressibly dreadful has been postponed, perhaps, more than avoided. Chamberlain and [French Premier Edouard] Daladier had Hitler in a hole but let him slip out, undoubtedly as a counterweight to Russia. No matter what we say of Stalin, the isolation of Russia is not just an isolation of him. It is a second quarantining, also, of October 1917. Stalin's policies have helped that, but [so] also [have] other historical factors.

Though Farrell had recognized that Hitler might be engaging in a colossal bluff, he did not simply condemn Chamberlain for failing to call it. Instead, he thought that the most important thing about the agreement was that war would have been worse. "War would have been immediate and close to universal fascism and with that, a close approximation to the destruction of nearly all human decency." But that was not to defend Chamberlain: "It is all a sad and messy business, it is a working out... of certain historic trends, rivalries, contradictions in Europe." And thanks to "economic rivalries," war remained likely, he believed. "The same economic rivalries that led to the last world war are threatening a worse war."

The Munich "peace" inspired much foreboding. It marked the death of European culture, said Farrell's friend Bill Troy, the astute literary critic, when he and Hortense visited Troy and his wife at their Connecticut home. "Bill says that anyone who talks of social revolution is as passé as a person debating medieval theological propositions," Farrell recorded in his diary. "He says that the most that it seems anyone can hope for at present is to save something of our civilization from barbarism." With the Soviet-backed concept of "collective security" apparently in tatters, Troy also reckoned that "the Communists' goose is cooked."

There soon was considerable talk—and not just by Trotsky and his followers—that Stalin would make a deal with Hitler. The *New York Times*'s Walter Duranty, who could be regarded as "a semi-official spokesman of the Kremlin," Farrell told his brother Jack, "wrote a dispatch pointing out that there was nothing in the way of such an understanding except Hitler's fanatic anti-Russian bias, and that even so, dictators can change their minds. This might have been a trial balloon.... If it does come about, of course, the comrades here are likely to be left sitting high and dry."

Some of the American comrades and their sympathizers became uneasy. The Communists "are very bewildered," according to Farrell's liberal friend Ferdinand Lundberg. "They don't know what to make of it all...following the defeat of their line, implicit in the Munich pact." In the *New Republic*, Malcolm Cowley mounted an attack on *Partisan Review* in which—rather astonishingly in light of his own past performance as literary editor—he lamented the absence of a *nonpartisan* literary magazine. This brazen maneuver won him a strong private rebuke from Edmund Wilson and public ones from Farrell and *Partisan Review*'s editors. ("Isn't this the same Malcolm Cowley," the latter asked, "whose use of his position on the *New Republic* to play Communist Party politics has long been a literary scandal?") At lunch with Fred Dupee, one of the *Partisan Review* editors, and others, Farrell learned that Cowley "is worried and upset.... Dupee says he has it that Cowley is trying to get off the Stalin bandwagon, and that first, he wants to smash at the left, and then fall back into the lap of the aesthetic boys." Others had already broken with the Stalinists, or were casting yearning glances toward the exit. When Cowley earlier in the year had circulated a statement endorsing the most recent Moscow show trials, Horace Gregory had refused to sign it and, as a result, was banished from the masthead of the *New Masses*, where he had been a contributing editor. Now, Farrell was told, Gregory "talks bitterly of the Stalinists, and [his wife] Marya hates them." Apparently novelist

Josephine Herbst was also "disgusted with the Stalinists." But she reportedly said "that she is lonely and that when she comes to [New York] she likes to go to cocktail parties… etc., and that, because of this she won't break with them."

Meanwhile, in Washington, the House Committee on Un-American Activities, headed by an anti–New Deal Democrat from Texas named Martin Dies, had been holding hearings on the Communist penetration of the Congress of Industrial Organizations (C.I.O.) and various other organizations. The committee's efforts to determine the accuracy of the many charges made by witnesses at its hearings were desultory at best. But that didn't bother many of the new committee's admirers. *Social Justice*, the publication of Father Charles Coughlin, the anti-Semitic radio priest, honored chairman Dies by naming him its "Man of the Week." Farrell held a different view: He believed that the Dies investigation "is likely to do great harm. Of course, the CP [Communist Party] has to bear part of the responsibility for it."

In Farrell's view, the fascist threat to America was serious and didn't come mainly from abroad. He was appalled by Kristallnacht and the Nazi pogrom against the Jews, but he considered the rise in anti-Semitism at home to be the much more immediate danger. "It is necessary to make people see that the menace of fascism is within our gates, and instead anti-fascist sentiment is confused by this trick of making war scares and making fascism something outside," he wrote to James J. Geller of the William Morris Agency in Beverly Hills (who had tried to interest Hollywood in *Studs Lonigan*). The urgent need was to meet the domestic fascist threat "head on."

And he would do his part, insofar as words could be pressed into service without abusing his art. During the coming year, he would pen *Tommy Gallagher's Crusade*, a novella about a young, unemployed New Yorker, the black sheep of a lower-middle-class, Irish-American family and a bitter, hate-filled recruit in the ragtag army of the anti-Semitic radio priest Father Moylan (read: Father Coughlin). Farrell's portrait of an American fascist was skillfully drawn and truthful. It was not at all anti-Catholic and, if it undeniably had a political point, it was not mere propaganda. "Tommy Gallagher will not get anywhere in the United States," Fred T. Marsh commented in reviewing this "all too true" story (published by Vanguard as a small book). "But he's a representative lad. He's a product of a poisonous spirit that is abroad throughout the world."

222

HERMAN SHUMLIN, THE PRODUCER of *Grand Hotel*, was putting on a play with a part that seemed tailor-made for Hortense Alden—but he didn't want her for it. Sam Jaffe, one of her co-stars in *Grand Hotel*, went with a colleague to see Shumlin and try to change his mind. Farrell fumed: "It is disgusting that this has to be done.... After all, he knows what Hortense can do, and he has gained most significantly from her abilities."

Farrell appears to have been unaware of how much Hortense's sudden exit from *Grand Hotel* in Chicago had infuriated Shumlin. Nor does he seem to have quite realized that his own open defiance of the Stalinists (which, to be sure, Hortense went along with) might well have hurt her theatrical career. Just the preceding month, Mary Hunter had told him "that through the Theatre Arts Committee, the Stalinists—under the guise of helping Spain—are sewing up the theatre, and that it is hard for others to get jobs." Shumlin, a member of the Theatre Arts Committee's executive board, was, at the very least, sympathetic to the Stalinists. Though he had been friendly with Hortense and Farrell, their political course can hardly have made him more inclined to hire the temperamental actress. Despite the appeals made in her behalf, Shumlin did not change his mind: she didn't get the part.

At about the same time, however, she was offered a small role in *Here Come the Clowns*, a drama by Philip Barry, a devout Catholic, about man's search for spiritual truth in a muddled world. Hortense and Farrell regarded the play as "hokum," but, as he noted, "she is certain that playing [the part] will not hurt her, and it will be psychologically good for her to be working again." The play, which opened on December 7, 1938, proved more popular with reviewers than with the public.

In mid-February, a few days before the last performance of *Here Come the Clowns*, Farrell told his diary of a more important drama: "Hortense and I are to have a baby. And we look forward to it as an experience that gives us the opportunity of enriching our lives. After learning that she was caught, we finally decided to go through with it."

FARRELL WAS A VORACIOUS AND SERIOUS reader. On January 20, 1939, he recorded in his diary that since the beginning of the year, he had finished reading, *inter alia*, the philosopher George Herbert Mead's *Mind, Self and Society from the Standpoint of a Social Behaviorist*; Volume One ("The Colonial Mind") of Vernon Louis Parrington's *Main Currents in American Thought*; and Boris Souvarine's *Staline*. And he had embarked on Tolstoy's *War and Peace* ("one of the greatest novels ever written," he would eventually decide), Boswell's *Life of Johnson* ("a magnificent book"), and Ignazio Silone's *School for Dictators*. In the months ahead, he would also turn his attention to logical positivist Rudolf Carnap's *Unity of Science* and *Logical Syntax of Language* ("I understood most of the former, but have to work more at this field to grasp it in the sense that it is assimilated"), Jaroslav Hasek's *Good Soldier Svejk*, Stendhal's *Charterhouse of Parma*, Joseph Conrad's *Youth*, John Dewey's *Logic: The Theory of Inquiry*, Saint Augustine's *Confessions*, and "perhaps the longest book ever written," Gibbon's *Decline and Fall of the Roman Empire*.

Farrell's continual quest was for knowledge, not confirmation of his prejudices. Though he had long since repudiated Catholicism, for instance, he had recently read Étienne Gilson's *Spirit of Mediaeval Philosophy* with interest. The distinguished Catholic historian of medieval philosophy was "a first-rate scholar and a man of rare intelligence," he judged. "But after reading two chapters.... I can see that I shall never agree with him.... Faith first, then rational thought, and finally vision. That is the pattern of Christian philosophy which he traces."

⎯⎯◈⎯⎯

THOUGH HE WAS NOT A pacifist, Farrell was passionately against the prospect of war. This in part resulted from the fact that despite his rejection of Stalinism and the Communist Party, he remained a revolutionary socialist. A decade later, looking back, he explained what his outlook had been:

> On principle, one cannot support a capitalist government. The War will solve no problems. What is important is the cause of the War and this is the world system under which we live, in which war is not an exceptional event. War is a normal consequence of the world system. This system is imperialist. The realpolitik of choosing the lesser evil is one that is opportunistic and a War which doesn't end in socialism and a revival of revolutionary energies which permit the masses to

enter politics, will lead to a Third World War. The fight for democracy can only be carried on by fighting for socialism.

Farrell's antiwar position was also, one suspects, an out-growth of his youthful, postwar stance against the Great War, the war of "steel and gold," as he supposed. In a sense, he was still objecting to the last war, just as generals are said to be always fighting it. The shades of Randolph Bourne and other heroic rebels who had refused to endorse "the war to make the world safe for democracy" paraded in moral triumph before his mind's eye.

Farrell resolutely resisted any tug of patriotism. "The recent trend of events in Europe," he observed, "has sickened many minds.... Many intellectuals are frightened and falling into becoming 'Americans' because they fear the future. Of course, this is not any approach to solving our problems."

In January 1939, when Sidney Hook and others gathered at Ben Stolberg's to talk about forming a "League Against Totalitarianism," Farrell adamantly insisted that their manifesto should include an antiwar clause. In the ensuing weeks and months, Hook managed to exclude Farrell and his like-minded allies, Meyer Schapiro and Phil Rahv, from playing any part in shaping the position of what became the Committee for Cultural Freedom. (Farrell was a little annoyed at the exclusion, feeling, as he told Ferdinand Lundberg, "that Sidney was forming an organization to defend democracy and that he had been undemocratic with close and good friends of his." But Farrell's annoyance did not last. "I find that Sidney is very appealing personally," he would note in his diary in June, "and it is impossible for me to get angry with him.")

The Committee for Cultural Freedom didn't have the field to itself. The American Committee for Intellectual Freedom and Democracy, a Communist front headed by anthropologist Franz Boas, rallied hundreds of scientists around a statement critical of oppression in Germany and Italy. But Hook's committee, with John Dewey as figurehead and a manifesto signed by 96 (later 142) writers, artists, scientists and scholars (including, Farrell noted, "many good names"), boldly added Russia to the list of totalitarian lands. This did not sit well with the *New Republic*'s editors ("In lumping together the Fascist powers with the USSR, the committee shows, we feel, a regrettable lack of historical perspective"), nor with the *Nation*'s Freda Kirchwey ("With all their faults the Communists perform necessary functions in the confused struggle of our time"). And Corliss Lamont, the indefatigible "liberal" Soviet apologist, was beside himself.

Hook was a "rabid Red-baiter and a leading partisan of Leon Trotsky," and he and "his fellow-Trotskyites" on the "decidedly phony" committee ignored "the fundamental differences between Fascism and Soviet Socialism," Lamont informed readers of the *New York Post.* In addition to "reducing illiteracy from 70 percent to less than 5 percent," emancipating woman and the family, freeing formerly enslaved national minorities, wiping out racial prejudice, making anti-Semitism a criminal offense, steadily raising the standard of living, and adopting a democratic constitution "with its epoch-making 'rights of man,'" Soviet Russia, he said, "has all along stood foursquare against war and Fascism, the brutal twin brothers that more than anything else lead to the enslavement of the mind and the degradation of culture." Replied Hook: There was not a single Trotskyite on the committee, and Russia was indeed a totalitarian state "because its press is not free, its schools are not free, its courts are not free. Art and science are censored by party dogma, all opposition parties are proscribed, and a minority party rules by purge, exile and execution squads. People may make excuses for these things whether they occur in Russia or Germany. To deny that they exist is unmitigated stupidity."

Farrell agreed, calling Hook's response "excellent." He was glad to see that the committee was having more of an impact than he had anticipated. But he declined several times to add his name to its manifesto. He had joined instead with Rahv, Phillips, Dupee, Macdonald, James Burnham (a colleague of Hook's in the Philosophy Department at NYU whom Farrell considered "the best of the intellectuals in the Trotskyite ranks"), Meyer Schapiro, George Novack and others to form a rival organization, one beating the drum for socialism as well as cultural freedom. "Shall we abandon the ideals of revolutionary socialism because one political group, while clinging to its name, has so miserably betrayed its principles?" asked the League for Cultural Freedom and Socialism in its manifesto.

THEY ARRIVED AT THE HOSPITAL sometime before six in the morning on August 1. Hortense had begun to have pains late the night before; she and Farrell had started timing the contractions in the early morning hours, and in the cab they had become more severe. At the hospital, Farrell was quickly shunted to the waiting room.

Gazing out the window, he saw that day was breaking, and he remembered how he had similarly watched the dawning of a new day at the American Hospital in Paris eight years before, when Dorothy was in labor. The outcome this time, he was sure, would be different. And their lives, of course, would be different. Jim Henle, the proud father of two boys, had advised him that having a child gives one something to live for.

Dorothy, who in the four years since Farrell had left her had not ceased to wonder how she had lost him or to hope that he would one day return, was now finally willing to give him a divorce, having learned in June from Phil Rahv that Hortense was pregnant. But when Dorothy told Farrell this, he was not certain he could believe her. "When Dorothy has deceived and lied to a person as much as she has to me," he wrote in his diary, "it is self-protection not to believe a word that she says." Nevertheless, Dorothy, who was now living in Chicago, was telling him the truth. She thought that with a child on the way, Farrell should be free to marry the mother.

In the hospital waiting room, Farrell read a chapter from Fielding's *Tom Jones* and then, tired, lay down. The minutes passed slowly. It had been a half-hour since their arrival. Suddenly the physician, Dr. Beckwith, appeared with the news: the baby had been born dead.

"It was a surprise, to say the least," he wrote in his diary some days later.

—————◆————

A "FANTASTIC FALSEHOOD"—that was what Granville Hicks, Clifford Odets, Robert Morss Lovett, Corliss Lamont, Herman Shumlin, Max Lerner (now teaching at Williams College), *Nation* associate editor I. F. Stone, mystery writer Dashiell Hammett, Hollywood screenwriter Donald Ogden Stewart and the rest of some four hundred avowed strugglers for democracy and peace branded the proposition that "the U.S.S.R. and the totalitarian states are basically alike."

The "400 suckers," as Farrell called them, were responding chiefly to the manifesto of Hook's Committee for Cultural Freedom, though they also obviously had the League for Cultural Freedom and Socialism in mind when they mentioned other, unnamed committees "which give lip-service to democracy and peace while actually attacking the Soviet Union and aiding reaction."

The "400"—only 167 of whom were ever revealed—could not match the intellectual distinction of John Dewey and the 141 others who signed the Hook committee's manifesto, or the intellectual firepower of the league's 29 advocates of revolutionary socialism. But the 400 did at least have their declared adversaries outnumbered. They had no intention of forming a committee or organization themselves, however. They simply wanted, they said, "to point out the real purpose behind all these attempts to bracket the Soviet Union with the fascist states, and to make it clear that Soviet and fascist policies are diametrically opposed."

Unfortunately for the 400, their timing was a bit off. Their joint letter, dated August 10, appeared in the *Daily Worker* on August 14 and in the issue of the *Nation* dated August 26. On August 22 came the news from Berlin that Germany and the Soviet Union had agreed on a non-aggression pact. In Moscow the next day, as Stalin looked on benignly, Soviet foreign minister Vyacheslav Molotov and German foreign minister Joachim von Ribbentrop signed the agreement (which had a secret protocol for dividing the spoils of Poland). Hitler's eastern front was now secure.

The agreement, though not all that surprising to Farrell and others who ever since Munich had recognized it as a real possibility, stunned many in Europe and the United States who had been sure that the Soviet Union, whatever else might truthfully be said about it, was a staunch enemy of fascism. At their home in Grafton, New York, Granville Hicks and his wife, Dorothy, listened intently to the shocking news coming from the radio in their kitchen. "Jesus Christ," Hicks exclaimed, "that knocks the bottom out of everything." Before long, he would leave the *New Masses* and resign from the party. He was not alone. "It looks as if there are going to be many breaks in the ranks," Farrell observed. "The party is apparently in turmoil, demoralized, and bewildered." Mike Gold, in this moment of profound crisis, decided to go on vacation.

Though the most distinguished among the party members and fellow travelers, including Edmund Wilson, Sidney Hook, Max Eastman, John Dos Passos and Farrell himself, had long since left the fold, many more writers now followed. Farrell would send sympathetic letters to some of them, those he considered "honest and misguided," but he believed that other "Stalinist intellectuals," such as Malcolm Cowley (who was slowly moving away from the radical movement), "should be driven out of public life—meaning out of positions of influence."

Despite the severe losses the party suffered after the Nazi-Soviet pact, historian Harvey Klehr has noted, it still would manage to retain "most of its membership, footholds in numerous organizations, and many friends and allies." One such friend, Frederick L. Schuman—a political scientist at Williams College who had been a graduate student and instructor at the University of Chicago when Farrell was there, had defended the Moscow show trials and had been one of the "400 suckers"—soon appeared in the pages of the *New Republic* with a cynical justification of Stalin's embrace of Hitler. But despite Stalin's apologists, the party's influence in the United States was never again to be what it had been. The party's support for the pact made it quite clear that loyalty to the Soviet Union was its paramount concern.

On September 1—scarcely more than a week after the signing of the pact—Germany invaded Poland. Two days later, Britain declared war, and then France followed suit. The Second World War had begun.

Farrell was determined not to be drawn into the maelstrom. "If one is to remain civilized, one must not give into this," he reflected. "One must preserve culture by keeping it a part of one's life. I am not going to let it get me. I am going to go on writing and studying. One is not less of a man or a humane person or a human being if one persists in saying, literature is not a less worthy pursuit than war and killing."

＝＞•0•＜＝

As the decade—the "Red Decade," in journalist Eugene Lyons's phrase—neared its end, Farrell looked back in an essay for Lyons's *American Mercury*, describing the arc from hope to despair that many writers and intellectuals had traversed. At the start of the 1930s, there had been the conviction that revolutionary change was both needed and imminent, with the Soviets pointing the way; at the end, the Russian Revolution had been betrayed and there was "anxiety, apprehension, even signs of panic."

Instead of opening the eyes of the writers and intellectuals, Farrell said, the radical movement, in many cases, had closed them. Edmund Wilson, who had "retained his judgment, perception, and independence" and had written "the finest" literary criticism of the decade, was an exception; so was "a younger critic," Philip Rahv. In sharp contrast, Farrell said, stood Granville Hicks and Malcolm Cowley. Hicks, who had joined the Communist Party, had "laid down the 'party line' in literature," while the fellow-traveling Cowley's literary criticism often had been "no more than an oblique application of the 'party line.'"

After the Comintern adopted the Popular Front policy in 1935, the cultural environment in America had changed. "A kind of literary Populism was born," in which the Left came to encompass "nearly everyone *but* radicals." In a window display for "the 'cultural' customers" outside, names of famous writers (not previously noted for radicalism) appeared, along with calls for "the defense of culture and democracy, not to mention the salvation of humanity. But what went on inside was another story," Farrell said.

> Under cover of this Popular Front movement was conducted one of the most pernicious literary witch-hunts in American literary history. Practically all American writers of liberal or radical persuasion who opposed the line (the Stalin murders and so on) were bitterly attacked, often slandered.... Sometimes these attacks were openly political. On other occasions, they took the form of gang-ups which pretended to be something other than what they were. The League of American Writers was one of the centers of this witch hunt. Many of its members are ornaments of present-day literature as viewed from the weekly literary supplements. And many of its members joined in the witch-hunt. When those who were thus attacked tried to defend themselves, some of these ornaments would declare with sudden "objectivity" that this was all factional politics. And they would go on affirming the approved line with appropriate gentility. Some of these ornaments are now declaring with characteristic objectivity that they never were fellow-travelers. But without them, this pernicious literary witch-hunt could not have been conducted with such immediate efficacy.

Still, the decade had produced some worthwhile works, in Farrell's view, and he listed some of them (his selection not at all based on whether the authors liked him or his politics). They included Nelson Algren's *Somebody in Boots*, Edward Dahlberg's *Bottom Dogs* and Henry Roth's *Call It Sleep*. Farrell pointed out how these works freshly reproduced the experience of hitherto voiceless immigrants:

> The 1930s in fiction attempted, briefly, to tell the story of the actuality of the American Melting Pot. Most of the younger writers of the

period come from social backgrounds new to American fiction, though not to American life. They have come from the bottom and the near bottom of American society. Their work reflects this background. Armenians, Negroes (such as those in Richard Wright's powerful book, *Uncle Tom's Children*), Italians, Jewish soda clerks, share-croppers, Maine Yankees, miners, Cape Cod Portuguese, pool-room habitués—such are the characters whom the newcomers... have sought to describe.

And what of the writers of the coming decade, the 1940s?

"The coming writer," Farrell opined, "stands amidst a kind of ruin. He must kindle excitement and enthusiasm for his work, confidence in himself, and he must forge his own perspectives. There are no literary movements now."

Chapter Thirteen

"The Wall of Isolation"

ARRELL AND HORTENSE, OUT walking one mid-June night in 1940, ran into Jack Sullivan. As the two old friends talked, the situation on the other side of the Atlantic was grim. Denmark, Holland, Norway and Belgium had fallen to Hitler's forces, and now it was France's turn; within days, the Germans would march in triumph through Paris. Sullivan demanded to know if Farrell's position was that it made no difference who won the war. Refusing to be "cross-examined" by the budding lawyer, Farrell finally submitted "that a victory by either side would be a reactionary victory, and looked at historically, would have bad consequences."

This was too much for Sullivan. He declared Farrell a "public enemy," along with the Nazis and the Communists.

Farrell was outraged.

Hortense walked away from them.

"Don't worry," Jack called to her, "I'm not going to spit in Jimmy's face."

"Not yet," said Farrell. "But you'll be doing worse soon, you're only starting."

The next day, writing in his diary, Farrell pronounced his friend "a mediocrity.... It will take better men than Jack Sullivan to bully and terrorize me."

In the face of common sense and the growing common danger, Farrell stubbornly maintained that ultimately it made no significant difference whether Nazi Germany or the democratic nations emerged victorious. The basic character of the British and American states had not changed since the First World War, he argued, and neither had that of the German state: Its character under Hitler was the same as it had been under Kaiser Wilhelm. The war, in Farrell's ideologically blinkered view, was a conflict of rival imperialisms. Fascism was an outgrowth of capitalism, and in opposing it the bourgeois democracies would also have to transform themselves into totalitarian states. Whichever side won, civilization appeared to him doomed, certainly for decades. "I can think of no alternative to the total state now but a democratic socialism." And—thanks largely, in his view, to Stalin's betrayal of the Russian Revolution—democratic socialism did not appear to be in the offing. The only hope was "a strong labor movement."

As Farrell closely followed developments in the world and at home in the new decade, he felt increasingly impotent and insignificant. "Patriotic feeling is growing," he noted with dismay in the spring of 1940. "The national defense appeal is spreading, and is popular. There is likely to be a shift in attitudes in America toward the war, and more and more, the feeling and conviction that American entry is inevitable grows in many minds. I have long felt that it is inevitable. I feel that I am an unimportant person whose voice is meaningless."

Other voices—those of chastened liberals and radicals who had rediscovered the virtues of American democracy and Western civilization, and saw more clearly than Farrell did the mortal peril that Hitler represented—carried much further. "Today," wrote Lewis Mumford in the *New Republic*, "liberals, by their unwillingness to admit the consequences of a victory by Hitler and Stalin, are emotionally on the side of 'peace'—when peace, so-called, at this moment means capitulation to the forces that will not merely wipe out liberalism, but will overthrow certain precious principles with which one element of liberalism has been indelibly associated: freedom of thought, belief in an objective reason, belief in human dignity."

Poet Archibald MacLeish, recently appointed the Librarian of Congress, thundered in the *Nation* against the "irresponsibles"—those American writers and scholars who were failing to defend in their work "the common inherited culture of the West" against the forces bent upon its destruction. "Where the modern scholar escapes from the adult judgments of the mind by taking the disinterested man of science as his model, the modern writer escapes by imitation of the artist. He practices his writing as a painter does his painting. He thinks...without responsibility to anything but truth of feeling. He observes...with honesty and truthfulness and without comment." That was inadequate, MacLeish maintained. The writer must carry "the weapon of his words...to the barricades of intellectual warfare" to defend Western civilization, "by which alone our scholars and our writers" have been sustained.

Soon, in another speech, MacLeish was claiming that the war novels of Dos Passos and Hemingway, *Three Soldiers* and *A Farewell to Arms*, had borne "bitter and dangerous fruit" in the form of a disillusioned younger generation. This was nonsense, as Farrell noted in his diary. These novels were symptoms of disillusion more than causes of it, and most American young people had never even read the books. Writers did matter, but their immediate influence was rarely as immense as MacLeish seems to have assumed.

Nevertheless, there was no stopping the reassessment of recent literature. "You know the picture of life you find in the novels of William Faulkner, Dos Passos, James T. Farrell, and so many others, who carry the day with their readers because they are writers of great power," literary critic Van Wyck Brooks was soon to tell his readers. "They seem to delight in kicking their world to pieces, as if civilization were all a pretence and everything noble a humbug.... I think our generation will be remembered as the one in which everyone hated, often without visible reason, the town in which he was born. And the writers of whom I am speaking were obsessed with ugly memories, ugly as to material things and mostly as to spiritual." It seemed to Brooks—not entirely without reason, be it noted—"that most of our current literature is written by adolescent minds."

Farrell and the others represented the "death-drive," Brooks warned. The great writers of the past, the creators of "primary" literature, he said, instead favored the "life-drive." They expressed in their works the "great themes [of] courage, justice, mercy, honor, love."

To Farrell and others of like mind, now suddenly put on the defensive, the words of Brooks, MacLeish and Mumford were signs of the gathering darkness of repression. Even that veteran radical Max Eastman, who had heroically opposed U.S. entry into World War I, was giving up on socialism as inconsistent with human nature, and—in the repellently bourgeois pages of the *Reader's Digest*—was (bravely and astutely) soon to pronounce Marxism a "pseudo science" and Lenin's great experiment a monstrous failure: "An honest, bold, noble attempt to produce through common ownership a Society of the Free and Equal produced a tyrant and a totalitarian state."

In the *New Republic, Partisan Review* and elsewhere, Edmund Wilson, Dwight Macdonald, Farrell and others would rise up to smite these outrageous Philistines. MacLeish, said Wilson contemptuously, "sounds as if he had never heard of the class war, which has certainly, since the Bolshevist revolution, presented itself as the fundamental conflict of the contemporary world." Brooks, declared Macdonald with equal disdain, "has become, doubtless with the best intentions, our leading mouthpiece for totalitarian cultural values." And Farrell, with pugnacious certitude, discerned in their arguments "a simple historic fact: the bourgeoisie cannot stand its own culture and its own past.... Now, from all sides, the Philistines are coming together, and they wail for a *Weltanschauung*.... What these men are really trying to do is to create a metaphysics of the war."

Before the German-Soviet Nonaggression Pact of 1939, Farrell's radicalism had made his criticism of the Stalinists more persuasive; now it was serving to mislead and isolate him. Sidney Hook and others argued with him about the war, but to no avail. At one point, an exasperated Hook told him that he and Meyer Schapiro (who shared, and no doubt reinforced, Farrell's position) were "political onanists." But Farrell stubbornly stuck to his antiwar guns.

As revolutionary socialists and anti-Stalinists opposed to the war, he and Schapiro were not entirely alone. There were, besides the editors of *Partisan Review*, the Trotskyists.

The "Old Man," as Trotsky was sometimes called by his acolytes, continued in Mexico to insist that Stalinist Russia, although a "degenerated workers' state," was still a workers' state, and therefore entitled to be defended unconditionally against all its capitalist enemies, whether fascist or democratic. Farrell considered this doctrine dubious, and—in light of the Nazi-Soviet pact, the joint occupation of Poland, and the invasion of Finland—so did Max Shachtman and many other American followers of Trotsky. At the April 1940 convention of the Socialist Workers Party, Shachtman, splitting with the orthodox Trotskyist leader James P. Cannon, led nearly half of the roughly eight hundred members out of the party and also took with him the vast majority of the young Trotskyists in the Young People's Socialist League (Fourth International). Shachtman formed his own Workers Party.

Farrell had friends in both camps, but little hope that the Trotskyists would accomplish much, separately or together. "There seems to be little future for the Trotskyites—split or no split—in the present world," he had noted in his diary in November 1939. "Trotsky will never come back, I think, as a figure who again comes to power."

In August 1940, the truth of that last observation was established beyond doubt. Farrell was in Mount Sinai Hospital in New York, recovering from an operation for the removal of a carbuncle from his neck. On this particular night he was asleep, with his bedside radio still on, when suddenly, at about thirty minutes past midnight, he woke up. "There was a news broadcast. About half of the words penetrated my mind." Then he grasped what was being said: *Trotsky had been stabbed by an assassin and was not expected to live.* Shocked, outraged and powerless to do anything about it, Farrell could not sleep anymore. He rang for the nurse, who gave him a pill. He still didn't sleep well, but kept tossing and turning.

In the morning, he wondered if it might have been a nightmare. But soon the newspaper arrived, dispelling that illusion. Trotsky had been fatally stabbed with an ice pick by a Kremlin agent who, in an elaborate ruse, had gained access to the villa in Coyoacán. Farrell, stricken, was plagued by the same sobering thought over the next few days: *Trotsky is dead.*

⟫•○•⟪

HORTENSE (WHO "NEVER REGARDED Farrell's Trotskyite views with any favor," according to Jim Henle) was pregnant again. She had learned this in March 1940.

Seven months earlier, not long after the loss of their child, she and Farrell had driven out to Brighton Beach with Mary Hunter to see a performance of Ibsen's *Ghosts* starring Alla Nazimova, Hortense's friend and former lover. Farrell was very impressed by her performance as Mrs. Alving. Surprised to see them, Nazimova went with her visitors after the show to a place on the Coney Island boardwalk, where they drank beer and talked. After Hortense told her of their recent loss, Nazimova took Farrell aside and told him: "You must make a new baby right away, or it will torment Hortense and be a nightmare to her all her life."

But the new baby was not "made" right away, possibly because of a slight reluctance on Farrell's part. When the doctor informed

Hortense that she was pregnant and that the baby would probably arrive in early October, she apparently waited a day or so before telling Farrell, perhaps a little fearful of his reaction. After hearing the news, Farrell noted in his diary: "This comes to us at a time when we are so insecure financially that it is going to be an added burden. But then there would always be some reason, if one wanted to find one. We are not without prospects." True, Hortense had been having little success getting acting roles. "In what should be her best years, [she is] finding that she cannot get a job," Farrell had written bitterly in his diary just days before. The two of them were writing a play together, though, in the hope (vain, as it turned out) of getting it produced, and he was also working on his next novel, *Father and Son.*

Just one week before the official publication of that novel (which Farrell was dedicating to the memory of his father), Hortense gave birth to their son, Kevin James Farrell. He arrived shortly after five in the morning of October 3. Hortense had been in labor for about two and a half hours, and knocked out for most of it. Farrell, waiting once again in the hospital's reception room, saw the infant before he was a half-hour old. Kevin weighed about seven and a half pounds. Farrell observed that the newborn's face was "chalky...and then, with more light, was red. It cried. A strange thing, to look at your son for the first time."

Farrell's excitement, joy and sense of having entered a new realm of being did not disappear when Kevin was taken away. "It is a strange feeling, even frightening to think that one is a parent of a newborn infant," he wrote two days later. "A human destiny that is a clean page to be written. And one has to take such a role in the writing of this page: at the same time that one takes such a role, one does not do the direct suffering for the consequences of that destiny."

Little more than three months later, in January 1941, Farrell and Hortense were married. His divorce from Dorothy had become final the previous June. (Some months before that, Farrell began to receive reports of Dorothy having been seen in New York and Chicago in the company of "Stuff" Smith, a black jazz violinist and band leader.)

The wedding took place near poet James Rorty's home in northern New Jersey. Jim and Marjorie Henle drove the happy couple there. The ceremony took place, not in the Rorty abode, but on a nearby mountain, just over the county line, so that the officiating justice of the peace would be acting within his own jurisdiction. On their way to the mountain site, Hortense shocked the official by telling him of the cute little baby she and the groom already had at home.

In the ensuing months and years, young Kevin would at times be a great delight to his parents. But he also would prove something of a trial, particularly for Hortense. "Why, it [the baby] doesn't leave you time for anything else!" she exclaimed in astonishment early on. Farrell, like most men then (and, indeed, for centuries before), regarded the care and feeding of his offspring as women's work. "Jim always avoided all domestic chores—in fact, apparently made no effort to be helpful in any way," Jim Henle recalled.

The burden, then, fell on Hortense, and she, unlike most women, was simply unequal to it. High-strung and intense, she could only scream or yammer when Kevin balked at being fed. She was utterly—and, as always, theatrically—at a loss. Although she was unable to find work as an actress and so remained at home, and although she and Farrell were worried about money, they had to hire a maid to feed their son.

And that wasn't the only problem. Even after Kevin passed the "terrible twos" and reached ages four, five, six, they found it difficult to control him. He behaved well at school, according to his teachers, but at home he was given to tantrums.

Determined to be a good mother, Hortense was extremely overprotective. A mere runny nose was sufficient reason for her darling boy to be kept home from school. "What that child went through!" said her friend Randolph Carter. "She was at him every minute.... He couldn't do this, he couldn't do that." Hortense allowed her exaggerated fears to rule. If Kevin went near water, she was sure he would drown. If he went near Carter's cat, she was afraid he would be suffocated by it. She never let up. "I think he had the most horrible childhood in the world with this woman," Carter said.

The parents came to wrangle frequently over the boy. "The behavior problem of Kevin continues, and Hortense and I often are at odds concerning it," Farrell wrote in his diary in September 1944. Five months later the situation was no better: "Hortense and Kevin have troubles. She can't convince him to help and be more cooperat[iv]e, and I can't convince her to take it more easy and more calmly, and there you are. Kevie has his will, and it is strong.

The hours we have spent discussing and also quarreling concerning him, and then, the hours on top of it."

⟫•◦•⟪

FARRELL BEGAN WRITING A COLUMN ("The Cultural Front") for *Partisan Review* in 1940. He seems to have been given it because some of the editors, Dwight Macdonald in particular, were unhappy with the fiction he was offering them. In the winter of 1938–1939, Farrell had been ready to call it quits with *PR* if the editors rejected the third story in a row that he had shown them. But by a three-to-two vote (with Rahv, Phillips and Dupee in the majority, and financial angel Morris siding with Macdonald), the editors had accepted "The Only Son," a clumsily written yet still effective story about a young man and his unhappy, hypocritical parents. It ran in the spring 1939 issue, and was the last piece of fiction by Farrell ever to appear in *Partisan Review*. Later that year, the editors arranged with him to write a regular column.

"Farrell would write such terrible stuff," Mary McCarthy told an interviewer more than four decades later (and six years after Farrell's death). "*PR* gave him a column so we wouldn't have to print his pieces." McCarthy, who had left Rahv to marry Edmund Wilson in February 1938, was not one of the editors, but she was contributing a "Theater Chronicle" column to *Partisan Review* (as Farrell himself had done in 1936), and there is little reason to doubt the accuracy of her description of what happened.

In his first effort (for which he received the grand sum of seven dollars), published in the March-April 1940 issue, Farrell undertook to explain why the leading fellow travelers and Communists who had lately jumped the Stalinist ship should not be welcomed with open arms. "It is difficult to consider the conduct of these men either noble or laudable. It required a historic earthquake to awaken their moral sensibilities. The murders of Stalin, the Stalinist methods of slander and character assassination, the role of Stalinism in the Spanish Civil War, the evidences of the totalitarian character of the Stalinist movement which no one could fail to perceive—all these failed to stir them." Stalinism remained a menace, both to "the genuine anti-war movement," because the Communists now pretended also to oppose the war, and to cultural life, over which Stalinism, despite the recent defections, continued to exert a powerful influence. (Stalin, Farrell said, "has shot much better men than Louis Fischer, Vincent Sheean, Malcolm Cowley, Granville Hicks, Ralph Bates, and Dr. Frederick L. Schuman. And Stalinism did not perish as a result of such murders.")

Farrell insisted that Hicks and the other new apostates had not "satisfactorily explained their sudden change of mind." Hicks, in an anguished statement in the *New Republic* attempting to explain his resignation from the party, seemed chiefly distressed by the antics of the American Communist leaders in trying to justify the Nazi-Soviet pact rather than by the larger meaning. Indeed, he said that despite having left it, he intended "to do my best to defend the Communist Party."

"One seeks in vain," Farrell said, "for an analytical and principled statement which will reveal why [the new apostates] lacked foresight and then suddenly possessed such remarkable hindsight." In fact, he added, "the only statement of a break which I have read that can be termed principled was one written in *The Socialist Call*, by Richard Rovere, a former editor of *New Masses*."

Rovere, a twenty-four-year-old protégé of Hicks, later to become an incisive liberal political journalist, had joined the Communist Party in 1936 in the belief that the Communists were working effectively to bring about socialism in America. He had seen no reason to break with the party over what "a brother party in Moscow" was doing, he explained, until it finally became clear to him that the "brother" party was actually "the domineering father, great Russian foreign policy its first household rule." But Rovere's faith in socialism was undiminished, and he was joining the Socialist Party. "If, as I believe, Leninist organizational theories lie behind most of the tragedies of the Soviet Union and the Comintern, then Socialism is in no way involved."

Impressed as Farrell evidently was by Rovere's intelligent and forthright piece, he and Rahv found Rovere himself "a distinct disappointment" when he came to visit them in Farrell's apartment that March. Despite what Farrell took to be his "principled" statement in the *Call*, Rovere was no theorist; in fact, as a young Communist he had found Marx and Engels boring, and Lenin even more so, and had scarcely read them. "He has no real perspectives, no ideas," Farrell recorded in his diary.

That Rovere, without the benefit of "principled thinking," saw so much more clearly than Farrell the Leninist source of the Stalinist malady shows how much the desire to be engaged in "principled thinking"—i.e., in theory—misled Farrell. His self-right-eousness, moreover, kept him from realizing sooner than he did that he was being misled, even as it also prevented him from hav-ing much sympathy for those such as Hicks who were slowly and painfully (and, to be sure, belatedly) extricating themselves from what Farrell called the Stalinist "political religion." Though he had apparently been eager at first to learn more of the thinking (mis-takenly assuming it to be "principled") behind Rovere's rejection of Leninism, Farrell seems to have been convinced that he himself had abandoned Stalinism at ("objectively") precisely the correct instant—that he had been right in his previous sympathy for it, and was then right in his opposition. In short, he was always right. That made it hard for him to forgive those who had been wrong for so long, or to have much patience for suggestions from ignorant hack journalists that the brutal suppression of the rebellion at the Kron-stadt naval base in 1921 had been as telling an infamy as the Moscow show trials. It was much easier to demand rather arro-gantly that all concerned follow his own example and engage in "principled thinking."

Farrell's second column for *Partisan Review* was about Broadway. But it never appeared. The column had not been a hur-ried effort: he had written five or six drafts before submitting it. "It never pays to dash off any piece of writing that one is doing," he reflected. "One should write it as if it were to last forever, no matter how fugitive it be." But the editors were unimpressed by the result. Macdonald phoned Farrell and informed him that they did not intend to run the column because they considered it superficial, loosely written, and saying nothing that had not been said before. This angered Farrell, who considered the piece at least adequate. "After all," he told himself, "it is only a column." A few days later, Rahv and Phillips came to see him, and after listening to them, he admitted there was justice in their criticisms and agreed to rewrite the column. But then he found that he could not bring himself to do it. Writing came easily to him; rewriting work that he had con-sidered finished did not. So, no column by Farrell appeared in the May-June issue.

His next effort, an extremely lame satire deriding the views on culture of MacLeish and company, should not have run either, but it did, in the July-August 1940 issue. Then, in the following issue, came a eulogy for Trotsky.

Finally, in the November-December issue, Farrell produced a

diatribe against Mortimer J. Adler, the neo-Thomist philosopher who had become a controversial figure at the University of Chicago (where he had the ear of President Robert M. Hutchins). In the course of a recent tirade against naturalism and positivism, Adler had said some inflammatory and foolish things. (Such as: "Democracy has much more to fear from the [positivist] mentality of its teachers than from the nihilism of Hitler.") Farrell responded with equal fervor in his column, calling Adler dull, pompous, weak in his reasoning, superficial in his scholarship, an "obscurantist and obfuscator" beyond compare, and "a provincial Torquemada" who lacked, for the moment at least, an Inquisition. While Farrell's intemperate *ad hominem* assault no doubt pleased Adler's enemies, it was hardly a model of dispassionate philosophical discourse; it was more the work of a Studs Lonigan, Ph.D. Though that probably didn't much bother his editors, the column proved to be Farrell's final one.

The editors were contemplating some changes in *Partisan Review*. In the September-October issue, they announced their intention of changing its name to *The Forties*, starting with the January-February 1941 issue. "We are making this change," they explained, "because the old name, pertinent when the magazine first appeared in 1934, has more recently led to many misunderstandings of the magazine's purpose and character." (They invited readers to suggest a better name. In the end, they kept the old one.)

Then, on December 10, 1940, after attending a lecture by Meyer Schapiro on Chartres, Rahv and Phillips accompanied Farrell and Hortense back to their apartment. "Quite casually," Farrell wrote in his diary the next day, "Philip suddenly said to me that *Partisan Review* would have to print my column only every other issue." It seemed the editors were now planning to have additional columns, by Macdonald and others, and so needed to cut back on his. Farrell responded by telling them to just eliminate his—that would give them the space they needed. They said he was making a mistake.

Farrell thought the whole affair "a shabby little business," as he recorded the next day.

> William and Philip laid the blame on Dwight. They said he is unconsciously jealous of me, and so on. I was not so much sore as I was disappointed. For six years, I have done everything in my power to try and build up the magazine. I fought the League of American Writ-

Top and left: Farrell's parents, James Francis Farrell and Mary Daly, some months before their wedding in April 1899. Right: Julia Brown Daly, Farrell's grandmother (whom he called "Mother"), about 1922.

Top: Farrell's Uncle Tom Daly, who took him fishing in Michigan in the summer of 1919; back in Chicago, meanwhile, a race riot occurred. Bottom: Farrell's Aunt Ella Daly, who called him "Little Brother" and loved him; but Jimmy, like his alter ego Eddie Ryan, was disturbed by his aunt's "drinking and cursing" (The Silence of History, *p. 130*).

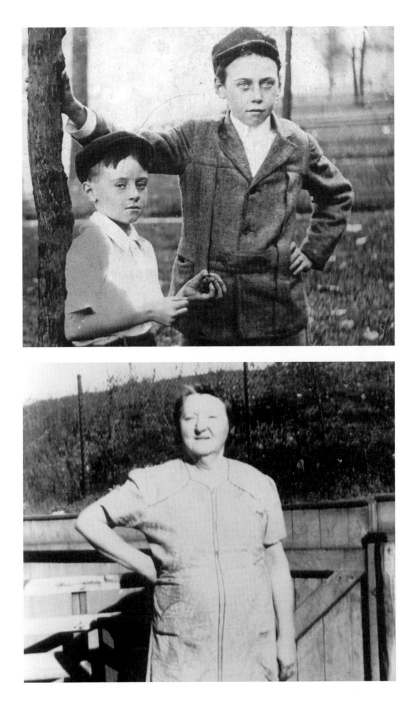

Top: Jimmy (left) with brother Earl in 1910. Bottom: Mary Daly Farrell, c. 1922, dressed "like the scrubwoman's cousin" (The Silence of History, *p. 130*).

*Top right: Farrell as a student at St. Cyril high school, where he acquired the
nickname "Jumps" and became "one of the best all-around athletes ever turned
out" at the school. Top left: Dorothy Farrell, who married Farrell twice, in 1931
and in 1955; at the University of Chicago, where they first met, said one in
their circle, "she absolutely worshiped the ground he walked on." Bottom: The
baronial mansion at Yaddo, a retreat for artists in Saratoga Springs, New York.
Farrell first went there as a guest in 1933. "It is the first time in my life," he
wrote Dorothy, "I can work under conditions that are describable as ideal."*

Top: Actress Hortense Alden, who met Farrell in 1935 and became his second wife. Middle: Farrell joined John McDonald (left) and Albert Glotzer (right) in Mexico in 1937 for the Dewey Commission's interrogation of Leon Trotsky. Bottom: Farrell and John Dewey (right) became friends in 1937. Farrell, who'd begun reading the philosopher years before, said in 1965 that Dewey was "the major influence on my writing."

Top: "In a literary, personal and psychological sense," Farrell once told editor Jim Henle (right), "you have meant perhaps more to me than any other human being in the world." Bottom: Farrell and Hortense Alden in Paris in 1938. The French, he found, "are more natural, more alive" than the English.

Top: The strain after the birth in 1947 of John Stephen shows on the faces of Farrell, Hortense, and Kevin. Bottom: This caricature of "James T. Farrell and His World" by John Mackey appears in The New Republic *of October 6, 1947.*

Top: Speaking in Paris in 1949, philosopher Sidney Hook (right) and Farrell criticized a Communist-inspired peace conference there. Bottom left: Cleo Paturis and Farrell in her office. Bottom right: At Farrell's grave, a monument in his memory to the families he immortalized in his fiction.

ers, and refused to cooperate with it, instead, cooperating with *Partisan Review*. I have tried to get it writers, readers, money. I've been willing to write often for it, and have written for it for nothing, or for a few pennies when I could have spent the same time either working on novels or stories, or writing elsewhere and making something. And despite this, they are either afraid of me, afraid of my name, don't like my work too much, or something. What? I don't know.... It so happens that I can bring them more readers than any other contributor whom they have got. But then, maybe they don't want readers.

Though *PR*'s editors did want readers, of course, Rahv and Phillips may not have been quite as keen on politics at the moment as Farrell, Macdonald and many *Partisan Review* readers were. Macdonald was pushing for major changes at the magazine. Despite what undoubtedly were his aesthetic reservations about Farrell's style as a writer, he shared his antiwar position and believed that *Partisan Review* should engage in uncompromising socialist criticism of the political and social order. And many *PR* readers wanted to see that sort of criticism. A reader survey some months later indicated that those who wanted more political articles outnumbered those who didn't by 4 to 1. In addition, Macdonald told Farrell that out of 250 responses from readers, 35 favored his column while 6 wanted it dropped—and that no other feature in the magazine received as many favorable votes. Macdonald also told him that he liked a lengthy piece about Lewis Mumford that Farrell did for the *Southern Review* and asked him why he never did anything like it for *PR*. ("I said that *PR* never wanted me to, nor was it really ever interested in my doing something like that for them. Rahv once told me that all I could have was three pages.")

Soon after the ax fell on him, Farrell surmised that the editors might be shifting away from politics and seeking to turn *Partisan Review* into "an aesthetic little magazine." Certainly, the cautious Rahv and Phillips were aware of the government crackdown on the *Masses* and other radical publications during World War I, and must have been somewhat apprehensive, as the war drew closer, that history was on the verge of repeating itself. Perhaps that was why they seriously considered giving *Partisan Review* the apolitical name of *The Forties* (which was not Macdonald's choice).

Whatever the true explanation for the editors' decision to rein in his column, Farrell realized that day in his apartment that they would not be "heartbroken" by its discontinuance. When he told Rahv and Phillips to just drop the column, one of them said that "well, it would be all right, I'd be able to write what I wanted when I had an idea of doing something for *PR*."

In his anger, Farrell soon vowed never to write for *Partisan Review* again (though he prudently did not foreclose the possibility entirely). In the years ahead, he was to appear a few times in the magazine. But his close relationship with *Partisan Review* and its editors was now at an end.

⟶►◦◄⟵

EDMUND WILSON DID NOT WANT to read *Father and Son*. He had read the first two volumes in the *Studs Lonigan* trilogy and, under their spell, had felt that he himself had grown up on the South Side of Chicago. But at some point in the third volume, he concluded that he had had enough. Wilson, who came from a privileged background, wanted to read no more about Irish families on the South Side, no more about those "unreflecting and limited people" (as he had described them in passing in his 1936 review of *A Note on Literary Criticism*). And after dutifully finishing *Judgment Day*, he hadn't. He had not read *A World I Never Made*. He had not read *No Star Is Lost*. And now he did not want to read the third volume in the series, *Father and Son*. But instead of passing the novel along to someone else to review, the eminent critic decided—in what must be counted an extraordinary display of arrogance and unashamed, almost boastful ignorance, only somewhat mitigated by the evidence of his friendly feelings toward Farrell—to ask the author directly, in the pages of the *New Republic*, just why it was that he kept inflicting these books "about Irish boys growing up in Chicago" on readers, and to invite him to respond. "Everybody," Wilson advised Farrell, "is interested to read a certain amount of this; everybody admires your honesty and courage; nobody will deny the importance of your work in the fiction of your generation. But this importance is not increased by your continuing to tell the same story."

Farrell, without apparent resentment, seized the opportunity not only to correct Wilson's misconceptions and misstatements, and to take a few swipes at Clifton Fadiman and others of his bêtes noires among the critics, but, more importantly, to express the intention behind his work:

> In my fiction, I seek to recreate a precise, detailed and objective pic-

ture of certain features of the so-called American Way of Life. I seek to answer the question: what happens to people? I hold a functional conception of character, viewing it as a social product embodying the reciprocal play of local influences on the individual, and of the individual on society. I am concerned with the concrete processes whereby society, through the instrumentality of social institutions, forms and molds characters, giving to the individual the very content of his consciousness.... Insofar as my books deal with boys growing up, the exploration of the psychology of boyhood affords me a better opportunity to reveal these processes concretely than does the depiction of adults. However, my books do not deal merely with boys growing up. They deal with one of the largest social groupings in America, and with both children and adults in that group. Anyone who thinks that my books about the O'Neill and O'Flaherty families are merely about a boy growing up has been patently misinformed or else he has misread these books.

Earlier in the year, Farrell had been heartened by some comments made by H. L. Mencken in an interview with the *New York Times*. "Wonderful stuff in those Chicago tales" of Farrell's, Mencken said. "Whoever doesn't like Farrell is an idiot or a liar." As to why what the interviewer called Farrell's "critical backing" had fallen off from what it had been three or four years earlier, Mencken put it down to politics. "Farrell refused to go along with Stalin's boys, and as a critic he took a fall out of new authors they were bringing up. So they ganged him."

This was quoted by Farrell in his response to Wilson, and would be quoted again and again by his staunch admirers down through the decades. But it was not wholly accurate. It was not Farrell's literary criticism that made him a renegade in the comrades' eyes, but rather his political apostasy on the subject of the Moscow show trials and Trotsky.

Mencken's support was naturally welcome to Farrell, but the great man's curmudgeonly comments could hardly be construed as literary criticism of a high order and, as a practical matter, his influence was far from what it had been in the 1920s. Edmund Wilson—whom Farrell had hailed for writing the finest literary criticism of the 1930s—was now a much more significant critic.

Had Wilson troubled to read any of the O'Neill-O'Flaherty novels, he would have discovered characters quite different from Studs Lonigan and a story quite different from Lonigan's, too.

In *Father and Son*, the third book in the O'Neill-O'Flaherty series, the time is 1918 to 1923, and Jim O'Neill and Danny O'Neill, estranged father and son, take center stage. As the novel begins, the O'Neill family has moved up—thanks to Jim's promotion at the express company—to an apartment with an indoor bathroom, hot and cold running water, steam heat, gas and electricity. And Jim, justly proud of that achievement, is in vigorous physical health. But the novel then chronicles his sad decline as he suffers several strokes, is reduced to a helpless paralytic, and then dies. Meanwhile, his son Danny, still living at the O'Flaherty's, is growing up. He enters high school, and his experiences there over the ensuing years closely parallel Farrell's own. Just before graduation, he goes to work at the express company. Danny and his father seem to grow closer, at least for a moment. But when Danny gets the news of his father's death, he reflects that he and his father "had never really known" each other, and he "felt empty more than he felt anything." He wonders if there was "something wrong" with him. He senses that "there was something tragic" about his father, that he "never had a chance."

"In *Father and Son*," wrote Pulitzer Prize-winning poet Stephen Vincent Benét in a searching appraisal in *Saturday Review*,

> James Farrell adds another panel to his set of honest and uncompromising murals of Irish-American life in Chicago.... [W]hat gives the book its major weight and impact is the interweaving of two themes. As Danny is going through school and making his first confused attempts to deal with life, the years of his father, Jim O'Neill, are declining.... The mixture of tenderness and irritation in Jim's attitude toward his family—his attempts to understand his sons—these are finely done. But what grows in the mind is the stature of the man himself. For Jim O'Neill is a man, not a symbol, a slogan, or a piece of propaganda. There is dignity in him. Through him you can see the hard life of the people, for he is one of the people. But his struggle is man's old struggle against time and fate—the struggle that ends in defeat with every death and continues nevertheless.

Although Benét thought that Farrell "has gone as far in depicting both Jim and Danny as honest and accurate realism can go," he still found "something lacking in the end of the book—in Jim O'Neill's death and Danny's feeling about it—the transforming touch that lifts work to greatness." The defect, he suggested, was perhaps due to Farrell's "method." But what Benét wanted was probably not so much beyond Farrell's method as it was beyond his experience:

Danny's lack of feeling when Jim O'Neill died undoubtedly mirrored Farrell's own lack of feeling when his own father died.

The daily *New York Times* review was mixed, but J. Donald Adams of the Sunday *Times* Book Review section phoned Jim Henle to tell him that he liked the novel. Farrell recorded this intelligence in his diary in mid-October, and kept looking for Adams's review each Sunday thereafter. Finally, on December 1 it appeared, but only as the lead item in a fiction roundup. Though the review was almost completely laudatory, Farrell, revealingly, was apoplectic at the perfunctory treatment.

> Adams did a double crossing act on us.... Somebody got to him: he lost his guts or something. Perhaps, it was the Church or indirectly, Catholic influences. If I am so good and so honest, why does he treat me this way? This question is logical. *The Times* has been doing this to me during my entire literary career. People like Adams are miserable hirelings.... I have no persecution complex; but my books get little help and less push than those of almost all of my contemporaries and many of my juniors. And they continue treating me just as they did with *Young Lonigan.*

In truth, Farrell did seem to have something of a persecution complex. He had no real cause to complain about many of the past *Times* reviews of his works, especially the very perceptive ones by Fred T. Marsh. And his denunciation of Adams in this instance seems more than a bit much, considering that the reviewer had praised him as "one of the most honest and unflinching of our novelists," and said, "His work grows in power and maturity, and in *Father and Son* we have the best book he has yet written."

Still, Farrell was looking for (in his word) "push." He wanted people to buy the books. "If [*Father and Son*] could have a sale of 20,000," he had reflected in September, "our financial problems would be settled for at least the coming year." By the end of October, it was apparent that the novel was selling slowly, with sales (including advance sales) at about 8,000. "I am beginning to think that it will not go more than 10,000 at the most," he said, concluding that *Father and Son* should do "a little better than *No Star Is Lost*, but that is the best that I now hope from it." He blamed the critics, though the reception accorded *Father and Son* had been better than that given the earlier novel. "Critics cannot, will not, do not want to read my books with an open mind. They do not want a write[r] to make a solid and patient effort to recapture reality."

Certainly, some of the reviewers seemed to have little use for his efforts. In the *New Yorker*, Clifton Fadiman made a complaint similar to Edmund Wilson's. "By this time," Fadiman said, "you'd figure that, what with the Studs Lonigan trilogy and two volumes of the story of the O'Neills, you had an adequate idea of Mr. Farrell's Chicago Irish, life being on the brief side and all that sort of thing. But in the grim lexicon of Mr. Farrell there's no such word as 'adequate,' so here's another O'Neill volume, *Father and Son*."

If critics were now inclined to neglect Farrell, John Chamberlain suggested in *Harper's*, "it is because his method does not make for surprises; one can review each Farrell book by saying something new about the Chicago Irish, or something new about the United States in which Danny O'Neill grows up, but there is nothing new to say about the Farrell technic, which was fixed in the *Studs Lonigan* trilogy. It is a good technic, for Mr. Farrell's purposes, which are not particularly concerned with advancing the art of the novel." Chamberlain deemed *Father and Son* "the tenderest of all Farrell's books: Danny grows as Farrell himself grows."

The best, most intelligent review that *Father and Son* received, at least in Jim Henle's opinion, was the one in *Partisan Review*. On that day in December 1940 when Farrell's close association with the magazine effectively came to an end, Rahv and Phillips, in an apparent effort to make amends, invited him to propose a reviewer for *Father and Son*. Farrell refused, "on principle." Subsequently the editors arranged with poet Weldon Kees to review the novel.

Kees, as it turned out, liked *Father and Son* very much. He hailed Farrell's "nearly impossible" accomplishment of creating, in Danny O'Neill, "a believable and three-dimensional autobiographical hero," one "very remote from the usual 'spokesman,'" such as Thomas Wolfe's Eugene Gant/George Webber. "[Farrell's] hero's jokes are bad, his taste worse; he is vain and his thoughts are ordinary, his opinions properly childish; the drunk he goes on is as honestly told as the exploits of Studs Lonigan. And yet Danny is highly sympathetic; the usual pat literary 'sensitivity' has been scraped off to reveal the human." On the series of novels of which *Father and Son* was the third, it was necessary to withhold final judgment, Kees said. "No one foresaw when reading the early volumes of the Lonigan trilogy—no one was capable of foreseeing—that the completed and collected work was to be far more powerful than even its three powerful sections.... What the O'Neill-O'Flaherty work will finally come to, with its wider canvas and its looser structure, it would be fantastic for anyone to predict. Mr. Farrell's effects are cumulative and not immediately apparent; in the meantime, while we wait, the individual volumes continue to be superbly readable."

=>-0-<=

THE UNITED STATES WAS NOW "the great arsenal of democracy," in President Roosevelt's phrase, providing aid to Britain while still holding back from war. With polls showing a majority of Americans wanting to risk war rather than let Hitler triumph, Max Eastman in May 1941 declared in the *New York Times* that "those honest radicals and progressives" who opposed this policy out of concern that it would mean turning American democracy into a fascist state were "not thinking practically." They were failing to grasp the "obvious fact" that this war was a struggle between democracy and tyranny, between modern democracy and totalitarianism.

Farrell seems to have been impervious to such arguments. Eastman's letter to the editor (which had taken up three full columns on the *Times's* editorial page) was "not a good letter," Farrell commented in his diary.

A year later, with America at war, Farrell would engage in an extensive exchange with Eastman in the pages of *Partisan Review*. "When Eastman tells us that we have lost faith in democracy," the novelist asserted, "he is using the wrong word: we have long ago lost faith in capitalism." Farrell also strongly objected to Eastman's contentions (in *Reader's Digest* of June 1941) that Lenin's great experiment was a monstrous failure, and that socialism was simply not in accord with human nature. "Just as it is now argued that human nature contravenes the principles of socialism, so was it once claimed that human nature contradicted the principles of democracy," Farrell remarked. In his estimation, Eastman, Brooks, MacLeish et al. were "Philistines...wail[ing] for a *Weltanschauung.*"

Eastman, for his part, described what he regarded as the real difference between Farrell and himself:

> In a period when certain means we had all agreed upon for emancipating the working class and therewith all society, have proven to lead in the opposite direction, we have remained loyal to the aim,

you to the means.... You do not care that much about the workers or about human freedom. You care more about your own emotional and intellectual life which had been organized around the means.

It was a harsh judgment, yet there was considerable truth in it. Farrell did seem to have an excessive regard for his own emotional and intellectual life. Ever since he had awakened to the world of ideas and learning at the University of Chicago, he had hungered insatiably for knowledge—of philosophy, of history, of literature, of everything. In 1940, wanting to learn mathematics in order "to go on in philosophy, and...to gain even a little sense of the science of our day," he studied it on his own, and then, in 1941, took a course in symbolic logic from a sympathetic professor at New York University. (Though he apparently didn't do very well in the course, the professor awarded him an "A" anyway.) But admirable as it may have been, there was a certain unreality about Farrell's grand intellectual ambition; it was far beyond any possibility of actual attainment.

In response to Eastman's criticism of the "muddled" thinking of radicals such as himself, Farrell simply denied the charge: "I am not muddled in the least," he declared indignantly in his diary. In truth, however, his thinking about the ongoing struggle between democracy and tyranny was indeed hopelessly confused. He could not accept the obvious facts of the situation.

Eight years after his *Partisan Review* exchange with Eastman, Farrell was to acknowledge that Eastman had been right. In a letter in 1950 to the magazine's editors, he apologized for his "unwarrantedly sharp" reply to Eastman and said: "On the basic questions which we were discussing, The Nature of Totalitarianism and of the War, I believe that he was more right and had more insight than I....At a time when it took great moral courage, Max Eastman wrote with frankness and honesty concerning the nature of totalitarianism." He sent a copy of this letter to Eastman, with a note saying it was meant as a tribute to him. "This," comments Eastman's biographer, "was a unique gesture in the history of radical letters."

But that was in the future.

On June 22, 1941, Germany attacked Russia. "Many people will hail the invasion of the Soviet Union," Farrell told Jim Henle. "I don't. Stalin or no Stalin, the invasion of Russia is likely to send up the fever chart of American fascism: to give them a better war cry....The main hope is that Stalin is dumped, and the revolutionary past of Russia, the spirit of 1917, should re-assert itself."

"29 Reds Indicted In 'Overthrow Plot,'" reported the *New York Times* in mid-July 1941. The "Reds" were James P. Cannon and other leaders of the Socialist Workers Party, along with the Trotskyist leaders of Minneapolis Teamsters Local 544. "It is a very serious business, and a big case," commented Farrell, who agreed to become chairman of a Civil Rights Defense Committee to aid the defendants. "If enough fuss is raised," Farrell told John Dos Passos, the committee's vice chairman, "the government may even back down on the case."

For some time, Farrell had regarded "a strong labor movement" as "the only hope for liberty," and it distressed him, as he surveyed the world scene, that virtually everywhere labor appeared "gagged and bound." Thus, during the interval between the Nazi-Soviet pact and the German invasion of Russia, he had been heartened by the series of strikes that Communist-led trade unions had carried out at defense plants in California, Wisconsin and elsewhere. The strikes, he was sure, were mainly over wages; the workers deserved raises, and if the Stalinists were leading the strikes, it was the fault of the other labor leaders, such as Phil Murray, president of the Congress of Industrial Organizations (CIO). That the effect of the strikes and the intent of the Communists were to hinder the growing U.S. defense effort did not disturb Farrell as it might have, had he not also been against the war.

With the German invasion of the Soviet Union, the American Communists' position shifted, of course. They now wanted the United States to enter quickly the conflict they had previously denounced as "imperialist," and soon they were insisting that "all disputes in industry must now...be solved without interruption of production." Meanwhile, the Trotskyists—the roughly 650 who belonged to Cannon's Socialist Workers Party, as well as the 400 or so in Shachtman's rival Workers Party—continued, in theory at least, to oppose the "imperialist" war. Cannon, still staunchly in favor of defending the "degenerated" Soviet Union, wanted American workers simultaneously to "overthrow the bourgeoisie at home" and, as the war was thus being transformed into a splendid

struggle for true democracy, to fight Hitler's forces as well. Shachtman, in the belief that the working class had "more to gain by
defeatism with regard to both imperialist camps" than by defense
of the Soviet Union, urged workers to opt for an imaginary "Third
Camp."

These ideological niceties were of little interest to Daniel J.
Tobin, the president of the International Brotherhood of Teamsters,
American Federation of Labor (AFL). To him, the lowercase communists who followed the late Trotsky's faltering light were no better
than the uppercase ones in thrall to Stalin, especially when they
controlled one of his own locals. Of unchallenged personal honesty, Tobin celebrated his sixty-sixth birthday in 1941. Just four
years younger than Farrell's father would have been, Tobin was
born in Ireland, immigrated to America when he was fourteen, and
later become an $11-a-week teamster in Boston. In 1907—two
years after the big strike in Chicago in which Farrell's father had
participated—Tobin had won the presidency of the teamsters'
union, and had held the position ever since. The conservative labor
leader was a "vehement" anti-Communist, noted *Fortune* magazine
in May 1941, and three years earlier, on the basis of an anti-Communist clause in the union's constitution, he had filed suit to oust
the Minneapolis local's militant Trotskyist leaders—the hard-bitten
Dunne brothers, Vincent R. (Ray), Miles and Grant. That was Tobin's
second attempt to get rid of the local's radical leadership, but it
proved a failure. Since the Trotskyists were hostile to the Communist Party, the court ruled they could not be expelled.

But now, with U.S. entry into the war ever more likely and
preparations for it mounting, the situation was different. After a
June 3 hearing in Washington before the International Executive
Board, Tobin demanded that Local 544 be placed under receiver-
ship, pending its reorganization under different leadership.
Refusing to go along, the Dunnes had Local 544 secede from the
AFL and join the rival CIO (which had been established in 1935
under the leadership of John L. Lewis, president of the United Mine
Workers).

At this point, Tobin called for help from the president of the
United States, complaining that because of his ardent support for
Roosevelt in the 1940 election and in the current national emer-
gency, "Bundists, Stalinists, Trotskyites" and other "subversive"
groups were seeking to damage his union of 530,000 members. The
White House immediately urged labor unions to refrain from "raid-

ing" each other, and two weeks later FBI agents and U.S. marshals swooped down on the Socialist Workers headquarters in the Twin Cities, seizing party literature, two red flags and a picture of Leon Trotsky. Then in July came the indictments, accusing the twenty-nine leaders of the Socialist Workers Party and Local 544 of violating an 1861 seditious conspiracy statute and the hitherto little-noticed 1940 Smith Act, which made it illegal to advocate the overthrow of the U.S. government by force.

Though the beleaguered Trotskyists had made no secret of their desire to overthrow capitalism when the long-awaited revolutionary moment at last arrived, or of their willingness to use force if necessary, it seemed not a little ridiculous, as journalist I. F. Stone noted in the *Nation*, "to equate the faint cannonading of Trotskyist popguns with the firing on Fort Sumter." Attorney General Francis Biddle, despite having authorized legal action against the Trotskyists, may well have agreed—but Roosevelt owed a political debt to "Big Dan" Tobin.

"If a conviction is gotten," Farrell told Dos Passos, "it is only a beginning. In due time, you and I will be hauled up, possibly, as culprits. Remember Brooks' little book, and MacLeish's charges against the writers. After all, Brooks said that you and I, along with Ernest, and William Faulkner have demoralized one-hundred-and-thirty-odd million Americans." Eager though he was to fight for the civil liberties of the indicted Trotskyists, Farrell was obliged to restrain himself somewhat. He had been found to have high blood pressure, and his doctor had advised him, especially in light of his father's early death, to quit smoking, reduce his intake of coffee and alcohol, and avoid undue excitement. "My doctor insists strongly that I not get too involved in any active fights because of my health," Farrell explained to Dos Passos, "but I will go down the line to the best of my ability on this case as a real civil liberties issue."

DETERMINED, DESPITE HIS CRITICS, to go his own way as a novelist, Farrell nevertheless managed in *Ellen Rogers*, published in September 1941, to produce a novel invulnerable to the accusations that he kept repeating himself, kept writing book after book (as Edmund Wilson put it) "about Irish boys growing up in Chicago," or that he was incapable of writing a novel with a plot. Yet still, the reviewers were not satisfied. "It would be pleasant to be able to record progress on the Farrell front," Clifton Fadiman announced in the *New Yorker*, "but it is a saddening fact that *Ellen Rogers* will probably rank among the feeblest of the author's books. One can hardly mention it in the same breath with the still unforgettable and monumental Studs Lonigan trilogy." ("He pays a great tribute to *Studs Lonigan*—but what did he say about *Studs Lonigan* when it was published?" Jim Henle angrily remarked to Farrell.) Fadiman conceded that the principal portraits in *Ellen Rogers* were "accurate and merciless," but complained—the busy reviewer's perennial gripe!—that at 429 pages, the book was too long.

While that apparently overburdened critic did not mention them, *Ellen Rogers* does have flaws that are more serious. To begin with, it is mistitled. Farrell may originally have intended young Ellen Rogers, a beautiful, blue-eyed blonde, fast and unsentimental, to be the main character, but the Jazz Age Nietzschean for whom she falls hard, the treacherous immoralist Ed Lanson (based on Farrell's old chum Paul Caron), soon takes over the novel. Ellen, who has taken pleasure in leading young men on and tormenting them, is no match for "Old Hellfire," as Lanson styles himself. A charming narcissist whom women find irresistible, he shamelessly manipulates them as he keeps adding to his score. The loss of him drives Ellen to suicide in Lake Michigan, even as he moves on to new conquests. Farrell brings Lanson brilliantly to life, through a portrait that is vivid and persuasive. And yet—despite the novelist's view of character as "a social product," as he had written in his response to Wilson—he fails to show how Lanson came to be the knave that he is.

Farrell was hopeful that the "new cast of characters" would stir interest in his latest book. "*Ellen Rogers* will have to be our main source of income for a while, now," he noted. The novel was published in a first edition of 15,000, and paper was purchased for an additional 6,000 copies, if necessary. By the end of September, however, Farrell had lowered his sights and was anticipating sales of about 10,000 (including the advance sale of 8,000). "Even this," he told Hortense, looking on the bright side, "means that since *No Star is Lost,* the gain is still slow but steady."

And there was a possibility of much greater gain. Even before publication, Hollywood had shown some interest in *Ellen Rogers*. Jim Geller of the William Morris Agency, who represented Vanguard Press and Farrell, had told the novelist that an RKO producer was eager to find out if it might be a good vehicle for the studio's actress Ginger Rogers.

Farrell had a contemptuous view of Tinsel Town. Just months earlier, he had declared in his diary that "the whole Broadway-Hollywood world" was filled with people who were "rude, dishonest, horrible climbers, exhibitionists, usually—but not always—talentless. Not serious people. What I mean is that as human beings, one cannot think much of them or want to associate with them." Still, these repellent wretches might be able to provide him with something that he, now with wife and child, was increasingly conscious that he lacked: money.

As he awaited word from the industry he scorned, Farrell and his family arranged to move into a more expensive apartment uptown, at 535 West 110th Street. Though in the spring of 1940 he and Hortense had left their Lexington Avenue apartment for a less noisy one on the building's fourth floor, they now, with the addition of Kevin, needed larger quarters. (The Upper West Side would prove not to their liking, however; after a little less than a year they relocated again, to an apartment at 340 East 58th Street.)

Soon after the move uptown, at Geller's invitation and the Morris agency's expense, Farrell flew to California, where he and Geller beat the Hollywood bushes for a few weeks in the hope of selling *Ellen Rogers* to the movies. Geller—whose past efforts to sell *Studs Lonigan* had been unsuccessful, and whom Henle and Farrell had temporarily dropped as their representative in 1940— may have been somewhat exaggerating the chances of selling *Ellen Rogers* in an effort to impress his clients with his tireless labors on their behalf. But whatever the prospects really were, Farrell's unconcealed contempt for Hollywood cannot have helped much. (When a screenwriter representing producer Sam Goldwyn talked about art and the importance of believing in the pictures one writes, Farrell told him: "Listen, I can go home and write novels I believe in, we're out here trying to sell you something.") In any case, the efforts of the author and his agent came to naught.

But Geller was not done. He arranged for Farrell to try out as a screenwriter at Twentieth-Century Fox. The deal, set ultimately by production head Darryl Zanuck, was that Farrell would work for two weeks, at $1,000 a week, outlining a new version of *Common Clay*, an old play about an Irish servant girl in Boston who becomes pregnant by the son of her rich Back Bay employer; if the outline proved acceptable, Farrell would continue for five more weeks at the same rate of pay. The novelist was very pleased by the money, "which sets one above the bastards treating one as dirt."

When Farrell's first day of work as a screenwriter *pro tem* arrived—Monday, October 6—he had mixed emotions. "But I feel I have a moral right to do it," he told his diary, "in the sense that in this period, I have a moral right to do something to take care of Hortense, Kevin, and myself, and that this need not interfere with my real work and its integrity." He also confessed that he was "not certain I can do the job I have undertaken. Jim Geller thinks I can. I can in time, but the first stages may be difficult. I will work seriously, methodically, as intelligently as I can." He resolved not to let his contempt for Hollywood prevent him from doing his best.

He was working with a young producer named Milton Sperling, another client of Geller's. A son-in-law of Harry Warner, of Warner Brothers, Sperling (who was also making $1,000 a week) struck Farrell as glib, pleasant and "not intellectually solid and precise. But then, who expects intellectual precision in a Hollywood studio, among producers."

And so, provided with an office and a secretary, Farrell turned his attention to *Common Clay.* "I am working on the rough outline of my story," he recorded in his diary on Thursday. "I am to have it in Sperling's hands by Saturday. By a week from Saturday, I should have one a little longer, and better, which is to go to Zanuck." He was optimistic about impressing Zanuck. "If I can't—well there is something wrong with me. Because the standards are not high here. Not at all. I shall write in clear, simple, lucid sentences, and that, in itself, should be sufficient. It is not often that they get anything that is really well-written out here." The next day, he was even more ebullient: "Writing for motion pictures is—whether Zanuck likes what I do or not—a cinch. There is really nothing to it. I, of course, have done in two days what is usually done in three weeks, and there are holes in what I've done. But I have blocked out the basis for a story."

After he turned in his rough outline, however, Sperling came up with some new thoughts for the drama. "Today will be a hard day," Farrell wrote in his diary early Tuesday. "I shall be dictating practically the entire day. I got a new line from Sperling, and I ought to get him something by Wednesday." Then they'd have a day to go over it before handing the result over to Zanuck. In the event, he turned in the manuscript to Sperling Thursday morning, then "hung around all afternoon, waiting to hear from him," he reported that evening to Hortense. "He has been busy, and so, I haven't heard from him. This is the typical Hollywood procedure, I presume."

It was some days before Zanuck's verdict was delivered. By then, the impatient Farrell, after consulting Sperling—but not his agent, Jim Geller—had returned to New York, but was ready to fly back to Hollywood on short notice if the decision was favorable. "I gave [Zanuck] the basis of a good picture, and Sperling was quite set on it, and said to me—and to others—that he wanted to go ahead," Farrell assured Geller. If that was so, then the writer's sudden flight east may have done him no good. For Zanuck decided not to pick up the option, averring that Farrell was a fine novelist, with deep psychological insight, but had no sense of dramaturgy.

Farrell reacted with wounded pride. "Hollywood is not as good as a whorehouse," he wrote to his brother Earl. "For what it is, a whorehouse is honest; Hollywood isn't. I was very glad to be back, and I am back at work, and it is better for me. Hortense and I live simply, and we can do that, and I can manage to go along, and remain free of that damned place." It was not his fault that he had been rejected, he insisted; it was Sperling's. "What happened," Farrell told Jim Henle, "was that Zanuck's thousand dollar a week, nepotistic hireling producer gummed me up with refusing to make up his mind, throwing out an intelligent line I proposed on the story, giving me three days to try and handle a phony, half-dated line, and then refusing [to] fight Zanuck on the matter."

"So, all in all," he wrote Earl, "I am frankly proud to announce that I am a failure in Hollywood, and when Hortense and I heard the news, we decided to go out and get a glass of sherry, and to celebrate this failure. I am back at work—writing what I can write honestly, and this is more important than making a lot of money in Hollywood's make-believe fakery." Soon he began taking what he probably didn't admit to himself was revenge: a short story, entitled "$1,000 a Week," about a writer's brief and unhappy experience in Hollywood.

<hr/>

WHEN HE WAS WRITING *Ellen Rogers*, Farrell had begun to drink very heavily. He had long been a tippler, and on more than one occasion in the past had a made a fool of himself when intoxicated. Once, in his University of Chicago days, seeking to impress a girl at the Cube and thinking he had failed, he did what even now he regarded as "the goofiest thing that I ever did in my life. I was drunk at a party. I challenged Leo [the girl's boyfriend] to fight. He said that he wouldn't fight unless I took my pants off. In a studio full of about fifty people, I took my pants off, and hauled off on him: at the same moment, Paul Caron hauled off on him from the other side. Then, I passed out."

As he grew older, Farrell's occasional antics under the influence became somewhat more refined. At parties he "used to perform a wonderful dance, parodying Communist ideology and the Communist effort to smuggle this ideology into every branch of 'culture,'" recalled Jim Henle.

> The dance was termed, if I recall correctly, "The Awakening Prole-tariat" and was performed *solo* with or without music. First Jim, his hair in disarray, his necktie askew, would portray the proletariat slowly being crushed to earth. When he was completely prostrate he would remain for a moment immobile and then slowly, muscle by muscle and joint by joint, begin to rise. In the process, he would manage to smooth his hair, adjust his necktie and when finally he stood erect, his right arm raised in a gesture of triumph—well, the effect was spectacular.

But the performances eventually ceased to be so amusing. Once Farrell started drinking beer or Scotch, he seemed unable to stop, Henle observed. By the time he was writing *Ellen Rogers,* in late 1940 and 1941, his drinking had become habitually excessive. Morton White, then a graduate student in philosophy at Columbia, had met Farrell through Meyer Schapiro and become a friend. Far-rell's heavy drinking, White recalled, "affected a good deal of one's relations with him, because…if he was incomprehensible about philosophy when he was sober, you can imagine what he was like when he was drunk."

"Why do I drink so much?" Farrell would remorsefully ask himself in the spring of 1942, after a particularly distressing episode. "I cannot figure it out except to say that once I start I like to go on. And then, God cannot predict what will happen." In this instance, he'd nearly wrecked a housewarming party to which he'd been invited by Boris Souvarine and his wife. A refugee from occu-pied France, Souvarine, whom Farrell had met in Paris in 1938, was the author of *Staline* (1935), a pioneering biography of the mur-derous Soviet dictator.

Penitent the next day, Farrell engaged in a remarkable exer-cise in introspective analysis as he sought to get at the roots of his problem. He thought "defiance" had something to do with it. "I am always wanting to be defiant, and I think that this goes back to my childhood and early youth—to Uncle Tom's strictness, his irrationality toward me, his keeping me so much in fear, apprehension." He also blamed the Church. "I have dropped God, all Gods, and that is forever. I shall never, as people predict, end up in the Church. But the Church has stigmatized me, left me with a kind of longing for more than life can give." He wanted to be "completely civilized," and he tried to be, but somehow he fell short. "I really am something of a Studs Lonigan, despite everything else, despite my efforts to be serious, think, think in a responsible manner and so on, and to be responsible about my work, my obligations—I still seem to have never gotten a little of Studs Lonigan out of me."

⋙─◉─⋘

NOW THAT RUSSIA WAS AT war with Germany, liberals could once again indulge in illusions about the benevolence of the Stalinist regime. While after the Nazi-Soviet pact, progressives at the *New Republic* and the *Nation* "had written honestly about the Soviet Union," historian William L. O'Neill has noted, they "put this knowledge aside" once Russia was invaded. A new Popular Front was created, this time with Washington's active encouragement. The commonsensical admonitions of such clear-sighted observers as Max Eastman—to support the "gangster-tyrant" Stalin's resistance to the more powerful "gangster-tyrant" Hitler, but be on guard "against the added strength this gives [Stalin's] American agents with their own more subtle plot against our way of life"—were little heeded.

Meanwhile, anti-Stalinist radicals such as Rahv were coming closer to recognizing the necessity of the war against Hitler. Near the end of a devastating attack in *Partisan Review* on the utter lack of realism in the antiwar position elaborated by Dwight Macdonald and art critic Clement Greenberg (who in a joint manifesto had insisted that winning "the war against fascism" required withholding "all support of whatever kind...from [Winston] Churchill and Roosevelt"), Rahv stated: "In a sense this war, even if it accomplishes the destruction of fascism, is not yet *our* war." His use of the word *yet* was quickly noted by Macdonald and Greenberg—and other *PR* readers.

"Rhetoric is more and more taking the place of thinking," Farrell wrote in his diary in November. "Phil Rahv's piece in the current *Partisan Review*, for instance, in which he comes out for Roosevelt and Churchill, is purely and sheerly and only rhetoric." In fact, however, Rahv's piece was not mere rhetoric—and it was Farrell himself (though not he alone) who was having difficulty thinking clearly about the war and the changed world in which it was being fought.

"More and more," he had written less than a fortnight earlier, "the wall of isolation will close around one, intellectually, politically, artistically." As this did indeed happen, he frequently lashed out bitterly in his diary at those on the other side of the wall:"I keep thinking of people I know—and I ask myself—is there any reason on earth why I should see most of them?"

In dramatic contrast, as Farrell saw it, stood the Trotskyist martyrs in Minneapolis (their number reduced by one after the suicide of Grant Dunne). Their case, he said in a foreward to a pamphlet penned by George Novack, "is the most important involving civil liberties since the trials of the I.W.W. [Industrial Workers of the World] members during the First World War. And it is similar to the I.W.W. cases in its fundamental point. Both constituted attacks on the labor movement....The basis of our liberties rests, formally, on the unconditional guarantees given us in the Bill of Rights. It rests actually on the freedom of labor."

The trial of the twenty-eight began on October 27. The Communists applauded the prosecution of the "fifth columnists" (not foreseeing that they themselves would one day suffer the same fate under the Smith Act). After hearing the testimony, the judge on November 19 dismissed the charges against five of the defendants. Ten days later, the case against the remaining twenty-three defendants went to the jury, which then deliberated for some 56 hours. On December 1 it returned with a verdict: all the defendants were found not guilty of violating the Civil War seditious conspiracy statute, but James P. Cannon, Ray Dunne, Farrell Dobbs and fifteen others were convicted under the Smith Act and faced up to ten years in prison. The jury recommended leniency. Sentencing was set for the following Monday.

That Sunday afternoon, a social gathering was held at the Socialist Workers Party headquarters in Minneapolis, where, as Farrell Dobbs later recounted, "many comrades and friends" showed up to express their solidarity with him and the others about to be sentenced. It was a pleasant, low-key affair. "Some played cards, chess, and checkers; others simply held relaxed conversations. A radio provided background music." Suddenly, "like a bolt from the blue" came a startling announcement on the radio: *The Japanese had attacked Pearl Harbor!*

In New York, Farrell learned the news in a telephone call from his brother Jack, and then gave himself over to listening to the radio. He had long anticipated America's entry into the war, and now it was coming about. He expected that soon "there will be clamping down, a total war economy, censorship and so on. Now, there will be real war conditions prevailing."

The next day, President Roosevelt pronounced December 7, 1941, "a date which will live in infamy," and Congress declared war; the federal judge in Minneapolis meted out prison sentences of 16 months to twelve of the Trotskyist defendants, and 12 months and a day to the other six; and Farrell received a telegram from his sister Helen, telling him that their Uncle Bill Daly had died.

Diagnosed in May as being in the third stage of syphilis, with general peresis, a brain disease, Daly, ever insistent on positive thinking, had refused to believe it and enter a hospital. (Told of this, Farrell had sent the family "a strongly insistent letter, even threatening never to help them again with money when they are in need, unless they take immediate steps to get him admitted to a hospital.") In August, Daly had been diagnosed with incipient tuberculosis and entered a TB hospital. Farrell had written to him in October from Hollywood; and later in the month in New York, he received some letters back. "They suggest that he is cracking pretty badly," Farrell noted in his diary. "He accuses Uncle Tom of being a cheat, a sneak and so on." Now, at sixty-two, Bill Daly—who used to say that you had to wade through his nephew's novels with boots on and who always hated "crepe-hanging"—was dead.

Farrell saw more than an individual tragedy in Daly's demise. "I could not have imagined a more terrible end for the O'Flahertys than the end which the Dalys are coming to," he had reflected in late October. "Their end is not to be described as something individual, exceptional, and accidental: it is an end delimited within the bounds of our civilization, our way of life."

———※◦❊———

DESPITE HIS HARSH APPRAISAL of American civilization, Farrell was invited in December 1941 to become a member of the National Institute of Arts and Letters. This prestigious body had been founded in 1898, apparently, as Max Eastman was to note, "by spontaneous combustion...a few artists and writers selecting themselves as worthy of the honor, and then voting in others up to the number of 250." (Though not themselves immortals, as Eastman explained in a sardonic report, the members of the institute had in 1904 "the power to confer immortality—which they did" by electing seven of their number to form an even more select and prestigious body, the Academy of Arts and Letters. "These seven elected other immortals to the number of 50.") So, by vote of the institute's members, Farrell—along with Katherine Anne Porter, Erskine Caldwell, Aaron Copland and eight others—was being invited to join them and become a near-immortal. In a letter to Henry Seidel Canby, secretary of the institute, he accepted. Subsequently he said that he did so because he thought the honor might be of "some protective help" in warding off efforts to censor his works, adding, "I see nothing unprincipled in this action."

Farrell did not, however, attend the institute meeting at which he was inducted. "Farrell, who professes to be a very revolutionary anti-philistine, satisfied a presumable conflict of motives by accepting the honor, but not coming up to receive it," Eastman wrote in his account of the ceremony for the *American Mercury*. "It is just as well," he added, "for Canby inducted him as 'John T. Farrell' and it would have been embarrassing to all if, after hearing himself described as a very-near immortal, he had had to say, on receiving a printed certification of it: 'The name is James....'"

Chapter Fourteen
"The Dividing Line"

THOUGH FARRELL HAD CLOSELY followed the progress of the conscription legislation in Congress, his poor eyesight and other infirmities, his age (thirty-eight) and his status as a husband and father made it most unlikely that he would be called up. Had he been drafted, however, one doubts that he would have resisted. Certainly, the Trotskyists did not. The Socialist Workers Party, despite the Smith Act prosecutions, came to favor the war as a way to defend the "degenerated workers' state" of the Soviet Union, and Shachtman's rival Workers Party, despite its antiwar position, did not encourage its members to refuse military service or to sabotage the war effort. Moreover, when a *Partisan Review* editor asked Farrell to cooperate with him in a fabrication to deceive his draft board, Farrell refused, and some years later he adverted in his diary to the man's "cowardice."

Farrell realized the war meant that American literature would not be the same. He wrote in his diary:

> The war is going to mark a sharp dividing line in our literature, and one of my tasks remains to fill out the other side of that dividing line, the side that is dying fast in the war. If I do that I have a better chance of making the jump over the dividing line myself, and perhaps, I shall also help new and younger writers who will be, almost completely, on the new side of the line. And I will help keep alive a sense of continuity.

Interviewed in the spring of 1942 by Robert Van Gelder of the *New York Times Book Review*, Farrell rather grandiosely declared, "I am working on a projected series of 25 volumes of fiction, of which I have completed 13. What I want to do is to make these works an integrated re-creation of what I've seen happen, or what I think can or might happen in American life."

Despite his lofty ambitions, the novel on which he was then

actually working, *My Days of Anger*—the fourth and, as it seemed, final volume in the O'Neill-O'Flaherty series, telling of Danny O'Neill's emergence from the "spiritually impoverished" environment in which he had been reared—was giving him a lot of difficulty. "No book I have written has given me as much trouble and worry, or will give me as much trouble and worry as *My Days of Anger* has and will give me," he confided to his diary. "It is going to be a truly major test of my will, talent, and insight."

And so it was. He was trying not just to bring to life the members of his family and the world of his youth, as he had done so well in the previous three novels in the series, but to show how the character based on his younger self had developed at the university and freed himself intellectually from his boyhood environment. This representation of interior growth was a much more demanding exercise in selective memory and imagination.

⟶▶·◦·◀⟵

LOOKING BACK, JIM HENLE reflected that the only thing about Farrell that disturbed him and that he really never understood was the fact that "his friendships were so often broken over quite impersonal matters that, one would think, could be discussed as calmly as one might debate about the weather." Henle himself was able to disagree with Farrell about political or literary matters without impairing their own close friendship (which was buttressed, of course, by their professional relationship). But that was an exception, he thought. And when he realized that "Jim's friendships...depended upon the friend never disagreeing with any of his views," Henle thereafter "never bothered to establish any but the most formal relations with the persons I met at his home, knowing it was only a matter of a comparatively short time until I would no longer meet them there."

Farrell knew a great many people. "He was a very warm person," recalled Al Glotzer, the baseball-loving Trotskyist from Chicago whom Farrell had met in Mexico and who moved to New York in 1940 and later edited the Shachtmanite *New International*. "He invited friends, new acquaintances to his house all the time."

But, as Henle noted, most of the friendships that Farrell formed from his wide circle of acquaintances proved impermanent. Ferdinand Lundberg, the Vanguard author best known for *America's Sixty Families* (1937), in which he claimed that a rela-

264

tively small group of wealthy families held sway over the economy and the body politic, is an example. In 1938, Farrell considered Lundberg not only "a good empiricist" (even if lamentably weak at theory), but also "a hell of a nice fellow" with "a keen sense of humor"—"quite a regular guy and honorable." Three years later, however, Farrell said he'd "decided there is no use whatsoever in making any effort or wasting any time" seeing such people as Lundberg or Sidney Hook, who disagreed with him about the war. "There is nothing to talk to them about. Of course, they are as little interested in seeing me as I am in seeing them."

He seems to have regarded a broken friendship almost as a sign of integrity. In his *Partisan Review* eulogy for Trotsky in 1940 he wrote approvingly: "Trotsky was a harsh opponent, never hesitating to break with friend after friend on issues of principle and policy. In this regard he did not differ from most men of strong convictions. In his thinking he was more inclined to draw sharp distinctions than to conciliate differences." For his own part, Farrell "would suddenly turn on someone who was a friend of his," and Hortense was much the same way, said H. D. (who wishes to remain anonymous). She and her husband, both writers with a daughter about the same age as Kevin, socialized very frequently with the Farrells during the 1940s. "When they became a friend of yours," she said, "it was a very passionate friendship, while it lasted." And during that time of intense friendship, Farrell "couldn't do enough for you." But then would come the break (though, in the case of H. D. and her husband, it apparently was *they* who finally terminated the relationship).

Even Farrell's long and close friendship with Meyer Schapiro was to be disrupted in 1946 by a disagreement over, of all things, the meaning of the Italian film *The Open City*. Farrell argued in print that the movie was Stalinist propaganda subtly promoting the notion that the masses should trust and follow the "leader," i.e., the Stalinist functionary or agent. Schapiro, in a published commentary on Farrell's review, maintained that the movie's portrayal of Communist collaboration with the Catholic Church against Nazi Germany—a portrayal that he said showed the reactionary church in a falsely favorable light—was an effort to prepare Italians for postwar Communist collaboration with the Christian Democrats. This difference in interpretation (which Farrell publicly poohpoohed in a letter-to-the-editor) hardly seemed adequate reason to break off "a rewarding friendship of some years standing," Henle observed. Yet it was reason enough for Farrell, who apparently felt embarrassed to be publicly "corrected" in this way by his more erudite friend. The two men would not revive their friendship (originally based in part on a shared enthusiasm for revolutionary socialism) until the 1970s.

Addressing in his diary (in mid-1942) "the coldness that has grown between myself and many persons who were friends of mine a few years ago"—among those he mentioned were Hook and Max Eastman—Farrell wrote: "It is not that I am cold. But rather that while I need friendship, I don't need it as many people do." In part, he believed, this was because from an early age he had had "to develop an inner resourcefulness."

"More than many friendships," the novelist mused, "I need contacts, associations. In most friendships, I feel that while I give more in the outpouring of energy, ideas etc., I usually give less in terms of emotions, and need the friend less than the friend needs me."

A decade later, Farrell would tell Henle that when he discovered that his feeling about a friend was one of "indifference," it was "total" indifference—and the end of the friendship. He explained:

> I don't know if I like this trait in myself, but it is one of the constituents of my character, and it is, really, better [and] more civilized than getting angry at people, punishing them, or having fanfare. Sometimes, I am surprised, myself, at how insights come together, and I just find out and know, hell, I am indifferent. It is like a small death. The death of friendship is a form of death. And yet it happens in life, and even should happen.

Though Farrell earnestly sought to understand the world around him and do what he could to change it for the benefit of the mass of mankind, he was basically absorbed with himself—with his emotions, principles and integrity—and with his art. Friendship per se did not ultimately count for much. Although this of course was a weakness, it was also a strength. It enabled him, for instance, to speak out against the Moscow show trials without worrying about what his friends might think. And it enabled him to keep going down a chosen path when all those around him fell away.

———⇒➤●◄═———

RUSSIA'S DECISIVE VICTORY IN the Battle of Stalingrad in the fall of 1942 shattered Hitler's image as an invincible military genius and was generally taken to be a turning point in the war. "The war is going into what seems like a climax stage," Farrell observed. "The German defeat at Stalingrad seems total." Despite his opposition to the war, he welcomed this development. He had come to think that Trotsky might well have been right in characterizing the Soviet Union as a "degenerated workers' state" that should be defended against imperialist foes. "The progressive possibilities of the Soviet Union have not been exhausted," he had reflected some months earlier, "and the results of the Russian Revolution have not been totally eliminated, despite Stalin. Therefore, perhaps it is a sound point to say— defense of the Soviet Union. Most certainly, if Hitler conquers it, the world will be much worse off."

Still, Farrell remained as much opposed to Stalinism as ever. The release of *Mission to Moscow*, a pro-Soviet propaganda film from Hollywood, afforded him and other anti-Stalinists a new opportunity to speak out against the dictator's crimes.

The Warner Brothers movie was based on a 1941 bestseller by Joseph E. Davies, a wealthy corporate lawyer who had been U.S. ambassador to the Soviet Union during 1936–1938. His book showed that one didn't have to be an intellectual to be flummoxed and taken in by Stalin. Attending the second Moscow show trial of Radek et al., the ambassador reluctantly concluded that "the state had established its case, at least to the extent of proving the existence of a widespread conspiracy and plot among the political leaders against the Soviet government." As for Stalin himself, Davies got "the impression of a strong mind which is composed and wise. His brown eye is exceedingly kindly and gentle. [*Perhaps Davies should have examined the other eye!*] A child would like to sit in his lap and a dog would sidle up to him." The befuddled diplomat immediately added: "It is difficult to associate his personality and this impression of kindness and gentle simplicity with what has occurred here in connection with these purges and shootings of the Red Army generals, and so forth." Hollywood's version of Davies's book did away with all such perplexing difficulties, leaving only the fatuity, which it considerably embellished.

Farrell attacked *Mission to Moscow* in the *New Leader*, a Social Democratic weekly:

> This film is a gross and shameless falsification of history. It misrepresents the Moscow trials, the history of Russian foreign policy in recent years, and the sequence of events which happened in America prior to Pearl Harbor. It re-stages the trials according to the

official version, and adds an invention which the O.G.P.U. ignored: it introduces Tukachevsky as a defendant who confesses to guilt....And then there is the Soviet-German non-aggression pact which is white-washed and slurred over.

⇒⦁◅

MY DAYS OF ANGER WAS published in October 1943. Running from 1924 to 1927, the novel takes Danny from work at the express company and study in night school to work at a gas station and classes at the University of Chicago, and finally to the verge of departure for New York, "his last step to freedom." In the course of his ascent to this point, Danny loses his virginity and his Catholic faith; rages against the world's injustice, against "this Godless, purposeless world"; turns to bohemianism, then sees through it; and vows fervently to become a writer and to change the world.

Drawing on incidents and scenes from his youth and inventing others, Farrell paints a psychologically acute portrait of adolescence, with its hurts and fears, its yearnings and confusions, its self-pity and grandiosity. But the realistic portrait is not entirely without flaw. Near the novel's end, Farrell writes of his protagonist:

> His heart was heavy. He had finally taken off a way of life, a world in itself, as if it were a worn-out suit of clothes. He was making a last break with his past. Nothing remained with him of that past now but scars and wounds, agonies, frustrations, lacerations, sufferings, death. These he would always carry with him, just as he would his own weaknesses and his own follies. But his anger had now cooled to irony; his hatred was not against people, but against a world which destroyed people.

In thus having Danny's anger "cooled," Farrell strikes a false note. Though the novel's title—*My Days of Anger*—does suggest that the anger didn't last forever, it is not plausible that an emotion so strong as to characterize this whole period of his life should have subsided so quickly. Certainly, the novelist's own ire had not turned to irony before his first published story, "Slob," appeared (in 1929). Consciously or unconsciously, Farrell may have been trying to refute the contention of critics such as Alfred Kazin that he "hated" his own people. But young Danny O'Neill would have been as unaware of the need for such a refutation as young Farrell himself had been.

Still, without quite realizing it, Farrell had hit upon the novel's chief defect: namely, the utter lack of irony regarding Danny's progress. It was not that Farrell couldn't look upon his youthful self with some detachment. At one point, for instance, when the writing of the novel was not going well, he told himself that "at the present moment, Danny O'Neill is an insufferable bore. I can see now clearly why he—myself—could not get a girl. I wouldn't say the girls were wrong in not giving him dates. I have to get on further to where he begins to expand, change, and have some 'exciting' adventures." The novelist was quite willing to show Danny in an unflattering light at times. But he was never able to laugh at his alter ego and his self-important anger, never able to see that waving one's fist at a godless universe swiftly becomes mere posturing, since it logically makes no difference.

The reader eventually loses sympathy for Danny, not because Danny indulges in self-pity, as adolescents are prone to do, but because the author presents Danny's self-pity as if it were objectively justified. On that, the author and his younger self were as one—and in a novel so dominated by the younger self this want of perspective is a serious defect. The failing, alas, was typical not only of the novelist but of the man. Farrell's inclination to self-pity was one of his least attractive traits.

He was not unaware of the tendency. Indeed, at one point in *My Days of Anger*, he writes:

> Today over coffee he [Danny] and Ed [Lanson] had argued heatedly about Dreiser and [novelist James Branch] Cabell, and Ed had said that Dreiser was a bad influence on him. Ed had accused him of having too much pity for mankind and had said the reason was that he pitied himself. Was it true? If true, was it wrong? Shouldn't all mankind be pitied? Laughter, scorn, irony—weren't these emotions of self-defense, defense mechanisms, blinders one put on to avoid looking at oneself and into one's nature, the way a hurt person licked his wounds?

Farrell had an excessive regard for his own emotions, combined with a strong need to see himself as alone and besieged, even when he wasn't. On getting back the essay on the Great War that Danny had submitted to Professor Paul Morris Saxon to gain admission to his English composition class, Farrell's alter ego reflects: "He had written this vitriolic essay out of feeling. But he was right. And *more important* [emphasis added], he had expressed his own emotions." Then, in response to the professor's stated reservations about whether he "*will ever think clearly enough, or invent dra-*

matically enough, to satisfy editors or publishers, and to reach a public [italics in original]," Danny decides to become a writer.

> This was a challenge. He set his chin. Yes, this day, January 9, 1927, was the day when he, Danny O'Neill, had finally discovered the weapons he would wield. Now he was setting out in earnest to be a writer. For good or for ill, he would go on. For good or for ill, this was the aim in his life.

In real life, Farrell had made his vow to become a writer when he saw his sketch about "Pie Juggling in the Loop" published in Professor James Weber Linn's newspaper column. But to acknowledge the full extent of the help he had received from the professor (who died in 1939) and its role in his decision to become a writer was still beyond Farrell. Hence, he changed this in the fictional account so as to make it seem—less plausibly—that Danny was all but alone, hurling defiance at Professor Saxon and the godless universe.

Despite its flaws, *My Days of Anger* succeeded—as *Judgment Day* had with the *Studs Lonigan* trilogy—in bringing the series to a satisfying conclusion. "When the four books come together," Farrell believed, "they will have a terrific wallop in them."

"But do you ever feel that you are writing almost in a vacuum, when you know that the mass of readers come from groups that don't care much to hear about the people you want to write about?" asked Robert Van Gelder, from the *Times Book Review*, in the spring of 1942.

"Of course," Farrell replied. "I know that women who belong to ladies' clubs don't want to be told that the life of the majority of people is banal, that it is gray, that it is dreary."

Critics were not much different in that regard, Farrell had come to believe. He expected *My Days of Anger* to get "a bad press," and after most of the reviews were in, he was sure that it had. "It gets disgusting to be ganged up on time after time, but then, it is part of what one must deal with. The expectation of being ganged up on, I now put that down as part of the given."

That was fantasy, the bitter, self-pitying fantasy of a man who felt himself increasingly isolated and unappreciated. To be sure, there were a few attacks (in the *New Republic* and elsewhere), but most of the reviews mingled praise and criticism. *My Days of Anger*, said Carlos Baker, the future Hemingway biographer, writing in the *New York Times Book Review*, "reveals in the author a heartening accession of philosophical gentleness and narrative power. It is in many ways a better book than Farrell has done before." "Like Dreiser before him, Farrell often moves at a deliberate and sometimes plodding pace," wrote Milton Rugoff in the *Herald Tribune*, "but, also like Dreiser, he goes where the crowd of novelists simply does not venture—into the unglamorous but immensely interesting country of the commonplace, the unheroic."

Ignoring the praise, Farrell explained away the criticism: "I can't escape the feeling that when most of the critics talk of my limitations, etc. etc., they really base most of their talk on their own acceptance of themselves as separated from the kind of people I write of, and with that, of seeing a quality of experience in their own lives, absent from that in the lives of my characters and so on."

But in apparently dismissing "all serious adverse criticism as so essentially without seriousness," Farrell was deceiving himself, critic Diana Trilling observed in the *Nation*. "The people he writes about could be rich and beautiful instead of poor and woeful and superstitious, and he would still be subject to the same criticism for the limits within which he has held his imagination."

Having read *A World I Never Made* years before, but not *No Star Is Lost* or *Father and Son*, Mrs. Trilling said that as she got into *My Days of Anger*, she "was struck by how vividly Farrell's characters had remained in my memory." But she faulted his "preference for the actionless, the plotless, and the unvarious. He seems to believe that to intensify by dramatic action or by the invention of plot is to falsify; but this is as if, telling the story, say, of Othello, he should think it more truthful to record a lifetime of Othello's emotional insufficiencies and racial inferiorities than to introduce an Iago to precipitate Othello's uneasy innocence into violence." Her point was legitimate, but she might have considered the possibility that the very absence of obvious plot helps to create the illusion of life in his novels and thus make his characters so vividly memorable.

Though there was no conspiratorial "ganging up" on Farrell, there *was* an injustice done. Neither Mrs. Trilling nor any of the other reviewers of the apparently final volume in the O'Neill-O'Flaherty series undertook, in any serious way, to read all four novels and appraise the series as a whole. Such an effort, in the absence of a freshly published omnibus volume, seems to have been beyond the reviewing conventions of the day; this failure meant that Farrell's true accomplishment—one that, at the very least, rivaled what he had achieved before with his *Studs Lonigan* trilogy—went largely unrecognized.

THE ATTEMPT TO KEEP WORK of his from the public that perhaps most surprised Farrell in 1944 came not from the police in New York or Chicago but from the very Socialist Workers Party he had been valiantly assisting in its struggle against the government.

Disturbed by two articles that had appeared in the party's monthly "theoretical" publication, *Fourth International*, Farrell (who, with his family, was ensconced for the summer in a rented house in Pleasantville, New York) on July 30 of 1944 penned a friendly letter of protest. He objected to an absurdly adoring account, in the February issue, of how James P. Cannon and his fellow martyrs went off to prison on the last day of December 1943, and also to a vituperative attack on Max Shachtman, the leader of the rival Workers Party, made in the guise of a book review in the May issue. "Gross sentimentality, unbending rigidity, unfair attacks on opponents—these are all dangerous. I hold them to be indefensible."

Cannon and his Socialist Workers Party found the criticism indefensible. The *Fourth International* refused to publish Farrell's letter (though it did appear in the party's *Internal Bulletin*, which went only to members). Cannon, from his prison cell, condemned the letter as "dishonest" and "rude and brutal" in tone. "Our party is too dignified, too sure of itself, to take any guff from anybody."

Farrell then gave the suppressed letter to Shachtman's *New International*, which published it in November 1944, and also to Dwight Macdonald's *politics*, which ran it in December. (Macdonald, with the aid of his wife's inheritance, had established his new magazine after losing out in a struggle with Rahv and Phillips over control of *Partisan Review*.) In an introduction to the letter in both journals, Farrell noted: "A large percentage of the leadership—and also an apparently large majority of the membership—of the Socialist Workers Party endorses the methods and attitudes embodied in the articles I criticized. I continue to consider them to be reprehensible."

He kept speaking out in behalf of the imprisoned Trotskyists (who were being released). But as Macdonald soon observed, Farrell, having been "a loyal and devoted fellow-traveller of the Trotskyists" for years, "has now transferred his allegiance to the rival Shachtman group, the Workers Party."

With the war ending in Europe—"Never in modern history has a nation been more overwhelmingly defeated than Germany is being defeated now," Farrell noted in his diary on April 29, 1945—there was talk in the Socialist Workers Party's *Militant* of "the coming revolution." But he was skeptical: "The German revolution has not as yet come, and the chances of it in the present situation are slim.... Stalinism stands over the workers of the world, and especially Europe, and Russian prestige must be tremendous."

———⟫•0•⟪———

H. L. Mencken, who believed that America's participation in the war had been "wholly dishonorable and ignominious," had Farrell and his brother Jack (now a psychiatrist on the staff of St. Elizabeth's Hospital in Washington, D.C.) to lunch at the Maryland Club in Baltimore on May 31, three and a half weeks after the German surrender.

"As he took us to his club," Farrell later recalled in print, "he half apologized, explaining that he had lambasted it and the other members but that he had found it more convenient to meet people for lunch there than at home. He was, needless to say, most gracious in his concern about what we ate and how we liked the food. He was a genuine gentleman...."

"Mencken was a good and fluent talker, and he had much to say that day." Among other things, he advised Farrell "that I was young, had a wonderful future, and would possibly still write my best books," but that "'to develop further as a writer,'" he should stay away from "'booze...women...and politics.'"

"Luncheon with Mencken was always a happy event," Farrell said.

Mencken came away from the meal with a slightly different impression, which he set down in his diary the next day: "Farrell has done some novels of excellent merit, all of them dealing with the poor Irish among whom he was brought up in Chicago, but he is not very good company, and I see him very seldom."

———⟫•0•⟪———

One Friday evening in December 1945, the flower of New York's anti-Stalinist Left intelligentsia appeared in a hall on the Lower East Side for a lecture-cum-discussion under the auspices of Dwight Macdonald's *politics* magazine. The lecture—on the heretical

273

proposition that "Socialism Should Be Utopian, Not Scientific"—
was given by Nicola Chiaromonte, an Italian writer and journalist
who had been a refugee in New York since 1947 and whose cultivated mind had a philosophic bent. Macdonald had taken him
under his wing and had received instruction from him in classic
Italian anarchism. Most others present that evening—including Farrell—were not inclined to do the same.

As he was soon to argue in a lengthy essay in *politics*,
Chiaromonte contended that Marxism, despite its pretensions, was
not "scientific" at all, but rather utopian in its expectation that a
"dictatorship of the proletariat" would somehow automatically
result in a classless society and the withering away of the state.
Despots have always invoked stupendous aims to justify their ruthless use of power, he pointed out, and the Marxist utopia "is the
vaguest, the most general, the least logically justified and least clear
Utopia in the history of socialism." Not Marxism, but "the *idea of
Justice*" was the only sound basis for socialism, and the sought-for
better society had to be described clearly and distinctly in advance.
"If, in Marxist terms, this has to be called 'Utopian' socialism,
then...there is no other form of socialism but the Utopian."

Nearly everyone present that evening rejected Chiaromonte's
thesis. Though his views were not offered in a dogmatic way, playwright Lionel Abel was to recall decades later, the response to them
was "violent in the extreme." Farrell—with what Abel described as
"the brutality of one who thinks he cannot possibly be wrong"—
declared: "At least Marxism isn't boring and you are." Others,
including Meyer Schapiro, a particular friend of Chiaromonte's,
joined in the assault. "If you follow Chiaromonte tonight," Schapiro
warned, "you won't know what to do in a week, month or year; you
won't even know what to do tomorrow morning." This grim pre-
monition, Abel remembered, "intimidated almost everyone who
might have wavered, or gone over to [Chiaromonte's] side."

The reception given Chiaromonte at the lecture made it quite
apparent, as Macdonald subsequently noted in *politics*, that "the
intellectual influence of Marxism, *qua* scientific socialism," was still
very strong among the anti-Stalinist intellectuals of the Left.

Farrell certainly remained under its spell. When Macdonald
casually stated in *politics* that Marxism's "inadequacies" might help
to account for the failure of Farrell and other Marxists to "speak
up" in his magazine, Farrell penned a long, rudely contemptuous
response. Playing on the nickname ("Flighty Dwighty") that some

had given the ideologically fickle Macdonald, Farrell wrote: "Constant readers of Dwight Macdonald cannot but be aware of the flighty character of his thinking. He is continually changing his mind." Macdonald, he said, "never seriously worked through Marxist ideas" and "has never worked out his critique of Marxism. For several years, for instance, he has been incidentally, casually, off-handedly declaring that Lenin is responsible for Stalin. This can be a very serious issue. But Macdonald has never even troubled to specify how and why Lenin is responsible for Stalinism. When he makes this charge, one doesn't even know what he is talking about." Nor did Farrell know what Chiaromonte meant by "Justice." The proponents of "Absolute Morality, Absolute Justice," he complained, did not define what they meant. "After two years, [*politics*] has not developed a rigorous and systematic analysis of world political events, an analysis which would open up perspectives for its readers." Macdonald and his contributors attacked Marxism but offered no "empirically verifiable" alternatives. Their only practical proposals came down to self-improvement. "One can try to better oneself without having to dredge the writings of Dwight Macdonald and Nicola Chiaromonte in order to try and make a little sense out of them."

Macdonald responded gracefully. "The difference between Farrell and myself," he said, "is that he has found certainty many years ago, while I am still looking.... Incidentally, I cannot see why Farrell, who can work up plenty of moral heat about the lies and injustices of Stalinism, should be so disturbed when *politics* talks in moral terms—unless because the blade is sometimes turned against his side.... [The] fact that we haven't yet found or worked out—and may never—a system better adapted to the needs of today than Marxism does not in any way make Marxism itself adapted to those needs."

Chiaromonte, too, soon weighed in: "Farrell asks us to deal with Marxism as if it were true, until something better is found. It can't be done, because the ideological machine to which James Farrell still professes allegiance has been in question at least since the day, October 25, 1917, when the ideology was first put to the test of historical vicissitudes."

Farrell's response: "The real issue...is Stalinism. Is or is not Stalinism a necessary consequence of Marxism? If Chiaromonte will deal with this issue in a forthright manner, then, we might have an issue worth discussing. But it is pointless to go on discussing with him, if he keeps writing in the spirit of this rejoinder.... Parts of his letter are scarcely above the level that we would expect from a gifted high school student." Farrell concluded by asking Macdonald if he were not "even a little embarrassed" to print Chiaromonte's letter.

Far from it, Macdonald said. "But I *am* embarrassed by the personal abuse which Farrell substitutes for argument, his tedious reduction of the whole issue between us to the question of whether Chiaromonte and myself are fools. It is impossible to discuss anything serious on this level."

Macdonald was right about that, of course.

⟫◦⟪

IN THE EARLY MORNING HOURS of December 29, 1945, Farrell was awakened by the loud ringing of the doorbell. It was a telegram telling him of the death of Theodore Dreiser the night before.

After an essay by Farrell on *Sister Carrie* had appeared in the *New York Times Book Review* in July 1943, the septuagenarian author, his works now fallen into general neglect, had written him a note of thanks, recalling the brief encounter they had had six years before in Philadelphia. He had been unsure of Farrell's name then, but he knew it now (though he probably had not read any of his books). Thus began a correspondence between the two naturalistic novelists.

The following May, when Dreiser had come east from Los Angeles to accept an award from the National Academy of Arts and Letters, Farrell (who had helped Sinclair Lewis in the fight he led to win the honor for Dreiser) had visited him in the Commodore Hotel, near Grand Central Station. When they shook hands, Farrell was to remember, "I saw that since 1936 he had become an old man. His face was thinner and quite wrinkled. His neck was wrinkled. He wore gray trousers and a white shirt, and stood a great deal of the time while we talked." They chatted for a few hours, mostly about literary matters. "He kept plying me with questions. Now and then he would make a remark about the past, and of how New York was different and was no longer of interest to him." Farrell asked him if he was going to finish the trilogy of novels about Frank Cowperwood (modeled on the notorious Chicago traction magnate Charles T. Yerkes); the first two volumes, *The Financier* and *The Titan,* had appeared in 1912 and 1914 respectively. "He said yes, and told me that he was working on it. I remarked that I would very much like to read it."

But first Dreiser was to finish *The Bulwark*, a novel having to do with religion that had been in the works for thirty-two years and whose forthcoming publication had been announced in 1920. After receiving one unenthusiastic appraisal of the manuscript, Dreiser in May 1945 solicited the opinion of Farrell, who had recently written appreciative essays on *An American Tragedy* and Dreiser's fiction for the *Times Book Review*. No doubt pleased to be asked, he gave generously of his advice and, while seeing need for some revision, returned a favorable verdict. That was not the end of *The Bulwark*'s complicated editorial history, but in June Dreiser turned to *The Stoic*, the novel, then two-thirds complete, that was the final volume in the Cowperwood trilogy. In October he wrote to Farrell that he had finished it, and in early December sent the manuscript to him. Farrell read thirty-three chapters the night it arrived, and the next morning dashed off a note to Dreiser telling him that "It reads excitingly, seems to me to be a solidly built story, and to have pace and progression." Later, on December 19, he sent a lengthy analysis, saying that the book was very impressive until it reached the end, and offering advice as to how the ending might be recast. Dreiser agreed that the last chapter needed to be rewritten. As to Farrell's recommendation that he eliminate a sketchy postscript on good and evil, intended as a coda to the trilogy, Dreiser said there was plenty of time to discuss that. But there wasn't. His comments came to Farrell in a letter that arrived after his death.

Farrell (who considered Dreiser's decision, some months before his death, to join the Communist Party simply "his way of repudiating the values of bourgeois America") penned a memorial essay on him for the *Saturday Review*. "We have lost a great writer. We have lost a man who made the way easier for many of us.... The man who contributed so much to the forging of our will to struggle to the bitter end has gone. Farewell, Theodore Dreiser; farewell and hail! You, creator of titans in fiction, were a greater titan yourself."

<hr />

JUST ABOUT FIVE MINUTES INTO the new year of 1946, Farrell's mother, Mary, had a stroke. The Farrells, including Jim, and the Dalys soon gathered at Helen's house in Chicago, where Mary had been living since 1938 and where she now lay dying. Thanks to Jim Farrell's generosity, she had round-the-clock nursing care. The night nurse was a heavy-set, middle-aged woman, and thinking her a good Catholic who might not approve of Farrell's novels, Helen hid her copies of her brother's books. As it turned out, the nurse brought her own copy of one of the novels and quietly read it as she sat beside the author's moribund mother. The day nurse was an attractive younger woman, and the men assembled in the house joked about who would get to drive her home.

Farrell's mother—whom he had rather harshly portrayed in his fiction—had been very pleased when he dedicated *$1,000 a Week and Other Stories* to her, and she had written to him telling him so. Then, when he and his difficult wife and their son had visited Helen and her second husband, Matt Dillon, for a week in June 1945, she had tried to stay out of the way, hoping to avoid any scenes with Hortense. But when they left, Farrell remembered, his mother had been on the platform at Englewood Station, waving, with tears in her eyes. He had somehow thought then that it might be the last time he would ever see her.

She died on January 9. As the novelist seems to have come reluctantly to apprehend, he and his mother had a good deal in common. Both were fundamentally well-meaning and free of racial or other prejudice; both cared very little about their personal appearance; both managed money poorly; both went their own way, regardless of what others thought; and both craved immortality, she in Heaven, he in the literary equivalent.

As was Farrell's wont, he soon sought to transmute the experience of his mother's death into fiction. Eventually, in 1978, the year before his own passing, *The Death of Nora Ryan* would be published. In the novel, Farrell's alter ego Eddie Ryan, upon learning of his mother's stroke, has trouble making up his mind as to whether even to go to her bedside in Chicago. "I wondered about that," Farrell's sister Helen acknowledged. When Danny O'Neill had gotten word of his father's death, he had "felt empty more than he felt anything." Farrell's other alter ego seems to have felt much the same way with regard to his mother. Clearly, Farrell's own feelings about the parents who had let him be reared by others were very ambivalent.

⟹•⟸

WHAT COULD ISIDOR SCHNEIDER have been thinking? Was the literary editor of the *New Masses* afflicted with the recently discovered malady of "Browderism" (named after Earl Browder, who had just been expelled from the Communist Party as a class enemy)? Whatever the explanation, there was a shockingly heretical essay by Albert Maltz in the February 12, 1946, issue of the normally reliable *New Masses.*

A top Hollywood screenwriter and a leading party theoretician, Maltz was so bold as to assert that the doctrine that "art is a weapon" had led to the condemnation of art that was not weaponry, and to the praise of weaponry that was not art. He confessed that he himself had found the doctrine so much a "straitjacket" that, as a writer, he had long since found it necessary "to repudiate it and abandon it." Writers "should be judged by their work, and *not* by the committees they join... ," he dared to suggest.

> The best case in point—although there are many—is James T. Farrell. Farrell is, in my opinion—and I have thought so ever since reading *Studs Lonigan* over ten years ago—one of the outstanding writers in America. I have not liked all of his work equally, and I don't like the committees he belongs to. But he wrote a superb trilogy and more than a few short stories of great quality, and he is not through writing.... Farrell's name was a bright pennant in the *New Masses* until he became hostile to the *New Masses.* Very well; for his deeds or misdeeds as a citizen, let him be editorially appraised. But his literary work cannot be ignored, and must not be ignored.

All this was too much, far too much, for the keepers of the orthodox flame. Maltz—who had won an Oscar for his 1942 documentary, *Moscow Strikes Back*—was immediately set upon in the pages of the *Daily Worker* by two of Moscow's reliable intellectual thugs, columnist Mike Gold and literary editor Samuel Sillen. "It has a familiar smell," said the ineffable Gold:

> I remember hearing all this sort of artistic moralizing before. The criticism of James T. Farrell, Max Eastman, Granville Hicks and other renegades always attacked the same literary "sins of the Communists," and even quoted Lenin, Engels and Marx to profusion.... Maltz's coy reference to the "political committees" on which James Farrell serves is a bad sign. Farrell is no mere little committee-server, but a vicious, voluble Trotskyite with many years of activity. Maltz knows this. Maltz knows that Farrell has long been a colleague of Max Eastman, Eugene Lyons and similar rats who have been campaigning with endless lies and slanders for war on the Soviet Union.

Sillen, driven to pen a six-part series of articles in response, discerned "a dangerous departure from Marxism" in Maltz's words.

"Albert Maltz seems to believe that he is merely criticizing a 'vulgarized approach' to literature," Sillen wrote in his second installment, "but he is in reality undermining a class approach.... Farrell embodies hatred and hostility to the working class, and Maltz glowingly predicts that 'he is not through writing yet,' as if that were something to cheer about."

Maltz's "bourgeois liberal" notion that a writer's work should be judged independently of his politics might have been tolerated during the Popular Front era or the years of wartime collaboration (at least so long as the writer involved was not, like Farrell, actively anti-Stalinist). But now the war was over and, as Winston Churchill was to observe in March in a speech in Fulton, Missouri, an "iron curtain" had descended in Eastern Europe. "Warsaw, Berlin, Prague, Vienna, Budapest, Belgrade, Bucharest and Sofia, all these famous cities and the populations around them lie in what I must call the Soviet sphere," he said, "and all are subject in one form or another, not only to Soviet influence but to a very high and, in many cases, increasing measure of control from Moscow."

From Moscow's point of view, then, this was no time for the American comrades to be indulging in heresy. It was rather a time for them to oppose vigorously all resistance to Soviet designs (a.k.a. "American imperialism") and to rid the party of "Browderism," whose eponym—that "unreconstructed revisionist," that "social-imperialist," that "enemy of the working class," that "renegade," that "apologist for American imperialism"—had dared to envision an era of class peace in postwar America.

Samuel Sillen flew out to Hollywood and called a special party meeting for the burning of the pariah Maltz. Leopold Atlas, a fellow screenwriter at Warner Brothers, later described the "nightmarish and shameful experience" to the House Committee on Un-American Activities:

> I remember that Albert tried to explain his thoughts on the article. I remember that almost instantly all sorts of howls went up in protest against it. I remember that I and one or two others made small attempts to speak in favor of Maltz, and we were literally shouted down....
>
> From one corner Alvah Bessie, with bitter vituperation and venom, rose up and denounced Maltz. From another corner Herbert Biberman rose and spouted elaborate mouthfuls of nothing, his every accent dripping with hatred. Others from every part of the room jumped in on the kill....

In the *New Masses* of April 9, 1946, Maltz abased himself and recanted his earlier article. "I consider now that my article—by what I have come to agree was a one-sided, non-dialectical treatment of *complex* issues—could not, as I had hoped, contribute to the development of left-wing criticism and creative writing. I believe also that my critics were entirely correct in insisting that certain fundamental ideas in my article would, if pursued to their conclusion, result in the dissolution of the left-wing cultural movement."

As for Farrell, whom he had previously long considered "one of the outstanding writers in America," Maltz now said that "my characterization of him was decidedly lax.... Farrell's history and work are the best example I know of the manner in which a poisoned ideology and an increasingly sick soul can sap the talent and wreck the living fibre of a man's work."

After reading Maltz's recantation, Jim Henle commented to Farrell: "It's so damned nauseating it makes me ashamed to be a human being."

<hr />

BERNARD CLARE, PUBLISHED IN May 1946 and the first in a series of novels that take the protagonist into the world of New York literati and radicals, had not come at all easily to Farrell. He'd made five false starts, and had often been discouraged. When he signed the contract with Vanguard in 1943, he had intended to tell the story of the corruption of his protagonist (first by Stalinism, then by capitalism) in one volume; the next year, he decided it would take three books, the first dealing with Bernard's youthful failure in New York. But if conveying Danny O'Neill's metamorphosis in *My Days of Anger* had been difficult, investing the experiences of the aspiring young writer Bernard Clare with significance turned out to be even harder. "Slowed down, blocked again on *Bernard Clare*," he noted in his diary in February 1945. He was afraid that what he had written was banal, but kept telling himself he had to risk it. "It is this fear of banality which often bothers and slows up writ[ing]. After so much stew, resolve, I'll do the best I can, and take what chances that involves. If it isn't too good, it's the best I could do, and I'll learn from it, and perhaps, then, I can do better the next time."

In revolt against his family and society, Clare (or Claire, as Farrell had dubbed him until Henle said the name had a Gallic ring and pointed out how County Clare in Ireland was spelled) has left Chicago behind and now, in 1927, is in New York, just as Farrell himself had been that year. Although picking up, in a way, where Danny O'Neill left off, Clare, unlike Danny, is only a partly autobiographical figure. Farrell moves him through the months from June to December, giving Bernard some of his own New York experiences and inventing others. At novel's end, Bernard, after having made a drunken fool of himself at a party, is set to return to Chicago. More mature than he was in June, he thinks he is ready now to harness his rebellious feelings and *write*.

Unfortunately, neither Bernard's sojourn in New York nor the would-be writer himself is particularly interesting. Some individual scenes are well done—such as the Sacco-and-Vanzetti demonstration in Union Square—but they don't seem to add up to very much. And Bernard, with his complaints about the "futility" and "emptiness" of life, his protests against "this goddamn society," becomes simply tiresome. The novel has far too much of the rebellious self and not enough of the world against which that self is rebelling. And as with *My Days of Anger*, the absence of irony, of mature perspective, is sorely felt.

Yet *Bernard Clare* did sell well—better than any of Farrell's previous works in hardcover. This must have been at least partly because of the lavish treatment the novel received from the influential *New York Times Book Review*. Under the headline "JAMES T. FARRELL'S HUMAN COMEDY," with the subhead "'Bernard Clare' Adds a New Chapter to an Important Study of Our Times," the whole front page was given over to the book. Accompanied by an illustration by "ashcan" artist John Sloan, the review by Harvard literary scholar F. O. Matthiessen began: "In the lean season of fiction through which we are now passing, James T. Farrell's continued dedication to naturalism is one of the few signs of vitality."

But careful readers of the review soon discovered that Matthiessen saw significant imperfections in the novel. He judged that the "most moving passages in this book are those that get farthest outside its hero's thoughts about his own problems....After the night in Union Square, which climaxes the first of the four sections, there is no progression of interest." Farrell needed to get away from "the too detailed obsessions of a Bernard Clare into other lives in the city surrounding him."

Other reviewers made similar criticisms. "One may ask, why the restriction, why the limitation to self, when naturalism can take empires for its subject?" novelist Isaac Rosenfeld wrote in the *New Republic*. Unless the succeeding volumes "broaden out," he warned, Farrell's "stature as a novelist must diminish."

The warning was prescient. Nearly four decades later, Mary McCarthy would recall for an interviewer that after *Bernard Clare* and the other novels in the trilogy, Farrell's "reputation sank."

The precipitous decline began with *Bernard Clare*. Reviewing the novel in *Partisan Review*, the astute critic Elizabeth Hardwick reluctantly concluded that "in the lazy clumsiness of the style, the banality of the incident, the poverty of the insight, *Bernard Clare* would be more appropriate as the hero's first fumbling effort than as James T. Farrell's 18th or so published book." The author, she said, had failed to give his aspiring artist "spiritual or intellectual boldness, delicacy of response, individuality of observation, or profundity of dedication—any of the traits that might make the reader believe the character has at least a potential capacity for the difficult creative task he has chosen.... If this story is a portrait of the artist as a young man, then Farrell's artist has sensation without intellect, honesty without subtlety, energy without discrimination."

Like Hardwick, Diana Trilling, writing in the *Nation*, was troubled by the author's failure to dissociate himself from the "confused and half-baked and self-pitying" Clare. "I think we must conclude," she said, "that Mr. Farrell's view of himself in relation to the world is fundamentally the same as Bernard's view of himself in relation to the world—a very narrow one." In Bernard's struggle to become a writer, he feels himself terribly weighed down by his humble background; even his nascent political radicalism "is deeply rooted in an emotion of social disadvantage," Mrs. Trilling observed. "For all his self-absorption, that is, Bernard estimates himself very low." The same, she suggested, was true of Farrell.

Her analysis was very acute, as is revealed in some remarks Farrell made in a 1944 letter to Felix Morrow, one of the imprisoned Trotskyists. "Writers like myself have no tradition to guide us," Farrell said. "We began with desire, rebellion, had to find our subject matter, and then, our way of writing. I read almost nothing until I was almost 21. One must see writers like myself in terms of America, not Europe. We had to grow up to everything painfully, grow up to James and Joyce and Proust and Kafka, grow up to Dewey and Marx, to theory, ideas, art. It took a long time. I still try to grow up."

For the epigraph of *Bernard Clare*, Farrell chose a quotation from Chekhov, one that he had originally thought of using for *My Days of Anger.* It said: *"What writers belonging to the upper class have received from nature for nothing, plebians acquire at the cost of their youth."* Though it could hardly be said that Farrell had been required to sacrifice his youth in order to make his way as a writer, Chekhov's wistful observation expressed Farrell's feeling that his social background had held him back. And no doubt, in certain ways it had. But it had also given him the South Side Chicago world of his childhood and youth that was his great subject. Alas, with *Bernard Clare* he had moved unwisely away from it.

⸺⸺►◦◄⸺⸺

PUBLISHING AFTER THE WAR WAS in the throes of change. The rise of the ravenous "reprint" business meant pure profits for Vanguard Press and Farrell. But, earnestly endeavoring to appraise the trend objectively in terms of the cultural common good, he feared the potential commercialization—the "Hollywoodization"—of literature. He wrote an illuminating essay on the subject, which New Directions, an independent press, published in the spring of 1946 in *New Directions Number 9* and then brought out as a pamphlet, *The Fate of Writing in America.*

The publishing industry had prospered greatly during the war. With the economy booming and millions of men away from home, there was a big demand for books from soldiers and civilians alike. Even before the war, publishers were trying to reach a larger readership with low-priced books, both clothbound and paperback; after Pearl Harbor, they expanded their efforts. The reprint houses, offering previously published works in low-priced editions, flourished. Pocket Books alone in one year sold thirty million 25-cent paperback reprints. In 1943, with no additional effort at all on his part, Farrell received a $3,000 advance—the equivalent of nearly $32,000 today—from the World Publishing Company to reprint the Studs Lonigan novels. ("My gross income this year is going to be better than it has been for a long time," he noted then with pleasure.) Hampered by government restrictions on paper, publishers were unable to fulfill the huge wartime demand. But it was clear that mass production and distribution of books was feasible and very remunerative.

Now, with the war over and the restrictions off, publishing was on the verge of becoming a big business. "The reprint houses are competing for distribution outlets, for authors and reprint rights, for motion picture tie-ups and for access to production facilities," Farrell wrote. "This rivalry is the central fact in the economics of the book business today." The market, almost as if it were developing "its own consciousness," was taking on greater importance than "the individual tastes of editors."

To produce low-priced books in vast quantity, a reprint publisher had to make a much larger investment than a trade publisher did, and so was much more averse to taking risks, Farrell observed. For the original publisher, reprint rights simply represented profits, without risk or cost. But this meant that "any book which stands a good chance of being reprinted is a better investment than one which doesn't." Thus the reprint publisher's preference for "safe" books was passed along, to some extent, to the trade publisher.

In the past, the keen economic competition among publishers had often translated into "the search for freshness, vigor, variety and originality in books," Farrell said. But in the reprint field, "standardization" was the likely result, as, for instance, in the extensive competition to obtain movie tie-ins. "The rise of the reprint houses is having the effect…of strengthening the ties between Hollywood and the book business," Farrell said. "For more than a decade films have influenced writing. Thanks to the prices it can pay, Hollywood has given a strong financial impulse to the publication of books which approximate the sentimental patterns of its films. Many writers have found it most convenient to adjust their conscience, their style and their themes to the dramaturgical conceptions of Hollywood."

In the long run, Farrell believed, quality would win out. Taste had improved in America. "More honest books sell in larger numbers than was the case a few decades ago. Many readers demand a greater seriousness from novelists today…. Far more people of the lower middle class and even workers are reading seriously than, say, in 1890." The masses would not be content forever with "standardized ideas and works of art."

For the individual writer of conscience, the challenge would be the same one Farrell's predecessors had to face: "the problem of success versus integrity."

But success and integrity were not necessarily in opposition—as Farrell evidently had come to appreciate. "We have bought a house—acre and a half of land, five room little house which we hope gradually to improve," he wrote from Wingdale, a town near

Pawling, New York, to his friend Morty White in June 1946. "It is up here, and has a lovely view, on a hill, with a view of hills and greenness so that one has a great feeling of space."

It was the only real estate that Farrell would ever own. He bought it impulsively for $8,250, apparently entirely with his own money and, according to Jim Henle's later recollection, "without consulting his attorneys or any of his friends, for it was obviously an injudicious step. The house was adequate for his needs, and the price—a rather substantial [sum] for any man living by the rattle of his typewriter—would not have been excessive had sufficient land been included. But…similar houses in the region usually included anything from a dozen to a hundred acres."

Unwise investment though it may have been, Farrell hoped that Hortense would be pleased to have a summer house of their own, that they would be happy in it. But she came—perhaps not immediately—to hate it.

———⟫•◦•⟨———

FARRELL WAS IN MINNEAPOLIS during July 1946, giving a series of lectures on Dreiser, Lewis and other American novelists to summer school students at the University of Minnesota. Also teaching there was critic Alfred Kazin, whose brilliant, wonderfully passionate study of the emergence of American realism and the history of modern American literature, *On Native Grounds* (1942), had established his reputation. Kazin had again adverted to Farrell's "hatred" of his characters, but he had much more to say about the novelist's work, and not just about its flaws (though he did not scant those). He called him "perhaps the most powerful naturalist who ever worked in the American tradition" and "the archetypal novelist of the crisis [of the early 1930s] and its inflictions."

Whatever Farrell—who read only parts of *On Native Grounds*—may have made of Kazin's criticism of himself and his work, he judged the book "very bad." Its author, he told one of the imprisoned Trotskyists in 1944, "has no capacity to deal with ideas." Still, he had once met Kazin at a gathering and found him "very sweet and sensible."

If Kazin in 1938 had perhaps allowed his desire for a unified resistance to Hitler by the Left to affect his judgment of *No Star Is Lost* and of Farrell's work in general, the dereliction was now in the past, back before the landmark Nazi-Soviet Pact. Now, at the University of Minnesota (Kazin would remind Farrell almost two decades later), they had a "remarkable easiness and intimacy with each other." When they parted, they were, if not exactly friends, at least on amiable terms.

⟹•○•⟸

TWO DAYS AFTER CHRISTMAS, 1946, Hortense and Kevin were on the 59th Street bus, returning from a visit to one of his school friends, when they saw fire engines speed past. The fire, as they soon discovered to their horror, was in their own apartment at 340 East 58th Street. Jim Farrell was at the second-floor window, with smoke billowing out from behind him. Trapped inside, he had shouted to passersby to turn in an alarm. The firemen extended a ladder to the window, rescued the writer and put out the blaze.

It had started in his workroom, and the damage there was extensive. More than a thousand pages of unpublished manuscripts, finished and partly finished, were destroyed, along with letters he had received and hundreds, perhaps thousands, of pages from his notebooks and diaries. Only charred fragments, about thirty pages, remained of the nearly hundred-page rough draft of the original ending to *Judgment Day*, detailing images, fantasies and thoughts in Studs's mind as he lay dying. Deciding this section was superfluous, Farrell and Henle had deleted it from the published book, but—until the fire—the novelist had hoped to revise it and publish it on its own someday. Other manuscript items lost in the fire included more than fifty stories-in-progress, several novelettes-in-progress, and various articles on subjects ranging from Irish culture to the American writers of the 1930s.

That night, with their apartment uninhabitable, Farrell stayed downtown somewhere while Hortense and Kevin went to the Central Park West apartment of Evelyn Shrifte, Henle's right-hand editor at Vanguard Press. Before long, the Farrells were temporarily ensconced in a hotel, the Park Central, at 7th Avenue and 55th Street; then, after a few weeks, they shifted to temporary quarters at 91 Charles Street. It would be several months before they were able to move back into their 58th Street home.

The cause of the fire was given out as electrical. Looking back some years later, however, Jim Henle said that although the fire was blamed on faulty wiring, he "saw no harm in stating at this late date I always believed it started from [Farrell's] cigarette ashes—he was smoking amid a pile of papers when he noticed [the] blaze."

A decade and a half after the conflagration, Farrell confirmed this version of events in a conversation with novelist Sloan Wilson. Offering some advice, Farrell told Wilson to stop drinking "'before you burn the house down.'" He confided that under the influence of alcohol, he had once fallen asleep while smoking and "'burned the house down.'"

Chapter Fifteen
Freedom

THE BELLS OF ST. MARY'S, a sequel to the Oscar-winning *Going My Way*, is a sentimental movie about a young priest, a beautiful nun and a dilapidated parochial school. The film "calls for, and deserves, the enthusiastic support of every Catholic moviegoer," proclaimed the reviewer for the *Sign*, a magazine published by the Passionist Fathers, an order of Catholic priests.

Jim Farrell disagreed. "The praise which so many Catholics have showered on this film suggests strongly the growing hollowness of conventional morality in our time," he declared in *Literature and Morality*, a collection of his essays published in June 1947. The nuns and priest in the movie, he pointed out, seem more interested in the new building that a rich, miserly unbeliever is erecting next door to their run-down school than in the children in their charge. Father O'Malley (Bing Crosby) and Sister Superior Benedict (Ingrid Bergman) also stoop to using two of the schoolboys as pawns in their own flirtatious rivalry. Did the Catholics who lavished praise on the film consider its moral implications? *The Bells of St. Mary's*, Farrell wrote, gives "the impression that hollow good cheer, and good will, will lead to valuable human results.... In the name of such optimism and sunshiny goodness, serious writers are attacked as cynics and denounced as nothing less then enemies of the human race."

Farrell's novels had long outraged many Catholics, of course. Once, in 1936, he and Hortense, on their way home from the theater, had stopped in a bookshop at Grand Central Station and learned that a few nights earlier a visiting Chicago priest had exploded with rage when he noticed copies of *A World I Never Made* in the store's window display. The irate priest was hardly alone among Catholics. Though the fulminations against Farrell's works seldom made their way into print, there were occasional hints of them in the Catholic press. Thus the *Catholic World*, a magazine published by the Paulist Fathers, offered this comment in 1938 on *No Star Is Lost*: "A successful achievement in almost unrelieved vulgarity, it should give immense satisfaction to readers who enjoy realistic talk on such subjects as vomit and urine."

But even then, more discerning Catholics were not so quick to dismiss Farrell. Barry Byrne, an architect reviewing *No Star Is Lost* for *Commonweal*, a lay Catholic weekly, wrote with candor and intelligence:

> While this is indeed a record of sordid lives, it is not a sordid record. The innate honesty of the author's purpose, as well as his Catholic tradition, saves it from such a charge.... That the life here pictured is a facet of life within Catholicism needs no emphasized assertion. The fact that these poor, tortured, sinful people remain within the Church, or in their absence from the offices of their faith, are tormented by an awareness of loss, is as it should be. Ours is a Church of branded sinners and unrecognized saints and it is our weakness that causes us intermittently to long for the flesh-pots of respectability.

As the years went by and Farrell continued to turn out books, sympathetic Catholics increasingly came forward to vouch for the moral passion behind them. Thus Harold C. Gardiner, the literary editor of the Jesuit weekly *America*, thought that Farrell was

> a writer with deeper and keener moral sensibilities than either Hemingway or [Sinclair] Lewis. He knows and parades...sin and its consequences; he admits on every page that sin is an evil—no, not in the sense that it offends God, but in its social repercussions: in the misery and poverty and cruelty that occasion it and which it, in turn, causes. There is a white-hot moral indignation in Farrell that goads him on to talking out these evils, as though he were hoping to exorcize himself and his characters by telling the whole sad and sordid story.

In Farrell's collection of essays *Literature and Morality*—which includes, *inter alia,* "The Fate of Writing in America" and other essays concerned with Hollywood's threat to culture—the author's moral passion was transparent. And writing in the *New Republic*, novelist Harry Sylvester (a frequent *Commonweal* contributor) commented:

> The most obvious irony in these essays is that of Farrell's relation to Catholicism, which he renounced some years ago. His values are largely Christian and many of them are indeed more basic than those

which contemporary Catholicism and Christianity in general now stress. He is concerned with those values which the Christian tradition embodies but largely fails to put into practice.

Reviewer Nancy Lenkeith saluted Farrell in *Commonweal* as "an honest writer, who serves his art and his reader with discernment," and astutely analyzed his outlook. "What Mr. Farrell wants is a broad human culture, a genuine culture of the people. He thinks that this is possible today, that our present economic prosperity makes it categorically imperative. Either the masses will be educated now, or culture will be lost to them forever. And before they can be educated, they must be understood, portrayed, and explained by the writer." This social function gives literature the sanction of morality. "Mr. Farrell's dynamism, the integrity of his anti-Stalinist convictions, and his spirit of self-sacrifice," she concluded, "are a challenge to Christian writers. Marxians are not the only ones who believe they have a kingdom to fight for."

After her generous and perceptive review appeared, Farrell contacted Lenkeith. She was a beautiful and intelligent young Catholic convert, then completing her doctorate at Columbia and working in publishing. As an established writer, he intrigued her. They became friends, of a proper sort.

She felt drawn to him, but whatever may have been in his mind, she had no interest in romance with a married man nearly twice her age. Their friendship lasted for several years—until, when they were no longer in close touch, and without her even being aware of it, he took offense at her alleged past "lack of understanding" of his difficult situation at home and, in his characteristic way, suddenly discovered his "total" indifference to her and effectively withdrew his friendship.

SOMETIME IN EARLY 1947, before the Farrells moved back into their fire-damaged apartment, Hortense discovered that she was pregnant. She was forty-seven years old, but she pretended, even to her doctor, to be forty-two—one year younger than Farrell. The fact, well known today, that the risk of birth defects increases with the mother's age was not common knowledge then.

During the ensuing months, Hortense's wrangling with Farrell diminished. Kevin's tantrums did not cease, but she seems more often to have left it to her husband to discipline him, something

Farrell disliked. One day, during an abbreviated summer stay at their cottage in Wingdale, when Kevin refused to put on his shoes before going out, Farrell sent him crying to his room. "Not asserting [authority] at times is a sidestepping of responsibility," Farrell reflected. "And yet, when I have to it is very unpleasant, and it causes me to think of my own childhood and sinks me into contradictions. These contradictions reveal how hard it is to grow up, how one dislikes growing up."

Back in New York a few weeks later, Farrell took his six-year-old son to Yankee Stadium to see his first major-league game. The Yankees, who were close to clinching the pennant, were playing the Red Sox. The game, scoreless until the eleventh inning, was a tense and exciting one.

Baseball games posed a slight problem for some radicals. When the band commenced playing "The Star-Spangled Banner," Trotskyist fans such as Farrell's friend Al Glotzer underwent a crisis of conscience: should they stand up and pay homage to capitalist, imperialist America? Glotzer, for one, did stand—but always uneasily, knowing that his party would not approve. Farrell, free of obligations to any party, apparently felt no such embarrassment. Once in 1943, pressed to buy war bonds and thus give support to the United States in a war he opposed, he had bought $200 worth, reasoning that no "fundamental principles" were involved and that if he didn't make the purchase then, he was likely to be "bothered" about it again in the future. "I'm not interested in 1917 gestures," he had told himself. He undoubtedly employed a similar rationalization, if he even found one necessary, when it came to standing at ballgames while the national anthem was played, and there is no indication that he ever felt any discomfort about doing so. This time, with his excited son beside him, he experienced a surge of patriotism.

"A welling of feeling, related to K[evin], when 'The Star-Spangled Banner' was played," he recorded in his diary the next day. "The crowd standing, the players out at attention, hats off. The thoughts that in such scenes, love of America wells up. Revolutionaries will so often repress such feelings. It is wrong. You can't repress. You can only work out. Love of country is often bound up with love of one's own past."

Farrell also reflected on how much better Hortense had been behaving lately than he had. "My moods have been more neurotic than usual, again and again this summer. Hortense has been, to the contrary, in very good shape. She looks wonderful, and has often been quite calm, and quietly affectionate. She has a sense of stability in her home, and handles her rankling disappointments re theatre with dignity."

Pregnancy seemed to agree with her, but it came to an end on September 21 with the birth of John Stephen Farrell. "The little boy was born with club feet, but it is correctible," Farrell wrote in his diary. "The first cast has been put on, already. He weighed five pounds and twelve ounces, and he seems cute." Hortense came home from the hospital four days before John Stephen did, and Farrell reflected that it was "one of the days which make one happy that one has a family." But soon Hortense was back in the hospital with puerperal fever (postpartum infection) and, by Farrell's later recollection, she almost died. A nurse attended to John Stephen at home, but Farrell found it a difficult time. "I have been depressed and repressed, gloomy. I may have been sick," he wrote.

At last, Hortense recovered and returned home. Kevin then "asked her if she liked him," Farrell wrote. "She said, I don't like you, I love you. Did she like the baby more. She said no, she loved them both, but she knew him longer and loved him first."

More than years separated the two brothers, though. For all the oppressive aspects of his upbringing, Kevin was a normal youngster; John Stephen was not. Just when his mental retardation became evident to his parents is unclear. A clinical report written long afterward stated that it was noted, along with his club feet, "soon after birth." But if "soon" meant "right away," as with the club feet, there is no indication of that in Farrell's diaries. Eventually, however, the boy's failure to develop normally became obvious. By mid-1949, when he was twenty-one months old, he still could not sit up without support and, in the words of the later medical report, "still had poor head control and did not turn over or crawl."

Hortense, in the description of her friend, playwright Randolph Carter, was "a very diligent mother." When John Stephen was four and a half months old, Farrell, writing in his diary, marveled at the way she "takes care of John. And Kevin. I have quarreled with her so much, but at the same time—the devotion and care and self-sacrifice she shows."

Motherhood must at times have seemed to Hortense the only great role left to her. Though she was an immensely gifted actress, she could not find work—with rare and unsatisfying exceptions, such as a short-lived role in the spring of 1948 as an aged Mary

Baker Eddy in a play by Carter—because she was so much a perfectionist, so imperious, so "difficult" (and because she shared
Farrell's outspoken anti-Stalinism, in a theatrical world that was
mostly sympathetic to the tyrant).

She could not justly blame her frustration as an actress on her
husband, who always encouraged her in her career. But she would
have been not fully human if she did not occasionally take that
frustration out on him. In addition, she had developed some minor
grievances against him over the years. She liked to entertain at
home, but usually found his political friends boring. When he
dragged home, as he did on occasion, a prototype for one of his
characters whom he happened to have run into at a bar—"both of
'em somewhat the worse for wear," as Henle put it—she was even
more disturbed. She liked to cook, but he was as indifferent to food
as he was to dress. And then there was his writing: it came first
with him and he seemed to be always at it. "Writers are hard to live
with," she would tell an interviewer decades later. An intelligent
and well-read woman, she often helped Farrell by critiquing his
fiction-in-progress and even functioning as an editor, cutting
superfluous scenes and trimming wordy passages. But as the years
went by and he kept turning out novels and short stories, Hortense
came more and more to detest his typical characters, just as she did
his family. "She felt she was more important than he was," Carter
said. "She never seemed to be swept away by his talent. And she
said she finally was absolutely sick of his writings. 'He's writing
more and more about those awful people.'"

For a while, John Stephen seemed to bring contentment to
the Farrell household. "In my forties, I have, all told, perhaps been
happier than in any other decade of my life," Farrell reflected in
February 1948, as he approached his forty-fourth birthday. But by
mid-year—perhaps they had begun by then to suspect the truth
about John Stephen—the happiness appears to have slipped away.
"It is going to be a bad day," he wrote in his diary in their summer
home in Wingdale. "But then, so many of our days are bad. There is
no one to blame. Things look differently to Hortense and to myself.
She seems to me to have deep anxieties, anxieties which are hard
to cope with, and it puts me, as I see it consciously, in the position
where I have to fight and push them off, and, in consequence, there
is a strain, an emotional drain. I get resentful and I notice an air of
hostility. Things are pushed onto Kevin, and we don't agree about
Kevin."

A year later, their situation was worse. Their terrible fears had been realized, and John Stephen's retardation established beyond all doubt. Pending his institutionalization, they had handed him over to "a colored family in Brooklyn," probably because Hortense simply could not bear having the poor, doomed child remain with them any longer, even for only a few months. "Now and then, thoughts of Johnny—usually of him lying in his crib," Farrell recorded in his diary in June 1949. "Parting with him was like death, and it was not death. H[ortense] said a while ago, still feels in somewhat of a stupor over it. I can still fill up myself."

Burdened since John Stephen's birth by medical expenses (including, at least for a time, the cost of a live-in nurse), Farrell worried about money. He tried to think of pieces that he could write quickly and sell, decided to do more lectures, and borrowed $2,500 against the Wingdale house. (He and Hortense would sell the property the next year for $5,000.) Meanwhile, he kept at what he called his "drudge-like work" on the trilogy he had begun with *Bernard Clare.*

Hortense left it to him to visit John Stephen and to make the arrangements for his admission to Letchworth Village, a facility for the retarded in Rockland County, New York. Farrell's young Catholic friend Nancy Lenkeith accompanied him and a female psychologist on a visit to John Stephen in Brooklyn. "He is the same little fellow," Farrell wrote afterward. "I guessed that his level [of development] is six months. I held him. He didn't recognize me. It doesn't seem to matter to him who holds him."

After John Stephen had left their home, his absence hung heavy over it. Hortense especially was often depressed and miserable—and, according to Farrell, irritable. They frequently quarreled over Kevin. "When the three of us are together alone," he recorded in his diary, "there isn't enough joy and spontaneity among us. Too much concern over K[evin] and K[evin]'s behavior. It is bad. I don't know what to do, and how to soften and lighten and brighten our family relationship." He allowed that he was "too self-centered" at times, but said that Hortense was "over-anxious."

Their arguments grew worse. Perpetually anxious and overprotective, Hortense resented Farrell for not sharing those anxieties and relieving her of the full burden of acting on them. He saw it all differently. "Several fights or quarrels about K[evin] in last week," he wrote in Wingdale near the end of July 1949. In an incident that morning, Hortense had told the eight-year-old to sit down while he was eating, and he stormed off to his father. "He came to me, angry and talking a mile a minute. She says he lied to me about her. She said he did a vicious thing. I was dragged in, and had to point out that it wasn't so serious, and this set things off. I am against H[ortense], I am an absolutist, I have to be right, I want arguments and so on. I haven't detailed the things said, but it was clearly overreaction." Farrell found the many such incidents very disturbing. "Often, I feel helpless. I don't know whether I am right or wrong, but my position is hopeless.... I fear we are on a bad merry-go-round."

A month later, on August 30, Farrell, accompanied by Jim Henle and Nancy Lenkeith, took little John Stephen Farrell to Letchworth Village. Long afterward, when she was a parent herself, Lenkeith would reflect that she should not have been there—the boy's mother should have. But Hortense must have thought it would be simply too much for her. For Jim Farrell, it appears to have been the last time he ever saw his son. If he did make any subsequent visits to Letchworth Village, they soon stopped. Since the boy did not recognize his parents and there was nothing they could directly do for him there, they no doubt concluded—as people in similar circumstances then often did—that there was no reason to put themselves through the ordeal of seeing him again.

John Stephen Farrell remained at Letchworth Village for nineteen years. By 1968, Letchworth had become overcrowded and he was transferred to another facility, the Wassaic State School. His condition was such that he needed "complete custodial care." He entered a group home in Clinton County, New York, in 1994, and died there five years later, at age fifty-two.

⟹•◦•⟸

PERHAPS EAGER TO SEE AN assembly of American workers that was more than an abstraction in a Marxist polemic, Farrell went south to Atlantic City in November 1947 to attend the eleventh annual convention of the United Auto Workers. For years he had invested his hopes in a strong labor movement; now, in the UAW under the adroit and resourceful Walter Reuther, he saw one emerging.

A former tool-and-die maker, Reuther had been catapulted to the UAW presidency the preceding year by his leadership of the union's strike against General Motors during the winter of 1945–1946. His liberal idealism, together with his strong anti-

Communism, undoubtedly made a favorable impression on Farrell. Despite having the presidency, though, Reuther was not yet in full command of the union, since his adversaries dominated the executive board. The Communists—who in 1946 had control of international unions representing about 15 percent of the total Congress of Industrial Organizations membership—had designs on the UAW from its inception, and the Communists in the union threw in with the anti-Reuther bloc. Even so, at the 1947 convention—with Farrell on hand and approvingly observing—not only was Reuther re-elected, but he and his allies won full control of the executive board. This victory, wrote economist and labor historian Philip Taft, "placed the United Automobile Workers' Union solidly in the anti-Communist camp."

Thus began what Jim Henle was to call Farrell's "love affair" with the UAW. He followed its internal struggles closely, attended many subsequent conventions, and became a fervent advocate of trade union educational efforts. "There does not seem to be a more democratic and honest leadership than Reuther's in the UAW," Farrell would comment two years later. "[It] is good for the union and its members, good for the trade union movement, good for the country."

As the Cold War began—with Stalin ruthlessly ensuring Soviet mastery over Eastern Europe and aggressively promoting the spread of Communism elsewhere, and with the United States under President Harry Truman committed to supporting "free peoples who are resisting attempted subjugation," such as those in Greece and Turkey—Farrell tried to figure out where he stood. It wasn't easy. Take, for instance, the Marshall Plan, the Truman administration's program of economic aid to war-ravaged Europe, first proposed in June 1947 and soon opposed by the Soviet Union: it was far from obvious to Farrell that this was a good thing.

Still, Farrell was gradually disenthralling himself from the Trotskyist, and indeed the Marxist, dogmas and shibboleths. He came to realize, as he later said, that the "rigidities" of Marxist scholasticism had constricted his thinking, and that by taking up theoretical questions that radical groups considered immensely significant he had "sometimes sacrificed my own inner independence." For example, the stupendous question of whether the Soviet Union should be deemed a "degenerated workers' state" or placed in some other theoretical category now seemed to him utterly trivial. "There are values, values of freedom, dignity, and honesty, which are important," he reflected, "and when Stalinism has for years ridden roughshod over these, it is clear that you can see the tendency."

At the end of the year, though still not ready to endorse the Marshall Plan, Farrell was able to affirm: "I am beginning to believe that it is a mistake to equate American imperialism and Stalinist imperialism." He was well aware, he quickly added, how shocking this would seem to some of his friends.

Yet he also saw developing in America "a wave of hysteria" about Communism, a new "Red Scare" in which Marx was deemed no different from Stalin, reactionary groups such as the American Legion beat the drums for war, and headline-seeking congressmen went haring off after subversive Hollywood actors and screenwriters. Indeed, in October 1947 a subcommittee of the House Committee on Un-American Activities (HUAC) began holding hearings on Communism in the motion-picture industry, with the result that Albert Maltz and some of his screenwriting comrades soon emerged as the "Hollywood Ten," brave martyrs who nobly refused to tell the truth about their political past. After they were black-listed for their sins, Farrell told Henle: "I think that the Hollywood producers are losing something when they kick out the Stalinist writers. The Stalinists have their backs bent, their spines properly adjusted, and their mentalities equally adjusted, etc. They can write anything in the most cynical fashion, without having any problems of conscience, etc., or at least with having fewer problems of conscience. In consequence, they will often make better employees than some of the other writers."

Despite his contempt for Maltz and his comrades, Farrell spoke out publicly and forcefully (albeit in an obscure publication called *The Western Socialist*) against their mistreatment by HUAC. "Should not the Bill of Rights imply that an American citizen has the political right, at all times, to keep silent as well as to talk?" he asked. "In addition to this, the Communist Party is a legal party in America." Although it was "shameful...to belong to such a totalitarian party," it was not "*legally* a crime."

Though smacking of the Star Chamber, the HUAC hearings were a far cry from the Moscow trials, Farrell noted. "These hearings are not trials which will end in death sentences, in bullets shot in the back of broken victims in Lubianka prison." Still, "the practices of the Stalinist police-state" should not be the measure of justice. He warned the committee against creating "an atmosphere truly menacing to all minority views, to all non-conformity, to all independent thinking in America." He also invited the witnesses and their champions to extend their outspoken concern to muzzled writers and artists in the Soviet Union and to "the millions of slave laborers who are rotting in the concentration camps" there.

Farrell saw little chance that Stalinism would rise to power in the United States, but he regarded Europe as a different story. Not only was Stalin stamping out democratic hopes in Eastern Europe, with the coup d'état in Czechoslovakia in February 1948 being only the latest instance, but in France and Italy the Communists had emerged from the war as a major political force.

By mid-April, Farrell had made up his mind about the Marshall Plan: he was for it, and said so in a letter to the Trotskyist editors of *Labor Action* (who printed the letter, though they didn't agree with him). "The capitalist reconstruction of Western Europe is far, far better than no reconstruction," Farrell observed. "I also think that if the Marshall Plan can be partially successful, war might be postponed....The simple fact is that today, only American wealth and power stands in the road of Stalinist expansion."

In a lengthy letter to the *New York Times*, Farrell (writing "as a Socialist") remarked that "America is a capitalist country," yet in "simple blunt fact" it is also "one of the freest countries in the world. The Soviet Union is the most unfree country." Averting their eyes from this, he said, many Americans—many intellectuals, liberals, professionals and educated persons—subscribed to what he called "the Stalinist myth," i.e., the false belief that the Soviet Union was a socialist state and that it represented the interests of humanity. According to Stalinist propaganda, the only alternative was reaction. This, Farrell pointed out, enabled extreme reactionaries to pose plausibly as champions of freedom. By defending the Stalinist myth, Stalinists and deluded liberals were driving the United States and the rest of the world into "the camp of bitter reaction." The fight against Stalinism, he concluded, was a struggle "for every possible human mind" and had to be waged by men with free minds. Winning this battle required that civil liberties in America, particularly freedom of speech, be bolstered and greater economic justice achieved.

About the reality of what had come to be called the Cold War, the events of the succeeding months left little doubt. In June, the Soviets blockaded Berlin, seeking to starve into submission the people in the Western sectors of the city, still in ruins from the war. The Western powers responded with the famous Berlin airlift. All through the summer, fall and winter, American and British pilots (some of whom lost their lives) flew in food and fuel to the beleaguered Berliners. To many Americans, a hot war seemed likely, sooner or later.

At home, twelve members of the American Communist Party's national board were indicted in July 1948 by a New York grand jury, charged with violating the Smith Act. The Justice Department apparently had acted at the behest of FBI director J. Edgar Hoover, who wanted a test case so that in the event of a U.S. confrontation with the Soviet Union, the FBI could use the Smith Act to round up and arrest Communists.

Although the wisdom of that precautionary action was debatable, it soon became clear that there was good reason for Americans to be seriously concerned about "the enemy within." Later that month, Elizabeth Bentley, an erstwhile wartime courier for a Communist spy ring, in testimony before the House Committee on Un-American Activities, named former high U.S. government officials as sources of information transmitted to the Soviets. Then in August came Whittaker Chambers, telling the committee how he and Alger Hiss, a former State Department official, had been in the Communist underground together. Some months later, Chambers would tell of espionage. "Apparently, many people think Hiss is innocent," Farrell would observe then. "I don't."

At a press conference, President Truman, adopting a reporter's phrase as his own, unwisely dismissed the hearings on Capitol Hill as a "red herring." Though the comment would come to haunt him, it did not affect his underdog re-election campaign, observes historian and Truman biographer Alonzo Hamby. "It was hard to use the Communist issue against Truman as long as Henry Wallace was running to his left."

Wallace, the embittered former vice president whom FDR (in characteristically complicated fashion) had dropped in favor of Truman in 1944, was now the presidential candidate of the Progressive Party. This organization was a creature of the Communist Party, although most Progressives were not Communists, nor was the candidate himself. "It is not true that Henry Wallace is an agent of Moscow," Dwight Macdonald wrote in a devastating appraisal published by Vanguard Press. "But it is true that he behaves like one."

Reviewing Macdonald's witty and caustic *Henry Wallace: The Man and the Myth* earlier in the year, Farrell pronounced it "fair, objective, and admirably scrupulous." But Macdonald's joyously slashing attack, while not unfair for the most part, hardly qualified as "objective." The review in which Farrell so mischaracterized Macdonald's polemical essay displayed not only what he thought of Wallace but also some of his own limitations. First, he failed to note the eccentric vantage point from which Macdonald mounted his assault, perhaps because he too had opposed World War II and was now in a somewhat confused state of mind on his way to "choosing the West." Second, Farrell did not convey to his readers the sheer pleasure that Macdonald's brilliant, high-spirited prose afforded. (For example: "Wallaceland is the mental habitat of Henry Wallace plus a few hundred thousand regular readers of *The New Republic*, *The Nation*, and *PM*. It is a region of perpetual fogs, caused by the warm winds of the liberal Gulf Stream coming in contact with the Soviet glacier.") The reason that the earnest Farrell didn't direct his readers' attention to this delight was probably that he had not felt it himself.

"It is hard to imagine Farrell really having fun with a book or laughing at a movie," James Burnham (no longer a Trotskyist since 1940) had written in a review of *Literature and Morality* the preceding year. "He doesn't seem to understand how a higher seriousness than that of Theodore Dreiser, whom he so much admires, can be expressed through an irony and indirectness that have no need to call attention to themselves by exposing a lacerated chest. He turns away from those pools in human experience so dark that only myth and symbol are 'realistic' enough to penetrate their depths." It was a just and penetrating criticism, both of Farrell the man and of his works.

But if Farrell, for all his praise of Macdonald's essay, did not seem to appreciate it fully, he certainly understood its prosaic content well enough. He had no difficulty seeing through the Wallace campaign. In that year's presidential contest he supported Socialist Norman Thomas, reluctantly running for a sixth time. The year before, Farrell had donated fifty dollars to the Socialists with some misgivings: "I do not think that the SP is a real advancing political force." But now he was "somewhat active" in Thomas's presidential campaign, seeing this as a way to promote the creation of a labor party, and also as "the best opportunity to fight the Wallace movement, especially among students." He spoke in Thomas's behalf at a luncheon in New York on October 16, at a mass rally in Philadelphia on October 28, and at a final rally for the ticket in New York on October 31. "Effort, honesty, sincerity and idealism went into [the Thomas] campaign," Farrell later said.

"And yet," he added, "on election night and on the next morning, I listened with a growing joy as I heard the results." Thomas got only a minuscule 139,521 votes, but Truman, whom everyone had expected to be trounced by Republican candidate Thomas Dewey, instead emerged victorious—and Farrell discovered that he was very glad. He realized now he should have supported Truman.

> I felt that I had made a mistake and I thought how wonderful it is to make a big mistake painlessly. How wonderful it is to be able to learn by trying, and not to be shot for one's mistakes, not to be imprisoned. How wonderful it is to follow one's own needs and one's own bent, and to know that you may correct your errors, frankly change your mind, and even have some sense of amusement at where you fell off the beam of reality and might have been even foolish.

⋙ ○ ⋘

LESLIE FIEDLER, A FLAMBOYANT young literary critic who regularly hurled his thunderously violent opinions at Montana State University students and the readers of *Partisan Review,* wanted Farrell slain. "[T]he writer in the forties is essentially concerned with establishing alternatives to naturalism," Fiedler declared in a 1948 *PR* symposium on "The State of American Writing." And helpfully, Farrell and others of "our leading naturalists have become middle-aged, ripe for ritual slaughter"—a death with honor (as he later explained), for the good of the community.

Fiedler defined literary naturalism, detailing its function and especially its limitations, in the *New Leader:*

> Naturalism is a literary approach based on a rigid philosophical determinism, which finds the individual insignificant or powerless or both (and therefore not responsible morally) in the face of his environment. Its method of exposition is typically documentary, marked by a profound distrust of style; and any selectivity it possesses is rather function of exhaustion than choice. It is dogmatically anti-tragic; tending on the one hand toward Sentimentalism through social pathos (this is the more typically American direction), and on the other toward a pseudo-scientific detachment. It is anti-mythic and anti-symbolic, finding truth in the specific rather than the general; and proposing the eye and ear as arbiters superior to

intelligence or imagination. Its historic function appears to have been the liberation for the artist of certain tabooed subject matter, and the final destruction of the convention of willful intrusion of the author into the frame of his illusion.

Farrell's novels seem to ill comport with Fiedler's definition. Studs Lonigan and Danny O'Neill grew up in essentially the same "spiritually impoverished" environment, yet the one's life was a descent, the other's an ascent. How could "a rigid philosophical determinism" produce those contrasting fates?

Still, Farrell himself had accepted the literary label of naturalism (without making a fetish of it), and he did indeed consider himself a philosophical naturalist. But his best novels, so full of life, transcended his philosophy, which did incline toward determinism. Naturalism, whether Deweyan or Marxist, is hard put to explain human consciousness or to acknowledge free will.

This last difficulty was evident in the title essay of *Literature and Morality*, in which Farrell assailed "The Other Margaret," a short story by Lionel Trilling. At the heart of the story, Farrell noted, is the problem of moral responsibility: "Is the individual responsible for his actions or is society responsible?" The story's answer is that ultimately, the individual is. Farrell would have none of it: the story was tendentious, the point of view reactionary. It was a mistake to treat the individual and society as "polar opposites," he maintained. "The self is a social product, not a separate, individual entity, superior to, anterior to, separable from, society. Nor can one consider society as outside of man, superior to man, or the sole responsible agent for what is called immoral action." In short, in his view, neither the individual nor society is responsible for the individual's actions; evidently, nobody is.

Six years before Fiedler, Philip Rahv had noted the decline of the naturalist method in fiction, amid charges that it "treats material in a manner so flat and external as to inhibit the search for value and meaning, and that in any case, whatever its past record, it is now exhausted." Fiedler maintained that "the rise of Freudian and post-Freudian psychology" had contributed to the decline. But even more significant, surely, were the horrors of World War II: the surrealist Nazi doctrine, the devastation of great cities, the slaughter of civilians and the genocide of six million Jews. In the face of these extreme manifestations of evil, naturalism's limitations became more apparent than ever. As philosophy and as literary method, naturalism, staying so close to the surface of life, now seemed utterly unequal to the challenge of plumbing the terrible depths of human nature.

Yet there was no need for a "ritual slaughter" of naturalists, certainly not in Farrell's case. He seemed to be slaying his reputation all by himself, first with *Bernard Clare* and now, in the spring of 1949, with *The Road Between*, the second novel in the series. *The Road Between*, wrote novelist Budd Schulberg in the *New York Times Book Review*, "may be a negative landmark in our national literature, warning us that we are approaching as complete a dead end as we may find in the ever-narrowing road of American naturalism."

Farrell's latest book was indeed a wretched failure, but that was not for want of effort on his part. He had worked hard on the novel, but had encountered great difficulties. "I have so often lost heart or almost lost heart on this *Bernard Clare* enterprise," he lamented at one point.

Though at times he admitted to himself that he was "tired," that there was no "spark" in his writing, he apparently could not quite bring himself to face the fact that, as an imaginative artist, he was worn out. In the less than two decades since he and Dorothy had returned from Paris, he had written more than twenty published books, including ten novels and seven distinct volumes of short stories. With his imagination and his phenomenal memory for detail, he had mined his boyhood and youth to great effect. And his naturalistic, almost reportorial technique had served his purpose well. His insistence on showing life as it was, without the contrivance of explicit, mechanical plot, was well suited to the green years of youth, when so much is uncertain, so much taken in without comprehensive interpretation.

But he was no longer dealing with the universal experience of childhood and youth, no longer recreating the vanished but vividly remembered world he never made; now he was trying to create a more fictional microcosm, to be experienced entirely from an adult perspective. The difference may not have been apparent to him when he began work on *Bernard Clare*, since it must have seemed to him that he was resuming where he had left off with Danny O'Neill. But that transient, illusory comfort was unavailable when he came to write the second Bernard novel, and he often found himself at a loss. He could conjure up isolated scenes and characters from his life and imagine others, but he couldn't make them add up to much, make them serve in a coherent way the themes he evidently had in mind.

In the novel, Farrell was seeking to show what a serious writer was up against in trying to be true to his calling and still earn a living, and he also was trying to show how someone sensitive to the misery of others and wanting the world to be different could be drawn during the Depression to the ruthless, exploitative Communist movement. But achievement of the first purpose is undercut by his dreary protagonist, whose name he changed from Clare to Carr. (After the earlier novel had appeared, a *Minneapolis Star* reporter by the name of Bernard Clare sued for libel; although a federal judge threw out the absurd lawsuit, Vanguard decided to change the fictional character's name in the next two novels, out of fear that this "simian in Minneapolis," as Henle called him, would strike again.) Despite the name change, the character is a no less tiresome fount of self-pity. And achievement of Farrell's second purpose is thwarted by the absence of any fully-realized character who is a Communist or even a passionate fellow traveler. It may be that Farrell was too aware of Communist perfidy, too conscious—now that he had seen through the Trotskyists—of the illusory promise of Bolshevism to convey adequately the allure of the revolutionary ideology that for so long had held him in its thrall. Moreover, his "blunt, pedestrian style," as Schulberg wrote, was "particularly ill-suited to an introspective, sensitive, intellectual subject."

But *The Road Between*—whose title had been suggested by Hortense, after Farrell and Henle had considered variants of *Two Cities* (Chicago and New York) and *Two Worlds*—is not entirely devoid of merit. Carr's wife, Elizabeth (modeled on Dorothy), is well done: "the best feminine character you have ever created," Henle told him. Her father, a Chicago undertaker, is also effectively portrayed, and surprisingly, with some sympathy. The scenes in Chicago with Elizabeth's family, or Carr's, have much more life than the scenes with the radicals in New York, and much more plausibility than the ones with editors in Gotham. For all his experience in New York, Farrell seems to have been truly at home only in the city of his birth, or more exactly in Chicago as it existed in his memory and imagination.

Farrell dismissed Schulberg's review as "a hatchet job" by "a fellow traveler." But on the subject of *The Road Between*, the reviewers were virtually unanimous.

"Even if the reviewers are correct on *The Road Between*," Farrell concluded, "it does not matter. To try and fail is to learn, and even if I failed—which I don't grant, I have still learned." But his education, such as it was, had come at considerable cost to his reputation.

ON APRIL 11, 1949, FARRELL'S phone rang. It was Sidney Hook, the combative philosopher and indefatigable champion of freedom, offering an invitation to fly with him to Paris later that month to help counter the next cultural blow in the Soviet "peace" offensive.

Only weeks before, Hook had been at the center of a vigorous effort to expose as a Communist-dominated sham an international cultural conference at the posh Waldorf-Astoria Hotel in New York. The successor to a Communist-inspired World Congress of Intellectuals that had been held the preceding August in Poland, the Cultural and Scientific Conference for World Peace, chaired by Harvard astronomer Harlow Shapley, had boasted as sponsors a glittering array of names, more than 575 in all (no mere "400 suckers" this time!), from Hollywood and Broadway and other cultural redoubts. There were Clifford Odets and Arthur Miller, Albert Maltz and Lillian Hellman, Leonard Bernstein and Isaac Stern, Albert Einstein and Henry Wallace, Budd Schulberg and many, many more.

But the Waldorf conference was still, as Hook said, "only a sounding board for Communist propaganda." The Soviets were eager to portray the just-signed North Atlantic Treaty, giving birth to NATO, as a threat to world peace by the war-mongering American imperialists. Joined by Farrell, Norman Thomas and others, Hook had organized the American Committee for Intellectual Freedom. Through statements to the press and a counter-rally at which Hook, Max Eastman, historian Arthur M. Schlesinger Jr. and others spoke, the committee helped to make the true purpose of the Waldorf affair apparent. Farrell (who privately grumbled about what he deemed Hook's "unprogrammatic anti-Stalinism" and the poor planning behind the effort to expose the conference) was not present on the climactic weekend; he was away from New York on a lecture tour.

But now Hook was offering him another chance. A Communist-inspired World Congress of Partisans of Peace, opening on April 20 in Paris and lasting six days, was to be followed at the end of the month by a non-Communist peace conference sponsored by *Franc-Tireur*, a Paris newspaper, and the Rassemblement Démocratique Révolutionnaire, a group of leftwing literati. Disenchanted with Stalinism and impressed by the example of the counter-rally staged by Hook's committee in New York, a *Franc-Tireur* editor, David Rousset, and his colleagues had organized an International Day of Resistance to Dictatorship and War, to be held in the French capital on April 30. They also ambitiously intended to lay the groundwork for the formation of a worldwide organization of the non-Communist Left.

Farrell and Hook left New York's LaGuardia Airport on the night of the 21st. (Neither man was aware that their travel expenses were being covertly paid by the U.S. Central Intelligence Agency, which, having observed with approval the Hook committee's effort to counter the Waldorf conference, had helped to bring about the impending counter-rally.) Earlier that day in Paris, new posters depicting the horrors of war and announcing the forthcoming Day of Resistance went up on walls and fences, competing for attention with Pablo Picasso's dove on the posters advertising the World Congress of Partisans of Peace then under way.

Three days later, in a joint statement to the press on behalf of the American Committee for Intellectual Freedom, Farrell and Hook, on the basis of reports they had read, charged that the meetings of the congress "have revealed the directing hand of the Cominform" (the Communist Information Bureau, which had been formed in 1947 as an instrument for Soviet coordination of European Communist activity). "There has been no talk of peace but only of Soviet peace. The actual wars throughout the world today waged by Communists in China and Greece have not even been mentioned. No specific proposals of a fair and reasonable character to further peace have come out of the Congress. All that has been heard is in effect a demand for capitulation to Soviet expansion everywhere." Farrell and Hook singled out as "especially disgraceful" the effort by American Communist delegates "to convince European public opinion that a Hitlerian regime exists in our country and that justice and liberty prevail only in the countries behind the Iron Curtain. Neither they nor anyone else has so much as mentioned the existence of concentration camps and total cultural terror in the Soviet Union."

The Day of Resistance did not live up to Farrell's and Hook's hopes, however. It consisted of two meetings: an afternoon session in the Grand Amphithéâtre of the Sorbonne, attended by some 125 delegates (most of whom were French), and a mass meeting in the evening, with some 12,000 Parisians in attendance, at the Vélo-drome d'Hiver, a sports arena that was the Parisian equivalent of New York's Madison Square Garden. Farrell, along with Hook, was among 25 delegates who gave short speeches in the afternoon at the Sorbonne on ways to promote peace.

"I favor the Marshall Plan and the North Atlantic Pact," Farrell (speaking in English) told his fellow delegates, "because I am con-vinced that the main danger [to peace] comes from behind the Iron Curtain.... If the authorities behind the Iron Curtain would establish democratic liberties, if they would establish free labor movements and if they would end a regime of concentration camps and slave labor, all of us would feel more confident about the future of peace and liberty." In the form of a personal testa-ment, he brought the news—which for many of the delegates *was* news—that America was not a fascist state:

> I come from one of the freest countries in the world. I have lived my entire life under conditions of freedom which were sufficient to per-mit me to educate myself, and to develop whatever potentialities I possess. I have always been able to read whatever books I wanted. I have always been able to express whatever thoughts I had, and to defend my convictions. When threats have been made to censor me in America, I have gone into the American courts and defended myself. I have won my cases. When the police of an American city seized books of mine without warrant and in disregard of due process of the law, I was able to go into the federal courts of the United States and to sue the police. The seized books are again on sale in that city. There is no cultural terror in the United States, and if you here, you people of Europe, believe that there is, you are allow-ing yourselves to be deceived.

He went on to point out that Truman had been elected by "millions of ordinary Americans," that the American labor move-ment was strong and had won "important victories" for workers, and that while "social evils" such as racial inequality did exist, many Americans were "determined to try to eradicate" them.

But the "prevailing mood" at the day-long peace conference, Sidney Hook later recounted, "was as anti-American as it was anti-Soviet." Before speakers could say a critical word about the Soviet Union, they seemed to feel obliged to attack American imperialism just as vehemently as the Communists did. "Most of the speakers were quite outspoken in their opposition to the Atlantic Pact, and pleaded for a neutrality between what they called the two blocs, as if the liberties of Western Europe were threatened equally by the Soviet Union and the United States."

A provocative explanation was soon provided by the French political philosopher Raymond Aron. Since the war, he wrote, French intellectuals have been confronted with the reality that their country is no longer "a power of the first rank" and that their political opinions "no longer count for anything beyond the borders of the country." For many of them, neutrality was the response, Aron noted.

> Never in the past did [the French intellectual] have to ask himself: Which camp do I like best, or dislike the least? He had always taken his stand for France, or for universal ideas valid for the world as well as France. Now he is asked (or he has the impression he is asked) to choose between the Soviet Union and the United States. He feels that he would be lowering himself to make this choice.

Other intellectuals, however, believed that making such a choice was crucial. That August, Melvin J. Lasky, American editor of *Der Monat*, a magazine published by the U.S. military government in Berlin, met with a few others in a Frankfurt hotel to develop a plan for an international conference of anti-Communist leftists to be held in Berlin in 1950. With the help of Michael Josselson, an Estonian-born American who, like Lasky, had stayed on after the war to work for the military government, but who now (unbeknownst to Lasky) was working for the CIA, the conference—covertly funded by the American intelligence agency—would indeed be held. Farrell was among the writers and intellectuals who would participate.

⸻ ⟫•0•⟪ ⸻

"JOURNEY'S END FOR JAMES T. FARRELL," read the headline over an editorial in the November 7, 1949, issue of the *Militant,* published by the Socialist Workers Party. Farrell happened upon the Trotskyist (Cannonite) paper one day at a newsstand on 42nd Street and read about his fall from grace.

Though Farrell "began his flight from Marxism later than many intellectuals of his generation," the *Militant* said, "he has caught up with and outstripped most of them." It was with the onset of the Cold War that he "began buckling under the pressure," according to the editorial. He "tried to cover his retreat by protests that he was a better Marxist than his critics in the Socialist Workers Party. But this lasted for only a short while. He soon began building his bridges back to the camp of capitalist respectability." His latest stop on the road to perdition was to give his support to the Liberal Party of New York State. Farrell had indeed joined the Liberal Party, formed in 1944 by David Dubinsky of the International Ladies' Garment Workers' Union and other anti-Communist labor leaders. The novelist had delivered a speech over the radio in October in behalf of Liberal candidates.

"Farrell has probably not reached the end of his political evolution," said the *Militant*, "but the rest of the story will have few real surprises....What counts is that he has made his peace with capitalism. The arms of reaction are the logical resting place for everybody who loses faith in the ability of the working class to shape its own fate and who rejects Marxism as the only progressive method of combating Stalinism."

Farrell later commented in his diary: "They live in a dream world."

After stopping at the newsstand, he proceeded to the New York Public Library where he came upon *Labor Action*, the publication of the rival Shachtmanite Trotskyists, the Workers Party. "They live in a dream world, too," he remarked.

THE NEWS ARRIVED IN West Berlin not long after Farrell did: North Korea had invaded South Korea. It gave an air of excitement and gravity to the Congress for Cultural Freedom, which drew more than one hundred writers, artists and scientists from twenty different countries to the divided city in the last week of June 1950. Did the Korean invasion presage Soviet military action in the split nation of Germany? The delegates could not be sure, but heartened by the tough, democratic spirit of the Berliners around them, they didn't lose their nerve.

Fearful that war would break out in Europe that summer, Hortense had remained in New York. Farrell had not tried to dissuade her from staying, although he did not share her fear. After a visit from Melvin Lasky in May, he had decided to go, wanting to do his part in "the struggle against Stalinism."

Despite what the Trotskyists may have thought, Farrell had

not abandoned his political idealism when he moved away from Marxism. Since then, not only had he gone to Paris for the International Day of Resistance to Dictatorship and War, but he had joined in a Workers Defense League campaign against forced labor in the Soviet Union; publicly protested the University of Michigan's suspension of the Workers Education Service, calling it an effort at "thought control and...infringement of academic freedom"; publicly urged establishment of a commission to investigate the apparent "frame-up" trial of Joseph Cardinal Mindszenty in Hungary; joined in a campaign against Jim Crow segregation in the armed forces, taking part in a demonstration outside the Waldorf; and spoken out in support of a legless World War II veteran in Illinois who had been dismissed from a minor governmental post because he belonged to the Socialist Workers Party.

This Farrell, the crusading Jim Farrell, Henle would write admiringly some years later,

> is the real Jim and it is the best Jim, which is to say it seems to me just about the best that humanity and human nature have to offer....
> [The] James T. Farrell sometimes seen on the streets—patently in need of a barber, just as his shirt may be yearning for the laundry—is an open invitation to caricature. But such a caricature would ignore the man who unselfishly has thrown himself (and his friends) into so many causes.

It was completely in character, then, for Farrell to be among the writers and intellectuals gathered in Berlin for the Congress for Cultural Freedom. Yet for the most part he remained on the periphery of events there. At the reception the first night, Marcia Burnham, James Burnham's wife, "said something to me about my being a world famous person and why didn't I circulate," he later recalled (without divulging his response). No doubt he felt somewhat ill at ease. He did not possess the refinement and self-assurance of the well-born and well-bred James Burnham (Princeton, 1927). Nor—though he seems never to have conceded this—did he have the analytical powers of Burnham, Sidney Hook and certain others at the congress. Farrell's strengths lay elsewhere, as his friend Arthur Schlesinger Jr., the brilliant historian who had first met him in Washington after the war, much later observed: "He was well-read and he was very honest and very earnest, very honest in his reactions, and passionate in his feelings. There was not a great subtlety of insight into certain people or situations. But he had a kind of good, honest, sensible reaction to things."

Whatever Farrell's own relative self-assessment on this occasion may have been, the apparent leaders of the congress—who along with Burnham and Hook included Lasky, the chief organizer; Arthur Koestler, the Hungarian ex-Communist author of *Darkness at Noon* (1941), a haunting novel about the Moscow trials; and Irving Brown, the European representative of the American Federation of Labor—evidently didn't consider his likely contribution to their work so valuable as to involve him in their nightly caucuses. "A manifesto is being drafted by Burnham, Arthur Koestler, Irving Brown, and Melvin Lasky, and they are going to have Sidney Hook look at it," Farrell noted in his diary early on. "When Arthur Schlesinger arrived, I told him this, and suggested that he have a look at it, because it is likely that he and I might not agree to all that is stated, and it is best that revisions be made that way. I suggested it to him because if they had wanted me to have a share in it, they'd have asked me."

The polymathic Koestler, now a vigorous Cold Warrior, was the most prominent figure at the congress. Delivering the final speech on the opening day before more than two thousand invited guests in Titania Palace, he urged that the congress be the turning point at which intellectuals awakened to the international emergency and took a firm stand against aggressive totalitarianism. "It is amazing to observe," he said, "how in a crisis the most sophisticated often act like imbeciles. Imbued with the mental habits of the neither-nor attitude, of looking for synthesis or compromise, they are incapable of admitting even to themselves that there are situations in which an unambiguous decision is vital for spiritual and physical survival."

Koestler's strong words aroused resentment among some delegates, but no opposition to his militant stance was boldly expressed. This would have been difficult to do in the presence of so many brave Berliners and with the attack on South Korea on everyone's mind. "The notion of many French and Italian ["third force" intellectuals] that America is dragging Western Europe into its imperial quarrels with Russia appears ridiculous in Berlin," noted François Bondy, a Swiss writer, in a report on the congress. "Here, everybody knows that it is Russia, not America, that aims to conquer Europe, and that without the American will to risk war Russia would have achieved this aim long ago."

Farrell came to detect "much smothered tension and anxiety at the congress," but he, too, felt the excitement. "There are writers and intellectuals here who would be killed or put into concentration camps if they were caught by the Communists," he pointed out. "This fact alone gives a significance to the congress." Koestler had brought his bodyguard with him, and detectives guarded certain other delegates as well.

When Koestler and Farrell were in a group together, Farrell at first thought that Koestler (whose "very clear thinking head" and value to the congress he recognized) was snubbing him. But after Hook told Koestler this, Koestler said he simply hadn't recognized Farrell, and then he became "very friendly." The two writers eventually revised their early impressions—Farrell's that Koestler was "too aggressive," and Koestler's that Farrell was "a timid man."

Farrell didn't see much of Hook at the congress. "The only time he showed much inclination to be with me," Farrell said, "was when I was to have lunch with [Ignazio] Silone." The Italian novelist—who had once held a high position in the Comintern and was now a socialist with the aura (albeit not the faith) of a gentle Christian—was, next to Koestler, the most prominent figure at the congress. Silone's party in Italy, the Socialist Party of Italian Workers, was opposed to the Atlantic Pact, and Silone, according to Bondy, "tried to keep the anti-Communism of the Berlin conference as tolerant, as moderate, and as 'third forcist' as possible." Hook joined Farrell's lunch with Silone in order to discuss with the latter the manifesto being drafted for the congress. "He and Silone talked German mostly," noted Farrell (who didn't know the language).

It was not the first time that Hook had upstaged him. Recalling Paris the year before, Farrell said that in joint press conferences Hook "takes over and you have to bust in on him" to make a point. Hook was inclined to engage in political "maneuvers" and to court publicity much more aggressively than he. Still, he added, Hook "is a fighter and, I think, brave."

Farrell had prepared a three-thousand-word address on freedom, culture and totalitarianism. But he didn't get to deliver the full speech. Inasmuch as nearly every delegate had a paper to present, considerations of time became paramount and Farrell was obliged to express his views far more succinctly. He told someone later that "I hadn't had much to do at Berlin, that I'd been frozen out" (though he said he'd managed to give Schlesinger some suggestions to include in *his* speech).

Among the heavyweights who were given time to express their views at length was James Burnham. Speaking with what one listener called "the dry and deliberately unemphatic smoothness of a Y.M.C.A. preacher," Burnham tore apart some of the neutralist Left's cherished notions, including the belief that the atomic bomb should always be opposed. "For five years," he said, "[America's atomic] bombs have defended—have been the sole defense of— the liberties of Western Europe."

"The paper was logical and to the point," Farrell thought. "But it was, to me, cold. And I had the feeling that some of the Europeans, especially the Western Europeans, would feel that Burnham was telling them—You are poor and powerless. You've got to come with us." When Farrell expressed this objection to Koestler, he replied that (in Farrell's paraphrase) it was "time to stop the old apologetic attitude Americans used to have."

Farrell felt lonely at the congress and not completely sure of his own views on all of the subjects under discussion. "I have not clearly held to my perspective," he reflected, "and have shifted my views, my interpretations, my alliances, one way, [then] the other way."

He made an effort to speak with ordinary Berliners. They seemed glad—as Koestler, Burnham and their allies at the congress were—that President Truman had responded with force to the invasion of South Korea. "A young German lad, a journalist," Farrell recorded in his diary, "said to me that the people in Berlin like the Americans and British now. He said that with the airlift they had learned that America keeps its word."

The plight of a young woman, a student, who had followed her fiancé out of the eastern zone, leaving her baby by another man behind in the care of a relative, evoked Farrell's sympathy. He gave the couple an honorarium he had received for making a broadcast over RIAS (Radio in the American Sector) and spoke with another American delegate to the congress about raising funds to bring the infant to West Berlin. "This American was not averse to giving money," Farrell wrote in his diary. "But he said that I knew that there were many, many tragedies, and that individual help didn't do much good." Farrell disagreed. "I have thought of this much. I think individual aid is as important, if not more so, as organizational aid. We have no solution to the problem of Berlin. I mean we of the congress. But we can give aid. The Berlin problem is one of human beings, of saving them. To save them, there must be aid."

With American help, Europe was being rebuilt. But the congress was more concerned with resistance to Stalin. Before a throng of fifteen thousand gathered in a public park in the British Sector of Berlin for the congress's closing ceremony, Koestler read aloud the "Manifesto of Freedom," affirming man's inalienable right to intellectual liberty and attacking both totalitarianism and neutrality. The manifesto was adopted by acclamation. *"Freunde,"* Koestler shouted, *"die Freiheit hat die Offensive ergriffen!"* ("Friends, freedom has seized the offensive!")

That was to prove the high point of Koestler's influence on the Congress for Cultural Freedom, which later that year was transformed into a permanent organization. The CIA's Michael Josselson, who at the conference had remained in the shadows (appropriately enough), taking in all that happened, sided more with Silone than with Koestler as to the proper approach for the organization to take in opposing communism. Josselson now became the congress's administrative secretary and its most important figure. Despite Koestler's role in the founding, his admirer Hook later recounted, "he withdrew from all activity within a year or two. He became convinced that it had become diverted from its educational-political task by its other cultural (art, music) activities." But others in the congress, like Josselson, regarded the Koestler type of harsh attacks on fellow travelers as counterproductive. "The alternative strategy adopted by the Congress for Cultural Freedom," its historian Peter Coleman has written, "was to build a kind of 'united front' with the democratic elements of the European Left and gradually win it over to the Atlanticist cause."

"Restless and anxious" in Berlin, Farrell was relieved to move on to other European capitals—Amsterdam, London, Paris, Copenhagen and Stockholm. He spent July and half of August in Europe, meeting with trade union leaders, government officials and writers, giving lectures and taking in as much as he could.

"Truman's decision seems to make him much more respected in Europe, and some call him a great man," he wrote Henle from Paris. For the moment, at least, neutralist sentiment had diminished. But some resentment toward the United States persisted. In Amsterdam, after encountering some hostility toward America and Americans, Farrell saw "that we can let ourselves be blackmailed, and abused in our efforts to sympathize and to understand." Like Koestler, he concluded that there was no need for Americans to be defensive or apologetic. "It seems to me that if a European says he doesn't want [the] Marshall Plan, then, the thing to do is to tell him not to take it. All right, we'll go home. If we take this attitude, we'll

get results. Tact, understanding, sympathy all go so far, and no further."

⟫⟶•⟵⟪

WHEN FARRELL WAS AWAY IN Europe that summer of 1950, Jim Henle
had found himself thrust into an intermediary role between the
writer and his wife. "In all my conversations with Hortense," he
advised Farrell by "confidential" letter, "I have stressed the need, on
your return, of dropping all old feuds and differences—that there is
nothing to be gained in her proving you to have been wrong or
vice versa. Also: a need for a united front in dealing with Kevin. I
could honestly and sincerely urge both these matters, for they
seem to me of supreme importance for Kevie's welfare."

It was sound advice but, alas, it had little effect. By the end of
the year, Farrell was grimly keeping "a purely factual diary about
events in the home here, especially with relationship to Kevin," and
had decided to yank his son out of the private school he was
attending in New York and put him in a boarding school in Massachusetts.

Hortense was not happy about this development; she was, as
many who encountered her noticed, a very nervous woman. Her
anxieties about Kevin, who turned ten that year, had not diminished as he grew older. She was upset when he went around the
apartment in his socks without wearing slippers, because she
feared he would catch cold; she was upset when his trousers were
cut slightly longer than she had prescribed, because she feared he
might trip and break a leg; she was upset when he immediately
drank the large glass of milk she regularly set before him, instead of
consuming it along with his meal; she was upset when he left his
toys and games scattered about the living room, and she screamed,
with odd hyperbole, that he was "urinating" and "defecating" all
over her home; she was upset when he was not in bed by nine
o'clock sharp, and she was upset when he spilled urine from the
milk bottle she left in his room each night so that he could relieve
himself without undertaking the perilous journey to the bathroom
and possibly awaking her.

Hortense had many fears, and most of them were undoubtedly rooted in her childhood. She once confided to a friend that
when she was a girl, her mother used to leave the house and keep
her locked in a closet for hours. But she seems almost never to

have trusted Farrell with such confidences. Indeed, she apparently went to elaborate lengths to hide her early background from him (and virtually everyone else). Her sister, for instance, was known to Farrell as "Bettina Alden," even though, since there is no indication that she was ever an actress or performer of any kind, it seems highly unlikely that she too would have taken Hortense's stage surname.

Hortense's apparent lack of trust in her husband, not to mention her extravagant promiscuity before she met him, could also probably be traced to her childhood. Her mother (she of the Boston Opera Company) had had hundreds of lovers, Hortense also confided to her friend. By now, Hortense herself had lost all interest in sex, and she told her husband on several occasions to go find some whores—she didn't care.

Meanwhile her friend, unbeknownst to her, relayed her confidences to Farrell. They prompted him to wonder: When Hortense complained, as she now did continually, that she had to be both mother and father to Kevin, that Farrell was not a *bad* father, he was *no* father—did she really mean, "I, Hortense, have no father"?

Whatever she meant, she was in a bad way. Her distrust of her husband, perhaps of men in general, seems to have turned into paranoia. She came to believe that he was plotting against her, that he was turning Kevin against her, that, out of hatred for her, he was deliberately destroying Kevin, sadistically "dismembering" him, making a Weary Reilley out of him, all in accordance with an evil "plan," a devilish "scheme."

Psychiatric help had been suggested for Hortense as early as June 1949. Two doctors who came then to discuss John Stephen's condition with his parents had each told Farrell privately that she needed psychiatric care. Eighteen months later, a psychiatrist who was treating Kevin suggested the same to Farrell. In all, he would record in his diary some days later, six doctors—three of them psychiatrists, including his brother Jack—had indicated to him that Hortense needed psychiatric treatment. So had his friend Bruno Bettelheim, the director of the Orthogenic School at the University of Chicago whom he had first met on a visit to Chicago five years before. But as Farrell told a neighbor and another woman who inquired, Hortense wouldn't agree to get that kind of help. "She says I am crazy and need it."

Farrell was not completely blameless in all this, of course. He was, as Hortense charged, reluctant to discipline Kevin, as he should have done in a firm, fair and consistent way; and it is apparent even from his own "factual" diary that, despite Henle's advice, he did not fully grasp the importance of a united parental front. Instead of going along with Hortense's harmless desire to have Kevin in bed by nine o'clock sharp, for instance, he stubbornly insisted that "a few minutes before [or] after made little difference"; so if he was reading to Kevin, he would "run a couple of minutes over, if I think that by stopping, I will frustrate him, or will break his interest and irritate him so that he goes to bed irritated." The "couple of minutes" apparently added up to as many as twenty-five at times. In most families, this might not have been consequential; in this one it was. There was "constant trouble here about Kevin's getting to bed"—and it seems to have been at least as much Farrell's fault as his wife's.

Nor did he refrain from disagreeing with her in front of Kevin, or even from (on rare occasion) speaking ill of her to him. Thus, on the day before Christmas that year, when Kevin asked his father why his mother was lying on the dining room floor (apparently it was initially in protest of excessive television watching), he told Kevin, "I don't know—she was disturbed." Then, after entering the incident in his diary, Farrell went downstairs to ask two neighbors "to please come upstairs and ask her not to lie on the floor"!

Still, however foolishly Farrell may sometimes have behaved, and whatever his defects and delinquencies as a parent may have been, it is clear that he was in a very difficult, if not impossible, situation. Indeed, they all were, the three of them trapped in a destructive triangle of pain, of incessant accusation and counteraccusation. "Often she would say Kevin had done something," he recorded. "I would question Kevin. Kevin would deny it, or at least, have an explanation. If I listened to him, she would attack me, scream, yell, interrupt. She demanded, over and over again, that I take her word, and never Kevin's." In anger, she sometimes called Kevin, to his face or in his presence, "a liar and a little liar...a dirty little liar."

In early January 1951, the two unhappy parents took their son to the boarding school in Massachusetts. "He didn't like to go," Farrell said, "and yet he went knowing it was best."

Days later, Hortense suggested to Farrell that they separate. He said that he wouldn't give up custody of Kevin. She said she would get a lawyer to talk with his lawyer. She seemed to him to want "that I separate and divorce from her, and give her custody of Kevin." But, he added in his diary that night, Bettelheim and two psychiatrists "all say that this would be dangerous for Kevin, and I think it would, myself, and have arrived at this conclusion, separate from their judgments."

In April, Farrell attended the six-day UAW convention in Cleveland, then stayed a few days with his brother Jack and his family in Silver Spring, Maryland, just outside of Washington. While there, he met a young woman named Adrienne and was attracted to her, but felt that he was "trying to wish myself into something. I just don't want to be alone, and to go on with the kind of life I am living." Back in New York, he found himself still entertaining thoughts of Adrienne, though they were hedged with doubts. Soon he made his final decision: to leave Hortense and his broken home. Toward the end of the third week in April, he moved into a hotel on East 40th Street; then, in June, he moved into an $18-a-week basement apartment on West 21st Street.

A separation agreement was worked out. Hortense got custody of Kevin but Farrell had the right to select his school and summer camp, provided he paid for them. In this way, he retained some influence over Kevin's life and didn't simply abandon him to the care of a woman whom he believed to be mentally ill. For Kevin's sake, he thought it best to avoid a full-fledged custody fight, which "could be dirty and bitter and nasty, with attendant publicity." He hoped that with him not there, Hortense would gain "a little more stability." That would be good not only for her but for Kevin: "It is Kevin's future. Kevin must work out his own relationship with Hortense. Part of reality for him is Hortense."

Life in the years ahead was at times not to be easy for Kevin. As a teenager, he would come to realize that his mother, as he later said, "was really kind of strange." But he would survive. In time he would become a physician, a specialist in burn and trauma surgery; at the present writing, he practices at a hospital in eastern Pennsylvania, where he lives with his family.

Hortense was bitter about Farrell, but took solace in the company of her friends. She appealed to them, Randolph Carter remembered, "because she was fun and screwball, in a way.... During that period after she separated from Jim, her whole circle was [the] gay theatrical and literary and artistic crowd. And she liked to go out to the bars, but not in a drinking way, just to socialize." She would appear in an off-Broadway production of Tennessee

Williams's *Garden District* in 1958, a television soap opera in 1962, and a one-act play by Carter in 1968. In the NBC soap opera, in which she played a possessive mother, she was such a pain to everyone else involved in the production, Carter said, that her character was soon written out of the script. In her final years in New York, having come to believe that virtually everyone close to her had betrayed her, she was almost a recluse in her apartment. "She had alienated everyone, including me," her longtime friend recalled.*

In July 1951, after seeing Kevin off to summer camp, Farrell, realizing that he "did not want to get involved with the details of homemaking—towels and sheets and defrosting refrigerators," left his basement apartment and moved into a $200-a-month, two-room studio apartment in the Hotel Chelsea, a once-elegant hotel on West 23rd Street that had been home to a good many writers and artists over the decades. "I did not move into the Chelsea because of its atmosphere or cultural environment," he later wrote. "I moved in because it was the first hotel I noticed when I went for a walk one day to find another place to live."

Eleven years later, a plaque designating the Chelsea a New York landmark would be placed near the hotel's entrance, and it would list a number of writers and artists who formerly had lived there, including O'Henry, John Sloan, Dylan Thomas, Thomas Wolfe and James T. Farrell. The *au courant* citizens who had selected the names for this honor evidently assumed, incorrectly, that like the others on their list, James T. Farrell, still remembered as the author of *Studs Lonigan*, was dead.

---

*Hortense Alden died in April 1978 at age 78 in Tucson, Arizona. She had developed "a terminal malignancy," Farrell explained to his old friend Dick Parker the year before, and their son Kevin, then a resident in surgery at the University of Arizona Hospital, had brought her to Tucson. "She was an extraordinarily beautiful woman, and a truly great actress—but with a destructive personality," Farrell told Parker. "It is very sad."

Part 3

Writing, Writing, Writing

Chapter Sixteen
"A Lost Soul"

"**S**EX IS ON MY MIND," Farrell recorded in his diary. Middle-aged and lonely, he yearned for a woman. His dreams of Adrienne, the young woman he had met when visiting his brother Jack's, had come to naught. She was "friendly and open," but unresponsive to his affectionate overtures. Back in Silver Spring in early May, he had taken her out to dinner one evening. "Don't you see," he finally said to her in a taxicab afterward, "I'm falling in love with you." The reaction: "She froze up, her lips tightened, she said she was upset, which she was." And so he abandoned his pursuit, "suddenly feel[ing] that I am a little in the dark concerning women."

Some months later, on a visit to Chicago with Kevin, Farrell saw Dorothy again. "She likes to talk of old times," he noted, and she and her sister, Virginia, "bent over backwards to be friendly. They were very nice to Kevin." Farrell confided to his diary that he was fond of Dorothy, but he also recalled the difficulty he had in knowing "when to believe and when not to believe her." Another visitor in her sister's home told Farrell that Dorothy seemed "radiant" when they discussed old times. "Dorothy still loves you," the woman said. Though he set down the remark in his diary, and may well have wondered how his life would have unfolded had he never left Dorothy, he was not inclined to reciprocate whatever interest she had. He was looking elsewhere.

At age forty-seven, slovenly in dress and unpolished in manners, his literary reputation in decline, the twice-married Farrell scarcely seemed the answer to a young woman's prayers. Yet he was a renowned author who had written a book commonly regarded as a classic; he was intelligent and not at all pretentious; he cared about humanity and was generous to individuals in trouble, and all in all he was, as many said, a very "sweet" man.

He had early on decided that he was not going to engage in

indiscriminate "petticoat chasing" at this point in his life. "I have reacted against...just making a date with a girl, taking her out, doing most of the talking and coming home more or less frustrated. And spending more money than I can afford." By now, he told himself, he had become accustomed to celibacy: "I have come to see that with experience, discipline, interest in work, ideas, people and life, this can be done—if it is necessary. It is necessary because I don't happen to meet the right girl or girls."

He did have scruples. "In New York," he noted in his diary, "two married girls—one with children, this would have produced complications. In time, I told myself that my interest was not sufficient to throw them and myself into complications. And in the case of the girl with children, this was doubly and *emphatically* a matter where moral choice was involved. It was a moral problem as well as a question of desire. And a third girl. She would fall in love with me, possibly deeply, and I wouldn't want a permanent relationship with her, and she would or could be hurt and wounded—a low ego. So again, I desisted."

That November, Farrell began dating a woman named Rosalyn Tureck, a pianist and harpsichordist who taught at the Juilliard School of Music, not yet at the height of her worldwide renown among music lovers as an interpreter of Bach. A disciplined musician, she was frequently practicing when not performing, but she managed to fit Farrell into her schedule.

"So far," he noted in his diary in mid-December, "my relation with Rosalyn has been good—untrying. By untrying, I mean that it has not been productive of anxiety, trouble, and has not been disturbing." That must have been a relief to him, after his recent experiences with other women. But their relationship was limited by the fact that they each were utterly devoted to their own very demanding careers. They continued to see each other off and on for several years, but—as he would write many years later in a novella, "Judith," based on their intermittent affair—he came "to realize that permanency would not work out satisfactorily for us."

<hr/>

FARRELL'S *THIS MAN AND THIS WOMAN*, published in October 1951, is a short novel about the disintegration of the marriage of a sixty-three-year-old expressman and his increasingly disturbed wife. Although Farrell drew on his ordeal with Hortense for the novel, it is not a portrayal of their marriage, nor is the wife a portrait of Hortense. *This Man and This Woman,* he later remarked, "relied not solely on experience but also on clinical insight." The novel shows how insanity can creep up on a person, and how hard it is for those close to the person to recognize it and deal with it. But by making his two main characters so unappealing, Farrell made it hard for the reader to see the universal in the particular. The novel comes to seem what Vanguard had only pretended *Young Lonigan* was: a fictionalized case study.

His friends Bruno Bettelheim and journalist William Shannon praised the grim minor work highly in letters to Henle. But few reviewers were enthusiastic. Without "the devastatingly detailed sociological background" that informed Farrell's earlier works, said the reviewer in *Commonweal,* the novel had no meaning. "Remove Mr. Farrell as sociologist and leave only Mr. Farrell as artist and you have *This Man and This Woman.*"

———————»·◦·«———————

ALTHOUGH SENATOR JOSEPH MCCARTHY would be likened by some critics to Studs Lonigan, and though it was easy to imagine him as a youth having been a member of a gang like Lonigan's, his origins, in mundane fact, were not urban but rural. Even so, McCarthy was a bully and a liar—and Farrell was on to him early in the game. "The main job in this country is fighting McCarthyism," he declared at a March 1, 1952, meeting of the American Committee for Cultural Freedom, an independent affiliate of the Congress for Cultural Freedom (and a successor to Sidney Hook's American Committee for Intellectual Freedom). "The effects of McCarthyism on culture may soon be alarming, and real intimidation already exists in colleges and small towns and among intellectuals. The Stalinist menace is largely licked in America, although not on the world plane....The most effective way of influencing European intellectuals is to show how we defend cultural freedom in our own country."

Dwight Macdonald, Richard Rovere and other anti-Communist liberals on the committee agreed, but not all the members did. Irving Kristol, who was shortly to become the committee's executive director (and would serve in that capacity for ten months), long afterward recalled the main divisions among the members:

> There was a small group on the right, led by James Burnham, who if not pro-McCarthy was certainly anti-anti-McCarthy. There was a

much larger group on the center-left, led by Arthur Schlesinger, Jr., and Richard Rovere, who believed the Committee should be, above all, actively anti-McCarthy. Somewhere in the middle were a handful of very articulate people, led by Diana Trilling, who were unhappy with the ideological posture of the congress in Paris, which was anti-Communist but which, in an effort to appeal to the anti-Communist left, was not simply or belligerently pro-American.

Like Sidney Hook, the committee's chairman and moving spirit, Kristol tried to mediate among the factions.

At the March 1 meeting, Farrell urged that the committee, during the summer, develop "a plan for opposing McCarthyism in culture" and for sending anti-McCarthy speakers to college campuses throughout the country. He himself would not be able to help in this effort, however, since he would be in Europe.

He left for Paris the following month. The Congress for Cultural Freedom (which paid his way) was sponsoring an international festival there, celebrating the "masterpieces" created in the first half of the twentieth-century by musicians, artists and writers fortunate enough to be able to work in freedom. Composer Nicholas Nabokov, the congress's secretary general, believed that such an exposition would cause "much more *retentissement* [stir] than a hundred speeches" on the evils of communism.

The French Communist paper *L'Humanité* sneered at the festival as an American concoction, "a caricature of culture" whose hidden purpose was to facilitate the ideological occupation of France by the United States. Other French papers were only a shade less captious. Yet the month-long exposition—with performances of some 100 symphonies, concertos, operas and ballets written by about 70 different twentieth-century composers, as well as an exhibition of 150 modern paintings and sculptures, not to mention a number of literary debates—proved very popular.

Farrell, who twice spoke publicly during the exposition for a total of about twenty minutes, skipped many of the events, as well as most of the parties and luncheons to which he was invited. He spent some days in London seeing his British publisher and others. He shared a room there with Victor Reuther, Walter's youngest brother, whom he had met in Paris (and who had urged him to write some articles for the labor press). Reuther, head of the CIO's Paris office, was working (with help, overt and covert, from the U.S. government) to support and develop strong anti-Communist trade unions in Europe. "He is one of the heroes of the American labor movement," Farrell told Henle. "His job over here is hard and lonely, but he is working quietly, patiently, solidly and sensibly and seriously."

Farrell was working, too, while in Europe. Before leaving New York, he had finished going over the manuscript of *Yet Other Waters*, the third and final Bernard Carr novel, with Henle's associate Evelyn Shrifte. Now he was working on a novel he was calling "Old Tom O'Flaherty" which he had begun the preceding year (and which would be published as *The Face of Time*). This novel, in which Farrell returned to the Chicago of his youth to focus on Danny O'Neill's grandfather (based on John Daly) and Danny's Aunt Louise (based on Farrell's Aunt Bessie), seemed almost to write itself. Back in February, Henle had been delighted after reading several hundred pages: "[To] say that I am pleased with it is putting it very mildly. It is just as good as *A World I Never Made,* and there just isn't any higher praise."

But with the deadly Carr trilogy still in mind, Henle had pointedly quoted back to Farrell his own recent words about his new novel-in-progress. Farrell had written to him: "The book has gotten too much hold on me, and I can't shake out of it, and, at the moment, do other things.... I can't—that is, I don't want to—take it in stride, doing a few pages a day, and forgetting it until the next day. But all day, I keep coming back to it."

Henle commented: "Now I know such feelings can't be commanded, but I respectfully suggest that when, in the future, a story doesn't seize you in this way, you should just drop it and try something else. That has been the trouble, I feel, with the Bernard Carr trilogy."

Farrell's work on the novel continued to go well in Paris, despite the festival's distractions. After the exposition ended, he remained in Europe for several months, moving about from one city to another, giving lectures and broadcasts, talking with officials, labor leaders, writers and intellectuals. "I am likely now to be at my book all summer," he wrote to Henle, "especially since I won't be able to give it long hours, since I shall be batting about Europe a great deal. But...I don't think that when you read it, you would realize if you didn't know, how it is being written, often in odd moments, and following changes of scenery and so on." Henle agreed.

At times, naturally, Farrell's thoughts turned to his private sorrows. Before he left New York, he had decided to surrender to

Hortense the limited influence he had retained over Kevin's schooling and summers, persuading himself that this was in the boy's best
interest as well as his own, because only then would his quarrels
with Hortense finally cease.

But his financial obligations to her and their two sons
remained, along with taxes and the burden of his own needs
(which now included regularly eating out, since he didn't know
how to cook). Though his expenses in Europe were largely being
covered by the fees he earned from lectures and articles and by
the U.S. government, he was concerned about money and the
future. He had had to borrow $2,000 from a bank the preceding
year, against royalties from the New American Library of World Literature on paperback reprints of his books. Now, in July, he
proposed to Henle that they work out a five-year contract with
New American Library, giving him a guaranteed annual minimum
advance in exchange for exclusive rights on all of his books. Henle
proceeded to arrange this. New American Library agreed to pay
$20,000 a year—$10,000 to him and $10,000 to Vanguard—for
four years, starting in March 1953, and if the accumulated $80,000
had been earned back by the reprint sales of his books by March
1957, to make an additional payment of $5,000 to him and $5,000
to Vanguard. With this arrangement, as well as a contract with Vanguard for three more novels after the one that would be published
as *The Face of Time*, Henle advised Farrell that he "should be
relieved of money worries." This would prove too optimistic a fore-
cast.

Meanwhile, Farrell had other worries. In June, he had written
Henle that "I think I have reached the point of accepting the way
that I now live...and of being a bachelor again, probably for good
and all. It isn't too hard or too bad." By early August, though, he was
reporting from Paris that "I relented a little on taking girls out
because it got too lonely working all day and trying to work at
night."

He had become reacquainted with a journalist whom he had
met at the Congress for Cultural Freedom in Berlin, a thirty-nine-
year-old French woman named Suzanne Labin. She had written a
critical biography of Stalin, and Farrell (who was soon pushing
Henle and others to publish translations of her books) was quite
taken with her. He was scheduled to make a trip to Toulouse, but
she offered to drive him before then to Italy, where he could visit
some Italian friends in Milan. At first he was reluctant, inasmuch as

she was married, "and why do things that are impossible and let her compromise herself." But he changed his mind, and they proceeded on the trip. It proved "a wonderful one." They made an idyllic crossing of the Alps, eventually reaching Milan. "Entering a foreign country by car is so different from going in by plane or train," he wrote to Henle. "And living in Europe this way, outside of American circles, is so productive of so much insight. And people are so casually friendly. And hotel people are very sophisticated and knowing. You ask for two rooms and they immediately say, in French, *'chambres communicants.'*"

They went on to Rome, where they and his Italian friends had lunch with Senator Paul Douglas, Democrat of Illinois, and his wife, who had been attending a meeting of the Inter-Parliamentary Union in Switzerland. Farrell's friends were impressed by the cultivated and intelligent American senator. He had been a professor of economics at the University of Chicago when Farrell was a student there. "I am very proud of Jim, and knew him years ago," Douglas told them.

The senator was licking his political wounds in Europe before returning to America to campaign for Adlai Stevenson, the patrician governor of Illinois who was now the Democratic presidential candidate. Estranged from Stevenson, Douglas had backed Senator Estes Kefauver of Tennessee for the presidential nomination. Many years later, Douglas—who in 1942, at age fifty, had enlisted as a private in the Marines and been wounded twice during the war—would note that while the high-minded Stevenson ran "an excellent campaign, appealing above all to intellectuals," he had little rapport with working people. But Farrell, following the presidential contest from afar, had nevertheless grown enthusiastic about Stevenson. "His statements and speeches are damned intelligent, and he has real political sophistication," he had written to Henle. Though discouraged by the demagogic Senator McCarthy's overwhelming victory in September in a Republican primary in Wisconsin, as well as by signs of the growing strength of Republican presidential candidate Dwight Eisenhower, Farrell continued to believe that Stevenson would triumph in November.

Leaving Suzanne in Rome with her husband, just returned from Argentina, Farrell moved on to London and then to Paris, sailing home from there in October on the *Queen Mary*. Henle did not meet him at the pier; he didn't want to take the chance that Hortense, who had been "very insistent" the last time that he not be there, might be on hand (with Kevin). "I have no real desire to see her again—I mean on this earth," he told Farrell. "I have no objection whatsoever to encountering her in Heaven, but I have had enough of her here."

Farrell arrived in New York shortly before the publication of *Yet Other Waters*, which he was dedicating to the memory of James Weber Linn. In middle age, Farrell had finally come to appreciate the teacher who had done so much for him.

Yet Other Waters, which principally concerns the Communists' attempted corruption of Bernard Carr and his growing disillusionment with their movement, is the best novel in the trilogy. The Communist scenes, derived from Farrell's own experience—including the violent disruption of the Socialists' meeting in Madison Square Garden, the picketing at Ohrbach's department store, and the first American Writers' Congress—are authentic and effective. And Farrell again brings Carr's wife, Elizabeth, to life. Nevertheless, the novel is not very good. Its disparate parts do not form a coherent whole, chiefly because Carr remains such a cipher. "As you know," Henle had written to Farrell in Paris, "I have never felt that these [Bernard Carr] novels have the inner life that your Studs Lonigan and Danny O'Neill novels possess. It is hard to explain wherein the difference lies, but one reads about Bernard Carr, whereas one lives with Danny O'Neill—and with Studs Lonigan, too."

<hr />

FARRELL SAW HENLE SOON AFTER his arrival in New York, but not until their next meeting did his friend and publisher give him the momentous news: he had sold Vanguard Press. The new owners were Henle's deputy editor, Evelyn Shrifte; her brother, Herbert Shrifte, who presided over H. Wolff, a large and very profitable bookbinding firm; and some anonymous associates. Evelyn Shrifte was now Vanguard's president. Henle, who was about to turn sixty-one, was staying on as a part-time consultant.

Miss Shrifte, who had come to admire the gentlemanly Henle almost to the point of adoration, had helped him edit virtually all of Farrell's published books, with her part in the labor increasing as time went on. A native New Yorker with striking red hair, she had gone to work at Vanguard in 1929, soon after graduating from Barnard College, at Columbia. Though she privately thought the

Bernard Carr novels were "terrible," that life seemed to depart from Farrell's fiction whenever he strayed from Chicago, she liked most of his earlier novels. And she liked Jim Farrell, the man. He could be irascible and combative at times, to be sure, but "generally," she said, looking back decades later, he was "a sweet person, a gentle person, really kind of like goofy Danny O'Neill, droopy-drawers Danny O'Neill. That was Jim, really, essentially. A very kind and generous fellow."

Yet the fact remained that Evelyn Shrifte was not Jim Henle, and Farrell's relationship with her, long and cordial though it had been, was not the same as his intimate friendship with Henle. As Shrifte, of course, well knew. "Jim [Henle] was always so interested in Jim's work," she recalled. "Jim Farrell used to call up Jim Henle every single morning, almost, and they would discuss the events of the day before or the political situation. It was almost as if—I don't know whether Jim Farrell thought of Jim Henle as a father or not, but every single day, he'd call up and talk and talk and talk, early in the morning."

And now Farrell's learned, witty and infinitely patient surrogate father was stepping down. He would still frequently be at Vanguard; he would still read Farrell's works-in-progress, and he would serve, in effect, as an intermediary for him with Shrifte. But their relationship would not be quite the same. Henle remained influential at Vanguard. Shrifte would almost invariably consult him in matters pertaining to Farrell and not seldom defer to his judgment, though she at times would also seek the advice of her brother and others. The essential fact remained that Henle was no longer making the final decisions and signing the checks.

It didn't take Vanguard's fading star writer long to notice a difference in its treatment of him. By January 24 he was complaining to Henle that editorial work on short stories he had submitted for a collection he expected Vanguard to publish that year had not been done. He said that a few weeks hence, when he returned from a lecture tour, he wanted to have lunch with Henle, Evelyn Shrifte and Herbert Shrifte, to talk about "how we are to get reorganized… because we are all wasting a lot of time, and we have to become more efficient." The book of short stories had to come out in the fall, he said, lest the book of essays that he and Henle had been discussing for some time, as well as other work, be "goofed up."

But Evelyn Shrifte had not committed Vanguard to publishing the short stories, and she, like Henle, was not keen on those he had submitted. Moreover, she thought it was a mistake to publish two titles by an author in the same year, especially since she and Henle were hopeful about the prospects of *The Face of Time*.

In February, with *The Face of Time* manuscript basically done, Farrell signed a contract with Vanguard for three more novels. Under this agreement, he would get an advance of about $5,000 a year for the next few years. With the $10,000 a year from New American Library, that brought his minimum annual income to $15,000—which is equivalent to more than $100,000 today and was far above what most Americans earned. The "paperback revolution" had brought Farrell affluence. But the ample income somehow was to prove insufficient for him. He was no more able to discipline his expenditures than he was his prose output.

Earlier in the year, he had been desperate for cash. The Hotel Chelsea, noted for its patience with the writers and other artists in residence, had had enough of Farrell and was threatening to evict him for nonpayment of rent.

Seeking to help him out, but unable or perhaps unwilling to turn over any more Vanguard money to him, Evelyn Shrifte called up a young literary agent named Stanley Colbert. He and his partner, Sterling Lord, had formed their agency in 1951 and were reputed to work hard for their clients. Perhaps with their help Farrell could earn some money from magazines. With Farrell quite likely in the room with her, Shrifte explained the situation to Colbert, who then invited her to send Farrell over. The forty-eight-year-old Farrell had long done without a literary agent, and as a world-renowned author he may have felt it a little humiliating to be asking a twenty-five-year-old such as Colbert for help. Nevertheless, he needed money, so he went.

Colbert, who had read *Studs Lonigan* as a boy, had been around enough writers to have no preconceptions about the legend who was on his way to the agent's East 36th Street office. When Farrell arrived, Colbert noticed that he had food stains on his collar and on his tie. "A slightly unkempt fellow" is how he later describe the novelist. "But he was James T. Farrell and he was a giant to me." The famed writer was soft-spoken and appeared less than self-assured: "He seemed a little beaten."

They talked about what Farrell had written that had not been published, "and he mentioned that he had done a whole batch of what he called 'boyhood baseball memories,'" said Colbert. Before they got much further, the agent was on the phone to Sid James, managing editor of the new "class" sports magazine, *Sports Illus-trated*, and telling him that possibly, just possibly, he might be able to induce the great author of *Studs Lonigan* to do a few pieces for him, not revealing that the ones he had in mind were already writ-ten. James, eager for "names" to dress up his new publication, went for it. And shortly, Colbert was giving Farrell an advance sufficient to cover his debt at the Chelsea. Farrell inquired about the com-mission. "That's one I owe you from reading your books," Colbert told him. "No commission on that one."

⟶➤◦◄⟵

IN THE SPRING, FARRELL WAS off to Paris again—and to Madame Suzanne Labin, who (in his later description) was "small, chic, blond and beautiful." Soon he was writing to Henle of his "love" for her and exuding contentment. "I am both happy and productive here, and healthy and eating well," he reported.

He was busily writing short stories, "finger exercises," he called them. In Rome the previous September, he had embarked on "an experiment of writing 50 stories laid outside of America as a means of assimilating some of my experiences (and with the will-ingness to write them and not care if they were good or bad)."

Farrell had had "the feeling of starting anew" the previous spring, when he was still writing *The Face of Time* (whose title is from W. B. Yeats's "Lamentation of the Old Pensioner": "I spit into the face of Time/That has transfigured me.") With the completion of that work, so unexpectedly transforming the Danny O'Neill tetralogy into a pentalogy, his masterwork—what a later critic would felicitously label his "Washington Park" novels (that is, the *Lonigan* trilogy and the pentalogy)—was finished. His earlier fresh start, after *My Days of Anger* seemed to have brought the O'Neill series to an end, had resulted in the disastrous Clare/Carr trilogy. That his vital artistic powers returned in *The Face of Time* must have given Farrell hope, yet it would have been only natural for him to have felt a certain anxiety about the future as well.

During the summer of 1952 he had entertained the idea of a novel based on his time in Paris with Dorothy, until Henle reminded him that he had already portrayed Dorothy in the Carr novels. Later that year, Farrell had revived an idea that had come to him after John Stephen's institutionalization, for a novel about "a defective child"; but after thirty-seven pages he had abandoned the project. Now, back in Paris in 1953, he occupied himself by writing short stories that he looked upon as mere "experiments," not caring (he told Henle) if any were ever published.

Meanwhile, he read galleys of *The Face of Time*. The year before, the galleys of *Yet Other Waters*, with many queries and comments from the editors written on them, had failed to reach the itinerant Farrell in Europe, and so, much to the editors' annoyance, a new set had had to be laboriously compiled and sent to him. To their relief, there was no similar mishap this time. But that was not the editors' only worry. Henle tactfully offered what he described as "some corny advice" to his slovenly writer with the hard-to-read handwriting:

> Please
>
> 1. Begin with a series of *sharp* pencils. When one becomes dull, change to another. When they all become dull, sharpen them.
>
> 2. Get at the proofs *promptly* but not *hurriedly*. Sit down and give yourself plenty of time.
>
> 3. When you write on the proofs, pls remember we have to *read* what you write.
>
> 4. When you write, rest the proof on a desk or other smooth, firm surface—not your knee.
>
> 5. Send the proofs back airmail first class. This is a *big* chance for $, for glory, and for Vanguard. *Please* give us all the time you can—i.e., time to germinate enthusiasm between having completed books and publication date.
>
> As you will see from glancing through these exhortations I am really a frustrated school teacher.

Henle's real frustration, of course, was with his brilliant but childishly careless "student."

⟶⊶ ⊷⟵

FARRELL WAS DISMAYED BY THE European non-Communist Left's failure to see through the Communist propaganda and inclination to believe that Julius and Ethel Rosenberg had been framed. In June, with the two convicted Soviet spies sentenced to death, the U.S. Supreme Court, having already refused to hear their appeal, denied a plea to stay the execution. The Communists portrayed the Rosenbergs as innocent martyrs and whipped up mass protests. Writing to Henle from Paris, Farrell said he would have liked, "out of simple humane feeling," to have seen them get a less severe sentence. "But

I would not raise my voice because of the campaign that the Communists have carried on, and because of the fact that the Rosenbergs have been a party to it."

"It is sad," Farrell reflected. "The feeling in Europe and in America is widening. The European papers give more space to McCarthyism than they will to anti-McCarthyism. This in turn may be to strengthen isolationist sentiment in America." He anticipated protests in front of the American embassy in Paris. "But I wonder—what demonstrations there were when millions were killed in Russia, for Trotsky, Zinoviev, Kamenev, and others...." He continued:

> What is bothersome in all of this and helpful to the growth of McCarthyism is that the attitudes of so many here—I mean in various European countries—are that when we take strong anti-Communist steps to protect ourselves, we are provocative etc. This creeps into the American press. And it only will serve to enrage Americans. Those of us who have, in small or bigger ways, struggled for a policy of strengthening the center and non-Communist Left in Europe are put in the middle, and, in part, by those whom we wished to see supported in Europe.

A few days later, with the Rosenberg executions imminent, Farrell wrote to his friend of the "terrific wave of sentiment and emotionalism...sweeping France—and apparently the rest of the world—but in France more so.... Our name is mud here, but France's name is probably mud, also, in America."

The next month, Farrell met an eminent American whose name was *not* mud in Europe. The visitor, on a world tour, was Adlai Stevenson. Farrell met the erstwhile presidential candidate at a reception and became, Stevenson's biographer John Bartlow Martin drily noted, "a lifelong—and prolific—correspondent."

<hr />

FARRELL'S MONEY WOES DID NOT cease because he was on the other side of the Atlantic. He soon feared that he might have to return earlier than planned. The bank from which he had taken a $2,000 loan had foreclosed on it, he complained to Henle, and his income taxes were higher than he had anticipated.

Henle (who pointed out that he must have known about his income taxes before he bought his ticket to Europe) tried repeatedly to explain the basic realities to him. He had $15,000 a year in income that he could count on. He gave $5,200 to Hortense for her and Kevin, and $800 or so more for Kevin's schooling and camp; he paid New York State $720 a year for its care of John Stephen (he had unsuccessfully tried to get the state to lower his monthly obligation), and he paid about $3,000 a year in income taxes. That left $5,200 a year—the equivalent of about $35,800 today—for himself. "This isn't altogether a gloomy letter," Henle concluded on one occasion. "As I said yesterday, you have $15,000 a year. This is more than 99½ per cent of the population receives."

But Henle might as well have been addressing a child. Instead of living within his means, Farrell kept looking to various will-o'-the-wisps that would let him continue living as he wished:

- He imagined—failing to remember the terms of his longterm contract with New American Library—that if that publisher would reprint *The Road Between* in paperback, it would fatten his wallet.

- He imagined that Stan Colbert and Sterling Lord (who met the novelist for the first time on a visit to Paris in June) might turn his trunkload of unpublished manuscripts into gold; but as Colbert told him, virtually all of the manuscripts were essentially first drafts and needed work, and there was no obvious market for them.

- He imagined that there was significant, if slumbering, demand in foreign lands not only for his books but for his articles, and that with "some satisfactory extra commission," Colbert could fulfill that demand; though as Henle pointed out to him, "you can't achieve financial security through the sale of articles to European journals."

The one obvious way for Farrell to supplement his assured income substantially was by commercial lecturing. Henle repeatedly recommended that course to him. But Farrell was reluctant to commit himself to it. "I risked not lecturing," he explained to Henle in September, "because it interferes with many other things, and would be a rough grind, and make me dependent for six weeks or more a year and forced to go where I was told."

Thus, James T. Farrell: whining about the money he didn't have, and whining about the "rough grind" of having to talk about life and literature for six weeks in places not of his own choosing in order to earn the money he didn't have. At nearly fifty years, Farrell was in many ways like a child. Yet that was not entirely without its advantages: it may well have been one of the keys to his ability to recreate the world of childhood and youth so convincingly.

The most recent manifestation of that ability—*The Face of*

Time—gave him hope of reviving his literary fortunes, a hope which Evelyn Shrifte and Jim Henle shared. "I have just reread from start to finish *The Face of Time*," Henle had written to Farrell in May, "and I want to tell you to your face what I have said behind your back—namely, that this is a truly magnificent novel." It was, he added later, "infinitely better" than the Carr novels. His only fear, previously expressed to Farrell, was that although the new novel "has all the pathos, humor, fire, vitality of your other Danny O'Neill books," readers other than himself might complain that it was not different enough from them, that they'd "'heard all this before.'" Time alone would reveal the public's reaction.

<hr />

FARRELL RETURNED FROM PARIS in early October. In the preceding weeks, he had been working on "Boarding House Blues," which, he reported to Henle, "threatens to become a novel," and on "New Year's Eve," about a party in 1929 in a fictional equivalent of the Coudich Castle in which his friend Mary Hunter had stayed. While noting that both stories were in need of "much revision," he eagerly sought Henle's opinion of them.

The editor thought that "Boarding House Blues," set in a boarding house on Chicago's North Side, was much too long, needed to be "drastically" cut, and should not be published as an independent volume. "You *do* have a wonderful setting here and wonderful characters," he told Farrell, "but we can stand just so much of them; I advocate hitting the reader hard and then getting away." Meanwhile, Farrell decided that "Boarding House Blues" was indeed a novel.

Henle was utterly unenthusiastic about "New Year's Eve": "The party, when all is said and done, is not precisely electric—a poor second (or third, or fourth) to the New Year's Eve party in *Young Manhood*. Ordinarily I don't make such comparisons (regarding them as not quite fair) but this invites them."

On the next to last day of September, Farrell informed the editor: "Today, I began a new novel *Tom Carroll*." The title character was a disillusioned, middle-aged ex-radical living in New York.

Henle cautioned Farrell that in trying to write two novels at once, he was not being fair to himself. "A novel, it seems to me, must be the product of condensation and distillation. How this process can be going on in your mind in two different directions at once I don't know and can't understand. Short stories? Yes, if you insist. Lovett referred to them, rather aptly, as sparks from your anvil, and (as sparks) they do not interfere with the condensation and distillation process."

A few weeks later, Henle had read a chunk of the "Tom Carroll" manuscript and was not impressed. "Somehow or other...the narrative—and the dialogue—are flat in a way that you never are flat writing about Chicago.... Re a guess on sales: As it now stands I think we'd be lucky to do as well with this manuscript as we did with *Yet Other Waters*. I wish to God I could assure you that you have another *Studs* or another *Face of Time* here, but I just can't feel that."

After *My Days of Anger*, Farrell had had great difficulty making headway on *Bernard Clare*—and that showed in the result. Now, with his masterly O'Neill-O'Flaherty saga finished for the second time, he was blocked once more. Unable to return again to the well of his boyhood and youth for a major novel, the author was floundering.

———————⸎———————

EVELYN SHRIFTE WANTED VERY MUCH to make *The Face of Time* a success. Toward that end, she had worked hard to put together a brochure that would remind booksellers and reviewers about all that Farrell had accomplished in the past, and thus, she hoped, get them to forget about his recent flops (sales of *Yet Other Waters* had been absolutely abysmal) and give *The Face of Time* the serious attention it deserved.

Among the contributors to the brochure, "The coming of age of a great book...," was Alfred Kazin. He stated: "I think that *Studs Lonigan* and the Danny O'Neill tetralogy are two of the most honest and important works of our time and that they will live long after a lot of the highly stylized but meretricious fiction we have been getting lately is forgotten."

Others who paid tribute to Farrell and his works included his friends Arthur Schlesinger Jr., Morton White, Bruno Bettelheim and Horace Gregory. The last-named old friend, now teaching at Sarah Lawrence College, would be persuaded to do even more for the cause. In an essay that appeared in New American Library's *New World Writing—Fifth Mentor Selection*, a paperback published the following spring, the poet would liken Farrell's works to those of

Dickens: "The analogy holds in respect to Farrell's productivity, his passion for social justice, his humane temper, as well as the impact of his work upon the general reader; and like Dickens' writings, Farrell's writings in bulk have obvious flaws."

The comparison was an extravagant one. But Gregory's mention of Farrell's obvious flaws—he cited loose phrasing and repetitions—raises the question of why, if they were so obvious, Farrell's editors did not correct them. The answer has to do not merely with Jim Henle's human fallibility but with his conception of an editor's role. He firmly believed, as he would observe to Farrell a few years hence, that "the author, his typewriter, and—if you please—God should be the only ones responsible for the manuscript." It was a gentlemanly approach to the editorial calling, and Farrell's brash young agent, Stanley Colbert, for one, judged that the writer had been terribly coddled at Vanguard. Yet any advocate of more intrusive editing should be given pause by what Farrell, under Henle's deferential tutelage, had accomplished over the decades. It is very doubtful that *Studs Lonigan* or *A World I Never Made* would have been improved by aggressive editing, which is likely to have a leveling effect, elevating the wretched but lowering the exceptional.

The Face of Time, the latest exceptional book from Farrell, published in October 1953, is another case in point. Perhaps if the editing had been more aggressive, Farrell might have avoided having Mary O'Flaherty remembering her arrival at Ellis Island decades before the real Ellis Island first began to receive immigrants, and might have been spared having Jim O'Neill recall a *woman* on the streetcar accusing him of beating Danny, on that fateful journey when he took Danny to live with the O'Flahertys, instead of a *man* asking him, as in *A World I Never Made.* But these are trivial errors, and their correction would hardly have been adequate compensation for the damage that heavy editing by Henle, Shrifte or anyone else would probably have done elsewhere in the novel. For *The Face of Time* really is, as Henle said, magnificent. Even Nelson Algren, that tireless carper where Farrell was concerned (most recently having upbraided him for the "compassionless prose and belabored cataloging" in his 1950 short story collection, *An American Dream Girl*) relented long enough in his review of *The Face of Time*—before insisting that its length could have been cut by half—to pronounce it "easily the best written of Farrell's many novels. There is nothing faked here; every line of dialogue rings true."

What most distinguishes *The Face of Time* from its predecessors in the Danny O'Neill series, aside from the movement of Old Tom O'Flaherty and Aunt Louise to center stage, is not just the somewhat cleaner writing but the mellow tone. Age and no doubt his own recent family ordeal, as well as perhaps his previous abandonment of the stern Marxist utopia, had allowed Farrell to become more forgiving.

Farrell's old adversary Granville Hicks, in a remarkably warm, perceptive and generous review in the *Herald Tribune Book Review*, noticed this change of tone. "It is, astonishingly, a gentle book...," he wrote. "Perhaps I am disarmed by the elegiac note, but it seems to me that this is one of the best novels Farrell has ever written.... What he has given us is not tragedy but a deep sense of the way in which the human condition is bounded by diminution and loss."

And so he had. Yet *The Face of Time* sold scarcely more than six thousand copies.

⊸▸•◂⊶

AVOWEDLY "BROKE" WHEN HE returned from Europe, Farrell was soon making attempts to remedy his situation. The commercial fate of *The Face of Time* was already becoming apparent. ("The advance has been only moderate," Henle had informed him before he even left Paris. "The booksellers did so badly with *Yet Other Waters* that it was impossible to generate much enthusiasm.") Not for the last time, Farrell came up with a host of suggestions as to how his publisher—in this case, his paperback-reprint publisher, New American Library—might do a better job of marketing his books. He offered the ideas to Henle for possible presentation to Victor Weybright of New American Library. Farrell wanted, as he explicitly said, "special consideration." He naively believed that he was owed this because in agreeing to New American Library's generous financial arrangement (which he himself had suggested in the first place), he and Vanguard had "sacrificed our bargaining position"! Weybright could hardly have gone along with that logic.

Within a few days, Farrell was on a new tack, complaining to Henle about his "desperate" financial situation, and proposing that he be released from his contract with New American Library long enough to allow his agent, Colbert, to sell a short story collection, *French Girls Are Vicious*, to another publisher and so get him a quick advance of $3,000 to $5,000. "Why should I just let myself take this continual pounding and harassing?" he asked Henle. "Why should I just go on, letting myself get nervous, driving myself, hitting a stone wall, and getting out of it only the satisfaction of doing what I consider to be my duty and my responsibility and the satisfaction also of doing my work. Great as that is, there is more to life than it." Though he was not to be released from his contract, Vanguard did finally agree to publish *French Girls Are Vicious.*

A few days later, Farrell's spirits lifted. He was cheered by a review of *The Face of Time* in the daily *New York Times.* "I again predict that we are over the hump," he exulted to Henle.

Despite such transient encouragements, Farrell remained discontented. In an unsent letter to Henle in January 1954, he wrote: "I am in a vise. On the one hand, I am told—not without reason—that I write too much; on the other hand, it is the main resource I have as a means of trying to make the money I need in order to get out of the hole I am in." Though prone to self-pity, Farrell did try (not entirely successfully) to keep his plight in perspective, as he indicated in the same letter: "If all of this is anybody's fault, it is mine. It isn't the fault of the publishing business. But if I get out of this goddamned trap it will be a near miracle and a piece of rare good fortune."

Henle continued to urge Farrell, who had moved from the Chelsea to the more costly Hotel Dryden on East 39th Street, to curb his expenditures. "Surely," he told him, "there are places where you can live far less expensively than at the Dryden—places in this country or places abroad. But if you go abroad I'd certainly urge you to go tourist and to do everything as inexpensively as possible."

Henle and Shrifte also arranged, at Farrell's request, to have his New American Library payments made to him on a monthly basis (instead of semiannually). This, he thought, would enable him to "more easily live on my budget, and I could meet current expenses with less need for loans." They also arranged for some of his income to be deferred so that some of his tax liability for 1954 would be postponed. In short, they did what they reasonably could to help him.

———————⟫•0•⟪———————

IN APRIL 1954, FARRELL WAS off to Europe again, for the third year in a row. He spent the spring and summer in Paris—following in the press the progress of the Army-McCarthy hearings being televised back home; interviewing Suzanne Labin in connection with a book of hers that Vanguard planned to publish; reviewing galleys for his own *Reflections at Fifty,* a collection of essays (which he was dedicating to Madame Labin); and struggling once more to write the novel about "a defective child," which he was calling "Moonlight on the Mountain."

He was having difficulty with the principal characters in the novel. Henle, after reading a large chunk of manuscript, urged him to get the background and personality of each one fixed in his mind before proceeding further. "I think the sureness with which you approached the Lonigans and the O'Neills was due not merely to the fact that they were in your blood, so to speak, but also because you could see them as well as *feel* them. You were never in the least doubt about them, and from the moment one of them comes on the scene he is fixed, indelible, credible, utterly convincing."

Henle had long thought that a novel based on Farrell's ordeal with John Stephen would be very painful to write—and to read. But Farrell felt driven to transmute the searing experience into literature. "I am tearing at myself in my book, Jim," he wrote Henle, "but won't give up on it, at least not as yet."

Farrell now had several people helping to bring some order to his affairs. One was a young New York lawyer named Ria Simon, who at his request was handling his payments to Hortense and his other regular obligations. "I handled all his money," she recalled. She opened a separate account, paid his bills and gave him money when he needed it. "And that's what he wanted. He didn't want to be able to spend freely, because he overspent all the time."

Another person helping him was literary agent Sterling Lord. He and Stanley Colbert ended their partnership that summer, and Lord, on a coin toss, took over the agency. A midwesterner in his mid-thirties, he had been handling Farrell's freelance work for *Sports Illustrated* and other magazines since their meeting in Paris the year before. "I was trying to get him into as many magazines as possible," Lord remembered. "Not just for the money. With most people, at that time, when I'd tell people I'm representing James T. Farrell, they'd say, 'Oh, God, I thought he was dead.' I kept hearing that. So I thought, well, exposure would help." But the money was important, too, at least to Farrell, so much so that on occasion he allowed work of his to appear in magazines he did not esteem, such as a publication called *Manhunt.*

Despite the extra money he earned, Farrell was ill-suited to freelancing. He was not a glib or clever writer, nor was he a hack. He found it very hard to write to the market or to a formula. "I never have sold to the big mass circulation magazines," he would reflect the next year. "They do not care for my writing it seems, and I do not know how to write for them."

Though his situation was somewhat improved, Farrell was not happy. In his correspondence with Henle, he didn't hesitate to make various suggestions, demands and complaints. One grievance in particular gnawed at him: that under the new regime at Vanguard, decisions affecting him were not being made in a timely way. Thus in September 1953 he had suggested that a selection of his best short stories be issued by a reprint publisher, but no decision had been made, as he complained to Henle in May: "Evelyn told me she would let me know and decide, and I never heard."

Some of Farrell's complaints amounted to childish carping about petty matters. Once, with the author making a great many changes and corrections—some illegible, all costly—on the galleys of *Reflections at Fifty*, and also griping that an article of his had not been found in the bulging files of his material that he kept at Vanguard and sent to him right away, even Henle lost patience. Telling him that the extensive revisions were "especially deplorable in the case of a book that represents a certain financial loss, no matter what it may mean in prestige," he added: "I don't think you do well to complain about little matters under these circumstances.... Evelyn (and Herbert) have cooperated so wonderfully in so many ways that you do ill to raise tiny pin-pricks of this kind and complain that 'things keep getting goofed up.'"

Farrell apologized. But he continued to harbor the suspicion that at the new Vanguard he and his works were not valued sufficiently, that not enough effort was being made to promote his books, that somehow "things keep getting goofed up."

The suspicion did not yet consume him, however. He was a delegate to the PEN Club Congress in Amsterdam in June; then went on to Antwerp to cover the first tournament of the European Baseball Federation for *Sports Illustrated*. In August he went with Suzanne on a Mediterranean cruise. He lectured in Copenhagen in September, and in Sweden in October.

Almost every American he met "has something of the same story to tell me," he wrote to Henle from Paris at the end of July. "All over the world, we are disliked. Almost, anyway. In the face of worldwide peril to every decent value, and in the face of the fact that, mistakes or not, we have basically tried to build up a defense of a free world, this is disgusting and terrible." Later, writing Henle from Sweden in October, he said that he kept being asked about McCarthy. "It seems to me that he has sunk and is not the danger he was a year ago and seven months ago. Over here, many people gave us up as free people, and only yesterday I was asked...if writers dare to write what they think."

That month, he returned to New York, to Vanguard Press and the expensive Hotel Dryden. In December, he was elected chairman of the American Committee for Cultural Freedom.

DOROTHY WAS NOW LIVING IN New York. She worked for a firm that manufactured safety glasses, arranging displays of the product at industrial expositions. One day, Farrell called her up at work. "I was surprised," she remembered decades later. "And I said, 'All right, I'll meet you.' And I met him. And we went back together."

But not right away. "He was after me and I liked James, I liked him, I really liked him," she said. "He was after me all the time, he'd call me every day at my job, my new job. And I said, 'James, I'm not going out with you unless I'm married to you. That's all.' So he said, 'Then, we'll get married.'"

Evidently he had come to realize that there was no future in his transatlantic affair with Suzanne Labin; nor did he see any in his intermittent relationship with musician Rosalyn Tureck.

"I think he really got lonely enough that he wanted somebody to look after him," said Ria Simon, who arranged his divorce from his second wife so that he could remarry his first. "I don't think he was madly in love with [Dorothy]. But I think he wanted somebody—and she was a nurturer, she was a caretaker, she would take care of him to the best of her ability. She was flaky...but nice, pleasant, likeable. You couldn't not like Dorothy. She was very likeable. And she was right for him. She did take care of him. He did a lot of obnoxious things to her, but she did take care of him."

Meanwhile, his suspicion that the new regime at Vanguard was *not* taking care of him had deepened. Even the sale of the *Studs Lonigan* movie rights to producer Lew Kerner and United Artists in February 1955 ended up stoking his discontent with his publisher. In an emotional letter (undated and probably unsent) to

Jim Henle and his wife, Farrell, after noting his greatly valued friendship with Henle, complained of indecision and delay and of not being consulted about matters affecting him:"I think I had the right to assume that Vanguard Press would publish any books I felt should be published; I don't think I was unjustified in assuming this. However, after publication of *The Face of Time*, I have met with delay, resistance and negativism."

His immediate problem seemed to be that the editing of *French Girls Are Vicious*, his latest short story collection, due to be published in the spring, now had to happen in a rush and at a time when he wanted to be doing other work."The simple and truthful fact," he said, "is that Evelyn had the manuscript in her hands for over a year and didn't read it. She clearly indicated that she didn't care for the book. Nevertheless, she insisted on publishing it, and wouldn't allow me to have anyone else publish it.... On the one hand, I'm told that I'm loved at Vanguard Press and am a great writer; on the other hand, I receive only the shabbiest treatment."

He was distressed, too, by the "bitterness" toward him that he detected at a conference on the sale of the *Studs Lonigan* movie rights for a five-figure sum (probably $20,000). "Vanguard Press threw every obstacle they could in the way of my selling *Studs Lonigan* to the movies, at a time when the sale could be a salvation to me.They acted as though I were damn near an intruder concerning the rights to my own book." He cited a proposal by Evelyn Shrifte "that we get the absolutely impossible guarantee that the producer put three million dollars into the picture" as among the obstacles put in the way of the sale. But Farrell had his eyes on the cash that he would get right away (60 percent of the sale price), while Shrifte appears to have had the longer-term interest of Vanguard (and of Farrell himself) in mind.An inferior, low-budget film of *Studs Lonigan* would be unlikely to earn them much money or give much of a boost to sales of his novels.

His unsent letter to Jim and Marjorie Henle was typewritten, single-spaced and more than eight pages long. He had numerous minor grievances against the new Vanguard Press—including inattention to his birthday, a lapse he deemed "highly significant," since "so much used to be made of it."

Soon, Farrell did send a letter of complaint directly to Evelyn Shrifte, saying that he wanted to leave Vanguard and find a new publisher. Needless to say, Shrifte—who had worked on virtually all of his books, had striven earnestly to promote *The Face of Time*, and regarded Farrell himself fondly—was shocked and hurt. Henle, too, was shocked. They soon got together with their aggrieved and agitated author, and soothed his feelings sufficiently to enable them all to carry on, almost—but of course not quite—as before.

Farrell's overblown complaints about Shrifte and the new Vanguard, though perhaps not entirely unjustified, seem to have been largely an outgrowth of his literary frustrations and money woes. Later that year, in a memorandum probably prepared in connection with his divorce from Hortense, he detailed his grim financial situation. "Since 1949, I have pulled out of debt about eight or nine times," he wrote. "I have done it by work and by [the] unearned advances" from New American Library and Vanguard.

His contract with New American Library, which was providing him with $10,000 a year and Vanguard with a like sum, would expire in 1957. Though the firm had sold roughly five million paperback copies of his books, competition in the field had intensified and sales of his books had "taken a sharp decline" in the previous year. At the moment, his and Vanguard's unearned advances from New American Library amounted to at least $25,000. (The following April, Henle would pass on to him the bad news that, according to the latest report from New American Library, they were actually more than $50,000 in the red!) Farrell hoped that a *Studs Lonigan* movie might stimulate sales of his books. But unless the New American Library advances were earned back by the royalties on his paperbacks, it appeared that his long-term contract with the publisher would not be extended or renewed.

In addition, Farrell noted, there was his contract with Vanguard for three novels, which was providing him with $5,000 a year. This contract would expire at the end of 1956. And though he had finished a first draft of "Moonlight on the Mountain" in December 1954, he had yet to produce even one of the three novels required to satisfy the contract.

His last four novels—*The Road Between, Yet Other Waters, This Man and This Woman,* and even *The Face of Time,* so highly regarded by Henle, Hicks and others—had not sold well, and his unearned advances on them from Vanguard now totaled some $10,000 (including about $6,000 against *Yet Other Waters* alone). He figured (much too optimistically) that "Moonlight" needed only about six months more of intensive work, but he knew that his novel about a retarded child held no promise of "a big sale."

In short, the situation facing Farrell was that the public was not exactly clamoring for even the best of his novels, he was experiencing much difficulty turning more of them out, and the opposite of prosperity appeared to be just around the corner.

But at least he now had Dorothy, who had moved in with him at the Hotel Dryden (and would soon find a cheaper place for them on West 24th Street, and then, for their new home as man and wife, larger and no more expensive quarters at 252 West 85th Street). "Now every other problem of my life is solved," he had written to Henle after his "shocking" letter to Shrifte. "Dorothy and I are very happy. She takes wonderful care of me."

They were remarried on September 10, 1955, in a friend's home in Montclair, New Jersey, by a Presbyterian minister whose son Dorothy knew. Afterward there was a reception, courtesy of Dorothy's sister and her husband, at the Drake Hotel in New York. Farrell's brother Earl was there. So was Jim Henle, who a few days later wrote to Farrell: "The reception was so much fun and Dorothy and you were both so very happy that it was a genuinely happy occasion." Though he didn't tell him then, Henle had privately wondered if Farrell "wouldn't have spared [himself] a great deal of pain and anxiety, of nervous strain and worry, of sturm und drang und general hell if [he] had never obtained a divorce" from Dorothy in the first place.

BERTRAND RUSSELL WAS ONE OF several world-renowned thinkers who lent their names to the Congress for Cultural Freedom, serving as "honorary chairmen." Though opposed to Soviet totalitarianism, Lord Russell was under the impression that freedom was also in a bad way in the United States. Indeed, he stated in March 1956 that America had come to resemble "other police states such as Nazi Germany and Stalin's Russia." He made that bizarre comparison in a published letter in which he expressed his outrage at the continued incarceration of Morton Sobell, who five years earlier had been sentenced to thirty years in prison after having been found guilty of conspiring with the Rosenbergs to steal nuclear secrets and transmit them to the Soviet Union. The octogenarian British lord was sure that Sobell was an innocent victim of American injustice.

To the American Committee for Cultural Freedom, which Farrell chaired, it seemed that the outrageous injustice was being committed by the congress's honorary chairman himself. In a published letter to Russell, signed by Farrell (but written by Diana Trilling), the committee's executive board strongly objected to Russell's "extraordinary lapse from standards of objectivity and justice" and denounced his attack on American justice as "a major disservice to the cause of freedom and democracy...and a major service to the enemies we had supposed you had engaged in combat." This prompted Russell to indicate he would resign his honorary chairmanship.

It was then the turn of Michael Josselson, the congress's executive director, to be angry—with the American committee. Although Josselson privately characterized Russell as "an old fool," he thought the philosopher's resignation would be a coup for the Communists. To avoid that, he instructed Sidney Hook, it would be necessary for the congress's executive committee in Paris to rebuke its American affiliate. "You don't seem to realize," he told Hook, "what Russell's name on our masthead has meant to our international reputation, nor how very severely the loss of his name will affect the Congress and our friends who work for the Congress in non-committed areas where his name has helped offset some of the initial reluctance of people to associate with us."

This issue—whether anti-Communist liberals should mute their convictions to win over the uncommitted—would implicitly present itself to Farrell again and again in the ensuing months as he encountered anti-American sentiment on an extensive tour abroad for the congress. Indeed, the experience—together with his weakness for drink—would lead to his public embarrassment and his resignation from the American committee.

Farrell had been reelected chairman of the committee at the end of October, despite his stated desire to step down. In the months before then, he had been quite active in public controversies—charging Nobel laureate Linus Pauling and 359 others who were urging the Supreme Court to strike down the Internal Security Act of 1950 (the "McCarran Act") with naively misconstruing the nature of the Communist movement, and objecting to the omission of important anti-Communist works in a Fund for the Republic "Bibliography on the Communist Program in the United States." Farrell agreed to continue as chairman of the committee, though he apparently would have preferred, at least on a conscious level, to concentrate on his writing as he settled into his new married life.

He was still having difficulty with the novel about a retarded child, which he was now calling "Invisible Swords." Henle considered the first four chapters of the second draft "a tremendous improvement," but advised him that "the married couple doesn't yet ring true." Later, after reading more chapters, Henle told him that "you still have a terrible—and appalling—problem in the first part of the book. It just washes back and forth like the tide—it has no *current* at all."

Given his literary perplexities and his financial worries—the latter perhaps exacerbated by the news that Dorothy was pregnant—Farrell may well have found relief in turning to the world of public affairs. In February he had interviewed Adlai Stevenson in Chicago for what would be a wholly admiring portrait of the once and future presidential candidate.

In early April, Farrell set down some thoughts about the future of the American Committee for Cultural Freedom in light of Soviet leader Nikita Khrushchev's recent "secret speech" denouncing Stalin and his purges. In a letter to Diana Trilling (who chaired the group's administrative committee), Farrell proposed that the American committee adopt a new statement of policy, reaffirming its fundamental purposes and seeking to dispel the confusion and doubt being fostered by the new Soviet stance. "Mr. Khrushchev and the other Russian leaders can now prove themselves; all they need to do is to put firm chains on the dogs of terror and repression."

Later that month Farrell departed for the West Coast. He spent a week as a visiting writer at the University of Washington in Seattle, lectured at Reed College in Portland, and saw his sister Mary in Beverly Hills. Then he embarked on his congress-sponsored tour of Australia, India, Israel and points between.

He arrived in Sydney on May 1 and spent virtually the whole month in Australia, lecturing and giving informal talks as the guest of the Australian Committee for Cultural Freedom. He began his stay with a press conference and, according to a published account by Richard Krygier, secretary of the Australian committee, "very promptly showed the main trait in his character—the utter sincerity and integrity of his approach to every problem raised."

Krygier made the same point in a "confidential" letter to Michael Josselson, but added, with more candor, some others. Farrell's "whole visit could not be classed as a success," he said, "because the financial results show the difficulty in getting a man, comparatively little known at present in Australia, across." In Perth, for instance, Farrell had drawn only 265 people to a hall that, on an earlier tour by British journalist Malcolm Muggeridge, had been filled with about 1,000.

There was another problem, Krygier said: "the drinking problem." According to Luna Wolf, who had become his part-time secretary in late 1953, Farrell had for the most part been on the wagon until he got back together with Dorothy. "But then when he remarried her," she said, "they had parties, and...he would drink." Krygier told Josselson:

> Well, it was on and off. At some stages, Jim proclaimed his decision to stay on the wagon, and did, for a day or so. On other occasions, he had a few beers, but kept it down pretty well. On some, one or two, he really did have a few drinks, but managed to deliver his speech, so that I don't know how many people knew what I did. However, in one case, the fact [is] that [after] he had had a few bottles of beer (and Australian beer is twice as strong, and the bottles twice as big as in America) he became more than usually sensitive about some remarks about the United States, and offended quite a few people at a private gathering. He then apologised profusely, and improved the general impression, but the apologies didn't work with some guests.

And yet, he added, "Jim is a great guy, and he really tried his best. He worked very hard, he accepted every commitment and engagement; he went out of his way to help other people, to help everybody who called on him, and for friendliness he was really without equal."

Farrell himself apparently believed his visit was successful. "My lectures have all gone well," he wrote Henle on May 12, "and the one yesterday at the University of Sydney was exceptionally well received by the students."

Peter Coleman, a future editor of *Quadrant*, one of the congress's distinguished magazines, "had expected a great deal" from Farrell's visit, as he would later recall in a memoir. He had read the recently published *French Girls Are Vicious* and especially liked the story, "They Ain't the Men They Used to Be," which, Coleman observed, "is about an old baseball fan who, now that the great contests are over, has nothing more to live for—but at another level it is also an autobiographical comment on anyone who puts his faith in creeds like Stalinism or Trotskyism."

Coleman met Farrell at a sparsely-attended reception in Canberra. "A heavy-set, broad-chested Irish-American," the Australian would remember, "he was a drunk and a womanizer (although he had recently remarried his divorced first wife)." Krygier, accompanying the visitor, "would promptly quaff the drinks that the waiter kept pouring for Farrell," hoping in this way to keep him from "becoming drunk, aggressive and a militantly patriotic Americanizer. It did not always succeed."

That night, Farrell addressed a tiny audience on the subject of American literary realism. "He came most to life," Coleman would recall, "when he talked about a novel that I had not heard of: Harold Frederic's *The Damnation of Theron Ware*, about a small-town Protestant minister who destroys himself in his doomed attempts to cope with modernity." It seemed that Farrell "was really talking about himself, an Irish boy from the south side of Chicago, and his inability to cope with the intellectual currents of his time."

Farrell's Australian tour was a flop, Coleman judged. "Old enemies, *the frightened philistines* of the left, boycotted him and the conservatives had little interest in him in the first place. But part of the problem was Farrell's moodiness—aggressive, uncertain, alcoholic. He was a lost soul." When he left Australia near the end of May, he was "depressed by his own performance and by the anti-Americanism that seemed a datum among the *bien pensants.*"

Farrell wrote from Sydney about the anti-Americanism he was encountering, in a letter to the editor of *Quest*, the magazine sponsored by the Indian Committee for Cultural Freedom:

> One of the hopes which many of us entertained was that common bonds of feeling would exist between the people of America and other lands. This hope appears to be fading. The American people, in increasing numbers, are becoming disillusioned, and even angry.... If the disillusionment deepens, the consequences on American foreign policy will be felt. And if this happens, I wonder if our anti-American friends will be satisfied. Is this what they want? Briefly, do they want the American people to turn isolationist? Because this can happen.

Farrell continued on to Singapore, staying overnight, and thence to India, where he met with writers in Bombay, interviewed Prime Minister Jawaharlal Nehru twice (in Bombay and New Delhi), and again encountered anti-Americanism—as well as much else. "I can perhaps never forget the poverty I saw," he would later write, "the people sleeping almost like flies in the streets of Bombay, some because of the heat, but others because they were homeless." Then, it was on to Karachi, Beirut and Tel Aviv—but not without incident.

Along the way, during a stopover in Istanbul on June 24, after what he later admitted was "too much beer," he wrote and dispatched a ranting letter to the *Chicago Tribune*, a newspaper notorious for the isolationist and reactionary outlook of its late owner, Colonel Robert R. McCormick. In his missive Farrell boozily declared:

> The American people must know this. [W]e will take not one word of insult, not one expression of hatred, and we will no longer give one cent or one drop of blood of our boys, our sons, unless it is in a partnership of freedom. And if we cannot achieve that, then we should retire to our own shores, and if necessary fight it out to the death with communism. But the time has come, and more than come, when we honest Americans, myself [*sic*] who is anti-*Chicago Daily Tribune*, have taken enough, given enough, and have had enough of the blood of our boys spilled on foreign soil. From here on in, we should have a truly honest partnership in freedom, or else go it alone.

When word of what Farrell had done reached Diana Trilling, Sidney Hook and other members of the American Committee for Cultural Freedom, and they read the letter, they were appalled by its intellectual crudity, its barroom bathos and bombast, and by the irresponsibility of their chairman in having it published—and in the *Chicago Tribune*, of all places! With the letter's publication, Mrs. Trilling would later tell the *New York Times*, Farrell's usefulness to the American committee came to an end. Members of the committee decided to seek Farrell's resignation at their next meeting, to be held after Labor Day.

Meanwhile, Farrell was in Israel, where instead of anti-Americanism he found a brave and free people, committed to building and defending their young democracy. In a June 25 letter to Henle—after irately complaining about the insufficient assistance he was receiving from officials in U.S. embassies—Farrell repeatedly went into sentimental raptures about the Israeli people. "The Israeli are something to be proud of—not simply because they are Jews—but because they are giving the finest example of democracy the world has ever seen, Jim. They'll win, or die fighting in the greatest exhibition of courage and gallantry the world has ever seen....The Jews, Jim, of Israel are the advance guard of honor, dignity and freedom. And we must stand with them. *We must not let them down.*"

While he was in Israel in July, Farrell received some bad news from home: Dorothy, some five months pregnant and staying in

Chicago, had suffered a miscarriage. "It made us both sad and disappointed," Farrell later wrote, "but it's life, and one must accept the dictates of biology."

He departed Israel for home in early August, making a stopover in Paris. There he talked with Michael Josselson, the executive director of the Congress for Cultural Freedom. Farrell's encounters with anti-Americanism, especially in Asia, had left him uncertain about the best approach for the congress and its affiliates to take there, but had also convinced him that the staunch anti-Communism he and others on the American Committee for Cultural Freedom had advocated was inadequate. Josselson and the congress's Paris office, Farrell now believed, at least recognized the complexity of the situation.

He landed at Idlewild Airport in New York on August 9, and before long went on to Chicago to comfort his wife and bring her back to New York.

While Farrell had been abroad, the distress his fellow members of the American Committee for Cultural Freedom felt at his *Chicago Tribune* letter was probably not apparent to him (though it is possible the subject came up in his conversation with Josselson). Once back home, he seems to have gotten wind of their dismay and of their plans to seek his resignation.

Farrell, who would soon report to Henle that he had quit drinking again, knew he had been "a damned fool" to fall off the wagon. He would tell the *New York Times* that his letter was "indefensible" and did not represent his true views. "I shouldn't make a mistake like that at my age, but I presume I'll never live it down." Yet he showed no remorse about the embarrassment his letter had caused to the other members of the committee and to the cause they all served. It was merely *his* "mistake."

Someone less self-centered, feeling some shame at his misbehavior, might simply have apologized to his fellow committee members, told them what he had learned and concluded from his travels, and quietly tendered his resignation. But Farrell could not do that. One suspects that it would have made him feel less than equal to the others on the committee.

Moreover, as a result of the anti-American sentiments he had encountered abroad, he was now convinced (when sober) that it was the committee itself that was misguided, that the Paris office was right to object to its uncompromising anti-Communist stance. He did not doubt the purity of his intentions. He had never been much inclined to question his own motives or to recognize in them the tinge of self-interest. He was utterly sincere, but unusually naive. And so, with a conscience undoubtedly clear, he decided to beat the committee to the punch and cast his resignation as a matter of lofty principle—by his action deliberately weakening the committee of which he was chairman in its ongoing struggle with Josselson and the congress's Paris office.

Late in the evening of August 27, Farrell sent a two-sentence telegram of resignation to the American committee and phoned the *New York Times* with the news. *Times* reporter Max Frankel then called Diana Trilling at her summer place in Connecticut. She promised to look into the matter the next afternoon and get back to the *Times*, which she did. By then Farrell had written a two-page letter to Norman Jacobs, the committee's executive director, explaining his decision.

Besides saying he needed to give more time to his work and personal affairs, he cited a number of differences with the committee over policy. Most of these were manifestly spurious. He charged that the American committee had been unable "to sink our roots deeply into American life, and to make ourselves a national organization with chapters in many key regions of the country." Mrs. Trilling told *Times* reporter Peter Kihss that the committee's executive board had decided against seeking a mass membership. (And at the time, according to Hook, Farrell himself "had fervently concurred" with that decision.) Farrell said the committee's major effort on the domestic front should be to improve "the cultural climate" in the face of "growing apathy and complacency," and asserted that the committee had not done enough to fight censorship, "a perennial problem" and "one of our big issues." Mrs. Trilling commented that the committee had successfully contested many civil liberties cases and had frequently spoken out against censorship.

Only with respect to the relationship between the American committee and the congress's Paris office—an issue on which Mrs. Trilling deemed it "senseless" to comment to the *Times*—did Farrell's remarks seem at all pertinent. "I led the struggle against the Paris office," he asserted. "But my direct experiences during my recent travels have convinced me that I was wrong, and that others on the Committee were wrong. I cannot say with definiteness that the Paris office is always sound, but, especially in Asia, they are dealing with problems which are extremely difficult. The views which many of us have held on anti-Communism are simply irrelevant to the Asians." They are convinced that Americans have "a rigid, hysterical, one-track fear of Communism," he said, and many Asians have concluded that their best course is "to flirt with Communism, insult us and perhaps get more money out of us. This might make many Americans indignant, and at times makes me indignant. At the same time, we are concerned with the soul of a continent, and we must find a new approach or retreat. We must find new ways of dealing with the Asians, especially with the Indians."

Farrell's newfound position—apparently shared already by some committee members—was hardly grounds for resignation. By the same token, neither was it, in itself, cause for Mrs. Trilling and her colleagues to become distressed. What really bothered them (besides his earlier *Chicago Tribune* pratfall) was the fact that he had gone to the press with his resignation.

Why had Farrell phoned the *Times*? He may have acted on impulse. He often did, and that might explain why his letter of resignation was written the day after he sent his telegram, and why he phoned so late, making it unlikely the story would appear in the next day's paper. He also may have been motivated partly by a desire for revenge, seeking to publicly embarrass the committee and those who wanted to oust him because of his trivial *Chicago Tribune* "mistake." And finally, now that he considered Josselson and Paris right, or at least more right than the committee, he apparently thought that by acting as he did he would help Paris to prevail. Thus, that evening of the 27th, after talking with the *Times*, he sent a telegram to Josselson. It read:

ISSUED STATEMENTS NEW YORK TIMES RESIGNING AMERICAN COMMITTEE DEFENDING YOU IN TOTAL ACCORD WITH YOU ACTION FAIT ACCOMPLI HAVE BROKEN UP AMERICAN COMMITTEE YOUR ADVANTAGE REGARDS TAKE CARE OF YOUR HEALTH HAVE KEPT MY WORD LOVE=JIM FARRELL.

In a letter to Josselson a few days later, Farrell explained: "I don't know whether or not you'll agree with the way in which I did it, but I have been thinking about it for a long time, and once I made up my mind, I decided to act quickly and resign. I did not have the taste nor the time to have to resign after making a long fight on this issue. Fights like this are time-consuming and useless." As for the *Chicago Tribune* letter, Farrell told him not to "worry too much about [it]. I have explained it, and it does not bother anybody but the Committee, and it bothers them for polemical reasons."

But Josselson soon wrote back saying that while he had no quarrel with his letter of resignation, which was in accord with the views Farrell expressed in Paris, "permit me to say in all friendship that I think you made a mistake in making the letter available to the press.... What this amounts to now is a washing of the Committee's dirty linen in public and this can only harm us." He urged him to make no further public statements.

Chapter Seventeen
"Dark Hours"

H OME AGAIN AND FREE of further obligation to the organized defenders of cultural freedom, Farrell was hard at work on a journalistic volume unsought by Vanguard or anyone else—a book about Israel, based on his six-week visit there. He felt compelled to write it. But, with his monthly payments from New American Library soon to cease, he also felt an urgent need to earn more money.

Casting about for possible sources of income, he imagined that he might have "a second future in writing about baseball," even though *Sports Illustrated's* enthusiasm for his contributions had waned as the magazine established itself. He asked Evelyn Shrifte and Vanguard to free him from his contract sufficiently to let him do two books—a collection of his baseball writings and a novel about the Chicago Black Sox—for A. S. Barnes, a publisher of sports books.

He was not ready, Farrell told Henle, to resume work on "Invisible Swords" (or, "The Invisible Sword," as he also called it). He had "hit a block" and needed more "distance," but was sure the novel would come in time; perhaps he would have it for Vanguard by the end of 1957. In the meantime, he wondered if he should do a fourth Bernard Carr volume—an idea that Henle and Shrifte quickly squelched. Advancing a counter-suggestion (and putting aside his own previously expressed reservations), Henle proposed that he turn to his Paris novel. Farrell responded by writing more than one hundred pages, but then reported that the novel was "not in good shape."

Shrifte and Vanguard—apparently without a word of reproach to Farrell about his failure thus far to deliver even one novel in compliance with their three-novel contract—agreed to allow him to do the two sports books for Barnes. "I am most grateful to you and Evie

357

for letting me do this," he told Henle. "The decision concerning it, on my part, is neither a matter of choice or wish, but of necessity. I'm in a hole, and if I do not get out of it, I can't meet my obligations, pay my rent, eat and work with any peace of mind." He then pushed for an immediate decision by Vanguard on publishing the Israel book; if Vanguard was not interested (and it proved to be not especially), he asked to be allowed to publish it elsewhere (giving Vanguard 15 percent of any advance and all royalties). "I believe that this is fair, and along with the Barnes deal, would give me the basis on which to work next year."

Farrell was making other efforts that he hoped would pay off. He was writing newspaper editorials for the Alburn Bureau, a Minneapolis-based operation that supplied editorials to small-town newspapers. Run by a journalist named Leo Sonderegger, the Alburn Bureau paid Farrell very little, but he had hopes of syndication. He also intended to take Henle's long-standing advice and, after the Israel book was finished, do some commercial lecturing.

All in all, Farrell was now working some sixteen hours a day, he told Henle. "And I am happy at it. Curiously, Jim, I have found great happiness with Dorothy, and a home, and I have attained a greater discipline than I ever did." The situation was perhaps less satisfying to his wife, however. Farrell would work through the night, not going to bed until six or seven in the morning—and Dorothy would usually stay up with him. Though he realized that this "change in my life is not good for her," he said he found "that I work better this way."

Despite the forbearance and even compassion shown toward him by Shrifte and Vanguard, Farrell continued to feel neglected. Thus in the letter to Henle that autumn in which he thanked him and Shrifte for letting him do the Barnes books, he felt obliged to add this postscript:

> I want to be frank. I do feel—rightly or wrongly—that while the affection felt for me remains at Vanguard, I am not considered any more to be such an asset. I mean in financial terms. Secondly, and whether or not I am right or wrong, that by following my own inner impulse, I am not writing what is considered as good as my early work. This may be so. I can't repeat it. I'm not a pole vaulter. But I feel that I have a hell of a lot which I want to say, including more fiction. Concerning my writing, I always think this—I can't fail, I can only find a temporary or fixed limitation, and if I do, then, I have to hit a new line which must come from inner impulse.

Farrell recognized the difficult situation in which he now found himself, but recognition alone could not alter it. He seems to have craved limitless reassurance and support from Vanguard, an illusory comfort that Henle and Shrifte could not provide.

And so his discontent grew. Vanguard had let him contract with New American Library for an original paperback collection of short stories; in March 1957 he complained to Henle about the "delay" by Vanguard in deciding whether to publish the book in hardcover. The sooner a decision was made, he believed, the sooner the book could be published and the sooner it would start bringing in money for him. Vanguard did decide to publish *A Dangerous Woman and Other Stories*, provided that the royalties were applied to Farrell's debt to Vanguard. "This isn't as big a concession as it sounds," Henle noted, "as we can't hope to sell many copies of a hard-bound collection of short stories (at a price of $3.50 or so) against the competition of a paperbound edition." (The hardcover would be published in September; over the next three months fewer than a thousand copies would be sold.)

Farrell welcomed the decision to publish the book and was willing to make the concession—but Vanguard's insistence upon it provoked a 2,500-word eruption of resentment. "Jim," he wrote to Henle, "this is my honest feeling: I feel and have come to believe that Vanguard—not you—is more interested in getting back the unearned advances I have received from them, than they are in my future as a writer. Had Vanguard and NAL stood by me one more year"—meaning, apparently, had they given him one more annual combined infusion of $15,000—"I should not have had to do all the work I am now doing, and I should have finished my novel. But that's that, and it is not for me to tell Vanguard how to run its business." He then reiterated his complaints about indecision and delay, but added some heartfelt words to Henle personally:

> There is really nothing more to say, except to add that as long as I live, I'll always be grateful for your friendship and the many kinds of help you have given me in my career. I want you to know, Jim, that in a literary, personal and psychological sense, you have meant perhaps more to me than any other human being in the world. However, you are no longer Vanguard, and while Evie is a lovely person, Vanguard functions on a different basis....
>
> When you were the head of Vanguard, things were different. I always knew where I was. I always received prompt and direct answers, and I had the feeling that we were working for the long

run, and if I seriously and deeply wanted a book published, you would publish it.... Now, more concern is felt for the immediate reaction of reviewers for whom I have contempt than for my own feelings. There is no feeling of abuse or resentment here. Rather, I feel resigned, and I expect only inefficiency, delay and little help from Vanguard in the future.

After receiving this lengthy communication the next day, Henle dashed off a quick note, promising a more detailed response later: "The big mistake," he said, "was to draw so much money ahead and live on the future instead of your current earnings."* One week later, Henle gave his detailed—and quietly devastating—analysis:

> As I wrote to you, I regret terribly that matters haven't worked out as we both—and as Evelyn—would have wanted them to. This was partly, as I said, my responsibility. Because of this I think I am more upset than anyone else at Vanguard over the financial aspect, for I was the prime-mover here in what has proved to be an unfortunate contract. For I'm sure you won't forget that you agreed to deliver the manuscripts of three novels, and to date Vanguard hasn't received one. Certainly any visitor from Mars, told the bare facts of the contract, of the sums advanced, of the manuscripts not delivered, would come to the conclusion that, no matter what queries hadn't been answered promptly, Vanguard had treated you pretty g.d. well, especially as there has never been—until this moment—any allusion to the non-delivery of the manuscripts.
>
> Don't you think the situation would have been different if you had remained at home one or two of those summers? To be sure you continued to work while you were traveling, but it wasn't concentrated work of the type you put into your earlier novels....
>
> And...I think you know Vanguard has lost substantial sums on every title by you it has issued in recent years—this began while it was still under my control. No one said anything about this to you— just as we didn't bother you about the promised manuscripts—and Vanguard was perfectly willing to accept this situation because it (and this emphatically includes Evelyn) believed in you and your work.

---

*In a postscript added after he'd read Farrell's letter more thoroughly, Henle told him that he was "deeply moved by your expressions of affection. Nothing will ever alter the high opinion I hold of you and of your work. I've never met a man fairer in *every* way (including political argument, where few persons are fair)—you are devoted to the truth and have sought for it ever since I've known you (and before). And I'll never forget the way you wore out shoe leather—when you were living on $10 or $15 a week—trying to do and *doing* favors for others."

As a matter of fact, I think Evelyn has dealt with you not only fairly but with extreme generosity and always with affection for the worker and respect for the work. Damned if I know what else she could have done except to have answered some queries more promptly.

His grievances thus put in adult perspective, Farrell now backed off, expressing his appreciation of Henle's long letter and saying that "right or wrong, fairness or unfairness, do not always reside on one side or another. Also, I don't see the point of digging up again what has already happened; I'd rather look ahead."

Henle replied that he was "enormously pleased" by that response. "The word," he said, "is full steam ahead!"

——➤·◦·◄——

FARRELL FINISHED *MY BASEBALL DIARY* in May 1957; it was published six months later. The collection of writings (both fictional and nonfictional, many previously published) charmingly evokes the sport as it was when the author and organized baseball were young. He believed the nostalgic volume would prove popular and predicted that ten thousand copies would be sold.

That volume written—and with his agent, Sterling Lord, looking for a publisher for the Israel book—Farrell turned his attention to the second sports book for Barnes, the novel about the Black Sox. When it was done, he told Henle, he hoped to resume work on "Invisible Swords" and finish that novel for Vanguard by the end of the following year, 1958. But the Black Sox novel, unlike *The Face of Time*, did not "write itself." After reading his first, rough draft in the fall, John Lowell Pratt, president of Barnes, expressed disappointment. Henle, to whom Farrell had also shown the draft, said the novel's world seemed two-dimensional.

Farrell recognized that the book still needed much work. "I am inventing almost all of my characters," he had explained to Henle, "and it takes me more time to get into them than it did with the *Lonigan* and O'Neill books.... But I think I'll get it.... I am going ahead, daily, not fearing to be dull, laying it out. We'll see what I can do. Jim, you can only fail, and I do get some things."

Further discouragement arrived unexpectedly in November when, shortly after publication of *My Baseball Diary*, Farrell learned that he had inadvertently libeled a retired American League umpire. He had written that the man "was found broke and dead in a cheap hotel,"

361

but it transpired that he was alive and a respectable citizen of Chicago. It was a different umpire who had met the sad end described in the book.

Farrell's memory was so prodigious that he was prone to rely on it excessively, habitually dispensing with the research (or, when functioning as a journalist, the note-taking) that a conscientious writer less gifted in recall would do routinely. As a result, he and Barnes were now threatened with a lawsuit.

Barnes halted distribution of the book and prepared an erratum notice to be inserted in stores' existing copies. Sales of *My Baseball Diary* would not exceed the 2,100 sold to bookstores in advance of publication (and that figure included a few hundred destined to be returned to Barnes). The threat of a lawsuit was to hang over Farrell and the publishing company for months. Though the retired umpire would file a suit seeking $250,000 in damages, in the end he decided not to press the case. Quite possibly he discovered that neither the Barnes firm nor Farrell was in financial shape to make the suit worthwhile. In December 1957 it was reported that a creditors' committee was considering plans for "the orderly liquidation of the current liabilities" of Barnes; three months later, the news would appear that Pratt had sold the controlling stock of the company to Thomas Yoseloff Inc., and that Yoseloff was now chairman of the board of directors, with Pratt staying on as president. Despite Farrell's careless libel and the change in ownership, the firm still wanted the Black Sox novel.

Meanwhile the quest for a publisher for his Israel book had not gone well. Farrell's artless impressions of the people of the young Jewish state held little appeal for commercial publishers. However, Raphael Patai, a biblical anthropologist who was director of research for the Theodor Herzl Foundation, was interested. In February he met Farrell and Dorothy for lunch. Patai also brought along his estranged wife, whom he was trying to win back. An attractive, intelligent and talented woman of about forty, Irene Patai taught English in a public school on Long Island. She had published a well-received first novel two years before, and she much admired Farrell's work. He was taken with her right away. More important for Farrell's immediate purpose, though, was Raphael Patai's eagerness for the foundation to publish his book. Farrell's sympathetic work, focusing on Israel's treatment of immigrants, would appear in the fall under the title, *It Has Come to Pass*. It received a few favorable reviews in the *Herald Tribune* and elsewhere, but caused little stir.

In May, Farrell—upset because he believed that Barnes, on the excuse of the threatened libel suit, was withholding royalties (a trifling sum) due him from *My Baseball Diary*, as well as his half of $5,000 Barnes received from the advance sale to Pocket Books of reprint rights to the Black Sox novel—delivered the final installment of the second draft of the novel. But Pratt still didn't like much of what he read; he proposed a meeting.

"Naturally, I am prepared to discuss the novel and to fulfill the contract," Farrell responded, "but my heart is not in this work, and I shall do it to keep my word and as a matter of honor. I do think that in terms of my attitude, the best thing all around would be for you and Mr. Yoseloff to give me, through Sterling, a chance to get another publisher to buy the contract."

After more letters back and forth, Farrell and Barnes were at an impasse. Farrell asked Vanguard to take over the Black Sox novel—but then to set it aside for a while because he felt he "should come out next with a more important novel." Then he resumed work on "Invisible Swords."

"I appeal to you to give yourself a chance on this novel [*Invisible Swords*]," Henle urged him in late July, having received the first eighty-two pages of his Paris novel from him only about five weeks before. "You certainly won't be giving yourself a chance if you work on two or three major projects at the same time. You have to *live* with these persons...."

———➤◦◀———

DOROTHY VISITED HER AILING mother in Chicago that August. She also did some research there for Farrell, gathering material, it seems, for a piece about baseball in Milwaukee for *Holiday* magazine. Late in the month she interviewed his uncle Tom Daly about old minor league baseball teams in that Wisconsin city. Farrell intended to travel to Milwaukee a few weeks later, and she was to join him. But their plans were shattered by a discovery that Farrell made back in their New York apartment.

While Dorothy was away, Farrell later testified, he came upon a hidden trove of "hundreds of love letters," some of them recent, written to her by jazz violinist Hezekiah "Stuff" Smith. "The love letters reflect a continuing two-way correspondence and numerous secret visits between my wife and her lover, throughout the period of our remarriage," Farrell stated. "The addresses on the envelopes reveal that [Dorothy] made use of a number of secret addresses and P.O. Box numbers to conceal this correspondence." With the letters, according to Farrell, was an issue of *Jet* magazine, dated January 8, 1953, containing a picture of Dorothy and Smith, along with this statement: "Smith's present wife is Dorothy Butler Farrell, divorced wife of famed novelist James T. (Studs Lonigan) Farrell, whom he married 15 years ago following a meeting at Chicago's old three Deuces night club."

Dorothy, interviewed many years later, said she was never married to Smith, but acknowledged having had an affair with him when she was separated and divorced from Farrell. "I did have an affair with him. So what?.... When I went back with James, that was long over." Smith did continue to write to her, she acknowledged, and she did have her own post office box.

Even supposing that Dorothy was carrying on an extramarital affair, Farrell was hardly in a position to object. He had not been a model of marital fidelity himself. As recently as his 1956 world tour, his conduct had prompted independent observers such as Peter Coleman to characterize him as a "womanizer." Sidney Hook, who had been with Farrell in Europe several times, would write, some years after the novelist's death, that when Farrell had too much to drink "he would chase any skirt in sight."

Still, Farrell felt betrayed. What seems to have bothered him most was his belief that Dorothy was "lavishing vast sums of money" on Smith, while he was desperately struggling to earn enough for them to live in relative comfort and for him to meet his other obligations and to write as he wished.

Farrell had ample reason to be concerned about money. Without the regular payments from Vanguard and New American Library, his income had plummeted. In subsequent legal documents, based on his tax returns, he would report that his net income had gone from $14,158 in 1956 to $5,943 in 1957 and $4,189 in 1958. But Dorothy had some money of her own. After selling a house she owned in Chicago for $25,000 in 1957, she received monthly mortgage payments. Her brother-in-law, a wealthy banker in Chicago, handled the money for her and Farrell was unable to touch it. This may have bothered him, Dorothy suggested. If so, it could only have intensified his rage at her alleged gifts to Smith of money that he had earned.

Whether or not Dorothy was relatively innocent in all this, Farrell leapt to the conclusion that she was guilty. After discovering her hidden letters, he called her up in Chicago. Then, as he later testified (in connection with an alimony suit Dorothy brought), he "confronted her" with them. "She gave me no explanation or justification for her conduct." Dorothy, however, said long afterward that he "never did anything of the sort" in his phone call. But both were in agreement that he told her not to come back to their apartment, that she was no longer welcome, and that he was changing the locks.

"I nearly went crazy," she remembered. "I yelled, I yelled."

She borrowed some money from her sister and took a plane to New York. On September 6, a Saturday, she showed up at the door of what had been their home at 252 West 85th Street. The locks had indeed been changed. "I rang the bell," she said. "He finally came to the door." And then, as she entered, her husband did something that she never would have expected of him. "He picked me up and threw me into the hall.... I was mad as hell. I was furious. I was distraught." She went to a friend's place on West End Avenue and stayed there. On Tuesday she returned to the apartment with a locksmith and got in. Farrell was not there; after borrowing some money from Henle, he had gone to Milwaukee.

"Your loan helps me much," he wrote Henle from Wisconsin. "Luna was wonderful. Ria was very good. One or two others."

Before he left, Luna Wolf, his secretary, or Ria Simon, his lawyer—or perhaps both—evidently told him the seemingly fantastic story that they had come to believe in 1956: that Dorothy had feigned pregnancy so she could take the money supposedly going to her doctor and send it instead to Smith. Once, in the Farrells' apartment, Luna Wolf said, when the writer was on his extensive trip abroad for the Congress for Cultural Freedom and Dorothy was not around, the elderly black woman who did cleaning for them had told her: "It's pillows. She is not pregnant. You wait, just before Jim comes back from that trip, she's going to lose the baby." The subsequent miscarriage—which, it should be emphasized, Dorothy decades later insisted was genuine and occurred in Henrotin Hospital on Chicago's Near North Side—persuaded Luna Wolf and Ria Simon that what the cleaning woman had said was true. They had debated whether to tell Farrell on his return, but decided to say nothing. Now, two years later, they told him.

"Dorothy was playing me and at least half insincere from the beginning" of their remarriage, he told his brother Jack. "We're checking the pregnancy story—my live hypothesis is that it was false."

Farrell also told Jack of a "wholesome girl" he now loved. Her name, though he did not divulge it, was Irene Patai. After they first met in February, she recalled, he then "kind of latched onto me," beginning right away by writing to her, and not letting up. "At first, it was really very exciting. Here was this famous author whose work I just devoured, and he was so interested in me."

When Farrell returned to New York, he stayed with her brother, a dentist, for some days, then checked into a hotel at 42nd Street and Lexington Avenue. Not long thereafter, he signed a one-year lease on a large, "bright and cheerful" one-room apartment at the Beaux Arts Hotel, 310 East 44th Street, near the United Nations. The hotel was no longer in the luxury class, but the apartment wasn't cheap. It would be home for him for some years to come. From there in mid-October, he wrote Henle of his conviction that from the time they first got back together, Dorothy "was playing a double game, and but for her, I'd still be financially solvent and more advanced in my career....As for the 1956 stillborn baby, it seems quite definitely to have been a phony. When I questioned her about it in her lawyer's office, she finally asked, with insolence, 'So what.'"

⸺≫-◦-≪⸻

OCTOBER *21, 1958:* THE DATE would come to be charged in Farrell's mind with almost as much significance as March 16, 1927, that day more than three decades earlier when he had melodramatically vowed he would be a writer, accepting only the constraints of "honor, truth, sincerity, honesty."

It was a vow he had single-mindedly kept over the decades, as though he had given the God in Whom he did not believe his solemn word. Thus, in the midst of detailing his financial woes in 1955, he had explained that he was "morally committed to myself to completing" his "life work"—all his many novels and stories written and yet to be written. But ever since *The Face of Time*, which he considered his best book but which had not sold well, he had found it exceedingly difficult to make any progress.

The prevailing opinion was that the best work of "the author of *Studs Lonigan*" had been written long ago. "My past, and *Studs* most especially killed *The Face of Time*," he had told Henle in April, adding that he was still trying "to figure out how I can assassinate 'the author of *Studs*.'" But in his post-*Face* novelistic efforts he had been floundering. His literary problems had been compounded by his financial ones. His obligation to Vanguard remained unfulfilled. His experience with Barnes had not worked out well. And, to add to his woes, his marriage, which had given him such happiness, had suddenly exploded.

All these torments might have led him, Job-like, to question his continuing "moral commitment." After all, he had made good on his original vow: he had become a writer. And not only that, he had produced a work generally recognized as a classic, as well as many other novels, some of them—those in the O'Neill-O'Flaherty series—perhaps even more powerful. Surely he had done enough to win release from his self-imposed obligation. But in permanent thrall to a romantic conception of the writer, he couldn't even entertain the thought of casting off his burdens that way.

Instead, in the early morning hours of October 21, 1958, while he was at work on a novel he had started after the break with Dorothy, "The Story of a Marriage" (which was based on theirs), Farrell began to experience a rebirth—or more accurately, the fantasy of a rebirth—in which all the literary difficulties he had experienced in recent months and years, all the erratic jumping from one prospective novel to another, all his thwarted efforts were washed away. In their place would come what he called "The Universe of Time" (or, alternatively, "A Universe of Time"), a series of novels so massive, so grand, so imposing that no serious publisher or editor could do anything but fall back in awe, then bow in reverence. "The Story of a Marriage" would inaugurate the series.

Yoseloff, chairman of the board at Barnes, had decided that the firm would have no more to do with the Black Sox novel or its author, and so Farrell no longer needed Vanguard (which had yet to give him a reply to his June request) to buy out the contract for the novel. "Since Yoseloff doesn't want it," he told Sterling Lord, "we don't have to sell it. I want to do other work, and come naturally to the baseball novel in a let up. My new series is major work—the biggest literary creation of my career.

"Vanguard has delayed on deciding on my request for help when it looked as if I needed money to defend myself," he continued. "I can chance it and not rush. I've not broken the contract on the baseball novel. But I don't want to force myself on fiction. And other work is more important." The fact that his lectures were "going very well" undoubtedly fortified him in this stance. Between early November and mid-April, he expected to earn between $3,500 and $4,000 from his speaking engagements.

Farrell gave Henle a chunk of his first draft of "The Story of a Marriage," telling him that the series (whose name, if it had yet occurred to him, he did not divulge) would run to three or four volumes. In response, Henle told him that what he read interested him "enormously," but he wondered if anyone who didn't know Farrell would have the same reaction.

Then, on November 13, in two unsent letters to Henle, Farrell tried to explain in full his grandiose vision as it had thus far evolved:

> The canvas on this work is more vast than any I have ever thought of, and the series will run from 1928 to the present period. As I write, I'll write away from autobiography and into fiction, invention, and I'll use the 'I' in draft one, experimentally. I'll have the 'I' talk of what other characters think. I'm evolving my own method for this work. In the first draft, I am using the name Danny O'Neill etc., but I'll most likely decide to change the names and I might even invent a city which will still be Chicago. *The Story of a Marriage* has been dropped [as a title]. The title for the whole series is now, tentatively, *The Universe of Time*. People, characters living in our segment of time, and time, the characters, the flow of time, this will be part of the whole meaning of the work. The[re] will be from three to five books, or possibly seven. Then again, I may condense it into one or two volumes. I'm allowing myself to be discursive, and letting the book follow the flow of the unconscious. Also I'm working into a treatment of time—which has been so significant as a matter of feeling etc. in my work. The evolving concept is Proustian, and in a sense, this is my [*Á la recherche du temps perdu*].

He figured that the project—"my major literary effort, the biggest one of my whole career"—would take six to ten years. "The books will be panoramic, and will take in many environments, and a swarm of characters." The first volume, his novel-in-progress based on his marriage to Dorothy, would end on the eve of the couple's departure for Paris, or else would include their year in Paris—he hadn't made up his mind.

But he soon decided that he had to cut himself free from Vanguard. In two unsent letters to Henle the next day, November 14, he tried to explain that "I need a new start with a new publisher and that Vanguard Press will not be able to handle my new series of books, *A Universe of Time*, and my other unpublished writings or writings to come in the way I think absolutely necessary if I am to survive and not kill myself with overwork."

It bothered him that he was written about these days as if all his accomplishments were in the past—as if no more was expected of him, as if his life as a writer were effectively over. He had to overcome this perception if he was "to escape from my present morass." Although he had been "indifferent to publicity" in the past, and had never given "two hoots in hell for prizes or immediate recognition," he now realized that the publishing world had changed. "Vanguard cannot publish all that I want published, and do what I now consider to be necessary." He needed a new publisher, he said, one able to mount a major publicity campaign that would bring him the Nobel Prize for Literature. "I have now decided that with my new series, I am going after the Nobel Prize and I want it."

The publicity campaign he envisioned would have to prepare critics and the public for his new series; help him "to reactivate the influence I can exert whenever I please to in the literary world" and emphasize "my work as a whole as a lifetime project which will now be completed, and when completed, it will constitute the most massive fictional recreation of our times that anyone has ever attempted and completed."

His decision to seek another publisher, Farrell said in one of his unsent letters, "is a decision I have made alone here in my room, and I have consulted no one in reaching it, not even Irene. I haven't approached any publishers nor has Sterling, and I do not know if I can, at the present time, get the contract I want. However, I want to try."

<hr/>

ALTHOUGH FARRELL TOLD HIMSELF that he wanted to leave Vanguard, he apparently was not entirely sure. He didn't tell Henle or Vanguard about it for three weeks. And his "final decision" was precipitated by the offer Vanguard made in response to a proposal that Sterling Lord had put forward on his behalf. Lord's proposal: that Vanguard give Farrell a $25,000 advance, spread over five years, for novels in his new "Universe of Time" series.

On Monday, December 1, Henle—who had warned Farrell in October that if Vanguard gave him an advance, it would be for the Black Sox novel—wrote to Lord with Vanguard's response. "What you have in mind," he said to Farrell's agent, "is that Vanguard advance further money to obtain novels on which it already has made a very substantial advance and to which it has every legal and moral claim. This, however, does not meet Jim's present situation, and we want to assist all we can." Henle spelled out the firm's offer: Vanguard, in essence, would advance Farrell $3,000 a year for two years against completed manuscripts and future earnings of his previously published books. "The first manuscript to be delivered would be a properly revised Black Sox novel." And if Farrell failed to deliver it in "publishable" form during the first year, he would not get the second $3,000 advance. In view of "all the circumstances," Henle considered this "an exceedingly fair arrangement."

Farrell was incensed by both the letter and the offer, which seemed dismissive of his towering vision of his future as an artist. On Thursday, December 4, he wrote five letters to Henle expressing his outrage, though without mailing any of them. "I should be angry with and deeply offended by you and by Vanguard Press. I am not," he insisted. But "a farce is being carried on at my expense, the expense of my peace of mind, my health, my career, and my creative life. All perspective has been lost, and I do not want this business to go on or else it will destroy something I have always prized most highly—our friendship." Evelyn Shrifte was "a very nice person" and her brother was "a fine fellow," but they had nothing to tell him about writing or what book he should write. He wanted to be released from Vanguard. And if Vanguard did not release him he would "fight and fight bitterly, determinedly, and to the very end."

Farrell had not abandoned Vanguard when Henle was having financial difficulties in 1939 or when Henle sold the firm in 1952. "But now I am in trouble," he observed:

> I am and I have been risking my health for months in my effort to work. I have lost weight and I continue to lose weight. Stripped, I now weigh less than 160 pounds. I have worked for twenty four and forty eight hour stretches with no sleep or with only a few hours sleep, working on the first volume of my new series of books. And Vanguard Press talks of moral and legal rights, hurts my pride with insulting terms, proves it has neither faith nor trust in me, and wants to put me under conditions that will make it impossible for me to earn my living next year, not to speak of ignoring the fact that I have begun a big book. I want to and I will write the books I plan in the series called *A Universe of Time*. And Vanguard Press, represented by Jim Henle, the man who published *Studs Lonigan*, and to whom *Studs Lonigan* is dedicated, and, also, the man who published the

Danny O'Neill books asks me to write a secondary baseball novel and under terms which could harm my career and even lead to the wrecking of my health. The least that is due to me, besides an immediate release, is an apology from Vanguard Press. I won't do it, Jim.

Farrell would subsequently comment (in a note apparently intended for scholars who might later examine them) that the unsent letters were written "under stress, and I think that there is much that is uncharitable in them." But he would never acknowledge that Vanguard's offer was not altogether unreasonable—in light, as Henle said, of "all the circumstances."

⇒►○◄⇐

HE TELEPHONED HENLE ON Friday, December 5, and asked to be released from his Vanguard contract so he could seek a different publisher. Henle, recalling Lord's recent proposal, thought that what Farrell really wanted was backing for his new series of novels. He invited him to submit the manuscript of the first novel in the series, or as much of it as he had completed, and promised an answer from Vanguard within ten days. But Farrell was not interested.

On Monday, Farrell wrote to Henle, and this time he mailed the letter. In it, he cut the cord:

Jim, I asked for a release from the contract and a chance for a new start. You are trying to hold me against my will and wishes, against my best interests, and in disregard of the fact that I can wreck my health if I must go on as I have been. And you must know that a man cannot give his best when he is held against his wishes. Why are you doing this?...

Jim, it is not nice to have to assimilate my disappointment. I'll do it. But I am very disappointed. And you will be retired in ten years, Jim. I might not have this work finished until then. You are not fair to me. And the coldest note of all is your repeated insistence on Vanguard's moral and legal rights. You can't back me with what I need. You lack the means to handle this series as it ought [to] be handled. You have a set up whereby I must go to you and you must go to the owners who love me, but who cannot deal with me except through you. And you don't want to allow me to try and make a fresh start.

The next day, Farrell wrote to Evelyn Shrifte, asking her to release him: "Why do you insist and persist in holding me against my wishes, and when I am in a very bad situation?"

371

He also penned another (unsent) letter to Henle, saying that he was being "humiliated" and trying to explain why he felt he now had to leave Vanguard: He had grown beyond *Studs Lonigan* and the Danny O'Neill books, he said, but Evelyn Shrifte and her brother could not fully grasp that; nor would they understand his new novels, with their complex philosophical explorations of time; and if the first novel didn't sell well or ran into opposition, Vanguard would quickly lose faith. "I need freedom from my past in order to be above it," he said, and he would not let even "old or close associations" stand in his way.

On Wednesday, December 10, Farrell received a "Special Delivery" letter from Henle, written the same day, telling him that his letter of Monday (the only one of the many written to Henle lately that Farrell had mailed) "came as a big surprise. I had assumed that all you were interested in was getting the backing you want on your new series of novels. That was certainly the impression Evelyn and I received when Sterling asked for a $25,000 advance spread over five years. From your present letter, however, I take it you do not want to continue with Vanguard under any circumstances whatever." Henle added in a handwritten postscript: "Had you determined to leave Vanguard when Sterling presented those terms?"

That night, Farrell wrote (and apparently sent) a letter to Henle in reply, saying that he hadn't fully made up his mind when Sterling made the proposal.

> The determination to leave Vanguard came after Sterling presented the terms, and the clinching reason was the letter you sent Sterling with an offer, ignoring the terms he proposed, treating my new work as though it were unimportant, insisting on getting the baseball book in one year with money offered me which wouldn't have helped me get anywhere but into a deeper pit, and with a dangling $3,000 the next year if I finished the baseball novel. This showed me that my problems, my difficulties, my writing at this stage, the character of the literary eclipse I'm in, the necessary means to be taken to get out, and the prospects and possibilities of my future are all so completely misunderstood at Vanguard that it is hopeless.

The next day, Thursday, December 11, Farrell wrote another letter to Henle covering much the same ground, though with more venomous abandon. "The owners of Vanguard Press," he said, "do not have sufficient literary taste, literary judgment, understanding

of what creative writing is, or experience of the world to understand my writing today." They confused Farrell with the young
author of *Studs Lonigan*, not appreciating how much he had
grown since then, how much he had read and experienced, how
much his thinking had progressed. Nor could they grasp how an
author, "when he is almost on the sheriff's hands, when he is overworked and underweight, when he has little personal life, or
relaxation," could declare: "I will spend ten years in transcending
myself." As for Vanguard's claim on him, Farrell said:

> It made a hell a lot of money out of my books.... The owners of Van-
> guard Press take no risks, of money, health, welfare and future, in any
> way comparable to the risks I am taking. I risked my health, and
> about a year ago I told myself—this can be my health and a prema-
> ture death to get my work done and finish a novel. And I was doing it
> to get one in. I am risking my health now—putting it flat on the line
> to do my new series. Anything you or the owners of Vanguard Press
> say to me about money, moral rights and legal rights leaves me
> unperturbed.

But perturbed he was. Indeed, his agitation and distress
reached their height that day. He imagined himself dying as a result
of the dispute; at his funeral service Henle would be handed a letter that Farrell had written and, after reading it, abruptly leave.
"That will be good," Farrell would say in this "posthumous" letter.

> It can mean nothing to me at that time, but your presence might
> offend [those] who were close to me and who loved me, and who
> knew how you and Vanguard made me oppose you, work at the risk
> of my health and possibly my life in order to prevent myself from
> being destroyed by Vanguard Press, with you acting as their agent or
> employee, and for a salary. I write in dark hours of my career, when I
> yet may be destroyed as a writer, as a moral being, and even by
> death. And you and your employers are not helping me or letting me
> alone—they are helping to press me closer to possible destruction.

Farrell imagined telling Henle in this letter that he would be
remembered by posterity only so long as Farrell himself was, and
that from the day he wrote these words until the day he died, he
would be embarrassed on any occasion when he had to see Henle,
embarrassed by his "pettiness":

> You, once owner of Vanguard Press, are now an employee.... You are
> paid to be my enemy. And in your present employment situation,

your relationships are singularly disgusting. I have come to the conclusion that if you had been a man of honor, you would have
resigned.

IN THE END, VANGUARD AGREED to release Farrell. He was free to find
another publisher.

"The whole affair amazes me," Henle wrote him in a very brief
letter, three days before Christmas. "I feel Vanguard has overfulfilled
all its obligations to you. I wonder how you feel about your obligations to Vanguard."

Chapter Eighteen
Crazy Gallantry

W HEN LUNA WOLF, HIS part-time secretary, came to see Farrell in his one-room apartment at the Beaux Arts Hotel,
as she did several times a week, he was *always* writing.
"I would come sometimes in the morning," she recently
remembered, "and he would have obviously been sitting there for
two days, 48 hours. Sometimes he stank." Dressed in dirty pajamas,
he would almost be falling asleep, with the room an utter mess, lit-
tered with paper and reeking at times, the remains of hamburger
meals delivered from a nearby White Tower strewn about. "Write,
write, write, write, write. He was obsessed.... It was very strange."
She came to think that Farrell had every attribute of genius except
perhaps one: genius. "Whatever he did, it was always connected
with his writing.... It was not anything that he could control. It just
came pouring out, pouring out, pouring out."

By the time he took up residence in the Beaux Arts Hotel and
then took his delusive, tortured leave of Vanguard Press, however,
the strangeness of his behavior went beyond mere compulsiveness
as a writer.

In her innocence, Luna Wolf did not suspect the influence of
drugs. But as Irene Patai was to discover, the novelist was then
given to taking "uppers" (amphetamines) and "downers" (valium)—
and had been taking them during the time when he was remarried
to and living with Dorothy. He was not using the drugs for amusement or recreation. The amphetamines were to enable him to stay
up through the night, writing, writing, writing, so as to produce
more books that would earn more money and allow him to fulfill
his literary destiny, while the valium was to bring him "down," as
necessary, and to relieve his anxieties about his financial and literary problems. Irene Patai went with him once to a pharmacy in
Greenwich Village where he obtained the drugs. "He'd go in there

and somehow he'd get this stuff," she remembered. "And I often had the feeling it wasn't legal. I just had a feeling."

One side effect of amphetamines is loss of appetite, which would explain the extensive weight loss of which he complained. The change in his physical appearance was, as a matter of fact, quite dramatic. In a photograph taken in 1957 to accompany a newspaper profile, he appears in his Chicago hotel suite, clad in pajamas and wielding a pen, looking like the vigorous, if somewhat eccentric, fifty-three-year-old man he was; in a second photo, taken for the same purpose in the Beaux Arts Hotel in New York three years later, his haggard appearance gives the impression of an old man.

Another, albeit less common, side effect of amphetamines is feelings of suspicion and paranoia. Such irrational feelings seem evident in certain of his unsent December 1958 letters to Henle ("You are paid to be my enemy"). And that, alas, would not be the last occasion on which he would manifest such delusions.

———⟫•०•⟪———

IT DIDN'T TAKE STERLING LORD very long to get Farrell a new contract. By late January 1959, he had arranged with Ken McCormick, editor-in-chief of Doubleday, to pay the $4,244 that the novelist owed Vanguard on his unfulfilled contract and take him on.

McCormick, whose acquaintance with Farrell antedated World War II, was a legendary figure in the publishing world. He had been promoted to editor-in-chief only seven years after joining the giant publishing house in 1935, and had edited many well-known authors. "I think that Ken McCormick was a very great man," said Sally Arteseros, who joined Doubleday in the summer of 1959 and later would work as an editor on many of Farrell's books. "[McCormick] was a very optimistic man, a very inclusive man. He was a very great editor-in-chief. He created a wonderful spirit of cooperation. He was a minister's son. I think that he felt that Farrell could do it again"—that is, produce another *Studs Lonigan.*

McCormick and Doubleday gave Farrell a contract that was, to all appearances, better than the one Lord had sought for him from Vanguard. It provided an advance of $30,000 for four novels, with $9,000 (including the $4,244 for Vanguard) being paid immediately and the rest in $600 monthly installments for 35 months. A final draft of the first novel had to be produced by April 1, 1960.

Farrell thus appeared to get what he so desperately wanted:

the opportunity for a fresh start, the chance to begin immediately creating his "Universe of Time."

He soon discovered, however, that working with Ken McCormick and Doubleday was not quite the same as working with Jim Henle and Vanguard. McCormick kept the relationship more strictly professional. Though cordial and encouraging, he also was politely demanding and insistent.

At Vanguard, Henle and Farrell had been intimate friends. Henle—as McCormick himself recalled in an interview decades later—"was endlessly patient with [Farrell], endlessly." Henle had not discouraged Farrell's frequent phone calls, letters and visits; and Henle and others at Vanguard had routinely complied with the author's requests to hunt down facts, articles and books he wanted. Doubleday and its editor-in-chief were not so obliging. When, on one occasion, Luna Wolf made such a request, McCormick replied that he was "absolutely floor[ed]" by it. "The kind of books and materials that Jim wants," he told her, "are largely what he should find in the Public Library."

That McCormick and Doubleday did not indulge him as Henle and Vanguard had was undoubtedly annoying to Farrell. But what mattered most to him was his work itself—and during the summer of 1959 he came to believe that McCormick and Doubleday were threatening it. The editor—in what Farrell characterized as an "ultimatum"—asked him to reshape the novel on which he was working, removing a whole section that McCormick thought could be made, with further effort, into a second novel. Farrell balked. The novel left, he said, "will not be powerful enough" to lead off the "Universe of Time" series.

"I expect a breakup with Doubleday," Farrell confided two weeks later to Edgar Branch, a professor of English at Miami University of Ohio, who that year published a bibliography of Farrell's writings. "What they demand, I can't do." Four days later, however, the situation had changed: "Things seem to be straightened out with Doubleday," he wrote Branch. "I'll start revising for publication the first volume as I wrote it sometime next month and I should have a novel done this fall."

<hr />

MERV BLOCK, A REPORTER FOR the *Chicago American*, had profiled Farrell two years earlier when the latter was in town to deliver some lectures at the University of Chicago. Then, Block later recalled, he had seemed "subdued [but] okay." This time, interviewing him again in November 1959, Block saw a different, very agitated man. "For three hours," he wrote in the newspaper, "Farrell paced back and forth in his Blackstone hotel room like a caged literary lion, a prisoner, as he sees it, because 'the snobs in the east and publishers decided to lock me up as Studs Lonigan.' When Farrell did stop ambling, he stood rocking and swaying, seemingly unable to come to a dead stop. Verbally, too."

Farrell had developed the odd habit of rocking on the balls and heels of his feet, rocking in place, back and forth. "It made me uncomfortable," Block recalled. "I think it probably made other people uncomfortable, too."

Farrell and the reporter stayed in touch during the next few years, while Farrell entertained the hope—in which he was to be disappointed—of becoming a columnist for Block's newspaper. Block saw him occasionally not only in Chicago but in New York, at the Beaux Arts Hotel. "It seemed to me that he slept very little," Block remembered. "He'd be up late. And he'd be pacing, in his stocking feet, perhaps even barefoot." And he would rant, endlessly. When he stopped pacing, he would rock, back and forth, back and forth. "He really was troubled, some might even say disturbed," Block reflected. "This was a man who needed help."

Even before Farrell reached that low point, serving as his literary agent was a trying experience at times for Sterling Lord. Once, he remembered, after Farrell had expressed a desire to do some writing for television, he arranged a meeting with "one of the very active television producers here in town." The producer was interested in Farrell, but at the meeting, Lord said, "Jim proceeded to sit there and tell him, in effect, how he didn't have any respect for television"—or, by none too subtle implication, for the producer and his work. "Nobody can take that. So nothing happened as a result. Jim never quite understood why."

Farrell could be "very crude," as Lord said he discovered early on in their relationship when he invited the novelist to a party in his apartment. In mixed company, with four or five women and a like number of men present, Farrell "explained to us all how he hadn't masturbated for five years, [and had] been without a woman." Lord, a fastidious man, was offended by this and embarrassed for his guests, and he never again invited Farrell to his apartment or even to lunch.

"He must have driven Sterling crazy at [times]," observed Ria Simon, Farrell's lawyer. "Because Sterling was the opposite of Farrell. Neat, precise, proper. Suit, tie, the whole bit. White shirt.... Must have driven Sterling crazy." And Farrell, she agreed, "could be rather crude. Although, for the most part, with me—with women, I think, in general—he tried not to be." She remembered the novelist as "more sloppy than crude. And more pain in the neck, when he was sloppy, because you didn't know what to do with him. He would ramble on and on and on and on," sometimes incomprehensibly, as if he were "half asleep." Annoying as that was, "you couldn't say anything to him," for fear of upsetting him. "He could be very difficult."

Farrell, Lord came to realize, "was like a child in many ways." He was "a very warm person," and, for all the difficulties he presented, he could be as "endearing" as a child. But he also could be as exasperating as one. He not only blurted out what he supposed to be the simple truth at inappropriate moments, but was self-centered and incessantly demanding. He tended, Lord said, to convey "the feeling of being helpless" and of urgently needing others to do things for him. The novelist frequently called or wrote to Lord, wanting to find out what the agent was doing for him and to chat about ways of promoting him and his work. He did not seem to grasp that his rambling was wasting his agent's time (to his own possible disadvantage).

In 1959, after Farrell had signed with Doubleday, he became especially demanding, Lord remembered. "He wasn't getting the same kind of tender loving care from Ken that he'd got from the Vanguard people—and so more burden was put on me."

By late in the year, Farrell had grown dissatisfied with his agent. In a remarkably condescending and peremptory letter, especially considering that Lord had brought him together with Doubleday, he informed him "that a change is necessary, and I must make it in the interest of my work and for financial reasons. There are a number of details of business that I cannot get free of because you don't understand them and don't do what I ask, and in consequence you cost me money that I cannot afford, and time. From here on, I shall pay you a commission on what you actually sell and handle completely, and I shall handle other matters myself or through Luna." These other matters included his continuing business with Vanguard, involving royalties and the like, and also his dealings with certain foreign publishers.

His letter got the result that might have been expected: Lord told him the next day that while he would continue to service the contracts he had negotiated for him in the past, he could no longer "continue to represent you as a literary agent."

Within months, Farrell also would get rid of Ria Simon as his lawyer. "He started to get a little bit paranoid," she remembered. When she went off with her husband on their annual vacation without telling Farrell, leaving it to her law partner to handle a motion at a hearing in connection with Dorothy's alimony action, Farrell felt betrayed and abandoned. "And that," she said, "was the end of our relationship."

<hr />

"'I WANT TO SPEND THE rest of my life with you,'" Irene Patai remembered Farrell telling her. As she got to know the famous author better, that prospect had less and less appeal. "Oh, he was a charmer, when he wasn't taking [the uppers and downers]. But he always took them." On one occasion, he agreed to come to the high school where she taught on Long Island, to talk to her colleagues. "And they were all excited. Here was *Farrell* coming." But when he showed up, "he had had his downers…and he could hardly get the words out. Took him almost 40 minutes before he could really talk."

She had been drawn to the older man at first, but as time went by she came to see him as "sort of a pathetic figure in a way" and realized that "I really wasn't madly in love with him." They would see each other from time to time in the years immediately ahead, but by about the end of 1959, if not before, it must have become obvious to him that he would not be spending the rest of his life with her.

Farrell soon turned his attention to another, even younger woman, a beautiful and ambitious young Indian actress named Surya Kumari. A Brahmin from Madras in South India, she was in her mid-twenties. She had come to New York on her own and in 1961 would appear in an off-Broadway production of Rabindranath Tagore's *The King of the Dark Chamber*. Farrell was smitten with her. But what did she see in this troubled man who was some three decades her senior? Perhaps she saw a famous American writer who seemed sweet and eager to help her and might be useful in her career. "She is dedicated to her career," Farrell would write, "which is not the pursuit of dollars but the desire to sing and perform, and to make known what she can of the culture of India."

———≫-0-≪———

A LOW-BUDGET MOVIE VERSION of *Studs Lonigan* was made and released by United Artists in 1960. Philip Yordan, a Chicago native, was the producer and screenwriter. As a rendition of Farrell's work, Yordan's film is a travesty. Still, it may have been what critic Pauline Kael some years later said it was: "an honorable low-budget try by a group of people trying to break the Hollywood molds." The photography is impressive, certain scenes are inventive, and Jack Nicholson and Frank Gorshin are interesting as Weary Reilley and Kenny Killarney. A handsome young actor named Christopher Knight was miscast in the title role. His character, however, fares better in the end than Farrell's Studs did: he doesn't die—an uplifting Hollywood touch.

Farrell publicly dissociated himself from the film before it even came out. But at least he got some additional money out of it. When the rights had been sold to producer Lew Kerner and United Artists in February 1955, it had been for a period of only five years; consequently, in 1959, with no film yet in the works, an extension was needed. Farrell balked at that, since it seemed that the producer had no intention of making the major motion picture previously envisioned. But then, faced with the threat of a "quickie" movie being shot in a period of only a few weeks—a cinematic potboiler that would have been even worse than the low-budget film that Yordan was to make—and needing money, Farrell gave in, selling the rights a second time for $5,000.

———≫-0-≪———

FARRELL CAME TO ENVISION HIS "Universe of Time" series—which he now likened not to Proust's masterwork but to Balzac's "La Comédie humaine"—as consisting of at least twenty-one books, divided into four series: "When Time Was Young" (six novels), "Paris Was Another Time" (three), "When Time Was Running Red" (six), and "A Universe of Time" (six). The four novels promised to Doubleday were part of the first series.

Despite this grandiose scheme (which he would further develop over the ensuing decades), Farrell, for all his attention to the subject of time, seems to have had nothing original or especially compelling to say about it. There was too much naive philosophizing in his work, Ken McCormick found. But that was far from the editor's main problem: he was having great difficulty just getting a completed manuscript from the author. Farrell "had endless ideas" but found it hard to turn them into reality on the page, McCormick recalled. And instead of revising what he had written, he would "start off in another direction entirely."

In August 1960, McCormick's frustration with him—and this was not the first time—boiled over. Sternly reminding the author what their professional relationship entailed, he wrote Farrell:

> The last time we met in my office, which was mid-June, I told you how dissatisfied I was with the state of our affairs. I told you what was wrong with Volume I, and asked you to send me a letter...which would convince me that you were going to do something about getting Volume I into shape. I received no letter.... I had warned you that unless you satisfied me, I'd have to cut off your payments at the beginning of August. We've given you $2400 over the contract commitment for Volume I, and we still haven't got Volume I. Volume II, in complete satisfactory form, is to be in by November. This is highly improbabl[e] when we don't have Volume I.

And he reminded Farrell that the novelist had invited him "to severely edit the manuscript and try to put it in some form." McCormick said that he was attempting to do just that. But he needed Farrell's help, naturally.

Four days later, McCormick received a nineteen-page letter from Farrell—which, because of the author's terrible handwriting, he couldn't decipher. The next month, however, the two men got together in person and talked calmly about their situation. Farrell outlined the promised tetralogy as he then saw it. They agreed, as McCormick would subsequently write to him, "that you would look at our revised version of the first book and see whether you approve. If you don't approve, you were then going to revise it on your own and then let us see it. If at that time we cannot have a meeting of minds then it's understood that you will sell the property to another publishing house and repay us."

<hr />

FARRELL SEEMED SO INTELLIGENT and erudite to her, standing there on a Sunday night that August in her friend Maureen's apartment at the

Beaux Arts Hotel, with a cigarette in his left hand, his right hand firmly gripping his bent left elbow, and gently rocking back and forth, back and forth as he explained the vast literary project on which he was embarked. An obviously lonely man suddenly given an audience, he spoke a lot that evening, his talk ranging widely from the French Revolution to the Russian, from George Herbert Mead to Ty Cobb. "I couldn't believe anyone was that smart," Cleo Paturis later recalled.

She herself was no dummy. In 1944, at age seventeen, she had escaped from the broken home of her mother in Wilmington, North Carolina, and come north to New York; where (with the financial aid of her father, an affluent Greek immigrant, back in Wilmington), she learned how to type, which enabled her to earn a living and be free of her family and everyone else. She then held a succession of jobs, frequently entering an enterprise as a typist and soon becoming a writer—then getting bored and moving on. She was at the time working as a market reporter for *Earnshaw's*, a trade magazine devoted to children's wear.

Farrell had been invited to the small gathering in Maureen's apartment at the last moment, after the others—including Cleo and her companion, Ted, an editor at a well-known publishing house, and Maureen and her male friend, a portrait painter—had finished their Chinese-takeout dinner and were about to have coffee and dessert. Maureen, a writer who had just found a new job, was in an exultant mood. She had arranged the evening to show her gratitude to Cleo, who had lent her the money to pay her rent some weeks earlier, after she had lost her old job. Now, as she went toward her small kitchen pantry, Maureen turned around and asked the others if they would mind if she asked James T. Farrell, the writer, to join them. He lived next door, she explained, and was down on his luck, apparently broke, writing all day, every day, often not even stopping to eat. Sometimes at night, to relieve his loneliness, she said, he would go down to the lobby to watch the people there. He was a fascinating man, she told her guests, and he loved sweets, and she would like to ask him to join them. And so, with their permission, she did—and Cleo's life was changed forever as a result. It would not happen right away, indeed not for several years, but in time she would succeed Hortense and Dorothy as the most important woman in Farrell's life.

She came away that night in awe of this lonely but utterly determined, even fanatic author, whose major works she had read and admired. "This is the most incredible man," she said to Ted as they left the Beaux Arts.

The next morning, Maureen phoned her to say she had neglected to mention that Farrell was a womanizer and that he had asked for Cleo's phone number. "Well, I admire him tremendously, but my God!" Cleo said.

Farrell phoned and asked her to dinner. She told him: "Mr. Farrell, obviously, with all your insight, you didn't case the situation." She explained that she was "rather seriously involved" with Ted and didn't accept invitations that didn't include him. "Consider him included," Farrell replied. So she accepted.

After their dinner (Ted picked up the tab), Farrell invited them back to his apartment to see his manuscripts. When they got there and saw the papers strewn about everywhere, pages and pages and more pages, none of them numbered, Cleo was shocked: "I have never seen such disorder in my entire life." She told him he needed a secretary; he said he had one but couldn't afford to pay her much, so she only worked part-time. Cleo volunteered her own services (and Ted's) to help him straighten out the mess. Farrell immediately accepted, urging them to start the very next night.

About three weeks later, Ted said to her, "You know, I thought this was a good idea in the beginning, but I didn't know we were going to marry the guy." Cleo replied that they didn't have to go to the apartment every night but she couldn't just desert Farrell. "The guy's in trouble," she said. But there was more to it than that. She liked to listen to Farrell: "I learn so much. 'Cause he's so lonesome, he follows you around and talks." And she liked going through his papers and reading his unpublished fiction. "This is my idea of heaven."

Before many more weeks had passed, she suggested to Ted that perhaps what they had thought might be love had really been only mutual loneliness—and so, feeling guilty because she knew that she was adding to the already considerable burden of his woes, she brought their affair to an end.

<hr />

"THEY SAY I'M WASHED UP," Farrell told a *New York Post* reporter in October:

> They tell me I should have quit writing years and years ago. That's what the editors and the publishers tell me, that I'm finished. See,

they'd like me to die. I finished "Studs" when I was 30 and they think I should have conveniently died then.

"Studs" was my monument, they think. Now that he's got his monument, they think, he ought to die. But I won't die; I'll keep writing. I've got 40 books written right here in this apartment. Forty books. No one will publish them. The editors read them and say they're boring. No one would read those books, the editors tell me.*

The "editors" of Farrell's discourse seem to have been largely a product of his imagination, though the sentiment attributed to them was probably a common one in the publishing world, at least to the extent that that world now took any notice of him at all. But it was not the only sentiment about Farrell that editors held. The *Post* reporter was evidently unaware—because the novelist did not tell him—that he was under contract with Doubleday for four new books, and that Doubleday's editor-in-chief was impatient to have one of them to publish.

⟹➤◆◄⟸

SIX MONTHS AFTER THAT particular ranting outburst, novelist Sloan Wilson checked into the Beaux Arts Hotel, not knowing how long he would stay or what he would do next. He had enjoyed great success with *The Man in the Gray Flannel Suit* (1955) and had been able to sell the movie and other rights to *A Summer Place* (1958) for about $700,000 before it was even published (and before the circling reviewers moved in for the kill). But now he was in the midst of a painful divorce from his wife of more than twenty years, was worried about its impact on his three children, and was feeling very glum.

The hotel surrealistically reflected his mood. The woman at the desk who had given him the registration form to sign, he noticed, had a badly deformed hand. And shortly afterward he had come down to the hotel bar and found it filled with the loud, twittering voices of fashionably dressed men whom he took to be

---

*Farrell was a prolific writer, but it is doubtful that he had forty completed book-length manuscripts in his apartment, and even more doubtful that any editors had read them, pronounced them boring and refused to publish them. Certainly, neither Jim Henle nor Evelyn Shrifte nor Ken McCormick had done so (though McCormick had turned down a prose poem and had declined to publish in hardcover a collection of his short stories that New American Library was bringing out in paperback).

homosexuals. He found the scene depressing. "To me," he remembered decades later, "it seemed the whole world was deformed. Everything was deformed and lousy."

Leaving the bar after a few drinks, he went to the elevator and stepped inside. There was one other occupant, an older man with a haggard, vaguely familiar face. He was carrying a stack of paperbacks whose author—it suddenly dawned on Wilson—was the man clutching them. When Wilson had been a youth in prep school, *Studs Lonigan* had opened his eyes to an urban world he had never known, a world at times sordid but always fascinating; since then, he had read many other Farrell works. Wilson admired the writer enormously. He introduced himself, and when the elevator reached Farrell's floor, the older novelist invited Wilson to follow him to his room.

Once inside (which now, doubtless thanks to Cleo Paturis, seemed to the visitor rather neat), Farrell stood by his desk in the center of the room, holding his stomach and rocking back and forth. Wilson asked him if he was all right; Farrell said yes; he'd had an operation a while ago, but he was all right.* Then Farrell inquired about Wilson's condition, observing that he looked like hell for his age (which was nearly forty-one). "I hate to see a writer go down the drain," Farrell told him. "I know your stuff. I'm tough and you're sentimental, but we're both real writers. There are not many of us left."

This accolade lifted Wilson out of his gloom: "I could not have been more pleased if I had been awarded the Nobel Prize," he would later say.

Their conversation (as Wilson would reconstruct it) continued:

"Now, why do you walk around looking so down-at-the-mouth?" Farrell asked.

"I'm in the middle of a divorce."

"Oh, that. I've been through two or three. After a while you begin to lose count."

"I guess I haven't begun to get the knack of it yet."

"You're a writer, aren't you? Haven't you learned anything yet? Women will go to you because of your intensity. They will leave you for the same reason. You will always have a woman but it will never be the same one for long."

---

*Farrell underwent surgery for stomach ulcers in November 1952 at Beth Israel Hospital in Manhattan.

The prospect of an endless succession of transient liaisons, with no hope of anything more permanent, was a sad thought to Wilson. But Farrell presented himself as a man immune to such sentimentality. He urged Wilson not to let anything happen to his "vitality."

"I've hung onto mine," he boasted. "You know, when I went into that hospital for my operation, a lot of people figured that I had cancer. All my former wives and agents got in touch with my lawyer to make sure that I had written a will. I have trunks full of manuscripts for posthumous publication and everyone wanted a share. Do you know what I did?"

"What?"

"I told my lawyer to tell them I had written no damn will because I had no intention of dying. I went into the hospital, let them cut me open, and four days later I laid the night nurse!"

"That's vitality," Wilson said, though he didn't believe Farrell's boast.

Before long, Wilson returned to his own room.

He saw Farrell again and again over the next few days, until finally—much as he admired the novelist, much as he saw him as "a lion at bay" who had been treated shabbily by the public and the book trade—he could take no more. "I finally couldn't stand his nonstop talking. And he just talked, actually continuously, about himself. And you'd just have to sit still and listen and nod and say, 'I understand.' About two or three evenings of that, and you could [find it] pretty hard to go on."

And he also found Farrell's sophomoric sexual boasting hard to take. Farrell was a short, unimposing, middle-aged man "with a high squeaky voice"—not at all "the masculine figure he tried to present" himself as being. "He was an awfully nice man and a brilliant man, of course, but he had a thing about proving himself a sexual Tarzan."

Once, during Wilson's brief stay at the Beaux Arts, he introduced Farrell to the young woman, a former showgirl and model, who would later become Wilson's second wife (in a union that lasted until his death in 2003). Farrell was obviously impressed by Betty Stephens's beauty. After a few minutes he departed, saying he had a date of his own. Wilson was quite sure that Farrell really didn't—"and there was a great pathos in that to me, when he went off."

In fact, there *was* a young woman whom he might have been

387

going to visit: Surya Kumari. How strong his hold was on her, however, was open to question. A year or so later, Farrell would invite Jay Robert Nash, an editor who had resurrected Ben Hecht's *Literary Times* and persuaded Farrell to contribute, to meet his girlfriend. At the appointed hour, the two men ascended the three flights to her apartment, with Farrell "chatting amiably" as they went. "At the third landing," Nash later recalled in print, "he paused and stared at me. His mouth turned into a hard grimace. His hands went out to the lapels of my coat and he grabbed them fiercely, drawing me toward him. His words shot out like bullets barking from a .45 automatic: 'If you make a pass at my girl, I'll kill you!'" After Nash smilingly told him not to be silly, Farrell's mood quickly shifted, and he took Nash inside for a brief visit to the shrine of Surya Kumari's beauty; then, with Farrell's eager approval, the editor left. As Nash headed toward the stairs, he heard the novelist bolt the door and slide on the chain lock. "James T. Farrell was taking no chances."

"When I first met Jimmy," Cleo Paturis said, "Jimmy was in love with Surya." But one day when Cleo was in his apartment typing, he returned from a party to which he had taken Surya and told Cleo that the actress had asked him to pretend he was not with her, lest important others at the gathering get the wrong impression. "I can't believe this man is so smart about so many things and he's such a fall guy for every dumb woman," Cleo told her friend Ted.

⇒►•◄⇐

EVEN WITH ALL HIS OWN difficulties, Farrell was often willing to lend a hand to younger writers who sought his aid. Eliot Asinof, then a forty-two-year-old novelist and former minor-league baseball player, is a case in point. He had signed a contract to write a nonfiction book about the Chicago Black Sox scandal before learning that Farrell had already written a book on the subject. "And I said, well, I'm not going to compete with that," he remembered. "So I called him." Six years earlier, Farrell had reviewed Asinof's first novel, *Man on Spikes*, lauding it as "a good baseball novel and a good novel," but the two men had never met. When Asinof phoned, Farrell recognized his name right away and invited him over.

At the Beaux Arts, Asinof told Farrell about his proposed book about the Black Sox scandal and asked him whether he had indeed written a book about the subject, and if so, what was happening with it. Farrell asked why he wanted to know. Asinof explained that he didn't want to compete with him.

"And [Farrell] said, 'You're telling me that you're [not] going to write this book because I have already written something like it?' I said, 'That's right.' And he said, 'I'll tell you what. My book is no good at all. Besides, it's a novel. And I will give you my book, and you can use anything in it that you wish, and what's more, I'm going to tell you everything that I know. Now, get out your damn pencil and let's go to work.' And it was the damndest thing I ever had been through in all my life."

For the next hour and a half or so, to Asinof's amazement, out poured from Farrell's phenomenal memory names and dates and figures pertaining to the Chicago White Sox of 1919. And names of people for him to see, "all of which were sensational helps."

"I went to Chicago as soon as I left him," Asinof recalled. After he returned, he met with Farrell again, "and kept meeting with him. He was a constant help throughout the book. And he read parts of the manuscript and made certain suggestions. He was just a real good friend." (And when *Eight Men Out* was published in 1963, Farrell gave it an admiring review.)

GENEROUS WITH ASSISTANCE TO others as Farrell could be, it was he himself who was truly in need of help. He had come to regard himself as a victim of large malign forces beyond his control.

In November 1961 he penned an open letter to Soviet leader Nikita Khrushchev, requesting "a rectification in the press of your country for attacks upon me for my defense of the victims of a great injustice…the Stalin purge." (The month before, at the twenty-second party congress in Moscow, Khrushchev, who had attacked Stalin's crimes in a "secret" speech in 1956, had condemned them again, vehemently and publicly). In his letter, Farrell claimed that he had "suffered for over twenty-five years in my literary career as a consequence of the attacks, some of them foul, made upon me, solely because I would not defend the official version of the [Moscow show] trials."

When the open letter appeared in *Thought*, an Indian publication, Farrell accompanied it with a note that mixed truth with self-pitying, somewhat paranoid fantasy:

The sales of my books declined sharply—I had had, up to that time, only one book, *A World I Never Made*, which reached the best-seller lists. *No Star Is Lost* was returned from book stores by carton-loads. Some literary people who had not liked *Studs Lonigan* became converted to my trilogy, this seemed a means to attack my O'Neill-O'Flaherty books.

In time, others picked up this line on me, and I sustained attack after attack, as my books appeared.

I have tried again and again to explain these facts to publishers and editors, but in vain. They would not even listen to me.

Here is the root of my financial and literary troubles. Now, the publishers and literary people in America who adopted the content of a savage political attack on me, for having taken and held to a position of truth about the Moscow trials, stand exposed as dupes....

For a quarter of a century, I have withstood the attacks which were motivated by my stand on the Moscow trials. Over and over again, the same generalizations were printed about me as a writer. And the critical—not economic—success of *Studs Lonigan* gave a cover to this kind of attack. I should have been ruined, from the standpoint of my career as well as my health, had I not fought back.

Not long after the letter to Khrushchev, the aggrieved Farrell picked up his pen again, this time to complain about some published praise of him as one of the greatest American writers of the pre–World War II era. "I am not only a writer of the '30s and the '40s," he lectured the *Oakland* (California) *Tribune*. "I am a writer of the '50s, of 1960, 1961, and of tomorrow." In fact, he claimed, his "most productive and creative period has been from 1950 until now." But he could not get much of what he wrote during these years published: "I have had a harsh and pitiless struggle—which I shall win."

Someone showed the letter to Ken McCormick, who read it attentively and then dropped Farrell a note. "We're just as interested in you as a writer of the '60's as you are," he said. "Won't you please let me have the first volume of the tetralogy so that we can publish in Fall '62?"

One line in Farrell's published letter, McCormick told him, had him "a little concerned." After mentioning that he was "now preparing volume one" in his "Universe of Time" series for publication, Farrell had added: "I am to sign a contract for six works of fiction from among my finished and almost finished manuscripts." (Two such books, he noted, *Boarding House Blues*, the novel on which he had begun work in 1953, and *Side Street and Other Stories*, had been published as paperback originals in 1961.)

An exasperated McCormick commented: "Aren't you obligated to us for four works of fiction, and shouldn't you fulfill that obligation? Please do."

McCormick had become so desperate for Farrell to complete the first volume that some months earlier he had offered to pay Luna Wolf to do the "final typing," i.e., the final editorial work that Farrell was supposed to do. Previously, she remembered, the manuscript would come to Farrell from the Doubleday copy editor with instructions to shorten this and that; instead, "it would end up longer, because he could not cut.... Finally, Ken was just in despair, because [the book] had been delayed and delayed and delayed," and he asked her to do the job. She agreed.

She had come to do other editing for Farrell in the course of her part-time employment by him. In 1958 a paperback volume of H. L. Mencken's *Prejudices: A Selection* had appeared, with the selection purportedly made by Farrell, who also supplied an introduction. In reality it was Luna Wolf who did the work: the disorganized Farrell was incapable of the systematic editorial work involved in making such a selection. Likewise with a paperback selection of Theodore Dreiser's writings that would be published by Dell in December 1962. "'Don't think I don't know what you did here,'" she remembered Dick Huett, Dell's editor-in-chief, gratefully telling her.

And so with Luna Wolf's help, Farrell was able to turn in the final pages of his first novel for Doubleday, *The Silence of History*, in March 1962. "I couldn't be more pleased," McCormick told him on receiving them.

=━━━➤●◄━━━=

WAITING IN PENN STATION FOR the gate to be opened to let them board a train for Washington and an extraordinary evening in the Kennedy White House, Diana and Lionel Trilling were suddenly joined on the morning of April 29 by an unwelcome apparition, the embarrassingly seedy figure of James T. Farrell.

Carrying a suitcase in one hand and a worn, bulging briefcase in the other, he wore a shabby, rumpled suit that might once have been brown, but now was of indeterminate color; his tie was drastically askew; his shirt was dirty and had a missing button. He seemed to Mrs. Trilling not only seedy but "wild... insane, sober but insane." My God, she and her husband wondered, had Farrell, too, been invited to the White House dinner that night honoring America's Nobel laureates? And even worse, did they have to spend the next several hours on the train in his disreputable company?

Farrell was indeed on his way to the glittering White House event, thanks no doubt to his friend Arthur Schlesinger Jr., who was now special assistant to President John F. Kennedy. That the first major novelist of the Irish Catholic experience in America should be invited to the White House occupied by the first Irish Catholic president seems quite fitting, even if the novelist had rejected Catholicism and was neither a model of sartorial elegance nor, one imagines, the sort of man with whom Kennedy (any more than the Trillings) would have cared to spend much time.

But Farrell didn't let on at the train station that he was bound for the White House; nor did the Trillings reveal that they were. Farrell said that his bulging briefcase contained publishers' royalty statements. "He felt," Mrs. Trilling later recalled, "that he was being very much cheated by the income-tax people, and he was going to Washington to take up the matter." That may actually have been his intent. His federal income tax returns for 1955 and 1957 had been audited, and he was experiencing, or was soon to experience, tax problems again.

When Farrell indicated this reason for traveling to Washington, Mrs. Trilling heard Lionel "heave a sigh of relief: he wasn't going to the White House; he was going to the Treasury Department." Now, Mrs. Trilling reproached herself for having vetoed her husband's proposal that they reserve chairs in the pricey club car; in consequence, she supposed, they would have to ride all the way to Washington in their coach car with the shabby and tiresome Farrell. But they were spared that indignity. When the Trillings turned to board the first coach car, Farrell, surprised and a little embarrassed, told them he had reserved a chair in the club car. He hadn't been sleeping well lately and needed to rest, he explained. "I could feel humiliation racing through every inch of my husband's body," Mrs. Trilling recalled. "He was riding in a coach while this poor, bedraggled devil who looked as if he had not had a bed to sleep in for a year or a change in underwear for a month was travelling in a chair."

As the train sped on to Washington, Farrell may have called to mind another possible motive for his trip: the hope that his presence at the White House dinner might somehow bring him nearer to the Nobel Prize, not merely to past Nobel Prize winners. His desire and determination to win the prize had not flagged since he first set his mind on it during the maelstrom of his affairs in the fall of 1958; nor would it in the ensuing years. He would arrange for Edgar Branch, the professor who was his admiring bibliographer, and others to nominate him many times, and Adlai Stevenson, Senator Paul Douglas and other famous persons he knew would write letters in his behalf. The idea of Farrell being awarded the Nobel Prize for Literature was not inherently preposterous. Writers of lesser achievement—even American writers of lesser achievement, such as Pearl Buck—had won it. Later in 1962, in October, that year's winner would be announced: John Steinbeck. Once, in 1940, Jim Henle had quoted to Farrell what a friend had told him: he'd heard Steinbeck self-deprecatingly but seriously say that Farrell was a greater novelist than he.

Yet if Farrell was entitled to consider himself a potential Nobel laureate, his naked ambition for the prize was a bit unseemly and even pathetic. Journalist Dan Wakefield was to see this when, working on a piece about John Dos Passos that would appear in the April 1963 *Esquire*, he interviewed Farrell in his room at the Beaux Arts Hotel. Pacing back and forth in his pajamas, Farrell "suddenly stopped and crawled under the bed to search for some old papers and letters," Wakefield recalled in a memoir. "With his bare feet sticking out the side of the bed, I heard him say, 'Don't you see, Dos has lived a world so different from these contemporary writers. His interest isn't just himself, it's the world.' I admired Farrell's respect and loyalty but cringed when he showed me a map of the world with marks on various countries indicating support for his own candidacy for the Nobel Prize. (He was running for laureate!) Then he pointed out other countries and said, 'Dos has a lot more backing there than I do.'" Wakefield thought: "My God...will it come to this? Will my friends and I, twenty or thirty years later, be scrambling under hotel beds for evidence of our standing in the world literary market? Show me the way to Walden Pond!"

The White House on the evening of April 29, 1962, was a far cry from Walden Pond. With 49 Nobel Prize winners and 124 other scientists, writers, editors and educators on hand, it was, President Kennedy famously remarked, "the most extraordinary collection of talent, of human knowledge, that has ever been gathered together at the White House, with the possible exception of when Thomas Jefferson dined alone."

And among those present was Farrell, who, to the relief of the Trillings, was suitably attired. Irene Patai and his journalist friend Bill Shannon, Patai remembered, had "pitched in and helped him buy a proper outfit." When Diana Trilling heard Farrell's name being announced over the loudspeaker, she looked and saw the shabby man of that morning wondrously transformed. "He had on an absolutely clean shirt, his suit was pressed and sparkling clean, every shirt stud was in place. He looked dreamy, and I felt horribly ashamed of us for not having wanted to tell him that we were going to the White House and asking whether that was where he was going, too. What was amazing was that he had had the delicacy not to ask us, for fear that we hadn't been invited and would feel bad."

Though Farrell would never win the Nobel Prize, his great literary achievement, his steadfast fidelity to his own high aspirations, his cherished integrity, his lonely struggle against the Stalinists, and his efforts for freedom at home and abroad had won him, at least that once, a place of honor among what might be regarded, in Jefferson's phrase, as the nation's natural aristocracy.

It was only for an evening, of course. But the next day's *New York Times* carried a front-page story about the event, and when, high up in the story, a brief roll of the writers present was called, the name of James T. Farrell headed the list, followed by Robert Frost, John Dos Passos, Pearl Buck, Katherine Anne Porter and Van Wyck Brooks.

For one brief shining moment, it appeared that Farrell was not so down-and-out after all.

———→»-0-«←———

ON THE RECOMMENDATION OF Dell's Dick Huett, Luna Wolf was hired as an editor by McGraw-Hill, which was launching a paperback division. She badly needed the job, being divorced now and about as broke as Farrell. But when she told him in June 1962 that she was leaving his (lately unpaid) employ after nine years, "he was furious," she remembered. "He was absolutely [furious]. He said, 'All right, leave the sinking ship! Go ahead! Go ahead!' And I kept trying to tell him, 'I have to eat.' [But] it didn't matter."

She had never held Farrell in awe, either as a man or as a writer. She had just turned thirty when she left his employ, and she did not find this slovenly man who had come to seem much older than his years physically attractive, though she never doubted that had she wished, "he would have slunk in bed with me." She never understood what other women—attractive women, too—saw in him. And she found his obsession with writing "very strange."

Yet she liked Farrell. "I mean I was crazy about him," she said. "I really liked him very much. Otherwise, I wouldn't have stayed with him that long."

She loved the Danny O'Neill books. "There was a lot of the child in [Farrell], all along," she said. "And I think when that spoke, then he was very good. And when he tried to do something else, he wasn't that good."

She understood his great flaw as a writer. "He was an extremely creative writer," she said, "but he was not a great stylist. That's always a problem with his writing. It's a shame. Because he could have been right up there. It's terrible that he had this flaw. He was a writer who, in a way, couldn't write." And yet, she added: "He wasn't a great writer, but he was a great author, in a way."

By the time Luna Wolf left Farrell for McGraw-Hill (where she would edit a collection of his essays), Cleo Paturis had quit her job at *Earnshaw's* to become the service editor for Dell Publishing's *Modern Romances* and *Modern Screen* magazines. She was in charge of their medical advice columns, and for the first time in her life she "really started making money." And thanks to a very competent associate editor, she began to enjoy some free time. She would drop by Farrell's apartment, take away a chunk of disorganized manuscript pages in a shopping bag and then, during her free hours, sort the pages out and type them up. Before long she recruited a friend named Penny Potenz, a receptionist at another firm who was an excellent typist and seldom busy, to assist her in this service to American literature.

One day Cleo stopped by Farrell's apartment and he was writing a letter. "And I said, 'You better give it to me to type. No one can read your letters. And more and more I'm hearing about how crazy you are because your handwriting is so bad.'" When he was done, he handed over the letter and she took it back to her office.

The letter was a reply to a high school sophomore whose English teacher had assigned *Studs Lonigan* to his class, but whose outraged mother had said he was too young to read it. The teacher had suggested the boy write to the author, expecting that he would provide persuasive arguments to win over the mother. Instead, Cleo discovered on reading the reply, Farrell told the youth that he agreed with his mother! While some high school students were mature enough to read *Studs Lonigan*, not all were; he thought it irresponsible for a teacher to assign the book to an entire class. He suggested that the teacher might better assign a novel by Sir Walter Scott.

When Cleo read Farrell's letter, she started crying. "I thought…here is a man that so many people have neglected for so long and they say he's through and everything. And here he's got a chance at making a bravado" (by reproving the putatively unenlightened mother). "And his absolute integrity and his rational brain will not let him give in to that easy reward." Farrell, she marveled, is something else. "And that was the first time that I ever thought I might be falling in love with him."

<hr>

FARRELL MUST HAVE FOUND THE publication of *The Silence of History* in February 1963—his first novel between hard covers since *The Face of Time* in 1953—immensely satisfying, after all his many literary and personal difficulties during the intervening ten years. Whatever his critics might say, *The Silence of History* (dedicated to Surya Kumari) was, at the very least, unmistakable proof that he was not dead.

But the novel also offered clear evidence—from which the author appears to have averted his eyes—that his grandiose hopes for an artistic rebirth were to go unfulfilled. For in *The Silence of History*, Farrell was, in essence, back at the same old stand: South Side, Chicago, and the University of Chicago in the mid-1920s, with Danny O'Neill (renamed Edward A. Ryan) and the familiar cast of family members (also renamed). Ryan's impulsive decision to quit his promising gas-station job, a decision that he comes to understand was rooted in the need to take a chance on his inner freedom and destiny, serves as the novel's armature.

Names of the reappearing characters aside, what was new in the book—such as the embarrassing babble about time ("All that he had of Time was now, and now, and now, and now") and the inexplicable shifts in narration from the third person to the first—was not good, and what was good—the engaging portrayal of the earnest Ryan's thirst for knowledge and interior growth—was not especially new. It was a different portrait of the artist as a young man, but not all that different.

Even so, *The Silence of History* received a warmly sympathetic front-page appraisal in the *New York Times Book Review*. The reviewer was Robert Gorham Davis, an English professor at Columbia and Farrell's immediate predecessor as chairman of the American Committee for Cultural Freedom. In time, he suggested, Farrell would be rediscovered and given his due as "a sort of William Dean Howells of Jackson Park" who faithfully recorded "the day-to-day, almost hour-by-hour suffering, sentimentality, dignity, coarseness and despair of an important part of the nation's population at a time of decisive change in its psyche."

Other reviewers were less kind. *Newsweek*, for instance, complained about "the interminable pages of this pitiable novel" and pronounced Eddie Ryan to be "a numbing bore, and so is the novel."

Despite such brickbats, by May 24, little more than three months after publication, 9,769 copies of *The Silence of History* had been sold—a modest triumph for Farrell, even if one that he largely owed to Davis and the influence of the *New York Times*.

⟹➧⊙◅⟸

THE DECLINE OF FARRELL'S reputation had not erased the indelible impression that *Studs Lonigan* had made on some readers. One of these was Louis Terkel. As a young man in Chicago during the 1930s, he had become so enamored of Farrell's creation that he acquired the nickname "Studs"—and kept it as he later embarked on his broadcasting career. Now in March 1963, with *The Silence of History* just published, Studs Terkel was in Farrell's hotel room in Chicago, meeting the author for the first time and taping an interview with him for his radio show on WMFT. This figure who had loomed so large in Terkel's life as a young man appeared before him "pretty battered and smacked about," he later recalled, "but still having a certain, I guess the word would be *fever*, a certain fever. He had that fever."

The interview was more feverish monologue than normal dialogue. Farrell talked virtually nonstop about himself and his work, about how he usually didn't sleep at night and sometimes worked for 20 or 24 hours straight, about *The Silence of History* and the "Universe of Time" series which would run to at least 25 volumes, about how he had 36 books published and "40 or 50 books in manuscript almost ready" and "20,000 pages of fiction, unpublished," and "almost 10 complete novels to publish, they're almost ready, some are ready." When he'd told an interviewer from *Esquire* that a man shouldn't be written off until he's dead he had been "giving a warning," not pleading for sympathy. He didn't care about critics, he told Terkel, he didn't care about success and he wasn't afraid of failure. "I know what I'm doing in my books, and if nobody reads them, I'll go on and write 'em just my way." He wasn't dead, but, he revealed, he'd written his own obituary, a poem he recited that had him dying of "a deprivation of time." He could "run as fast as when I played football 30 years, 40 years ago," he asserted—and then, to prove it, started running about the hotel room!

"He was fighting mortality," Terkel said, "and had to make his point, that he was going to write as many novels and books as he possibly could, all on the theme of time. Beating the clock."

Terkel was sorry to see this writer he admired—who was "almost in a class by himself as a chronicler of life, certainly of working class, lower middle class, Irish Catholic families on the South Side of Chicago"—now so "beaten down." Yet there was more than pathos evident in the man and his frantic defiance of fate and time. Farrell was "sad," Terkel observed, "but in a crazy way, gallant, too."

⫸●⫷

NEARLY SIXTY YEARS OLD NOW, his hair gray and cut short, Farrell gave a lecture in September 1963 at St. Peter's College, a Jesuit institution in Jersey City, New Jersey. Later he would become an adjunct professor there for the 1964-1965 academic year.

His lecture—characteristically long and rambling, earnest and revealing, fascinating in some places and obscure in others—was about the writer and his world, that is, of course, about himself and his world. Here were the figures from his childhood who were so immensely important to him—his grandmother, his aunt who worked as a cashier in a hotel, his uncle who was a shoe salesman; and the literary characters he had created, Studs Lonigan and Danny O'Neill. And he spoke of the writer's continuing struggle to learn and grow, so "that out of this day-by-day living and gaining impressions, you try to develop your own way of seeing life, particularly in a new world." He explained:

When I say new world, I mean also a new world for literature. There

398

had never been characters like mine put into American literature before. Many things are in there for the first time, so that there was writing that was new. You have to begin by being realistic—at least in most cases it's necessary—just like you have to name first. It's the beginning of an attempt to master the material, to master the world, as it were, from the standpoint of your own consciousness.

Though a reader of this or others of Farrell's talks might wish he had been more orderly and disciplined in the presentation of his ideas, students and others who saw and heard him were often captivated, in part no doubt by his transparent sincerity and honesty.

Farrell told his auditors at the Catholic college that he had come to realize that his own Catholic schooling had been very valuable to him. "I used to be a very intense critic of parochial schools. I was wrong. I'm not a religious person, but I learned four things and absorbed four things," he said:

> (1) that truth is possible, it's possible to think of the world in terms of order; (2) I was never told a lie; I was given a conception of the meaning of the truth as important; (3) I got a sense there was something before me and something after me, that there was a depth of experience, and that I was living in a continuity where there was depth of experience and where there was an idea of greatness and grandeur and also of mystery and reality—where you face tragedy, you face yourself. You ask yourself if you sin or not. That can have the effect of making you see rather realistically. (4) I got the idea that there are things so important in this world that it's your duty to die for them if necessary, and that the values are more important than you.
>
> I had those feelings and they are, as best as I could put them, in my work.

———»-0-«———

WHEN DOUBLEDAY JUNIOR EDITOR Tom McCormack brought the galleys of *What Time Collects*, the second novel in the "Universe of Time" series, to the Beaux Arts Hotel, he was worried about what the author's reaction would be.

Farrell had turned in the final chapters of his 1,100-page manuscript to Ken McCormick some months before. McCormick was a "terrific editorial manager" (in the younger editor's view), but not ordinarily a "hands-on" editor, though he had done a good deal of work on *The Silence of History.* This time he turned the manuscript over to Tom McCormack and asked him to fix it.

"No one had told me the difference between an editor and a rewrite man," McCormack wrote later, "so I toiled manically for six weeks, cutting 400 pages, rearranging sections, rewriting sentences, rendering 200 straight-narrative pages into scenes because the great man, then in [his] twilight, had simply forgotten to write dialogue." When he was finished, Ken McCormick, seeing "the enormity of what I did," and not having the time to scrutinize the work in any detail, had the rewritten manuscript sent straight to the copy editor and then—without showing the edited version to Farrell—had it put directly into type.

In February 1964 it fell to Tom McCormack to bring the galleys to the author at his hotel. In an accompanying note, Ken McCormick told Farrell that "it really isn't necessary for you to look too closely [at the galleys] or even look at all, because all the queries have been answered by us. We are working on a tight schedule [and] it's absolutely urgent that no changes be made at this stage unless they constitute a dire emergency."

Inside the apartment, Tom McCormack later remembered, Farrell took the galleys, "sat me down and went to his desk to address his novel. He read exactly six pages. Then he turned to me. *This is it*, I felt, and I could see the headline: NOTED AUTHOR RUBS OUT SNOT-NOSED TAMPERER." But the noted author, "in his tough-guy Chicago voice," simply said: "You're good, kid." Farrell said no more about the book and read no more of the galleys. Instead he rambled on about the Black Sox scandal until McCormack retrieved the galleys and departed.

McCormack was elated for a while. But he soon realized that no one—seemingly not even the author—would ever know all he had done with what he regarded as 1,100 pages of "chaos." And what had he really accomplished? One thing he was sure of was that he had not turned the chaos into a great book: "I never worked harder in my life, but all I managed to do was make it publishable."

What Time Collects presents middle-class Protestants in a medium-sized midwestern city during the 1920s, and through them a bleak view of marriage. Despite the novel's shortcomings, Granville Hicks said in his *Saturday Review* column in June 1964, it "has a kind of solidity that one has to respect. Farrell understands the Midwestern middle class as it was when he was growing up.... He also understands the importance of Fundamentalist Protestantism in the lives of these people, and he analyzes with greater precision than Sinclair Lewis ever did the nature of hypocrisy. And no one has ever shown more clearly the causes and consequences of the double standard." In addition, Hicks said, "Farrell gives life to his characters. He goes at it clumsily, to be sure...but he does create a sense of reality."

"What is it," Hicks asked in conclusion, "that has allowed Farrell once more to rise above his deficiencies as a writer, which are so gross, and to produce a novel that can be read with admiration, if not with much pleasure? Why is he at 60 one of the substantial figures in modern American literature? There is one word that explains his whole career—integrity. He has never been anything but himself."

Farrell was not happy with Hicks's nuanced judgment. "Don't bother reading that bastard's review," he told Jay Robert Nash, the *Literary Times* editor whom he'd met for lunch. "He's done what he always does to my books—condemned it, attacked it, blasted the hell out of it." After they left the restaurant, according to Nash's account, Farrell—running, as he was inclined to do when the spirit moved him—led him to a coffee shop several blocks away. From a pay phone inside he challenged Hicks to come down from his apartment across the street "'to settle this once and for all.'" Hicks did not show up. Nash wasn't sure that Farrell had even been talking with him.

THE DEMOCRATIC NATIONAL CONVENTION was being held in Atlantic City, New Jersey, during the fourth week of August 1964, and Farrell invited Irene Patai to spend a day there with him. ("He was alone, I was alone, we were going our separate ways," she said. "But he wanted me to go with him, and I went with him.") With the nomination of President Lyndon B. Johnson a foregone conclusion, the convention promised little in the way of high drama. But Senator Hubert H. Humphrey, whom Farrell knew somewhat and admired, was the leading candidate to be Johnson's running mate; other political figures of his acquaintance would be in attendance, and of course there would be parties galore.

On Tuesday morning, Irene Patai showed up at Farrell's apartment in the Beaux Arts Hotel, only to learn that he had no suit to wear because his best suit was at the dry cleaner. "So I went and got the suit from the cleaner's," she would remember, "and he got himself dressed up, and we got on the train." Once aboard, he insisted on showing her how well he managed to write while traveling. "So he took out all his materials to write and he ordered a cup of coffee. And as he's holding this [while] the train is going, the coffee spills on his suit. So there he was, poor guy, messed up—which was not unusual for Farrell."

In Atlantic City they found his friend Max Kampelman, whom he had first met in the summer of 1946 at the University of Minnesota. The political scientist had subsequently gone to work for Hubert Humphrey in Washington. On Farrell's first encounter with Humphrey, in 1950, he had judged him a "yokelish, simple sort of fellow," but the novelist came to know better and became a champion of the loquacious anti-Communist liberal. On one occasion in Washington, Farrell had introduced Irene Patai to Humphrey; her first novel, *The Valley of God*, had concerned the prophet Hosea, and he knew all about Hosea and seemed quite interested. But now the senator, who had arrived in Atlantic City over the weekend, was busy with more urgent matters, and Kampelman, who had not known that Farrell was coming to Atlantic City, had no more tickets to the various events to give out. "'Well, we'll go to the convention,'" Irene Patai remembered Farrell saying. "So we go marching along on the boardwalk til we get there, and they wouldn't let us in. So back we go to Max Kampelman and we see the darn thing on TV, which we could have done at home just as well or maybe better."

Then came the discovery that "we couldn't go home. There was no train going home, there was no bus going home. We were stuck." Making the best of it, they went looking for a party. But "nobody would let us in. No one gave a damn that he was Farrell. We went from state to state. Each state had its own room at the hotel. And we just couldn't get in."

During his and Irene Patai's dispiriting quest at the hotel, Walter Reuther passed by. "'Walter, I can't get in anywhere,'" Farrell said. "'Too bad,'" Reuther replied—"and off he went." Finally, though, she and Farrell reached the room reserved for Minnesota delegates. "By this time," she recalled, "I was ready to shriek. I say to the young man guarding the door, 'Do you know who this is? This is James T. Farrell, the writer of *Studs Lonigan*.' And the kid says, 'Farrell! You're really Farrell? What did you mean when you wrote...?' And, of course, in we went. And then everybody made a fuss over him."

Farrell and Irene wound up staying in different places overnight. The next day, she called his room and eventually—"I guess he had taken his downers and didn't have any uppers"—he came down, a forlorn figure.

They took a bus back to Manhattan, with Farrell sleeping most of the way. From the bus station, they took a cab. "I left him off at the Beaux Arts. He looked at me and said, 'We had a wonderful time, didn't we?'"

Five months later, Farrell attended one of the five inaugural balls held in Washington on the evening of January 20, 1965, after President Johnson and Vice President Humphrey were sworn into office. This time, Farrell asked his seventeen-year-old niece, Margaret, one of his brother Jack's daughters, to accompany him. They went to the ball at the Armory, she remembered; her uncle was an excellent dancer and they had a good time.

⊶·o·⊷

LATER THAT YEAR, CLEO PATURIS and Farrell commenced their affair. By year's end, she recalled, "we were in love." In her past romantic entanglements, she had always shied from making a total commitment, and this one was at first no exception. She didn't move in with him at the Beaux Arts Hotel. Indeed, she refused to "throw my cards in with him til he got off" the drugs—the amphetamines and the valium. And he did stop using them. (She didn't have to get him to stop excessive drinking: he had done that on his own before she ever met him.) She found his utter devotion to his writing initially reassuring, thinking that even if she were eventually to leave him, he would have his work. But by 1966 "we both knew we were irrevocably connected."

They began living together in the latter part of 1966, moving into Tudor City, a middle-class enclave of apartment housing from the 1920s just a few blocks south of the Beaux Arts. They occupied two studio apartments, which were separated by a third one. "They were all we could get," she said. One of their two apartments "was fixed up for him to work in and to rest during the day and all. The other was a bedroom. And we cooked in his apartment sometimes, sometimes in mine."

Even Farrell's friends thought that living with him would have been difficult for anyone. "He would have been impossible," Arthur Schlesinger said. "Cleo was an angel, a saint, to put up with him."

But she herself did not find living with Farrell hard. On the contrary, she found him fascinating. She adored his nobility of spirit. She *liked* to listen to his rambling discourse. "Everybody always says that to me," she observed. "They always say, 'Wasn't he difficult?' He was the easiest person in the world to live with. He couldn't have been more thoughtful, he couldn't have been more thoughtful. I mean, Jim Farrell—if [I'd] come home from work and if it had been a bad day, he would have known, because he would have called enough times during the day. And I'd come home and I'd start into the kitchen, and there'd be a bunch of flowers there and a note about how much he loved me. And he'd say, 'I'm taking you out.' Now, it might be to McDonald's; I'm not saying that he went to Lutèce's. But I mean he couldn't have been kinder. He was always very sweet to me."

That September, a prose-poem version of Genesis, which he had written in 1959 (and which Ken McCormick had rejected), was published by The Smith, an independent press, under the title *When Time Was Born*. (It was his second book published that year. In January, his third book for Doubleday had appeared: *Lonely for the Future*, a novel based on the Slow Club episode in 1927.) He dedicated *When Time Was Born* to Cleo Paturis.

Farrell had found love again. But about the literary world at large—all those reviewers, editors, and publishers who he still imagined were blocking his way—he remained defiant.

"They can fight me as they wish," he declared in an "Introduction" (dated December 10, 1965) to his prose poem. "They can blacklist me as they wish. They can reject me as they wish.

"I guarantee to survive, and, I guarantee that my bones, dissolving into chalky dust, will fight them from the grave."

Chapter Nineteen

"A Ministering Angel"

C LEO RESCUED HIM—not so much the writer Farrell, as the man. In her eyes, he was an authentic hero. "He never, ever cared if he heard applause," she said. "He loved it if he heard it; but when he didn't hear it, it was all right, too. He was very strong. He really felt that he was doing something important. And he lived his life as he wanted to live. To me, he was, and is, a hero, because the odds were against him all the time. All the time."

He would have continued to write, even if Cleo had never crossed his path. Indeed, he was so compulsive about writing that he wondered if he might be suffering from what psychiatrists call obsessive-compulsive disorder.

Cleo could hardly have changed that compulsiveness. But she did rescue the man from the melancholy depths to which he had sunk, and she did make it easier for the writer to work productively. She came to Farrell "like a ministering angel" (in Arthur Schlesinger's phrase). She was his devoted lover and his fierce champion. And though she was not a wealthy woman, the income from her work as a magazine editor—starting in 1967, at *American Girl*, a magazine published by the Girl Scouts of the U.S.A.— enabled him to cease worrying about money. She brought order, tranquility and happiness into what had been his frenzied, chaotic, lonely existence.

Though Farrell did not require applause, Cleo said, "he needed someone to say, 'This is the time to eat breakfast,' 'This is the time to eat lunch,' ... that kind of thing." But while she served that function, she always minimized her effect on him. "People think Jim's been 'saved' by an honest woman," she told an interviewer in 1979. "Nonsense! Jim never needed saving. He was always a great man, a great writer with enough energy for 10 authors."

"[Cleo] just made a new man of him." This was the opinion of

405

Evelyn Shrifte, whom Cleo began having to dinner parties a few years after she and Farrell moved in 1969 to an apartment uptown, at 308 East 79th Street in Yorkville. "It was absolutely amazing," Shrifte said. "I didn't know it was the same Jim Farrell. What she did with his library alone was miraculous, every book in its place, and dinner parties that she made for his friends, and she was a very good cook indeed. And just everything was like a perfect kind of marriage. It really was wonderful."

After they left their studio apartments in Tudor City and moved to 79th Street, Farrell began introducing Cleo to others as "Mrs. Farrell," though legally, Dorothy still retained that title. Farrell did consider seeking a divorce from Dorothy; but he and Cleo came to fear that if he did, Dorothy might seek the back alimony of about $85 a week to which she was entitled but which she had never collected. "'Jimmy, we're talking about my money now,'" Cleo remembered saying to him. "'I'm the one that makes the income; I'm the one who works.' And I said, 'I would rather we live on that money. I can't afford to pay [her] that money.'" For that very practical reason, they did not pursue a divorce. "'You'll have to stay married to her,'" Cleo said—"And he laughed."

But there was no doubt about whom he was really married to.

"Cleo, to me, did more for Jimmy than all the other women who [had been] around him," Farrell's sister Helen said. Farrell first introduced Cleo to her on a visit to Chicago during the Christmas holidays in 1970. "She brought order in his life," Helen explained. "She made him realize that you do save money; before that, money just went through his hands. She sort of organized his work. She claims that he would have [written] whether he ever knew her or not. But I think she was very instrumental in aiding him in his career." Their sister Mary agreed: "[Cleo] just really kept him in line and just did everything for him. And made a good home for him. And made everything wonderful. He was very happy with her. *Finally.* Settled down and had a good relationship."

Cleo described a typical day with him. She would rise at 6:30 and fix his breakfast: orange juice, corn flakes with sliced banana (the latter for his high blood pressure), and an English muffin. She would have a glass of orange juice; then, while he ate, she would shower and dress. "And then he would walk me to Second Avenue to catch the bus. And I would get on the bus and then he would hit the back of the bus" with his hand, call out her name, and throw kisses to her. She would throw kisses back; if she didn't, she knew he would feel hurt. The high school youths who rode the bus found their daily romantic display quite amusing.

She would get to her midtown office at *American Girl* magazine at about 7:45 and begin work. At about 8:30 her phone would ring: "It would be Jimmy. He'd say, 'Did I tell you that...' He called at least six times a day." He usually didn't get down to work until after the mail arrived around 10 A.M. Then he would write, and keep writing, often skipping lunch, until Cleo came home about 5 P.M. She would prepare dinner and summon him when it was ready. Afterward he would deal with his correspondence, while she cleaned up in the kitchen and then settled down with the newspaper he'd read in the morning hours.

During the baseball season, they would watch the Yankees or Mets games on TV. "As a matter of fact, Jim said there were two things that he most loved about me," Cleo recalled. "One was that I was the least petty person that he had ever known in his whole life. I don't know what that sprang from, but he always kept saying that. The other was how quickly I caught on to baseball."

Farrell always said he loved her. She knew he didn't have the intense romantic feeling for her that he once had had for Hortense. ("Hortense was the love of his life," she noted matter-of-factly.) Yet the two of them were very comfortable with each other, they enjoyed each other's company—and they were happy. His autumnal years with Cleo seem to have been among the happiest years of his life.

AFTER TOM MCCORMACK LEFT Doubleday for Harper & Row, Ken McCormick brought in associate editor Sally Arteseros, then in her twenties, to work on Farrell's books. *Lonely for the Future* was the first. In contrast to the seeming indifference he had shown to all the alterations that McCormack had made in *What Time Collects*, Farrell in 1965 balked at many of Arteseros's suggested changes in *Lonely for the Future*—his closer attention perhaps being a sign of his improving condition under Cleo's influence.

Arteseros had read Farrell in a college course, and as she dealt with his work at Doubleday she initially felt "a certain amount of awe." The generational gap was vast, she was inexperienced as an editor, and he frequently resisted her suggestions. It is possible that "towards the end, with the last few books, he may have accepted some of my editing," she said. "But I could not claim to be Farrell's editor. I was his in-house shepherd, but I wasn't his editor. I think that Cleo became his editor in the last years, and before that, maybe Luna Wolf."

There would be six more books for Doubleday. Four were novels: *A Brand New Life* (1968), in which Anne Duncan Daniels, a leading character from *What Time Collects*, goes to Chicago and eventually encounters George Raymond from *Lonely for the Future*, a character based (as Ed Lanson in *Ellen Rogers* had been) on Farrell's old Nietzschean chum Paul Caron; *Invisible Swords* (1971), his novel long in the works about the birth of a retarded child; *The Dunne Family* (1976), based on the Daly family during the Depression; and *The Death of Nora Ryan* (1978), based on the death of his mother. Doubleday also would publish two collections of his short stories—*Childhood Is Not Forever* (1969) and *Judith and Other Stories* (1973). (Several other books by Farrell were published by independent presses.)

None of the novels would escape the confines of the minor, but perhaps *Invisible Swords* came closest. Robert Phillips, a young and knowledgeable critic writing in *Saturday Review*, called it Farrell's "most ambitious book in years" and "one of [his] most powerful novels." Yet despite its strengths and virtues, *Invisible Swords*, too, ultimately falls short.

"I think that when I knew him, his best years [as a writer] were behind him," Sally Arteseros said. Still, she liked his Doubleday novels, particularly *The Death of Nora Ryan* and the novella "Judith." "I think that he had his moments and I think that there was great truth in [his books]."

None of Farrell's Doubleday books caused the cash registers in bookstores to ring nonstop, though some of the titles did better than others. By February 1979, more than eight months after publication of *The Death of Nora Ryan*, 8,109 copies had been sold, for instance. In contrast, by January 1973, about twenty-one months after publication of *Invisible Swords*, only 3,430 copies had been sold. While Doubleday would of course have preferred that his books have broad popular appeal, that was not then a necessity for the publisher, Arteseros pointed out. "There wasn't the desperate need to have every book sell very well and make a lot of money that [exists] today."

Doubleday thus came to be content with Farrell. "We love publishing you, Jim!" Ken McCormick told him in 1968. And Farrell, their rocky start a thing of the past, had become quite content with Doubleday, at least for the moment.* He dedicated *Invisible Swords*, published in March 1971, to McCormick, who retired as editor-in-chief later that year.

━━━━━━●━━━━━━

IN THE TUMULTUOUS YEAR OF 1968, in which Senator Eugene J. McCarthy of Minnesota challenged President Johnson over the Vietnam war, Johnson dramatically disclosed his decision not to seek another term, and Senator Robert F. Kennedy was assassinated, Farrell's political sympathies came to be with Vice President Hubert Humphrey and his candidacy to succeed Johnson. The novelist lent his name to a National Citizens Committee for Humphrey and served as an alternate delegate on a slate pledged to him from Manhattan's 17th District—until the Democratic primary that June, when McCarthy delegates swept the district.

Farrell had known McCarthy somewhat for many years and thought well of him, but did not agree with his "antiwar" stance. "I defended LBJ and practically broke with Gene McCarthy," he recalled two years later in a letter to his sister Helen. "I was one of the first to speak of, and to speak to Gene about the Presidency. But when the time came, I was in disagreement with him. I am not for the war to continue, but I do not want a one-sided peace."

In late 1965, Farrell had joined Dos Passos and some fifty other writers and intellectuals on a committee inspired by the Johnson administration, the "Committee for an Effective and Durable Peace in Asia." Two years later, he was on the "Citizens

---

*His contentment did not last. In a May 3, 1977, letter to Richard Parker, Farrell said: "I never turn in a manuscript any more until it is ready for publication, because if I do, the fools, idiots and miedocrities [*sic*] who are called editors and senior editors try to monkey with it. They have all kinds of foolish suggestions to make a book sell, and it is all a cariacature [*sic*], because the publishers then don't sell the book, anyway. I hope that it is the last book that I shall have published with Doubleday, and might even write to have my books published after I am dead. Such is my estimation of publishers." A year later, in a May 17, 1978, letter to another friend, Farrell said, "Doubleday printed a first edition of 6,000 copies of Nora Ryan, and it went into a second edition on the day of publication, but th[o]se are confidential figures. They publish me by semi-conspiracy. I don't now have a publisher, since I refused to sign a two book contract with Doubleday and have to decide what I shall do and what I shall prepare for publication next. I easily have more than fifteen books that could be put in final shape for publication, and am going on writing."

Committee for Peace with Freedom in Vietnam," chaired by his friend, former Senator Paul Douglas, and claiming to speak for the "silent center" in America.

According to Charles Tyroler, a Democratic strategist who recruited prominent writers to sign manifestoes backing administration policy in Vietnam, Farrell was "deeply disturbed that college students were siding with Hanoi instead of the White House."

In his lectures at various institutions, and as an adjunct professor at St. Peter's College during 1964–1965, a writer-in-residence at Richmond College, Virginia, during 1969–1970, and a writer-in-residence at Glassboro State College, New Jersey, in 1973, Farrell had ample opportunity to observe what was happening on campuses. "I support the policy of the United States in its present commitment," he wrote in the *New York Times* in November 1967, the month that McCarthy announced his presidential candidacy. "And for my political views I have been insulted by mail and by students during lectures. All of whom are terribly concerned about the freedom of people all over the world—unless they have another view, obviously."

In 1972 he looked askance at the Democratic presidential nominee, Senator George McGovern of South Dakota, who had supported Henry Wallace in 1948 and now favored immediate U.S. withdrawal from Vietnam. "Almost every day, my opinion of McGovern gets worse," Farrell told Helen that August. Like more than 60 percent of the electorate, he voted in November for President Richard Nixon, considering him the lesser evil.

Five years later, he and Cleo joined the Social Democrats, U.S.A., heir to the Socialist Party of Norman Thomas and Eugene V. Debs—and Max Shachtman! The Shachtmanite Workers Party had been reborn in 1949 as the Independent Socialist League, which in 1958, after explicitly abandoning Leninism, had submerged itself in the Socialist Party. Shachtman, who by 1951 had ceased calling himself a Trotskyist, had in some respects lagged behind Farrell in his rightward political evolution, but eventually came to much the same position. In 1972, with the Socialist Party divided over the Vietnam war, and later the McGovern candidacy, Shachtman and his forces were in control. They successfully pushed for the party to merge with the Democratic Socialist Federation, a small splinter group of elderly social democrats. After Shachtman's death that November (and McGovern's defeat), the Shachtmanite majority of the Socialist Party–Democratic Socialist Federation voted to adopt a new name: *Social Democrats, U.S.A.*

Instead of fielding independent candidates, the Social Democrats worked in close alliance with organized labor to influence the Democratic Party. "Socialists have rejected the conventional 'radical' approach of building upon the vague social discontents of marginal groups," Carl Gershman, executive director of Social Democrats, U.S.A., explained in 1975. "They have become valued allies of labor in the drive to enlarge the political role of the working class." Standing foursquare against Communist tyranny and aggression abroad, and for achieving socialism at home through democratic means, the Social Democrats provided a congenial political home for Farrell, who even in his seventies never ceased striving for a better world.

⟶▶•◀⟵

IN MAKING IT POSSIBLE FOR Farrell to write without having to worry about other matters, Cleo did a fine thing—or so it seemed until he developed a prolonged "writer's block" in 1973. "I was a basket case," Cleo remembered, "because Marya Zaturenska and Horace Gregory told me that the reason he had a writer's block is that I had taken the guesswork out of his life.... I absolutely wanted to jump off the roof. And I said to him, 'Jimmy, I never meant to hurt your writing.'"

He didn't blame her, however, and was stoic about his problem. "I accepted the fact that the block might be permanent," he would later recall. "I didn't panic but spent most of my days reading. Old books that I had read before. New books. Magazine articles. Then, after about six months, I awakened one morning, sat down at my desk, and started writing again. I have written every day since."

Thanks to Cleo, however, he had come to realize, once again, that there was more to life than *writing, writing, writing.*

Starting in 1969, they went to Paris every year in the spring (and some years they went twice, as in 1977, when he was honored with a *soirée de James T. Farrell* in June at the Pompidou Center). In the City of Light, Farrell renewed his old friendship with Mary McCarthy, who was now married to an American diplomat and living there. McCarthy and Farrell "were very good friends," almost like "an older brother and a sister," Cleo remembered.

411

Farrell also visited Chicago irregularly but virtually every year. "I am not a New Yorker," he said once. "I am a Chicagoan living in New York." He went sometimes with Cleo, when her job permitted; more often he went on his own, usually (after 1971) staying, with the Carmelite priests at Mount Carmel High School. Returning to his old school in the fall of that year with some folks who were making a documentary film about him and wanted to photograph him there, Farrell met Father David Dillon, then the school's vice principal. The priest told him that he had recently read *Studs Lonigan* and invited him to visit his alma mater whenever he was in town. Thus began a warm friendship between Farrell and not only Dillon but several other priests at the school.

"He stayed on the first floor here [in] this building," remembered Father Leander Troy, who was then the school's librarian and had begun collecting Farrell's books even before he met the novelist. "We had a room there for him. All he had in there was a chair and a bed and a desk. He could pop down the hall to the dining room. He generally had breakfast with us. [A] lot of times it would be in the warm weather, school was out, and the fellows weren't on such a strict schedule. So we could chat there. He chatted away. He loved to talk. All his experiences, people he knew, and he'd tell us stories." The priests were avid listeners.

Farrell also corresponded with Fathers Dillon and Troy. On several occasions, he asked Troy to say a memorial Mass for someone who had died and send a Mass card to the deceased's husband or other relative who was Farrell's friend. Farrell evidently did this simply because he thought the friend would appreciate it, not because his own faith had returned. (Troy never ventured to inquire into that possibility.) Still, Father Melvin James, who was at St. Anselm's Church in the late 1960s and was associate pastor there in the late 1970s, remembered several visits Farrell made to his old church, which was then serving the black community. "He liked to look around and say a prayer," Father James recalled. *Say a prayer?* "Well, he kneeled down. I don't know what he said. [Laughs] But he'd sit in the pew and he'd kneel down." Some of Farrell's siblings came to think during the 1970s that he might be on his way back to the faith.

"He hated to hear anything bad about the church," said Bill Lederer, a Chicago playwright. "He had this secret love for it." Once, Lederer remembered, he was with Farrell in a Chicago restaurant, "and he saw a priest and nun smoking and drinking. And here is this devout atheist saying, 'My goodness, I hate to see that in public: nuns and priests smoking and drinking.'"

As it happens, Lederer is a nephew of William "Studs" Cunningham, Farrell's model for Studs Lonigan. When Farrell was giving a talk in Chicago, in 1960 young Lederer approached him afterward. "I said, 'Mr. Farrell, my name is Bill Lederer. My mother's maiden name was Loretta Cunningham.' And I saw him freeze, literally freeze. And all I could see was the whites of his eyes. And he said, 'Well, how's Marty?' That was my mother's brother, Marty Cunningham, who's in the book." The encounter was fleeting, but a dozen years later Lederer wrote Farrell a letter, telling him that he had been named after his uncle Bill Cunningham "and my nickname in the old neighborhood was Studs," and that though his family "is still bitter about your book," which they refused to read, he himself had read it in 1951 as an Army draftee on a transport going overseas. "It moves me deeply. It speaks to my roots," Lederer wrote.

Farrell saw Lederer in Chicago several times after that. "When he met me for the first time," Lederer remembered, "he said I looked just like Studs and he started to cry, just like a child. I think he was a lonely guy."

Once, Lederer drove Farrell out to his old neighborhood on the South Side. "And he'd start talking with the residents [who] had been long gone, of course, and I thought, my God, he was transported in time. And it was strange. He actually started to talk about them, and I didn't know whether he was talking to me or these imaginary characters."

Lederer liked Farrell, but he was amazed that this supposed hard-boiled naturalist who looked at life as it was seemed in actuality to be "a real sentimentalist." Lederer also couldn't help but notice Farrell's odd behavioral tics, his "rolling his tongue, and licking his lips, and rocking" back and forth on the balls and heels of his feet. "And he would talk in truncated sentence form, [leaving] off in the middle of a sentence and then start[ing] up on something else.... [But] then sometimes he would key in on a thing, and boy, he'd catch it, from a real fine philosophical viewpoint."

For several months, the relationship between the author of *Studs Lonigan* and the nephew of Studs Cunningham was rather intense, at least on Farrell's part. "I was getting letters [from him] once, twice a week, [and] he sent me four or five novels," Lederer remembered. "I just couldn't keep up with the guy."

But after the two men appeared together before the students in an English class at Mount Carmel High School, their relationship cooled.

"They asked Farrell why did he write," Lederer recalled. "And he said, 'For immortality, something to go on after I die.' And then they asked me, and I said, 'Well, I never have become as famous as Mr. Farrell, so I don't know about the immortality stuff. But I know that when I'm writing my best, I feel that it's larger than me, that I'm in touch with Being or God or something larger than myself.' Well, from that point on, in my relationship with Farrell—this was after he'd embraced me and there was all this stuff—the iron curtain went down. He was cordial to me from then on, [but] he was never open, he was very guarded. I had a feeling that as long as I was at his feet as a disciple, we'd get along fine. But as soon as I showed anything from myself, he would feel threatened." Lederer wrote Farrell "two or three letters" after the novelist returned to New York that time, but "he didn't answer 'em, so I sort of gave up on the guy."

⟫•0•⟪

IN JANUARY 1973, JIM HENLE died at the age of eighty-one.

A few years before, Cleo had invited Henle to a book party for Farrell. She could tell later that Farrell was annoyed with her for doing so. But at the party, Henle, who had Parkinson's Disease, walked in "trembling all over," Cleo said, "and my Jimmy just went over and just waited on him hand-and-foot, and never left his side." Though still feeling—childishly and absurdly—that Henle had "betrayed" him, Farrell nonetheless, according to Cleo, "loved that man."

A few weeks after Henle's death, Farrell set down on paper a remembrance, recalling him as a witty, intelligent man and "a good editor" who respected his writers and their work. He made "intelligent suggestions" but didn't insist on them, and "believed it was wrong...to try to force a writer to change his or her book for commercial reasons."

It is possible that Farrell prepared the remembrance with a memorial meeting in Henle's honor in mind. If so, his ambivalence about Henle, which was not unlike his ambivalence about his father and mother, may have kept him from delivering the eulogy. When the meeting was held in February 1973, Farrell failed to show up, even though it had been announced in the *New York Times* the preceding day that he (along with journalist Bill Shannon) was to be a speaker.

"Jim Henle was not only my publisher but for years one of my closest friends," Farrell had written in the remembrance. "But we both lived beyond that era when publisher and author could sustain a true and profound friendship. Before Jim Henle died, I had changed publishers. Our relationship was based on business, on the twenty-seven books of mine he had published, and on nostalgia for what had been between us."

Farrell's first surrogate father, Tom Daly, had died a dozen years earlier, in August 1961, just a few weeks short of his ninetieth birthday. He spent his final years in Oak Forest Infirmary, Cook County's "old people's home," southwest of Chicago. Daly had mellowed a lot, according to Farrell's sister Helen, and become "a real kindly, nice old man, very dignified and all, and lovable." The nurses called him "The Mayor," because his last name was similar to that of Chicago's mayor at the time. Daly's sister Ella had been scheduled to enter Oak Forest along with him in April 1959. At seventy-five, she was quite sick, with heart problems. But two days before the planned move, she died. She and later her brother were buried in Calvary Cemetery in Evanston, in the ground that held the remains of other family members.

LITTLE MORE THAN A YEAR after Henle's death, Farrell had what Cleo called "his coming-out party." After they moved to their East 79th Street apartment in 1969, she had had an open house for friends nearly every Sunday. But this event—a seventieth-birthday party for Farrell at the National Art Museum of Sport, an anteroom of Madison Square Garden, on February 27, 1974 —was far grander. A few weeks later, in the *New Yorker* it was "The Talk of the Town."

Some two hundred people attended the bash. "I took his address book and invited everybody," Cleo said. Among those present were his brother Jack, from Maryland; his brother Earl, from Chicago; his old friends Horace Gregory and Marya Zaturenska; novelist Kurt Vonnegut and his companion, photographer Jill Krementz; essayist and novelist Elizabeth Hardwick; Professor Edgar Branch and his wife, Mary Jo; Evelyn Shrifte; and many, many others.

"We served hot dogs, because it was in the new sports

museum," Cleo said. "[But] so that we wouldn't look cheap, [we] had the best French champagne. And had a beautiful cake.... It was a great party. We had such fun."

"When we finally succeeded in getting the guest of honor to ourself for a moment or two," the anonymous *New Yorker* writer (Jervis Anderson) reported, "we asked him what his thoughts were on reaching his 70th birthday. He reflected, and turned quite serious. 'Seventy is too short a time in which to live,' he said. 'There's too much to know, too much to do, too much to think, too much to feel.'"

He did not begrudge the precious hours given to his birthday party, however. "He loved it," Cleo said. "He loved things like that. And"—despite his relative isolation when she had first known him—"he was such a social animal."

Two years later, Cleo—independently of Doubleday and remaining in the background—organized a "salute" to Farrell, a $50-a-plate dinner at the St. Regis Hotel in midtown Manhattan, honoring him on the occasion of the publication of what was reckoned to be his fiftieth book, *The Dunne Family* (which he dedicated to her). A multitude of literati and others whose current value on the celebrity market in many cases exceeded his own showed up on the evening of September 15, 1976, and paid him tribute. "I love Jim Farrell, the way the saints, discovering their métier, love J.C.," said novelist Norman Mailer, whose reading of *Studs Lonigan* as a young man had helped him decide to become a writer. Arthur Schlesinger Jr., Bill Shannon, Robert Gorham Davis, Meyer Schapiro, former Senator Eugene J. McCarthy, composer Virgil Thompson, Yiddish writer Isaac Bashevis Singer, and Kurt Vonnegut, as well as Ken McCormick—and Dorothy Farrell—were among those on hand. A photograph taken then suggests that Farrell was immensely pleased.

⟫⟩·0·⟨⟪

LESS THAN TWO MONTHS AFTER that joyful tribute to him, and unbeknownst to Cleo, Farrell resumed taking amphetamines. His physician, Dr. Edward Jacobs, had died a year earlier, and he began seeing Dr. Robert D. Seely in November 1976. Dr. Seely started prescribing amphetamines for Farrell that month and continued doing so right up to the end. Over 34 months, the doctor issued 36 prescriptions for dexedrine (or dexamyl, which is dexedrine mixed with amobarbital, a sedative, for "double trouble," as they say on the street). On November 12, 1976, he prescribed 30 tablets of five milligrams each, to be taken one a day; nine days later, he prescribed another 30 tablets; before long, he prescribed 60 tablets, increasing the dosage to two a day; then, in February 1977, he upped it to three 5-milligram tablets a day. Farrell had hypertension, and amphetamines can boost blood pressure, but even after Dr. Seely learned in December 1978 of angina and the death of muscle tissue in the heart, he continued to prescribe them.

"For what medical condition did the patient need dexedrine, that you were aware of?" Dr. Seely would be asked in legal proceedings after Farrell's death.

"He [Farrell] told me that for a considerable period of time that he had been taking dexedrine and he needed dexedrine to function, to continue as a writer and could not get along without it," Dr. Seely would testify. The physician also indicated that he took Farrell's (alleged) word for this, did not ask him who had prescribed the medication or try to find out what the records of the late Dr. Jacobs showed, and had no physical evidence that Farrell could not function without the drug.

"So that throughout the entire time that you prescribed the dexedrine, which you did prescribe for Mr. Farrell," the doctor would be asked, "it was based solely on what you say Mr. Farrell told you; is that correct?"

"Yes," Dr. Seely would reply.

Cleo—who would not discover Farrell's secret until after his death, when a bill arrived in the mail from a neighborhood pharmacy—said that she is sure that he was not on amphetamines when he was seeing Dr. Jacobs, who lived in the same building as they did. "I know he was off of it for Dr. Jacobs. I went back, I did all of the legwork. Jacobs was dead, [so] I contacted his wife. I got the medical records. He was off of it."

After Farrell began seeing Dr. Seely, Cleo came to be somewhat suspicious of his new physician. But she had no inkling that he was prescribing amphetamines or that Farrell was taking them, though she did learn at some point that Seely was prescribing valium, which Farrell used occasionally to help him sleep.

"Jimmy was so protective" of his relationship with Seely, she recalled. "I could not talk to Seely, I could not do this, I could not do that." She had taken over so many aspects of his life, but he refused to let her take over this one. "He just didn't want me to take charge of his relationship with his doctor. Period. And I thought: okay."

The fact that Cleo remained unaware of his use of amphetamines when they were living together suggests that the dosage must have been much lower than it had been when she first knew him. And the fact that he did not experience any great loss of weight and become again the gaunt figure he had been when she first knew him (a time when he had not been eating at all well) indicates the same.

There can be little doubt as to *why* Farrell had wanted the amphetamines from Dr. Seely: to help him with his writing. To the very end, his writing was almost everything to him.

"DO YOU MIND IF I'M comfortable?" Farrell would ask his sister Helen almost as soon as he and Cleo crossed the threshold of the Dillons' modest cottage in St. Petersburg, Florida. Receiving permission, he'd go put on his pajamas and then rejoin the others. Later, fortified with a Coke and cigarettes, he'd work past midnight at the typewriter Helen and Matt Dillon had rented for him.

The Dillons had moved from Chicago to St. Petersburg in 1969, and Farrell and Cleo, starting in 1971, joined them there annually, Cleo staying a week, Farrell two or three. They came not only to visit with Helen and Matt but to watch one or more of their favorite teams in spring training—the Chicago White Sox (in Sarasota), the New York Yankees (in Fort Lauderdale), and the New York Mets (in St. Petersburg).

One year, Farrell went to twelve exhibition games in Florida; that same year, during the regular season, he saw, by his own estimate, "35 to 40" baseball games. In New York, he was able to get in free at both Yankee Stadium and Shea Stadium. "I get let in free, fed, and sit in the press box and have a good time," he told Dick Parker, his old friend from St. Cyril's who was now an Egyptologist at Brown University.

Farrell liked to hang out with the sportswriters and ballplayers, and they liked seeing this literary giant who was so enthusiastic about baseball and knew so much about it. "Because he has loved baseball since childhood," *Chicago Sun-Times* sportswriter Bill Gleason, a friend and admirer, wrote in one column, "Farrell, a realist in his fiction, sometimes imagines himself as a baseball writer. He has written tens of thousands of words about baseball for magazines, but his fantasies take him into major league press boxes, covering game after game through an entire season."

Once, when someone asked Farrell why he had become a novelist, Ralph Kiner, the Mets broadcaster and former Pittsburgh Pirates slugger who was standing next to him, interjected : "I'll tell you why James T. Farrell wrote books. He wanted to play second base for the Chicago White Sox, and couldn't." Everyone laughed, but Farrell, remembering his boyhood, knew, as he later wrote, that "it wasn't altogether a joke."

In the winter of 1978, some months after he and Cleo had moved into a more luxurious apartment at 345 East 73rd Street, Farrell one night began talking about baseball and how he couldn't wait for spring training to begin, couldn't wait to see the guys again. "Well, why do we have to wait until March?" Cleo said. "Why don't we have a baseball party?" So she called up Ralph Kiner, former Mets star Ron Swoboda, "and a whole bunch of baseball guys, and I went to the delicatessen and I bought a great big tray of corn beef." On the day of the party, she and a few female friends hid in the bedroom, while just outside, the twenty or so "baseball guys" (including Farrell's old friend Al Glotzer, no longer a Trotskyist but still an ardent baseball fan) talked about their favorite subject. When Cleo heard—and peeking out, saw—Ron Swoboda demonstrating how he held the bat when he hit the double that gave the Mets the winning run in the 1969 World Series, she knew the party was a success. "And Jimmy was in heaven."

One summer day later that year, Farrell went out to Central Park, carrying his Louisville Slugger bat, a Roberto Clemente model. "The Young People's Socialist League team had a game scheduled, and I thought they might let me hit a few," he would tell sportswriter Gleason. The young ballplayers politely let the old switch-hitter have his swings. "But I was hitting right-handed to right field and left-handed to left field," Farrell said, "so I knew it was time to retire."

He gave away his bat to one of the kids.

———⇒•⇐———

STUDS LONIGAN CAME TO television in March 1979 in the form of a six-hour miniseries, shown by NBC over three successive Wednesday nights. It was good television drama, evidencing respect for the viewers' intelligence as well as for the original novels. The adaptation—by Reginald Rose, a playwright from TV's so-called "Golden Age"—was literate. The acting—with Colleen Dewhurst and Charles Durning as the Lonigan parents, and Harry Hamlin (and young Dan Shor) as Studs—was fine.

Even Farrell himself was impressed by the production. At first apprehensive, he was relieved after watching the first installment. "I did not think that *Studs Lonigan* had been cheapened. The television series was done with care and attention." But, he quickly added, "there was a difference between my book and the work that was shown."

There was indeed. The harsh realism of his trilogy had been toned down. "The South Side is so clean it could almost be a new Disney park—Palookaland—and the gritty scenes are tough only in comparison to the romantic moments, which blush into soft filter as if setting us up for a soap commercial," wrote a Chicago reviewer.

To make the miniseries, Lorimar Productions spent more than $5 million, and, it was reported, faced a deficit of more than $500,000, which the producer, Harry R. Sherman, feared would not be earned back. Because United Artists (under whose aegis the low-budget 1960 movie of *Studs Lonigan* had been made) still owned the rights to the trilogy, Lorimar had to turn over a percentage of its worldwide syndication revenues to United Artists. For the same reason, neither United Artists nor Lorimar was obligated to pay Farrell anything in connection with the TV production. In response to "a moral appeal" from his lawyer, however, the author was cut in as (in his words) "a nonconsulting consultant."

It was partly because of the payments he received in that capacity that, as Farrell told Dick Parker, "we are threatened with becoming rich." During the late 1970s, Farrell "started making money," Cleo recalled. Besides the income from the TV show, he also got $25,000 from the Franklin Library, which in 1979 issued a limited collector's edition of *Young Lonigan*—each copy on gilt-edged paper, bound in green leather and signed by the author. In addition, he "started getting a lot of money for lectures" in the late 1970s, Cleo said. Instead of $350 or $500 per talk, he was getting $2,000 or $3,000.

The TV miniseries brought Farrell a good deal of publicity, including a profile in *People* magazine. But his good fortune antedated the television drama. "Suddenly, when it looked like my career in the public sense was cooked, and wouldn't be resuscitated until after I go Yonder, things began changing," he told Parker in 1977. It had begun, he said, with the "salute" to him the preceding year. Since then, "things have changed, and I have even been making money for a change and was able to help a lot of people who needed money more than I needed it in a bank or an investment." He had made a donation to Mount Carmel, he told his former classmate, and hoped to make "a bigger one, in memory of Bob Lusk...and our friends and comrades of those callow days." ("However," he added, "they were less callow for you than for me. You were more mature and brighter than I in high school.")

Even before the 1976 "salute," Farrell had become an object of official veneration. He received an honorary degree in 1968 from Miami University (where Professor Branch taught); the Roswell and Wilma Messing Jr. Award in 1973 from the Associates of the Saint Louis University Libraries; and an honorary degree from Columbia College in 1974. Three years later, the National Endowment for the Arts awarded him a $7,500 grant. In 1979 he picked up the University of Chicago Alumni Association's Professional Achievement Award (and spoke on the same day at a ceremony in Rockefeller Memorial Chapel, honoring his old teacher James Weber Linn); he also received honorary degrees from Bradley University in Peoria, Illinois, and the University of Illinois at Chicago.

The honor that meant the most to Farrell, however, came from the American Academy of Arts and Sciences. It was the Emerson-Thoreau Medal for 1979, given for distinguished achievement in the broad field of literature. The prize had first been awarded to Robert Frost in 1958, and subsequent recipients had included T. S. Eliot, Mark Van Doren, Lewis Mumford, Edmund Wilson and Saul Bellow. Harvard Professor Daniel Aaron, chairman of the Emerson-Thoreau committee, had proposed Farrell for the honor, and the other committee members—Bellow, Irving Howe, Roy Lamson, Howard Nemerov, Wallace Stegner and Eudora Welty—agreed. (Farrell was surprised by the supportive votes of Bellow and Howe, who, he told Father Troy, "previously had been critical of me, silent often on my work etc." He reflected: "I must be very old, since I am getting honored and awarded—and various and sundry—including former enemies, or near enemies—are approving of me and aiding in honoring me.")

In presenting the award at a ceremony in Boston on April 18, 1979, Professor Aaron, the author of *Writers on the Left* (1961), noted how often Farrell had been "summoned to the bar by his peers and ordered to justify himself," first by the Stalinists during the 1930s, then, after the war, by the antinaturalists (even though, by their own criteria, Farrell didn't really qualify as a "naturalist"). But Farrell "has never needed help in defending himself against his faultfinders...," Aaron said.

> He has refused to be constrained or intimidated or bribed by political parties or literary coteries, and at a time when such words as 'reality' or 'truth' are drained of meaning, and when it is no longer possible, at least according to some of the poststructuralist dicta, for fiction to be mimetic, he continues to depict the world of his experience, a world very real to him. The writer, he says, has a duty to tell the truth about his world. He has no obligations to make money, to be glamorous: "God never told me to be rich."...
>
> In nominating him for the Emerson-Thoreau award, the committee is giving belated but well-deserved recognition to James T. Farrell, novelist, critic, journalist, a brave man, a good writer, the discloser of heretofore undisclosed scenes of American life.

After the meeting, Farrell was one of the last to leave the academy's house. As he made his way out, a priest whom he had noticed standing and waiting while people filed out, approached him and offered congratulations on behalf of himself and Cardinal John J. Wright, who headed the Roman Curia's Sacred Congregation of Clergy in the Vatican, charged with the supervision of priests throughout the world. The priest, one Father Murray, told Farrell that the Boston-born cardinal had read his work when young, as had Murray, and that he regretted not being able to attend the award ceremony. This news, which Farrell soon related to Father Troy, evidently added to the great pleasure he felt on getting the Emerson-Thoreau award from, as he proudly said, "one's peers."

——➤•◀——

THE YANKEES WERE TO PLAY in Kansas City against the Royals on the night of August 21st, a Tuesday, and Farrell told Cleo that he wanted to watch the game on TV when she called to say that her friends, Jack and Kathleen Flanagan, had invited them for dinner. *American Girl*, of which Cleo had been the top editor since 1972, had folded a few weeks before, and she had gone to see Jack Flanagan about a job. Kathleen Flanagan told Cleo it would be fine to end the evening early, before the game started.

Mrs. Flanagan served a delicious German chocolate cake for dessert, and Farrell and Cleo split a piece of it. After dinner, outside the Flanagans' apartment at 66th Street and Park Avenue, Cleo suggested that they walk home to 73rd. "It will be a nice little walk." Farrell said he was really tired. Cleo said she had never heard him say that before. He said that his arm was shaking. She was sure it was from too much typing. They took a taxi home.

He got into his pajamas, she got into her nightgown, and they slipped into bed and watched the ballgame, which began at 8:30. The Yankees didn't do much until the ninth inning, when they were behind 2-1; with the bases loaded and two out, their designated hitter hit a single, putting them ahead, and then their shortstop blasted a three-run home run, his second homer of the year, to crush the Royals, 6-2.

The game over, Farrell turned to Tacitus, the Roman historian. After a while, Cleo remembered, he said to her: "You've got to read this."

"If I read everything you told me I had to read," she replied, "I could never, ever get a job or anything else."

"Yeah, but Cleo, you won't believe how fascinating it is to read about how they passed laws in ancient Rome." And soon he whispered to her, "You know, you really would like to read it."

She tried to go to sleep, but couldn't. He asked her if his reading light was bothering her. It wasn't that; she said she thought she might be worried. He told her they had nothing to worry about any more.

Before long, they both fell asleep.

About 1:30 or 2 A.M., she remembered, she heard "a funny noise" coming from Farrell.

"Jimmy," she said.

No answer.

"If you don't answer me, I'm going to get terribly nervous."

No answer.

"That's the damndest noise. What in the world are you doing?"

She turned on the light, then jumped up and shook him. But he wouldn't open his eyes. She began administering mouth-to-mouth resuscitation. At some point, she paused, reached outside the bedroom door and pressed the buzzer for the doorman, shouting into the intercom: "Get me help! Farrell's had a heart attack."

Help soon came, but to no avail.

James T. Farrell was dead.*

⟫-0-⟪

NOVELIST KURT VONNEGUT AROSE to speak at the brief service Friday afternoon in the Frank E. Campbell funeral home on Madison Avenue at 81st Street, with people spilling out onto the street. His companion, Jill Krementz, had been very helpful to Cleo in coping with the demands suddenly imposed upon her and had told Cleo that Vonnegut would be hurt if she did not invite him to speak at the funeral service.

He began by expressing some bewilderment that he had been asked to speak, inasmuch as he had not known the deceased all that well. Nevertheless, he gamely proceeded, saying (according to an edited version of his remarks that he subsequently published) that perhaps he had been chosen "as a representative of the generation of American writers most influenced by James T. Farrell.... Here is what he did for me and many like me when I was very young: He showed me through his books that it was perfectly all right, perhaps even useful and beautiful, to say what life really looked like, what was really said and felt and done—what really went on."

Vonnegut took disapproving note of the fact that a cross was hanging not far from the casket—Cleo, in her grief, had not even noticed it—and he said that it was "a nice try by whoever put it there, but it is surely known in heaven that James T. Farrell of Chicago and New York was not among our leaders in organized tub-beating for Jesus Christ."

Though Farrell had remained an avowed atheist and might have deemed the presence of the cross unfitting, one doubts that he, in his maturity, would have shared Vonnegut's evident discomfort. Just a few months before, he had written enthusiastically to

---

*It is possible that Farrell's fatal heart attack was brought on by his use of amphetamines. In 1980, as executrix of Farrell's estate, Cleo Paturis filed a civil suit against Dr. Seely, accusing him of medical malpractice resulting in Farrell's death. Six years later, after pretrial depositions were taken but before the case went to trial, Dr. Seely settled the suit out of court for what a confidential source said was a considerable six-figure sum.

Dick Parker about how "thrilled" he was by Pope John Paul II's bold and stunningly successful visit to Communist Poland. "It constitutes one of the biggest, one of the greatest blows for freedom, for a fundamental humanism, struck in our time, and even in our century.... The action of Pope John [Paul] is, I believe, going to cause a revival of Catholicism, and that will not hurt our world. The previous statement is an understatement."

At Cleo's invitation, Carl Gershman, executive director of the Social Democrats, U.S.A., also spoke at the service, and Bayard Rustin, the civil rights leader and chairman of the Social Democrats, sang. In addition, actor Kevin McCarthy read a statement from his absent sister, Mary McCarthy, who wanted to pay her respects to her "valiant and valued old friend and fellow-writer." Farrell, she said, had the rare quality, particularly among writers, of being "at ease with himself.... He never seems to have had any problem with touching bottom in himself. Impossible to imagine Farrell affected, Farrell hypocritical, false, insincere. To praise him for his integrity is almost a waste of breath, for he was cut from the whole cloth—one guesses—to start with and had no temptations to wear a coat of many colors or be a chameleon taking on the color of his environment.... He was an important figure in our literary and moral history who will be remembered with pride and love, for he was a completely lovable being as well as an author and influence."

A few months before Farrell died, A. Philip Randolph, the great civil rights and labor leader, had died at the age of ninety, and Farrell, who had worked with him in the late 1940s on a committee to end segregation in the armed forces, paid him tribute in *New America*, the publication of the Social Democrats. "His struggles were for goodness," Farrell wrote. "His life aims were to make goodness prevail in our world. And yet his ideals were realistic rather than utopian. Unlike those who carry the fight for goodness into, to paraphrase Theodore Roosevelt, 'the lunatic fringe' of goodness, Phil Randolph was totally free of sentimentality in politics—that sentimentality which often renders men foolish and creates demagogues."

Quoting those last remarks in his eulogy of Farrell, Carl Gershman, who had come to know him well, added: "Jim Farrell, too, was free of such sentimentality. It may also be said that he was totally unpretentious, despite his fame and immense literary achievement; that he was totally uncorrupted, despite his success; that he was without cynicism, despite his deep understanding of mankind's capacity for cruelty and dishonesty; and that he was irrepressibly buoyant in his attitude toward life, in his work, in his human relationships, in his pursuit of truth, and in his struggles for justice as he saw it. There was in Jim Farrell, as he said there was in Phil Randolph, 'a magnificence of spirit; and yet a simplicity.' "

The service over, the polished mahogany casket containing his body was flown to Chicago. Although Cleo, like Farrell, was an avowed atheist, she decided that he should be buried with his grandmother in Calvary Cemetery, the Catholic cemetery in Evanston. With the help of his sister Helen and the Reverend Conan Hartke, one of his friends at Mount Carmel High School, it was arranged. Though the offer of a Mass was declined, there was a brief ceremony at the site on Saturday, with family members and others (including Dorothy) gathered. Father Hartke, assisted by Father Troy, presided.

The deceased author, declared Father Hartke—perhaps remembering the reluctance of many of his fellow Catholics to accept as accurate the portrayal of their community in *Studs Lonigan* and *A World I Never Made* and others of his novels — "was not a liar. He told the truth as he perceived it and observed it. We should all be so able to give the truth so faithfully." The 25th Psalm and the Lord's Prayer were read.

And so James Thomas Farrell, an honest writer dead at seventy-five from "a deprivation of time," joined his beloved grandmother and the other Dalys and Farrells in the consecrated ground.

Acknowledgments

I ACQUIRED MANY DEBTS IN the making of this biography. My first is to Cleo Paturis. Along with the keys to the Farrell archival kingdom and permission to quote from his works, she gave me her time and her memories, and never once tried to dictate what I should write.

Next, I must thank Dorothy Farrell, who also gave very generously of her time and memories, allowing an inquisitive stranger to probe deeply and at length into her life with James T. Farrell, with all its ups and downs. She, too, never tried to dictate what I should write.

I regret that Farrell's sisters, Helen and Mary, did not live to see the completed biography. Helen Farrell Dillon was the family historian and, like her novelist brother, had a keen memory. In lengthy interviews in her Florida home, and also by telephone and letter, she told me what she knew—and my account of Farrell's boyhood is much richer for it. Mary Farrell Bertrand, in a long interview in her Los Angeles home and in subsequent letters, was also very generous and helpful, giving me some invaluable details and insights into life in the Farrell and Daly households.

Many others with memories of Farrell helped enormously, letting me interview them in person or by phone, or providing copies of relevant letters and other documents. They include: Stanford S. Apseloff, Sally Arteseros, Eliot Asinof, Irene Auvil, Mervin Block, Luna Wolf Carne-Ross, Randolph Carter, Stanley Colbert, Peter Coleman, Olga Corey, "H. D.," Katherine Dunham, Dr. Kevin Farrell, Dr. Margaret Farrell, Dennis Flynn, Carl Gershman, Albert Glotzer, Elinor Rice Hays, Peter and Theda Henle, Nancy Horneffer, Father Melvin James, S.V.D., Alfred Kazin, Ruth Kenny, Loretta Cunningham Lederer, William Lederer, Sterling Lord, Thomas J. McCormack, Kenneth McCormick, Richard Parker, Arthur Schlesinger Jr., Evelyn Shrifte,

Ria D. Simon, Ellen Skerrett, Dick Starkey, Studs Terkel, Diana Trilling, Father Leander Troy, O.C.C., Morton White, Sloan Wilson and Mary Hunter Wolfe. Some of those people have since died, but my gratitude to them all is undiminished.

Still others who helped in various ways, large and small, include: Michael D. Aeschliman, Jean Ashton, Timothy Barton, John Blades, Helen Blanchard, Marshall Brooks, Robert J. Butler, Paul M. Caron, Catherine Clarke, Clare Conerty, Marcella Crosse, Matt Dillon, Scott Donaldson, Karen D. Drickamer, Melissa Dunlap, Alan Ehrenhalt, Clifton P. Fadiman, Johanna Fallon, James Finn, Carol Gelderman, John Grande, Father Andrew M. Greeley, Peggy Greenfield, Howard Hansen, William Healy, Fred Hobson, Lisa Hope, Father Robert G. Humbert, S.J., Averil Kadis, Max Kampelman, Mike Kelly, James Laughlin, Lawrence W. Lichty, Brenda Macon, Dr. Howard Markel, Patricia Mauf, Anne McCormick, Harold L. Miller, Marion Mixon, George E. O'Brien Jr., Alexandra Oleson, Mary Ann Papageorgiou, Beatrice Parker, Gladys Parker, Richard Popp, Leslie J. Reagan, Christine Ruggere, Julie A. Satzik, Sandra Stencel, Maxine Hunsinger Sullivan, Tom Terranova, John Tytell, Amy Viens and Mary Ruth Yoe.

At the University of Pennsylvania's Rare Book and Manuscript Library, where the massive Farrell archive (more than a thousand boxes of material) is located, Nancy Shawcross, curator of manuscripts, and John Pollack, public services specialist, along with director Michael Ryan, were unfailingly helpful. Librarians at other institutions (some of whom are named in the preceding paragraph) also aided my research, including those at the Library of Congress, the National Archives, the U.S. Labor Department's Wirtz Labor Library, Columbia University's Rare Book and Manuscript Library, New York University's Fales Library, the University of Chicago's Regenstein Library, the Chicago Historical Society, George Washington University's Gelman Library, the American University Library, the Enoch Pratt Free Library, the Morris Library at Southern Illinois University at Carbondale, the Iron Range Research Center (Chisholm, Minnesota), the State Historical Society of Wisconsin, the Oakland (California) Public Library, Catholic University of America's Mullen Library, Marymount University's Reinsch Library (Arlington, Virginia), and the Arlington County Public Library. The Federal Bureau of Investigation, in response to my Freedom of Information Act request, provided a 64-page file on Farrell.

Professor Edgar Branch's *James T. Farrell* (1971), in the Twayne series on authors, and his several articles on various aspects of Farrell's early life were very useful to me, particularly in the initial stages of my research. His published bibliography of Farrell's works (updated several times in *The American Book Collector*) was a great help. Professor Branch's more recently published works appeared after I had virtually completed my own research, but they too were useful, allowing me to check some of my findings and to add some pertinent details to my account of Farrell's life. In the early stages of my research, I also found useful Professor Alan Wald's *James T. Farrell: The Revolutionary Socialist Years* (1978), which is written from the point of view of a latter-day Trotskyist.

Mark Wukas, a talented young Chicago writer who learned of my biographical project, volunteered to do some legwork for me in that city, simply out of admiration for Farrell and fellow feeling for Chicago writers in general. He proved as good as his word, obtaining for me some useful details and documents. I am grateful for his selfless labors.

Steve Lagerfeld, editor of *The Wilson Quarterly*, also worked selflessly (and on his summer vacation!) to help me trim the manuscript. Steve and Jay Tolson, his predecessor as editor of the *WQ*, were staunch supporters of my project from the beginning. Other friends and colleagues at the Woodrow Wilson International Center for Scholars who lent aid and support included Jim Carman, James Morris, Blair Ruble and Seymour Martin Lipset.

My thanks to Hilton Kramer, editor of *The New Criterion*, for pointing me toward Encounter Books. Peter Collier, my editor there, made scores of helpful suggestions for improving the manuscript. The late Clyde Taylor, of Curtis Brown Ltd., was my agent from the very beginning of this project in 1992, and when some unanticipated difficulties appeared midway, he stayed with it, and with me, until his death in early 2001. I shall always be grateful for his unwavering support. Mitchell S. Waters, of Curtis Brown, then became my agent and saw the project through to publication.

The book could not have been written without the support and sacrifices of my wife, Susan Landers, to whom it is dedicated. Whatever its merits may be, it is a very inadequate tribute. The long journey toward publication was made lighter by the presence of our children, Alyssa and Christopher, both now grown to adulthood. Perhaps they, and our son-in-law, Alex Plummer, will find lessons of their own in the life of James T. Farrell.

Notes

Introduction

ix   *"among the memorable people":* Joseph Warren Beach, *American Fiction, 1920-1940* (New York: Macmillan, 1941), 304.

ix   *"You forget":* Carl Van Doren, "The City Culture," *Nation,* 24 October 1936.

ix   *"Nothing in modern sociology":* Gerald Green, 18 September 1976 letter to KM.

x   *"Sooner or later":* Morley Callaghan, "James T. Farrell: A Tribute," *Twentieth Century Literature,* February 1976.

x   *"head out into":* Tom Wolfe, "Stalking the Billion-Footed Beast," *Harper's,* November 1989.

xi   *"In spite of"*: Arthur Schlesinger Jr., in *the coming of age of a great book...* (New York: Vanguard Press, 1953), 3.

xi   *"changed my life"*: Norman Mailer, in "The Books That Made Writers," *NYT Book Review*, 25 November 1979; Hilary Mills, *Mailer: A Biography* (New York: Empire Books, 1982), 44. See also Peter Manso, *Mailer: His Life and Times* (New York: Simon & Schuster, 1985), 45–46, 68, 101; Carl Rollyson, *The Lives of Norman Mailer: A Biography* (New York: Paragon, 1991), 14–15; and J. Michael Lennon, "A Conversation with Norman Mailer," *New England Review*, Summer 1999, 141.

xi   *"[Farrell] taught me"*: Pete Hamill, "Farrell," in *The Big Book of American Irish Culture*, ed. Bob Callahan (New York: Viking, 1987), 132.

xi   *"a paperback, falling apart"*: Frank McCourt, *'Tis* (New York: Scribner, 1999), 73.

xi   *"do[ing] battle so that others"*: JTF, *My Days of Anger* (New York: Vanguard Press, 1945), 401.

xii   *"I think our generation"*: Van Wyck Brooks, "Fashions in Defeatism," *SR*, 22 March 1941.

xii   *"People look back"*: Ross Klavan and David Feinberg, "The Mugging of James T. Farrell," *Village Voice*, 12 March 1979.

xii   *"a lonely road"*: Murray Kempton, *Part of Our Time: Some Ruins and Monuments of the Thirties* (New York: Simon & Schuster, 1955), 143.

xiii   *"would be more appropriate"*: Elizabeth Hardwick, "Fiction Chronicle," *PR*, Summer 1946.

xiii   *"unreflecting and limited people"*: Edmund Wilson, "Novelist Bites Critic," *Nation*, 24 June 1936; Edmund Wilson, "James Farrell on James Farrell," *NR*, 28 October 1940.

xiii   *"He writes about"*: Quoted by William V. Shannon, *The American Irish* (New York: Macmillan, 1963), 251.

xiv   *"those awful people"*: HA, quoted by Randolph Carter, interview.

xiv   *"gray" and "dreary"*: JTF, in Robert van Gelder, "An Interview with Mr. James T. Farrell," *NYT Book Review*, 17 May 1942.

xiv   *"Do writers"*: Edna O'Brien, *James Joyce* (London: Weidenfeld & Nicolson, 1999), 130.

xiv   *"Obviously"*: JH, "The Record of a Friendship" (unpublished notes about JTF, n.d., provided to RKL by JH's son Peter Henle).

PART ONE: YOUNG FARRELL

Prologue: The Wound

3   Sources: JTF, "The World I Grew Up In," *Commonweal*, 25 February 1966, 606–11; JTF, "[Chronology for Edgar Branch]," circa 1962, Box

443, JTFUP; JTF, *True* [unpublished autobiography], Box 460, JTFUP; HFD, interview; HFD, 12 October 1992 letter to RKL; MFB, interview. In "The World I Grew Up In," JTF writes that he returned home after the baby was born and then went back to live with the Dalys in "about 1907"; in *True,* he says that occurred "around 1907 and 1908." The confusion likely arose because although HFD was born on June 16, 1906, two years were later shaved off her age.

4   [Footnote] *"the conception":* Edmund Wilson, *The Wound and the Bow* (1941; London: Methuen, 1961), 257; David Castronovo, *Edmund Wilson* (New York: Ungar, 1987), 44.

Chapter 1: The Farrells and the Dalys

5   *When their first child:* Baptismal certificate issued by St. John Church, 18th and Clark Streets, for William Earl Farrell, baptized 29 April 1900; marriage certificate issued by St. John Church for James Farrell and Mary Daly, wed 19 April 1899; 1900 Census (E.D. no. 109, Sheet no. 8); HFD, interview; JTF, *True,* Box 460, JTFUP. The 1900 Census indicates that by that June, the Farrells were living at 2127 Archer Avenue. The Lakeside City Directory for 1900 confirms that James G. [*sic*] Farrell, a "driver," was living at that address. The Lakeside City Directories for 1896, 1898 and 1899 indicate that a James Farrell, "driver" or "teamster," was living next door, at 2125 Archer Avenue. Information about the occupants of the buildings is from the 1900 Census. Timothy Barton, a preservation specialist in the landmarks division of the city's department of planning and development, provided details about the buildings themselves.

5   *Trains rumbled by: Talbot's Industry and Railroad Map of Chicago* (1904); *Blanchard's Map of Chicago with the New Street Names* (1901); Greeley-Carlson Company's *Second Atlas of the City of Chicago,* vol. 1 (Chicago: R. R. and R. H. Donnelly, 1891); James R. Barrett, *Work and Community in the Jungle: Chicago's Packinghouse Workers, 1894-1922* (Urbana: University of Illinois Press, 1990), 67.

5   *the vice district:* Lloyd Wendt and Herman Kogan, *Bosses in Lusty Chicago: The Story of Bathhouse John and Hinky Dink* [original title: *Lords of the Levee*] (1943; Bloomington: Indiana University Press, 1967), 282; Finis Farr, *Chicago: A Personal History of America's Most American City* (New Rochelle, N.Y.: Arlington House, 1973), 299. See also Emmett Dedmon, *Fabulous Chicago: A Great City's History and People* (New York: Atheneum, 1981), Chapter 20.

6   *more than one-third:* Charles Shanabruch, *Chicago's Catholics: The Evolution of an American Identity* (Notre Dame, Ind.: University of Notre Dame Press, 1981), 235.

6   *Once, no more than:* Bessie Louise Pierce, *A History of Chicago,* vol. 1, *The Beginning of a City, 1673-1848* (New York: Knopf, 1937), 44; Evelyn M. Kitagawa and Karl E. Taeuber, *Local Community Fact Book, Chicago Metropolitan Area, 1960* (Chicago: Chicago Community Inventory, University of Chicago, 1963), 78; Sibylle Allendorf, "The Loop," in Chicago Fact Book Consortium, *Local Community Fact Book, Chicago Metropolitan Area, Based on the 1970 and 1980 Censuses* (Chicago: University of Illinois at Chicago, 1984), 89; Carl Sandburg, "Chicago," in his *Complete Poems* (New York: Harcourt, Brace & World, 1950), 3; Harold M. Mayer and Richard C. Wade, *Chicago: Growth of a Metropolis* (Chicago: University of Chicago Press, 1969), 12, 14; Dedmon, *Fabulous Chicago,* 4-5; Harry Hansen, *The Chicago* (New York: Farrar & Rinehart, 1942), 29-30; Dominic A. Pacyga and Ellen Skerrett, *Chicago: City of Neighborhoods* (Chicago: Loyola University Press, 1986), 512.

6   *The Irish laborers:* Glen E. Holt and Dominic A. Pacyga, *Chicago: A Historical Guide to the Neighborhoods* (Chicago: Chicago Historical Society, 1979), 113; Pacyga and Skerrett, *Chicago: City of Neighborhoods,* 453; Hansen, *The Chicago,* 134; Kerby A. Miller, *Emigrants and Exiles: Ireland and the Irish Exodus to North America* (New York: Oxford University Press, 1985), 274.

6   *Even before the canal:* Irving Cutler, *Chicago: Metropolis of the Mid-Continent,* 2nd ed. (Dubuque, Iowa: Kendall/Hunt, 1976), 17, 179; William Cronon, *Nature's Metropolis: Chicago and the Great West* (New York: W. W. Norton, 1991), 63-68, 91-92.

7   *James Farrell of County Tipperary:* JTF, "Farrell, James T., the man I know best," 14 August 1964, Box 578, JTFUP, 9; JTF, "[Introspective remarks concerning my cultural background and literary motivation]," Box 258, JTFUP; HFD, interview; MFB, interview; MFB, letter to RKL, 28 June 1993; EB, *James T. Farrell* (New York: Twayne, 1971), 17; Miller, *Emigrants and Exiles,* 280, 291; Cecil Woodham-Smith, *The Great Hunger* (1962; New York: Old Town Books, 1989), 407, 411; Carl Wittke, *We Who Built America: The Saga of the Immigrant* (1939; Cleveland: Case Western Reserve University, 1967), rev. ed., 165-66; Terry L. Jones, *Lee's Tigers: The Louisiana Infantry in the Army of Northern Virginia* (Baton Rouge: Louisiana State University Press, 1987), xi-xii, 6, 14, 229-31.

7   *The war over:* EB, *James T. Farrell,* 17; JTF, "[Introspective remarks]"; HFD, interview; 1880 Census (E.D. 155, Page 45); Eric L. Hirsch, *Urban Revolt: Ethnic Politics in the Nineteenth-Century Chicago Labor Movement* (Berkeley: University of California Press, 1990), 92; Shanabruch, *Chicago's Catholics,* 234.

7   *Hostility toward the Irish:* Lawrence J. McCaffrey, "The Irish-Amer-

ican Dimension," in Lawrence J. McCaffrey, Ellen Skerrett, Michael F. Funchion and Charles Fanning, *The Irish in Chicago* (Urbana: University of Illinois Press, 1987), 7-8; *The Chicago Evening Post,* 9 September 1868, quoted by Wittke, *We Who Built America,* 172; Hirsch, *Urban Revolt,* 123.

7   *Such attacks only:* Ellen Skerrett, "The Catholic Dimension," in McCaffrey *et al., The Irish in Chicago,* 28, 33-34.

8   *This conflagration:* David Lowe, ed., *The Great Chicago Fire* (New York: Dover, 1979), 1, 5; Pacyga and Skerrett, *Chicago: City of Neighborhoods,* 207; Ellen Skerrett, "The Development of Catholic Identity among Irish Americans in Chicago, 1880 to 1920," in *From Paddy to Studs: Irish-American Communities in the Turn of the Century Era, 1880 to 1920,* ed. Timothy J. Meagher (Westport, Conn.: Greenwood Press, 1986), 118.

8   *On March 23, 1871:* Baptismal Certificate for James [F.] Farrell, from St. Columbkille Church; Rev. Msgr. Harry C. Koenig, S.T.D., ed., *A History of the Parishes of the Archdiocese of Chicago* (Chicago: Archdiocese of Chicago, 1980), 1645; Death Certificate for Honora Farrell, from County Clerk, Cook County, Illinois. (The handwritten death certificate, obtained by MFB in 1978, mistakenly gives Honora Farrell's first name as "Herman." The County Clerk's office in 1993 was unable to locate that certificate; nor was it able to find a death certificate in Honora Farrell's correct name, although a certificate was found for a woman by that name who died in 1912.) JTF says (Box 258, JTFUP) that "After the Civil War, my grandfather is supposed to have gone to Kentucky, where my father was born." His father's baptismal certificate, however, indicates that he was born in Chicago.

8   *married again:* 1880 Census (E.D. 155, Page 45); EB, *James T. Farrell,* 17; JTF, "[Introspective remarks]"; JTF, "[Autobiography: My Father]," Box 351, JTFUP; HFD, interview; MFB, interview.

⎯⎯➤⎯◉⎯◄⎯⎯

8   *crowded with teamsters:* John R. Commons, "The Teamsters of Chicago," in *Trade Unionism and Labor Problems,* ed. Commons (Boston: Ginn & Co., 1905), 56; *CT,* 14 May 1905; Robert D. Leiter, *The Teamsters Union: A Study of Its Economic Impact* (New York: Bookman Associates, 1957), 22; John Cummings, "The Chicago Teamsters' Strike—A Study in Industrial Democracy," in *The Journal of Political Economy,* vol. 13 (Chicago: University of Chicago Press, 1905), 543; *Magazine of the International Brotherhood of Teamsters,* June 1905, 9-10; Victor Soares, "Reforming a Labor Union," *The World To-Day,* January 1906, 97; HFD, interview; MFB, interview.

8   *The express business:* Frank Haigh Dixon, "Publicity for Express Companies," *Atlantic Monthly,* July 1905, 5, 7; Peter Z. Grossman, *American Express: The Unofficial History of the People Who Built the Great Financial Empire* (New York: Crown, 1987), 39–40, 135.

9   *Farrell's daily routine:* HFD, interview; MFB, interview; Edwin Griswold Nourse, *The Chicago Produce Market* (Boston: Houghton Mifflin, 1918), 7–9, 15–17.

9   *Teamsters worked hard:* Commons, "The Teamsters of Chicago," 43–44, 47–48; Leiter, *The Teamsters Union,* 19.

9   *Teamsters were used:* Commons, "The Teamsters of Chicago," 36–38; *Magazine of the International Brotherhood of Teamsters,* June 1905, 9.

9   *A writer named:* Ernest Poole, "How a Labor Machine Held Up Chicago, and How the Teamsters' Union Smashed the Machine," *The World To-Day,* July 1904, 896; Christine Scriabine, "Upton Sinclair and the Writing of The Jungle," *Chicago History,* Spring 1981, 27.

10   *fit that mold:* JTF, "The man I know best," 8–9; JTF, "The World I Grew Up in," *Commonweal,* 25 February 1966, 607.

10   *"My father was":* JTF, "[Autobiography: My Father]," Box 351, JTFUP. See also JTF, *True.*

10   *the dubious character:* See Commons, "The Teamsters of Chicago," 36–42; Leiter, *The Teamsters Union,* 18–26; Cummings, "The Chicago Teamsters' Strike," 536–73; Soares, "Reforming a Labor Union," 92–97; Poole, "How a Labor Machine Held Up Chicago," 897–904; Selig Perlman and Philip Taft, *History of Labor in the United States, 1896–1932,* vol. 4, *Labor Movements* (New York, Macmillan, 1935), 61–70.

10   *"cordially hated":* Soares, "Reforming a Labor Union," 93.

10   *an utter failure: CT,* 21 July 1905; Allan H. Spear, *Black Chicago: The Making of a Negro Ghetto* (Chicago: University of Chicago Press, 1967), 39–40; Ray Ginger, *Altgeld's America: The Lincoln Ideal versus Changing Realities* (1958; Chicago: Quadrangle Books, 1965), 294–95. On the strike, also see *Magazine of the International Brotherhood of Teamsters,* June 1905, 3–11; *CT,* 7, 24–28, 30 April, 3–4, 17, 21–22, 25 May, 13–14 June, 16 August 1905; *Chicago Record-Herald,* 24–25 April 1905.

10   *"My father":* HFD, interview.

10   *A few years later:* The Lakeside City Directories for 1908 and 1909 list James Farrell of 2430 LaSalle Street as a bartender. The 1910 Census (E.D. 252, Sheet no. 2)—done, in this case, in April—lists James F. Farrell of the same address as a teamster. JTF was told in 1956 by a man named Harry Read that his father had once gone into the saloon business (JTF, 15 March 1956 letter to JH). JTF at first thought that "what Read says about my father does not ring true, although

there is circumstantial evidence" (JTF, 26 March 1956 letter to JH). But later he apparently came to believe it: "In 1900, for a few weeks, he seems to have been a bourgeois. He and a pal opened up a saloon. He borrowed fifty or a hundred dollars off a friend. That launched him as a man of property. The property did not remain as such. It was liquid, and he knew what he would do with the liquid property. I am convinced that he, and his partner, drank up the liquid assets. He went back to a horse and wagon." (JTF, "[Autobiography: My Father]," Box 351, JTFUP.) The 1900 Census, previously cited, lists Farrell as a teamster. The Lakeside City Directory for 1901 lists a James Farrell in the "saloon" business, but it is evidently a different man since his home address is different. It seems doubtful that JTF's father, a teamster, could have gotten enough capital to start a business; supposing that he somehow did, it seems unlikely that he would have abandoned the venture after only "a few weeks." On the other hand, it is plausible that, as the documentary evidence suggests, he may have tried bartending for someone else for a few years; and that may eventually have given rise to the inflated version.

━━━━►●◄━━━━

11   *Before her marriage:* HFD, interview. See Thomas J. Schlereth, *Victorian America: Transformations in Everyday Life, 1876-1915* (New York: HarperPerennial, 1991), 72-74.

11   *She began having children:* HFD, interview; MFB, interview; JTF, Diary, 22 May 1939. Records of JTF's birth and baptism apparently do not exist. He himself believed he was baptized in St. James Church (Box 639, JTFUP). However, in January 1937, after his passport application ran into difficulties because of the absence of a birth certificate, he had a lawyer get affidavits from his mother, uncles, midwife Lottie Klein and others. According to them ("Farrell, James T. (State Dept.)" folder, Box 47a, VPCU), he was baptized at St. John Church. The sworn statements also indicate that the Farrell home at the time was at 269 West 22nd Street; however, the Lakeside City Directory for 1905 says it was at 369. (Through what was probably an error by the lawyer or his secretary, JTF's birth date—February 27, 1904—was wrongly given in the sworn statements as February 28, 1904. His mother and the others apparently didn't notice.)

11   [Footnote] *Some scholars:* EB, *James T. Farrell,* 18; Alan M. Wald, *The New York Intellectuals: The Rise and Decline of the Anti-Stalinist Left from the 1930s to the 1980s* (Chapel Hill: University of North Carolina Press, 1987), 82.

11   *Looking back nearly:* JTF, *True;* MFB, interview.

12   *A year or so after:* HFD, interview; MFB, interview; Schlereth, *Victorian America,* 225.

12   *Jim Farrell occasionally:* HFD, interview; Schlereth, *Victorian America,* 227–28.

12   *seldom inebriated:* JTF, "World I Grew Up In," 610; HFD, interview; MFB, interview.

12   *In allowing her:* HFD, interview; MFB, interview; baptismal certificates of Richard Joseph Farrell, John Henry Farrell, Mary Elizabeth Farrell; Koenig, *A History of the Parishes,* 39.

12   *a poor job:* HFD, interview; MFB, interview.

13   *a fictional portrait:* JTF, *A World I Never Made* (New York: Vanguard Press, 1936), 21.

13   *all in a line:* HFD, interview.

➤➤-◦-◄◄

14   *One afternoon, Jimmy Farrell:* JTF, *True;* JTF, "The man I know best," 8; JTF, "[Autobiographical: My Grandmother]," JTFUP Box 349.

14   *The old woman:* HFD, interview; MFB, interview; letter from HFD to RKL, 30 June 1993; letter from MFB to RKL, 28 June 1993; JTF, "World I Grew Up In," 607, 610; JTF, *True;* JTF, *My Baseball Diary* (New York: A. S. Barnes & Co., 1957), 39; JTF, [December 1936] letter to HA. The census data conflict: In the 1900 Census (E.D. 108, Sheet no. 2), Julia Brown Daly was said to have been born in September 1850 and to have immigrated in 1860, and John Daly was said to have been born in March 1845 and to have immigrated in 1861; in the 1910 Census (E.D. 355, Sheet no. 7), in which the Dalys were enumerated on April 22, Julia Daly's age was given as 58 and her husband's as 65, and both were said to have immigrated in 1870; in the 1920 Census (E.D. 108, Sheet no. 2), in which the Dalys were enumerated on January 9, Julia Daly's age was given as 76 and she was said to have immigrated in 1869. However, Julia Daly was more or less consistent in what she told her grandchildren about when she left Ireland and how old she was when she did. The 1906 Lakeside City Directory for Chicago indicates that both Tom and Bill Daly were commercial travelers. According to the 1910 Census, Tom was a commercial traveler selling wholesale shoes, Ella ("Helen J.") was a hotel cashier, and Bessie ("Elizabeth") was a stenographer.

➤➤-◦-◄◄

15   *The Grand Boulevard community:* Annie Ruth Leslie, "Grand Boulevard," in Chicago Fact Book Consortium, 103; Pacyga and Sker-

438

rett, *Chicago: City of Neighborhoods,* 335-41; Holt and Pacyga, *Chicago: A Historical Guide,* 86-88; Wim de Wit, "Apartment Houses and Bungalows: Building the Flat City," in *Chicago History,* Winter 1983-1984, 18.

15 *Sometimes, Jimmy's grandfather:* HFD, interview.

15 *When Jimmy was six:* JTF, *My Baseball Diary,* 1-3. JTF gives the priest's name as "Dondaville," but Koenig, *A History of the Parishes,* 1657, and the Chicago Archdiocese's Archives & Records Center indicate it was Dondanville.

16 *Visits from parish priests:* HFD, interview; MFB, interview.

16 *"If there was anything":* JTF, 14 December 1954 letter to JH.

16 *"No one could curse the Devil...":* JTF, "World I Grew Up In," 610.

16 *"would stir things up":* MFB, interview.

17 *In December 1910:* JTF, "[Chronology for Edgar Branch]," circa 1962, Box 443, JTFUP; HFD, interview. That the ground was frozen is an inference by RKL.

17 *Earlier that year:* Lakeside City Directories for 1909-1912; 1910 Census (E.D. 355, Sheet no. 7); HFD, interview; EB, *James T. Farrell,* 18; JTF, *True.*

—➤•◄—

17 *Tom Daly, a bachelor:* 1900 Census (E.D. 108, Sheet no. 2); Lakeside City Directories for 1899-1900; Lakeside Chicago Business Directory for 1901; HFD, interview. The Lakeside City Directory for 1906 lists both Tom and Bill as commercial travelers, while the directories for 1907-1910 do not list Bill at all. HFD said she believed that Bill got married and moved to Madison before she was born.

17 *at selling shoes:* Lakeside City Directories for 1901-1904; Lakeside Chicago Business Directories for 1901-1903; "Upham Brothers Co. a Big Factor in the Growth of the Town," *Stoughton* (Mass.) *Sentinel,* 17 June 1911 (copy of this article provided to RKL by Peggy Greenfield of Plainville, Mass., a design consultant who has done extensive research on the Upham firm).

17 *commercial traveler's job:* Timothy B. Spears, "'All Things to All Men': The Commercial Traveler and the Rise of Modern Salesmanship," *American Quarterly,* December 1993, 540-42, 546.

18 *a success:* JTF, "World I Grew Up In," 610; JTF, *True;* HFD, interview.

18 *"He had, as many":* MFB, interview.

18 *When Tom Daly was home:* JTF, Diary, 31 July 1947; JTF, *True.*

19 *Like his mother:* JTF, "World I Grew Up In," 610; MFB, interview.

19 *loved young Jimmy:* HFD, interview; MFB, interview.

—➤•◄—

19 *worked as a cashier:* 1910 Census (E.D. 355, Sheet no. 7); HFD, interview.

19 *the Grand Pacific:* Herman Kogan and Robert Cromie, *The Great Fire: Chicago 1871* (New York: Putnam's, 1971), 143–45, 212; Dedmon, *Fabulous Chicago,* 100; Mayer and Wade, *Chicago: Growth of a Metropolis,* 121; Perry Duis, "Whose City? Public and Private Places in Nineteenth-Century Chicago," *Chicago History,* Spring 1983, 14; David Lowe, *Chicago Interiors* (Chicago: Contemporary Books, 1979), 14–15; Frank A. Randall, *History of the Development of Building Construction in Chicago* (Urbana: University of Illinois Press, 1949), 76–77.

20 *an attractive woman:* HFD, interview; MFB, interview.

20 *At the Grand Pacific:* HFD, interview; MFB, interview. Walter Van Brunt, ed., *Duluth and St. Louis County, Minnesota,* vol. 2 (Chicago: American Historical Society, 1921), 746–47, has information about Cook.

20 *a Chicago lumberman:* Hines, who headed the Edward Hines Lumber Co. of Chicago, also was president of the Virginia and Rainy Lake Lumber Co. in Minnesota. Hines, Cook and his partner, William O'Brien, and the Weyerhaeuser companies had formed the Minnesota firm in 1908 to log timber in the northeastern corner of the state. For background on the enterprise, see Duane A. Krenz, "An Historical Geographic Study of the Virginia and Rainy Lake Company, the Last Major White Pine Operation in the Great Lakes Region," a Master of Science thesis, Mankato State College, September 1969. The unpublished thesis can be found at the Iron Range Research Center, Chisholm, Minn.

20 *Cook's later testimony:* CT, 26 April, 28 June 1911; Ralph W. Hidy, Frank Ernest Hill and Allan Nevins, *Timber and Men: The Weyerhaeuser Story* (New York: Macmillan, 1963), 195–96, 206; CT, 26 April, 28 June 1911.

21 *Detectives:* Ella Daly, October [1935] letter to JTF; HFD, interview. After testimony on 5 April 1911, by an upright Chicago businessman named Clarence Funk implicated Hines and blew open the case, Hines set some private detectives on his trail. (See CT, 6 April, 27, 28 June 1911.)

21 *With the ouster:* CT, 14 July 1912; NYT, 14 July 1912. Cook, who (according to Van Brunt, *Duluth and St. Louis County,* 747) in 1911 organized the Trout Lake Lumber Co., producing lumber in Tower, Minnesota, extended his interests the next year to South Carolina; a decade or so later, he and his wife moved there. He died on October 31, 1950. The page-one obituary the following day in the *Duluth News-Tribune* got his name wrong.

21 *For a long time:* HFD, interview; MFB, interview.

21   *seldom went to church:* JTF, "World I Grew Up In," 610.

21   *She drank:* HFD, interview; MFB, interview.

Chapter 2: Jimmy—and Studs

23   *In September 1911:* JTF, "[Chronology for Edgar Branch]"; Rev. Msgr. Harry C. Koenig, S.T.D., ed., *A History of the Parishes of the Archdiocese of Chicago* (Chicago:Archdiocese of Chicago, 1980), 216; JTF, "World I Grew Up In," *Commonweal*, 25 February 1966, 610-11.

23   *a new outbreak:* James Hennesey, S.J., *American Catholics:A History of the Roman Catholic Community in the United States* (New York: Oxford University Press, 1981), 182-83; Shanabruch, *Chicago's Catholics: The Evolution of an American Identity* (Notre Dame, Ind.: University of Notre Dame Press, 1981), 56-58.

23   *"Baltimore Catechisms":* Hennesey, *American Catholics,* 176.

23   *First Holy Communion:* JTF, "[Chronology for Edgar Branch]"; JTF, "World I Grew Up In," 611.

23   *In 1911, he saw:* JTF, *My Baseball Diary,* (New York:A. S. Barnes & Co., 1957), 27, 32-33, 45.

24   *The next spring:* JTF, "World I Grew Up In," 611.

24   *Helen Farrell:* HFD, interview.

25   *"They who of all others":* New World, 22 September 1906, quoted by Ellen Skerrett, "The Catholic Dimension," in Lawrence J. McCaffrey, Ellen Skerrett, Michael F. Funchion and Charles Fanning, *The Irish in Chicago* (Urbana: University of Illinois Press, 1987), 48; HFD, interview. Moving Day, when leases expired, came in Chicago on May 1 or October 1. See "Hail! Moving Day," editorial, *Hyde Park Herald,* 28 September 1928.

25   *James H. Mullen:* HFD, interview; Lakeside City Directories for 1912-1916.

25   *Moving day:* 23 June 1972 letter from JTF to Father David Dillon, Mount Carmel High School, Chicago (copy provided by Father Leander Troy).

26   *a nickname:* William Lederer, interview; JH, 7 March 1956 letter to JTF; JTF, 12 March 1956 letter to JH.

26   *Decades later:* HFD, interview; MFB, interview.

26   *Cunningham's father:* Loretta Cunningham Lederer, interview; William Lederer, interview; Lakeside City Directories, 1897-1917; Thomas J. Schlereth, *Victorian America:Transformations in Every-*

day Life, 1876-1915 (New York: HarperPerennial, 1991), 72-73; 1910 Census (E.D. no. 406, Sheet no. 7); 1920 Census (E.D. no. 367, Sheet no. 9). The four Cunningham children besides William were Mary, who was 17 years old in 1915; Frances, 15; Loretta, nine, and Martin, six. All but Mary would appear as Lonigan children in *Studs Lonigan,* and she would lend her name to the Lonigan mother.

26   [Footnote] *born on:* William P. Cunningham was baptized at Holy Cross Church on 65th Street on September 28, 1902, and his baptismal certificate gives his date of birth.

26   *The two boys:* William Lederer, interview; Loretta Cunningham Lederer, interview; HFD, interview; Ruth Kenny, interview; JTF, 17 January 1973 letter to William Lederer (copy provided by Lederer). The Lakeside City Directory for 1917 (the last directory published before 1923), indicates the Cunninghams were living then at 5733 South Wabash Avenue; by the 1920 Census, they were living at 5730 Michigan Avenue.

27   *"one of the best fighters":* JTF, 15 January 1946 letter to JH, quoted by EB, *Studs Lonigan's Neighborhood* (Newton, Mass.: Arts Ends Books, 1996), 40; EB, "James T. Farrell's 'Studs Lonigan,'" *American Book Collector,* June 1961, 13-14.

27   "Studs Lonigan, on the verge": JTF, *Studs Lonigan* (1935; New York: Vanguard Press, 1978) [including *Young Lonigan* (YL), *The Young Manhood of Studs Lonigan* (YMSL), and *Judgment Day* (JD)], YL, 3.

27   *Cunningham—short, stocky:* Loretta Cunningham Lederer, interview; William Lederer, interview; Ruth Kenny, interview; HFD, interview; Robert G. Humbert, S.J., Senior Alumni & Development Officer, Loyola Academy, interview. Ruth Kenny's late husband, Ed Kenny, was a friend of Cunningham's in grammar school days. Kenny's son-in-law, Cunningham's nephew Bill Lederer, said that Kenny once told him that after grammar school, Studs fell in with a bad crowd.

28   *seldom saw each other:* EB, *Studs Lonigan's Neighborhood,* 39.

---

28   *During the winter of 1916-1917:* JTF, "[Chronology for Edgar Branch]"; HFD, interview.

29   *"wearing a man's":* JTF, *No Star Is Lost* (New York: Vanguard Press, 1938), 167.

29   *her brother Bill:* HFD, interview; MFB, interview.

---

29   *the White Sox players:* Richard Lindberg, *Who's on Third? The Chicago White Sox Story* (South Bend, Ind.: Icarus Press, 1983),

38-39; Richard Whittingham, *The White Sox: A Pictorial History* (Chicago: Contemporary Books, 1983), 21.; Joseph L. Reichler, ed., *The Baseball Encyclopedia* (New York: Macmillan, 1985), 2596; JTF, *My Baseball Diary*, 57-66.

30   *"I went home thrilled":* JTF, *My Baseball Diary*, 66.

30   *"Liberty":* HFD, interview. She recalls that both Airedales were named Liberty; JTF, in *My Baseball Diary*, 66, gives the name of the one that ran away as Gerry.

30   *Three days:* St. Anselm Church records.

━━━━◆━━━━

30   *the cottage:* HFD, interview; Annie Ruth Leslie, "Fuller Park," in Chicago Fact Book Consortium, 101; EB, *James T. Farrell* (New York: Twayne, 1971), 19.

31   *regard as excessive:* HFD, interview; MFB, interview; JTF, "Farrell, James T., the man I know best," 14 August 1964, Box 578, JTFUP, 8.

31   *That year did, however:* HFD, interview; JTF, "[Factual Data on J.T.F.]," 2 September 1961, Box 466, JTFUP.

31   *time of great change:* Grossman, 148-56; John F. Stover, *American Railroads* (1961; Chicago: University of Chicago Press, 1976), 185-89. American Railway Express was initially known as Federal Express.

31   *On Wednesday:* HFD, interview.

31   *Diphtheria, which mainly threatens:* Roderick E. McGrew, *Encyclopedia of Medical History* (New York: McGraw-Hill, 1985), 93-98; Dr. Lawrence C. Kleinman, "To End an Epidemic: Lessons from the History of Diphtheria," *New England Journal of Medicine*, 12 March 1992, 773-76; Chicago Department of Health, *Report and Handbook of the Department of Health of the City of Chicago for the Years 1911 to 1918 Inclusive* (1919), 382, 388, 1434-1435.

32   *By Tuesday:* HFD, interview; MFB, interview.

32   *a special effort:* Chicago Department of Health, 374. In "The man I know best," 9-10, JTF remembered having gone, like his brothers and sisters, to the hospital; his sisters, however, say that he did not, but remained at home at the Dalys'.

32   *gave birth:* MFB, interview; HFD, interview.

━━━━◆━━━━

33   *"Nothing seemed...":* JTF, *Reflections at Fifty and Other Essays* (New York: Vanguard Press, 1954), 156.

33   *From early spring:* JTF, *My Baseball Diary*, 76-81.

33   *"His intensity":* JTF, *The Silence of History* (New York: Doubleday, 1963), 89.

33   *"As you know, Jim":* Andrew H. Dugar, 23 November 1947 letter to JTF.

33   *"Mostly the tough boys":* JTF, 15 December 1959 letter to EB.

33   *"I used to watch":* JTF, 24 January 1973 letter to William Lederer (copy provided by Lederer). See also, JTF, "[The old 'Studs Lonigan Neighborhood' and Its Significance]," Box 258, JTFUP.

33   *That fall:* JTF, *Reflections at Fifty,* 156–58; JTF, "[Chronology for Edgar Branch]"; EB, *Studs Lonigan's Neighborhood,* 56.

34   *"I sat":* JTF, *Reflections at Fifty,* 157.

·····

34   *many racial clashes:* Chicago Commission on Race Relations, *The Negro in Chicago: A Study of Race Relations and a Race Riot* (1922; New York: Arno Press, 1968), 54–55, 289; William M. Tuttle Jr., *Race Riot: Chicago in the Red Summer of 1919* (New York: Atheneum, 1970), 237; *Chicago Herald and Examiner,* 23 June 1919.

34   *One stiflingly hot Sunday afternoon:* Tuttle, *Race Riot,* 3–10; Chicago Commission on Race Relations, *The Negro in Chicago,* 1, 4, 11–12, 601.

35   *"Day and night":* Tuttle, *Race Riot,* 10; Chicago Commission on Race Relations, *The Negro in Chicago,* 108.

35   *was spared:* Chicago Commission on Race Relations, *The Negro in Chicago,* 8–9, map following 8; HFD, interview.

35   *to Grand Junction:* HFD, interview; EB, *Studs Lonigan's Neighborhood,* 52, 60n20.

35   *Clarence "Clackey" Metz:* Chicago Commission on Race Relations, *The Negro in Chicago,* 24–25, 659–60; Tuttle, *Race Riot,* 41–42; *Chicago Herald and Examiner,* 30 July 1919; *CT,* 1 August 1919; Stanford S. Apseloff, *James T. Farrell: A Visit to Chicago* (Kent, Ohio: Kent State University Libraries, 1969), 16; JTF, "The Fastest Runner on Sixty-first Street," in *An American Dream Girl* (New York: Vanguard Press, 1950), 14–27.

35   *belatedly eager:* JTF, *Studs Lonigan,* YMSL, 73–74. If the fictional riot kept to the same timetable as the actual one, then Lonigan and his pals were assembling on Thursday, July 31, 1919.

·····

36   *a vocation:* JTF, *True;* HFD, interview.

36   *Quigley Preparatory Seminary:* Shanabruch, *Chicago's Catholics,* 212–13; Edward R. Kantowicz, *Corporation Sole: Cardinal Mundelein and Chicago Catholicism* (Notre Dame: University of Notre Dame Press, 1983), x, 16–17.

36   *"It was the first time":* JTF, 15 January 1946 letter to JH, quoted by
      EB, *Studs Lonigan's Neighborhood,* 80n63 (see also 76); JTF, "Sis-
      ter," Box 7, JTFUP. By Farrell's recollection, he "later on...took
      Loretta out twice." But she claims they never went out (Loretta
      Cunningham Lederer, interview).

36   *That September:* JTF, "A Catholic High School Education," Box 8,
      JTFUP.

Chapter 3: Growing Up

37   *Resolved:* JTF, *Reflections at Fifty and Other Essays* (New York:
      Vanguard Press, 1954), 159-61; JTF, *My Baseball Diary* (New York:
      A. S. Barnes & Co., 1957), 93-97; JTF, "A Catholic High School Edu-
      cation," Box 8, JTFUP; *New World,* 26 September 1919.

37   *"I was the first speaker":* JTF, *Reflections at Fifty,* 160.

————◦—◦◦═══

38   *a small regional school:* Father Leander Troy, O. Carm., interview;
      New World, 26 September 1919; JTF, "Some Notes on My MIS-educa-
      tion at a Catholic High School," Box 28, JTFUP (henceforth:
      "MIS-education").

38   *Jimmy's first two years:* JTF, *Reflections at Fifty,* 158-59, 161-63;
      Dolan obituary, *NYT,* 23 January 1951; *New World,* 26 September 1919.

38   *"a man of energy":* JTF, "MIS-education."

38   *"All over again":* JTF, *Reflections at Fifty,* 162.

════◦—◦═══

39   *One night in June 1920:* Chicago Commission on Race Relations,
      The Negro in Chicago:A Study of Race Relations and a Race Riot
      (1922; New York:Arno Press, 1968), 125-26, 131.

39   *Farrell wrote:* JTF, *Studs Lonigan,* YMSL, 169-70.

39   *fifty-eight bomb explosions:* Chicago Commission on Race Rela-
      tions, *The Negro in Chicago,* 122-23.

39   *Hundreds of thousands:* Chicago Commission on Race Relations,
      The Negro in Chicago, 79-87; Spencer R. Crew, "The Great Migra-
      tion of Afro-Americans, 1915-40," *Monthly Labor Review,* March
      1987, 34; Allan H. Spear, *Black Chicago: The Making of a Negro
      Ghetto* (Chicago: University of Chicago Press, 1967), 130-32.

40   *"The Negroes suffered":* John P. Roche, *The Quest for the Dream*
      (1963; Chicago: Quadrangle, 1968), 81.

40   *rejected the newcomers:* Spear, *Black Chicago,* 97.

40   *When the Farrells:* MFB, interview; HFD, interview.

40   *"As early as May 11, 1850":* Carl Wittke, *The Irish in America*
      (1956; New York: Russell & Russell, 1970), 125.

40   *the "Merry Clouters":* JTF, 17 February 1925 letter to Andy [Dugar]; JTF, "The Merry Clouters," in *Guillotine Party and Other Stories* (New York: Vanguard Press, 1935), reprinted in *The Short Stories of James T. Farrell* (New York: Vanguard Press, 1937; reprint: New York: Halcyon House, 1941), 82–107.

41   *a telephone clerk:* JTF, "[Chronology for Edgar Branch]."

41   *"It ain't true, Joe":* JTF, *My Baseball Diary,* 105–8.

41   *meant "golden flame":* Father Leander Troy, interview.

41   *"The [St. Cyril] teams had a habit":* JTF, "MIS-education."

42   *"Danny's Uncle": St. Cyril Oriflamme,* February 1921, 7–9, in "St. Cyril College Yearbooks with Commentary on Them by JTF" folder, JTFUP Box 52.

42   *"tried to stimulate":* JTF, *Reflections at Fifty,* 163.

42   *Less than a block away:* Richard Parker, interview; Father Leander Troy, interview.

42   *"I was slow in developing":* JTF, *Reflections at Fifty,* 162; JTF, *True.*

42   *"After a lapse": New World,* 6 September 1921.

42   *"more or less of a star":* JTF, "MIS-education."

42   *"applause for their play": New World,* 25 November 1921.

43   *in a single game:* JTF, *My Baseball Diary,* 83; JTF, *Father and Son* (New York: Vanguard Press, 1940), 233.

43   *"I daydreamed":* JTF, *Reflections at Fifty,* 158.

43   *drinking became:* JTF, "MIS-education."

43   *"partly drunk":* JTF commentary (1952), Box 52, JTFUP (henceforth: JTF, St. Cyril commentary).

43   *"his usual spectacular game": St. Cyril Oriflamme,* October 1922, Box 52, JTFUP.

43   *began not showing up:* JTF, "[JTF educational formative years]," Box 184, JTFUP.

43   *That fall, in a game: St. Cyril Oriflamme,* October 1922; *New World,* 1 December 1922; JTF, 17 November 1972 letter to Father Leander Troy (copy provided by Troy); JTF, 24 January 1973 letter to William Lederer (copy provided by Lederer); JTF, 3 September 1925 letter to Andrew Dugar; MFB, interview.

43   *He objected:* JTF, "MIS-education."

44   *"school spirit": St. Cyril Oriflamme,* January–February 1923; JTF, St.

Cyril commentary; "The St. Cyril High School Yearbook," June 1923, Box 52, JTFUP; JTF, "MIS-education." For fictional rendition, see JTF, *Father and Son,* 506–9. If that fictional account is a reliable guide, then it appears that Jimmy later had to pay the school the tuition owed. Tom Daly's inability, or unwillingness, to pay the tuition for Jimmy's final year at St. Cyril's suggests that Upham Bros. by then may have begun to encounter the difficulties that (according to a one-paragraph item in the 24 March 1927 *Stoughton Sentinel*) prompted it to suspend operations in 1927.

44 *"a scandal":* JTF, "MIS-education"; Charles W. Stein, ed., *American Vaudeville as Seen by Its Contemporaries* (New York: Knopf, 1984), 127. Although JTF does not say when the "scandal" occurred, it seems likely that it happened in his third or fourth year, most probably the latter.

44 *"Bumming":* JTF, "MIS-education."

45 *a stroke:* HFD, interview; MFB, interview.
45 *an encounter:* JTF, *Father and Son,* 407–8.
46 *wood alcohol:* JTF, St. Cyril commentary.
46 *"Why did you do it":* Quoted by MFB, in 28 June 1993 letter to RKL.
46 *"My father made me":* JTF, St. Cyril commentary. Jimmy's sister Mary, in a 1993 letter to RKL, expressed doubt that their father intervened in this way. However, the available evidence from the *New World* (a weekly newspaper the elder Farrell might well have seen) and the *St. Cyril Oriflamme* suggests that his father probably did direct him to quit playing sports—and that Jimmy circumvented the order.

46 *"one of the best":* "The St. Cyril High School Yearbook," June 1923.
46 *high school fraternity:* EB, *James T. Farrell* (New York: Twayne, 1971), 21.
46 *Trianon Ballroom:* St. Cyril Oriflamme, March–April 1923, Box 52, JTFUP, and JTF, St. Cyril commentary; Dominic A. Pacyga and Ellen Skerrett, *Chicago: City of Neighborhoods* (Chicago: Loyola University Press, 1986), 344.
47 *"When ten different girls":* JTF, "Senior Prom," in *A Dangerous Woman and Other Stories* (New York: Vanguard Press, 1957), 65–79.
47 *like young Farrell himself:* JTF, *My Baseball Diary,* 243.

47　*Graduation: New World,* 22 June 1923; HFD, interview; MFB, interview; "St. Cyril College Yearbook," June 1923; Father Leander Troy, interview.

48　*had begun work:* JTF, 7 January 1976 letter to EB.

━━━➤►·0·◄◄━━━

48　*That November:* HFD, interview; MFB, interview; [May–June] 1993 letter from MFB to RKL.

Chapter 4: A Modern Man

50　*"think of writing":* JTF, "Farrell, James T., the man I know best," 14 August 1964, Box 578, JTFUP, 1.

50　*began to read serious books:* JTF, "My Early Reading," Box 259, JTFUP.

50　*"the crime of the century":* See Paula S. Fass, "Making and Remaking an Event: The Leopold and Loeb Case in American Culture," *Journal of American History,* December 1993, 919–51. JTF read news accounts of the case (JTF, "[Leopold-Loeb Case]," Box 641, JTFUP).

50　*"Every night":* JTF, "The man I know best," 1.

51　*That September:* EB, *James T. Farrell* (New York: Twayne, 1971), 22.

51　*in his right eye:* JTF, Diary, 26 May 1951.

51　*a false diagnosis:* JTF, "Reflections at Sixty," in *James T. Farrell—Selected Essays,* ed. Luna Wolf (New York: McGraw-Hill, 1964), 197.

51　*"I was struggling":* JTF, *Reflections at Fifty and Other Essays* (New York: Vanguard Press, 1954), 128, 130. See also JTF, "Some Correspondence with Theodore Dreiser," in *The Stature of Theodore Dreiser,* ed. Alfred Kazin and Charles Shapiro (1955; Bloomington: Indiana University Press, 1965), 39–42.

51　*"Next Saturday evening":* JTF, 17 February 1925 letter to J. ["Red"] Conners; *St. Cyril Oriflamme,* November 1922, Box 52, JTFUP. Father Hilary Doswald was principal of Mount Carmel High School, formerly St. Cyril's.

51　*"the main things":* JTF, 17 February 1925 letter to Andy Dugar.

51　*Caron:* MFB, interview; HFD, interview; JTF, 3 January 1973 letter to William Lederer (copy provided by Lederer).

51　*read the last chapter:* JTF, 6 April 1976 letter to Robert J. Butler, reproduced in Robert James Butler, "The Christian Roots of Farrell's O'Neill and Carr Novels," *Renascence,* Winter 1982, 99. The letter is one of two JTF sent to Butler with the same date (copies provided by Butler).

51　*"profoundly stirred":* JTF, "Some Correspondence with Theodore Dreiser," 40–41.

52   *In February 1925:* JTF, 16 February 1925 letter to University of Chicago registration office.

52   *quit the express company:* EB, *James T. Farrell,* 23; JTF, *True,* Box 461, JTFUP; JTF, "[Factual Data on J.T.F.]."

52   *to work his way up:* JTF, "Introduction" written for publication in pamphlet form of "Truth and Myth about America," a speech he delivered in Paris on 30 April 1949, Box 52, JTFUP (henceforth: "Truth and Myth" introduction draft). The autobiographical material in this draft did not survive in the printed introduction to JTF, *Truth and Myth about America* (New York: Rand School Press, 1949).

52   *"I went back":* JTF, Diary, 29 June 1942. Cf. JTF, *My Days of Anger* (New York: Vanguard Press, 1945), 86-89.

<hr />

52   *he stood:* The figure given for Farrell's height is based on various estimates, especially one by Albert Glotzer in conjunction with a photograph of the two men standing next to each other in 1937; Albert Glotzer, interview. The "shabby blue suit" and horn-rimmed glasses are from a description of himself in 1927 that JTF gave in "Truth and Myth" introduction draft. The loosely knotted tie and collar slightly askew are from a description by a college friend, MHW, interview. She and others described his odd way of walking. (In JTF, *My Days of Anger,* 222, his alter ego Danny O'Neill "strolled on, his gait rolling, ungainly.") The briefcase is from the "Truth and Myth" introduction draft: "When I started to school, I took pride in thinking that I was carrying a briefcase. It made me feel important." The route from home to campus is based on his alter ego Eddie Ryan's in JTF, *The Silence of History* (New York: Doubleday, 1963), 53, where the quoted passage about "many associations" is also to be found.

53   *The university:* William H. McNeill, *Hutchins' University: A Memoir of the University of Chicago, 1929-1950* (Chicago: University of Chicago Press, 1991), 3; Edward Shils, "The University, the City, and the World: Chicago and the University of Chicago," in *The University and the City: From Medieval Origins to the Present,* ed. Thomas Bender (New York: Oxford University Press, 1988), 212-13, 217.

53   *"a new model":* Frederick Rudolph, *The American College and University: A History* (New York: Knopf, 1965), 351-52.

53   *school of sociology:* McNeill, *Hutchins' University,* 10-11, 13; Shils, "The University, the City, and the World," 222. See also Robert E. L. Faris, *Chicago Sociology, 1920-1932* (Chicago: University of Chicago Press, 1970).

53   *not unusual:* McNeill, *Hutchins' University,* 6-7.

53   *Tuition:* Maxine Hunsinger Sullivan, university registrar and director of student information system, 10 June 1993 letter to RKL.

54   *"diabolical" institutions:* James W. Sanders, *The Education of an Urban Minority: Catholics in Chicago, 1833-1965* (New York: Oxford University Press, 1977), 38.

54   *he reported:* EB, "American Writer in the Twenties: James T. Farrell and the University of Chicago," *American Book Collector,* vol. 11, no. 10 (Summer 1961), 27.

54   *Farrell's courses:* University of Chicago transcript of Farrell's courses and grades. (Subsequent references to course and grades are also from the transcript.) Farrell also registered for a Home Study course in English that summer but failed to complete the work.

54   *Tennessee schoolteacher:* See Frederick J. Hoffman, *The 20's* (New York: Collier Books, 1962), 313-15; Page Smith, *Redeeming the Time: A People's History of the 1920s and the New Deal* (New York: McGraw-Hill, 1987), 854-64; and Garry Wills, *Under God: Religion and American Politics* (New York: Simon & Schuster, 1990), 97-107.

54   *"Illusions have been lost":* Joseph Wood Krutch, *The Modern Temper* (1929; New York: Harcourt Brace, 1956), 7.

---

55   *One Saturday morning:* JTF, "The man I know best," 6-7; EB, "American Writer in the Twenties," 25; *CT,* 8 November 1925.

55   *had entertained the hope:* JTF, 3 September 1925 letter to Andy Dugar; EB, "American Writer in the Twenties," 25; Bill Gleason, "Jim Farrell Sets the Record Straight," *Chicago Sun-Times,* 19 February 1973.

56   *She was working now:* HFD, interview; David Lowe, *Chicago Interiors* (Chicago: Contemporary Books, 1979), 16-17.

56   *to his own employer: Stoughton Sentinel,* 17, 24, 31 March, 14 April 1927; HFD, interview; JTF, "[Factual Data on J.T.F.]."

56   *"a great sadness":* JTF, "The man I know best," 7.

---

56   *was transferred:* JTF, 17 November 1925 letter to "Red" Conners; JTF, "[Factual Data on J.T.F.]"; HFD, interview; Lakeside City Directory for 1928; JTF, "[Autobiographical: 1926]," Box 351, JTFUP. The new apartment was at 5932 Calumet Avenue.

56   *Traffic was light:* EB, "American Writer in the Twenties," 26; JTF, "Truth and Myth" introduction draft.

56 *"pulling the pumps":* JTF, "[Autobiographical: 1926]," Box 351, JTFUP.

56 *Babbitt:* EB, "American Writer in the Twenties," 26; JTF, "Truth and Myth" introduction draft.

57 *gone without:* EB, "American Writer in the Twenties," 25.

57 *"a hymn of hate":* Arnold Kettle, *An Introduction to the English Novel* (New York: Harper & Row, Perennial Library, 1968), 216.

57 *"an excellent novel":* JTF, 2 January 1926 note, in "Notes from Notebook of 1930 and 1926 note," Box 5, JTFUP.

---

57 *Father Michael Gilmartin:* Ellen Skerrett, "Sacred Space: Parish and Neighborhood in Chicago," in *Catholicism, Chicago Style,* ed. Ellen Skerrett, Edward R. Kantowicz and Steven M. Avella (Chicago: Loyola University Press, 1993), 161–62; Rev. Msgr. Harry C. Koenig, S.T.D., ed., *A History of the Parishes of the Archdiocese of Chicago* (Chicago: Archdiocese of Chicago, 1980), 72–74; Loretta Cunningham Lederer, interview; Dominic A. Pacyga and Ellen Skerrett, *Chicago: City of Neighborhoods* (Chicago: Loyola University Press, 1986), 363.

58 *"St. Patrick's":* JTF, *Studs Lonigan,* YMSL, 240.

58 *Something lasting behind:* In JTF, 17 March 1958 letter to JH, JTF claims that "Lizz" (evidently referring to his real mother, not the character based on her) "ordered a window to Jim's memory in the new church and never shelled out for it…. Lizz had the window put in the new church, stained glass and all to Jim's memory, and it was Lizz who never paid our Rev. Father for it." There is no such window dedicated to the elder Farrell in the church, but there is the Station of the Cross dedicated to him and his mother. If there was a substitution, JTF does not seem to have been aware of it. Given Mary Farrell's piety, it seems unlikely that she failed to pay the promised amount; but if she did find herself unable to pay the full sum, it appears— since the inscribed plaque is with the Station of the Cross—that Father Gilmartin did not hold her delinquency against her.

---

58 *He had read:* JTF, 7 February 1979 letter to Robert James Butler, cited by Butler in "The Christian Roots," 84–85, 98n9; JTF, 26 February 1979 letter to Butler (copy provided by Butler).

59 *"a slough of gloom":* JTF, *The Silence of History,* 133.

59 *"Faith is":* JTF, "[Why Farrell Lost Faith]," Box 670, JTFUP; EB, "American Writer in the Twenties," 27.

59 *described it happening:* JTF, *My Days of Anger,* 211–14.

59   *"one fell swoop":* JTF, 21 March 1946 letter to H L. Mencken, quoted by EB, "American Writer in the Twenties," 27.

60   *"I'm not going":* JTF, *My Days of Anger,* 218.

60   *"A bombshell like that":* MFB, 8 April 1995 letter to RKL.

60   *"a verbal bombshell":* JTF, *My Days of Anger,* 225.

60   *"I opposed":* JTF, "[My Decision to Become a Writer]," Box 622, JTFUP.

60   *That same year:* JTF, 6 April 1976 letter to Robert J. Butler, reproduced by Butler in "The Christian Roots," 99.

60   *"a challenging statement":* Hoffman, *The 20's,* 277-78.

61   *"That man is":* Bertrand Russell, "A Free Man's Worship," in *Why I Am Not a Christian* (New York: Simon & Schuster, 1957), 107.

━━━━➤➖•➖◄━━━━

61   *"I overturned":* JTF, "Truth and Myth" introduction draft.

61   *went to work:* JTF, "Calico Shoes," Box 28, JTFUP; JTF, 21 September1926 letter to "Red" Conners; JTF, "Truth and Myth" introduction draft; JTF, "Chicago Reflections and Memories," Box 499, JTFUP; Chicago Fact Book Consortium, 153.

Chapter 5: To Be a Writer

63   *"seemed sophisticated":* JTF, "James Weber Linn—A Memoir," *Chicago,* October 1955, 57.

63   *"My heroes":* JTF, "Truth and Myth" introduction draft.

63   *Linn's aunt... older brother:* Allen F. Davis, *American Heroine: The Life and Legend of Jane Addams* (New York: Oxford University Press, 1975), 83-84, 256.

64   *"a rather big man":* JTF, "Farrell, James T., the man I know best," 14 August 1964, Box 578, JTFUP, 2.

64   *"greatest inspiration":* J. D. Thomas, "The Wisdom of Teddy Linn," *University of Chicago Magazine,* May 1958, 18.

64   *first day of class:* JTF, "James Weber Linn—A Memoir," 57; JTF, "Truth and Myth" introduction draft; JTF, "The man I know best," 2; *Who's Who in America, 1924-25* (Chicago: A. N. Marquis Co., 1924), 1993; *Who's Who in America, 1938-39* (Chicago: A. N. Marquis Co., 1938), 1540; Linn obituary, *NYT,* 17 July 1939.

65   *"courage, confidence":* James Weber Linn, "Amos Alonzo Stagg," *University of Chicago Magazine,* November 1931, 11.

65   *"We sit by the fire":* James Weber Linn, "Round about Chicago: Victorian, No Doubt," *Chicago Herald & Examiner,* 4 October 1929.

━━━━➤➖•➖◄━━━━

65   *sexually experienced:* DBF, interview.

65   *"the Rubicon of sex":* JTF, *My Days of Anger* (New York: Vanguard Press, 1945), 34–36.

65   *"awkward, not completed":* JTF, *Lonely for the Future* (New York: Doubleday, 1966), 256–57.

65   *the later version:* JTF, *Lonely for the Future,* 45–49. For the earlier version of the episode, see JTF, *My Days of Anger,* 260–62

66   *would contract gonorrhea:* Dr. Robert D. Seely, pretrial deposition, 29 April 1983, 40–41, in New York Supreme Court, County of New York case of Cleo Paturis, as executrix of estate of James T. Farrell, plaintiff, against Robert D. Seely, M.D., defendant (henceforth: "Seely case").

—————»·●·«—————

66   *"a striking blonde":* CT, 2 March 1927. See also *CT,* 4 March 1927.

66   *idea of "Slow Clubs":* George F. Kearney, "Slow Clubs—A New-Old Idea for Recreation," *Playground,* May 1927, 77; Weaver Pangburn, "Report on Study of Slow Clubs, Philadelphia," *Playground,* July 1927, 210; "'Slow' Clubs That Are Not Slow," *Literary Digest,* 2 April 1927, 36.

66   *the main force:* MHW, interview; DBF, interview.

67   *At one Oasis gathering:* JTF, 7 June 1957 letter to EB; *Chicago Daily News,* 15 March 1927; *Hyde Park Herald,* 11 March 1927. Farrell gives a fictional rendition of the debate in *Lonely for the Future,* 50, 83–85. In his 1957 letter, Farrell gives Midney's name as "Frank Medney"; the *Chicago Daily News* makes it "Frank Midney," and the *Hyde Park Herald* has "George Midney." Farrell misremembers the name of the hotel as the "Drake Hotel"; the news accounts indicate it was the Essex Hotel. Farrell also refers to the bohemian club as "Uasia," while news accounts and an undated letter from Caron to Sullivan indicate it was the Oasis. Farrell may have misremembered the name, or, not remembering, accepted a misreading of his own handwriting; or he may have actually referred to the club in 1927 as "Uasia," perhaps as a result of a faded club sign in which the "O" in Oasis had come to look like a "U," and the final "s," like an "a."

67   *reluctant:* See JTF, *Lonely for the Future,* 126–27.

67   *"REAL REVOLT":* CT, 15 March 1927. Sullivan's first name is mistakenly given as "Dennis." See also *CT,* 18 March 1927.

67   *"slowed down" youth:* JTF, 7 June 1957 letter to EB.

67   *"for good measure":* JTF, *Lonely for the Future,* 215.

68   *"It ended in":* JTF, 7 June 1957 letter to EB.

68   *"a remarkable fighter":* JTF, 3 January 1973 letter to William Lederer (copy provided by Lederer).

68   *"a picture of Satan":* Undated letter from Paul Caron to Jack Sulli-

van. The contents of the letter indicate it was written not too long after a 19 September 1927 letter from Caron to Sullivan.

68   *shed his Catholic faith:* JTF, "[Factual Data on J.T.F.]."

68   *"H.R.H. 'Hellfire' Caron":* Paul Caron, 30 July 1925 letter to JTF. Caron tells him that he came to Dallas "on impulse." In a later, undated letter to JTF, he reports that he is "'on the road'" and "selling school book covers as an advertising medium."

68   *"anything I thought of":* JTF, "James Weber Linn—A Memoir," 58.

69   *"This column today":* James Weber Linn, "Round about Chicago: Pie Juggling in the Loop," *Chicago Herald & Examiner,* 16 March 1927.

69   *"a kind of pledge":* JTF, "[My Decision to Become a Writer]," JTFUP Box 622. See also JTF, "Chicago Reflections and Memories," Box 499, JTFUP

69   *Soon thereafter:* JTF, *Reflections at Fifty and Other Essays* (New York: Vanguard Press, 1954), 165-66; Kim Townsend, *Sherwood Anderson* (Boston: Houghton Mifflin, 1987), 233-34. It is unlikely that Farrell let much time elapse between his reading of Anderson's *Tar: A Midwest Childhood* (New York: Boni & Liveright, 1926) and his attempt in April 1927 (according to JTF, "Chicago Reflections and Memories") to imitate it.

70   *"I went back":* JTF, "Chicago Reflections and Memories."

70   *quit his job:* EB, "American Writer in the Twenties: James T. Farrell and the University of Chicago," *American Book Collector,* vol. 11, no. 10 (Summer 1961), 27.

70   *"I was 23":* JTF, "The First Time I Saw New York," *New York Sunday Herald Tribune,* 6 October 1962, 9.

71   *"world's greatest city":* JTF's account of his first night in New York, in James Weber Linn, "Round about Chicago: His First Night," *Chicago Herald & Examiner,* 25 August 1927.

71   *Linn's readers were informed:* James Weber Linn, "Round about Chicago: Picks and Choices," *Chicago Herald & Examiner,* 6 August 1927.

71   *found work:* JTF, *Literary Essays 1954-1974* (Port Washington, N.Y.: Kennikat Press, 1976), 93-94; Paul Caron, 19 August 1927 letter to Jack Sullivan; JTF, "My first demonstration, 1927," Box 210, JTFUP.

72   *Nicola Sacco and Bartolomeo Vanzetti:* See Francis Russell, *Sacco & Vanzetti: The Case Resolved* (New York: Harper & Row, 1986); Page Smith, *Redeeming the Time: A People's History of the 1920s*

and the New Deal (New York: McGraw-Hill, 1987), Chapter 6; Arthur M. Schlesinger Jr., *The Crisis of the Old Order, 1919-1933* (Boston: Houghton Mifflin, 1957), 139-41; Frederick J. Hoffman, *The 20's* (New York: Collier Books, 1962), 400-8.

72 *"an unseen force":* JTF, "Truth and Myth" introduction draft.

72 *Earlier: NYT,* 23 August 1927.

72 *"silence of a church":* JTF, *Bernard Clare* (New York: Vanguard Press, 1946), 82-83.

73 *"a cold passion":* JTF, "My first demonstration, 1927."

73 *"all right we are":* John Dos Passos, *The Big Money* (1937), in *U.S.A.* (New York: Harcourt, Brace & Co., 1937), 462.

73 *assassinated:* Francis Russell, *Sacco & Vanzetti,* 26-27.

73 *"I was shocked":* JTF, 1976 letter to Francis Russell, quoted by Russell, *Sacco & Vanzetti,* 29.

---

73 *a "real" writer:* JTF, "Max Bodenheim," Box 372, JTFUP.

74 *By mid-September:* Paul Caron, 19 September 1927 letter to JTF.

74 *"I was able to sell enough":* JTF, *Literary Essays 1954-1974,* 94.

74 *"More than anything else":* JTF, "Some Correspondence with Theodore Dreiser," 42.

75 *"Callico Shoes":* JTF, "The First Time I Saw New York," 9.

75 *"tried to get going":* JTF, "Chicago Reflections and Memories."

75 *thanking him:* Paul Caron, undated (New Year's Eve) letter to JTF.

75 *rang in the new year:* JTF, "The First Time I Saw New York," 9; EB, "American Writer in the Twenties," 27.

Chapter 6: Dorothy—and Lonigan

76 *The Cube: Hyde Park Herald,* 10 February, 8 June 1928; "The Art Colony," *University of Chicago Magazine,* May 1961, 7-10; Mary Ruth Yoe, "Looking Back: Life Is Long, Art Is Short," *University of Chicago Magazine,* December 1991, 48; Dale Kramer, *Chicago Renaissance: The Literary Life in the Midwest, 1900-1930* (New York: Appleton-Century, 1966), 8. While the *Hyde Park Herald* refers to the "South Side Art Colony," John Drury, *A Century of Progress Authorized Guide to Chicago* (Chicago: Consolidated Book Publishers, 1933), 183, calls it the "Jackson Park Art Colony." That is also the way MHW (MHW, interview) remembers it.

76 *Bodenheim was due: Hyde Park Herald,* 22 June 1928, 7, 19, 27 July 1928.

76 *posted on a tree:* DBF, interview.

77 *"die in the gutter":* JTF, "Max Bodenheim," Box 372, JTFUP; JTF, "[Max Bodenheim's Murder]," Box 398, JTFUP. It is possible that

JTF's conversation with Bodenheim occurred on another occasion, but from the available evidence, it seems likely that it was on the one described.

77   *Dorothy Butler resided:* DBF, interview; MFB, interview; MHW, interview; HFD, interview; JTF, 26 March 1938 letter to Jack [Farrell]; *CT,* 25 January 1925. Patrick Butler died on January 23, 1925. Although the *CT* death notice indicates the family address as 1405 E. 55th Street, DBF said that their home was not there, but at 5600 Blackstone Avenue.

77   *entered the University of Chicago:* Information supplied by the university Registrar's Office, 14 June 1993.

78   *a much more worldly background:* MHW, interview.

78   *"Jimmy the Genius":* EB, "American Writer in the Twenties: James T. Farrell and the University of Chicago," *American Book Collector,* vol. 11, no. 10 (Summer 1961), 28.

78   *turn on the Victrola:* DBF, interview.

78   *"a divine dancer":* MHW, interview.

---

79   *fell and broke:* HFD, interview; MFB, interview; MFB, 9 July 1995 letter to RKL.

79   *the Stevens:* Frank A. Randall, *History of the Development of Building Construction in Chicago* (Urbana: University of Illinois Press, 1949), 274; John Ashenhurst and Ruth L. Ashenhurst, *All About Chicago* (New York: Houghton Mifflin, 1933), 83–84; "The Stevens Personnel," *The Hotel World,* 7 May 1927, 54.

79   *a wholesale shoe firm:* The Chicago telephone directories for November 1928, Winter 1929–1930 and Winter 1930–1931 list Daly as working at a wholesale shoe firm at 209 South State Street.

79   *on relief:* HFD, interview; JTF, 1 September 1935 letter to Tom Daly.

79   *May 1928:* JTF, 9 January 1976 letter from JTF to EB; Chicago City Directory for 1928.

79   *ceased, or at least:* HFD, interview.

---

80   *His first* Maroon *contribution:* JTF ("Dorothy Butler"), "Modernism Marks American Exhibit at Art Institute," *Daily Maroon,* 9 November 1928; EB, *A Bibliography of James T. Farrell's Writings, 1921–1957* (Philadelphia: University of Pennsylvania Press, 1959), 40.

80   *Soon, writing in the* Maroon: JTF, "A Criticism of the University Library Department," *Daily Maroon,* 14 December 1928; JTF, "The

Filling Station Racket in Chicago," *Debunker,* January 1929, 91–93; JTF, "A Note on Some Ancient History Called 'Porgy,'" *Daily Maroon,* 23 January 1929.

80 *campus correspondent:* JTF, "[Memories of my days as a Reporter on the Chicago Herald-American]," Box 212, JTFUP; JTF, "[Autobiographical: Campus Reporter, c. 1927]," Box 372, JTFUP; JTF, "[As Campus Reporter—1929]," Box 499, JTFUP; JTF, "[My Days as a Newspaper Man]," Box 464, JTFUP; JTF, "[Campus reporter]," Box 256, JTFUP; JTF, "Memoirs of a Cub Reporter Who Covered St. Valentine's Day," Box 305, JTFUP; Mervin Block, "Writer Farrell Recalls Early Days in City," *Chicago American,* 19 November 1957; JTF, 26 February 1952 letter to JH.

80 *"This part-time job":* JTF, "[As Campus Reporter—1929]."

81 *"I had to arrange":* JTF, "Memoirs of a Cub Reporter Who Covered St. Valentine's Day."

81 *"Verbal as he was":* MHW, interview.

81 *at the end of August:* JTF, 5 September 1931 letter to Whit Burnett; JTF, 7 June 1957 letter to EB; Michael Sadleir, *Studs Lonigan by James T. Farrell: An Appreciation by Michael Sadleir* (London: Constable & Co. Ltd, 1936), 16. A copy of Sadleir's work is in Box 46, VPCU.

---

81 *"Coudich Castle":* Drury, *A Century of Progress,* 183; MHW, interview; EB, "American Writer in the Twenties," 28.

81 *lost her virginity:* DBF, interview. Although she did not remember just when this occurred, it seems likely, or at least plausible, that it happened before she dropped out of college and embarked upon an extensive deception of her mother.

81 *winter quarter of 1929:* Information supplied by university Registrar's Office, 14 June 1993.

81 *didn't tell her mother:* DBF, interview; MHW, interview.

---

82 *died at home:* Death notices published on 11 and 12 March 1929, in *Chicago Daily News* and in *CT;* Loretta Cunningham Lederer, interview. Cunningham's sister's account of the circumstances of his death receives some corroboration from a very similar account given by Farrell in an unpublished novel, *The Distance of Sadness.* (The account is in Chapter 40, which is in CP's possession.)

82 *"I casually ignored":* JTF, 15 January 1946 letter to JH, quoted in EB, *James T. Farrell* (New York: Twayne, 1971), 48–49.

82 *"I never talked"*: JTF, 5 October 1959 letter to EB.

82 *"probably could have handled"*: JTF, 15 December 1959 letter to EB.

82 *"He went to Loyola"*: JTF, "Studs," in *The Short Stories of James T. Farrell* (New York: Vanguard Press, 1937; reprint: New York: Halcyon House, 1941). In a 1993 interview, Loretta Cunningham Lederer denied that the quoted passage accurately reflected her brother. One suspects, nevertheless, that it did, for Farrell seems to have stuck rather closely to the known facts in this story, much more closely than he did in *Studs Lonigan.*

83 *Two of his friends:* JTF, 6 February 1976 letter to EB.

83 *"I wrote stories"*: JTF, "How *Studs Lonigan* Was Written," in *The League of Frightened Philistines* (New York: Vanguard Press, 1945), 84–85.

84 *Lovett:* Robert Morss Lovett, *All Our Years: The Autobiography of Robert Morss Lovett* (New York: Viking Press, 1948), 123, 171–93.

84 *had first become aware:* EB, "American Writer in the Twenties," 29; Robert Morss Lovett, May 29, 1929 letter to JTF. Evidently, Farrell not only had written a column for the *Maroon* but also had sent a manuscript on the subject to the *New Republic.* Rejecting it, the editors sent the manuscript on to Lovett, who then contacted Farrell.

84 *"a play of negro sentiment"*: JTF, "Athenaeum: A Note on the Dramatic Association," *Daily Maroon,* 16 May 1929.

84 *four Negro plays: Hyde Park Herald,* 21 December 1928; MHW, interview; Katherine Dunham, interview.

84 *"a kind of large and brooding walrus"*: JTF, "Robert Morss Lovett," Box 516, JTFUP.

84 *"I had already begun"*: JTF, "How *Studs Lonigan* Was Written," 85.

━━━━➤●◄━━━━

84 *"Whoever reads"*: JTF, "Slob," *Blues,* June 1929, 114–16.

86 *"I read"*: Clifton P. Fadiman, 19 June 1929 letter to JTF.

86 *"Students passed us"*: JTF, *Reflections at Fifty and Other Essays* (New York: Vanguard Press, 1954), 59.

86 *correspondence with Fadiman:* JTF, 24 June & 10 July 1929 letters to Fadiman; Fadiman, 27 June & 16 July 1929 letters to JTF.

88 *took off for New York:* EB, *James T. Farrell,* "Chronology"; JTF, 9 January 1976, 7 June 1957 letters to EB. See various undated letters from Caron and Sarajo Loeb to Farrell and others.

88 *had worked hard:* JTF, *Reflections at Fifty,* 59–60.

88 *Once, on a very hot day:* DBF, interview.

88 *"The scene with the tree"*: Don Harrison, "Farrell a Fan," *St. Lauderdale Sun-Sentinel,* [?] April 1979.

458

88 *girl named Helen Shannon:* EB, "James T. Farrell's 'Studs Lonigan,'" *American Book Collector,* June 1961, 13; EB, *Studs Lonigan's Neighborhood* (Newton, Mass.: Arts Ends Books, 1996), 71, 79n35.

———»•0•«———

89 *"Boy Scout":* JTF, "Memories of John Dewey," transcript of tape recording of talk given 5 November 1965, Special Collections, Morris Library, Southern Illinois University at Carbondale.

89 *"harsh realization":* JTF, "Half Way from the Cradle," *Earth,* June 1930. A copy is in "Farrell, James T. 1932/33" folder, Box 47a, VPCU.

89 *"the major influence":* JTF, "Memories of John Dewey."

89 *"The poignancy":* John Dewey, *Human Nature and Conduct* (1922; New York: Modern Library, 1930), 216-17.

90 *"impressions":* John Dewey, "Impressions of Soviet Russia," *NR,* 14, 21, 28 November, 5, 12, 19 December 1928.

90 *"Liberals in Chicago":* JTF, "Liberals in Chicago," *Plain Talk,* November 1929; Lovett, *All Our Years,* 149. The payment of $100 is mentioned in JTF, 7 June 1957 letter to EB.

90 *"A sense of socialism":* JTF, "Truth and Myth" introduction draft. He seems to have originally put this thought down in his "Thought Diary" in the spring of 1928.

———»•0•«———

91 *"This is rot!":* Samuel Putnam, *Paris Was Our Mistress: Memoirs of a Lost and Found Generation* (New York: Viking Press, 1947), 108-9, 229; Hugh Ford, *Published in Paris: American and British Writers, Printers, and Publishers in Paris, 1920-1939* (Yonkers, N.Y.: Pushcart Press, 1975), 161-62.

91 *paid $25:* JTF, 7 June 1957 letter to EB.

91 *"I saw the merit":* JTF, "Personal Reflections—1942," Box 8, JTFUP; EB, "James T. Farrell's 'Studs Lonigan,'" 11.

92 *"I cannot cotton":* Clifton P. Fadiman, 4 February 1931 letter to JTF.

92 *Back came the manuscript:* Harry Block, 12 March 1931 letter to JTF.

92 *"obviously could not be published":* Joseph Brewer, 31 March 1931 letter to JTF. See also Brewer's 6 April 1931 letter to JTF.

92 *"From 1928 to 1931":* JTF, "Farrell, James T., the man I know best," 14 August 1964, Box 578, JTFUP, 11.

92 *pregnant:* DBF, interview; EB, *A Paris Year: Dorothy and James T. Farrell, 1931-32* (Athens, Ohio: Ohio University Press, 1998), 18-19.

93 *one night:* MHW, interview.

93 *this time:* DBF, interview.

93   *"I wanted to go":* DBF, interview.

93   *a cult book:* Richmond Barrett, "Babes in the Bois," *Harper's,* May 1928, quoted by Kenneth S. Lynn in *Hemingway* (New York: Simon & Schuster, 1987), 336.

93   *cover stories:* DBF, interview. Farrell provides a fictional version of the subterfuges they used in *The Dunne Family* (Garden City, N.Y.: Doubleday, 1976), 100.

94   *April 13, 1931:* Marriage certificate, Cook County, Ill.

94   *Later that same day:* JTF, Diary, 8 April 1941; EB, *A Paris Year,* 23.

94   *"balmy":* MHW, interview.

94   *In New York:* JTF, 9 January 1976 letter to EB.

94   *Walt Carmon:* Walt Carmon, 2 & 13 May 1931 letters to JH, "Farrell—New Masses" folder, Box 46, VPCU; EB, "James T. Farrell's 'Studs Lonigan,'" 11.

94   *a visit to Horace Gregory:* JTF, 9 January 1976 letter to EB; Horace Gregory, *The House on Jefferson Street: A Cycle of Memories* (New York: Holt, Rinehart & Winston, 1971), 200; DBF, interview. In his memoir, Gregory conflates the visit by Farrell alone to his house in 1931 with a visit by Farrell and Dorothy on their return from Paris in 1932.

94   *SS* Pennland: DBF, interview; EB, *James T. Farrell,* 24; "Shipping News," *New York Sun,* 17 April 1931; "Shipping News and Detailed Marine Intelligence from All Parts of the World: Outgoing Passenger and Mail Ships," *New York Herald Tribune,* 17 April 1931.

Chapter 7: Paris

95   *arrived in Cherbourg:* DBF, interview; JTF, "Return to Paris," *New Leader,* 7 May 1949, 8.

95   *"strange and mysterious beings":* JTF, "Paris Lovely in Spring, But Ideas Growing Stale," *New Leader,* 9 July 1949, 4.

95   *soon found:* Samuel Putnam, *Paris Was Our Mistress: Memoirs of a Lost and Found Generation* (New York: Viking Press, 1947), 109-10.

95   *ceased to be "the center":* Malcolm Cowley, *Exile's Return* (New York: W. W. Norton, 1934), 284.

95   *Putnam took Farrell:* Noel Riley Fitch, *Sylvia Beach and the Lost Generation* (New York: W. W. Norton, 1983), 316.

96   *"a new America":* Putnam, *Paris Was Our Mistress,* 110.

96   *"Realism in America":* transition eds., "Suggestions for a New Magic," June 1927, in *In transition: A Paris Anthology* (New York: Doubleday Anchor, 1990), 23.

96   *"sacramental significance":* Hugh Ford, *Published in Paris: American and British Writers, Printers, and Publishers in Paris, 1920-1939* (Yonkers, N.Y.: Pushcart Press, 1975), 319-20.

96 *began to run out:* EB, *A Paris Year: Dorothy and James T. Farrell, 1931-32* (Athens, Ohio: Ohio University Press, 1998), 42-43; DBF, interview.

96 *"everyone talks":* JTF, 27 May 1931 letter to Walt Carmon, quoted in EB, *James T. Farrell* (New York: Twayne, 1971), 25.

96 *lunch with Ezra Pound:* JTF, *Literary Essays 1954-1974* (Port Washington, N.Y.: Kennikat Press, 1976), 86.

97 *"Certainly the stuff":* Ezra Pound, 16 February [1931] letter to S[am Putnam].

97 *his generosity:* Ernest Hemingway, *A Moveable* Feast (New York: Scribners, 1964), 107. See also John Tytell, *Ezra Pound: The Solitary Volcano* (New York: Doubleday, 1987), 115, 128-29, 135, 193.

97 *Pound arranged:* Ezra Pound, postcard, postmarked "6 V 1931," to JTF; JTF, 20 October 1975 letter to EB; EB, "James T. Farrell," in *American Writers in Paris, 1920-1939,* ed. Karen Lane Rood, vol. 4 of *Dictionary of Literary Biography* (Detroit: Gale Research Co., 1980), 129; JTF, *Literary Essays 1954-1974,* 87. The three stories, besides "The Scarecrow," that Pound liked were "Meet the Girls!" "Honey, We'll be Brave" and "Looking 'Em Over." Farrell says, inaccurately, that Pound "compared... 'The Scarecrow,' with the writings of Henry James."

97 *perhaps even more frustrating:* See Jacob Schwartz, 1 & 17 December 1931 letters to JTF (in folder with Ezra Pound letters to JTF, JTFUP); JTF, 12 November 1931 and [?] & 9 January 1931 [actually, 1932] letters to Pound.

97 *Pound tried to assist:* Ford, *Published in Paris,* 220; Tytell, *Ezra Pound,* 221.

97 *sent "The Scarecrow":* Peter Neagoe, 16 June, 5 August 1931 letters to JTF; Ford, *Published in Paris,* 311-12; Mark Fritz, "Peter Neagoe," in *American Writers in Paris, 1920-1939,* ed. Rood, 295-98.

97 *also heard from Bob Brown:* Bob Brown, 3 June 1931 letter to JTF. For background on Brown and his Reading Machine, see Ford, *Published in Paris,* 302-11, and Joseph M. Flora, "Bob Brown," in *American Writers in Paris, 1920-1939,* ed. Rood, 60-64.

98 *"You have the idea perfectly":* Bob Brown, 12 June 1931 letter to JTF. See also Bob Brown, 22 July 1931 letter to JTF.

98 *Brown admitted:* Bob Brown, 7 & 12 January 1932 letters to JTF.

98 *"Well, our friend Farrell":* JH, 12 May 1931 letter to Walt Carmon, in "Farrell—New Masses" folder, Box 46, VPCU.

99 *moved to Sceaux-Robinson:* JTF, 20 October 1975 letter to EB; JTF, "Return to Paris"; DBF, interview; EB, *A Paris Year,* 47-48.

99 *a contract:* Contract for *Young Lonigan* in "Farrell, James T. — Contracts" Folder, Box 47b, VPCU.

99 *Not long after:* In a 14 May 1931 letter to Walt Carmon ("Farrell—

New Masses" folder, Box 46, VPCU), Henle says he is enclosing a carbon of his letter to Farrell; in a 7 June 1931 letter to JTF, Ella Daly asks: "Did you hear Paul Caren [*sic*] passed away, Mary called up I mean Mary Farrell, & said Jimmy Golden's cousin told her." Farrell may have learned of Caron's death from some other source, but it would appear that this bad news probably reached him after Henle's good news did.

99   *a cancerous tumor of the brain:* JTF, 3 January 1973 letter to William Lederer (copy provided by Lederer).

99   *Farrell wept:* JTF, 24 January 1973 letter to William Lederer (copy provided by Lederer).

99   *"Paul kept talking":* JTF, 3 April 1936 letter to HA.

99   *"Mother & I":* Ella Daly, 30 May 1931 letter to JTF. See also Ella Daly, June 1931 & 1 July [1931] letters to JTF; JTF, 9 January 1976 letter to EB.

99   *"Your letter received":* Ella Daly, 1 July [1931] letter to JTF.

99   *always good at wheedling:* HFD, interview.

99   *Menckens would soon:* DBF, interview.

100   *"that I was hoping":* JTF, "Return to Paris."

100   *"get up early":* DBF, interview.

100   *add a new first chapter:* EB, "James T. Farrell," in *American Writers in Paris, 1920–1939,* ed. Rood, 129.

100   *"The Madhouse":* JTF, 31 October 1931 letter to Helen (Farrell) and Lawrence Townley.

100   *Farrell and Dorothy decided:* EB, *A Paris Year,* 79–80, 177n116; DBF, interview.

100   *"Amen I say":* JTF, 15 September 1931 letter to Theodore [Marvel].

101   *"I was foolish":* JTF, 5 September 1931 letter to Whit Burnett.

101   *Putnam and Pound might be sympathetic:* Humphrey Carpenter, *A Serious Character: The Life of Ezra Pound* (New York: Delta, 1988), 489; Peter Neagoe, ed., *Americans Abroad* (The Hague: Servire Press, 1932), 322.

101   *"The communists":* JTF, 5 November 1931 letter to Mary Farrell (MFB).

101   *"The boy is":* JH, 28 September 1931 letter to Walt Carmon, in "Farrell—New Masses" folder, Box 46, VPCU.

102   *"When I had left Chicago":* JTF, "Return to Paris."

<hr/>

102   *In November:* DBF, interview; EB, *James T. Farrell,* 25; EB, *A Paris Year,* 99–102; JTF, "Return to Paris"; JTF, 29 October 1975 letter to EB; Joan Mellen, *Kay Boyle: Author of Herself* (New York: Farrar, Straus & Giroux, 1994), 150.

102 *The advances from Henle:* EB, *A Paris Year,* 43, 165-66n51; EB, "James T. Farrell," in *American Writers in Paris, 1920-1939,* ed. Rood, 128.

102 *Getting him to pay:* JTF, 15 September 1931 letter to Theodore [Marvel]; JTF, 9 November 1931 letter to JH.

102 *"I don't know what to say":* JTF, 9 November 1931 letter to JH.

103 *"If Henle is":* Peter Neagoe, 20 November 1931 letter to JTF.

103 *"It took so long":* DBF, interview.

103 *"He recalled her moaning":* JTF, "Soap," in *Americans Abroad,* ed. Neagoe, 146-47.

104 *Four days after Sean's birth:* JTF, "Return to Paris"; EB, *A Paris Year,* 105-6.

104 *a party thrown:* JTF, 12 January [1932] letter to "Little Sister" [MFB]; Mellen, *Kay Boyle,* 150; EB, *A Paris Year,* 112-16. Farrell told EB in 1976: "There was no incident of my handing the baby clothes back in such a way that everybody laughed."

104 *"There were hard days":* JTF, "Return to Paris."

104 *"the breadline":* JTF, 12 January [1932] letter to "Little Sister" [MFB].

104 *Henle, on his own initiative:* JTF, 29 October 1975 letter to EB.

105 *Farrell had Vanguard:* JTF, [?] January 1931 [actually, 1932] letter to Ezra Pound.

105 *The poet thought:* Ezra Pound, 3 February 1932 letter to JTF.

105 *"As to the Irishness":* JTF, 17 February 1932 letter to Ezra Pound.

105 *a cheaper apartment:* DBF, interview.; EB, *A Paris Year,* 123-24.

105 *Henle liked:* JTF, [?] January 1931 [actually, 1932] letter to Ezra Pound.

105 *When his shoes wore out:* JTF, "Return to Paris"; DBF, interview.

106 *her mother sent:* EB, *A Paris Year,* 136, 189n65.

106 *was apparently instrumental:* Robert Morss Lovett, *All Our Years: The Autobiography of Robert Morss Lovett* (New York: Viking Press, 1948), 123. In his memoir, Lovett mistakenly recalls Thrasher's name as "Trotter."

106 *Farrell wrote the sociologist:* JTF, 15 March 1932 letter to Frederic M. Thrasher.

106 *the help of Mrs. Butler and Travelers Aid:* JTF, 20 October 1975 letter to EB; JTF, 29 September 1953 letter to JH; JTF, "Return to Paris"; DBF, interview; EB, *James T. Farrell,* 26; EB, *A Paris Year,* 136, 141-45, 165-66n 51, 189n68; "Shipping News," *New York Sun,* 16 April 1932; "Shipping News and Detailed Marine Intelligence Received from All Parts of the World: Incoming Passenger and Mail Ships," *New York Herald Tribune,* 17 April 1932.

106 *"It was there":* JTF, "Return to Paris."

PART TWO: NOVELIST AND RADICAL

Chapter 8: A Revolutionary Writer

109   *"This novel":* Quoted by Guy Henle, "Vanguard Press: Sixty-two Influential Years," *Columbia Library Columns,* November 1990, 9.

109   *published just days:* EB, *James T. Farrell* (New York: Twayne, 1971), "Chronology" and 27.

109   *"I have a feeling":* Quoted by Herman Kogan, "Jim Farrell at 60: 'Much More to Do,'" *Chicago Daily News Panorama,* 14 March 1964.

109   *"who took all kinds":* JTF, *Studs Lonigan,* YL, 64.

110   *"like their case histories":* "Fiction for Scientists," *Chicago Herald & Examiner,* 14 May 1932.

110   *"The artistic powers":* "Chicago Streets," *NYT Book Review,* 1 May 1932.

110   *"a classic":* "Some of the Most Recent Spring Fiction," *New York Herald Tribune Books,* 22 May 1932.

110   *"Mr. Farrell's unblinking":* Horace Gregory, "Unspectacular Realism," *The Nation,* 20 July 1932.

110   *"a grave injustice":* Edward Dahlberg, "Apprentice Gangster," *NR,* 20 July 1932.

111   *"My book is out":* JTF, 10 May 1932 letter to Helen Townley [HFD].

111   *420 copies:* JH, 18 March 1948 letter to JTF.

111   *1,742 copies:* JTF, 19 January [1932] letter to "Little Sister" [MFB].

111   *The next two volumes:* "Vanguard's First Ten Years," *PW,* 13 June 1936, 2,350.

---

111   *an apartment:* DBF, interview.

111   *until recently:* Whittaker Chambers, *Witness* (New York: Random House, 1952), 268, 271; Allen Weinstein, *Perjury: The Hiss-Chambers Case* (New York: Knopf, 1978), 71.

111   *Garland Fund:* Guy Henle, "Vanguard Press: Sixty-two Influential Years," 3-4; Theodore Draper, *American Communism and Soviet Russia* (New York: Vintage Books, 1986), 204; Gloria Garrett Samson, *The American Fund for Public Service: Charles Garland and Radical Philanthropy, 1922-1941* (Westport, Conn.: Greenwood Press, 1996), xiii-xiv, 1-3, 134-35, 150, 159, 165, 167-68, 186, 205, 210; John McAleer, *Rex Stout: A Biography* (Boston: Little, Brown & Co., 1977), 196; Daniel Aaron, *Writers on the Left: Episodes in American Literary Communism* (New York: Columbia University Press, 1992), 100-2; Joseph Freeman, *An American Testament* (New York: Farrar & Rinehart, 1936), 338-39; Joseph Freeman, "Ivory Towers—White and Red," *NM,* 11 September 1934, 22; Page

Smith, *Redeeming the Time: A People's History of the 1920s and the New Deal* (New York: McGraw-Hill, 1987), 3; Jack Alan Robbins, "Editor's Introduction," in *Granville Hicks in the* New Masses, ed. Jack Alan Robbins (Port Washington, N.Y.: Kennikat Press, 1974), xii.

112   *"He affected":* Freeman, *An American Testament,* 257.

112   *"that the white that I see":* The Spiritual Exercises of St. Ignatius (New York: Doubleday Image Books, 1989), 140-41.

112   *having outmaneuvered:* Robert Conquest, *Stalin: Breaker of Nations* (New York: Penguin Books, 1991), 131, 139-40; Harvey Klehr, *The Heyday of American Communism: The Depression Decade* (New York: Basic Books, 1984), 11.

112   *a transformation:* Klehr, *The Heyday of American Communism,* 71; Thomas Kennerly Wolfe Jr., "The League of American Writers: Communist Organizational Activity among American Writers, 1929-1942," Ph.D. dissertation, Yale University, 1956, 43. Citing a 1955 interview he had with Joseph Freeman, Wolfe writes: "In 1929 the Communist Party instructed the Communist faction within the editorial board of *New Masses* to bring the magazine under Communist Party discipline."

112   *In May 1928:* "Vanguard's First Ten Years," *PW,* 2, 348-49.

112   *Born in Louisville:* Peter Henle, interview; "James Henle, 81, Former Head of Vanguard Press, Is Dead," *NYT,* 11 January 1973; James Henle, "Nobody's Sister," in William L. O'Neill, ed., *Echoes of Revolt: The Masses, 1911-1917* (Chicago: Ivan R. Dee, 1989), 191-92.

113   *talked on the phone:* Evelyn Shrifte, interview.

———➤➤-●-◄◄———

113   *didn't like the bedbugs:* DBF, interview.

113   *"evicted":* In a 1958 essay on Nathanael "Pep" West, in JTF, *Literary Essays, 1954-1974,* 77, JTF says: "When my wife and I were evicted from our apartment (a not too uncommon experience during the Depression), Pop [*sic*] let us stay in a suite of rooms for two weeks." James F. Light in *Nathanael West: An Interpretative Study* (Evanston: Northwestern University Press, 1971), 73, quotes JTF as saying that West gave them rooms "when we had no money and no place to go." Jay Martin, in *Nathanael West: The Art of His Life* (New York: Farrar, Straus & Giroux, 1970), 159, states: "When James T. Farrell and his wife were evicted from their hotel, West gave them two rooms for two weeks."

113   *"He did it simply":* Quoted by Light, *Nathanael West,* 73-74.

113   *One afternoon:* JTF, Diary, 15 February 1950; Murray Kempton, *Part of Our Time: Some Ruins and Monuments of the Thirties* (New York: Simon & Schuster, 1955), 130, 132; Chambers, *Witness,* 261-64.

114   *"A writer always":* JTF, 6 July 1932 letter to "Mr. Gray."

114   *"extraordinary":* Horace Gregory, in "More Good New Fiction," *New York Herald Tribune Books,* 26 February 1933.

114   *"In* [Young Lonigan]*":* Fred T. Marsh, in "'Gas-House McGinty' and Other Recent Works of Fiction," *NYT Book Review,* 5 March 1933.

115   *only 819 copies:* JTF, 30 January 1934 letter to Mary Farrell [MFB].

115   *"I am exceedingly soured":* JTF, 11 June 1932 letter to Mary Farrell [MFB].

115   *"He would do battle":* JTF, *My Days of Anger* (New York: Vanguard Press, 1945), 401.

115   *that extremist sect:* Klehr, *The Heyday of American Communism,* 91, 161-65; Harvey Klehr and John Earl Haynes, *The American Communist Movement* (New York: Twayne, 1992), 73-74.

116   *"generally quite sympathetic":* JTF, 11 June 1932 letter to Mary Farrell [MFB].

116   *had marched with the Communists:* JTF, "Truth and Myth" introduction draft; *NYT,* 2 May 1932.

116   *That the economic crisis:* JTF, "Plekhanov and Marx," in "The Bear Garden," *New York Sun,* 15 October 1932.

116   *More than fifty:* Klehr, *The Heyday of American Communism,* 80-81; Klehr and Haynes, *The American Communist Movement,* 66-67.

117   *did not support:* EB, "The 1930's in James T. Farrell's Fiction," *American Book Collector,* March–April 1971, 10.

━━━━◆━━━━

117   *"frequently can see":* JTF, "In Which the Gospel of Illusion Is Preached as a Cure for World Ills," *New York Sun,* 19 December 1932.

117   *"Christian radical":* Arthur M. Schlesinger Jr., "Reinhold Niebuhr's Role in American Political Thought and Life," in Schlesinger, *The Politics of Hope* (Boston: Houghton Mifflin, 1962), 106-7.

117   *In* Moral Man: Reinhold Niebuhr, *Moral Man and Immoral Society* (New York: Touchstone/Simon & Schuster, 1995), xii–xvi, 60-61, 179, 221.

118   *"risk the welfare":* Niebuhr, *Moral Man and Immoral Society,* 199.

118   *perhaps seven million:* Robert Conquest, *The Harvest of Sorrow: Soviet Collectivization and the Terror-Famine* (New York: Oxford University Press, 1986), 303.

118   *the great amount of force:* Niebuhr, *Moral Man and Immoral Society,* 218.

118   *soon repudiated:* Schlesinger, "Reinhold Niebuhr's Role," 112.

━━━━◆━━━━

118   *when Adolf Hitler:* Klehr, *The Heyday of American Communism,* 13, 97–98.

119   *"Socialists, stay":* NYT, 2 May 1933.

119   *"the only thing":* Edmund Wilson, *The Thirties* (New York: Washington Square Press, 1980), 346.

119   *"a rich proletarian background":* Edwin Rolfe, "Farrell's Progress," *NM,* July 1933, 29.

119   *as he then assumed, final:* JTF, undated letter to Victor Weybright, quoted by EB in *James T. Farrell,* 173; JTF, 3 August 1933 letter to DBF. (Relevant section of August 3 letter was evidently written that August but later in the month.)

119   *read Marx's* Capital: JTF, "Truth and Myth" introduction draft.

119   *more than seventy-five book reviews:* EB, *A Bibliography of James T. Farrell's Writings, 1921–1957* (Philadelphia: University of Pennsylvania Press, 1959), 48–55. The review quotes that follow were from: JTF, "Small Town Portraits," *New York Sun,* 6 January 1933; JTF, "The Book of the Day: The Essays of a Man Who Gloried That His Life Had Been Lived Quietly," *New York Sun,* 18 December 1933; JTF, "Stony Broke," *NR,* 11 October 1933; JTF, "The Book of the Day: The Tragic Story of an American Family That Points Its Own Moral," *New York Sun,* 31 May 1933; JTF, "A Working-Class Novel," *The Nation,* 20 December 1933.

120   *"I have fears":* JTF, 3 August 1933 letter to DBF; DBF, interview.

120   *a retreat for artists:* Description of Yaddo and background details are drawn from: Jean Nathan, "Yaddo," *NYT,* IX, 19 September 1993; Stephen Altman, "Paradise Regained," *Cultural Post,* National Endowment for the Arts, March–April 1977; Laura Furman, "The Benign Ghosts of Yaddo," *House & Garden,* June 1986; "Yaddo and Substance," *Time,* 5 September 1938; "Six Decades at Yaddo," Yaddo's 60th-anniversary publication in 1986; "Elizabeth Ames, Creator of Yaddo, Upstate Cultural Haven, Dies at 92," *NYT,* 30 March 1977.

121   *"The place":* JTF, 13 August 1933 letter to DBF.

121   *had warned him:* MHW, interview.

121   *"very charming":* JTF, 13 August 1933 letter to DBF.

122   *"Against the backdrop":* Horace Gregory, *The House on Jefferson Street: A Cycle of Memories* (New York: Holt, Rinehart & Winston, 1971), 201.

122   *"I didn't hint":* JTF, 13 August 1933 letter to DBF.

122   *"disconsolate and then confident":* JTF, 14 August 1933 letter to DBF.

122 *come to realize:* JTF, undated letter to Victor Weybright, quoted by EB in *James T. Farrell,* 173; JTF, "Epilogue" (1978), in *Studs Lonigan,* 469–70. The letter to Weybright indicates his realization came in 1934. The evidence in his letters from Yaddo in 1933 and January 1934 suggests that the realization probably came in 1933.

122 *intensive labor:* JTF, 3, 15 & 27 August 1933 letters to DBF.

122 *"I don't know":* JTF, 27 August 1933 letter to DBF.

122 *worried about Dorothy:* JTF, 15, 20 & 27 August 1933 letters to DBF.

122 *"Dear it's this way":* JTF, 27 August 1933 letter to DBF.

123 *in mid-September:* Elizabeth Ames, 21 August 1933 letter to JTF.

123 *returned to Yaddo:* Elizabeth Ames, 30 October, 3 & 11 December 1933 letters to JTF.

━━➤◦◄━━

123 *"We're all settled now":* JTF, 25 January 1934 letter to HFD.

123 *In the novel:* Direct quotes are from JTF, *Studs Lonigan,* YMSL, 34, 56–60, 146, 240, 411.

123 *"The book is rough":* Lewis Gannett, "Books and Things," *New York Herald Tribune,* 30 January 1934.

123 *"[The] adjective 'clinical'":* John Chamberlain, "Books of the Times," *NYT,* 31 January 1934.

123 *"It is too early":* JH, 2 February 1934 letter to JTF.

124 *"power and truth":* "Hard-Boiled Study of Adolescence," *NYT Book Review,* 11 February 1934.

124 *overlooked Danny O'Neill: Studs Lonigan,* YMSL, 371.

125 *"Farrell is writing":* Fred T. Marsh, "Farrell's Best Novel," *NR,* 21 March 1934.

125 *"It is true":* Edward Dahlberg, "Portrait of the Gangster," *NM,* 20 February 1934.

━━➤◦◄━━

125 *mass meeting:* NYT, 16, 17 & 18 February 1934; EB, "The 1930's in James T. Farrell's Fiction," 10.

126 *"Chairs were flung": New York Herald Tribune,* 17 February 1934.

126 *"that the Communist psychology": NYT,* 17 February 1934.

126 *"What the hell":* JTF, *Yet Other Waters* (New York: Vanguard Press, 1952), 276.

126 *"Open Letter to the Communist Party":* "To John Dos Passos," *NM,* 6 March 1934, 8.

126 *"ubiquitous 'decoration'":* Eugene Lyons, *The Red Decade: The Stalinist Penetration of America* (New York: Bobbs-Merrill, 1941), 198. Cf. Robert Morss Lovett, *All Our Years: The Autobiography of Robert Morss Lovett* (New York: Viking Press, 1948), 297–302.

126 *V. F. Calverton's* Modern Monthly: Leonard Wilcox, *V. F. Calverton* (Philadelphia:Temple University Press, 1992), 179–82.

126 *"act of insane hooliganism":* "An Open Letter to American Intellectuals," *Modern Monthly,* March 1934, 87–92.

126 *flagrantly untrue account:* "No Provocation Can Halt the March of Working Class Unity Against Fascism," *DW,* 19 February 1934.

127 *visited Leon Blum:* Alfred H. Hirsch, "Censorship in Prison," *NM,* 1 May 1934;Terry Cooney, *The Rise of the New York Intellectuals: Partisan Review and Its Circle, 1934-1945* (Madison,Wis.: University of Wisconsin Press, 1986), 108; JTF, 30 April 1934 letter to Joseph H.Wilson, warden, Comstock Prison, N.Y.

127 *Farrell's name appeared:* "An Open Letter to Thomas Mann," *NR,* 27 June 1934, 185. Farrell's name was apparently affixed to the letter without his permission (see JTF, Diary, 29 December 1938), but he does not seem to have publicly objected at the time.

127 *picket line of literati: NYT,* 26 September 1934;Wolfe, "The League of American Writers," 74–75; Edwin Rolfe, "The Second Macaulay Strike," *NM,* 23 October 1934, 20–21; "On the White Collar Front," *NM,* 19 June 1934.

127 *"It is quite apparent":* JTF, "'Daily Cannot Exist on Faith Alone, Says Farrell on D.W. Drive," *DW,* 22 October 1934.

127 *George Novack:* Alan M.Wald, *James T. Farrell: The Revolutionary Socialist Years* (New York: New York University Press, 1978), 48–49.

128 *Trotsky:* Joel Carmichael, *Trotsky: An Appreciation of His Life* (New York: St. Martin's Press, 1975), 368–69, 408, 410–11.

128 *"lone oppositionist":* Quoted by Wald, *James T. Farrell,* 50.

128 *Farrell, who had previously read:* Wald, *James T. Farrell,* 50, 52.

128 "New Masses *criticisms":* JTF, "James T. Farrell," in "Authors' Field Day:A Symposium on Marxist Criticism," *NM,* 3 July 1934, 28–29.

128 *"offers further testimony":* Herman Michelson, "Farrell Between Books," *NM,* 30 October 1934, 21.

128 *"This killing":* Robert Conquest, *The Great Terror:A Reassessment* (New York: Oxford University Press, 1990), 37.

129 *"a good year":* Granville Hicks, "Revolutionary Literature of 1934," *NM,* 1 January 1935, 36–37.

129 *The New England-born son:* Leah Levenson and Jerry Natterstad, *Granville Hicks: The Intellectual in Mass Society* (Philadelphia: Temple University Press, 1993), 1, 3, 18, 25, 42–43, 64.

129 *"The capitalist system":* "Call for Congress of American Revolutionary Writers on May 1," *DW,* 18 January 1935.

130 *Soviet Writers' Congress:* Wolfe, "The League of American Writers," 88; Moissaye J. Olgin, "A Pageant of Soviet Literature:The All-Union

Writers' Congress in Moscow," *NM,* 16 October 1934; Moissaye J. Olgin, "One Literature of Many Tongues: The All-Union Writers' Congress in Moscow," *NM,* 23 October 1934.

130 *Earlier in the month:* Elizabeth Ames, 2 September 1934 letter to DBF.

130 *at the Brevoort Hotel:* JTF, "[Autobiographical: Writing *Judgment Day,* c. 1934]," Box 356, JTFUP.

━━➤━◦━◄━━━

130 *"Come on along with me":* Quoted by Martin, *Nathanael West,* 258; JTF, 24 January 1973 letter to William Lederer (copy provided by Lederer); JTF, "[Autobiographical: Writing *Judgment Day,* c. 1934]."

130 *ninety-two women: NYT,* 21 January, 7 & 17 February 1935.

130 *"The girls":* "Writers in Union Square," *NM,* 5 February 1935.

131 *After eight hours:* Wald, *James T. Farrell,* 31.

━━➤━◦━◄━━━

131 *Farrell and 215 other:* Milton Howard, "5,000 Greet Writers Who Pledge Fight on Fascism, War: 400 Authors Gather in Parley to Discuss Their Role in Fight," *DW,* 29 April 1935; Henry Hart, "Introduction," in *American Writers' Congress,* ed. Henry Hart (New York: International Publishers, 1935), 12.

131 *Mecca Temple:* The Guilds' Committee for Federal Writers' Publications, Inc., *New York City Guide,* American Guide Series (New York: Random House, 1939), 179–80.

131 *"the father of":* Olgin, "A Pageant of Soviet Literature."

131 *"the brutality of our society":* Howard, "5,000 Greet Writers."

132 *Trachtenberg...had convened:* Wolfe, "The League of American Writers," 88–89, 91–92. See also *American Writers' Congress,* ed. Hart, 187; Klehr, *The Heyday of American Communism,* 352.

132 *As the implications:* Klehr, *The Heyday of American Communism,* 167, 169–71.

132 *"our literary movement":* Freeman, "Ivory Towers—White and Red," 23.

132 *"While recognizing":* "Text of Speech by Browder at American Writers Congress," *DW,* 29 April 1935.

132 *"made a few sarcastic":* John Chamberlain, "The Literary Left Grows Up," *SR,* 11 May 1935, 3.

133 *papers on various aspects:* The quotations are from the essays by the respective authors in *American Writers' Congress,* ed. Hart.

133 *One paper that went unread:* Townsend Ludington, *John Dos Passos: A Twentieth Century Odyssey* (New York: Dutton, 1980),

338-46; Hart, "Introduction," *American Writers' Congress,* ed. Hart, 17.

133   *"To fight oppression":* John Dos Passos, "The Writer as Technician," in *American Writers' Congress,* ed. Hart, 81. At least one sentence in Dos Passos' paper that was particularly disturbing to Cowley and others was dropped from the revised version included in the collection of essays from the congress published later in the year.

134   *Farrell spoke:* EB, *James T. Farrell,* "Chronology"; JTF, "The Short Story," in *American Writers' Congress,* ed. Hart, 103-14.

134   *"the creation":* JTF, "What is a Proletarian Novel? Discussion, James T. Farrell:," *PR,* April-May 1935, 13-15.

135   *enormously impressed:* Michel Fabre, *The Unfinished Quest of Richard Wright,* 2nd ed., trans. Isabel Barzun (Urbana, Ill.: University of Illinois Press, 1993), 118.

135   *"a very serious":* Quoted in *American Writers' Congress,* ed. Hart, 184.

135   *The new organization: American Writers' Congress,* ed. Hart, 184-85, 188; Klehr, *The Heyday of American Communism,* 352.

135   *"We have to create":* Quoted in *American Writers' Congress,* ed. Hart, 189.

135   *"gaily disruptive":* JTF, Diary, 7 December 1950.

136   *arose and suggested: American Writers' Congress,* ed. Hart, 192.

———◆———

136   *The sun was bright: NYT,* 2 May 1935.

136   *Farrell again marched:* JTF, "Truth and Myth" introduction draft.

136   *"I saw massed thousands":* "Writers Who Marched in the Parade Express Solidarity with Workers," *DW,* 3 May 1935.

Chapter 9: "A Kind of Inevitability"

137   *he found Hortense Alden:* DBF, interview.

137   *a glamorous woman:* Randolph Carter, interview.

137   *her son didn't know:* Dr. Kevin Farrell, interview.

137   *as Farrell himself evidently was:* In JTF, Diary, 2 October 1939, he refers to Hortense's sister as "Bettina Alden."

138   *won a beauty contest: Newark Star-Eagle,* 2 February 1917; *Newark Evening News,* 2 February 1917. See also *Dramatic Mirror,* 17 February 1917, 25; *New York Dramatic Mirror,* 13 January 1917, 25. For Boston Opera Company, see Quaintance Eaton, *The Boston Opera Company* (New York: Da Capo Press, 1980).

138   *city directory: R. L. Polk & Co.'s Trow General Directory of New York City Embracing the Boroughs of Manhattan and the Bronx, 1917.*

138   *sixteen years old:* Her birthday was on February 12. See JTF, Diary,

12 February 1940; "Alden, Hortense" entry in *The Biographical Encyclopaedia and Who's Who of the American Theatre,* ed. Walter Rigdon (New York: James H. Heineman, 1966), 238.

138   Tumble In: "Alden, Hortense" entry in *Who's Who in the Theatre,* ed. John Parker (New York: Pitman Publishing Corp., 1939), 210-11. Reviews of *Tumble In* appeared in the *Washington Post,* 17 February 1919, and *NYT,* 25 March 1919.

138   *Theatre Guild:* Norman Nadel, *A Pictorial History of the Theatre Guild* (New York: Crown, 1969), 1-5.

138   *"can do a character part":* "In the Spotlight," *Theatre Magazine,* August 1921, 80.

138   *"the flirtatious Emelia":* NYT, 22 March 1925.

138   *Her sister:* Bettina ["Alden"], 18 June [1978] letter to JTF.

139   *for two seasons: The Biographical Encyclopaedia and Who's Who of the American Theatre,* ed. Rigdon, 238; "Hortense Alden, 76, [*sic*], Long-Time Actress Toured with Lunt," *NYT,* 3 April 1978.

139   *Alla Nazimova:* "Nazimova, Alla" entry in Alice M. Robinson, Vera Mowry Roberts and Milly S. Barranger, ed., *Notable Women in the American Theatre: A Biographical Dictionary* (Westport: Greenwood Press, 1989), 687.

139   *"made memorable":* Nadel, *A Pictorial History of the Theatre Guild,* 102.

139   *her lover:* Randolph Carter, interview; Ria D. Simon, interview. That the affair commenced on this occasion is an inference by RKL.

139   *a new lover: Clifford Odets:* Margaret Brenman-Gibson, *Clifford Odets: American Playwright: The Years from 1906 to 1940* (New York: Atheneum, 1981), 156-61.

139   *whose friendship:* Charles DeFanti, *The Wages of Expectation: A Biography of Edward Dahlberg* (New York: New York University Press, 1978), 119, 133.

139   *"was an unadulterated dizzard":* Edward Dahlberg, *The Confessions of Edward Dahlberg* (New York: Braziller, 1971), 291. Dahlberg did not identify her by name.

139   *"a handsome and complaisant stenographer":* Percy Hammond, "The Theaters: Lifting One's Hat to 'Grand Hotel,'" *New York Herald Tribune,* 14 November 1930.

139   *In a single week: NYT,* 15 November 1931.

139   *beneath a drawing: NYT,* 22 February 1931.

140   *F. Scott Fitzgerald:* F. Scott Fitzgerald, "My Ten Favorite Plays," a feature in an unidentified, undated newspaper. The item makes reference to Fitzgerald's "latest novel... 'Tender Is the Night,'" which appeared in 1934. Hortense Alden preserved the clipping, which Randolph Carter made available to RKL.

140   *561 performances: NYT,* 6 December 1931.

140   *Yet within days:* Randolph Carter, interview.

140   [Footnote] *fleetingly unfaithful:* See JTF, Diary, 24 June 1939 and
       31 December 1939; EB, *Studs Lonigan's Neighborhood* (Newton,
       Mass.: Arts Ends Books, 1996), 88. DBF (interview) said she does not
       recall the episode. On Nora Kaye, see her *NYT* obituary (1 March
       1987). There are apparently no letters to JTF from Nora Kaye (or
       Nora Koreff, as her name was at birth) in JTFUP. A query sent by
       RKL in 1995 to her last husband, Herbert Ross, went unanswered.

⋙●⋘

141   *"It's like building blocks":* Evelyn Shrifte, interview.

141   Judgment Day *takes:* Direct quotes in next four paragraphs are
       from JTF, *Studs Lonigan,* JD, 27, 307–8, 131, 434, 440, 441, 448.

142   *"for sheer terror":* William Troy, "Portrait of an Age," *The Nation,* 1
       May 1935.

142   *"Mr. Farrell's art":* Lewis Gannett, "Books and Things," *New York
       Herald Tribune,* 27 April 1935.

142   *"shocked":* Fanny Butcher, "Critic Conducts an All-Chicago Novel
       Column," *CT,* 11 May 1935.

142   *"Judgment Day should illuminate":* Josephine Herbst, "Studs Loni-
       gan in Conclusion," *NM,* 21 May 1935.

143   *"acceptance of the Marxist analysis":* Harold Strauss, "Mr. Farrell's
       'Judgment Day' and Other Recent Works of Fiction," *NYT Book
       Review,* 28 April 1935.

⋙●⋘

143   *"Reverting to his old role":* James MacGregor Burns, *The Cross-
       winds of Freedom* (New York: Knopf, 1989), 75.

144   *"I watched one circus":* JTF, 6 June 1935 letter to HA.

144   *a nominal Republican:* Richard Rovere, *Senator Joe McCarthy*
       (London: Methuen & Co., 1960), 205; Eugene Lyons, *The Red
       Decade: The Stalinist Penetration of America* (New York: Bobbs-
       Merrill, 1941), 264.

144   *"probably the most able":* JTF, 6 June 1935 letter to HA.

144   *"Roosevelt is suave":* JTF, 7 June 1935 letter to HA.

145   *"Comrade Jerry":* JTF, 8 June 1935 letter to HA.

145   *"one of those sportland places":* JTF, 11 June 1935 letter to HA.

145   *"He has got something":* JTF, 11 June 1935 letter to HA.

145   *"Just when he seemed":* JTF, 13 June 1935 letter to HA; *NYT,* 13
       June 1935.

145   *"And so—Darling":* JTF, 8 June 1935 letter to HA.

145   *"I know little of music":* JTF, 14 June 1935 letter to HA.

145 *"I find that I talk too much":* JTF, 12 June 1935 letter to HA.
146 *"I like fireworks":* JTF, 14 June 1935 letter to HA.

——➤◦◄——

146 *in a car driven by:* JTF, "June 20," 1935 letter to HA; Elinor Rice Hays, interview. The letter is dated "Friday-June 20" but Friday was June 21.
147 *"Dorothy was quite lovely to me":* JTF, "June 21," 1935 letter to HA. The letter is dated "June 21/35, Saturday," but Saturday was June 22.
147 *unsuspecting:* DBF, interview.
147 *"Yaddo. Well darling":* JTF, 24 June 1935 letter to HA.
148 *"Another Washington Circus":* JTF, "Another Washington Circus," *NM,* 2 July 1935.
148 *"very elegant":* JTF, 21 June 1935 letter to HA.
148 *"one of the most important executives":* Quoted by JTF in 24 June 1935 letter to HA.
148 *advised Nathanael West:* Jay Martin, *Nathanael West: The Art of His Life* (New York: Farrar, Straus & Giroux, 1970), 261.
148 *MGM offered:* EB, *James T. Farrell* (New York: Twayne, 1971), 26.
148 *"that enormous room":* JTF, 24 June 1935 letter to HA.
148 *"crazy Irishman":* JTF, 8 June 1935 letter to HA.
149 *"It has become the orphan":* JTF, 25 June 1935 letter to HA.
149 *"Sometimes I wish":* JTF, 24 June 1935 letter to HA.
149 *On Friday:* JTF, 26 June 1935 letter to HA.
149 *for Paris and Hitler's Germany:* Elinor Langer, *Josephine Herbst: The Story She Could Never Tell* (Boston: Little, Brown, 1984), 186–88.
149 *"Don't mention":* JTF, 24 June 1935 letter to HA.

——➤◦◄——

149 *"Darling":* JTF, 10 July 1935 letter to DBF.
150 *Dorothy never saw it:* DBF, interview.

——➤◦◄——

150 *returned to Yaddo:* JTF, 16 August 1935 letter to HA.
151 *They were in bed:* DBF, interview.
151 *"Dorothy and I":* JTF, 16 August 1935 letter to HA.
152 *"She does not see":* JTF, 17 August 1935 letter to HA.
152 *"was very shocked":* JTF, 18 August 1935 letter to HA.
152 *"what did most":* JTF, Diary, 6 September 1951.
152 *"tried to make herself":* MHW, interview.

152   *"While she is":* Elizabeth Ames, undated 1935 letter to JTF.

153   *"Dorothy talked to [Peter]":* JTF, 19 August 1935 letter to HA.

153   *"Dorothy is now nice":* JTF, 19 August 1935 letter to HA.

153   *"If I had some strychnine":* DBF, interview.

⟹•⟸

153   *It was quiet:* Details drawn from JTF letters to HA, 20–27 August 1935.

153   *"I am sad":* JTF, 20 August 1935 letter to HA.

154   *"the family saga":* JTF, 2 February 1934 letter to Mary Farrell (MFB).

154   *"I am still plugging":* JTF, 23 August 1935 letter to HA.

154   *"imprisoned":* JTF, 23 August 1935 letter to HA.

154   *He tried repeatedly:* JTF, 23 & 24 August 1935 letters to HA.

154   *"wonderful":* JTF, 26 August 1935 letter to HA.

⟹•⟸

154   *his hitherto small readership:* "Vanguard's First Ten Years," *PW,* 13 June 1936, 2350.

154   *"sometimes unbearably brutal":* Henry Seidel Canby, "James T. Farrell's Indelible Portraits," *SR,* 7 December 1935.

Chapter 10: "A Betrayal of Honest Writers"

156   *Edmund Wilson came:* JTF, Diary, 28 January 1936.

156   *139 Lexington Avenue:* JH, 14 January 1936 letter to JTF.

156   *which Wilson had visited:* Edmund Wilson, *The Thirties* (New York: Washington Square Press, 1982), 519–90; Jeffrey Meyers, *Edmund Wilson: A Biography* (Boston: Houghton Mifflin, 1995), 161–65. For Wilson's series of articles on his journey, see *NR,* 25 March, 1, 15, 19 April and 13 May 1936.

156   *"take Communism away":* Quoted by Arthur M. Schlesinger Jr., *The Crisis of the Old Order, 1919-1933* (Boston: Houghton Mifflin, 1957), 213–14.

156   *the sudden flood:* Robert Conquest, *The Great Terror: A Reassessment* (New York: Oxford University Press, 1990), 44–45, 47–49, 71, 77–78; Isaac Deutscher, *Stalin: A Political Biography* (New York: Vintage, 1960), 369–70.

156   *Although he believed:* Edmund Wilson, "Introduction, 1971," to his *To the Finland Station: A Study in the Writing and Acting of History* (New York: Farrar, Straus & Giroux, 1972), v.

157   *"we shall be able to show":* Edmund Wilson, "Russian Paradoxes," *NR,* 13 May 1936.

157   *whose second wife:* Meyers, *Edmund Wilson,* 134-35.

---

157   *"are losing one hope":* JTF, "'Present-Day America Lives in Spivak's Book,' Says Farrell," *DW,* 8 August 1935.

157   *"the rigidity":* JTF, Diary, 7 January 1936.

158   *"leftward movement":* JTF, Diary, 12 January 1936.

158   *Popular Front:* Irving Howe and Lewis Coser, *The American Communist Party: A Critical History* (New York: Praeger, 1962), 319; Thomas Kennerly Wolfe Jr., "The League of American Writers: Communist Organizational Activity among American Writers, 1929-1942," Ph.D. dissertation, Yale University, 1956, 103.

158   *a $2,500 Guggenheim fellowship:* JTF, Diary, 18 March 1936; EB, *James T. Farrell* (New York: Twayne, 1971), "Chronology."

158   *he decided to set down:* JTF, Diary, 9 January 1936.

158   *"genuine sincerity":* JTF, "A Poor 'Revolutionary' Novel," *New York Herald Tribune Books,* 29 December 1935.

158   *"Stumbling Stumbling":* JTF, 23 January 1936 unsent letter to Stanley Burnshaw, Box 68, JTFUP.

158   *"Jim Farrell's review":* Margaret Wright Mather [Granville Hicks], "That's Their Story," *NM,* 21 January 1936, 27.

159   *"I argued out":* JTF, Diary, 17 January 1936.

159   *"manifestoes and burlesques":* JTF, Diary, 20 January 1936.

159   *whose* Let Freedom Ring: "Writers Urge New Yorkers to See Play," *DW,* 14 November 1935, 1. See also JTF, "The Theater: 'Let Freedom Ring,'" *NM,* 19 November 1936.

159   *"This convinces me":* JTF, Diary, 22 January 1936.

---

160   *"a fellow named Moscowitz":* JTF, Diary, 9 January 1936.

160   *vice president in charge:* David A. Cook, *A History of Narrative Film* (New York: Norton, 1981), 274-75.

160   *"Cagney is absolutely made":* JTF, Diary, 30 May 1936.

160   *had been huskier:* JTF, 2 April 1936 letter to HA; William Lederer, interview.

160   *when the movie industry:* See Edward R. Kantowicz, *Corporation Sole: Cardinal Mundelein and Chicago Catholicism* (Notre Dame: University of Notre Dame Press, 1983), 208-12; William M. Halsey, *The Survival of American Innocence: Catholicism in an Era of Disillusionment, 1920-1940* (Notre Dame, Ind.: University of Notre Dame Press, 1980), 119-21; Cook, *A History of Narrative Film,* 264-67.

160 *"an underlying moral code":* Philip Rahv,"'Notes on the Decline of Naturalism,'" in *Documents of Modern Literary Realism,* ed. George J. Becker (Princeton, N.J.: Princeton University Press, 1963), 587. Rahv's essay was originally published in *PR* in 1942.

---

161 *"a betrayal":* JTF, Diary, 2 February 1936.

161 *"Robert Cantwritewell":* John Chamberlain, *A Life with the Printed Word* (Chicago: Regnery Gateway, 1982), 43.

161 *"this broken down hulk":* JTF, Diary, 1 February 1936.

161 *modest first step:* Irving Howe and Lewis Coser, *The American Communist Party: A Critical History* (New York: Praeger, 1962), 325.

---

161 *Farrell had been involved:* JTF, 11 August 1951 letter to JH; JTF, "Studs Lonigan," *PR,* February–March 1934, 16–23.

161 *ordered the John Reed Clubs:* Harvey Klehr, *The Heyday of American Communism: The Depression Decade* (New York: Basic Books, 1984), 351. See Orrick Johns, "The John Reed Clubs Meet," *NM,* 30 October 1934, 25–26; Richard Wright, in *The God That Failed,* ed. Richard Crossman (New York: Bantam, 1965), 122.

161 *its principal editors:* Terry Cooney, *The Rise of the New York Intellectuals: Partisan Review and Its Circle, 1934–1945* (Madison, Wis.: University of Wisconsin Press, 1986), 82; James Gilbert, *Writers and Partisans: A History of Literary Radicalism in America* (New York: Columbia University, 1992), 142–43.

162 *"a burlesque":* JTF, "Theatre Chronicle," *Partisan Review and Anvil,* February 1936, 28–29.

162 *"It seems a pity":* Michael Gold, "Papa Anvil and Mother Partisan," *NM,* 18 February 1936, 22.

162 *Farrell's friend Josephine Herbst:* An undated copy of her original letter is in Box 68, JTFUP. The published letter appears in *NM,* 10 March 1936.

162 *After the* New Masses *editors:* Elinor Langer, *Josephine Herbst: The Story She Could Never Tell* (Boston: Little, Brown, 1984), 199.

163 *"couldn't talk to us":* JTF, Diary, 8 March 1936.

---

163 *"The Cunninghams are quite sore":* JTF, 2 April 1936 letter to HA.

163 *still saying this:* Loretta Cunningham Lederer, interview.

163 *"what an insult":* JTF, 2 April 1936 letter to HA; JTF, 3 April 1936 letter to JH.

164   *"more and more respectable"*: JTF, 2 April 1936 letters to HA; JTF, 3 April 1936 letter to JH.

164   *"Some lawyers in town"*: JTF, 1 April 1936 letter to HA.

164   [Footnote] *became good friends:* William Lederer, interview.; Loretta Cunningham Lederer, interview; William F. Roemer Jr., *Roemer: Man against the Mob* (New York: Donald I. Fine, 1989), 257.

165   *Frank Egan:* JTF, 10 July 1929 letter to Clifton P. Fadiman; EB, *Studs Lonigan's Neighborhood,* (Newton, Mass.: Arts Ends Books, 1996), 34.

165   *people seemed to be "sore"*: JTF, 3 April 1936 letter to JH.

165   *Kenny, Farrell learned:* JTF, 1 April 1936 letter to HA.

165   *found it a strain:* JTF, 2 April 1936 letters to HA.

165   *"a sense of the way"*: JTF, 3 April 1936 letter to JH.

165   *"I did not stay long"*: JTF, 7 April 1936 letter to HA.

166   *"something terribly pathetic"*: JTF, 4 April 1936 letter to HA.

166   *"just hugs his radio"*: JTF, 1 April 1936 letter to HA.

166   *"She has no teeth"*: JTF, 13 April 1936 letter to HA.

166   *"Two days after"*: MFB, interview.; JTF, 11 December 1938 letter to MFB; JTF, 12 December 1938 letter to HFD.

167   *"celebrities are forever"*: JTF, 6 April 1936 letter to HA.

167   *"an intellectual Jewish girl"*: JTF, 1 April 1936 letter to HA.

167   *even less happily:* JTF, 8 April 1936 letter to HA.

167   *less intelligent:* JTF, 13 April 1936 letter to HA.

167   *"definite class differences"*: JTF, 7 April 1936 letter to JH.

167   *"representative of many workers"*: JTF, 6 April 1936 letter to HA.

167   *"grant very enthusiastically"*: JTF, 13 April 1936 letter to HA.

168   *published in May:* EB, *James T. Farrell* (New York: Twayne, 1971), "Chronology."

168   *"quite a remarkable event"*: Edmund Wilson, "Novelist Bites Critic," *Nation,* 24 June 1936.

168   *"the school of revolutionary sentimentalism"*: JTF, *A Note on Literary Criticism* (New York: Vanguard Press, 1936), 29, 31, 46, 57.

169   *"Mr. Hicks"*: JTF, "Mr. Hicks, Critical Vulgarian," *American Spectator,* April 1936, 21-26.

169   *"The truth is"*: R. N. Carew Hunt, *The Theory and Practice of Communism: An Introduction* (London: Geoffrey Bles, 1951), 43-44.

169   *descriptive categories:* JTF, *A Note on Literary Criticism,* 77-94.

169   *"The class struggle"*: Ibid., 125-26.

170   *"When revolutionary novels"*: Ibid., 150.

170 *"is the first lengthy statement"*: Alan Calmer, "Down with 'Leftism'!" *Partisan Review and Anvil,* June 1936, 7–9.

170 *"the boys"*: JTF, Diary, 15 June 1936.

171 *"In other words"*: JTF, Diary, 31 May 1936.

171 *"To accept his analysis"*: Isidor Schneider, "Sectarianism on the Right," *NM,* 23 June 1936, 25.

171 *"In the course of his book"*: Granville Hicks, *NM,* 14 July 1936, 23.

---

171 *Farrell attended:* JTF, Diary, 7 & 22 June 1936.

171 *knew—and disliked:* JTF, 14 February 1953 letter to JH.

171 *"We drank beer"*: JTF, "Introduction" to H. L. Mencken, *Prejudices: A Selection* (1955), xii.

172 *"the greatest American novel"*: JTF, *A Note on Literary Criticism,* 80.

172 *"I went there"*: JTF, "Some Correspondence with Theodore Dreiser," in *The Stature of Theodore Dreiser,* ed. Alfred Kazin and Charles Shapiro (1955; Bloomington: Indiana University Press, 1965), 36–37; and JTF, *Reflections at Fifty and Other Essays* (New York: Vanguard Press, 1954), 124–25.

172 *"the stream of American life"*: JTF, Diary, 24 June 1936.

172 *"The enthusiasm"*: JTF, Diary, 29 June 1936; *NYT,* 29 June 1936.

172 *Under pressure from Moscow:* Klehr, *The Heyday of American Communism,* 191–95.

173 *"Drank too much beer"*: JTF, Diary, 3 June 1936.

Chapter 11: Renegade, in a World He Never Made

174 *"Over a hundred people"*: JTF, Diary, 20 August 1936.

174 *"humbug"*: *NYT,* 16 & 20 August 1936; Isaac Deutscher, *The Prophet Outcast: Trotsky: 1929–1940* (London: Oxford University Press, 1963), 332.

174 *already troubled:* JTF, Diary, 14 August 1936.

174 New York Times *correspondent: NYT,* 17 August 1936. On Duranty, see S. J. Taylor, *Stalin's Apologist: Walter Duranty: The* New York Times's *Man in Moscow* (New York: Oxford University Press, 1990).

174 *Rahv and Phillips:* Cooney, 39, 41; William Phillips, *A Partisan View: Five Decades of the Literary Life* (New York: Stein & Day, 1983), 20, 29; JTF, Diary, 16 October 1937.

175 *"had this view"*: JTF, Diary, 20 August 1936.

175 *"is practicing"*: JTF, Diary, [21] August [1936].

175 *"dragging* Partisan Review": JTF, Diary, 14 August 1936.

175 *"Looks to me"*: JTF, Diary, 17 September 1936.

175 *By early September:* JTF, Diary, 5 September 1936.

175   *covertly backing:* Harvey Klehr, *The Heyday of American Commu-nism: The Depression Decade* (New York: Basic Books, 1984), 195.

175   *a "dull" meeting:* JTF, Diary, 8 October 1936.

176   *"The Socialist Party":* JTF, "I Support Thomas," *SC,* 24 October 1936.

176   *arrest of Soviet propagandist: NYT,* 8 October 1936.

176   *"the subject of the Russian trials":* JTF, Diary, 10 October 1936.

176   *a Farrell satire:* JTF, "Comrades: Nu-Style," *SC,* 10 October 1936.

176   *"I suspect":* JTF, Diary, 14 October 1936. Some months later, how-ever, perhaps wanting to be seen as being on the "right" side in connection with the attempt to suppress *A World I Never Made,* the Workers Bookshop ordered 250 copies of the novel (JTF, Diary, [{?} February 1937]).

---

177   *"As Mr. Farrell":* Carl Van Doren, "The City Culture," *The Nation,* 24 October 1936.

178   *"His book has abundantly":* Bernard DeVoto, "Beyond Studs Loni-gan," *SR,* 24 October 1936.

178   *"had never really known":* JTF, *Father and Son* (New York: Van-guard Press, 1940), 599.

179   *"This is a dirty book":* Lewis Gannett, "Books and Things," *New York Herald Tribune,* 22 October 1936.

179   *"profoundly shocking":* F. B. [Fanny Butcher], "'Studs Lonigan' Author Writes a New Shocker," *CT,* 24 October 1936.

179   *had come to be counted:* See, e.g., Henry Seidel Canby, "James T. Farrell's Indelible Portraits," *SR,* 7 December 1935; and Alfred Kazin, "Danny O'Neill of Chicago," *New York Herald Tribune Books,* 25 October 1936.

179   *Naturalism:* See Malcolm Bradbury, *The Modern American Novel* (New York: Penguin, 1992); and Philip Rahv, "'Notes on the Decline of Naturalism,'" in *Documents of Modern Literary Realism,* ed. George J. Becker (Princeton, N.J.: Princeton University Press, 1963). For some ruminations by Farrell, see JTF, "On the Premises of Natu-ralism and of Revolutionary Literature," June 1936, Box 62, JTFUP.

179   *"you have certainly":* JH, 2 November 1936 letter to Gail Borden, *Chicago Times.*

180   *"Do you feel that":* JH, 13 November 1936 letter to JTF.

180   *"Ella was livid":* MFB, interview.

---

180   *an encyclical: NYT,* 3 July 1936.

181   *"outside assaults":* JTF, Diary, 3 July 1936. Two years later, the Catholic hierarchy formed the National Organization for Decent

Literature, which would find some of JTF's works objectionable. See Jonathon Green, *The Encyclopedia of Censorship* (New York: Facts on File, 1990), 204.

181   *a movie Studs saw:* JTF, *Studs Lonigan,* YMSL, 139-47.

181   *"potentially a threat":* JTF, "The Pope Needs America," *Nation,* 17 & 24 October 1936.

181   *"The course of the writer today":* NYT, 8 November 1936; JTF, Diary, 8 November 1936.

———※◦◄———

182   *interned in Norway:* Deutscher, *The Prophet Outcast,* 336-50.

182   *American Trotskyists:* Harvey Klehr and John Earl Haynes, *The American Communist Movement* (New York: Twayne, 1992), 91; Klehr, *The Heyday of American Communism,* 172-73; Peter Drucker, *Max Shachtman and His Left: A Socialist's Odyssey through the "American Century"* (New Jersey: Humanities Press, 1994), 82-83; Leonard Wilcox, *V. F. Calverton* (Philadelphia: Temple University Press, 1992), 195; Alan M. Wald, *The New York Intellectuals: The Rise and Decline of the Anti-Stalinist Left from the 1930s to the 1980s* (Chapel Hill: University of North Carolina Press, 1987), 110.

182   *"impassioned":* JTF, 21 October 1936 letter to Elizabeth Ames.

182   *"Not much achieved":* JTF, Diary, 13 November 1936. See *NYT,* 1 February 1938, for a list of members of the American Committee for the Defense of Leon Trotsky.

182   *"the issues transcended":* Sidney Hook, *Out of Step: An Unquiet Life in the Twentieth Century* (New York: Harper & Row, 1987), 224-25.

182   *a cocktail party:* JTF, Diary, 18 November 1936.

183   *somebody had told her:* JTF, Diary, 17 November 1936; MHW, interview; Michael Straight, *After Long Silence* (New York: W. W. Norton, 1983), 210-11; Gene Smith, "American Characters: Martha Dodd's Shining Season," *American Heritage,* July–August 1997.

183   *"novelist friend":* Mary McCarthy, *On the Contrary: Articles of Belief, 1946-1961* (New York: Noonday Press, 1962), 95; Carol Gelderman, *Mary McCarthy* (New York: St. Martin's Press, 1988), 69-70, 74-76; Carol Brightman, *Writing Dangerously: Mary McCarthy and Her World* (New York: Clarkson Potter, 1992), 130-32; Elisabeth Niebuhr, "The Art of Fiction XXVII: Mary McCarthy—An Interview," in *Conversations with Mary McCarthy,* ed. Carol Gelderman (Jackson, Miss.: University Press of Mississippi, 1991), 12-13.

184   *"very distinguished":* JTF, 15 September 1967 letter to Mary McCarthy, quoted by Frances Kiernan, in *Seeing Mary Plain: A Life*

of *Mary McCarthy* (New York: Norton, 2000), 113.

185 *"The local boys":* JTF, Diary, 17 November 1936.

———◆◆◆———

185 *Farrell left New York:* JTF, Diary, 18 November 1936; JTF, 22, 23 & 28 November 1936 letters to HA; Jane DeHart Mathews, *The Federal Theatre, 1935-1939: Plays, Relief, and Politics* (Princeton, N.J.: Princeton University Press, 1967), 12, 40, 87; Jerre Mangione, *The Dream and the Deal: The Federal Writers' Project, 1935-1943* (Philadelphia: University of Pennsylvania Press, 1983), 8, 39-40.

185 *"I shall try":* JTF, 22 November 1936 letter to HA.

185 *in a play that:* The play was *But Not for Love.* See Burns Mantle, ed., *The Best Plays of 1934-35 and the Year Book of the Drama in America* (New York: Dodd, Mead, 1935), 414.

185 *exceedingly amateurish production:* See JTF's Diary entries during July 1936.

185 *briefly brighten:* JTF, Diary, 20 February 1937. See also JTF, Diary, 22 & 23 February, 11, 12, 13, 14, 16 & 17 March 1937; and Burns Mantle, ed., *The Best Plays of 1936-37 and the Year Book of the Drama in America* (New York: Dodd, Mead, 1950), 472.

185 *had become acquainted:* DBF, interview.

185 *playful parodying:* JTF, *Literary Essays 1954-1974* (Port Washington, N.Y.: Kennikat Press, 1976), 88.

186 *his opinion that:* Carlos Baker, ed., *Ernest Hemingway: Selected Letters, 1917-1961* (New York: Scribner's, 1981), 533.

186 *"the most simplified":* JTF, 8 December 1936 letter to HA.

186 *"The explanation":* Ibid. Cf., Elizabeth Bishop, 26 January 1940 letter to Frani Blough Muser, in Elizabeth Bishop, *One Art: Letters,* ed. Robert Giroux (New York: Noonday Press, 1994), 87.

186 *"During the course":* JH, "The Record of a Friendship" (unpublished notes about JTF, n.d., provided to RKL by JH's son Peter Henle).

187 *"a dead town":* JTF, 5 December 1936 letter to JH.

187 *"I couldn't find":* JTF, 10 December 1936 letter to HA.

187 *"migratory intellectuals":* Michael Gold, "Migratory Intellectuals," *NM,* 15 December 1936.

187 *"being an Irishman":* SC, 26 December 1936; *NYT,* 19 & 23 December 1936.

———◆◆◆———

188 *seized by police:* "Farrell Novel Seized," *PW,* 23 January 1937, 328; *CT,* 15 January 1937; *NYT,* 15 January 1937; JTF, Diary, 3 January 1937; Heywood Broun and Margaret Leech, *Anthony Comstock:*

Roundsman of the Lord (New York: Boni, 1927), 150-54.

188 *"is humming"*: JTF, Diary, 18 January 1937.

188 *"[Farrell] has done"*: H. L. Mencken, 21 January 1937 letter to JH, in "Farrell (Promises of Statements in Fight with Sumner—'A World I Never Made'" folder, Box 46, VPCU.

189 *"utterly incomprehensible"*: Lionel Trilling, 19 January 1937 letter to JH. For Trilling's earlier assessment of Farrell's work, see his "Studs Lonigan's World," *The Nation,* 23 October 1935.

189 *"just about impossible"*: JTF, Diary, 28 January 1937.

189 *"And so," Farrell noted:* JTF, Diary, 1 February 1937.

189 *"No other American writer"*: NYT, 30 January 1937.

189 *"a sociological novel"*: "Memorandum in Behalf of Defendant," Stern & Reubens, in *People of the State of New York vs. The Vanguard Press, Inc.*, in "Farrell (Mag. Curran's Decision in 'A World I Never Made' Case)" folder, Box 46, VPCU.

190 *At the two-day hearing:* JTF, Diary, 2 & 3 February 1937; *NYT,* 4 February 1937.

190 *"superb"*: JH, "The Record of a Friendship."

190 *"coarse words"*: "Magistrate's Decision," in *People of the State of New York vs. The Vanguard Press, Inc.*, Box 46, VPCU; *NYT,* 12 February 1937.

190 *police in Philadelphia:* Henry S. Huntington, "The Philadelphia Book Seizures," *Nation,* 21 August 1948; *Philadelphia Evening Bulletin,* 21, 23 & 24 March, 7 April, 17 & 18 May 1948, 18 March 1949; *Philadelphia Inquirer,* 23 & 24 March, 7, 9, 16, 18 & 19 May 1948, 19 March 1949; *PW,* 3, 10 & 17 April, 15, 22 & 29 May, 25 December 1948, 2 April 1949; *NYT,* 7 & 25 May 1948, 19 March 1949; JTF, *Reflections at Fifty and Other Essays* (New York: Vanguard Press, 1954), 188-223; JTF, Diary, 10 April 1949. In his "The Record of a Friendship," JH asserted: "'Raids' had been cooked up by a Catholic group adroit enough to persuade a few Protestant clergymen to run interference for them." But he did not say what led him to that conclusion and offered no evidence for it. JTF also apparently blamed the Catholic hierarchy: See Stephen Menick, "Studs, Reds, 44 Acts of Faith—and Big Jim Farrell Ain't Done Yet," *Village Voice,* 20 September 1976.

191 *Farrell wanted very much:* Hook, *Out of Step,* 227.

191 *"had the intellectual breadth"*: JTF, 16 April 1937 letter to Margaret Marshall, quoted in Alan M. Wald, *James T. Farrell: The Revolutionary Socialist Years* (New York: New York University Press, 1978), 70.

191 *The son of:* Drucker, *Max Shachtman and His Left,* 6-7, 39-40, 48, 64-65, 88.

191 *"His pamphlet":* JTF, "'Behind the Moscow Trial,'" *SC,* 2 January 1937.

191 *The second Moscow show trial:* Robert Conquest, *Stalin and the Kirov Murder* (New York: Oxford University Press, 1989), 95; Robert Conquest, *The Great Terror: A Reassessment* (New York: Oxford University Press, 1990), 147-48.

192 *"exterminating the agents":* NYT, 6 February 1937.

192 *"The bitterness involved":* JTF, Diary, 7 February 1937.

192 *"deep and earnest thought":* Mauritz A. Hallgren, letter to the editor, *NYT,* 5 February 1937. See also *NM,* 9 & 16 February 1937.

192 *"slashed to pieces":* Hook, *Out of Step,* 229.

193 *"Why does Moscow":* NYT, 10 February 1937.

193 *One week later:* NYT, 17 February 1937; Hook, *Out of Step,* 228-29.

193 *"An Open Letter":* Corliss Lamont *et al.,* "An Open Letter to American Liberals," *Soviet Russia Today,* March 1937, 14-15; *NM,* 16 February 1937.

194 *"The condition of the world":* JTF, Diary, 7 February 1937.

194 *"The confusion":* JTF, Diary, 9 February 1937. See also JTF, "Dewey in Mexico," in JTF, *Reflections at Fifty,* 102.

194 *vetoed his selection:* Hook, *Out of Step,* 227; Albert Glotzer, *Trotsky: Memoir and Critique* (Buffalo, N.Y.: Prometheus Books, 1989), 239.

194 *"falling heavily":* JTF, Diary, 22 March 1937.

194 *whitewashing:* Malcolm Cowley, "The Record of a Trial," *NR,* 7 April 1937.

195 *Farrell joined:* JTF, Diary, 28 March 1937; Glotzer, *Trotsky,* 255-56; Alan Wald, "Memories of the John Dewey Commission: Forty Years Later," *Antioch Review,* Fall 1977, 443; Wald, *The New York Intellectuals,* 130.

195 *"I thought":* JTF, "The Influence of Dewey on Me," Box 283, JTFUP; JTF, "[Influence of J. Dewey on JTF]," Box 340, JTFUP; JTF, Diary, 3 March 1937.

195 *"He amazed everyone":* JTF, "Dewey in Mexico," 105-6.

195 *Dewey liked Farrell:* Wald, "Memories of the John Dewey Commission," 446.

195 *"a great man":* JTF, fragment of [(?) April 1937] letter to someone in Chicago, probably his sister Mary or brother Jack, Box 68, JTFUP.

196 *"In and out":* JTF, "Dewey in Mexico," 106; *NYT,* 18 April 1937.

196 *"it was affecting":* Quoted by Wald, "Memories of the John Dewey Commission," 449.

196 *"Jim got the chills":* Albert Glotzer, interview.

196 "Either Lenin's": *The Case of Leon Trotsky* (1938; New York: Merit

Publishers, 1968), 462. This book provides a complete transcript of the Coyoacán hearings.

196 [Footnote] *"truly serious"*: *The Case of Leon Trotsky,* 416; *NYT,* 19 April 1937; JTF, 18 April 1977 letter to Albert Glotzer, quoted by Glotzer, *Trotsky,* 267; Albert Glotzer, interview.

197 *"an extremely fertile"*: JTF, fragment of [(?) April 1937] letter to someone in Chicago, probably his sister Mary or brother Jack, Box 68, JTFUP.

197 *"Stalinist bureaucracy"*: *The Case of Leon Trotsky,* 282, 476, 514.

197 *"was a man of genius"*: JTF, "Dewey in Mexico," 109.

197 *a fanatic:* JTF, Diary, 13 December 1937.

197 *"to...protect"*: JTF, Diary, 30 March 1937.

197 [Footnote] *Trotsky had brutally suppressed:* Irving Howe, *Leon Trotsky* (New York: Viking, 1978), 79–81; Conquest, *The Great Terror,* 412; Deutscher, *The Prophet Outcast,* 163; Hook, *Out of Step,* 244; *The Case of Leon Trotsky,* 429.

198 *"Trotskyist robbers of the pen"*: *NYT,* 27 April 1937.

198 *"no retreating"*: JTF, Diary, 30 April 1937.

198 *"scribblers"*: V. J. Jerome, "No Quarter to Trotzkyists—Literary or Otherwise," *DW,* 20 October 1937.

198 *to be publicly announced:* Conquest, *The Great Terror,* 182.

198 *"Though the liquidation"*: Ronald Hingley, *Russia: A Concise History* (New York: Thames & Hudson, 1991), 180–81.

198 *The third one:* See Conquest, *The Great Terror,* Chapter 12.

199 *"the great lesson"*: Agnes E. Meyer, "John Dewey, Great American Liberal, Denounces Russian Dictatorship," *Washington Post,* 19 December 1937.

199 *that summer:* Drucker, *Max Shachtman and His Left,* 95.

199 *"neither head nor tail"*: JTF, Diary, 29 July 1937.

199 *"I'm going to write novels"*: JTF, "A Memoir on Leon Trotsky," *University of Kansas City Review,* Summer 1957.

Chapter 12: "Amidst a Kind of Ruin"

200 *"an opposition"*: JTF, Diary, 31 May 1937.

200 *the meager output:* JTF, "The Last Writers' Congress: An Interim Report on Its Results," *SR,* 5 June 1937.

200 *When one speaker:* Kenneth Burke, "Revolutionary Symbolism in America," in *The Writer in a Changing World,* ed. Henry Hart (New York: Equinox Cooperative Press, 1937), 89–94; Philip Rahv, "Two Years of Progress—From Waldo Frank to Donald Ogden Stewart," *PR,* February 1938; Harvey Klehr, *The Heyday of American Communism: The Depression Decade* (New York: Basic Books, 1984), 352–53.

201 *the 1937 Congress:* Thomas Kennerly Wolfe Jr., "The League of

American Writers: Communist Organizational Activity among American Writers, 1929-1942," Ph.D. dissertation, Yale University, 1956, 159, 166-67; Carol Brightman, *Writing Dangerously: Mary McCarthy and Her World* (New York: Clarkson Potter, 1992), 137; Henry Hart, ed., *The Writer in a Changing World,* 199, 208, 225, 252; Kenneth S. Lynn, *Hemingway* (New York: Simon & Schuster, 1987), 449-50; Klehr, *The Heyday of American Communism,* 354-55.

201 *"Mary and Eleanor and Dwight":* William Phillips, *A Partisan View: Five Decades of the Literary Life* (New York: Stein & Day, 1983), 50-51; Granville Hicks, *Part of the Truth* (New York: Harcourt, Brace & World, 1965), 147-48.

201 *"All in all":* JTF, Diary, 8 June 1937.

201 *"cunning and unscrupulous":* Philip Rahv, "Where the News Ends," *New Leader,* 10 December 1938. ("Where the News Ends" was the standing head for a column by Eugene Lyons, for whom Rahv was pinch-hitting.)

202 *wavered back and forth:* JTF, Diary, 18 January 1937.

202 *"exuberant, boyish":* William Phillips, interview.

202 *"The cat came out":* JTF, Diary, 22 January 1937.

202 *"that they're fairly rapidly":* JTF, Diary, 23 March 1937.

202 *Phillips had met:* William Phillips, "How 'Partisan Review' Began," *Commentary,* December 1976.

202 *expelled from the party:* JTF, Diary, 10 June 1937.

202 *told Farrell about this:* JTF, Diary, 31 May 1937.

203 *"Not that I care":* JTF, Diary, 20 June 1937; JTF, 11 August 1951 letter to JH.

203 *Max Eastman—the handsome:* John P. Diggins, *Up from Communism: Conservative Odysseys in American Intellectual History* (New York: Harper & Row, 1975), Chapter 1.

203 *"the repressive features":* "Trotsky and Labor Unity," *SC,* 26 December 1936.

203 *Rahv was expelled:* JTF, Diary, 16 October 1937.

203 *"a bright and clever girl":* JTF, Diary, 22 January, 7 February 1938.

204 *"We were interested":* William Phillips, interview.

204 *"whose choice of vocation":* Mary McCarthy, *Mary McCarthy's Theatre Chronicles 1937-1962* (New York: Farrar, Straus, 1963), 81-82.

204 *the erstwhile Exeter and Yale aesthete:* Michael Wreszin, *A Rebel in Defense of Tradition: The Life and Politics of Dwight Macdonald* (New York: Basic Books, 1994), Chapter 1.

204 *"Lillian Lugubriously Sighed":* Otis Ferguson, "Lillian Lugubriously Sighed," *NR,* 10 November 1937; JTF, Diary, 4 November 1937; Otis Ferguson, 9 August [1933] letter to JTF. On Ferguson, see Alfred Kazin, *Starting Out in the Thirties* (Boston: Little, Brown & Co., 1965), 29-31.

205 *excited just to meet:* Kazin, *Starting Out in the Thirties*, 51-52; Alfred Kazin, 6 November 1965 letter to JTF; Alfred Kazin, interview. In his 1965 memoir, Kazin says the meeting was on the day in 1935 when Farrell "finished" *Judgment Day.* Farrell, in a 1965 letter to Kazin, as well as in a 25 February 1976 letter to EB, said he did not recall meeting Kazin on the day he finished that novel. Kazin, in his 6 November 1965 reply, said, "I'm not surprised that you don't remember our first meeting in the '30's; I was completely unknown, my name meant nothing to you then, and our meeting was very brief. But brief as it was, it made a very great impression on me. I've always remembered that first meeting at the Brevoort— and it all happened exactly as I said.... The only bit of poetic license in the passage—and this was unconsciously dramatic rather than anything else—was to say that it was the day you had finished your book; it was the day the mss. came back from the typist—I remember so vividly the look of the freshly typed pages, turned back." See also EB's letter and Kazin's reply in *NYT Book Review,* 21 October 1979. In "[Alfred Kazin]," Box 567, JTFUP, Farrell claims that he first heard of Kazin in 1938; but that was a lapse of memory on Farrell's part. Kazin reviewed *A World I Never Made* in the *New York Herald Tribune Books* in 1936 and his collected short stories in the same publication in 1937, and Farrell almost certainly saw the reviews when they were published. "BOOKS gives Kazin my books all the time," he complained in his diary, 14 September 1938, after reading the critic's review of *No Star Is Lost.*

205 *"the strident stories":* Alfred Kazin, "The Bitter Bread of James T. Farrell," *New York Herald Tribune Books,* 16 May 1937.

205 *"a personal grievance":* Kazin, "Danny O'Neill of Chicago."

206 *"a little awkward":* Fred T. Marsh, "Mr. Farrell's Stories," *NYT Book Review,* 16 May 1937.

206 *"No Quarter to Trotzkyists":* V. J. Jerome, "No Quarter to Trotzkyists—Literary or Otherwise," *DW,* 20 October 1937.

206 *"That we do not consider":* editors, "Ripostes," *PR,* December 1937.

206 *Chicago novelist Nelson Algren:* Bettina Drew, *Nelson Algren: A Life on the Wild Side* (New York: G. P Putnam's Sons, 1989), 54, 82-84, 90-92, 103-4; JTF, Diary, 14 November 1937; Bill Granger, "Nelson Algren, a Neglected Poet of Chicago's Mean Streets," *CT Magazine,* 4 May 1997.

206 *"the cost of capitalistic society":* Hart, ed., *American Writers' Congress,* 110.

207 *"almost insane":* JTF, Diary, 5 May 1935, quoted by Drew, *Nelson Algren,* 91; JTF, Diary, 17 January 1943, 7 December 1950. On this episode, see also Elizabeth Ames, 4 May 1935 telegram and 7 May 1935 letter to JTF.

207 *"Algren sure wants":* JTF, Diary, 14 November 1937.

207 *"James 'Tuffy' Farrell":* Jack Conroy, letter to the editor, *NR,* 1 December 1937.

207 *"that pretentious windbag":* William H. Walker et al., letter to the editor, *NR,* 12 January 1938; Lewis Fried, "Conversation with Jack Conroy," *New Letters,* Fall 1972, 50-51.

207 *"genuine crackpot":* JTF, Diary, 30 November 1937. "Macdonald is a genuine crackpot all right," Farrell wrote. "There is a curious contradiction in him, his embracing of Marxism on the one hand, and his possession of a kind of snobbish Dial—T. S. Eliot—Burke—Cowley—Cantwell etc. Aesthetic on the other.... He argues on everything, and not with great cogency."

207 *"the literary lynching":* Dwight Macdonald, letter to the editor, *NR,* 16 February 1938.

208 *also protested:* Fred Dupee, letter to the editor, *NR,* 16 February 1938.

208 *"personal and scurrilous attack":* editors, "Mass Criticism," *PR,* March 1938.

208 *"a genuine influence":* JTF, Diary, 14 November 1937.

208 *"weak" response:* JTF, Diary, 26 January 1938.

━━►●◄━━

208 *Soon after he finished:* JTF, Diary, 11 May 1938.

208 *"slow and dull":* JTF, Diary, 12 May 1938.

208 *"[the] sense":* JTF, Diary, 15 May 1938.

208 *in no danger of attack:* JTF, Diary, 29 April 1938.

208 *"another War":* JTF et al., "War and The Nation," *The Nation,* 22 January 1938. The letter protesting *The Nation*'s "ambiguous policy of 'collective security,'" was signed by Farrell, Sidney Hook, Suzanne La Follette, Dwight Macdonald, Mary McCarthy, A. J. Muste, Philip Rahv, James Rorty, Meyer Schapiro, Norman Thomas, Lionel Trilling and Edmund Wilson, among others.

208 *the "May crisis":* William L. Shirer, *The Rise and Fall of the Third Reich: A History of Nazi Germany* (New York: Simon & Schuster, 1960), 361; A. J. P. Taylor, *The Second World War: An Illustrated History* (New York: G. P. Putnam's Sons, 1975), 31.

208 *outwardly calm:* JTF, 23 May 1938 letter to Felix Kolodziej.

209 *The BBC asked:* JTF, Diary, 24 May 1938.

209 *arrived in London:* JTF, 26 May 1938 letter to JH.

209 *"tremendously thrilled":* JTF, 27 May 1938 letter to JH.

209 *"I dread":* JTF, 3 June 1938 letter to JH.

209 *"an intelligent and likeable fellow":* JTF, 26 June 1938 letter to Sidney Hook.

209 *"really serious talk":* JTF, Diary, 2 June 1938.

209   *"and me, with my bad teeth":* JTF, 26 June 1938 letter to Meyer Schapiro.

209   *walking stick:* JTF, Diary, 21 May 1938; JTF, 18 June 1938 letter to George [Novack].

209   *"reserved" and "Puritanical":* JTF, 12 June 1938 letter to Jack [Farrell].

209   *"too literal and dull":* JTF, Diary, 17 June 1938.

210   *saw Sylvia Beach:* JTF, Diary, 15 & 18 June 1938.

210   *"pushy upstart":* Noel Riley Fitch, *Sylvia Beach and the Lost Generation* (New York: W. W. Norton, 1983), 382.

210   *having returned to the states:* Samuel Putnam, *Paris Was Our Mistress: Memoirs of a Lost and Found Generation* (New York: Viking Press, 1947), 157.

210   *"An intellectual desperado":* JTF, Diary, 12 June 1938.

210   *"A woman who":* JTF, Diary, 8 August 1937.

210   *could not "find a berth":* Elizabeth Ames, 2 August 1937 letter to JTF.

210   *"a failure":* JTF, "The Professor," in *Can All This Grandeur Perish? and Other Stories* (New York: Vanguard Press, 1937), 87, reprinted in JTF, *The Short Stories of James T. Farrell.*

211   *did not "like or respect":* JTF, 17 October 1938 letter to Felix Kolodziej.

211   *given up trying to defend:* JTF, 11 November 1938 letter to Felix Kolodziej.

211   *"In a sense":* JTF, "Introduction," in JTF, *Studs Lonigan* (New York: Modern Library, 1938), xi.

211   *"My experiences here":* JTF, 12 June 1938 letter to Jack Farrell.

211   *"the deepest":* Henry Adams, *Mont Saint Michel and Chartres*, in *Henry Adams*, vol. 1, *Novels, Mont Saint Michel, The Education* (New York: Library of America, 1983), 439.

211   *"It is probably":* JTF, 22 June 1938 letter to Jack Farrell; JTF, 23 June 1938 letter to JH.

211   *"a genuine student":* JH, "The Record of a Friendship."

211   *"A mouth":* William Barrett, *The Truants: Adventures among the Intellectuals* (New York: Anchor Press/Doubleday, 1982), 53, 150; Deborah Solomon, "Meyer Schapiro," *NYT Magazine,* 14 August 1994.

211   *"I felt":* JTF, 23 June 1938 letter to Meyer Schapiro.

212   *Society of the Little Flower: NYT,* 23 January 1951.

212   *"I went":* JTF, 2 July 1938 letter to JH. See also JTF's 3 July 1938 letter to JH, his 4 July 1938 letter to Meyer Schapiro, and HA's 2 July 1938 letter to Marjorie and Jim Henle.

212   *time to leave:* JTF, 22 July 1938 letter to JH.

212   *"Dublin is not a lovely city":* JTF, 28 July 1938 letter to JH.

212   *"The people are the main interest":* JTF, 30 July 1938 letter to Felix Kolodziej.

212   *worked on his father's farm:* JTF, Diary, 20 October 1939.

213   *"pretty much succeeded":* JTF, 3 July 1938 letter to George Novack.

213   *"one of the loveliest sights":* JTF, 4 August 1938 letter to JH; JTF, 30 July 1938 letter to JH; JTF, 6 August 1938 letter to George Novack.

213   *Abbey Theatre:* JTF, Diary, 9 August 1938.

213   *which had been robbed:* JTF, Diary, undated [July 1938]; JTF, 12 July 1938 letter to JH; JTF, 12 July 1938 letter to George Novack.

213   *"rather lonely":* JTF, 11 August 1938 letter to JH. See also JTF, 8 August 1938 letter to JH, and JTF, Diary, 12 August 1938.

213   *"Chica Dove":* JTF, 14 August 1938 letter to HA ("Chica Dove").

213   *"to make a round or two":* JTF, 20 August 1938 letter to Jack Farrell.

213   *"Ireland is very parochial":* JTF, 14 August 1938 letter to Jack Farrell.

214   *"You might think":* JTF, 24 August 1938 letter to Jack Farrell.

214   *"What I saw":* JTF, 24 August 1938 letter to MFB.

214   *who had roused Dublin's workers:* Kerby A. Miller, *Emigrants and Exiles: Ireland and the Irish Exodus to North America* (New York: Oxford University Press, 1985), 369.

214   *"a tired and embittered old man":* JTF, 25 August 1938 letter to Alfred [Rosmer?].

214   *"I want you to meet":* Eric Pace, "Studs Lonigan's Creator, Reaching 70, Savors New Life Style," *NYT,* 28 February 1974.

214   *"Besides being such interesting company":* JTF, Diary, 26 August 1938.

214   *Farrell left Ireland:* JTF, Diary, 27 August 1938.

214   *disturbing news:* JTF, Diary, 30 August 1938; *NYT,* 28, 29, 30 & 31 August 1938.

215   *"Stars, I have seen":* A. E. Housman, *More Poems* (1936), VII. The title of *A World I Never Made* was taken from A. E. Housman, *Late Poems* (1922), XII. See *The Collected Poems of A. E. Housman* (New York: Holt, Rinehart & Winston, 1965), 111, 166.

215   *"The painful truth":* Alfred Kazin, "Continuing the Saga of Danny O'Neill," *New York Herald Tribune Books,* 18 September 1938.

216   *"photographic realism":* George Stevens, "Life and Danny O'Neill," *SR,* 17 September 1938.

216   *"do not develop":* Clifton P. Fadiman, "James T. Farrell," *New Yorker,* 17 September 1938.

217   *"a gang up on me":* JTF, Diary, 14 September 1938.

217   *"shared [Cowley's] feeling"*: Kazin, *Starting Out in the Thirties,* 138.

217   [Footnote] *The political sympathies:* Alfred Kazin, "American History in the Life of One Man," *New York Herald Tribune Books,* 4 June 1939; JTF, Diary, 27 May, 1, 6, 8 & 16 June 1939; JTF, "Dos Passos and the Critics," *American Mercury,* August 1939.

217   *had been offended:* JTF, 17 October 1938 letter to Felix Kolodziej.

217   *"the mean streets"*: Robert Morss Lovett, "Farrell at the Crossroads," *NR,* 21 September 1938.

218   *"It looks as if"*: JTF, Diary, 15 September 1938.

218   *"a tremendous piece of work"*: Ralph Thompson, "Books of the Times," *NYT,* 15 September 1938. For Thompson's view of JTF's short stories, see *NYT,* 7 May 1937 and 6 October 1937.

218   *"I must interpret"*: JTF, Diary, 15 September 1938.

219   *Dick Parker:* JTF, Diary, 17 September 1938; Richard A. Parker, interview.; Richard A. Parker obituary, *Brown Alumni Monthly,* October 1993.

219   *moved into a new apartment:* JTF, Diary, 4 & 8 September 1938; JTF, 12 September 1938 letter to Felix Kolodziej.

220   *" 'Peace' now"*: JTF, 30 September 1938 letter to Jack Farrell.

220   *a colossal bluff:* JTF, 28 September 1938 letter to Jack Farrell.

220   *"It is all a sad and messy business"*: JTF, Diary, 2 October 1938.

220   *"economic rivalries"*: JTF, 7 October 1938 letter to Tom Daly.

221   *"Bill says"*: JTF, Diary, 2 October 1938.

221   *"a semi-official spokesman"*: JTF, 21 October 1938 letter to Jack Farrell. For Duranty's dispatch, see *NYT,* 11 October 1938.

221   *an attack:* Malcolm Cowley, "*Partisan Review,*" *NR,* 19 October 1938. See also his "Red Ivory Tower," *NR,* 9 November 1938.

221   *a strong private rebuke:* Edmund Wilson, 20 October 1938 letter to Malcolm Cowley, in Edmund Wilson, *Letters on Literature and Politics, 1912-1972* (New York: Farrar, Straus & Giroux, 1977), 309-10.

221   *public ones:* JTF, "*Partisan Review* Omnibus" (letter), *NR,* 30 November 1938; editors of *PR,* "A Letter to the *New Republic,*" *PR,* Fall 1938. An edited version of the letter appeared in *NR,* 9 November 1938.

221   *"is worried and upset"*: JTF, Diary, 20 October 1938.

221   *"talks bitterly"*: JTF, Diary, 2 December 1938.

222   *House Committee on Un-American Activities:* Walter Goodman,

The Committee: The Extraordinary Career of the House Commit-tee on Un-American Activities (New York: Farrar, Straus & Giroux, 1968), 24-35.

222   *"is likely to do great harm"*: JTF, 21 October 1938 letter to Jack Farrell.

222   *He was appalled*: JTF, Diary, 12 November 1938; JTF, 10 October and 4 November 1938 letters to HFD.

222   *"It is necessary"*: JTF, 21 November 1938 letter to James J. Geller.

222   *"Tommy Gallagher will not get anywhere"*: Fred T. Marsh, "Parable of the Times," *NYT Book Review*, 12 November 1939.

=====>•<=====

223   *"It is disgusting"*: JTF, Diary, 29 October 1938.

223   *"that through the Theatre Arts Committee"*: JTF, Diary, 12 September 1938.

223   *a member of the Theatre Arts Committee's executive board*: Eugene Lyons, *The Red Decade: The Stalinist Penetration of America* (New York: Bobbs-Merrill, 1941), 296.

223   *offered a small role*: JTF, Diary, 22 October 1938. See Burns Mantle, *The Best Plays of 1938-39* (New York: Dodd, Mead, 1939), 216, 285-317, 436, 467.

223   *"hokum"*: JTF, Diary, 19 November 1938.

223   *"she is certain"*: JTF, Diary, 7 November 1938.

223   *"Hortense and I"*: JTF, Diary, 15 February 1939.

=====>•<=====

224   *he recorded*: JTF, Diary, 20 January, undated fragment [Jan. 1939], 9 March, 31 May, 3, 25, 28 & 30 September, 29 October, 6, 11 & 15 December 1939.

224   *"a first-rate scholar"*: JTF, Diary, 28 October 1938.

=====>•<=====

224   *"On principle"*: JTF, "Truth and Myth" introduction draft.

225   *"The recent trend"*: JTF, Diary, 5 December 1938.

225   *Farrell adamantly insisted*: JTF, Diary, 15 January, 26 May 1939; Sidney Hook, *Out of Step: An Unquiet Life in the Twentieth Century* (New York: Harper & Row, 1987), 259-62, 271-74; *NYT*, 15 May 1939.

225   *"that Sidney was forming"*: JTF, Diary, undated fragment [April or May 1939]. Later in the year, in privately considering Hook's *John Dewey: An Intellectual Portrait*, Farrell would contrast Hook's view of democracy with Dewey's: "Democracy to Sidney is becoming an

instrument for fighting Stalinism. It is much much more real with Dewey." JTF, Diary, 29 October 1939.

225 *"I find that Sidney"*: JTF, Diary, 20 June 1939.

225 *"many good names"*: JTF, Diary, 15 May 1939.

225 *"In lumping together"*: "Liberty and Common Sense," *NR,* 31 May 1939.

225 *"With all their faults"*: Freda Kirchwey, "Red Totalitarianism," *The Nation,* 27 May 1939.

226 *a "rabid Red-baiter"*: Corliss Lamont, "Mr. Corliss Lamont Replies to the Freedom Committee," letter to the editor, *New York Post,* 2 June 1939.

226 *Replied Hook:* Sidney Hook, "Soviet Union a Totalitarian Dictatorship Just as Is Germany," letter to the editor, *New York Post,* 7 June 1939.

226 *"excellent"*: JTF, Diary, 8 & 9 June 1939.

226 *declined several times:* JTF, Diary, 26 May 1939, and undated fragment, April or May 1939.

226 *"the best of the intellectuals"*: JTF, 21 November 1938 letter to Felix Kolodziej.

226 *"Shall we abandon"*: "Still Another Committee," *NR,* 14 June 1939; JTF, Diary, 3 & 18 March 1939; The League for Cultural Freedom and Socialism, "Manifesto and Appeal," *The Nation,* 15 July 1939.

————————

226 *They arrived:* JTF, Diary, 6 August 1939.

227 *something to live for:* JTF, Diary, 24 February 1939.

227 *Dorothy, who:* JTF, Diary, 8 November 1937, 24 & 30 June 1939, 21, 27 & 28 February 1940; DBF, interview; Tim Page, ed., *The Diaries of Dawn Powell, 1931-1965* (South Royalton, Vt.: Steerforth Press, 1995), 175-76.

227 *"a surprise"*: JTF, Diary, 6 August 1939.

————————

227 *"fantastic falsehood"*: Jay Allen et al., "To All Active Supporters of Democracy and Peace," *The Nation,* 26 August 1939; Lyons, *The Red Decade,* 346-51.

227 *"400 suckers"*: JTF, Diary, 21 September 1939.

228 *only 167:* Hook, *Out of Step,* 269. One name, oddly, appeared both among the signers of the Hook committee's manifesto and among the four hundred who condemned it: poet William Carlos Williams.

228 *"Jesus Christ"*: Leah Levenson and Jerry Natterstad, *Granville Hicks: The Intellectual in Mass Society* (Philadelphia: Temple University Press, 1993), 119; Hicks, *Part of the Truth,* 176.

228   *"It looks as if":* JTF, Diary, 24 August 1939.

228   *Mike Gold... decided:* JTF, Diary, 25 August 1939.

228   *sympathetic letters:* JTF, Diary, 27 September 1939.

228   *who was slowly moving away:* William L. O'Neill, *A Better World: The Great Schism: Stalinism and the American Intellectuals* (New York: Touchstone, 1982), 21; Malcolm Cowley, *"—And I Worked at the Writer's Trade": Chapters of Literary History, 1918-1978* (New York: Viking, 1978), 153, 157-58.

229   *"should be driven out":* JTF, Diary, 22 September 1939.

229   *"most of its membership":* Klehr, *The Heyday of American Communism,* 409.

229   *Frederick L. Schuman:* Frederick L. Schuman, "Machiavelli in Moscow," *NR,* 29 November 1939, and "Machiavelli Gone Mad" (letter), *NR,* 27 December 1939; O'Neill, *A Better World,* 27; Hook, *Out of Step,* 269; *Who's Who in America,* 37th ed., 1972-73, vol. 2 (Chicago: Marquis Who's Who, 1972), 2,817. See also JTF, Diary, 29 & 30 September 1939; Frederick L. Schuman, "Leon Trotsky: Martyr or Renegade," *Southern Review,* Summer 1937, 51-74, and related correspondence from JTF and others, 199-208; and Sidney Hook, "Liberalism and the Case of Leon Trotsky," *Southern Review,* Autumn 1937, 267-82, and related correspondence from JTF and others, 406-16. Also: Frank N. Trager, "Frederick L. Schuman: A Case History," *PR,* May-June 1940.

229   *"If one is to remain":* JTF, Diary, 2 September 1939.

229   *Farrell looked back:* JTF, "The End of a Literary Decade," *American Mercury,* December 1939.

Chapter Thirteen: "The Wall of Isolation"

232   *one mid-June night:* JTF, Diary, 12 June 1940.

232   *stubbornly maintained:* JTF, Diary, 7 September 1940.

232   *conflict of rival imperialisms:* JTF, "The Cultural Front," *PR,* March-April 1940.

233   *"I can think of no alternative":* JTF, Diary, 1 June 1940.

233   *Stalin's betrayal:* JTF, 7 July 1941 letter to Felix Kolodziej.

233   *"a strong labor movement":* JTF, Diary, 19 June 1940.

233   *"Patriotic feeling":* JTF, Diary, 16 May 1940. See also JTF, Diary, 14 May 1940.

233   *"Today," wrote Lewis Mumford:* Lewis Mumford, "The Corruption of Liberalism," *NR,* 29 April, 1940.

233   *the "irresponsibles":* Archibald MacLeish, "The Irresponsibles," *The Nation,* 18 May 1940.

234   *"bitter and dangerous fruit":* Archibald MacLeish, "Post-war Writers and Pre-war Readers," *NR,* 10 June 1940.

234   *nonsense:* JTF, Diary, 24 May 1940.

234   *"You know the picture of life":* Van Wyck Brooks, "Fashions in Defeatism," *SR,* 22 March 1941; Van Wyck Brooks, "What Is Primary Literature?" *Yale Review,* September 1941.

234   *giving up on socialism:* Max Eastman, "Socialism Doesn't Jibe with Human Nature," *Reader's Digest,* June 1941.

235   *"sounds as if":* Edmund Wilson, "Archibald MacLeish and 'the Word,'" *NR,* 1 July 1940.

235   *Brooks, declared Macdonald:* Dwight Macdonald, "Kulturbolschewismus Is Here," *PR.* November–December 1941.

235   *"a simple historic fact":* JTF, in Allen Tate et al., "On the 'Brooks-MacLeish Thesis,'" *PR,* January–February 1942.

235   *Sidney Hook and others:* JTF, Diary, 2 February, 16 November 1940; 2 March, 5 April 1941.

235   *"political onanists":* JTF, Diary, 6 October 1940.

235   *"degenerated workers' state":* Robert J. Alexander, *International Trotskyism, 1929-1985: A Documented Analysis of the Movement* (Durham, N.C.: Duke University, 1991), 794–95; Isaac Deutscher, *The Prophet Outcast: Trotsky: 1929-1940* (London: Oxford University Press, 1963), 203–4, 459.

235   *Farrell considered this:* JTF, Diary, 9 October, 29 December 1939; 16 January, 14 February, 13 March 1940.

235   *did Max Shachtman:* Peter Drucker, *Max Shachtman and His Left: A Socialist's Odyssey through the "American Century"* (New Jersey: Humanities Press, 1994), 108–9, 120, 127, 145; Albert Glotzer, *Trotsky: Memoir and Critique* (Buffalo, N.Y.: Prometheus Books, 1989), 283–89; Alexander, *International Trotskyism,* 797, 805.

236   *"There seems to be little future":* JTF, Diary, 11 November 1939.

236   *in Mount Sinai Hospital:* JTF, Diary, 24, 25, 26 August, 17 September 1940; JTF, "A Memoir on Leon Trotsky." See also JTF, "The Cultural Front: Leon Trotsky," *PR,* September–October 1940.

⟹•⟸

236   *"never regarded":* JH, "The Record of a Friendship" (unpublished, n.d.).

236   *Seven months earlier:* JTF, Diary, 18 August 1939.

237   *"This comes to us":* JTF, Diary, 22 March 1940.

237   *"In what should be":* JTF, Diary, 16 March 1940.

237   *their son, Kevin:* JTF, Diary, 4 [*sic*] October 1940; Dr. Kevin Farrell, interview. The diary entry is misdated; it evidently was written on 3 October 1940.

237   *"It is a strange feeling":* JTF, Diary, 5 October 1940.

237   *were married:* JTF, Diary, 11 January 1941.

237   *final the previous June:* JTF, Diary, 27 June 1940.

237   *Some months before:* JTF, Diary, 19, 31 March 1940. See Tim Page, ed., *The Diaries of Dawn Powell, 1931-1965* (South Royalton, Vt.: Steerforth Press, 1995), 175-76.

238   *Hortense shocked:* JH, "The Record of a Friendship."

238   *a great delight:* See, e.g., JTF, Diary, 27 November 1942, 31 May 1944.

238   *"Why, it [the baby]":* JH, "The Record of a Friendship."

238   *had to hire a maid:* CP, interview; Theda Henle, interview; JTF, Diary, 23 February, 10, 15 April, 8 May, 7 July, 4, 6 October, 20, 28 December 1941; 21 April, 7, 12 June 1942; 21 January, 3, 4, 10, 13 February 1943; 4, 5 March 1951.

238   *behaved well at school:* JTF, Diary, 1 February 1945.

238   *A mere runny nose:* JTF, Diary, 15, 16 November 1943.

238   *"What that child":* Randolph Carter, interview.

238   *"The behavior problem":* JTF, Diary, 22 September 1944.

238   *"Hortense and Kevin":* JTF, Diary, 15 February 1945.

━━━▶◦◀━━━

239   *ready to call it quits:* JTF, Diary, 30 December 1938; 3 January 1939; JTF, "The Only Son," *PR,* Spring 1939.

239   *regular column:* JTF, Diary, 8 December 1939. Originally, the column was to be called "The Literary Front," but the name was changed to "The Cultural Front," which, by coincidence or not, was the name of a regular column he had written for the Socialist Party's *Socialist Call* in 1937.

239   *"Farrell would write":* Quoted by Carol Brightman, *Writing Dangerously: Mary McCarthy and Her World* (New York: Clarkson Potter, 1992), 130. The interview was conducted by Brightman on 31 July 1985. Asked nine years later about McCarthy's comment, William Phillips said: "I don't remember that as a strategy. Mary had a way of making up witty things. So I don't know. May have been true, may not have been true." (Phillips, interview)

239   *"It is difficult":* JTF, "The Cultural Front," *PR,* March–April 1940; JTF, Diary, 20 March 1940. Sidney Hook took a similar view of the recent defectors from Stalinism: see his "Unreconstructed Fellow-Travelers," *SC,* 13 January 1940.

240   *"to do my best":* Granville Hicks, "On Leaving the Communist Party," letter to the editor, *NR,* 4 October 1939.

240   *"a brother party":* Richard H. Rovere, "On Joining the Socialist Party," *SC,* 27 January 1940. See also Richard Rovere, *Final Reports:*

Personal Reflections on Politics and History in Our Time (New York: Doubleday, 1984), 42–43, 59–68, and Richard H. Rovere, *Arrivals and Departures: A Journalist's Memoirs* (New York: Macmillan, 1976), 53–60.

240 *"a distinct disappointment"*: JTF, Diary, 24 March 1940.

241 *"It never pays"*: JTF, Diary, 20 April 1940.

241 *"After all"*: JTF, Diary, 22, 24, 25 April 1940.

241 *an extremely lame satire*: JTF, "The Cultural Front," *PR*, July–August 1940.

241 *a eulogy*: JTF, "The Cultural Front: Leon Trotsky."

242 *a diatribe*: JTF, "The Cultural Front: Mortimer J. Adler: A Provincial Torquemada," *PR*, November–December 1940.

242 *a recent tirade*: Mortimer J. Adler, *Philosopher At Large: An Intellectual Autobiography* (New York: Macmillan, 1977), 188–90; Hook, *Out of Step*, 335–39.

242 *"We are making this change"*: Editors, "To Our Readers," *PR*, September–October 1940.

242 *"Quite casually"*: JTF, Diary, 11 December 1940.

243 *Macdonald was pushing*: Michael Wreszin, *A Rebel in Defense of Tradition: The Life and Politics of Dwight Macdonald* (New York: Basic Books, 1994), 92–94; Terry Cooney, *The Rise of the New York Intellectuals: Partisan Review and Its Circle, 1934–1945* (Madison, Wis.: University of Wisconsin Press, 1986), 185.

243 *A reader survey*: "Results of the P.R. Questionnaire," *PR*, July–August 1941; JTF, Diary, 24 April 1941.

243 *he liked a lengthy piece*: JTF, Diary, 17 February 1941. See JTF, "The Faith of Lewis Mumford," *Southern Review*, Winter 1941.

243 *"an aesthetic little magazine"*: JTF, Diary, 12 December 1940.

243 *crackdown on the* Masses: John Patrick Diggins, *The Rise and Fall of the American Left* (New York: W. W. Norton, 1992), 102–3.

244 *soon vowed*: JTF, Diary, 3 January 1941. See JTF, "'The Cultural Front,'" letter to the editor, *PR*, January–February 1941.

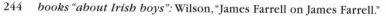

244 *books "about Irish boys"*: Wilson, "James Farrell on James Farrell."

245 *"Wonderful stuff"*: "Mr. Mencken on Literature and Politics," *NYT Book Review*, 11 February 1940.

246 *"had never really known"*: JTF, *Father and Son* (New York: Vanguard Press, 1940), 599–601.

246 *"In* Father and Son": Stephen Vincent Benét, "Chicago's Danny O'Neill," *SR*, 12 October 1940.

247 *was mixed*: Ralph Thompson, "Books of the Times," *NYT*, 10 October 1940.

247 *liked the novel:* JTF, Diary, 16, 18, 22 & 30 October, 1 November 1940.

247 *"Adams did a double crossing":* JTF, Diary, 25 November 1940.

247 *"one of the most honest":* J. Donald Adams, in "Mr. Farrell's 'Father and Son' and Other Recent Fiction," *NYT Book Review,* 1 December 1940.

247 "If [*Father and Son*]": JTF, Diary, 19 September 1940.

247 *"I am beginning":* JTF, Diary, 30 October 1940. See also Diary, 8, 18 October 1940.

247 *"Critics cannot":* JTF, Diary, 1 November 1940.

248 *"By this time":* Clifton Fadiman, "Books," *New Yorker,* 12 October 1940.

248 *"it is because":* John Chamberlain, "The New Books," *Harper's Magazine,* January 1941.

248 *best, most intelligent review:* JTF, Diary, 29 April 1941.

248 *"on principle":* JTF, Diary, 11 December 1940.

248 *"nearly impossible":* Weldon Kees, "To Be Continued," *PR,* May–June 1941.

---

249 *"the great arsenal of democracy":* James MacGregor Burns, *Roosevelt: The Soldier of Freedom* (New York: Harcourt Brace Jovanovich, 1970), 28.

249 *polls showing:* Quincy Howe, "American Foreign Policy and Public Opinion," *Yale Review,* December 1941.

249 *"those honest radicals":* Max Eastman, "Vicarious Belligerence Viewed as No Policy for Us," letter to the editor, *NYT,* 11 May 1941.

249 *"not a good letter":* JTF, Diary, 13 May 1941.

249 *"When Eastman tells us":* JTF, in JTF and Max Eastman, "As to Values and Facts: An Exchange," *PR,* May–June 1942.

250 *to learn mathematics:* JTF, Diary, 18 February, 11 March, 21 June, 30 October 1940; 18, 19 February, 12, 18 March, 8 April, 18, 20, 21 May, 7 August 1941; "James Farrell, 63, on Eve of 20th Novel, Is Busy Writing His 21st," *NYT,* 3 December 1967.

250 *"I am not muddled":* JTF, Diary, 13 June 1941.

250 *"unwarrantedly sharp":* JTF, 31 January 1950 letter to the editors of *PR,* quoted by William O'Neill, *The Last Romantic: A Life of Max Eastman* (New York: Oxford University Press, 1978), 218.

250 *"Many people will hail":* JTF, 22 June 1941 letter to JH.

---

251 *"29 REDS": NYT,* 16 July 1941.

251 *"a very serious business":* JTF, 25 July 1941 letter to John Dos Passos.

251 *"a strong labor movement":* JTF, Diary, 19 June 1940.

251 *had been heartened:* JTF, Diary, 12, 13 June 1941. On the strikes, see Max Kampelman, *The Communist Party vs. the C.I.O.* (New York: Praeger, 1957), 25–28; Irving Howe and Lewis Coser, *The American Communist Party: A Critical History* (New York: Praeger, 1962), 397–98; Bert Cochran, *Labor and Communism: The Conflict That Shaped American Unions* (Princeton, N.J.: Princeton University Press, 1977), 162–66.

251 *"all disputes":* DW, 8 December 1941, quoted by Howe and Coser, *The American Communist Party,* 398.

251 *Meanwhile, the Trotskyists:* Alan M. Wald, *The New York Intellectuals: The Rise and Decline of the Anti-Stalinist Left from the 1930s to the 1980s* (Chapel Hill: University of North Carolina Press, 1987), 165, 197–99; Drucker, *Max Shachtman and His Left,* 136–37, 144–45.

252 *born in Ireland:* Tobin obituary, *NYT,* 15 November 1955; *Current Biography 1945* (New York: H. W. Wilson, 1946), 612–14.

252 *won the presidency:* Robert D. Leiter, *The Teamsters Union: A Study of Its Economic Impact* (New York: Bookman Associates, 1957), 26.

252 *a "vehement" anti-Communist:* "The I.B.T.C.W.H. of A.," *Fortune,* May 1941.

252 *the hard-bitten Dunne brothers:* See Walter Galenson, *The CIO Challenge to the AFL: A History of the American Labor Movement, 1935–1941* (Cambridge: Harvard University Press, 1960), 478–86; Thomas L. Pahl, "G-String Conspiracy, Political Reprisal or Armed Revolt? The Minneapolis Trotskyite Trial," *Labor History,* Winter 1967; Philip Taft, *Organized Labor in American History* (New York: Harper & Row, 1964), 445–46; Page Smith, 705–6; Thomas R. Brooks, *Toil and Trouble: A History of American Labor* (New York: Dell/Delta, 1964), 165–68; Farrell Dobbs, *Teamster Bureaucracy* (New York: Pathfinder Press, 1977), 9, 90–94, 105.

252 *"Bundists, Stalinists":* NYT, 14 June 1941.

253 *two weeks later:* NYT, 28 June 1941; Dobbs, *Teamster Bureaucracy,* 137.

253 *"to equate":* I. F. Stone, "The G-String Conspiracy," *The Nation,* 26 July 1941.

253 *may well have agreed:* See Cabell Phillips, "No Witch Hunts," *NYT Magazine,* 21 September 1941; Michal R. Belknap, *Cold War Political Justice: The Smith Act, the Communist Party, and American Civil Liberties* (Westport, Conn.: Greenwood Press, 1977), 38.

253 *high blood pressure:* JTF, Diary, 1 June, 30 July 1940; 3, 26 January, 19 March, 23 May 1941.

━━◆━◆━◆━━

253 *"It would be pleasant":* Clifton Fadiman, "Books: Mr. Cain and Mother Love—Entries from Mr. Farrell and Mr. Lanham," *New Yorker,* 27 September 1941.

254 *"He pays a great tribute":* JH, 25 September 1941 letter to JTF.

254 *"our main source of income":* JTF, Diary, 5, 21 August 1941.

254 *"Even this":* JTF, 29 September 1941 letter to HA ("Chica Dove").

254 *an RKO producer:* JTF, Diary, 3 July 1941. See also James J. Geller, 30 June 1941 letter to JTF.

255 *"Broadway-Hollywood world":* JTF, Diary, 20 April 1941.

255 *more expensive apartment:* In his Diary, 28 August 1941, JTF says they found "a desirable apartment," four rooms, at 100th Street and Broadway, and notes that while the rent, $80, is "steep for us," they would probably take it. However, letters from JH to JTF, starting with 9 September 1941, indicate the apartment they finally took was further uptown, at 535 West 110th Street. The rent was probably no less steep.

255 *a less noisy one:* JTF, Diary, 20, 25 April, 2 May 1940; JTF, 8 May 1940 letter to John A. Farrell.

255 *not to their liking:* H.D., interview. JH's 11 and 24 August 1942 letters to JTF indicate the addresses and roughly when the move back downtown took place.

255 *Farrell flew to California:* JTF, Diary, 31 August, 6 September 1941; JTF, 29 September, 1, 4 October 1941 letters to HA ("Chica Dove").

255 *had temporarily dropped:* JTF, Diary, 2, 14 May, 17 October 1940.

255 *"Listen":* JTF, 1 October 1941 letter to HA ("Chica Dove").

255 *He arranged:* JTF, 4 and 5 October 1941 letters to HA ("Chica Dove"); JTF, 4 October 1941 letter to JH.

256 *"But I feel":* JTF, Diary, 6 October 1941.

256 *"not intellectually solid":* JTF, 6 and 7 October 1941 letters to HA ("Chica Dove").

256 *"I am working":* JTF, Diary, 9 October 1941. Typescripts of Farrell's *Common Clay* outlines are in Box 5, JTFUP.

256 *"Writing for motion pictures":* JTF, Diary, 10 October 1941.

256 *"a hard day":* JTF, Diary, 14 October 1941.

256 *"hung around":* JTF, 16 October 1941 letter to HA ("Chica Dove").

257 *"I gave [Zanuck]":* JTF, 21 October 1941 letter to James J. Geller.

257 *a fine novelist:* JTF, 23 October 1941 letter to Alla Nazimova; JTF, 23 October 1941 letter to James J. Geller; JTF, 25 October 1941 letter to JH; JTF, 27 October 1941 letter to Felix Kolodziej.

257 *"a whorehouse":* JTF, 23 October 1941 letter to Earl Farrell.

257 *"What happened"*: JTF, 25 October 1941 letter to JH.
257 *"$1,000 a Week"*: JTF, Diary, 31 October, 10 November 1941. The story appears in *$1,000 a Week and Other Stories* (New York: Vanguard Press, 1942).

---

257 *"the goofiest thing"*: JTF, Diary, 6 August 1941.
258 *"used to perform"*: JH, "The Record of a Friendship."
258 *"affected a good deal"*: Morton White, interview.
258 *"Why do I drink so much?"*: JTF, Diary, 8 April 1942. See also JTF, Diary, 7 April 1942. On Souvarine, see O'Neill, *The Last Romantic,* 267; Pierre Ryckmans, "Malraux," *Quadrant,* October 1997; JTF, 12 July 1938 letter to George Novack; JTF, 23 July 1938 letter to Meyer Schapiro.

---

259 *"had written honestly"*: William L. O'Neill, *A Better World: The Great Schism: Stalinism and the American Intellectuals* (New York: Touchstone, 1982), 50, 58.
259 *"gangster-tyrant"*: Max Eastman, "Stalin's American Power," *American Mercury,* December 1941. A condensed version of the article appeared in *Reader's Digest,* December 1941.
259 *"In a sense"*: Philip Rahv, "10 Propositions and 8 Errors," *PR,* November–December 1941. Clement Greenberg and Dwight Macdonald's reply to Rahv appears in the same issue; their original article, "10 Positions on the War," was in *PR,* July–August 1941.
259 *"Rhetoric"*: JTF, Diary, 11 November 1941.
260 *"More and more"*: JTF, Diary, 31 October 1941.
260 *"I keep thinking"*: JTF, Diary, 11 November 1941.
260 *the Trotskyist martyrs*: Dobbs, *Teamster Bureaucracy,* 162, 184, 208, 238-39; Thomas L. Pahl, "G-String Conspiracy"; *NYT,* 2 December 1941.
260 *"the most important"*: Quoted in "New Pamphlet on SWP Prosecution Now on Sale," *Militant,* 11 October 1941.
260 *"many comrades"*: Dobbs, *Teamster Bureaucracy,* 241.
261 *"clamping down"*: JTF, Diary, 8 December 1941.
261 *Diagnosed in May*: JTF, Diary, 23 May, 6 August 1941; JTF, 7 October 1941 letter to HA ("Chica Dove"); HFD, interview.
261 *"cracking pretty badly"*: JTF, Diary, 30 October 1941.

---

262 *"by spontaneous combustion"*: Max Eastman, "The Library: Close-

up of Our Own Immortals," *American Mercury,* July 1942.

262 *he accepted:* JTF, 16 December 1941 letter to Henry S. Canby.

262 *"some protective help":* JTF, Diary, 4 July 1942.

Chapter 14: "The Dividing Line"

263 *conscription legislation:* See JTF, Diary, 8, 9 June, 3, 26, 27 August, 8, 10, 12, 14, 16, 17 September, 23, 30 October 1940; 12, 14, July, 9 December 1942.

263 *the Trotskyists did not:* Robert J. Alexander, *International Trotskyism, 1929-1985: A Documented Analysis of the Movement* (Durham, N.C.: Duke University, 1991), 809.

263 *a* Partisan Review *editor:* JTF, Diary, 27 September 1947.

263 *"The war is":* JTF, Diary, 2 May 1942.

263 *Interviewed:* Robert van Gelder, "An Interview with Mr. James T. Farrell," *NYT Book Review,* 17 May 1942. See also JTF, Diary, 20 April 1941.

264 *"No book":* JTF, Diary, 12 June 1942.

---

264 *the only thing:* JH, "The Record of a Friendship" (unpublished, n.d.).

264 *"a very warm person":* Albert Glotzer, interview.

265 *"a good empiricist":* JTF, 2 December 1938 letter to Felix Kolodziej.

265 *"decided there is no use":* JTF, 14 November "1951" [1941] letter to Felix Kolodziej.

265 *"Trotsky was":* JTF, "Leon Trotsky," *PR,* September–October 1940.

265 *"would suddenly turn":* H.D., interview.

265 *in the case of H.D.:* JTF, Diary, 22 May 1951.

265 *was to be disrupted:* JH, "The Record of a Friendship."

265 *Farrell argued:* JTF, "The Problem of Public Sensibility: A Review of the Film, 'The Open City,'" *New International,* August 1946; Meyer Schapiro, "A Note on 'The Open City': Some Comments on Farrell's Review," *New International,* December 1946; JTF, "Correspondence," *New International,* January 1947.

266 *until the 1970s:* CP, interview.

266 *"the coldness":* JTF, Diary, 16 July 1942. See also JTF, Diary, 14 July 1942.

266 *"indifference":* JTF, 13 July 1952 letter to JH.

---

266 *Russia's decisive victory:* J. A. S. Grenville, *A History of the World*

in the Twentieth Century (Cambridge, Mass.: Harvard University Press, 1994), 300-1.

267   *"The war is going"*: JTF, Diary, 3 February 1943.

267   *"The progressive possibilities"*: JTF, Diary, 24 April 1942.

267   *"the state had established"*: Joseph E. Davies, *Mission to Moscow* (New York: Simon & Schuster, 1941), 43, 356-57.

267   *"This film is"*: JTF, "A Movie, a Lie, and a Moral," *New Leader*, 15 May 1943.

━━►═◄━━

268   *"his last step"*: JTF, *My Days of Anger*, (New York: Vanguard Press, 1945), 400.

268   *"this Godless, purposeless world"*: Ibid., 249.

268   *"His heart was heavy"*: Ibid., 401.

269   *"at the present moment"*: JTF, Diary, 28 March 1942.

269   *"Today over coffee"*: JTF, *My Days of Anger*, 312.

269   *"He had written"*: Ibid., 297-300

270   *"When the four books"*: JTF, Diary, 12 October 1943.

270   *"But do you ever"*: Van Gelder, "An Interview with Mr. James T. Farrell."

270   *"a bad press"*: JTF, Diary, 8 October 1943.

270   *"It gets disgusting"*: JTF, Diary, 14 November 1943.

270   *a few attacks*: See, e.g., Isaac Rosenfeld, "The Angry Man," *NR*, 8 November 1943.

270   *"reveals in the author"*: Carlos Baker, "Another Milestone in the Long Saga of Danny O'Neill," *NYT Book Review*, 24 October 1943.

270   *"Like Dreiser"*: Milton Rugoff, "Danny O'Neill Grows Up," *New York Herald Tribune Weekly Book Review*, 24 October 1943.

271   *"I can't escape"*: JTF, Diary, 17 December 1943.

271   *"all serious adverse criticism"*: Diana Trilling, "Fiction in Review," *The Nation*, 18 December 1943. The review also appears, in revised form, in Diana Trilling, *Reviewing the Forties* (New York: Harcourt Brace Jovanovich, 1978).

━━►═◄━━

272   *not from the police*: In 1944, New York police investigated a complaint by "a Brooklyn mother" against *Young Lonigan*, and Chicago police briefly seized copies of *A World I Never Made*. See JH, *"MEMO RE YOUNG LONIGAN (TOWER EDITION)*," 29 February 1944, Box 46, VPCU, and *"MEMO RE STUDS LONIGAN*," 2 March 1944, Box 46, VPCU; *PW*, 11 March 1944; JTF, "Lonigan, Lonergan, and New York's Finest," *The Nation*, 18 March 1944; *NYT*, 5, 6 March 1944; *Time*, 3

April 1944; *Chicago Sun,* 31 October 1944; JH, "*MEMO,*" 26 October 1944, Box 46, VPCU.

272   *a friendly letter of protest:* JTF, "Letters from J. T. Farrell," *New International,* November 1944; JTF, "James T. Farrell and the S.W.P.," *politics,* December 1944. The articles criticized by JTF were: Joseph Hansen, "How the Trotskyists Went to Jail," *Fourth International,* February 1944, and Harry Frankel, "A Defamer of Marxism," *Fourth International,* May 1944.

272   *in a rented house:* JTF, Diary, 31 May, 27 September 1944.

272   *found the criticism:* For Cannon's comments, originally published in his party's *Internal Bulletin,* see *New International,* August 1945. See also Alan M. Wald, *James T. Farrell: The Revolutionary Socialist Years* (New York: New York University Press, 1978), 125–29.

272   *after losing out:* Terry Cooney, *The Rise of the New York Intellectuals: Partisan Review and Its Circle, 1934–1945* (Madison, Wis.: University of Wisconsin Press, 1986), 190–91; Michael Wreszin, *A Rebel in Defense of Tradition: The Life and Politics of Dwight Macdonald* (New York: Basic Books, 1994), 122–23.

272   *kept speaking: Militant,* 4 November 1944, 10 February 1945. See also *Militant,* 27 January 1945, and *NYT,* 3 February 1945.

272   *"a loyal":* Dwight Macdonald, "Revolution, Ltd.: A Text with Comments," *politics,* July 1945.

273   *"Never in modern history":* JTF, Diary, 29 April 1945.

---

273   *"wholly dishonorable":* Quoted by Fred Hobson, *Mencken: A Life* (New York: Random House, 1994), 471.

273   *"As he took us":* JTF, *Literary Essays, 1954–1974* (Port Washington, N.Y.: Kennikat Press, 1976), 11–13.

273   *"Farrell has done":* Charles A. Fecher, ed., *The Diary of H. L. Mencken* (New York: Knopf, 1990), 368–69.

---

273   *a lecture-cum-discussion:* "Announcement," *politics,* November 1945; Dwight Macdonald, "politicking," *politics,* January 1946; Lionel Abel, *The Intellectual Follies: A Memoir of the Literary Venture in New York and Paris* (New York: W. W. Norton, 1984), 186–88; Wreszin, *A Rebel in Defense of Tradition,* 166–67; William Barrett, *The Truants: Adventures among the Intellectuals* (New York: Anchor Press/Doubleday, 1982), 31, 90–91. Abel recalled the session at which Chiaromonte "developed what was to me a surprising thesis" as having taken place in 1946 in "a quite crowded basement

somewhere in the Village," but the *politics* "Announcement" in the November 1945 issue indicates the "discussion meeting"—the third in a series of six—was set for December 14, 1945, in the Stuyvesant Casino, on Second Avenue near Eight Street (on the Lower East Side), and it evidently took place as scheduled. Abel was to deliver the sixth lecture (on January 4, 1946) and, according to Macdonald's "politicking" article, was involved in planning and organizing the series. In that same article, Macdonald wrote, in apparent reference to the session featuring Chiaromonte: "The question of the Utopian as against the historical-materialist approach roused especially violent feelings, with the Anarchists almost the only defenders of the Utopian approach (and even they did not go so far as Chiaromonte)." It is possible that Chiaromonte and his thesis were thrown to the lions twice, but it seems more likely that the session Abel remembered is the one on December 14, 1945.

274   *a lengthy essay:* Nicola Chiaromonte, "On the Kind of Socialism Called 'Scientific,'" *politics,* February 1946. The Chiaromonte quotes are from this essay.

274   *"Flighty Dwighty":* Albert Glotzer, interview.

275   *"Constant readers":* JTF, "New Roads: Discussion," *politics,* March 1946. Macdonald's response immediately followed Farrell's letter.

275   *"Farrell asks us":* Nicola Chiaromonte, "New Roads: Discussion," *politics,* May 1946. Farrell's response and Macdonald's comments immediately followed Chiaromonte's letter.

⟫─0─⟪

276   *Note:* Except as otherwise indicated, this section is drawn from JTF, "Some Correspondence with Theodore Dreiser," which appears in very slightly different versions in *The Stature of Theodore Dreiser,* ed. Alfred Kazin and Charles Shapiro (1955; Bloomington: Indiana University Press, 1965), 36–50, and in JTF, *Reflections at Fifty and Other Essays* (New York: Vanguard Press, 1954), 124–41.

276   *Farrell on* Sister Carrie: JTF, "James T. Farrell Revalues Dreiser's 'Sister Carrie,'" *NYT Book Review,* 4 July 1943.

276   *to accept an award:* Richard Lingeman, *Theodore Dreiser: An American Journey, 1908–1945* (New York: Putnam's, 1990), 444–48; W. A. Swanberg, *Dreiser* (New York: Scribner's, 1965), 494–500.

277   *But first Dreiser:* Lingeman, *Theodore Dreiser,* 455–66; Swanberg, *Dreiser,* 507–11, 519.

277   *appreciative essays:* JTF, "Some Aspects of Dreiser's Fiction," *NYT Book Review,* 29 April 1945, and "'An American Tragedy,'" *NYT Book Review,* 6 May 1945.

277   *turned to* The Stoic: Lingeman, *Theodore Dreiser,* 472–74.

277   *"his way":* JTF, "Theodore Dreiser: In Memoriam," *SR,* 12 January 1946. The essay is reprinted in JTF, *Literature and Morality* (New York: Vanguard Press, 1947).

———◦———

277   *a stroke:* HFD, interview.

278   *Jim Farrell's generosity:* HFD, interview; JTF, 4 November 1953 letter to JH.

278   *very pleased:* JTF, Diary, 6 April 1942.

278   *on the platform:* JTF, Diary, 10 March 1951.

278   *As the novelist seems:* See JTF, *The Road Between* (New York: Vanguard Press, 1949), 151, 415.

278   *to transmute:* JTF, "The Death of Lizz O'Neill," Box 143, JTFUP.

———◦———

279   *"Browderism":* See Harvey Klehr, *The Heyday of American Communism: The Depression Decade* (New York: Basic Books, 1984), 410–11.

279   *shockingly heretical essay:* Albert Maltz, "What Shall We Ask of Writers?" *NM,* 12 February 1946. See also Isidor Schneider, "Probing Writers' Problems," *NM,* 23 October 1945, and "Background to Error," *NM,* 12 February 1946.

279   *"a familiar smell":* Mike Gold, "Change the World: The Road to Retreat," *DW,* 12 February 1946. See also Gold's *DW* columns of 23 February, 2, 16 March 1946. For other attacks on Maltz by various hands see *NM,* 26 February, 12 March, 19 March, 12 April 1946. For Farrell's comments, see JTF, "Stalinist Literary Discussion: An Answer to Maltz and The New Masses," *New International,* April 1946.

279   *"a dangerous departure":* Samuel Sillen, "1. Mischarting the Course," *DW,* 11 February 1946. Sillen's series of articles continued on succeeding days through 16 February 1946.

280   *"iron curtain":* Quoted by David McCullough, *Truman* (New York: Simon & Schuster, 1992), 489.

280   *"nightmarish and shameful":* Quoted by Victor S. Navasky, *Naming Names* (New York: Penguin, 1981), 291. See also Murray Kempton, *Part of Our Time: Some Ruins and Monuments of the Thirties* (New York: Simon & Schuster, 1955), 201.

281   *"I consider now":* Albert Maltz, "Moving Forward," *NM,* 9 April 1946.

281   *"so damned nauseating":* JH, 18 April 1946 letter to JTF.

———◦———

281 Bernard Clare: JTF, Diary, 12 August, 3 September 1943, 30 March 1944, 15 October 1947; JTF, 13 September 1944 letter to Oscar Schoenfeld; EB, *James T. Farrell* (New York: Twayne, 1971), 105-6; Alan M. Wald, *The New York Intellectuals: The Rise and Decline of the Anti-Stalinist Left from the 1930s to the 1980s* (Chapel Hill: University of North Carolina Press, 1987), 251-52.

281 *"Slowed down":* JTF, Diary, 4 February 1945.

281 *"It is this fear":* JTF, Diary, 26 February 1945. See also JTF, Diary, 7 January, 4, 22 February, 6 March 1945.

281 *or Claire:* JH, 25 August 1944 letter to JTF.

282 *sorely felt:* But see JTF, "Farrell Analyzes Bernard Clare," *Chicago Sun Book Week,* 8 September 1946.

282 *did sell well:* JH, 19 January, 13, 30 June 1946 letters to JTF; William V. Shannon, *The American Irish* (New York: Macmillan, 1963), 257. Shannon, who was a friend of Farrell's, states that *Bernard Clare* sold 39,000 copies.

282 *"In the lean season":* F. O. Matthiessen, "James T. Farrell's Human Comedy," *NYT Book Review,* 12 May 1946.

282 *"One may ask":* Isaac Rosenfeld, "Work in Regress," *NR,* 27 May 1946.

283 *"reputation sank":* Carol Brightman, *Writing Dangerously: Mary McCarthy and Her World* (New York: Clarkson Potter, 1992), 130.

283 *"in the lazy clumsiness":* Elizabeth Hardwick, "Fiction Chronicle," *PR,* Summer 1946.

283 *"confused and half-baked":* Diana Trilling, "Fiction in Review," *The Nation,* 1 June 1946.

283 *"Writers like myself":* JTF, 14 September 1944 letter to Felix Morrow.

284 *he had originally thought:* JTF, 12 December 1941 letter to John Switalski.

=▶·◀·◀=

284 *the "Hollywoodization":* JTF, *The Fate of Writing in America* (Norfolk, Conn.: New Directions, 1946). The essay first appeared under the title, "Will the Commercialization of Publishing Destroy Good Writing? Some Observations on the Future of Books," in *New Directions Number 9,* published by New Directions in the spring of 1946. See PW, 24 August 1946.

284 *The publishing industry:* Besides JTF, *The Fate of Writing in America,* see Malcolm Cowley, "The Literary Business in 1943," *NR,* 27 September 1945, and "Books by the Millions," *NR,* 11 October 1943, and also Robert Dahlin, "Men (and Women) Who Made a Revolution," *PW,* July 1997.

284 *"My gross income":* JTF, Diary, 10 March 1943. See also JTF, Diary, 4 October 1943.

285 *"We have bought":* JTF, 12 June 1946 letter to Morton G. White (copy provided by White).

286 *for $8,250:* JTF, 4 November 1953 letter to JH. A 4 June 1946 letter from JH to JTF discusses the pros and cons of seeking a mortgage—just eight days before JTF's letter to White reporting his purchase. No evidence that he got a mortgage has turned up.

286 *"without consulting":* JH, "The Record of a Friendship." Henle mistakenly recalled the size of the property as a quarter of an acre. A July 1946 survey of the property, in Box 52, JTFUP, as well as Farrell's 12 June 1946 letter to White, shows it was about 1.5 acres.

286 *to hate it:* JTF, 4 November 1953 letter to JH.

⟫•❮

286 *in Minneapolis:* See "Appearances at Universities" folder, Box 47a, VPCU. Farrell gave talks at the University of Minnesota during July 15–20, 1946, on Dreiser, Jack London, Sinclair Lewis, Hemingway and Fitzgerald.

286 *"perhaps the most powerful":* Alfred Kazin, *On Native Grounds* (New York: Reynal & Hitchcock, 1942), 381.

286 *"very bad":* JTF, 13 September 1944 letter to Oscar Schoenfeld. See also JH, 10, 16 November 1942 letters to JTF.

287 *"remarkable easiness":* Alfred Kazin, 6 November 1965 letter to JTF. According to Farrell's later recollection (JTF, Diary, 25 September 1950; see also JTF, "[Alfred Kazin]," Box 567, JTFUP), Kazin came up to him in Minneapolis in July 1946 and "in effect, apologized" for having said in his 1938 review of *No Star Is Lost* that Farrell hated his people. It was he, Kazin, who had been "full of hatred," as he had subsequently learned from psychoanalysis. Asked by RKL about all this in a 1994 interview, Kazin said, "I don't remember any of that."

⟫•❮

287 *Two days after Christmas:* JTF, Diary, 28 December 1947.

287 *on the 59th Street bus:* Dr. Kevin Farrell, interview.

287 *shouted to passersby:* JH, "The Record of a Friendship."

287 *the damage there:* Vanguard Press news release, and related materials, Box 178, JTFUP; *NYT Book Review,* 19 January 1947; JTF, "Epilogue," in *Studs Lonigan* (Vanguard Press), 470.

287 *That night:* Evelyn Shrifte, interview.

287 *ensconced in a hotel:* JH, 11, 21 January, 3 February, 21 March, 2 April 1947 letters to JTF; JTF, 18 January 1947 letter to JH.

287 *electrical:* JH, "The Record of a Friendship"; Dr. Kevin Farrell, interview; Neda M. Westlake, "The James T. Farrell Collection at the University of Pennsylvania," *American Book Collector,* June 1961.

287 *"saw no harm":* JH, "The Record of a Friendship."

288 *" 'before you burn' ":* Sloan Wilson, *What Shall We Wear to This Party? The Man in the Gray Flannel Suit Twenty Years Before and After* (New York: Arbor House, 1976), 270; Sloan Wilson, interview.

Chapter 15: Freedom

289 *The film "calls for":* Jerry Cotter, "Stage and Screen," *Sign,* December 1945.

289 *"The praise":* JTF, "Observations on The Bells of St. Mary's," in his *Literature and Morality* (New York: Vanguard Press, 1947), 101-2, 104.

289 *Once, in 1936:* JTF, Diary, 14 November 1936.

290 *"A successful achievement":* "New Books: Shorter Notices," *Catholic World,* November 1938.

290 *"While this is":* Barry Byrne, review of *No Star Is Lost,* in *Commonweal,* 25 November 1938.

290 *"a writer":* Harold C. Gardiner, "Tenets for Reviewers: II," *America,* 27 November 1943.

290 *"The most obvious irony":* Harry Sylvester, "Righteous Anger," *NR,* 6 October 1947.

291 *"an honest writer":* Nancy Lenkeith, "The Writer as Citizen," *Commonweal,* 8 August 1947.

291 *Farrell contacted:* Nancy Lenkeith, interview. On Lenkeith and her friendship with Farrell, see JTF, Diary, 2 December 1947, 2, 8, 13 April, 5 July, 5, 16, 22 November 1949, 13 April and 30 December 1950, and JTF, 13 July 1952 letter to JH.

—————⇥•⇤—————

291 *Hortense discovered:* JTF, Diary, 10 March 1951.

291 *even to her doctor:* "Letchworth Village—Clinical Summary" on John Stephen Farrell, 4 September 1968. Hortense's birthdate in this document is given as February 12, 1905, as presumably it was in the previous medical records pertaining to John Stephen.

292 *sent him, crying:* JTF, Diary, 1 August 1947.

292 *scoreless: NYT,* 18 August 1947.

292 *a crisis of conscience:* Albert Glotzer, interview.

292 *no "fundamental principles":* JTF, Diary, 17 September 1943.

292 *"A welling of feeling":* JTF, Diary, 18 August 1947.

292 *"My moods":* JTF, Diary, "18" [19] August 1947.

293 *"The little boy":* JTF, Diary, 25 September 1947.

293 *"one of the days":* JTF, Diary, 29 September 1947.

293   *puerperal fever:* JTF, Diary, 3 October 1947, 10 March 1951, 4 November 1953.

293   *"I have been depressed":* JTF, Diary, 10 October 1947.

293   *Kevin then "asked her":* JTF, Diary, 11 October 1947.

293   *"soon after birth":* "Letchworth Village—Clinical Summary."

293   *"a very diligent mother":* Randolph Carter, interview.

293   *"takes care of John":* JTF, Diary, 8 February 1948.

294   *"both of 'em":* JH, "The Record of a Friendship."

294   *She liked to cook:* Randolph Carter, interview.

294   *"Writers are hard":* Margaret Brenman-Gibson, *Clifford Odets: American Playwright: The Years from 1906 to 1940* (New York: Atheneum, 1981), 156-57.

294   *"In my forties":* JTF, Diary, 5 February 1948.

294   *"It is going to be":* JTF, Diary, 19 June 1948. If they were worried then about John Stephen's lack of development, they seem to have kept it to themselves. In a 30 July 1948 letter to JH, Farrell writes simply: "Johnny's feet are further improved now. Everything goes along, and another day starts."

295   *terrible fears:* JTF, Diary, 10 March 1951.

295   *"a colored family":* JTF, Diary, 17 June 1949.

295   *Burdened:* JTF, Diary, 10 February, 11 June 1948, 17, "18" [20], 24 June 1949; JTF, 4 November 1953 letter to JH. In the letter to Henle, Farrell calculated that he had spent $5,000 on medical expenses for John Stephen from when he was born to when he was institutionalized. Besides the medical expenses, there was the cost of other help. "I always urged [Hortense] to get as much domestic help as she needed," Farrell writes in his Diary, 10 March 1951. "When Johnny was with us, I paid Mrs. Dunn $175 a month [JTF says he paid her $200 a month, in the 1953 letter to JH] and board to take care of Johnny, and then, when I was going into debt, $150 a month and keep, and most of that time, except when we were in Wingdale, Hortense had cleaning women to help. Back during the war, there was a period when I hired Mrs. Clark to feed Kevin, and when we, also, had a fulltime maid. If I recall correctly, there was a period when I was paying around $200 a month for help for Hortense."

295   *would sell the property:* JTF, Diary, 11 March 1950.

295   *"drudge-like work":* JTF, Diary, 17 June 1949.

295   *left it to him:* JTF, Diary, 1 August 1949.

295   *"He is the same":* JTF, Diary, 30 July 1949.

295   *"When the three of us":* JTF, Diary, "18" [20] June 1949.

295   *"too self-centered":* JTF, Diary, 8 April 1949.

295   *"Several fights":* JTF, Diary, 30 July 1949.

296   *A month later:* "Letchworth Village—Clinical Summary"; Nancy Lenkeith, interview.

296   *"complete custodial care":* "Letchworth Village—Clinical Summary."

296   *entered a group home:* John Grande, client records administrator, Hudson Valley (formerly Letchworth) Developmental Disabilities Services Office, Thiells, N.Y., 7 March 2003 phone conversation, and 17 January 1996 letter to RKL. John Stephen Farrell died on October 16, 1999.

———≫•◦≪———

296   *to Atlantic City:* JH, 12, 14 November 1947 letters to JTF; JTF, Diary, 28 November 1949. The convention was held November 9-14, 1947.

296   *had been catapulted:* Thomas R. Brooks, *Toil and Trouble: A History of American Labor* (New York: Dell/Delta, 1964), 212-17; Philip Taft, *Organized Labor in American History* (New York: Harper & Row, 1964), 566-71; Max Kampelman, *The Communist Party vs. the C.I.O.* (New York: Praeger, 1957), 45-46, 73-76.

297   *"love affair":* JH, "The Record of a Friendship."

297   *trade union educational efforts:* See JTF, "A Note on Trade Union Education," *New Leader,* 18 December 1948, and JTF, Diary, 28, 29, 30 November, 1 December 1949.

297   *"There does not seem":* JTF, Diary, 5 July 1949.

297   *to supporting "free peoples":* Truman's 12 March 1947 message to Congress proposing U.S. support for the hard-pressed Greek and Turkish governments, quoted in Eric F. Goldman, *The Crucial Decade—and After: America, 1945-1960* (New York: Vintage, 1960), 59-60.

297   *Marshall Plan:* See JTF, Diary, 4 July, 13 October, 29 December 1947, 16 March, 19 April 1948, and JTF, 8 December 1947 letter to JH.

297   *"rigidities":* JTF, "Truth and Myth" introduction draft.

297   *"There are values":* JTF, Diary, 5 July 1947. See also JTF, Diary, 10, 24 August 1947.

298   *"I am beginning":* JTF, Diary, 29 December 1947.

298   *"a wave of hysteria":* JTF, Diary, 31 August, 19 October 1947, 13 February 1948.

298   *began holding hearings:* Walter Goodman, *The Committee: The Extraordinary Career of the House Committee on Un-American Activities* (New York: Farrar, Straus & Giroux, 1968), 207-25.

298   *"I think that":* JTF, 9 December 1947 letter to JH. See Goodman, *The Committee,* 217-18.

298   *"Should not the Bill of Rights":* JTF, "On the Washington Un-American Hearings," *Western Socialist,* February 1948.

299   *saw little chance:* JTF, Diary, 16 March 1948.

299   *had made up his mind:* JTF, Diary, 19 April 1948.

299   *"The capitalist reconstruction":* JTF, letter to the editor, *Labor Action,* 17 May 1948.

299   *"America is a capitalist country":* JTF, "The Stalinist Myth," letter to the editor, *NYT,* 18 April 1948.

299   *blockaded Berlin:* Alexandra Richie, *Faust's Metropolis: A History of Berlin* (New York: Carroll & Graf, 1998), 657–73; John Lukacs, *A History of the Cold War* (New York: Doubleday, 1961), 74.

300   *indicted: NYT,* 21 July 1948; Richard Gid Powers, *Not Without Honor: The History of American Anticommunism* (New York: Free Press, 1995), 225–26.

300   *Elizabeth Bentley: NYT,* 1 August 1948.

300   *Whittaker Chambers:* Sam Tanenhaus, *Whittaker Chambers* (New York: Random House, 1997), 212–23. 311–13.

300   *"Apparently, many people":* JTF, Diary, 14 December 1948.

300   *"red herring":* Quoted by Alonzo L. Hamby, *Man of the People: A Life of Harry S. Truman* (New York: Oxford University Press, 1995), 453.

300   *a creature of the Communist Party:* Irwin Ross, *The Loneliest Campaign: The Truman Victory of 1948* (New York: New American Library, 1968), 142–43.

300   *"It is not true":* Dwight Macdonald, *Henry Wallace: The Man and the Myth* (New York: Vanguard Press, 1948), 175.

300   *"fair, objective":* JTF, "An Objective Study of Henry Wallace of Iowa," *Philadelphia Sunday Bulletin Book Review,* 15 February 1948.

301   *"choosing the West":* See Dwight Macdonald, "I Choose the West," in his *Memoirs of a Revolutionist* (New York: Meridian Books, 1960), 197–201.

301   *"Wallaceland":* Macdonald, *Henry Wallace,* 24.

301   *"It is hard to imagine":* James Burnham, "Serious, Social, Moral," *NYT Book Review,* 13 July 1947.

301   *donated fifty dollars:* JTF, Diary, 10 August 1947.

301   *"somewhat active":* JTF, "Truth and Myth" introduction draft.

301   *spoke in Thomas's behalf:* EB, *A Bibliography of James T. Farrell's Writings, 1921–1957* (Philadelphia: University of Pennsylvania Press, 1959), 99–100.

302   *"Effort, honesty":* JTF, "Truth and Myth" introduction draft.

⟫●⟪

302   *"[T]he writer in the forties":* Leslie A. Fiedler, in "The State of American Writing, 1948: A Symposium," *PR,* August 1948.

302   *"Naturalism is a literary":* Leslie A. Fiedler, "Two Notes of Definition: Naturalism and Ritual Slaughter," *New Leader,* 18 December 1948.

303   *consider himself:* See, e.g., JTF's contribution to symposium, "Religion and the Intellectuals III," *PR,* April 1950.

303   *"Is the individual":* JTF, "Literature and Morality: A Crucial Question of Our Times," in his *Literature and Morality,* 3–14.

303   *"treats material":* Philip Rahv, "'Notes on the Decline of Naturalism,'" in *Documents of Modern Literary Realism,* ed. George J. Becker (Princeton, N.J.: Princeton University Press, 1963).

304   *"may be a negative":* Budd Schulberg, "'Literary Limbo,'" *NYT Book Review,* 3 April 1949.

304   *"I have so often":* JTF, Diary, 15 October 1947.

304   *"tired":* JTF, Diary, 11, 13 October 1947.

304   no *"spark":* JTF, Diary, 3 March 1948.

305   *a* Minneapolis Star *reporter:* See press release by Vanguard Press, and Judge Gunnar H. Nordbye, "Order Granting Motion of Defendant Farrell for Summary Judgment," in "Bernard Clare Case—Decision" folder, Box 46, VPCU; Bernard G. Clare obituary, *Minneapolis Star,* 1 March 1966; *PW,* 5 April 1947; JTF, 6 August 1948, 4 November 1953 letters to JH; JH, 20 August 1946, 18 March 1947 letters to Laurence Pollinger, and 19 March, 9 April, 6 November 1947 letters to JTF.

305   *whose title:* JTF, Diary, 13 December 1948; JH, 5, 16 November 1948 letters to JTF.

305   *"the best feminine":* JH, 25 March, 23 August 1948 letters to JTF. Also, see JH, 21 July 1952 letter to JTF, and undated [August 1952] fragment (mistakenly filed with 1955 JH letters in JTFUP) of letter from JTF to JH.

305   *"a hatchet job":* JTF, Diary, 2, 3 April 1949.

306   *"Even if the reviewers":* JTF, Diary, 18 June 1949.

———→•◦◄———

306   *Farrell's phone:* JTF, Diary, 13 April "1948" [1949].

306   *"only a sounding board":* New York Herald Tribune, 20 March 1949. For background on the Waldorf conference, see Sidney Hook, *Out of Step: An Unquiet Life in the Twentieth Century* (New York: Harper & Row, 1987), 382–96; William Barrett, "Culture Conference at the Waldorf," *Commentary,* May 1949; Irving Howe, "The Culture Conference," *PR,* no. 5, 1949; *New York Herald Tribune,* 22–29 March 1949; and *NYT,* 21 February, 4, 17–30 March 1949. The sponsors are listed in *NYT,* 24 March 1949.

306   *privately grumbled:* JTF, Diary, 2 April 1949.

306   *lecture tour:* JTF, Diary, 12 March 1949.

307   *a non-Communist peace conference: NYT,* 19, 22, 30 April 1949.

307   *Neither man was aware:* Michael Warner, "Origins of the Congress for Cultural Freedom, 1949–50," in U.S. Central Intelligence Agency,

Studies in Intelligence, 1995 ed., vol. 38, no. 5. The article, by a CIA staff historian, is an excerpt from a larger classified draft study and is available on the World Wide Web at <www.odci.gov/csi/studies/95unclas/war.html>.

307 *a joint statement:* "Statement by James T. Farrell and Sidney Hook for Americans for Intellectual Freedom," 24 April 1949, Box 52, JTFUP. The phrase "total cultural terror" is apparently what was meant by the phrase in the press release, "total cultural total terror." Hook used the phrase "total cultural terror" in another statement he made that day, according to *NYT,* 1 May 1949.

307 *Communist Information Bureau:* Harvey Klehr and John Earl Haynes, *The American Communist Movement* (New York: Twayne, 1992), 114.

308 *"I favor the Marshall Plan":* JTF, "Truth and Myth about America," advance text, 30 April 1949, Box 178, JTFUP.

308 *"prevailing mood":* Sidney Hook, "Report on the International Day against Dictatorship and War," *PR,* July 1949. See also Hook, *Out of Step,* 397-401. For his speech, see Hook, "Science, Freedom and Peace," *New Leader,* 25 June 1949.

309 *"a power of the first rank":* Raymond Aron, "Politics and the French Intellectuals," *PR,* July-August 1950.

309 *That August:* Peter Coleman, *The Liberal Conspiracy: The Congress for Cultural Freedom and the Struggle for the Mind of Postwar Europe* (New York: Free Press, 1989), 15-16.

309 *With the help:* Warner, "Origins of the Congress for Cultural Freedom, 1949-50."

<hr />

309 *"Journey's End": Militant,* 7 November 1949. The year before, in an editorial in its 18 October 1948 issue, the *Militant* called Farrell "[o]ne of the most vociferous of the disoriented intellectuals supporting Norman Thomas."

310 *joined the Liberal party:* EB, *James T. Farrell* (New York: Twayne, 1971), "Chronology"; Taft, *Organized Labor in American History,* 481-82; J. David Gillespie, *Politics at the Periphery: Third Parties in Two-Party America* (Columbia, S.C.: University of South Carolina Press, 1993), 97; JTF, Diary, 29 October, 5 Novemnber 1949.

310 *"They live":* JTF, Diary, 12 November 1949.

<hr />

310 *news arrived:* JTF, Diary, 25, 26 June 1950.

310 *Congress for Cultural Freedom:* For details on the Berlin congress, see Coleman, *The Liberal Conspiracy,* 1-2, 15-32; *NYT,* 26-30 June

1950; François Bondy, "Berlin Congress for Freedom," *Commentary,* September 1950; Sidney Hook, "The Berlin Congress for Cultural Freedom," *PR,* no. 7, 1950, and *Out of Step,* 432–60; Peter de Mendelssohn, "Berlin Congress," *New Statesman and Nation,* 15 July 1950.

310   *Fearful that war:* JTF, Diary, 9 May 1950.

310   *After a visit:* JTF, Diary, 11 May 1950.

311   *forced labor:* JTF, Diary, 3, 5, 7, 12 March 1948; *NYT,* 29 February, 6 December 1948.

311   *University of Michigan's:* JTF, "Academic Freedom," letter to the editor, *NYT,* 23 October 1948.

311   *"frame-up" trial:* JTF, "Conduct of Cardinal's Trial," letter to the editor, *NYT,* 9 February 1949.

311   *campaign against Jim Crow:* JTF, Diary, 13 October, 26 December 1949; 6 January 1950; EB, *James T. Farrell,* "Chronology."

311   *legless World War II veteran: Labor Action,* 2 May 1949.

311   *"is the real Jim":* JH, "The Record of a Friendship."

311   *"said something to me":* JTF, Diary, 2 July 1950.

311   *well-born and well-bred:* John P. Diggins, *Up from Communism: Conservative Odysseys in American Intellectual History* (New York: Harper & Row, 1975), 163.

311   *"He was well-read":* Arthur M. Schlesinger Jr., interview.

312   *"A manifesto":* JTF, Diary, 26 June 1950.

312   *"It is amazing":* NYT, 27 June 1950.

312   *"The notion":* Bondy, "Berlin Congress for Freedom."

312   *"much smothered tension":* JTF, Diary, 1 July 1950.

312   *"There are writers":* JTF, Diary, 26 June 1950.

313   *his bodyguard:* Coleman, *The Liberal Conspiracy,* 24; JTF, Diary, 28 June 1950.

313   *snubbing him:* JTF, Diary, 26 June, 2, 3 July 1950.

313   *"The only time":* JTF, Diary, 2 July 1950.

313   *three-thousand-word address:* See JTF, "Draft of Speech for Berlin Congress," Box 14, JTFUP.

313   *"I hadn't had much":* JTF, Diary, 7 July 1950.

314   *"the dry":* de Mendelssohn, "Berlin Congress."

314   *"For five years":* Coleman, *The Liberal Conspiracy,* 31.

314   *"The paper was":* JTF, Diary, 2 July 1950.

314   *"I have not clearly held":* JTF, Diary, 30 June 1950.

314   *"A young German lad":* JTF, Diary, 3 July 1950.

314   *The plight:* JTF, Diary, 2, 3 July 1950.

314   *Before a throng:* Coleman, *The Liberal Conspiracy,* 1, 32; *NYT,* 30 June 1950; Arthur Koestler, "The Congress for Cultural Freedom," in Arthur and Cynthia Koestler, *Stranger on the Square* (New York: Random House, 1984), 97.

315   *The CIA's Michael Josselson:* Warner, "Origins of the Congress for Cultural Freedom, 1949–50."

315   *"he withdrew":* Sidney Hook, "Cold Warrior," *Encounter,* July–August 1983.

315   *"The alternative strategy":* Coleman, *The Liberal Conspiracy,* 34.

315   *"Restless and anxious":* JTF, Diary, 30 June 1950.

315   *other European capitals:* JTF, Diary, 8 May, 21 June, 1, 2, 3, 6, 7, 8, 9, 10–11, 11, 12, 13, 14, 15, 16, 17, 18, 19 July 1950; JH, 3, 15, 17 August 1950 letters to JH.

315   *"Truman's decision":* JTF, 7 July 1950.

315   *"that we can let":* JTF, Diary, 18 July 1950. See also JTF, 18 July1950 letter to JH.

316   *"In all my conversations":* JH, 26 July 1950 letter to JTF. See also JH, 24 July 1950 letter to JTF.

316   *"a purely factual":* JTF, Diary, 13, 16 December 1950; Dr. Kevin Farrell, interview.

316   *not happy:* JTF, Diary, 17 December 1950.

316   *a very nervous woman:* Nancy Lenkeith, interview; JTF, Diary, 26 February, 5 March 1951.

316   *She was upset:* JTF, Diary, 14, 17, 24 December 1950, 5 March 1951.

316   *confided to a friend:* H.D., interview; JTF, Diary, 13 March 1951.

317   *lost all interest:* H.D., interview.

317   *told her husband:* JTF, Diary, 5 March 1951.

317   *did she really mean:* JTF, Diary, 13 March 1951.

317   *that he was plotting:* JTF, Diary, 14, 19, 30 December 1950, 8 January 1951.

317   *Psychiatric help:* JTF, Diary, 19 December 1950, 5 March 1951.

317   *Bettelheim:* See Bruno Bettelheim, 5, 19 July 1945 letters to JTF.

317   *"She says I am crazy":* JTF, Diary, 11 January 1951.

318   *"a few minutes":* JTF, Diary, 14 December 1950.

318   *"I don't know":* JTF, Diary, 24 December 1950.

318   *"Often she would say":* JTF, Diary, 8 March 1951.

318   *"He didn't like to go":* JTF, Diary, 5 January 1951.

318   *that they separate:* JTF, Diary, 8 January 1951.

319   *In April, Farrell:* JTF, Diary, 1, 4, 7, 9, 10 April 1951. The UAW convention was held April 1–6.

319   *"trying to wish":* JTF, Diary, 10 April 1951.

319   *still entertaining thoughts:* JTF, Diary, 17, 21, 22 April 1951.

319   *a hotel on East 40th Street:* JTF, Diary, 22 April 1951; JH, 18, 23 April 1951 letters to JTF.

319   *an $18 dollar-a-week:* JTF, Diary, 14 June 1951.

319   *"could be dirty":* JTF, Diary, 28, 29 May 1951.

319   *"was really kind of strange"*: Dr. Kevin Farrell, interview.

319   *"because she was fun"*: Randolph Carter, interview; *The Biographical Encyclopaedia and Who's Who of the American Theatre,* ed. Walter Rigdon (New York: James H. Heineman, 1966), 238; HA obituary, *NYT,* 3 April 1978.

320   [Footnote] *Hortense Alden died:* HA obituary, *NYT,* 3 April 1978; JTF, 26 May, 19 July 1977 letters to Dick Parker (copies provided by Parker).

320   *"did not want"*: JTF, "Remembering the Chelsea," *Playboy,* December 1974; JTF, Diary, 7, 8. 10 July 1951.

PART THREE: WRITING, WRITING, WRITING

Chapter 16: "A Lost Soul"

323   *"Sex is"*: JTF, Diary, 10 June 1951.

323   *lonely:* JTF, Diary, 10, 17, 22 April, 16 May, 17 June 1951.

323   *"friendly and open"*: JTF, Diary, 4 May 1951.

323   *"She likes to talk"*: JTF, Diary, 3, 6 September 1951.

324   *"petticoat chasing"*: JTF, Diary, 16 May 1951.

324   *began dating:* JTF, Diary, 24, 25, 30 November 1951.

324   *Rosalyn Tureck:* See Charles Moritz, ed., *Current Biography Yearbook, 1959* (New York: H. W. Wilson, 1960), 456–58; Nicolas Slonimsky, ed., *Baker's Biographical Dictionary of Musicians,* 8th ed. (New York: Schirmer, 1992), 1,913; "Pianist Abroad," *Time,* 29 July 1957; Allan Kozinn, "Rosalyn Tureck's 40-Year Search for Bach," *NYT,* 9 October 1977; Allan Kozinn, "On Stage: Rosalyn Tureck," *Avenue,* December–January 1980. In 1996, Ms. Tureck initially agreed to answer written questions about Farrell from RKL, but then did not respond to the letter in which questions were put to her.

324   *"So far"*: JTF, Diary, 16 December 1951. See also JTF, Diary, 11, 13, 15, 23 December 1951 and 5 June 1954.

324   *"to realize"*: JTF, "Judith," in his *Judith and Other Stories* (New York: Doubleday, 1973), 33.

═══◈═══

325   *"relied not solely"*: JTF, undated [1958?] letter to JH.

325   *praised the grim minor work highly:* Bruno Bettelheim, 23 October 1951 letter to JH, in response to JH, 28 September 1951 letter to Bettelheim; Shannon, quoted by JH in 15 November 1951 letter to JTF.

325   *But few reviewers:* See *SR,* 20 October 1951; *NYT Book Review,* 28 October 1951; *New York Herald Tribune Book Review,* 14 December 1951; *Chicago Sun,* 6 April 1952.

325   *"the devastatingly detailed"*: William P. Clancy, "Books," *Common-*

weal, 9 November 1951. For another appraisal of Farrell as sociologist rather than artist, see Frank O'Malley, "The American Novel through Fifty Years, XI. James T. Farrell," *America,* 23 June 1951.

⟫•0•⟪

325   *likened to Studs Lonigan:* See, for example, Emmet John Hughes, *The Ordeal of Power: A Political Memoir of the Eisenhower Years* (New York: Atheneum, 1963), 90.

325   *"The main job":* Minutes, American Committee for Cultural Freedom, 1 March 1952, Folder 8, Box 12, RHR.

325   *"a small group":* Irving Kristol, *Neoconservatism: The Autobiography of an Idea* (New York: Free Press, 1995), 21.

326   *for Paris:* JH, 14, 15, 23 April 1952 letters to JTF; JTF, 30 May 1952 letter to JH.

326   *"much more* retentissement": Peter Coleman, *The Liberal Conspiracy: The Congress for Cultural Freedom and the Struggle for the Mind of Postwar Europe* (New York: Free Press, 1989), 33.

326   *"a caricature":* NYT, 1 May 1952. For details on the festival, see Coleman, *The Liberal Conspiracy,* 45–46, 55–57; Genet [Janet Flanner], "Letter from Paris," *New Yorker,* 31 May 1952; and *NYT,* 17, 18 February, 30 March, 7, 11 May 1952.

326   *"one of the heroes":* JTF, 7 May 1952 letter to JH. See also JTF, 3 May 1952 letter to JH, and Nelson Lichtenstein, *The Most Dangerous Man in Detroit: Walter Reuther and the Fate of American Labor* (New York: Basic Books, 1995), 328–32.

327   *finished going over:* JH, 11 April 1952 letter to JTF.

327   *which he had begun:* JTF, 16 October 1951 letter to JH.

327   *"[To] say that":* JH, 13 February 1952 letter to JTF.

327   *"The book has gotten":* JTF, 3 February 1952 letter to JH, quoted in JH, 13 February 1952 letter to JTF. See also JH, 4 March 1952 letter to JTF.

327   *Farrell's work on the novel:* JTF, 3 May, 9 June 1952 letters to JH.

327   *Henle agreed:* JH, 3 July 1952 letter to JTF.

327   *to surrender to Hortense:* JTF, 26 March, 2 April, 9 June, 5, 14 August, 13 October 1952 letters to JH; JH, 3 April 1952 letter to JTF.

328   *regularly eating out:* JTF, undated fragment of letter, c. 1953, from JTF to JH (copy provided to RKL by DBF).

328   *had to borrow $2,000:* JTF, 8 August 1951 letter to JH; JH, 16 August 1951 letter to Clifford G. Phillips, Corn Exchange Bank Trust Co., New York, N.Y.; JH, 5 September 1951, 2 May 1952 letters to JTF.

328   *a five-year contract:* JTF, 9 July 1952 letter to JH; JH, 30 July, 6, 7, 14, 20, 24 August 1952, 15 June 1953 letters to JTF.

328   *"should be relieved"*: JH, 9 October 1952 letter to JTF.

328   *"I think I have reached"*: JTF, 9 June 1952 letter to JH. See also JTF, 3 May 1952 letter to JH.

328   *"I relented a little"*: JTF, 4 August 1952 letter to JH.

329   *"and why do things"*: JTF, 14 August 1952 letter to JH.

329   *"a wonderful one"*: JTF, 26 August 1952 letter to JH.

329   *had lunch with:* JTF, 15 August, 19 September 1952 letters to JH; Paul H. Douglas, *In the Fullness of Time: The Memoirs of Paul H. Douglas* (New York: Harcourt, Brace, Jovanovich, 1972), 561-68; *Current Biography 1949* (New York: H. H. Wilson, 1950), 166-68.

329   *"His statements"*: JTF, 5 August 1952 letter to JH.

329   *would triumph:* JTF, 19 September 1952 letter to JH.

329   *Leaving Suzanne:* JTF, 22 September 1952 letter to JH; JH, 17 October 1952 letter to JTF.

329   *"very insistent"*: JH, 10 October 1952 letter to JTF.

330   *arrived in New York:* JH, 17 October 1952 letter to JTF; EB, *James T. Farrell* (New York: Twayne, 1971), "Chronology."

330   *"As you know"*: JH, 30 July 1952 letter to JTF.

⟫∘⟪

330   *Farrell saw Henle:* JTF, 11 December 1958 "Not to be delivered" letter to JH.

330   *presided over H. Wolff:* Stanley Colbert, interview.

330   *some anonymous associates:* Evelyn Shrifte, interview; Guy Henle, 10. Even four decades later, the associates remained anonymous. "I took over with a group of people," Miss Shrifte told RKL in 1992. "But those names are anonymous; they cannot be revealed."

330   *striking red hair:* JH, "The Record of a Friendship" (unpublished, n.d.).

331   *"terrible"*: Evelyn Shrifte, interview.

331   *"how we are to get"*: JTF, 24 January 1953 letter to JH.

331   *the book of essays:* See JH, 30 July 1951 letter to JTF.

331   *not keen:* JTF, undated [1955] letter to JH and Marjorie Henle, SLNYU; JH, 13, 14 April, 18 May 1953 letters to JTF.

332   *a mistake to publish:* Evelyn Shrifte, interview.

332   *signed a contract:* JH, 15 June 1953, 4 April 1957 letters to JTF; JTF, "Memorandum on My Finances," 1955 (copy provided to RKL by HFD). The 2 February 1953 date of the contract is mentioned in a subsequent amendment, dated 15 November 1956, providing an exemption.

332   *desperate for cash:* Stanley Colbert, interview.

⟫∘⟪

333 *"small, chic":* JTF, "Interview with Suzanne Labin," Box 63, JTFUP. Farrell wrote several versions of the 1954 interview.

333 *"love":* JTF, 21 May 1953 letter to JH.

333 *"an experiment":* JTF, 10 December 1958 letter to JH.

333 *"Washington Park" novels:* Charles Fanning, *The Irish Voice in America: Irish-American Fiction from the 1760s to the 1980s* (Lexington, Ky.: University Press of Kentucky, 1990), 260.

333 *a novel based on:* JTF, 15 July 1952 letter to JH; JH, 21 July 1952 letter to JTF.

333 *"a defective child":* JTF, 22 September, 13 October 1952 letters to JH. See also JTF, 8 August 1951 letter to JTF, and JH, 7 August 1951, 2 [5?], 22 September 1952 letters to JTF.

334 *the galleys of* Yet Other Waters: JH, 13 June, 3, 15, 18, 22 July 1952 letters to JTF; JTF, 9, 11, 13, 15, 31 July 1952 letters to JH.

334 *"some corny advice":* JH, 4 June 1953 letter to JTF.

<hr>

334 *"out of simple":* JTF, 16 June 1953 letter to JH.

335 *"terrific wave":* JTF, 18 June 1953 letter to JH.

335 *"a lifelong—and prolific":* John Bartlow Martin, *Adlai Stevenson and the World: The Life of Adlai E. Stevenson* (New York: Doubleday, 1977), 71; Evelyn Shrifte, 18 July [1953] letter to JTF; JH, 27 July 1953 letter to JH.

<hr>

335 *soon feared:* JH, 2 June 1953 letter to JTF.

335 *foreclosed:* JTF, 4 September 1953 letter to JH.

335 *who pointed out:* JH, 22 June 1953 letter to JTF.

335 *tried repeatedly:* JH, 2, 4, 15, 16, 18, 22 June, 28 August, 14, 15 September 1953 letters to JTF; JTF, 4 November 1953 letter to JH.

336 *"This isn't altogether":* JH, 16 June 1953 letter to JH.

336 *reprint* The Road Between: JH, 15 June 1953 letter to JTF.

336 *who met the novelist:* JTF, 25 June 1953 letter to Stanley Colbert, SLNYU; Sterling Lord, 31 July 1953 letter to JTF.

336 *essentially first drafts:* Stanley Colbert, interview. See also Stanley Colbert, 1 June 1953 letter to JTF.

336 *"some satisfactory extra":* JTF, 12 September 1953 letter to JH.

336 *"you can't achieve":* JH, 1 September 1953 letter to JTF.

336 *repeatedly recommended:* JH, 2, 4 June, 12 August 1953 letters to JTF.

336 *"I risked not lecturing":* JTF, 4 September 1953 letter to JH. See also JTF, 9 July 1952 letter to JH, and JTF, handwritten draft reply to JH, written on JH, 7 August 1952 letter to JTF.

337 *"I have just reread":* JH, 14 May 1953 letter to JTF.

337 *"infinitely better":* JH, 25 May 1953 letter to JTF.

337 *has all the pathos":* JH, 6 August 1952 letter to JTF.

━━━━➤●◄━━━━

337 *returned from Paris:* JTF, 29 September 1953 letter to JH.

337 *"threatens to become":* JTF, 12 September 1953 letter to JH.

337 *"much revision":* JTF, 18 September 1953 letter to JH.

337 *"You* do *have":* JH, 25 September 1953 letter to JTF.

337 *was, indeed, a novel:* JTF, 25 September 1953 letter to JH.

337 *"The party":* JH, 28 September 1953 letter to JTF.

337 *"Today, I began":* JTF, 29 September 1953 letter to JH.

337 *"A novel":* JH, 13 October 1953 letter to JTF.

338 *"Somehow or other":* JH, 5 November 1953 letter to JTF.

━━━━➤●◄━━━━

338 *absolutely abysmal:* JH, 15 June, 28 August 1953 letters to JTF.

338 *"I think that* Studs Lonigan": Alfred Kazin, in *the coming of age of a great book...*, 5.

338 *would be persuaded:* JH, 26 October 1953 letter to JTF; JTF, 30 October 1953 letter to JH.

339 *"The analogy holds":* Horace Gregory, "James T. Farrell: Beyond the Provinces of Art," *New World Writing—Fifth Mentor Selection* (New York: New American Library, April 1954).

339 *"the author":* JH, 15 June 1955 letter to JTF.

339 *terribly coddled:* Stanley Colbert, interview.

339 *the real Ellis Island:* Roger Daniels, *Coming to America: A History of Immigration and Ethnicity in American Life* (New York: HarperCollins, 1990), 272.

339 *"compassionless prose":* Nelson Algren, "Case Studies of Dreams," *SR,* 9 December 1950.

339 *"easily the best written":* Nelson Algren, "New Chicago Cantos," *SR,* 14 November 1953.

340 *"It is, astonishingly":* Granville Hicks, "Pre-Tetralogy Danny O'Neill," *New York Herald Tribune Book Review,* 8 November 1953.

340 *six thousand copies:* JH, 28 September 1953 letter to JTF; JTF, 12 January "1953" [1954], 4 February 1954 letters to JH; JTF, "Memorandum on My Finances."

━━━━➤●◄━━━━

340 *"broke":* JTF, 29 September 1953 letter to JH.

340   *"The advance":* JH, 28 September 1953 letter to JTF.

340   *"special consideration":* JTF, 30 October 1953 letter to JH.

340   *"desperate":* JTF, 3, 4 November 1953 letters to JH. At least one of these letters (two of them dated 4 November) may not have been sent.

341   *Vanguard did finally agree:* JH, 4 January 1954 letter to JTF.

341   *"I again predict":* JTF, 6 November 1953 letter to JH.

341   *"I am in a vise":* JTF, unsent 12 January "1953" [1954] letter to JH.

341   *"Surely":* JH, 15 January 1954 letter to JTF.

341   *"more easily live":* JTF, 3 November 1953 letter to JH. See also JH, 27 January 1954 letter to JTF; JH and Evelyn Shrifte, 11 February 1954 letter to JTF; JTF, 18 May 1954 letter to JH.

=»·0·«=

341   *off to Europe again:* JTF, 30 April, 1, 8, 29 May, 16 June, 15 July 1954 letters to JH; JH, 23 April, 12 May, 8 July 1954 letters to JTF; Seon Givens, 3 June 1954 letter to JTF.

342   *"I think the sureness":* JH, 26 April 1954 letter to JTF. See also JTF, 1 May 1954 letter to JH.

342   *very painful:* JH, 7 August 1951, 2 [5?] September 1952 letters to JTF.

342   *"I am tearing":* JTF, 12 July 1954 letter to JH.

342   *"I handled all his money":* Ria D. Simon, interview; Ria D. Simon, 26 April, 19 May 1954 letters to JTF; JH, 19 May 1954 letter to JTF.

342   *He and Stanley Colbert:* Stanley Colbert, interview; Sterling Lord, interview; JTF, 29 July 1954 letter to JH; JH, 29 July 1954 letter to JTF.

342   *"trying to get him":* Sterling Lord, interview.

343   *"I never have sold":* JTF, "Memorandum on My Finances."

343   *"Evelyn told me":* JTF, 22, 29 May 1954 letters to JH; JH, 15 September 1953 letter to JTF.

343   *"especially deplorable":* JH, 8 July 1954 letter to JTF; JH, 12 July 1954 letter to JH.

343   *a delegate:* JTF, 1, 14 June, 31 July, 3 August, 3 October 1954 letters to JH; JTF, "Baseball in Europe," *Sports Illustrated,* 20 September 1954; JH, 24 June, 9 August 1954 letters to JTF; Evelyn Shrifte, 15 August 1954 letter to JTF.

343   *"has something":* JTF, 31 July 1954 letter to JH.

344   *"It seems to me":* JTF, 3 October 1954 letter to JH.

344   *elected chairman:* NYT, 19 December 1954.

=»·0·«=

344   *"I was surprised":* DBF, interview.

344 *"I think he really"*: Ria D. Simon, interview.

344 *the* Studs Lonigan *movie rights:* Ria D. Simon, 11 May 1959 letter to Robert S. Benjamin, c/o United Artists, New York, SLNYU

345 *"I think I had the right"*: JTF, undated [1955] letter to JH and Marjorie Henle, SLNYU. A 16 March 1955 letter from JTF to JH seems to indicate that the undated letter was not sent, and the 16 March letter also probably was not sent, since both the original and a carbon are in Farrell's archive.

345 *a five-figure sum:* According to JTF, "Memorandum on My Finances," the sale was for a five-figure sum, which may well have been $20,000 (unfortunately, the first digit was not entirely legible on HFD's copy of the memorandum), and 10 percent of the net profits. Of the cash up-front, Farrell figured he would get 60 percent, less taxes. In an unpublished fictional rendition by JTF, according to a synopsis by CP that she provided to RKL, the total of cash up-front is given as $20,000.

346 *shocked and hurt:* Evelyn Shrifte, interview; Evelyn Shrifte, 16 March 1955 letter to JTF. In her reply, she refers to Farrell's 9 March letter to her. See also JTF, 14 March 1955 letter to JH.

346 *"Since 1949"*: JTF, "Memorandum on My Finances."

346 *the bad news:* JH, 19 April 1956 letter to JTF.

347 *a cheaper place:* DBF, interview; JTF, 9 June, 30 September 1955 letters to JH.

347 *"Now every other problem"*: JTF, 16 March 1955 letter to JH.

347 *remarried:* DBF, interview; Wedding invitation, SLNYU.

347 *"The reception"*: JH, 12 September 1955 letter to JTF.

347 *"wouldn't have spared"*: JH, 15 October 1958 letter to JTF.

⟫⟩•◦•⟨⟪

347 *he stated in March 1956:* Coleman, *The Liberal Conspiracy*, 165–66; *NYT,* 6 April 1956.

348 *Diana Trilling:* EB, *A Bibliography of James T. Farrell's Writings, 1921–1957* (Philadelphia: University of Pennsylvania Press, 1959), 118.

348 *"You don't seem to realize"*: Coleman, *The Liberal Conspiracy*, 166.

348 *reelected chairman: NYT,* 3 November 1955.

348 *quite active: NYT,* 16, 18 September, 29, 30 October, 2, 14 November 1955. See also *DW,* 18 November 1955.

349 *was now calling:* JTF, 14 January 1956 letter to JH.

349 *"a tremendous improvement"*: JH, 23 November 1955 letter to JTF.

349 *"you still have"*: JH, 10 April 1956 letter to JTF.

349 *Dorothy was pregnant:* Mary Jo Branch, 24 February 1956 letter to JTF.

349 *interviewed Adlai Stevenson:* JTF, "A Talk with Adlai Stevenson," *New York Post,* 4 March 1956.

349 *"Mr. Khrushchev":* JTF, 17 April (drafted 5–6 April) 1956 letter to Diana Trilling (copy provided to RKL by Coleman).

349 *for the West Coast:* [University of Washington] English Dept., "NOTICE," 10 April 1956, Box 115, JTFUP; Printed note in "World Trip-Flight Itineraries, Announcement of Arrivals, etc." folder, Box 115, JTFUP; JH, 19 April 1956 letter to JTF; Evelyn Shrifte, 26 April 1956 letter to JTF.

349 *"very promptly showed":* H. R. Krygier, "Visit by James T. Farrell," *Free Spirit* (published by the Australian Committee for Cultural Freedom), June 1956 (copy provided to RKL by Coleman).

349 *a "confidential" letter:* H. R. Krygier, 18 June 1956 letter to Michael Josselson (copy provided to RKL by Coleman).

349 *"But then when":* Luna Wolf Carne-Ross, interview.

350 *"My lectures":* JTF, 12 May 1956 handwritten response to JH, on JH, 7 May 1956 letter to JTF. See also JH, 21 May 1956 letter to JTF.

350 *"had expected a great deal":* Peter Coleman, *Memoirs of a Slow Learner* (Sydney, Australia: Angus & Robertson, 1994), 82–84.

351 *"One of the hopes":* JTF, "Anti-Americanism," letter to the editor, *Quest* (published by the Indian Committee for Cultural Freedom), August–September 1956. See also letters by D. D. Karve in *Quest,* October–November 1956, and by JTF in *Quest,* December 1956–January 1957; and essay, "James T. Farrell," by editor Nissim Ezekiel, in *Quest,* June–July 1956.

351 *staying overnight:* JTF, 12 May 1956 handwritten response to JH, on JH, 7 May 1956 letter to JTF.

351 *to India, where:* JTF, "Exporting Dreams," unpublished essay (copy provided to RKL by Mervin Block); "Mr. James T. Farrell's Itinerary in Bombay," Box 115, JTFUP; USIS Bombay, "Teletype Sent," 5 June 1956, Box 115, JTFUP; JH, 5, 7, 12 June 1956 letters to JTF; JTF, 28 August 1956 letter to Norman Jacobs (copy provided to RKL by Coleman; another copy is in Box 115, JTFUP).

351 *"I can perhaps":* JTF, *It Has Come to Pass* (New York: Theodor Herzl Press, 1958), 257.

351 *a stopover:* Alan M. Wald, *The New York Intellectuals: The Rise and Decline of the Anti-Stalinist Left from the 1930s to the 1980s* (Chapel Hill: University of North Carolina Press, 1987), 272.

352 *"too much beer":* NYT, 29 August 1956.

352 *"The American people":* JTF, "From Novelist Farrell," letter to the editor, *CT,* 30 June 1956.

352 *When word:* Sidney Hook, *Out of Step: An Unquiet Life in the Twentieth Century* (New York: Harper & Row, 1987), 429–30; Diana Trilling, interview.

352   *Farrell's usefulness:* Statement given to *NYT* on 29 August 1956 by
      Diana Trilling, attached to "A Report on the Circumstances Sur-
      rounding James Farrell's Resignation" made by her to the members
      of the Board of Directors of the American Committee for Cultural
      Freedom (copies of the report and statement provided to RKL by
      Coleman).

352   *"The Israeli are":* JTF, 25 June 1956 letter to JH.

352   *received some bad news:* JH, 25 July 1956 letter to JTF; DBF, inter-
      view.

353   *"It made us":* JTF, 31 August 1956 letter to Michael Josselson (copy
      provided to RKL by Coleman).

353   *a stopover in Paris:* JTF, *It Has Come to Pass,* 287.

353   *talked with Michael Josselson:* Michael Josselson, 6 September
      1956 letter to JTF; JTF, 28 August 1956 letter to Norman Jacobs
      (copies of both letters provided to RKL by Coleman).

353   *landed at Idlewild:* Evelyn Shrifte, 7 August 1956 telegram to *NYT*
      et al., in "World Trip-Flight Itineraries, Announcement of Arrivals,
      etc." folder, Box 115, JTFUP.

353   *went on to Chicago:* JH, 15 August 1956 letter to JTF.

353   *gotten wind:* Hook, *Out of Step,* 430; Diana Trilling, "A Report."

353   *"a damned fool":* JTF, 14 October 1956 letter to JH.

353   *"indefensible":* NYT, 29 August 1956.

354   *Late in the evening:* Diana Trilling, "A Report"; Diana Trilling, inter-
      view; *NYT,* 29 August 1956. The *Times* story was picked up by *CT,*
      29 August 1956.

354   *"to sink our roots":* JTF, 28 August 1956 letter to Norman Jacobs.

355   *a telegram to Josselson:* Coleman, *The Liberal Conspiracy,* 169.
      Coleman supplied RKL with a copy of the telegram, which is
      quoted here in full (and in abbreviated form in his own book).

355   *"I don't know":* JTF, 31 August 1956 letter to Michael Josselson
      (copy provided to RKL by Coleman).

356   *"permit me to say":* Michael Josselson, 6 September 1956 letter to
      JTF (copy provided to RKL by Coleman).

Chapter 17: "Dark Hours"

357   *hard at work:* JTF, 14 October, 1 November 1956 letters to JH.

357   *"a second future":* JTF, 18 October 1956 letter to JH.

357   *"hit a block":* JTF, 23 November 1956 letter to JH.

357   *more "distance":* JTF, 14 November 1956 letter to JH.

357   *fourth Bernard Carr:* JTF, 18 October 1956 letter to JH; JH, 24
      October 1956 letter to JTF.

357   *turn to his Paris novel:* JH, 22 November 1956 letter to JTF.

357   *"not in good shape":* JTF, 1 December 1956 letter to JH.

357   *"I am most grateful":* JTF, 23 November 1956 letter to JH.

358   *Alburn Bureau:* JTF, 14 October, 1 December 1956 letters to JH. Farrell has Sonderegger's name slightly wrong; it is given correctly in a letter from Sonderegger to Sterling Lord, SLNYU.

358   *some sixteen hours:* JTF, 23 November, 1, 3 December 1956 letters to JH.

358   *"And I am happy":* JTF, 14 November 1956 letter to JH.

358   *"change in my life":* JTF, 1 December 1956 letter to JH.

358   *"I want to be frank":* JTF, 23 November 1956 letter to JH.

359   *the "delay":* JTF, undated [c. 12 March 1957] letter to JH.

359   *Vanguard did decide:* JH, 25 March 1957 letter to JTF.

359   *published in September:* EB, *James T. Farrell* (New York: Twayne, 1971), "Chronology"; JH, 2 January 1958 letter to JTF.

359   *eruption of resentment:* JTF, 27 March 1957 letter to JH.

360   *"The big mistake":* JH, 28 March 1957 letter to JTF.

360   *"As I wrote to you":* JH, 4 April 1957 letter to JTF.

361   *"right or wrong":* JTF, 8 April 1957 letter to JH.

361   *"enormously pleased":* JH, 10 April 1957 letter to JTF.

⟞⟝⬦⟞⟝

361   *Farrell finished:* JTF, 21 May 1957 letter to JH; EB, *James T. Farrell,* "Chronology."

361   *ten thousand copies:* JTF, 16 August "1947" [1957] letter to JH.

361   *Farrell turned:* Sterling Lord, 15 July 1957 letter to JTF; JTF, draft letter to JH, handwritten on JH, 24 June 1957 letter to JTF; JTF, 7 August 1957 letter to JH.

361   *disappointment:* John Lowell Pratt, 15 October 1957 letter to JTF; JH, 13, 26 August 1957 letters to JTF; JTF, handwritten on JH, 23 October 1957 letter to JTF.

361   *"I am inventing":* JTF, 16 August "1947" [1957] letter to JH.

361   *inadvertently libeled:* Ria D. Simon, 21 November 1957 letter to John Lowell Pratt; John Lowell Pratt, 22 November, 2 December 1957 letters to JTF; John Lowell Pratt, 9 December 1957 letter to A. G. Geocaris; JH, 2 January 1958 letter to JTF; *CT,* 5 March, 22 July 1958; *NYT,* 5 March 1958; John Lowell Pratt, 21 April 1958 letter to Sterling Lord, SLNYU; Sterling Lord, 12 May 1958 letter to John Lowell Pratt, SLNYU.

362   *the note-taking:* HFD, interview.

362   *sales of* My Baseball Diary: JTF, 5 May 1958 letter to Sterling Lord, SLNYU.

362   *it was reported:* PW, 9, 16 December 1957, 10 March 1958.

362   *quest for a publisher:* JTF, 17 February, 5, 17 March 1958 letters to JH; Sterling Lord, 22 May 1958 letter to JTF; Irene Patai Auvil, interview.

362   *a few favorable reviews:* See *Herald Tribune Book Review,* 1 February 1959; *Christian Science Monitor,* 29 June 1959.

363   *In May, Farrell:* JTF, 5 May 1958 letter to Sterling Lord, SLNYU; Sterling Lord, 16 April, 12 May 1958 letters to John Lowell Pratt, SLNYU; John Lowell Pratt, 21 April 1958 letter to Sterling Lord, SLNYU.

363   *"Naturally, I am":* JTF, 21 May 1958 letter to John Lowell Pratt, SLNYU.

363   *After more letters:* See JTF, 12 June 1958 letter to Thomas Yoseloff, SLNYU; John Lowell Pratt, 13 June 1958 letter to JTF, SLNYU; JTF, 17 June 1958 letter to John Lowell Pratt, SLNYU; John Lowell Pratt, 18 June 1958 letter to JTF.

363   *Farrell asked Vanguard:* JTF, 11 December 1958 letter to JH; JH, 13 July, 13 August 1958 letters to JTF.

363   *"should come out":* JTF, unsent 4 December 1958 letter to JH.

363   *"I appeal":* JH, 28 July 1958 letter to JTF.

363   *the first eighty-two pages:* JH, 20 June 1958 letter to JTF.

---

363   *Dorothy visited:* JTF, in legal document connected with an alimony suit brought by DBF against him in November 1959, JTFUP (document and related ones filed with DBF letters to JTF); DBF, interview; DBF, transcript of her conversation with Tom Daly about baseball in Milwaukee, 26 August 1958, Box 162, JTFUP. Only some of the documents in the alimony case survive, and most of those that do are incomplete. Dorothy Farrell recalled in interviews that her research was for the "baseball book" Farrell was writing. But JTF, 11, 20 September 1958 letters to JH indicate he was in Milwaukee on assignment for *Holiday* magazine. The assigned piece apparently was not published, however. No *Holiday* article is listed in EB, "A Supplement to the Bibliography of James T. Farrell's Writings," *The American Book Collector,* Summer 1961.

364   *"I did have":* DBF, interview.

364   *"he would chase":* Sidney Hook, *Out of Step: An Unquiet Life in the Twentieth Century* (New York: Harper & Row, 1987), 429.

364   *"lavishing vast sums":* JTF, in legal document connected with DBF alimony suit, JTFUP.

364   *for $25,000:* JTF, 7, 12 August 1957 letters to JH; a legal document connected with the DBF alimony suit, JTFUP; DBF, interview.

365   *she showed up:* JTF, in legal document connected with DBF alimony suit, JTFUP. According to this document, Dorothy appeared first at the apartment on September 6, 1958, and returned on September 9. She herself remembered returning "the next day."

365 *"Your loan":* JTF, 11 September 1958 letter to JH.

365 *the seemingly fantastic story:* Luna Wolf Carne-Ross, interview; Ria D. Simon, interview.

365 *insisted was genuine:* DBF, interview.

365 *"Dorothy was playing me":* JTF, 20 September 1958 letter to Jack Farrell (mistakenly marked "Henle" by someone and filed with the Henle letters, JTFUP).

366 *then "kind of latched on to me":* Irene Patai Auvil, interview.

366 *When Farrell returned:* Irene Patai Auvil, interview; JH, 6 October 1958 letter to JTF; JTF, 11 October 1958 letter to JH.

366 *hotel was no longer:* CP, interview; The Guilds' Committee for Federal Writers' Publications, Inc., *New York City Guide,* American Guide Series (New York: Random House, 1939), 210; Sloan Wilson, *What Shall We Wear to This Party? The Man in the Gray Flannel Suit Twenty Years Before and After* (New York: Arbor House, 1976), 271.

366 *"was playing a double game":* JTF, 16 October 1958 letter to JH.

---

366 October 21, 1958: JTF, "Introduction," *When Time Was Born* (New York: The Smith, 1966).

366 *"morally committed":* JTF, "Memorandum on My Finances."

366 *his best book:* JTF, 15 April 1958 letter to JH.

366 *"My past":* JTF, 25 April 1958 letter to JH.

367 *"Since Yoseloff":* JTF, 6 November 1958 letter to Sterling Lord, SLNYU.

368 *Farrell gave Henle a chunk:* JTF, 11 November 1958 letter to JH; JH, 12 November 1958 letter to JTF.

368 *"The canvas on this work":* JTF, unsent 13 November 1958 letters to JH.

368 *"I need":* JTF, unsent 14 November 1958 letters to JH.

---

369 *Lord's proposal:* JTF, 10, 11 December 1958 letters to JH; JH, 10 December 1958 letter to JTF.

369 *"What you have in mind":* JH, undated [1 December 1958] letter to Sterling Lord, in "Farrell Miscellaneous" folder, Box 47b, VPCU. (Date of that letter is evident from JTF, 8 December 1958 letter to JH.)

370 *"I should be angry":* This and the other quotes are from one or another of five unsent letters from JTF to JH, dated 4 December 1958.

370 *financial difficulties in 1939:* See JTF, Diary, 6, 7, 12, 16, 22, 26, 28 July 1939.

371 *"under stress":* JTF, note with his unsent December 1958 letters to JH.

━━▶◦◀━━

371 *He telephoned:* JTF, 8 December 1958 letter to JH, SLNYU; JTF, 11 December 1958 letter to JH; JH, 10 December 1958 letter to JTF.

371 *"Jim, I asked":* JTF, 8 December 1958 letter to JH, SLNYU.

372 *"Why do you":* JTF, 9 December 1958 letter to Evelyn Shrifte.

372 *"humiliated":* JTF, 9 December 1958 letter to JH.

372 *"came as a big surprise":* JH, 10 December 1958 letter to JTF.

372 *hadn't fully made up:* JTF, 10 December 1958 letter to JH.

372 *"The owners of Vanguard Press":* JTF, 11 December 1958 letter to JH.

373 *"That will be good":* JTF, unsent 11 December 1958 letter to JH.

━━▶◦◀━━

374 *"The whole affair":* JH, 22 December 1958 letter to JTF.

Chapter 18: Crazy Gallantry

375 *"I would come":* Luna Wolf Carne-Ross, interview.

375 *was to discover:* Irene Patai Auvil, interview; CP, interview.

376 *loss of appetite:* Jack M. Gorman, M.D., *The Essential Guide to Psychiatric Drugs* (New York: St. Martin's, 1990), 109.

376 *In a photograph:* The 1957 photo appears with Mervin Block, "Writer Farrell Recalls Early Days in City," *Chicago American,* 19 November 1957; the 1960 photo appears with Gene Smith, "Portrait of the Artist As a Middle-Aged Man," *New York Post,* 9 October 1960.

━━▶◦◀━━

376 *he had arranged:* JH, 30 January 1959 letter to JTF; KM, 3 February 1959 letter to JTF; Sterling Lord, 10 February [1959] letter to JTF; Sterling Lord, 16 February 1959 letter to Evelyn Shrifte.

376 *McCormick:* JTF, Diary, 27 September, 6 October 1940; KM, interview; KM obituary, *NYT,* 29 June 1997.

376 *"a very great man":* Sally Arteseros, interview.

376 *a contract:* From Sterling Lord's record of sales; JTF, 1 August 1959 letter to KM, SLNYU.

377 *"was endlessly patient":* KM, interview.

377 *"absolutely floor[ed]"*: KM, 15 October, 5 November 1959 letters to Luna Wolf; KM, 22 October 1959 letter to JTF.

377 *"ultimatum"*: JTF, 1 August 1959 letter to KM, SLNYU.

377 *removing a whole section*: KM, 4 August 1959 letter to JTF.

377 *"I expect"*: JTF, 14 August 1959 letter to EB.

377 *"Things seem to be"*: JTF, 18 August 1959 letter to EB.

---

378 *"subdued [but] okay"*: Mervin Block, interview. See Block, "Writer Farrell."

378 *"For three hours"*: Mervin Block, "A Writer Haunted by a Book," *Chicago American,* 21 November 1959.

378 *"one of the very active"*: Sterling Lord, interview.

379 *"He must have driven"*: Ria D. Simon, interview.

379 *"that a change"*: JTF, 21 December 1959 letter to Sterling Lord, SLNYU.

380 *"continue to represent"*: Sterling Lord, 22 December 1959 letter to JTF.

380 *"He started to get"*: Ria D. Simon, interview. See Ria D. Simon, 27 May 1960 letter to JTF.

---

380 *"'I want to spend'"*: Irene Patai Auvil, interview.

380 *Surya Kumari*: JTF, 2 December 1974 letter to EB; Mervin Block, 4, 17 April 1960 letters to JTF. See JTF's writings about Surya Kumari in Boxes 232, 250, 359 and 645, JTFUP. Also see *NYT,* 10 February 1961 for a picture of Surya Kumari, accompanying a review of an off-Broadway production of *The King of the Dark Chamber.*

380 *"She is dedicated"*: JTF, Box 250, JTFUP.

---

381 *movie version*: *NYT,* 3 April, 15 December 1960; *SR,* 16 July 1960.

381 *Philip Yordan*: Ephraim Katz, *The Film Encyclopedia* (New York: Harper & Row, 1979), 1254.

381 *"an honorable low-budget try"*: Pauline Kael, *5001 Nights at the Movies: A Guide from A to Z* (New York: Holt, 1985), 566.

381 *Farrell publicly dissociated*: JTF, letter, *NYT,* 10 April 1960. See also JTF, letter, *SR,* 8 October 1960.

381 *selling the rights*: Ria D. Simon, interview. See Ria D. Simon, 11 May 1959 letter to Robert S. Benjamin, c/o United Artists, New York, and Ria D. Simon, 30 December 1959 letter to JTF.

---

381   *came to envision:* Block, "A Writer Haunted"; Cindy Hughes, "Farrell Working on 20 Novels," *New York World Telegram & Sun,* 14 July 1961; JTF, "James T. Farrell Answers His Critics," *Oakland* (Calif.) *Tribune,* 21 January 1962.

382   *"had endless ideas":* KM, interview.

382   *"start off":* KM, quoted by Richard Schickel, "James T. Farrell: Another Time, Another Place," *Esquire,* December 1962.

382   *"The last time":* KM, 15 August 1960 letter to JTF.

382   *a nineteen-page letter:* Ursula Sommer, assistant to KM, 19 August 1960 letter to Luna Wolf.

382   *"that you would look":* KM, 20 September (dictated 17 Sept.) 1960 letter to JTF.

383   *"I couldn't believe":* CP, interview. Details are also drawn from a fragmentary, unpublished memoir by CP, "JTF *BIO SECTION II JIM & CLEO,*" written after Farrell's death and provided by her to RKL.

384   *"They say I'm":* Gene Smith, "Portrait of the Artist."

386   *"To me":* Sloan Wilson, interview. Details are also drawn from Sloan Wilson, *What Shall We Wear to This Party?* 268–71, 317.

386   [Footnote] *Farrell underwent surgery:* CP, interview; JH, 10, 13, 14, 19 November, 2 December 1952 letters to JTF; JH, 25 November 1952 letter to Dave H. Morris Jr., The Browning School, New York; JH, 18 December 1952 letter to Isidor Cohen; JH, "The Record of a Friendship." See also JTF, 19 September 1952 letter to JH; JH, 7, 9 October 1952 letters to JTF.

388   *"chatting amiably":* Jay Robert Nash, *The Innovators: Sixteen Portraits of the Famous and the Infamous* (Chicago: Regnery Gateway, 1982), 205–6. Nash does not identify Surya Kumari by name. His essay on Farrell, Nelson Algren and Jack Conroy also appeared in the *Chicago Reader,* 12 February 1982.

388   *"When I first":* CP, interview.

388   *"And I said, well":* Eliot Asinof, interview.

388   *"a good baseball novel":* JTF, "Here's One for Baseball Fans," *New York Post,* 22 May 1955.

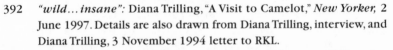

389   *"a rectification":* JTF, "Open Letter to Khrushchev," *Thought,* 2 December 1961.

389   *condemned them again: NYT,* 18, 19 October 1961; Martin Malia, *The Soviet Tragedy: A History of Socialism in Russia, 1917-1991* (New York: Free Press, 1994), 339.

390   *"I am not only":* JTF, "James T. Farrell Answers His Critics."

390   *"We're just as interested":* KM, 1 February 1962 letter to JTF. *Boarding House Blues* was published in June 1961, and *Side Street and Other Stories* in September 1961, both by Paperback Library, Inc. The same publisher in December 1962 would bring out another Farrell collection of short stories, *Sound of a City,* as a paperback original.

391   *"final typing":* KM, 12 December 1961 letter to JTF.

391   *"it would end up":* Luna Wolf Carne-Ross, interview.

391   *other editing:* The two books were: H. L. Mencken, *Prejudices: A Selection,* made by James T. Farrell and with an Introduction by him (New York: Vintage, 1958), and Theodore Dreiser, *Theodore Dreiser,* edited by James T. Farrell and with an Introduction by him (New York: Dell, 1962).

391   *"I couldn't be":* KM, 6 March 1962 letter to JTF.

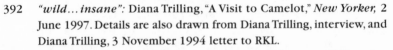

392   *"wild...insane":* Diana Trilling, "A Visit to Camelot," *New Yorker,* 2 June 1997. Details are also drawn from Diana Trilling, interview, and Diana Trilling, 3 November 1994 letter to RKL.

392   *had been audited:* Ria D. Simon, 27 May 1960 letter to JTF. See also JTF, 21 July 1963 letter to Arthur M. Schlesinger Jr. (mislabeled 21 July 1962, in Box 505, JTFUP) and KM, 6 June 1963 letter to JTF.

393   *He would arrange:* [Luna Wolf?], 28 February 1962 letter to EB; JTF, 8 June 1963 letter to EB; EB, 9 January 1963, 10 February 1964 letters to JTF; JTF, 2 March 1972, 10 December 1975, 14 February 1976 letters to Father Leander Troy (copy provided to RKL by Troy); JTF, 24 January 1973 letter to William Lederer (copy provided to RKL by Lederer); JTF, 24 November 1977, 21 February 1978 letters to Father Dave Dillon (copy provided to RKL by Troy).

393   *not inherently preposterous:* For background on Nobel Prize, see Blake Morrison, "So You Want to Win a Nobel Prize," *NYT Magazine,* 1 October 1995.

393   *would be announced: NYT,* 26 October 1962.

393   *Jim Henle had quoted:* JH, 20 June 1940 letter to JTF; JTF, Diary, 21 June 1940.

393   *"suddenly stopped":* Dan Wakefield, *New York in the Fifties*

(Boston: Houghton Mifflin, 1992), 327.

393   *"the most extraordinary":* Arthur M. Schlesinger Jr., *A Thousand Days: John F. Kennedy in the White House* (Boston: Houghton Mifflin, 1965), 733. The Kennedy quote is given differently in Marjorie Hunter, "49 Nobel Prize Winners Honored at White House," *NYT,* 30 April 1962.

394   *"pitched in":* Irene Patai Auvil, interview.

---

394   *"he was furious":* Luna Wolf Carne-Ross, interview.

395   *a collection of his essays:* Luna Wolf, ed., *James T. Farrell—Selected Essays* (New York: McGraw-Hill Paperbacks, 1964).

395   *she "really started":* CP, interview.

---

396   *in February 1963:* EB, *James T. Farrell* (New York: Twayne, 1971), "Chronology."

396   *inner freedom:* JTF, *The Silence of History* (New York: Doubleday, 1963), 363.

396   *"All that he had":* Ibid., 3.

397   *"William Dean Howells of Jackson Park":* Robert Gorham Davis, "New Chapter in the Farrell Story," *NYT Book Review,* 12 May 1963.

397   *"the interminable pages":* Newsweek, 25 February 1963.

397   *9,769 copies:* Lisa Drew, secretary to KM, 31 May 1963 letter to JTF.

---

397   *acquired the nickname:* Studs Terkel, interview. He has given various accounts of just how and when he came to be called "Studs." See Bruce Cook, "'Studs': Chicago As It Was," *National Observer,* 13 April 1974; Roger Ebert, "Farrell: Only Studs on Everyone's Mind," *Chicago Sun-Times,* 26 August 1979; Tony Parker, *Studs Terkel: A Life in Words* (New York: Holt, 1996), 173; and Herbert Mitgang, "Studs Terkel: Voice of America," *Doubletake,* Fall 1997.

397   *The interview:* "Studs Terkel with James T. Farrell," audiotape, 9 March 1963.

398   *an interviewer from* Esquire: Schickel, "James T. Farrell: Another Time, Another Place."

---

398   *his hair gray:* Stanford S. Apseloff, *James T. Farrell: A Visit to Chicago* (Kent, Ohio: Kent State University Libraries, 1969), 10.

398   *a lecture in September:* KM, 4 October 1963 letter to JTF.

398   *an adjunct professor:* Charles Fanning, "Farrell, James T(homas)," in *Great Writers of the English Language: Novelists and Prose Writers,* ed. James Vinson and D. L. Kirkpatrick (London: Macmillan, 1979).

398   *"that out of this":* JTF, "A Novelist's Reflections on Writing and His World," *Catholic Messenger,* 31 October 1963.

⇒•●•⇐

399   *"terrific editorial manager":* Thomas McCormack, interview.

400   *"No one had told":* Thomas McCormack, *The Fiction Editor, the Novel, and the Novelist* (New York: St. Martin's, 1988), 94–95.

400   *"it really isn't necessary":* KM, 24 February 1964 letter to JTF. See also KM, 7 August, 10 October 1963 letters to JTF, and Joan Kord, secretary to KM, 9 September 1963 letter to JTF.

400   *"has a kind of solidity":* Granville Hicks, "Literary Horizons: The Longevity of Integrity," *SR,* 20 June 1964.

401   *"Don't bother reading":* Nash, *The Innovators,* 206–7. Nash's account mistakenly refers to a Hicks review of *The Silence of History.* Hicks indicates in his review of *What Time Collects* that he had not read *The Silence of History.*

⇒•●•⇐

401   *"He was alone":* Irene Patai Auvil, interview.

402   *had first met:* Max M. Kampelman, *Entering New Worlds: The Memoirs of a Private Man in Public Life* (New York: HarperCollins, 1991), 56.

402   *"yokelish, simple sort":* JTF, Diary, 17 February "1949" [1950].

402   *arrived in Atlantic City: Washington Post,* 23 August 1964.

403   *They went to the ball:* Dr. Margaret Farrell, interview; *Washington Evening Star,* 20 January 1965.

⇒•●•⇐

403   *"we were in love":* CP, interview.

403   *latter part of 1966:* Paul H. Douglas, 14 July, 1 December 1966 letters to JTF. The first letter is addressed to JTF at the Beaux Arts Hotel, and the second, at 5 Tudor City Place.

403   *a middle-class enclave:* Norval White, *New York: A Physical History* (New York: Atheneum, 1987), 177; Elliot Willensky and Norval White, *AIA Guide to New York City*, 3rd ed. (New York: Harcourt Brace Jovanovich, 1988), 255.

403   *"He would have been impossible":* Arthur M. Schlesinger Jr., interview.

404   *That September:* EB, *James T. Farrell,* "Chronology."

404   *"They can fight":* JTF, "Introduction," *When Time Was Born* (New York: The Smith, 1966).

Chapter 19: "A Ministering Angel"

405   *"He never, ever":* CP, interview.

405   *obsessive-compulsive:* JTF, *True,* Box 460, JTFUP. He wrote: "It may be that I am compulsive. (The word is compulsive-obsessive, [*sic*] clinically). I feel that I must write so much."

405   *"a ministering angel":* Arthur M. Schlesinger Jr., interview.

405   *a magazine editor:* CP, interview; *American Girl,* November 1967, July 1972. Her name first appears on the magazine's masthead as "Beauty and Home Services Director" in November 1967, and as "Editor" in July 1972.

405   *"People think":* Stefan Kanfer, "As 'Studs Lonigan' Goes on TV, James T. Farrell Still Sings of the City of the Big Shoulders," *People,* 12 March 1979.

405   *"[Cleo] just made":* Evelyn Shrifte, interview.

406   *"Cleo, to me":* HFD, interview.

406   *"[Cleo] just really":* MFB, interview.

406   *a typical day:* CP, interview; CP, pretrial deposition in Seely case, 29 April 1983, 20-22.

407   *among the happiest:* See JTF, 13 July 1978 letter to Dick and Gladys Parker (copy provided to RKL by Richard Parker), and JTF, 23 April 1979 letter to Father Leander Troy (copy provided to RKL by Troy).

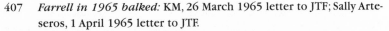

407   *Farrell in 1965 balked:* KM, 26 March 1965 letter to JTF; Sally Arteseros, 1 April 1965 letter to JTF.

407   *"a certain amount":* Sally Arteseros, interview.

408   *Several other books:* These included *New Year's Eve/1929* (New York: The Smith, 1967), a novel, and *Olive and Mary Anne* (New York: Stonehill, 1977), a collection of five tales. Two collections of his essays, one edited by Luna Wolf, the other by Jack Alan Robbins, also would appear.

408   *"most ambitious book":* Robert Phillips, review of *Invisible Swords* in *SR,* 12 June 1971.

408   *8,109 copies:* The sales figures were provided to RKL by Sally Arteseros.

408   *"We love publishing you":* KM, 30 August 1968 letter to JTF.

409   [Footnote] *His contentment:* JTF, 3 May 1977 letter to Richard Parker (copy provided by Parker); JTF, 17 May 1978 letter to Father Leander Troy (copy provided by Troy).

409   *lent his name: NYT,* 30 April, 12 May, 19 June 1968.

409   *"I defended LBJ":* JTF, 4 October 1970 letter to HFD (copy provided to RKL by HFD).

409   *In late 1965:* Douglas Brinkley, "The Other Vietnam Generation," *NYT Book Review,* 28 February 1999; Membership Roster of Citizens Committee for Peace with Freedom in Vietnam, included with letters to JTF from Paul H. Douglas, JTFUP; Harry McPherson, *A Political Education* (Boston: Atlantic-Little, Brown, 1972), 403.

410   *"deeply disturbed":* Quoted by Brinkley, "The Other Vietnam Generation."

410   *writer-in-residence:* Charles Fanning, "Farrell, James T(homas)," in *Great Writers of the English Language: Novelists and Prose Writers,* ed. James Vinson and D. L. Kirkpatrick (London: Macmillan, 1979).

410   *"I support":* JTF, "Today's Disobedience Is Uncivil," *NYT Magazine,* 26 November 1967.

410   *who had supported:* Theodore H. White, *The Making of the President—1972* (New York: Atheneum, 1973), 120, 122, 245.

410   *"Almost every day":* JTF, 21 August 1972 letter to HFD (copy provided by HFD).

410   *he voted:* CP, interview; William Lederer, interview.

410   *joined the Social Democrats:* "News on the Democratic Left," *New America,* June 1977, 12; Carl Gershman, interview; CP, interview; JTF, 13 June 1979 letter to Dick Parker (copy provided by Parker).

410   *The Shachtmanite Workers Party:* Peter Drucker, *Max Shachtman and His Left: A Socialist's Odyssey through the "American Century"* (New Jersey: Humanities Press, 1994), 219, 221, 222, 262, 275, 300, 304-8, 309, 311, 313n45; Maurice Isserman, *The Other American: The Life of Michael Harrington* (New York: PublicAffairs, 2000), 293, 295, 300-1; *NYT,* 31 December 1972; various articles, *New America,* 31 December 1972. See also "Social Democrats Express Solidarity with AFL-CIO," *New America,* 31 January 1973.

411   *"Socialists have rejected":* Carl Gershman, "Socialism: The Diamond, Not the Dung," *NYT,* 1 February 1975.

411   *"I was a basket case":* CP, interview.

411   *"I accepted the fact":* JTF, "Learning to Live with Studs Lonigan," *CT Book World,* 4 March 1979.

411   *Starting in 1969:* CP, interview; JTF, 4 December 1976, 9 June 1977

letters to Father David Dillon (copies provided to RKL by Father Leander Troy); Eric Pace, "Studs Lonigan's Creator, Reaching 70, Savors New Life Style," *NYT,* 28 February 1974; JTF, 13 July 1975 letter to Richard Parker (copy provided to RKL by Parker).

412 *"I am not a New Yorker":* Roger Ebert, "Farrell: Only Studs on Everyone's Mind," *Chicago Sun-Times,* 26 August 1979.

412 *Returning to his old school:* Father Leander Troy, interview.

412 *he asked Troy:* JTF, 4, 14 February 1976, 22 October 1976 letters to Father Leander Troy (copies provided to RKL by Troy).

412 *"He liked to look around":* Father Melvin James, interview.

412 *Some of Farrell's siblings:* MFB, interview.

412 *"He hated":* William Lederer, interview.

413 *"and my nickname":* William Lederer, 26 October 1972 letter to JTF (copy provided to RKL by Lederer).

413 *"When he met me":* William Lederer, interview.

——⇒•०•⇐——

414 *Jim Henle died: NYT,* 11 January 1973.

414 *"trembling all over":* CP, interview.

414 *a remembrance:* JTF, "*I Remember James Henle,*" in "James Henle, 1969–78" folder, Henle 7 Box, JTFUP.

414 *failed to show up:* Peter Henle, interview.

415 *had been announced: NYT,* 15 February 1973.

415 *Tom Daly.* HFD, interview.

——⇒•०•⇐——

415 *"his coming-out party":* CP, interview.

415 *"The Talk of the Town":* Anon. [Jervis Anderson], "Farrell's Party," *New Yorker,* 18 March 1974.

416 *a "salute":* CP, interview; "Salute to James T. Farrell," 15 September 1976, program given out at dinner. See Box 830, JTFUP.

416 *$50-a-plate:* JTF, 17 October 1976 letter to Father David Dillon (copy provided to RKL by Father Leander Troy).

416 *"I love Jim Farrell":* Lisa Anderson, "Eye: Studs and Fans," *Women's Wear Daily,* 17 September 1976.

416 *A photograph taken then:* The photograph, by Jill Krementz, appears in Kanfer, "As 'Studs Lonigan' Goes on TV."

——⇒•०•⇐——

416 *resumed taking amphetamines:* Dr. Robert D. Seely, pretrial deposition in Seely case, 29 April, 16 December 1983, 10 January 1984, 25–26, 101–6, 145–47, 223–26.

416   *had died a year earlier:* Obituary of Dr. Edward Jacobs, *NYT,* 25 November 1975.

417   *hypertension:* Seely, pretrial deposition in Seely case, 137–39, 173, 186–94.

417   *"For what medical condition":* Ibid., 111.

417   *took Farrell's (alleged) word:* Ibid., 114–17, 121–22, 125–26.

417   *"So that throughout":* Ibid., 123.

417   *a bill arrived:* CP, interview. A copy of the bill was provided by CP to RKL.

417   *"I know he was off":* CP, interview.

417   *she did learn at some point:* CP, pretrial deposition in Seely case, 35–36. See also Seely, pretrial deposition, 115–17, 143–45.

417   *"Jimmy was so protective":* CP, interview.

—————————⊷•⊶—————————

418   "Do you mind": HFD, interview.

418   *Cleo staying a week:* CP, interview.

418   *twelve exhibition games:* JTF, 29 March 1978 letter to Dick Parker *et al.* (copy provided to RKL by Parker).

418   *"35 to 40":* JTF, quoted by Bill Gleason, in "Farrell: On the Beat," *Chicago Sun-Times,* 7 March 1979.

418   *get in free:* JTF, 21 August 1972 letter to HFD (copy provided by HFD to RKL).

418   *"I get let in free":* JTF, 26 May 1976 letter to Richard Parker (copy provided to RKL by Parker).

419   *Once, when someone asked:* JTF, "Baseball: A Fan's Notes," *American Scholar,* Summer 1979.

419   *a more luxurious apartment:* CP, interview; JTF, 25 October 1977 letter to Father David Dillon (copy provided to RKL by Father Leander Troy); JTF, 17 May 1978 letter to Father Troy (copy provided to RKL by Troy).

—————————⊷•⊶—————————

420   *"I did not think":* JTF, "TV's 'Studs': The Author's View," *Washington Post,* 23 March 1979.

420   *"The South Side":* David Elliott, "NBC'S Well-Laundered Studs Lonigan 'Epic,'" *Chicago Sun-Times,* 7 March 1979. Cf. John J. O'Connor, "TV: 'Lonigan' on NBC," *NYT,* 7 March 1979.

420   *spent more than $5 million:* "A Costly 'Studs' Takes Shirt off Lorimar's Back," *Variety,* 20 September 1978.

420   *"a moral appeal":* JTF, 3 May 1977 letter to Richard and Gladys Parker (copy provided to RKL by Richard Parker).

421   *official veneration:* Fanning, "Farrell, James T(homas)"; JTF, 2 March

1973, 8 April 1979 letters to Father Leander Troy; JTF, 25 October 1977 letter to Father David Dillon; and copies of various certificates and related material (provided, along with copies of the cited letters to him and Dillon, to RKL by Troy).

421   *had first been awarded:* Victor F. Weisskopf, president, American Academy of Arts and Sciences, 2 February 1979 letter to JTF. The American Academy of Arts and Sciences, in Boston, should not be confused (though it often is) with the American Academy of Arts and Letters, in New York. The latter is the organization of "immortals" and "near-immortals" (to use Max Eastman's derisive terminology) to which Farrell had been elevated in 1942; he seldom attended its meetings.

421   *"previously had been critical":* JTF, 23 April 1979 letter to Father Leander Troy (copy provided to RKL by Troy).

422   *"summoned to the bar":* Daniel Aaron, in "The Emerson-Thoreau Award Ceremony," *Bulletin* of the American Academy of Arts and Sciences, October 1979.

422   *After the meeting:* JTF, 23 April 1979 letter to Father Leander Troy (copy provided to RKL by Troy).

422   *Cardinal John J. Wright:* James Hennesey, S.J., *American Catholics: A History of the Roman Catholic Community in the United States* (New York: Oxford University Press, 1981), 286.

422   *"one's peers":* JTF, in "The Emerson-Thoreau Award Ceremony."

---

422   *The Yankees were to play:* NYT, 21, 22 August 1979.

422   *Farrell told Cleo that he wanted:* CP, interview; CP, pretrial deposition in Seely case, 29 April 1983, 39, 70–84.

424   [Footnote] *filed a civil suit:* Plaintiff's "Verified Complaint" in Seely case, filed 15 April 1980; CP, interview; New York Supreme Court, New York County records in Seely case (Index no. 7284/80); confidential source.

---

424   *Novelist Kurt Vonnegut:* CP, interview; Eric Pace, "James T. Farrell, Realistic Novelist, Dies; Author of Studs Lonigan Trilogy Was 75," *NYT,* 23 August 1979; Peggy Constantine, "James Farrell Is Buried after Evanston Rites," *Chicago Sun-Times,* 26 August 1979.

424   *"as a representative":* Kurt Vonnegut, *Palm Sunday* (New York: Dell, 1984), 143–44.

425   *"thrilled":* JTF, 13 June 1979 letter to Dick Parker (copy provided to RKL by Parker).

425   *bold and stunningly successful:* Jonathan Kwitny, *Man of the Cen-*

tury: The Life and Times of Pope John Paul II (New York: Holt, 1997), 323-25.

425 *"valiant and valued"*: Mary McCarthy, "For Jim Farrell's Funeral," *New York Review of Books,* 8 November 1979.

425 *"His struggles"*: JTF, "A Rare Quality of Greatness," *New America,* July-August 1979.

425 *"Jim Farrell, too"*: Carl Gershman, "James Farrell: A Magnificence of the Spirit," *New America,* October 1979.

426 *Cleo...decided:* CP, interview.

426 *offer of a Mass:* Father Leander Troy, interview.

426 *"was not a liar"*: Constantine, "James Farrell Is Buried after Evanston Rites."

Works of James T. Farrell
That Appear in An Honest Writer

Criticism
A Note on Literary Criticism

Essays
"Dos Passos and the Critics"
The Fate of Writing in America
"Liberals in Chicago"
Literature and Morality
"Mr. Hicks: Critical Vulgarian"
Reflections at Fifty

Journalism
It Has Come to Pass

Memoir
My Baseball Diary

Novels
Bernard Clare
Boarding House Blues
A Brand New Life
The Death of Nora Ryan
The Dunne Family
Ellen Rogers
The Face of Time
Father and Son
Gas-House McGinty
Invisible Swords
Judgment Day
Lonely for the Future
My Days of Anger

"New Year's Eve" [*New Year's
Eve/1929*]
No Star Is Lost
The Road Between
The Silence of History
Studs Lonigan
What Time Collects
A World I Never Made
Yet Other Waters
Young Lonigan
*The Young Manhood of Studs
Lonigan*

Poetry
When Time Was Born

Stories
"Boys and Girls"
"Calico Shoes"
"The Fastest Runner on Sixty-first
Street"
"Helen, I Love You"
"Jewboy"
"Judith"
"The Merry Clouters"
"$1,000 a Week"
"The Only Son"
"The Professor"
"The Scarecrow"
"Senior Prom"
"Seventeen"

"Slob"

"Soap"

"Studs"

"They Ain't the Men They Used
to Be"

"Tom Carroll"

Tommy Gallagher's Crusade

Short story collections

An American Dream Girl

Calico Shoes and Other Stories

*Can All This Grandeur Perish?
and Other Stories*

Childhood Is Not Forever

*A Dangerous Woman and Other
Stories*

French Girls Are Vicious

Guillotine Party and Other Stories

Judith and Other Stories

$1,000 a Week and Other Stories

The Short Stories of James T. Farrell

Side Street and Other Stories

Index

543

249-50, 308; *see also* Hitler, Adolf

"Fastest Runner on Sixty-first Street, The" (JTF), 35

Fate of Writing in America, The (JTF), 284-85

Father and Son (JTF), 43, 45, 237, 244; plot, 245-46; reviews, 246-49; sales, 247

Faulkner, William, ix, xii, 154, 253

Ferguson, Otis, 204-5, 207, 210

Fiedler, Leslie, 302-3

Fischer, Louis, 240

Fitzgerald, F. Scott, 140

Flanagan, Jack, 422-23

Flanagan, Kathleen, 422-23

Fontanne, Lynn, 139

Forsythe, Robert, 161

Foster, William Z., 117

Fourth International (Socialist Workers Party), 272

Frank, Waldo, 135, 201

Frankel, Max, 354

Franklin Library, 420

Franks, Bobby, 51

Freeman, Joseph, 112, 113, 129, 132, 135

French Girls Are Vicious (JTF), 340-41, 345, 350

Freud, Sigmund, 50

Frost, Robert, 394, 421

Gannett, Lewis: on *Judgment Day*, 142; on *World I Never Made*, 179; on *Young Manhood of Studs Lonigan*, 124

Gardiner, Harold C., 290

Garland, Charles, 111

Garland Fund, 111, 112

Garner, John Nance, 145

Gas-House McGinty, 69, 100, 114-15, 119, 149, 165

Geisel, Theodore ("Dr. Suess"), 113

Geller, James, 222, 254-57

German-Soviet Nonaggression Pact, 228-29, 235, 240, 251, 259, 268, 286

Gershman, Carl, 411, 425

Gilmartin, Michael (Fr.), 57-58

Gilson, Étienne (*Spirit of Medieval Philosophy*), 270

Gleason, Bill, 418-19

Glotzer, Albert, 196, 264, 292, 419

Gold, Michael (Itzok Granich), 94, 111-12, 113, 129, 131-35, 159, 161, 162, 163, 168, 170, 202, 228; attacks Trotskyists, 187, 279

Goldwyn, Sam, 255

Gorky, Maxim, 131

Gorshin, Frank, 381

Grange, Red, 55

Green, Gerald, ix

Greenberg, Clement, 259

Gregory, Horace, 94, 122, 129, 135, 163, 221, 338-39, 411, 415; on *Gas-House McGinty*, 114; on *Young Lonigan*, 110

Guggenheim fellowship, 158

Guillotine Party and Other Stories (JTF), 154

Hallgren, Mauritz, 192

Hamby, Alonzo, 300

Hamill, Pete, xi

Hammett, Dashiell, 227

Hardwick, Elizabeth, 415; on *Bernard Clare*, 283

Harmsworth, Desmond, 97

Harper, William Rainey, 53

Hartke, Conan (Fr.), 425-26

Hathaway, Clarence, 126, 129

Hecht, Ben, 388; *Count Bruga*, 74

"Helen, I Love You" (JTF), 106, 114

Hellman, Lillian, 193, 306

Hemingway, Ernest, ix, xii, 93, 161, 188, 201, 234, 253, 290; JTF meets, 185-86

Hemingway, Pauline, 186, 187